# Recovering Agency:
# Lifting the Veil
of
# Mormon Mind Control

by

LUNA LINDSEY CORBDEN

Recovering Agency: Lifting the Veil of Mormon Mind Control

Version 1.0 Release 7.22.2014: Original
Version 1.1 Release 10.23.2014: Typo corrections
Version 1.2 Release 10.07.2015: Typo corrections
Version 1.3 Release 03.23.2021: Name change

Copyright ©2013-2014 by Luna Flesher Lindsey
Internal Graphics ©2014 by Luna Flesher Lindsey
Cover Art ©2014 by Ana Cruz
All rights reserved.

This publication is protected under the US Copyright Act of 1976 and all other applicable international, federal, state and local laws. No part of this book may be used or reproduced in any manner whatsoever without written permission, except in the case of brief quotations embodied in critical articles, professional works, or reviews.

www.recoveringagency.com
www.corbden.com
ISBN-10: 1489595937
ISBN-13: 978-1489595935
First digital & print publication: July 2014

# Table of Contents

| | |
|---|---|
| FOREWORD | VII |

**PART 1: IN THE BEGINNING**

| | |
|---|---|
| IT STARTED IN A GARDEN… | 2 |
|   *Free Will vs. Determinism* | 3 |
|   *Exit Story* | 5 |
|   *The Illusion of Choice* | 9 |
| WHAT IS MIND CONTROL? | 13 |
|   *What is a Cult?* | 16 |
|   *Myths of Cults & Mind Control* | 17 |
| ALL IS NOT WELL IN ZION | 21 |
|   *Is Mormonism A Danger To Society?* | 22 |
|   *Why Should We Mourn Or Think Our Lot Is Hard?* | 26 |
|     Self-esteem | |
|     Square Peg, Round Hole Syndrome | |
|     Guilt & Shame | |
|     Depression, Eating Disorders, & Suicide | |
|     Codependency & Passive-Aggressive Culture | |
|     Material Loss | |
| DON'T JUST GET OVER IT—RECOVER! | 36 |
|   *Though hard to you this journey may appear…* | 40 |
|   *Born Under the Covenant* | 41 |
|   *We Then Are Free From Toil and Sorrow, Too…* | 43 |
| SLIPPERY SOURCES | 45 |
|   *Truth Is Eternal (And Verifiable)* | 45 |
|   *Truth Is Eternal (Depends on Who You Ask)* | 46 |
|   *By Their Fruits* | 48 |
|   *Unto Whom Much Is Given* | 49 |

**PART 2: THE SCIENCE OF BELIEVING** — **51**

| | |
|---|---|
| EXPLOITED HUMAN TENDENCIES | 52 |
| COGNITIVE CONSONANCE/ DISSONANCE THEORY | 54 |
|   *Dissonance in Mormon Life Five Fictional Case Studies* | 59 |
|   *Antidote–Cognitive Awareness* | 60 |
| WHEN PROPHECY FAILS | 62 |
| BIASES, BEHAVIORS, & OTHER BOOGEYMEN | 66 |
|   *Seek and Ye Shall Find - Confirmation Bias* | 67 |
|   *Six Compliance Practices* | 69 |
|     Reciprocation | |
|     Commitment & Consistency | |
|     Social Proof | |
|     Liking | |
|     Obedience to Authority | |
|     Scarcity | |
|   *Mirror Neurons* | 74 |
|   *Milgram Experiment* | 74 |

| | |
|---|---:|
| **PART 3: THOUGHT REFORM METHODS** | **76** |
| THE WHOLE ARMOR OF GOD | 77 |
|    *Breastplates, Shields, & Helmets of Faith* | *79* |
| LOVE BOMBING | 85 |
| DESTABILIZATION | 90 |
|    *Put Your Self on the Shelf* | *92* |
|    *Targeting Unstable Individuals* | *96* |
|    *Born in the Covenant* | *97* |
|    *Regaining the Self* | *100* |
| DECEPTION | 102 |
| SACRED SCIENCE: A CLOSED SYSTEM OF LOGIC | 111 |
|    *The Church Is Universally True (And Logical)* | *114* |
|    *The Prophets Speak for God* | *117* |
|    *Suppression of Dissent* | *121* |
|    *An Open System of Logic* | *125* |
| MYSTICAL MANIPULATION | 126 |
|    *Magical Thinking* | *130* |
|    *Wages of Sin and Miracles of Forgiveness* | *132* |
|    *Spiritual Surveillance* | *134* |
|    *Missions* | *136* |
|    *Prophecy* | *137* |
|    *Prayer* | *138* |
|    *Tithing* | *139* |
|    *Word of Wisdom* | *140* |
|    *Loops of Logic* | *141* |
|    *Grounded in Reality* | *142* |
| MILIEU CONTROL | 143 |
|    *Doctrine Correlation* | *146* |
|    *Outside Friends & Media* | *147* |
|    *The Family Milieu* | *150* |
|    *Miscellaneous Milieus* | *153* |
|    *Strengthening Church Members Committee* | *155* |
|    *Without Milieu Control* | *156* |
| DEMAND FOR PURITY: PERPETUAL INADEQUACY | 157 |
| DISPENSING OF EXISTENCE | 166 |
| DOCTRINE OVER SELF | 175 |
| LOADING THE LANGUAGE | 183 |
| TOTALIST REFRAMING | 189 |
| THOUGHT-TERMINATING CLICHÉS | 195 |
| SOCIAL PRESSURE | 201 |
| BELIEF FOLLOWS BEHAVIOR | 207 |
| PUBLIC COMMITMENT | 211 |
| CREATING DEPENDENCY | 218 |
| BLACK AND WHITE THINKING | 224 |
| ELITISM | 228 |
| US-VERSUS-THEM THINKING | 235 |
| INDIRECT DIRECTIVES | 244 |
| INFLUENCE THROUGH IDENTIFICATION & EXAMPLE | 250 |

| | |
|---|---|
| EMOTION OVER INTELLECT | 255 |
| INDUCED PHOBIAS | 264 |
| TRANCE INDUCTION & DISSOCIATIVE STATES | 271 |
| TIME CONTROL | 278 |
| THE DOUBLE-BIND | 283 |
| BLAME REVERSAL | 292 |
| GUILT & SHAME | 298 |
|    *Guilt* | *300* |
|    *Shame* | *301* |
|    *Understanding & Love* | *305* |
|    *Unintended Consequences of Shame* | *306* |
|    *The Shame of Sex* | *307* |
| CONFESSION | 308 |
| EUPHORIA INDUCTION | 313 |
|    *Ideals* | *315* |
|    *Loss of Individuality* | *315* |
|    *Trance Inducement* | *316* |
| PROSELYTIZING | 318 |
| BAIT, HOOK, LINE, & SINKER | 322 |
| **CONCLUSION** | **325** |
| FLEEING THE GARDEN | 326 |
| **APPENDIX** | **329** |
| RECOMMENDED READING | 331 |
|    *Cults & Mind Control* | *331* |
|    *Official LDS Sources* | *331* |
|    *LDS Controversies* | *331* |
|    *LDS Exit Stories* | *333* |
|    *Liberal Mormon Resources* | *333* |
|    *Support and Communities for Former Mormons* | *334* |
|    *What Now?* | *335* |
| INDEX | 337 |

# Foreword

I began writing *Recovering Agency* with one goal in mind: To help former Mormons understand and process their feelings of having belonged to the Church of Jesus Christ of Latter-day Saints. Additionally, I wanted to help members who are doubting and unsatisfied to cope when, for various reasons, they have to remain members of the Church.

In that sense, this is a self-help book for exmormons who are laboring to put their lives back together.

However, as my writing progressed, I realized I had a second audience. People who have never been LDS expressed eager interest. So I expanded my scope a little to include them. While the content is still aimed at former Mormons, I have added footnotes to explain LDS doctrines and practices that may be confusing to outsiders.

In that sense, this is an intellectual or academic work. My research was quite extensive, and I don't think anyone has ever correlated this kind of information in one place before. Anyone from the mildly curious to the seasoned cult researcher should find this book informative.

A third audience exists: True believing Mormons, i.e. those who are very happy with their beliefs and their membership in the Church. I did not set out to write for this set, yet many will read. For those with unwavering faith, my perspective may seem incomprehensible. Though you may not understand it, know that I wrote this book from a loving place and a sincere desire to help those who are hurting and confused.

If you truly believe that all people are the children of God, then your heart should go out to those who suffer, even if you can't fathom how the convictions that bring you joy could hurt others. I hope this book will help you understand their pain, and through your understanding, that it helps you love them more unconditionally.

Mind control techniques leverage natural human tendencies and mental shortcuts we all use to avoid the exhaustion that constant mistrust and skepticism would bring. This type of manipulation is used to varying degrees by many churches and other kinds of organizations, including businesses, political groups, and charities. The degree to which controlling tactics are used is what separates the freest groups from the most coercive. The LDS Church falls someplace on the unethical end of the spectrum, but it doesn't have to. Mormonism can still retain its unique identity as a religion without using coercive persuasion methods.

As this book goes to press, the LDS Church is in the news. Two prominent members of the Church have been notified of disciplinary action for opinions they have expressed online.[1] Their excommunication hearings are scheduled within weeks.

One, John Dehlin, runs the podcast and blog at MormonStories.org, which helps Mormons come to terms with difficult information they have discovered about the Church. He is also a vocal LGBT ally. In this book, I cite one of his studies about why Mormons leave.

The other, Kate Kelly, founded the organization OrdainWomen.org, which seeks to bring attention to women's issues within the Church and argues that women cannot be equal unless they are allowed to hold the Priesthood.

---

[1] Jennifer Dobner. "Two Prominent Mormon Activists Threatened with Excommunication." *Reuters*. June 12, 2014. http://www.reuters.com/article/2014/06/12/us-usa-utah-mormons-idUSKBN0EN02V20140612

And just yesterday, it came to light that other, less prominent LDS bloggers and online commenters have been contacted by their bishops and have been asked to stop making public commentary or they will face probation, disfellowshipping, or even excommunication.[1]

It is not known yet whether Dehlin and Kelly will be excommunicated. As of this writing, Dehlin's bishop has asked to deescalate. Kelly's bishop is standing his ground in spite of the negative media attention.

They have both drawn an outpouring of support from devout Mormons who believe the Church has gone too far. Even those who do not agree with their heterodox stances or unorthodox methods agree that they should have the freedom to publicly express their views and still remain members in good standing.

It is a time of much soul-searching for Mormons and, hopefully, for their Church and its leadership.

These events obviously serve as evidence for the claims I make in these pages–that the Church strictly controls freedom of thought and expression. But it also shows me something else. It reveals the great potential of what the Church *could* be, what it purports to be, and what it is when it is at its best.

Some LDS bloggers, who have taken stances similar to Dehlin and Kelly, describe how their bishops are reaching out to them with loving arms and assurance of continued acceptance. These bloggers describe family members who don't understand their views but who are being supportive and loving during this tumultuous and scary time. Other bloggers are bravely calling the Church to task on these silencing tactics and asking if this is really in the spirit of what God's earthly organization is supposed to be.

These particular leaders and members are showing the true love I think Mormon theology and culture is capable of inspiring. My faith in what is possible is renewed when I read these sincere posts by Mormons who would rather follow the compassionate teachings of Christ. They manage to hear his soft words, and practice them, over the loudly trumpeted compliance-seeking doctrines sung to the drumbeat of "obedience, obedience, obedience."

I am not Christian, nor do I align myself with any religious faith or organization, but I believe in taking beneficial meaning from all spiritual paths, Christianity and Mormonism included. In these pages, I describe in detail the negative power organizations have to control the hearts of men. But I also hope for that which is harder to see... that religious faith can inspire the best in people, in spite of any institution's attempts to control.

Over the past few weeks, as the Church tries to stamp out the voices of Dehlin and Kelly and other vocal members of the LDS bloggernacle, I've seen the best side of LDS faith– those loving members who support diversity of thought, freedom of mind, and most of all, those who love their brothers and sisters without conditions and without the rigid strictures on how they express themselves and what they express.

*That* is the dream Mormonism has to offer, though it is not always the reality.

To paraphrase Supreme Court Justice Louis Brandeis, "Sunlight is the best disinfectant." It is my sincerest hope that these pages shine a light on the ugliest parts of Mormonism, not to show that Mormonism is ugly, but so that those ugly parts can be cut away.

Just as Christ said, "And if thy right eye offend thee, pluck it out, and cast it from thee." (Matt. 5:29-30 KJV) As a Mormon, I used to think he referred to unrighteous friends and family, that I should stay away from them lest they lead me astray. But that doesn't make sense, given that Christ's central message focused on love and acceptance. In that same chapter, he tells his disciples to "agree with thine adversary quickly," to "turn the other cheek," and to "love your enemies." It makes more sense that he meant for "pluck it out" to

---

[1] Laurie Goodstein. "Mormons Say Critical Online Comments Draw Threats From Church." *The New York Times*, June 18, 2014. http://www.nytimes.com/2014/06/19/us/critical-online-comments-put-church-status-at-risk-mormons-say.html

apply to unloving *doctrines*, not *people*, that distract his disciples away from following his caring example.

(The King James Version uses the problematic and easily confused words, "offend" and "member": "...it is profitable for thee that one of thy members should perish," where it could easily be assumed that a *person* who leads one away from ideological purity should be cast off. But the New International Version specifically states "one part of your body", which is more metaphorical: "If your right eye causes you to stumble, gouge it out and throw it away. It is better for you to lose one part of your body than for your whole body to be thrown into hell." If the most important commandment is to "love one another as I have loved you", this whole verse more likely means we should cast away policies and cultural elements that hinder or obstruct unconditional love.)

Know that I do not hate the LDS Church, nor her people. It is an institution run by human beings, and as such, it is not above criticism, even if it purports to be an organization run by God. Criticism does not imply hate or anger or an attempt to destroy. If I ever take the time to criticize, be it a religion, a political party, or the work of a fellow writer, it is always in a constructive spirit.

The LDS Church, with its current policies, emphasis on ideological unanimity, promotion of coercive doctrines, and predominant conformity culture, harms many of its members. The leaders of the Church could benefit by reading these pages and then taking a good, hard look at how these findings might improve the lives of the souls they shepherd.

And should the Church remain manipulative and controlling, then at least this book will accomplish its original goal, which is to help those members and exmembers to grapple with those coercive mechanisms within their own minds, to come away more free than they started.

Many have asked me, "How do you know *you're* not brainwashed?" And the answer is, "I don't." Knowing a little about mind control, however, helps inoculate against many types of unethical persuasion. All readers of this book will be better educated to defend against *any* high-demand group.

In the words of the prophet Alma (Alma 32:34): If this is a good seed, it will enlighten your understanding and grow into a life-giving tree. I hope this seed does likewise.

Luna Lindsey Corbden

*To truth, in all her forms, no matter how bright, no matter how hard, no matter how lovely, no matter how horrifying. It is only by truth that we may be enlightened; especially when the truth looks nothing like what we expect.*

# Part 1: In the Beginning

*We are taught to cultivate our minds, to control our thoughts to thoroughly bring our whole being into subjection to the spirit and law of God, that we may learn to be one and act as the heart of one man, that we may carry out the purposes of God upon the earth.*

—**Prophet Wilford Woodruff**[1]

*The volition of [man] is free; this is a law of their existence, and the Lord cannot violate his own law; were he to do that, he would cease to be God... Every intelligent being must have the power of choice.*

—**Prophet Brigham Young**[2]

*Agency: Within your stewardship, complete independence to do what you're told.*
—**Orson Scott Card,**
***Saintspeak: The Mormon Dictionary***[3,4]

# It Started In a Garden...

Idyllic. Pastoral. Green and lush. Every tree bends arm to offer its fruits to the first two human beings. They labor not, they toil not, they *know* naught.

Adam and Eve were brought forth into existence in the midst of a perfect utopia. Of all the world's pains they were spared, perhaps the most merciful was that of complex choice.

Imagine such a state: innocent, trusting, childlike, naive. The whole sum of human decisions had been reduced to a simplistic dichotomy, a single commandment: Do not eat from The Tree of Knowledge of Good and Evil, yet in its own right, it was the Tree of Death, because those who partook of it would, in that same day, surely die.

One other tree stood to tempt Adam and Eve, yet in their ignorance, they weren't aware of the choice. In their immortality, this other tree, the Tree of Life, was redundant. Unneeded. Until after their one fateful action, it became forever barred to them.

Good and evil, life and death: this single option, stark, dramatic, world-changing. Better to remain safe, not to take those risks. Knowledge may be beautiful, exciting, growth-promoting, but it is also confusing, misleading, problematic, scary. Don't dare risk knowledge and the death that will surely follow.

The rest of their lives were filled with a lack of decisions, a lack of work, a lack of conflict. No forks in the road, no difficulties, no adventure. Peace, eternal boredom, and lonely solitude.

They never thought to question or criticize their state. Why should they? They had everything they needed.

Almost.

With no choices, Adam and Eve had no story. Their freedom was hampered by an absence of variety, of raw information, of conflict and contrast, of complex moral thought. Within these constraints of bliss, they could not progress.

And then something changed. Eve faced her one and only decision, the one pivot of agency she had available. It has been debated whether she acted from serpent-temptation,

---

1. *Journal of Discourses*. Vol. 6. p115 Privately Printed, n.d. http://jod.mrm.org/6/115
2. *Journal of Discourses*. Vol. 11. p272 Privately Printed, n.d. http://jod.mrm.org/11/272
3. *Saintspeak* is a satirical dictionary of LDS terms. It is meant to be funny, but in all humor there is a seed of truth. Card often manages to sum up my points perfectly.
4. Orson Scott Card. *Saintspeak, the Mormon Dictionary*. Salt Lake City, Utah: Orion Books, 1981.

outright rebellion, accident, or ennui. I like to think that with determination and purpose, she stepped forward, saying, "Why should God keep us confined?" Then she willfully, bravely, reached out and took a bite.

With that, her mind was suddenly filled with possibilities. She became open to the world outside the tamed garden. She discovered a vast Planet Earth, a living place, full of dangers, frightening choices, wild animals, and evil men.

She also learned it was a place of kindness, freedom, autonomy, and independence. As the sweetness still lingered on her tongue, she discovered that the bounds of human potential were limitless.

Eve grew up. Adam followed closely behind.

In that day, Adam did *not* die. The gates of the garden swung open, and he walked out a free man. Now with knowledge, he experience true liberty, to toil as he chose, to learn and grow, to go wherever he wished. Adam had matured, had thrown off the shackles of tightly controlled ignorance. He learned that day that there was more to existence than good versus evil, life versus death. He finally saw that sometimes there are no good options, or that some choices are neutral. That most decisions involve trade-offs.

On that day, Adam and Eve learned about moral ambiguity.

Together, arm in arm, they strode proudly into the dawn, ready to seed a humanity that would take after them, independent men and women, resistant to those who would control via enforced ignorance.

The day this couple ate the fruit, they knew only one act could allow them to progress, and it was only by making the *wrong* choice could they make the right choice. Only by defying God could they find liberation.

This is one of humanity's most ancient stories[1]. I might argue that it is the first dystopian novel, like *Nineteen Eighty-Four*, *V for Vendetta*, or *Fahrenheit 451*. It certainly follows the same plot: Oppressed people seem to live in a blissful utopia, but they are lied to by a controlling authority, until they uncover some piece of information or have an unauthorized insight, at which time they become heroes by attempting escape.

Whether the Garden story is dystopian depends on whether we frame God as the villain and see Adam's ejection from the Garden as a triumph. In religious tellings, God is the hero, and so we usually perceive a utopian story in which the ungrateful, rebellious antagonists stupidly throw away a pretty good thing. But then all dystopias seem like utopias to someone. It's all in whether or not you buy the propaganda.

Anyone who has left a controlling religious system may relate to Adam and Eve as heroes. I do. Like them, I threw off the shackles of my mind to join a frightening yet wonderful world of unrestricted knowledge and volition.

## Free Will vs. Determinism

*There are, of course, those who, in bitterness and disbelief, have rejected the idea of an independent spirit in man that is capable of free will and choice and true liberty.*
—**Howard W. Hunter**[2]

The nature of "free will" has been philosophically debated since before written records. Various cultures have placed emphasis on destiny, to the extent that they believed gods or spirits would accompany you to enforce your fulfillment of your ordained life mission. Our language still reflects this in words like "fate" and "fortune," which these days have been

---

1. This version of the Garden of Eden story is based on the LDS version, but told from a different point of view as a metaphor. Many of my readers will understand this, yet I point it out lest anyone think I am intentionally misconstruing LDS doctrine.
2. Howard W. Hunter. "The Golden Thread of Choice." In LDS General Conference, Oct 1989. https://www.lds.org/general-conference/1989/10/the-golden-thread-of-choice

downgraded to mean mere "luck."

In modern times, we value free will more highly, though the debate still rages on throughout our fiction, politics, philosophies, and religions. Will the hero buck his destiny and make a different choice at the end of the story? Are we driven by nature (genetics and temperament) or nurture (our environment and choices)? Can criminals be rehabilitated, or should they be locked away forever?

During the Enlightenment, scientists imagined the universe was a clockwork machine, governed by laws that operated predictably. If we understood every law of physics, chemistry, and biology, we could predict each toss of the dice. This scientific view of destiny was known as "determinism."

Yet the more science reveals in fields like mathematics, biology, and quantum physics, we find the question of free will is never answered. Our personalities seem to be some combination of genetics and environment, both nature and nurture. And the mathematics of chaos theory show that patterns repeat in a semi-predictable shape, yet all we can calculate are probabilities, and even then the more control we exert, the more likely that the whole system will collapse into disorder. Even the choices of low-level animals, like fruit flies, have been shown to be a combination of instinct and randomness.

Perhaps it is our fate to ask this question forever. We will just get better at asking it, thinking all the while we are *choosing* to ask it. But are we?

In a way, this book explores one aspect of this eternal question, which is: "What is freedom? When am I free to choose, and when am I being controlled?" Just like all other versions of this question, it seems to have a simple answer on the surface, except for the vast gray area between freedom and force.

Most people have a good idea what choice is. I've chosen my career, my car, my furniture, the people I surround myself with, the food I eat, the music I listen to, and what I do any given Friday night. If someone prevents me from choosing these things, I am no longer free.

If I wish to stand, and someone shoves me down, clearly my free will has been violated. Nor am I considered to be acting freely if someone puts a gun to my head and threatens to kill me. This is called duress. Threats remove liberty, as do threats to loved ones.

These are obvious forms of force. The rest of this book explores the gray area. There are no clear lines to be drawn, yet intellectual maturity allows us to fearlessly grapple with concepts that require a second look. I respect your intelligence and won't oversimplify anything just for the sake of an easy answer. This isn't the Garden anymore.

Cognitive scientists have studied these gray areas since prisoners of war returned from Korea in the 1950s singing the praises of communism. Later, the new religious movements of the 1960s and 70s offered further examples for study and insight. Controlled experiments in human behavior revealed even more. Science now knows much related to how we learn, enculturate, respond to authority, act in groups, resolve internal conflicts, are persuaded to new beliefs, and cling to old beliefs. Is it possible to control someone without ever laying a hand on her or holding a gun to her head? Research says, "Yes."

The Church of Jesus Christ of Latter-day Saints is a high-demand group, a deceptive religion that utilizes psychological manipulation via doctrine and culture to restrict the thoughts, behaviors, and emotions of otherwise good and intelligent members. In a word—though it is admittedly a highly-charged, loaded word—Mormonism is a cult.

What do I mean by cult? I will explore that in-depth in the next chapter.

This book is aimed primarily at exmormons seeking to understand their experiences, though members may also benefit. If you are a happy Latter-day Saint who finds the Church spiritually fulfilling in every way, then you may find little to relate to. But it will expand your understanding of those who aren't happy, those who do have doubts, and those who eventually leave.

Those who have never been LDS will see in detail how thought-reform techniques are applied in practice.

When, through the course of my life, I meet former members of Seventh-day Adventists, Jehovah's Witnesses, and fundamentalist Christians, I discover kindred spirits, joined in bonds that only a shared similar experience can generate. Ex-members of high-demand groups continue to have difficulties long after leaving. Exmormons are no different. This book is intended to help them recover from the emotional manipulation and spiritual abuse they may have suffered.

Margaret Singer is a leading cult researcher and clinical psychologist. She said, "Leaving a cult is for many one of the most difficult things they will ever do. And it's especially difficult to do alone."[1] Many exmormons will relate to this statement. I know I do.

# Exit Story

> *We are all condemned by birth to be indoctrinated, mystified, and shaped by authorities we did not choose.*
> —**Sam Keen,** *Hymns to an Unknown God*[2]

> *I ponder on what it would be like to experience personal freedom. I have always lived and grown up in the free country of the United States of America, but I myself have never been emotionally independent from the crippling shackles which have held me bound.*
> —**Diana Kline,** *Woman Redeemed*[3]

Exmormons find it healing to tell the stories of how they lost their faith. LDS exit stories are all over the internet and in books. My story isn't terribly sensational or all that different from anyone else's. But you may be interested in knowing who I am, so you can understand why I care so much.

My grandmother was the first Mormon convert in our family. She had a strong testimony[4] but rarely went to church. My mother and father converted shortly after they married.

I was born "under the covenant" in Salt Lake City and raised in Eastern Washington. My parents were very active[5], and we rarely missed attending church.

I was an intelligent, bright, curious child. While I found many sacrament meetings[6] and Sunday school lessons repetitive and boring, I thrilled at exploring the mysteries, delving into the scriptures, speculating endlessly about open-ended questions: Where is Kolob[7]? How did Nephi[8] get across the ocean? Is there scriptural evidence of dinosaurs? I couldn't imagine a version of natural history or human existence that didn't conform to scripture.

My father is a talented scriptorian, and I was set to follow in his footsteps. I proudly

---

1. Margaret Thaler Singer. *Cults in Our Midst*. 1st ed. San Francisco: Jossey-Bass Publishers, 1995. 280.
2. Sam Keen. *Hymns to an Unknown God: Awakening the Spirit in Everyday Life*. New York: Bantam Books, 1995. 79.
3. Diana Kline. *Woman Redeemed*. Bloomington, Ind.: AuthorHouse, 2005. 169.
4. A member's testimony is the degree to which they believe, or "know," the gospel to be true. It may or may not include a collection of spiritual experiences, answers to prayer, or just a feeling or knowledge. Members often "bear a testimony," which means they state aloud that they know the Church is true, and why.
5. Members who regularly attend church, keep the commandments, and fulfill their callings are considered "active." Those who do not, to one degree or another, are considered "inactive" or "less active." There is a stigma around being inactive, and efforts are made at the ward level to reactivate members who have strayed. Some inactives miss church due to neglect, i.e. they are still believers but are too busy, discouraged, ill, disinterested, etc. Others are inactive because they no longer believe, but have not yet taken their names off Church records to rescind their membership.
6. Each Sunday, members meet for a three hour "block" of meetings. These include Sacrament meeting, during which the ordinance of Sacrament (like Catholic Communion) is administered, church business is conducted, and doctrinal talks are given by fellow members of the Church. Another hour goes to Sunday School, and another hour goes to auxiliary meetings (Relief Society for the women, Priesthood for the men, Young Men and Young Women for the youth, and Primary for the children). Lessons are also taught in these auxiliaries.
7. Kolob is said to be the planet or star on or near which God lives. Abraham 3:2-18
8. Nephi was a prophet and hero in the Book of Mormon. Nephi and his family (under the direction of his father, Lehi) left Jerusalem to come to the Americas to avoid being destroyed when Babylon invaded Israel around 600BC.

memorized the Articles of Faith and Scripture Mastery verses, graduated from Seminary[1], and read the Book of Mormon[2] three and a half times.

I also took to heart concepts like obedience and faithfulness. I prided myself on how little I murmured against my parents, and how unfalteringly I abided the rules of the Church. I wore my dresses knee-length, waited to date until age 16, and almost never listened to pop or rock music. I judged family members and peers who scoffed at the rules. Sometimes I failed to meet a commandment out of laziness or exhaustion, such as skipping church or missing scripture reading on a given day, but it was never out of disbelief or rebellion. I followed this worldview the way I followed the laws of the land.

I always thought I had critical thinking skills, but therein lies the trick—everyone wants to think they're rational. And if someone you trust tells you your beliefs are rational, you will think they are. And I did.

How quickly the proud do fall.

When I turned eighteen, I got accepted to BYU with a scholarship, met a guy, fell in love, converted him to the Church, and married him outside the temple with the plan to get sealed[3] a year later when he became eligible. We moved to Provo, I got pregnant, dropped out, moved back home, and just over a year after my marriage I kicked him out, filed for divorce, and became a single mom.

I found it very hard to judge anyone after that, when I learned how tough and scary the real world is, especially for the unprepared. It was my first major shift out of a totalist mindset as my views softened.

I raised my child alone (with the help of my parents) for many years. While seeking a suitable eternal companion in the young single adult[4] ward[5], I steadily built a career in the computer industry (frowned upon for women), with the hopes that any day, against all odds, I'd meet Brother Right. I had more than odds to beat: I had a stigma because I was divorced and had a child.

In community college, I found more acceptance among non-Mormons. They didn't just tolerate my idiosyncrasies; they admired me for who I was. I shared interests with the local science fiction club. I made close friends there, and we all allowed for each other's beliefs. I met my first pagans, agnostics, atheists, and even a Buddhist. Somehow we all got along. I felt as if I didn't have to try to be anyone for them.

During those years, I hardly had time to be active at church, with motherhood, work, and going to school, and I didn't fit in there anyway. I strayed a little. But I tried to at least attend meetings on Sunday and be in the choir.

At some point the guilt settled in, and I felt the need to get my life back on track. I had graduated and was well into my career; I still wasn't married. I blamed myself for that. I prayed hard for guidance to know what I should do. Would I find a husband? Should I move to a new town? Should I continue to work in the computer field?

During fervent, frequent, desperate prayer, I finally received an answer. It was one of those spiritual experiences I had read about, with warmth, love, feeling the presence of God. And a promise: Repent, get worthy for the temple, make those covenants, and there

---

1. All high school students are asked to attend Seminary, an hour-daily religion class. Over four years, each of the major scriptures are studied: The Old Testament, The New Testament, The Book of Mormon, and Church History (Doctrine & Covenants, etc.).
2. This is the main book of scripture that sets Mormons apart from other Christians. According to LDS doctrine, it is named after one of the prophets who wrote it. Joseph Smith translated it from golden plates that were revealed to him by an angel. It tells the story of God's people who came from Jerusalem to the Americas.
3. Being sealed to a family member or spouse means you will be with them forever, assuming you remain worthy and keep all your covenants with God.
4. Members who are not married, and are over the age of 18, and under the age of 25ish, are considered "young single adults." The goal of most young single adults is to get married as soon as possible. When there are enough young single adults in an area, they are separated into their own congregation.
5. An LDS congregation is called a "ward." It generally consists of around 300-600 members. Ward boundaries are determined geographically. Smaller congregations are called a "branch." A group of wards (and branches) is called a "stake," as in "the stakes of Zion."

you will receive your answer.

So I did. And it wasn't easy getting there. I had alot of high bars to reach, standards that had come much more easily to me as a teenager. I met each challenge until I got my temple recommend[1].

Finally, in the Celestial Room[2], I sobbed and sobbed. My mother wondered if I was okay. Yes, I was. I got the answer, plain as day: Within the month you will meet your soulmate, your future spouse.

I met a man, we dated. I was sure it was him. Then months later I learned he'd already been engaged, the whole time, to another woman. After all that work and sincerity on my part, God broke his promise.

I became angry. I wasn't willing to accept the blame this time. I'd done everything that was asked of me.

At no time did I question the truth of the Church. I searched for some message just as I was trained. Perhaps, I thought, by failing to give me a straight answer, God was telling me to figure things out on my own. It was the only possibility that made any sense. The other options—that God didn't exist or that Mormonism was wrong—were unthinkable.

Fine, I decided. I would make choices for myself. I took off my garments[3] and decided to take nothing for granted from then on. I decided to stop believing so blindly. I still looked to God and the Church for answers, but when no answers were forthcoming, or when they didn't make sense, I decided to rely upon myself.

That led to me deciding to drink caffeine to medicate my ADHD, instead of taking the stronger drug, Church-approved Ritalin. I also decided to drink alcohol at social gatherings, because it alleviated my social anxiety. I started watching R-rated movies. I began to hold some minor heretical beliefs—like maybe our actions in this life really didn't decide our eternal fate. Maybe other religions held just as much truth as Mormonism. Maybe the power of the Priesthood was no different from everyday miracles that happened to everyone the world over.

During that short phase, I had one shoe in and one shoe out.

No amount of direct attack could shake my faith. Criticisms of Joseph Smith and polygamy? No problem. Kinderhook plates and Salamander papers? Blood Atonement?[4] All of it sounded like a bunch of anti-Mormon propagandistic lies. I never doubted the Church. Yes, sometimes I doubted the existence of God, but if there was a God, I couldn't fathom one that wasn't Mormon. The Protestant God seemed empty and the Catholic God seemed cruel. I knew nothing of any non-Christian concept of God... but why would they be any more right than the Mormons? I never allowed myself to think too critically of the Church, even when I was so angry. For the most part, the mind control methods were doing their job.

My serious doubts came from an entirely different direction.

I encountered several destabilizing paradigm shifts in quick succession. Among other things, I participated in political debates in online chat rooms. This particular group of people required proof for all claims. I was expected to provide sources for facts, and as I researched, I quickly discovered some of my "facts" were entirely incorrect. They would tolerate no logical fallacies, anecdotal evidence, or proof by analogy. Only reason and reliable data was permitted.

---

1. A temple recommend is a pass that states you are worthy to attend the temple. No one is allowed into the temple without a recommend. It requires multiple worthiness interviews with Church leaders.
2. The Celestial Room is an especially elegant room in the temple. You arrive there at the end of Endowment Ceremony, which symbolizes passing through the veil that separates heaven and the temporal world. The Celestial Room is considered to be a piece of heaven, the holiest place on earth.
3. When a member goes through the temple to receive his or her endowment ordinance, they receive special sacred underwear known as "temple garments" or just "garments." They cover the entire body, from the shoulder to the knees, which prevents the wearing of immodest clothing. Endowed members are commanded to wear them "both day and night." They are meant as a reminder of covenants and a protection to the wearer. The protection is intended to be spiritual in nature, though miracle stories are told of physical protection. By removing my garments, I figuratively disavowed my covenant.
4. Jim Day, Ph.D. "20 Truths about Mormonism." Accessed April 2, 2014. http://20truths.info/

In short, I learned the logic in which I took so much pride was not, in fact, logical. I had propagated untruths and unevenly applied my values. I discovered for the first time that I was wrong about a great many things.

As I learned the new rules, I managed to win many of the debates, but in the meantime, I experienced the feeling of disillusionment. Perhaps for the first time, I realized the world outside the Garden wasn't as the Church had described.

During those months, I read part of a sci-fi novel that challenged my political beliefs so much that I had to put it down. I began to wonder what else I might be wrong about.

It was in this state that I got my answer to whether the Church was true. It came to me like a bolt of lightning, like a testimony, a powerful knowledge of Truth with a capital "T", with the same power I'd always imagined I'd feel when I prayed to know if the Book of Mormon was true. Like most of my profound, peak experiences and spiritual epiphanies, it happened when I wasn't doing anything at all related to the Church.

I am a science fiction writer. In my curiosity, I read about artificial intelligence, and how someday we might make a computer mind more intelligent than humanity, and how such a mind might create something even smarter, and so on, until it achieves infinite intelligence and invents everything we've ever imagined, and then a whole lot more. This is an entire field of thought called Transhumanism.

Many authors take a dark view of this "Technological Singularity" in stories like *The Terminator* and *The Matrix*. But I am optimistic. A super-intelligent computer wouldn't necessarily be evil.

I came to many conclusions about the nature of this being—about how incomprehensible and unknowable such a creature would be. It would have purposes and designs far beyond our ken. It would pursue goals we couldn't fathom. No human could understand or predict its actions. I concluded that such a being would probably find us uninteresting and leave us alone.

I wrote my many complex thoughts in an essay[1], and only then did I make the connection.

The being I had described was identical to God.

In one instant, I came to realize that no man can know God. And that any man who made such a claim with certainty was lying. Even if God sent angels bearing messages to communicate his will, it would be interpreted through a human lens, muddied and distorted.

That didn't stop human prophets from trying. Their messages were simplistic, and the motives they ascribed to God were overly human. He's a Father, he's caring, he's jealous or angry. They claimed to know his will as if he were a giant, powerful human being in the sky.

We had assigned human motives to God. We had made God in *our* image.

How full of ourselves we are, to bring God to our level.

In that instant, I could no longer believe that Joseph Smith was a prophet. Nor could I believe that any other prophet had the slightest clue. All written scripture became worthless to me.

I became, in that moment, agnostic.

Yet I still doubted myself. I could be wrong. I could be confused. I could be deceived.

I decided to give it some time, to see if any new insights cleared things up. I avoided any kind of commitment to my new path. I prayed, but how could my prayers have any meaning after such an epiphany? If God's will is incomprehensible, praying for answers would attempt to put God in my tiny genie bottle, like a slave.

After three months, I had not changed my mind. No revelations came. Nothing could consolidate the gospel with this new, undeniable belief.

So I made the final leap. I knew if I did, I never would return. I haven't. That was January 2001. I was twenty-six. I resigned my membership three years later.

---

1. Luna Lindsey, writing as Becky Flesher. "Singularity and Why It Won't Be As Bad As All That," Fall 2000. http://users.owt.com/flesher/singularity.html

I might have left it at that. But in 2005, a friend of mine was living with a woman who claimed to have been raised in a small cult run by her abusive father. One day, this woman asked me if I'd been "deprogrammed" from Mormonism. Shocked, I told her, No, I didn't need deprogramming. I'd gone though the process of developing new beliefs and a foundation of values to live by. I was fine.

Over time, I thought more about it. Perhaps she was onto something. After all, in spite of therapy and self-help and journaling, I still had certain hang-ups I never seemed to get over. Maybe they had something to do with my unresolved feelings from Mormonism.

So I started reading about cults and mind control. I began interacting with exmormons and learning the hidden details about LDS history and the bad experiences of many members. I encountered angry people, hurt people, and depressed people. Without my Mormon blinders on, I could hear their stories without instant dismissal and judgment.

I came to see that I, too, bore a burden of unprocessed grief and toxic beliefs. I began to deprogram myself.

I didn't realize just how much fear I lived under until this phase. Fear of disaster, fear of the apocalypse, fear of Satan, fear of evil spirits, fear of sinning, fear of The World, etc. I began to work through them, and the anger, and the sense of betrayal. And the grief for all that wasted time, two and a half decades of my life, and thousands of dollars in tithing.

Ironically, the woman who suggested deprogramming ran a small cult herself. My friend eventually left her group and stayed at my house to piece her life back together. While she did, she benefited from my research.

In writing this book, I hope to help others the way I helped her and myself.

## The Illusion of Choice

*Once aware that their prey is bagged, the slickest operators then emphasize the victim's freedom of choice—after tactfully putting constraints on the alternatives.*
—**Philip Zimbardo, Ph.D. & Susan Andersen, Ph.D.,**
***Recovery from Cults***[1]

*I'm going to give you the choice I never had...*
—**Lestat,** *Interview with a Vampire*

My dad was an amateur illusionist, so I grew up knowing the fundamentals of stage magic. Once you learn a trick's secret, it's hard to not see it, no matter who performs it. It's also hard to not share it with others.

"Misdirection" is an illusionist technique used to distract the audience's eye away from sleight-of-hand or to alter assumptions that might otherwise dispel the illusion.

At what point in my life was I choosing to follow the commandments? When I was five and I bore my testimony after all the adults "encouraged" me? When I made myself wake up at 5:30am every winter morning to walk to Seminary in the bitter wind? When I went against my parents' wishes to rush into a marriage they didn't approve of, but that I thought God approved of? Or when I divorced him, which I also thought God wanted?

Was it when I followed what I earnestly thought was God's express will to go to the temple, where, without warning, I swore to give all I had to the Church, in exchange for promises that never materialized?

Or when I decided to finally leave it all?

One key to Mormon mind control is the illusion that you are freely choosing to believe and act. "Wherefore, men are free according to the flesh; and all things are given them

---

[1] Philip Zimbardo, Ph.D., and Susan Andersen, Ph.D. "Understanding Mind Control: Exotic and Mundane Mental Manipulations." In *Recovery from Cults: Help for Victims of Psychological and Spiritual Abuse*, edited by Michael D. Langone, Ph.D. New York: W.W. Norton, 1995. 115.

which are expedient unto man..." 2 Nephi 2:27

Freedom. We all want that. It sounds great, right? The promise of freedom is the perfect misdirection.

Steven Hassan, exit counselor and the author of several books on cults says, "With mind control, the 'agents of influence' are viewed as friends or mentors, which cause people to lower their defenses, making them more vulnerable to manipulation. The key to mind control's success lies in its subtlety, the way it promotes the 'illusion of control.' The individual believes he is 'making his own choices,' when in fact he has been socially influenced to disconnect his own critical mind and decision-making capacity... he believes that he has freely chosen to surrender his free will to God or to a leader or ideology."[1]

Not only does this deception give the Church plausible deniability (they're not forcing anyone) but it also traps members far more powerfully than physical bonds ever could. The captive becomes the most vocal defender of the captor.

My dad performed an illusion where he would "cut" a banana with a magic hacksaw that had no blade. He let the audience choose a banana from a bunch, then he dramatically sliced the unpeeled banana to no apparent effect. As he peeled it, the audience gasped in amazement when the pieces, one by one, fell away.

As his assistant, I got to know how the trick worked. Slicing the banana was the easy part. Before the show, with a banana still attached to the bunch, he would carefully pre-slice the banana using a needle and thread.

The difficult part of the trick lay in the misdirection. How do you keep the audience from suspecting you've tampered with the banana? By making a big show of letting them "choose."

In reality, he tricked them into selecting the right banana. He didn't give them an open-ended decision. Instead, he broke the bunch in two, held each up, singled out a random child, and said, "Pick one."

The child pointed a finger, left or right, but my dad actually drove the outcome. You see, he never specified the nature of the choice: Is this the bunch to keep, or the one to discard? My dad kept that under his control the entire time.

No matter which they picked, he kept the bunch with the tampered banana. Then he would break that half in half again, and call on someone else. No matter which they pointed at, he kept the bunch *he* wanted, until he was down to the last banana.

Meanwhile, the kids thought they had chosen. They had the *illusion* of choice.

"Cult leaders tell their followers, 'You have chosen to be here. No one has told you to come here. No one has influenced you,' when in fact the followers are in a situation they can't leave owing to social pressure and their fear. Thus they come to believe that they are actually choosing this life. If outsiders hint that the devotees have been brainwashed or tricked, the members say, 'Oh, no, I chose voluntarily.' Cults thrive on this myth of voluntarism, insisting time and again that no member is being held against his or her will."[2]

The Church frequently forces your hand by offering you choices while controlling the terms, much like the banana trick. For instance, we're told to never blindly trust the prophet. Instead, we're supposed to pray to verify for ourselves that the prophet is inspired.

But who defines these rules? It happens to be the prophet. He doesn't suggest the option of looking for the answers from a neutral source. Instead, he sends members to Church-approved sources and to the easily-manipulated emotional confirmation of prayer.

For so long I believed in the illusion that I could question the prophet. All along I accepted the premise that the prophet is inspired, God is real and inspires prophets, and prayer is the only way to verify prophetic pronouncements. The false choice was between "blind trust" and "trust after following the prophet's own instructions for how to verify his words."

---

1. Steven Hassan. *Releasing the Bonds: Empowering People to Think for Themselves.* 1st ed. Somerville, MA: Freedom of Mind Press, 2000. 40.
2. Singer, *Cults in Our Midst*, 1995. 72-73.

"Men are free to choose." Here's the catch. The rest of 2 Nephi 2:27 says: "And they are free to choose liberty and eternal life, through the great Mediator of all men, or to choose captivity and death, according to the captivity and power of the devil; for he seeketh that all men might be miserable like unto himself."

The bananas on the right or the bananas on the left?

Our choices are limited to two, and we are corralled into making the preordained one. Passages like these shut down the mind. No one wants to be evil. Everyone is afraid of death and misery. All people are attracted to goodness, happiness, and life. If these are presented as diametrically opposed choices, every middle option flees from our minds. We never think to bring our own banana to the magic show.

There are other, realistic, moral options, borrowed from other philosophies, such as:

- "An it harm none, do what ye will."
- "All things in moderation."
- "Acceptance of suffering helps end suffering."
- "Nothing is true for everyone. Take what works and leave the rest."
- "There is joy in asking the questions, even when there are no answers."
- "You're smart. Do your best to figure it out."
- "Don't sweat the small stuff. It's all small stuff."

There are dozens of different solutions to every problem. You can choose the right... or left, forward, backward, up, down, sideways, and every angle in between. Turning left gives you different scenery, not eternal death.

Freedom does come with responsibility. Consequences exist, although they might not be punishments or blessings from God. When you aren't automatically exalting or damning yourself for simple actions that non-Mormons make every day, you are free to research the facts leading to the full spectrum of possible risks and rewards.

"Mistakes" need not carry with them the heavy weight of "eternal", "evil", "wrong", "weak", "sinful", "unworthy." These labels lead to manufactured consequences like shame, the loss of blessings, lost favor from God, and spiritual death.

Is it any wonder many Mormons fear decision-making? If it's not as clear-cut as scriptures and Sunday School lead you to expect, it's hard to know what to do. When decisions seem two-dimensional, good or evil, there is pressure, an unnamed fear, as if letting go for just a moment will ruin some preordained destiny.

There are good reasons for this fear. In General Conference[1], Apostle Dallin H. Oaks said, "In terms of priorities for each major decision (such as education, occupation, place of residence, marriage, or childbearing), we should ask ourselves, what will be the eternal impact of this decision? Some decisions that seem desirable for mortality have unacceptable risks for eternity. In all such choices we need to have inspired priorities and apply them in ways that will bring eternal blessings to us and to our family members."[2]

The pressure is on and we feel like we ought to just know all the answers: "He hath given unto you that ye might know good from evil, and he hath given unto you that ye might choose life or death; and ye can do good and be restored unto that which is good, or have that which is good restored unto you; or ye can do evil, and have that which is evil restored unto you." Helaman 14:31

We are given these choices, but then we are corralled into choosing the tampered

---

1. Two weekends each year, all Mormons gather to watch or listen to General Conference. Some go to Salt Lake City to see it live; others go to their local church where it is streamed, or watch it online or on TV. General Conference consists of four sessions (2 hours each), plus one session specifically for men, and another just for women. Conference talks are given by the highest leaders in the Church, usually general authorities, apostles, and the prophet. Also twice a year, each stake gives its own conference called "Stake Conference." The contents of all General Conferences going back 30 years are available on the LDS.org website.
2. Dallin H. Oaks. "Focus and Priorities." In LDS General Conference, April 2011. http://www.lds.org/general-conference/2001/04/focus-and-priorities

banana. And when we don't automatically know the right answer, we feel unworthy.

These are just a few aspects of the complex web of mind control used to limit choice under the illusion of agency.

As an apostle, future prophet Howard W. Hunter, said, "To fully understand this gift of agency and its inestimable worth, it is imperative that we understand that God's chief way of acting is by persuasion and patience and long-suffering, not by coercion and stark confrontation. He acts by gentle solicitation and by sweet enticement. He always acts with unfailing respect for the freedom and independence that we possess. He wants to help us and pleads for the chance to assist us, but he will not do so in violation of our agency."[1]

These are admirable goals and complete deceptions. The Church's methods, while patient and long-suffering, are in fact choice-limiting, coercive, and in violation of free agency. The suppression of "stark confrontation" inhibits the free flow of opposing ideas and open debate, from which comes true freedom of thought.

There must be opposition in all things, including in free thought. Adam and Eve had to eat from the Tree of Knowledge before they could have agency. Yet a faithful Mormon is expected to be persuaded in a vacuum, casting aside all "contentious" debate, shelving serious doubts and questions, and shunning naysayers.

You cannot freely choose without considering all options. You cannot opt to believe when you cannot hear all the pros and cons. You cannot exercise agency while being prohibited from open deliberation. You cannot stave off fraud when you have been discouraged from researching alternate sources. And you cannot openly explore faith when you have been instructed to repress every doubt.

There's an exit sign hanging over the gate to Eden. Will you take it?

---

1. Howard W. Hunter. "The Golden Thread of Choice." In LDS General Conference, Oct 1989.

*I teach them correct principles, and they govern themselves.*
—**Prophet Joseph Smith**[1]

*I realized that the lies that had long preserved my false beliefs were the lies that I told to myself. I awoke to the fact that I am the master of my own deceit.*
—**Brad L. Morin, Suddenly Strangers**[2]

*Our culture had trapped us... Many Latter-day Saints lived in mental and social prisons that perpetuated precisely the kind of insanity with which I'd grown up. It wasn't slavery, but it was a powerful form of bondage: the belief that God had ordained a pattern of secrets and silence, that religious authority always trumped one's individual sense of right and wrong, that the evidence of the senses must bow to the demands of orthodoxy, no matter how insane. It was a kind of institutionalized madness, and its shackles were all the more confining for existing almost entirely in the human mind.*
—**Martha Beck, Leaving the Saints**[3]

*When finally you surrender to us, it must be of your own free will. We do not destroy the heretic because he resists us... We convert him, we capture his inner mind, we reshape him. We burn all evil and all illusion out of him; we bring him over to our side, not in appearance, but genuinely, heart and soul.*
—**George Orwell, 1984**

# What is Mind Control?

The terms "cult" and "mind control" are charged, full of assumption and emotion. How can we tell the difference between honest persuasion and manipulative exploitation?

Mind control is known by many names: brainwashing, coercive persuasion, thought reform, uninformed consent, exploitive persuasion, sociopsychological manipulation, exploitative manipulation, behavioral change technology, compliance-gaining influence, unhealthy group dynamics, and spiritual abuse.

Cults are also known as closed systems of logic, authoritarian structures, coercive organizations, high-demand groups, and ideological or psychological totalism.

If you were brainwashed, would you know it?

Author and former Moonie, Steven Hassan wrote, "I can't tell you how many times I've been on a talk show where the host asks a cult member, 'Are you brainwashed?' The cult member replies, 'No, of course not.' As if the cult member would actually say, 'Yes!' What the host fails to realize is that the mind-controlled member will not know that he has surrendered control until he is able to step away from the group and learn about cult recruitment and indoctrination."[4]

A former member of International Society of Divine Love, Joe Kelly, describes his experience: "It was easy to see how Maharishi, Swami Prabhupada, and Reverend Moon had duped and controlled their followers, but my Swami was different... I told myself that

---

1. *Journal of Discourses*. Vol. 10. Privately Printed, n.d. http://jod.mrm.org/1. 57-58.
2. Brad L. Morin, and Chris L. Morin. *Suddenly Strangers: Surrendering Gods and Heroes*. Chula Vista, CA: Aventine Press, 2004. 30.
3. Martha Nibley Beck. *Leaving the Saints: How I Lost the Mormons and Found My Faith*. 1st ed. New York: Crown Publishers, 2005. 239.
4. Hassan, *Releasing the Bonds,* 2000. 86.

we were a legitimate alternative religion."[1] In 2011, his leader, Prakashanand Saraswati, was convicted of 20 counts of child sexual abuse. Clearly, his Swami was not different.[2] Any Mormon reading about the Society of Divine Love would be quick to call it a cult. But he will probably have a hard time seeing his own subservience to a manipulative system.

Margaret Singer stated, "Brainwashing is not experienced as a fever or a pain might be; it is an invisible social adaptation. When you are the subject of it, you are not aware of the intent of the influence processes that are going on, and especially, you are not aware of the changes taking place within you...

"Thus, thought reform is a concerted effort to change a person's way of looking at the world, which will change his or her behavior."[3]

Another cult researcher, Geri-Ann Galanti, observes, "[Thought reform methods] are not easily recognized because they are techniques utilized by all cultures—directly and indirectly—to socialize children and acculturate immigrants...

"These techniques are used in socialization precisely because they are extremely powerful. They appear innocent, but when put to deceptive ends, they are no less potent.

"The confusion surrounding the brainwashing process stems from the fact that most people are looking for something overt and foreign... I went to Camp K [Moonies recruitment event] looking for something big and evil; what I found was very subtle and friendly, thus I didn't recognize its power."[4]

While the lines are sometimes blurry, ethical forms of influence include most kinds of therapy, education, mainstream religions, the military, and politics. When I visit my therapist, we both have the same goal. I give her money, and she listens to me and offers validation and, sometimes, good advice. The outcome is that usually I feel better and can manage my problems more effectively. The cost of the interaction is clearly stated up front, and she doesn't try to get anything else out of me. If I don't like the outcome, I am free to stop sessions at any time. I have no fear of doing so, and she won't try to keep me.

Even the military, which clearly uses brainwashing methods, is open about their goals. We all know military recruits will be programmed to unquestioningly follow orders so they can kill people and break things. This training occurs under very strenuous conditions where individual wills are broken down and new personalities are built up. Some may debate whether this is useful or not, or whether war is ethical, but military training methods are no secret.

Advertising is considered by some to be a form of coercive persuasion. Marketers take advantage of the mild trance state that comes from watching TV, and they associate unrelated positive imagery with the product. Advertisers will also often exaggerate to make their product seem more desirable.

These types of persuasive tricks, on their own, are not terribly effective at producing long-term loyalty. Laws are designed to prevent outright lies, so many companies are more or less honest. It's pretty easy to check claims against product reviews. And the mistake of buying an ineffective brand of laundry detergent costs only a few dollars.

In contrast, a high-demand group will pull all the stops to recruit and retain lifelong members. These groups use a legion of persuasive techniques in unison, techniques that strip away the personality to build up a group pseudopersonality. New members know very little about the group's purpose, and most expectations remain unrevealed. People become deeply involved, sacrificing vast amounts of time and money, and investing emotionally, spiritually, psychologically, and socially. Escape proves to be very difficult, and former members face a struggle to regain a sense of sanity.

In one sense, then, the line can be drawn at how totalistic the system is. Does it

---

1. Madeleine Landau Tobias, and Janja Lalich. *Captive Hearts, Captive Minds: Freedom and Recovery from Cults and Abusive Relationships*. Alameda, CA: Hunter House, 1994. 88.
2. "Hindu Guru Found Guilty on 20 Counts of Molesting Young Girls." *Austin-American Statesman*, March 4, 2011. http://www.statesman.com/news/news/local/hindu-guru-found-guilty-on-20-counts-of-molestin-1/nRX5s/
3. Singer, *Cults in Our Midst*, 1995. 61-62.
4. Geri-Ann Galanti, Ph.D. "Reflections on 'Brainwashing.'" *Recovery from Cults*, ed. Michael D. Langone, 1995. 101-102.

permeate every aspect of life and self? Hassan says, "...as employed by the most destructive cults, mind control seeks nothing less than to disrupt an individual's authentic identity—behavior, thoughts, emotions—and reconstruct it in the image of the cult leader [or group]... Cult mind control is a social process that encourages obedience, dependence, and conformity. It discourages autonomy and individuality by immersing recruits in an environment that represses free choice. The group's dogma becomes the person's only concern. Anything or anyone that does not fit into his reshaped reality is irrelevant."[1]

By contrast, "In a benevolent group, influence processes are positive and ethical and the locus of control remains within the individual. Influence is used only to promote independent thinking and decision-making, self-awareness, and self-control. Individuality, creativity, and free will are respected and promoted. People recognize and understand the influences around them. Access to diverse information sources is encouraged."[2]

Another author, therapist, and former cult member, John D. Goldhammer says, "Certainly many groups are helpful and constructive forces in society...*provided they maintain a balance of power between individual autonomy and the group.*"[3] Is the individual on equal footing with the group itself? Or is the ideology more important than the member?

As Galanti explains, "All forms of influence are not the same. Langone, for example, discusses a continuum of influence, ranging from choice-respecting influence (educative, advisory, and certain types of persuasion) to compliance-gaining influence... Although definitions of what is therapeutic vs. what is destructive will vary according to personal biases—for example, cult members would surely argue that what they do is for the benefit of the members—a strong case can be made that cults largely utilize indirect and deceptive techniques of persuasion and control to serve the interests of the leaders rather than those of the members."[4]

Informed consent is key here and separates unethical types of persuasion from the ethical. Persuasion comes from friends, family, corporations, politicians, religions, scientists, authors, and activists. The real question is: Are we being persuaded by facts, reason, research, and open access to information, or by manipulation and deception?

Consent through fraud is not consent at all. Hassan said, "Many cult leaders believe that it is necessary for them to practice deceptive recruitment and mind control techniques for ideological reasons. But if the effect of their actions is to make the person dependent and subservient, then I believe it is hurtful and people's rights are being violated."[5]

Mind control is as much about teaching members to control themselves as it is about exertion of external controls. I call this the "inner thought police."

Apostle Erastus Snow told this story about Joseph Smith: "...a certain lawyer...who came to see him...expressed astonishment and surprise at the ease with which he controlled the people, and said it was something that was not to be found among the learned men of the world. Said he: 'We cannot do it. What is the secret of your success?' 'Why,' said the Prophet, 'I do not govern the people. I teach them correct principles and they govern themselves.'"[6]

External constraints translate into self-suppression which leads to a totalist system blocking all avenues of escape. One member of a New Age spiritual cult described his internal struggle: "These images haunted my mind because I was starting to have thoughts of leaving. It was strange how charged these thoughts to leave were... The avalanche of consequences in my mind were unthinkable. My will to move on them was easily and quickly drowned in a sea of guilt, self-condemnation, and fear of hell. To leave was like walking off a cliff into a hellish abyss. I had to hide these thoughts not only from the other

---

1. Hassan, *Releasing the Bonds,* 2000. 38.
2. Hassan, *Releasing the Bonds,* 2000. 55.
3. John D. Goldhammer. *Under the Influence.* First Edition. Prometheus Books, 1996. 18.
4. Galanti, "Reflections on 'Brainwashing,'" *Recovery from Cults,* ed. Langone, 1995. 86.
5. Hassan, *Releasing the Bonds,* 2000. xx.
6. *Journal of Discourses.* Vol. 24. Privately Printed, n.d. http://jod.mrm.org/1 159 .

members, but from myself and God."[1]

Hassan observes, "What makes this all so insidious is that members often speak and act with the greatest sincerity because they have been subjected to the same mind control techniques that they use to recruit others."[2]

## What is a Cult?

Michael Langone, Ph.D., is a psychologist specializing in cult research. He is the director of the International Cultic Studies Association, and editor of *Cultic Studies Review*, a scientific journal. In the introduction to *Recovery from Cults*, he writes:

> A cult is a group or movement that, to a significant degree, (a) exhibits great or excessive devotion or dedication to some person, idea, or thing, (b) uses a thought-reform program to persuade, control, and socialize members (i.e., to integrate them into the group's unique pattern of relationships, beliefs, values, and practices), (c) systematically induces states of psychological dependency in members, (d) exploits members to advance the leadership's goals, and (e) causes psychological harm to members, their families, and the community.[3]

That may be hard to swallow all at once, but all these points will be addressed throughout these pages.

The defining characteristics can also be thought of in terms of isolation. To one extent or another, high demand groups isolate members, either physically or mentally, from the rest of society. "In order to manage [the conflicts between the group and society], cultic groups tend to become isolated, psychologically if not physically, governed by hidden agendas, and totalistic, that is, they will dictate, sometimes with excruciating specificity, how members should think, feel, and act."[4]

This brings to mind cult compounds, like the Branch Davidians in Waco, TX. Yet modern cults often try to fit into the mainstream as best they can. Most cults like to attract new members, and it helps to put on a good front.

"...the majority of cults today are not as isolated from the outside world as were cults in the 1970s... Typically believers continue working at their pre-cult jobs and more often tend to remain in contact with family and friends, even though this contact becomes more strained as the cult member's behavior, attitudes, and language begin to change."[5]

Many dysfunctional families display the same dynamics we see in larger groups, and often, thought-control methods are used in abusive homes. "Since the upsurge of both public and professional interest in the issue of domestic violence, there has been some recognition of the link between mind control and battering. Men or women who batter their partners sometimes use manipulative techniques similar to those found in cults. The most common include 'isolation and the provocation of fear; alternating kindness and threat to produce disequilibrium; the induction of guilt, self-blame, dependency, and learned helplessness.'... The similarities between cultic devotion and the traumatic bonding that occurs between battered individuals and their abusers are striking."[6]

Those more interested in how one-on-one relationships can employ mind control techniques can read *Captive Hearts, Captive Minds* by Madeleine Tobias and Janja Lalich, as it covers this issue more in depth. This may be of particular interest to Mormons who have also been in abusive relationships and were controlled not only by the Church, but also

---

1. Steve Sanchez. *Spiritual Perversion*. Austin, TX: Turn Key Press, 2005. 211.
2. Hassan, *Releasing the Bonds,* 2000. 4.
3. Michael D. Langone, Ph.D., ed. "Introduction." In *Recovery from Cults: Help for Victims of Psychological and Spiritual Abuse*. New York: W.W. Norton, 1995. 5.
4. Langone, "Introduction," *Recovery from Cults,* 1995. 5.
5. Lorna Goldberg, M.S.W., A.C.S.W. "Guidelines for Therapists." *Recovery from Cults,* ed. Langone, 1995. 236.
6. Tobias and Lalich, *Captive Hearts, Captive Minds*, 1994. 17-18.

by their spouse, who may have used LDS doctrine to enforce control. This will cause multiple layers of issues that will require special care to unravel.

## Myths of Cults & Mind Control

> *Unfortunately, our stereotypical misconceptions about the nature of brainwashing prevent us from recognizing it.*
> —**Geri-Ann Calanti, Ph.D.,**
> *Recovery from Cults*[1]

When discussing cults, it is important to dispel the biggest myths perpetuated by society. By looking at what a cult is *not*, we learn what a cult *is*.

Steven Hassan reveals, "When I was in the Moon cult [aka The Moonies], my friends and family told me time and time again that I had been 'brainwashed,' or that I was under 'mind control.' At the time, I thought 'mind control' meant being handcuffed, tortured, and interrogated under bright lights, and I knew that hadn't happened to me. So, when people called me a 'brainwashed robot,' I thought they were just persecuting me for my beliefs, and their negative comments wound up reinforcing my commitment to the group. Like any member of a destructive cult, I needed to learn what mind control really is, and how it is used, before I could understand that I had been subjected to it."[2]

> **Myth: Cults are weird or obvious. Cultists dress funny, talk funny, and have blissed-out, glassy stares.**

Media coverage exposes the most extreme cases and TV-ready images, so we tend to think all such groups are strange and easy to identify.

The most obvious example is Jonestown, where 912 men, women, and children were convinced to drink cyanide-laced Flavor-Aid. Another example is Heaven's Gate, where 39 members committed suicide, believing they were catching a passing space ship. The Branch Davidians were killed in a standoff with FBI agents in Waco, TX, while defending their beliefs and their prophet, David Koresh. Members of Aum Shinrikyo (now Aleph) in Japan are known for setting off a sarin gas bomb in a busy subway, killing 13 people and injuring 5,000.

The Unification Church, aka The Moonies, became known in the 1980s for its mass weddings. Eastern meditation groups, like Transcendental Meditation, often practice long hours of meditation, causing their members to appear "tranced-out." New Age and UFO cults often have unusual beliefs, which makes it easy to single them out for public scrutiny. A group based on Hindu beliefs, Hare Krishna (ISKCON), made the news in 1983 when the parents of a follower were awarded damages for falsely imprisoning and brainwashing their minor daughter.

To believe that all cultic groups fall into these sensational extremes is a dangerous fallacy. More often, successful groups blend into society by appearing mainstream, friendly, and normal. They project a positive image of strong moral values.

The most successful cults are the most subtle.

> **Myth: Brainwashing involves physical restraint, hypnotic wheels, flashing images, and a swinging lamp.**

---

1. Galanti, "Reflections on 'Brainwashing,'" *Recovery from Cults,* ed. Langone, 1995. 87.
2. Hassan, *Releasing the Bonds,* 2000. 33.

These images come from movie and TV writers who need dramatic imagery to keep us entertained. All those special effects would likely be counterproductive. Real-life mind control is not that exciting.

The term "brainwashing" comes from a Chinese word that literally translates to "cleanse brain." After the Korean War, some POWs returned sympathetic to the views of their captors and some did not. Those held by the Koreans had been tortured and starved, but did not show signs of sympathy for their captors. In contrast, those held by the Chinese allies had been treated much better, and this proved to be a far more effective indoctrination and interrogation tool.

The science shows we are much more likely to change our minds for those we like. Restraint devices are likely to scare people off. Those who wish to control must first earn trust.

Manipulators start by creating good feelings and positive opinions about the group. Potential recruits already agree with at least a few of the beliefs, so they slowly change some behaviors under slight social pressure. Over time, the will to use critical reasoning on doctrinal and group matters is stripped away. Misdeeds lead to shame, which is offset at other times by praise and elitism. Public commitments create deepening belief and dependence.

By this time, cult members have come to believe that their lives, identities, moral principles, and possibly their very souls are in danger if they do not obey and believe. This is enough to trap a person. No interrogation rooms or torture chambers are necessary.

> **Myth: Brainwashing requires hypnosis.**

Brainwashing does not require hypnosis. People are ready and willing to believe a good sales pitch without going into a trance.

And trances aren't all that mystical. It is very natural for the human brain to change states of consciousness. It does not require drugs, meditation, chanting, or swinging pocket watches.

Our mind is capable of tuning out unimportant or repetitive information so we can focus on more relevant cognitive tasks. We are in an altered state when we fall asleep and when we dream. We are prone to changing states when we read, learn, concentrate, watch TV, listen to music, drive, and create. Sometimes the conscious side of the brain wants to shut down for a little while and we "space out." We can become so involved in a story or focused on learning that we lose all awareness of the outside world. Music and creative activities can shift us into the right brain, which controls emotional, visual, and sensing functions, and makes us less critical.

Human beings are quite comfortable with most altered states because we experience them every day. It doesn't take much for a manipulator to subtly switch a person to a more emotional state, or cause someone to become absorbed in a story. While in these states, we're not at the total mercy of a would-be brainwasher, but we are more easily influenced, especially if the manipulator is someone we trust.

> **Myth: Only stupid, needy, mentally ill, uneducated, or spiritually weak people join cults.**

Anyone is susceptible to coercive persuasion. Not every group may be able to lure you in, nor are you always susceptible. But there are cultic groups that would appeal to you at the right time in your life.

Many cults target people who are in an unstable period. When someone is going through difficult times, normal defenses are down, and people are more open to deception and persuasive techniques. If someone offers hope, friendship, comfort, or answers to burning questions, people are more accepting of inspirational messages.

Teenagers and college-age adults are at the highest risk, because they are in transition and are seeking belonging and identity.

Cult followers are typically of above-average intelligence. Complex belief systems attract brilliant people, especially those who are driven to find meaning.

Hassan observes, "Most of the former cult members I have met are exceptionally bright and educated. They have an active imagination and a creative mind. They have a capacity to focus their attention and enter deep states of concentration. Most are idealistic and socially conscious. They want to make the most of themselves—and to make a positive contribution to the world...

"The more creative a mind a person has, the more his imagination can be used to control him. Indeed, bright people sometimes have even more sophisticated fantasies about the group and its doctrine than does the cult leader."[1]

### Myth: All cults are religious in nature.

A totalistic system can be built around any subject.

Researchers generally recognize four main categories of cults: Religious, political, self-improvement and large group awareness training (LGATs), and commercial cults.[2] The specific beliefs or dogmas of the group don't matter, because thought-reform methods can be built up around any subject. Generally cults appeal to the values of society, like peace and love, equality, God, money, personal growth, and political change.

Some political parties and activist groups are manipulative and deceptive. Some legitimate businesses are controlling of employees, as are many multi-level marketing groups. Any topic for which people are willing to organize is fair game.

### Myth: A cult is any pseudo-Christian or non-Christian faith.

Many people define cults as religious groups that are not Christian or include doctrines that are not in line with their interpretation of the Bible. Some believe any non-Christian religion is a cult.

This definition is not used by secular researchers who have studied cults with a scientific eye. It is doctrine-based and does not explain anything about the mechanisms of mind control or how it is psychologically and materially harmful to people. It assumes that one brand of biblical interpretation is more valid than another. It assumes all Protestant sects are completely free of manipulation and exploitation. These are inaccurate assumptions.

Mind control is not about the untruthfulness or strangeness of doctrines.

"From our perspective, a group or relationship earns the label 'cult' or 'cultic' on the basis of its methods and behaviors, *not* on the basis of its beliefs... *It is not the beliefs that we oppose, but the exploitative manipulation of a person's faith and trust in other human beings.*"[3]

### Myth: "Cult" means the same thing as "occult."

These words sound the same, but they do not mean the same thing, nor do they even have the same origin.

"Cult" can sometimes refer to any religion or set of beliefs. It comes from the Latin word for "worship", and we also find it in the words "culture" and "cultivate."

---

1. Hassan, *Releasing the Bonds,* 2000. 120.
2. Hassan, *Releasing the Bonds,* 2000. 5.
3. Tobias and Lalich, *Captive Hearts, Captive Minds,* 1994. 5.

Occult also comes from Latin, "occultus", meaning "hidden, concealed, secret." It refers to pagan forms of worship, magic, and divination. For many years, these activities were kept hidden from controlling religious bodies, and hence, the association to "that which is concealed."

Some Christians and those who believe these activities to be inherently evil will tend to associate the occult *and* cults with Satanism.

A study of the psychological effects of group manipulation has nothing to do with whether or not the group is Christian or related to the occult.

> **Myth: People can easily leave a cult whenever they want. No one is forcing them to be there.**

You wouldn't light yourself on fire, would you? Or drive your car into a wall, or cut off your arm, right? You are free to do these things, but probably don't out of fear.

Likewise, cult members believe they face real dangers if they leave, and this fear keeps them bound. Cultists may fear spiritual punishment, assault by spiritual forces (demons, evil spirits, God), financial failure, loss of friends and family, loss of support, loss of salvation, and loss of purpose. Sometimes cult members may even fear physical violence from fellow members.

Members may also be emotionally, financially, or psychologically dependent upon the group or leader. Some groups work to break down individuality and self-reliance, sometimes even regressing them to a childlike state.

Those who think about leaving face very real problems.

> **Myth: People who have left cults should just get over it.**

Unfortunately, it is not so simple. Former cultists had their entire lives, minds, and personalities deeply invested in a deceptive organization. Many former members suffer from psychological and even situational difficulties that will take time and effort to overcome. Some of these problems can include anxiety, depression, guilt, anger, eating disorders, panic attacks, indecisiveness, difficulty integrating into society, post-traumatic stress, recovery from physical and sexual abuse, inability to trust, sexual problems, confusion and disorientation, "floating" and dissociation, and lingering phobias.

Some former members suffer material loss for leaving, and may have left behind family and friends, which prevents closure.

> **Myth: Brainwashing is total. If some members are able to disagree, or if someone has left the group, that's proof they were never really brainwashed.**

No brainwashing method has ever been found to be total and complete. Abraham Lincoln said, "You can fool some of the people all the time, or all the people some of the time, but you cannot fool all the people all the time."

No matter how strong the methods, some members will eventually see through to the deceptions or become too miserable to stay.

*I was a wreck of stress. I kept going through the motions of my life, going to work, going home, going to the [SLF] school, going to work again. I tried to be positive, like I was okay, like I wasn't distressed by it all, like I knew what I was doing.*
—Steve Sanchez, ***Spiritual Perversion***[1]

*Partly because it was so much easier than feeling anything, and partly because I wanted desperately to please my father, I spent my early years almost completely oblivious to my own psychological state.*
—Martha Beck, ***Leaving the Saints***[2]

*Your worst enemy...was your own nervous system. At any moment the tension inside you was liable to translate itself into some visible symptom.*
—George Orwell, ***1984***

# All Is Not Well in Zion

Another ancient dystopian story is Plato's *Allegory of the Cave*. Like the Garden story, it depicts captivity, though in not such pleasant terms.

A group of prisoners are locked deep in a cave, chained to kneel before a wall lit by an unseen fire behind them. They can only see the shadows of figures moving in front of the fire. They have known no other life nor seen sights other than the shadow play before them.

One man is released. Now he can see the fires and the people with the shadow puppets, but the fire pains his eyes. The shadows seem more real and comforting to him than reality.

When he is shown the world outside, the sun blinds him and burns his skin. After awhile, he acclimates to the truth. Knowing freedom, he yearns to go back and explain it all to his friends. In this, he knows he is helpless to free his fellows. He lacks the language or context to explain this new world and how it is better than the cave.

So what's the big deal? Mormons are happy, clean, fun, moral, upright, gentle people. Why rock the boat? If mind control can improve lives, who is it hurting?

But too often the happiness, like choice, is an illusion made of pressed suits and modest dresses on cheerful families all striving blissfully for a life full of blessings. For too many Mormons, those outward smiles are mere shadow puppets on the cave wall.

In the ward, everyone thinks everyone else's family is happy and perfect. If you have any issue, it's temporary, or there's some sin that needs resolving. If you're miserable, there's something wrong with *you* and not anyone else. So you hide it. But maybe everyone

---

1. Sanchez, *Spiritual Perversion,* 2005. 156.
2. Beck, *Leaving the Saints,* 2005. 61.

else is hiding it, too.

Many individuals and families in the Church who seem happy, who seem perfect, are *not*. Outside the cave, it is easy to find accounts from current and former members who have been putting on a show.

Recall the Hans Christian Andersen story, *The Emperor's New Clothes*. The crafty con artist tailor sells the king a new magic outfit. Wise people will see the finest suit ever sewn; fools will see nothing. Word quickly spreads throughout the land and the people come to see the king, parade through the streets, absolutely naked in his new "clothes." In unison, everyone cheers for his beautiful outfit, afraid of being mocked for fools.

This story is real and everyone is naked. No amount of pretending will change that. Who is willing to admit that all is not well in Zion? Those who are brave enough to point out the issues and put on some real clothes are shunned by the many naked others. They are ousted from the group.

This chapter may seem overly negative to some readers. It lays out the case of why this book is needed and why the Church is not perfect like it is. Many believing Mormons may consider this chapter unfair, but to those who struggle, this chapter should validate and explain some of the things they may be feeling; it is a comfort to show they are not alone. For each statistic and example herein, there is a real person, a flesh and blood human being with legitimate suffering, in need of love and support.

This chapter also lays out the extremes on the fringes of the present Church (and her related splinter groups), and examines the potential dangers of a future that is as severe as the Mormon past.

The LDS church does come through on many of its promises and it is beneficial to members in many ways. Yet in spite of positive outward appearances, belonging to a high-demand group can cause a number of serious problems. John Goldhammer states, "Logically, people who are under mind control do not consciously realize [it]. But they can and do suffer from a myriad of physical, emotional, and psychological consequences that may be rationalized away as some personal fault or weakness, or a test of their faith, loyalty, dedication, and endurance."[1]

For many Saints[2], the costs of membership far outweigh the benefits.

## Is Mormonism A Danger To Society?

*One would think that the world had seen more than enough of what a well-disciplined mob can do in the hands of a single madman.*
—**Carl Jung, *The Undiscovered Self***

*The best lack all conviction, while the worst are full of passionate intensity. Surely some revelation is at hand; surely the second coming is at hand.*
—**William Butler Yeats, *The Second Coming***

The word "cult" conjures the worst in our imaginations.

Are Mormons poised to do something extreme, like the high-profile cult cases in the news? Will they pull a Jonestown mass suicide or an Aum Shinrikyo act of terrorism? Where are the group marriages, life on compounds, or the selloffs of property in preparation for the end times? And since they haven't done anything like that, doesn't it prove they're not a cult?

The answer to this, like the other topics in this book, is complex. Let's explore some of the ways in which Mormonism and its spinoff groups are presently and potentially

---

1. Goldhammer, *Under the Influence*, 1996. 175.
2. All members of the LDS Church are considered Saints, based on biblical usage of the term to refer to all Christ's followers.

dangerous.

In the Church's early history, Mormons were participants, both in perpetrating and being victimized by extreme acts, including unconventional sexual practices, confidence games, communal living, mass migration, establishment of a theocracy, destruction of a printing press, massacres, and religious assassinations. Today, Mormons are taught that the early Saints were merely being persecuted for standing up for their righteous beliefs. Yet there is much, much more to that story.

Indeed, if actions of the early Saints were news headlines today, Mormons would be unequivocally labeled a cult by just about everyone. American society at the time treated the Mormons with the same courtesy we treated the Branch Davidians in Waco, TX, for many of the same reasons: Joseph Smith and his followers broke written laws and social contracts.

These are not empty accusations. Many well-researched, evidence-based books and websites have been written to reveal the true events of LDS history. This book will generally avoid discussion of manipulation in Church history. Those early Saints are dead, and this book is to help the living. Anything else is an academic question, albeit an interesting one, perhaps worthy of its own book.

What about now? On the surface, there seems little chance Mormonism will fall back to the fringes of yesteryear. The mainstreaming approach garners respect and brings in new members. Nevertheless, the level of control exerted by the modern Church could, in theory, lead once again to extremes.

*Captive Hearts* tells us, "At any given time, a number [of cults] may be relatively harmless. But most—if not all—have the potentiality of becoming deadly..."[1]

I was ready to sell all I had to move to Missouri[2] the instant the prophet gave word. I had mentally prepared myself to live "the Principle", polygamy, had the prophet reinstated it. Would I have done anything more excessive based on direct or implied commandment?

Probably.

"I will go and do the things which the Lord hath commanded, for I know that the Lord giveth no commandments unto the children of men, save he shall prepare a way for them that they may accomplish the thing which he commandeth them." 1 Nephi 3:7

This is what Nephi tells his father, right before he kills a drunk man to get a book so that "an entire nation" would not "dwindle in unbelief." This story was taught to me from age three, in songs, storybooks, Primary[3] lessons, and later Seminary and firesides[4]. With examples like this, I grew up wondering if I could kill on God's command. I had certainly been prepared to die for the Church, like Joseph Smith, like the Mormon pioneers, like the Old Testament prophets.

So while the modern Church hasn't done anything too weird *lately*, leadership has the power to command large numbers of faithful members to do things which, to the outside world, would seem quite destructive.

And then there are the little programs that most members don't know about, like the West Ridge Academy and other reform schools that have direct ties to the Mormon Church, including a presiding Branch President[5], a Seminary teacher, missionaries, and funding.

---

1. Tobias and Lalich, *Captive Hearts, Captive Minds,* 1994. 180.
2. Joseph Smith prophesied that in the Last Days, New Jerusalem would be built in Missouri. D&C Section 103, Graham W. Doxey. "Missouri Myths." *Ensign*, April 1979. https://www.lds.org/ensign/1979/04/missouri-myths
3. Primary is the auxiliary for children aged 4-11.
4. Additional meetings are sometimes held, especially for teenagers and college-aged members, called "Firesides." These are often held Sunday evenings, and attendance is considered optional (but strongly encouraged). They are generally directed at a specific topic (like chastity), and often guest speakers come in from out of town.
5. A branch president is like a bishop, only over a smaller congregation.

Upon the recommendation of the ward bishop[1], parents pay tens of thousands of dollars to send their rebellious teen, and are warned not to listen to "lies" about their treatment. Cases of severe physical, psychological, and sexual abuse have been collected by former attendees.[2,3]

Other tangential programs have existed and continue to exist, such as Evergreen International (a conversion treatment center aimed at turning homosexual members straight)[4] and Youth Developmental Enterprises (work camps for LDS youth against which many allegations of abuse have been leveled).[5] Reports of abuse are often suppressed, inhumane practices excused, and ties disavowed.

Mormonism has inspired more than a hundred currently-operating spinoff religions[6], which consider the Book of Mormon to be scripture and which hold Joseph Smith as their founding prophet. Most are more high-demand than the mainstream Church. While the Church tries to distance itself from fundamentalists (FLDS), the fact remains that these offshoots are inspired by Smith's original teachings and rely on LDS doctrines. Those attempting to recover from FLDS groups will find much of value in these pages.

It is fertile ground for manipulative individuals. Many FLDS groups reference a Joseph Smith prophecy that the Church house will be set in order by a "mighty and strong" future prophet, which plays well into their narrative. Dr. Michael Welner, an associate professor of psychiatry at NYU School of Medicine, studied more than 60 leaders of fundamentalist Mormon sects. "In the course of my research, I interviewed a man who has taught in [LDS] fundamentalist circles [who] has met over a hundred people...who believed themselves, quite earnestly, to be the 'one mighty and strong.'... He himself believed for a time that he was the 'one mighty and strong,' then backed away from what he believed to be too much a calling for him."

He added, "It is in a culture where there is a prophet in the present day, and in which man and God communicate on a deeply personal level, that these experiences take place."[7]

Dr. Welner insists that such beliefs and behavior are not always psychotic, that traits similar to psychopathy can be a product of strong beliefs and cultural context. Moreover, "The power of religious ordination enables someone who is psychopathic to exploit the devout around them. How expedient a position to be a prophet, with unquestionable superiority and providence. For the wrong person, it is absolute power that corrupts absolutely."

Individuals within the mainstream LDS Church can also take the doctrine to extremes. One example is Glenn Taylor Helzer, who, in 2000, "twisted scripture to convince his brother Justin Helzer and friend Dawn Godman that bloodshed was necessary if he was to reach the highest echelons of the Mormon Church" and to usher in the Second Coming.[8] He then proceeded to murder five people.

---

1. The leader of a "ward," which is a congregation-sized group of Mormons. Bishops are laymen with no training, called of God, and do not receive a salary. Like most clergy, bishops take confessions, run meetings, and care for members. They are required to support themselves in addition to their leadership role. The bishop is assisted by two counselors, and this group is called "bishopric." He is also responsible for delegating work to other members who are also "called" to other positions, such as teachers and leaders of auxiliaries.
2. Chino Blanco. "Trapped in a Mormon Gulag." *Daily Kos*, Jan 5, 2009. http://www.dailykos.com/story/2009/01/05/680293/-Trapped-in-a-Mormon-Gulag
3. Eric Northwood. *Clearing Time: Fighting a Mormon Gulag*, 2011. http://vimeo.com/32268408
4. *Former LDS "Ex-Gay" Claims Evergreen Is a Suicide Mill*, 2010. https://www.truthwinsout.org/blog/2011/07/17561/
5. "Utah Boys Allegedly Victimized at Maui Land and Pineapple Camp in the 1980s." *Urban Honolulu News*, Jan 24, 2014. http://urbanhonolulu.hawaiinewsnow.com/news/business/295433-utah-boys-allegedly-victimized-maui-land-and-pineapple-camp-1980s
6. "Latter Day Saint Movement / Groups and Denominations - Active." Accessed Nov 8, 2013. http://ldsmovement.pbworks.com/w/browse/#view=ViewFolder&param=Groups%20and%20Denominations%20-%20Active
7. Michael Welner, M.D. "New Research Reveals Secrets About Psychology of Polygamous Sects and Their Leaders." *ABC News*, March 1, 2010. http://abcnews.go.com/Nightline/TheLaw/research-reveals-secrets-psychology-polygamous-sects-leaders/story?id=9955379
8. Malaika Fraley. "Grim Crime Scene Re-explored in Depth in 'False Prophet.'" *San Jose Mercury News*, March 16, 2008. http://www.culteducation.com/reference/childrenof_thunder/childrenof_thunder20.html

Other notorious latter-day prophets responsible for religious killings include Bruce Longo, Jeffrey Lundgren, the Lafferty brothers, and Ervil LeBaron. Christine Jonson was not a self-appointed prophet, but thought God told her to drown her two children. All of these events have occurred within my lifetime.

While anyone can go off the deep end, instances when insanity is inspired by LDS teachings cannot be easily dismissed. The scriptures contain too many stories about underdog prophets who triumph in the end. Leaders of spinoff groups can be very convinced and convincing in the context of prophets like Noah, Paul, Lehi, Jonah, Abinadi, or Joseph Smith himself.

On June 2, 2002, fourteen-year-old Elizabeth Smart was abducted from her home by Brian David "Emmanuel" Mitchell. She was held captive and repeatedly raped for nine months. The Elizabeth Smart case is particularly interesting for two reasons.

One, Mitchell (and his wife, Wanda Barzee) sincerely believed they followed the teachings of the Prophet Joseph Smith. In the LDS context of personal revelation and spiritual gifts, Mitchell thought he was a prophet. Following the examples set by the former prophets, he obeyed God's revelation, went against society's laws, and took an especially young second wife.

BYU professor Daniel Peterson studied Mitchell's writings and "called Mitchell's book 'an impressive production in many senses,' [and] said Mitchell uses scriptural language well and makes many references to both fundamentalist and mainstream beliefs of The Church of Jesus Christ of Latter-day Saints.

"'I don't share his belief, but there's a logic to them,' said Peterson... 'The logic makes sense when you buy into the presuppositions.'"[1]

Arguably, Mitchell would have abused people regardless of his beliefs. But the context of Mormon culture gave him spiritual justification.

Secondly, Elizabeth Smart's conditioning likely made her submissive and easily controlled by Mitchell. Mormonism puts people into a submissive and gullible state where they may be vulnerable to more extreme manipulators.

When the story first broke, reporters openly suspected Smart's family, questioning whether a 14-year-old girl would willingly go with a strange man without putting up a fight or trying to run away. When I heard this, I became livid. Of course she would willingly go with a strange man. I was also once a 14-year-old Mormon girl. I had been sheltered. I was naive. I had been taught to trust unquestioningly. I was particularly vulnerable to fear and had no defenses against those who might wish to abuse me, nor the understanding of what such abuse might entail. I had been taught that God works in mysterious ways and might have easily bought a well-crafted story by an assailant well-versed in scripture.

Worst of all, I was never taught I had the right to fight back.

With myself in her shoes, I could imagine a number of scenarios through which Elizabeth Smart would have gone quietly. It turned out I was at least partly right. She originally went with Mitchell because he threatened her sister. She stayed all those months in part because of the prior conditioning intended to keep her subservient.

In her own words: "I remember in school one time, I had a teacher who was talking about abstinence. And she said, 'Imagine you're a stick of gum. When you engage in sex, that's like getting chewed. And if you do that lots of times, you're going to become an old piece of gum, and who is going to want you after that?' ...for me, I thought, 'I'm that chewed-up piece of gum.' Nobody re-chews a piece of gum. You throw it away. And that's how easy it is to feel you no longer have worth. Your life no longer has value... Why would it even be worth screaming out? Why would it even make a difference if you are rescued? Your life still has no value."[2] This type of shaming object lesson is often taught in LDS

---

1. Pamela Manson. "BYU Prof Says 'There's a Logic' to Mitchell's Writings." *The Sale Lake Tribune*, Nov 30, 2009. http://www.sltrib.com/news/ci_13893835
2. *Child Trafficking Symposium: Elizabeth Smart*. Johns Hopkins Bloomberg School of Public Health, 2013. http://www.youtube.com/watch?v=ot3SdCip7XI&feature=youtube_gdata_player

Sunday School.

Smart now hopes to teach kids to fight back against assailants, something she said she was never taught to do: "...if you're given choices, if you're given skills, if you're given permission to fight back, to know that you are of value and to know that you don't *have* to live your life that way, you don't *have* to do what other people tell you, that you have value and you always will have value, nothing can change that, then that's what we should be doing."

## Why Should We Mourn Or Think Our Lot Is Hard?

*No one can ignore the truth, diminish their awareness by avoiding or trivializing the facts, betray their rational mind in the process, and not pay the price psychologically.*

—Blair Watson,
*The Psychological Effects of Mormonism*[1]

*I think I could—uh—be happier if I didn't—uh—did not believe the Church was—is true. I think if I didn't believe the gospel I could be—uh—would be off of this treadmill that is making me feel almost crazy...*

—Anonymous LDS woman,
quoted in *Mormon Women, Prozac and Therapy*[2]

There are many anecdotal stories, online and in books, about the negative effects of Mormonism in individual lives. I will not recount them here in detail. Instead I will give a high-level view of problems generated by high-demand group participation, and specifically in mainline Mormonism.

Most of these problems are hidden. To admit that more than a few stray sheep have significant issues would be to admit failure of the gospel. Nevertheless, "Cults attack and destroy a person's independence, critical thinking abilities, personal relationships, and general physical, spiritual, and psychological state of being."[3] Mormonism is no different.

Janja Lalich, Professor of Sociology and associate editor of the *Cultic Studies Journal*, writes of a political cult to which she belonged. "A well-respected doctor and party theoretician in his 50s said he was so tired he prayed daily for a heart attack to give him some release. A number of others said they secretly wished they would get killed in a car accident because they couldn't think of any other way of getting out."[4] Too many Latter-day Saints can relate.

Members oppress their inner selves. Major life decisions, like education, marriage, family planning, career, use of spare time, and development of talents are heavily influenced by generalized one-size-fits-all advice that doesn't account for individual preferences and situational details. In fact, the will of the group may be in direct conflict with individual interest. Minor personal decisions including diet, fashion, use of money, entertainment, and intellectual pursuits, are given disproportional weight and scrutiny.

Members can become overly dependent on the group and engage in approval-seeking behaviors. Members are encouraged to place their locus of control outside themselves, either in God, the doctrine, the leadership, or other members, thus allowing others to define their context and frame of happiness, accomplishment, validation, and worth.

---

1. Blair Watson. "The Psychological Effects of Mormonism: How Mormonism Affects People's Self-Esteem." 2008. http://members.shaw.ca/blair_watson/
2. Kent Ponder, Ph.D. "Mormon Women, Prozac and Therapy." 2003. http://packham.n4m.org/prozac.htm
3. Tobias and Lalich, *Captive Hearts, Captive Minds*, 1994. 6.
4. Janja Lalich. "A Little Carrot and a Lot of Stick: A Case Example." In *Recovery from Cults: Help for Victims of Psychological and Spiritual Abuse*, ed. Michael D. Langone. New York: W.W. Norton, 1995. 84.

Members become isolated through an over-focus on the Church. Conversations outside the meeting house are monopolized by Church topics. Nonmember friends and family feel alienated by overuse of Church terminology and a lack of topic diversity. Church members are kept childlike, blocked from exposure to a variety of ideas and people.

Moreover, members can be plagued with unexpressed feelings of depression, guilt, shame, exhaustion, phobias, magical-thinking, passive-aggressive behavior, and hidden familial abuse. They may suffer self-esteem issues or feel like they can never fit in. Others battle eating disorders, toxic perfectionism, and suicidal ideation.

## Self-esteem

*Self-Esteem reflects our deepest vision of our competence and worth.*
—**Nathaniel Brandon,**
***The Art of Living Consciously***[1]

*The degree to which Mormonism affects people's self-esteem is a function of the age when they began to be indoctrinated in it and the duration of that indoctrination process, the sensitivity of their psyche...and emotions, the degree of psychological and emotional health and interdependence,...enmeshment...with their family-of-origin, and other factors.*
—**Blair Watson,**
***The Psychological Effects of Mormonism***[2]

The Church regularly tears down individual identity and replaces it with the clone of a perfect Church member. This is a fundamental aspect of mind control, and it is not without cost. Self-esteem is a casualty, because you can only esteem your authentic self, not a pseudo-self created by an outside ideology.

For example, the word "worthy" is a loaded term used frequently in LDS culture. On the surface, it seems to mean one thing, but psychologically, it comes to mean another. Your worth, or value as an individual, is based on performance. The bishop regularly checks your purity in worthiness interviews. Other members judge your outward behaviors: Are you wearing the right clothes? Wearing garments? Following the Word of Wisdom[3]? Attending Church? Using clean language?

Because Heavenly Father and the Holy Spirit cannot stand to be in the presence of sin, your very acceptance by God is based entirely on performance-based purity. The psychological effect for many is that the locus of control, i.e. the source of your self-worth, moves out of your hands and into the hands of others, on whether or not they judge you worthwhile... or worthy.

Self-esteem also requires self-awareness. Continual repression of doubts and feelings that are not in line with Church teachings suppresses awareness. A personal blind spot develops to block more than just the proscribed topics.

Former member Blair Watson has written and presented extensively on the effects of Mormonism on self-esteem:

> When confronted by faith-disrupting facts, Mormons have a choice: Either they acknowledge the facts and question and doubt what they've been taught, or they

---

1. Nathaniel Branden. *The Art of Living Consciously*. New York: Fireside/Simon & Schuster, 1999. 175.
2. Watson, "Psychological Effects of Mormonism," 2008. http://members.shaw.ca/blair_watson/
3. The Word of Wisdom is a set of dietary recommendations (now considered commandments) given by Joseph Smith in 1833. (D&C 89). Modern interpretation means that Mormons refrain from alcohol, nicotine, caffeine, and nonprescription drugs. Chocolate is the main exception to the caffeine rule, and some Mormons allow for caffeine as long as it's in soft drinks (the original scripture does not list caffeine, only "hot drinks"). Since breaking the Word of Wisdom is an outwardly visible sin, it is often judged more harshly than less-visible commandments, such as caring for the needy.

> ignore or trivialize the facts that conflict with their religious faith.
>
> The psychological result of doing the latter is developing a reputation with [your] mind that [you] cannot fully trust it. If a person won't allow their mind to acknowledge and accept facts/realities that conflict with church teachings and widely-held Mormon beliefs, the individual ends up experiencing...a lack of confidence in their mind, its cognitive processes (e.g., their critical and rational thinking), and the judgments and conclusions that their mind produces. Religious people who do not fully trust their mind typically become psychologically dependent on authority figures (parents, church leaders, etc.) to tell them what is true, right, the will of God, how they should behave, etc.[1]

Self-esteem depends upon autonomy and flexibility to make personal decisions. When an outside organization carries undue influence, your sense of confidence suffers. Watson continues: "Being 'on purpose' has nothing to do with living the type of life that other people believe is right for you, or doing what a religious organization, family members, or other individuals say is the will of God for you. It's about being psychologically free enough from others' beliefs and in-tune with yourself to know what your destiny is and to live it."[2]

These factors have a powerful effect even on those who fit easily into the Church's mold. Others, who don't fit so well, are impacted even further...

## Square Peg, Round Hole Syndrome

*Sadly, members are taught to believe that Mormonism is right for every single human on the planet—that the Church is perfectly compatible with every person who has all the good traits of human nature. If a person has trouble fitting in, therefore, there is something seriously wrong with that person.*
—**Jack B. Worthy, *The Mormon Cult***[3]

*Some of the same beliefs and practices that are more good than bad for some LDS individuals are more bad than good for others."*
—**Kent Ponder, Ph.D.,**
***Mormon Women, Prozac and Therapy***[4]

Particularly vulnerable to self-esteem issues are those who struggle to fit in.

Many in the exmormon forums have said they felt like a square peg trying to fit into a round hole. I had used this analogy myself for many years before I finally left. The Church is a better fit for some than others, but it claims to be the straight and narrow gate to happiness and salvation for every human being.

Kent Ponder, in his essay on the high rates of Prozac usage among LDS women, uses a shoe analogy:

> If a church's 'belief shoes'...are all narrow, even though they vary in length, which women will think this *works*? Those with narrow feet, of course; they will benefit. Those with wide feet will be in pain and wondering why. When bishoprics and therapists have strong religious conviction that narrow shoes are God's only true shoes, they offer corn and bunion pads to pained women with wide feet.[5]

Ponder admits that many members gain a sense of security by strict adherence to rules and pre-made decisions. Indeed, the strong, loyal community resulting from such a

---

1. Watson, "Psychological Effects of Mormonism," 2008. http://members.shaw.ca/blair_watson/
2. Watson, "Psychological Effects of Mormonism," 2008. http://members.shaw.ca/blair_watson/
3. Jack B. Worthy. *The Mormon Cult: A Former Missionary Reveals the Secrets of Mormon Mind Control*. Tucson, Ariz.: See Sharp Press, 2008. 50.
4. Ponder, "Mormon Women, Prozac and Therapy," 2003. http://packham.n4m.org/prozac.htm
5. Ponder, "Mormon Women, Prozac and Therapy," 2003. http://packham.n4m.org/prozac.htm

totalistic environment has its advantages, especially to those who can walk the walk in those one-size-fits-all shoes.

Yet, according to a former member writing as Jack B. Worthy, "The Mormon community can be a source of serious misery for those with traits or personalities that clash with its clearly defined norms of acceptable behavior and its endless list of expectations."[1]

Particularly vulnerable are the socially-awkward; gay or transgender; exceedingly curious or scientifically-minded; neurodiverse individuals with bipolar disorder, autism and Asperger's syndrome, and anxiety disorders; eccentrics; certain types of artists and creative people; free-thinkers and intellectuals; non-conformists and free-spirits; single parents; divorced people; feminists; liberals; those who are uncomfortable with restrictive gender roles; converts; people from diverse racial and ethnic backgrounds; and unorthodox thinkers. This list is not exhaustive. Many people in these categories find ways to be happy in the Church, but for some, their struggles outweigh the benefits of membership, and they become inactive or leave.

The Church tells us it is a "choice" to be straight, obedient, submissive, faithful, conservative, healthy, and good mothers or fathers. The sad part is the extent to which square pegs tend to blame themselves, and can never be happy just being who they are, because the round hole is established as the ideal.

"Gay people are also misfits in Mormon culture. If a person is gay, this fact absolutely must be kept secret. Gay Mormons learn to hate themselves. Few are accepted by their families for who they are."[2]

The Church seems to be slowly changing its stance on homosexuality, but it is not changing quickly enough or in the right ways. In some cases, members still participate in institutionally-approved bullying, as gay members are shunned and mistreated by wards and families. Evergreen International is a Church-supported organization which still attempts to "cure" people of same sex attraction.[3] North Star is another organization for homosexual Mormons.[4] They advocate that homosexuals should enter a straight marriage with someone they do not love and are not attracted to.

This is self-denial in its most painful form. The message is, "If you can't become who the Church wants you to be, then at least pretend." The Church promises happiness and salvation through marriage and family, and to deny it to those born with same sex attraction, or to work around it by making people marry someone they cannot feel close to, is highly problematic.

In contrast to these organizations, Affirmation seeks to reconcile LDS faith with being true to your gender identity and sexual orientation.[5] This is the kind of open conversation the Church needs to have around these issues.

Creative souls may also be square pegs, like he who has "...a strong need to express himself or herself in unique and artistic ways. The repetitive lifestyle of Mormonism that demands conformity of dress and behavior, and major time commitments to Church activities, feels boring and bland to artists and non-conformists."[6]

While Mormonism encourages creative outlets, talents must be developed within a certain rigid structure. Music and other performance arts are highly encouraged, but usually channeled towards "uplifting" styles like hymns and classical music. Rock music, for example, is discouraged.

According to John D. Goldhammer, "Groups encourage what I call 'creativity in a box,' which means we can be creative as long as it furthers the group's agenda and purpose."[7]

Edgy expressions of art are highly frowned upon. Everything is expected to be "G"

---

1. Worthy, *The Mormon Cult*, 2008. 50.
2. Worthy, *The Mormon Cult*, 2008. 50.
3. "TheSSAVoice.com - Evergreen International." Accessed Nov 8, 2013. http://www.thessavoice.com/
4. "North Star International." *North Star International*. Accessed Nov 8, 2013. http://northstarlds.org/
5. "Affirmation: Gay & Lesbian Mormons." Accessed Nov 8, 2013. http://www.affirmation.org/
6. Worthy, *The Mormon Cult*, 2008. 50.
7. Goldhammer, *Under the Influence*, 1996. 42.

rated, faith-promoting, and all sweetness and light. It is difficult to say anything artistically new when confined by both spoken and unspoken expectations.

If you feel like a round peg in the Church's round hole, then more power to you. But don't take away power from others.

"Virtually every individual knows that it is irrelevant to wonder whether his or her native language is 'true.' Neither do they look for the true car or think they have found it; they look for a brand and model that suits their needs."[1] The Church is in a position to be the brand that meets everyone's needs. In order to do so, they would have to become less focused on a narrow ideal of perfection.

## Guilt & Shame

Totalistic systems establish a demand for purity, making it impossible to feel completely adequate. The result is a deep sense of guilt and shame which can have lasting effects. Members blame themselves for bad things that happen, fall into depression and self-loathing, and churn with anxiety for not measuring up.

Avoidance of shame can lead to denial of authenticity. The true inner personality, when it conflicts with doctrine, is tied up and stuffed into a well where its screams can't be heard.

Sexual shame and ignorance can prevent a healthy, responsible sex life. And ironically, shame can lead to addiction, often to the very thing you're most ashamed of. You then seek absolution. The imposed cycle of sin and repentance gives control to the Church, because you believe your behavior is shameful and the Church to be the sole mediator of God's compassion.

This dynamic will be discussed in greater detail throughout the book.

## Depression, Eating Disorders, & Suicide

> ...I did not pick up on Jane's mood of 'feeling down', as she described in the letter. To me, she appeared happy—just as everyone there seemed happy. ...what we see on the surface does not always reflect what is underneath. This is highly significant and part of how [the Moonies] 'hook' people.
> —**Geri-Ann Galanti, Ph.D., *Recovery from Cults***[2]

> I managed to act as happy as I should have been. I was pretty successful at hiding from everyone...the fact that beneath the surface, I was a slow-motion train wreck.
> —**Martha Beck, *Leaving the Saints***[3]

> It is no secret that many Mormon women are depressed.
> —**Blair Watson, *The Psychological Effects of Mormonism***[4]

I can still tell if someone is LDS. Something about their eyes, their carriage, and the famous Mormon accent. Sometimes they have a false smile that doesn't quite reach those world-weary eyes. I've smiled that smile before under the constant pressure to project happiness, regardless of how it feels inside.

Dr. Curtis Canning, President of the Utah Psychiatric Association, said, "In

---

1. Ponder, "Mormon Women, Prozac and Therapy," 2003. http://packham.n4m.org/prozac.htm
2. Galanti, "Reflections on 'Brainwashing,'" *Recovery from Cults,* ed. Langone, 1995. 95.
3. Beck, *Leaving the Saints,* 2005. 91.
4. Watson, "Psychological Effects of Mormonism," 2008. http://members.shaw.ca/blair_watson/

Mormondom, there is a social expectation—particularly among the females—to put on a mask, say 'Yes' to everything that comes at her and hide the misery and pain. I call it the 'Mother of Zion' syndrome. You are supposed to be perfect because Mrs. Smith across the street can do it and she has three more kids than you and her hair is always in place. I think the cultural issue is very real. There is the expectation that you should be happy, and if you're not happy, you're failing."[1]

This section will cite many statistics, but remember that behind each of these numbers are people: individuals with hard lives and demons to face. I care very deeply about their suffering, and I am motivated to help ease it in any way I can. The mind control techniques described in this book contribute to their pain. The facts are here to back up my claims and to offer validation to those who endure, to say, "You are not alone."

Any high-demand group will compound chronic negative emotions like depression, shame, and anxiety. Fundamentalists of any stripe face these issues and there are plenty to be found in every state. But Utah beats all.

An oft-cited pharmaceutical study claims, "Antidepressant drugs are prescribed in Utah more often than in any other state, at a rate nearly twice the national average."[2] 15% of randomly sampled Utahans used antidepressants in 2000. This rose to 18.36% in 2006. In both years, Utah was the top state in antidepressant use, though in 2006, use of antidepressants rose in most states, and the gap between Utah and other states decreased significantly.[3]

Mental Health America published a study in 2007 revealing the rate of depression by state. Utah ranked the highest. 10.14% of adolescent respondents had at least one "major depressive episode" in the previous 12 months, compared with the national average of 8.95%. Another 10.14% of adults answered the same, with the national average of 8.05%. 14.58% of Utah adults responded that they'd had "serious psychological distress" during the previous year, compared to 11.63% overall.[4]

Psychologist Matthew Draper argued in a presentation at the Utah Valley University Mental Health Symposium that these studies don't imply much, since they don't break state demographics down into active LDS vs. inactive LDS vs. non-LDS. He argues that if you look only at faithful attending members, and control for a number of factors, the gap disappears. This narrow category of Mormons are actually less likely to use antidepressants.[5]

To this I argue that with 62.2% of Utah's population being LDS,[6] the number of LDS antidepressant users cannot be so easily ruled out. Moreover, inactive Mormons are still affected by LDS doctrines and failures to meet social and religious expectations. His argument is a bit tautological: The most well-adjusted members are happy, and he conveniently ignores all who are not well-adjusted, and therefore, not happy.

Draper further breaks out active members into smaller groups, including, for instance, those who struggle with pornography, and finds higher antidepressant use among those who can't measure up. Draper's analysis seems to indicate that those who find the gospel easy, who have fewer "sinful" tendencies to repress, are happier.

So should we dismiss the larger number of Mormons who, for whatever reason, don't find it so easy? Should we ignore the source of their conflict and simply expect them to try

---

1. Julie Cart. "Study Finds Utah Leads Nation in Antidepressant Use." *Los Angeles Times*, Feb 20, 2002. http://articles.latimes.com/2002/feb/20/news/mn-28924
2. Cart, "Utah Leads Nation in Antidepressant Use," *Los Angeles Times*, Feb 20, 2002.
3. Emily Cox, Ph.D., Doug Mager, MA, and Ed Weisbart, MD. "Geographic Variation Trends in Prescription Use: 2000 to 2006." *Express Scripts*. (Jan 2008).
4. Tami L. Mark, Ph.D., MBA, David L. Shern, Ph.D., Jill Erin Bagalman, MSW, and Zhun Cao, Ph.D. "Ranking America's Mental Health: An Analysis of Depression Across the States: Mental Health America." *Mental Health America* (Dec 11, 2007). http://www.mentalhealthamerica.net/go/state-ranking
5. Matthew R. Draper, Ph.D., Brett Breton, Ph.D., Julie Ogilvie, Natalie Haight, and Kiley King. "Helping Depressed Mormon Clients: Looking for Aid in Mormon Doctrine and Theology." Utah Valley University, 2013.
6. Matt Canham. "Census: Share of Utah's Mormon Residents Holds Steady." *Salt Lake Tribune*, April 17, 2012. http://www.sltrib.com/sltrib/jazz/53909710-200/population-lds-county-utah.html.csp

harder?

Draper's slides reveal interesting data and case studies about the pressures of perfectionism, repression of sexuality and anger, and the belief that suffering is good for the soul. Draper credits these to false beliefs and misunderstandings of doctrine, which lead to unnecessary dissatisfaction and clinical depression.

I contend that most unhappy Mormons understand the doctrine just fine. (And if it's so hard to understand, and so detrimental when it is misunderstood, how can it be called "plain and precious truth"?)

Kent Ponder states, "The same LDS Church that works so well for many works very badly for many others, who become chronically depressed, *especially women*."[1] It is not necessary to prove that the LDS Church makes everyone unhappy, only that it makes some people unhappy. For those unhappy people, this is a very important issue indeed.

An unpublished Utah Valley University (UVU) study sampled 1,000 students at the school attended predominantly by Latter-day Saints. "The results...suggest that there is a culture of perfectionism...related to depression found at UVU... Aspects of perfectionism found included internally imposed standards, externally imposed standards and a high need for organization and competency. In addition, a person's perception of their spirituality or religious beliefs and experiences also played a role."[2]

They did find that, contrary to popular assumptions, men and women suffer depression at the same rate, though women are more likely to be diagnosed. Because of this perception, more is written about depressed LDS women. Eventually, more may be known about Mormon men with depression.

Kristine Doty, Director of Field Education at UVU, studies what she calls "toxic perfectionism." "Doty...said LDS women are frequently confronted by the perfect storm of unrealistic expectations, personal guilt and suppressed feelings."[3]

It is not a *lack* of faith or dedication that leads to this sort of perfectionist-fueled depression. As Ponder points out, "...very often the brightest women who most strongly believe the Church is true are the ones made most depressed by it."[4] If you don't believe in the need to be perfect, how could it depress you?

Perfectionist attitudes are planted from the pulpit and fertilized by LDS culture. Demand for perfection is directed at all members, but women are singled out for additional responsibilities with fewer rewards. For instance, Prophet Ezra Taft Benson (when he was still an apostle) defined women's roles in his conference talk, "The Honored Place of Women":

> Since the beginning, a woman's first and most important role has been ushering into mortality spirit sons and daughters of our Father in Heaven...
>
> Provide your daughters with opportunities to develop their own skills, by allowing them to bake, cook, sew, and arrange their own rooms.[5]

Speaking about his wife, Flora, Benson said, "Gladly losing herself in service to her husband and children, she has shown a courageous determination to magnify what she knows is the divine and glorious calling of being a worthy wife and mother."

Flora was good because she "lost herself" in service. To whom much is given, much is required, and members who believe this are likely to place unreasonable expectations on themselves. We can't accuse them of twisting or misunderstanding the gospel.

Since the Church promises happiness for righteous living, depression can be a cycle

---

1. Ponder, "Mormon Women, Prozac and Therapy," 2003. http://packham.n4m.org/prozac.htm
2. "Depression Study by UVU Professors Yields Insights on Cultural Impacts." *UVU Press Releases*. Accessed Nov 8, 2013. http://blogs.uvu.edu/newsroom/2010/10/14/depression-study-by-uvu-professors-yields-insights-on-cultural-impacts/
3. Ben Lockhart. "UVU Professor's Study Puts Focus on LDS Women and Depression." *DeseretNews.com*, January 31, 2013. http://www.deseretnews.com/article/865571984/UVU-professors-study-puts-focus-on-LDS-women-and-depression.html
4. Ponder, "Mormon Women, Prozac and Therapy," 2003. http://packham.n4m.org/prozac.htm
5. Ezra Taft Benson. "The Honored Place of Woman." In LDS General Conference, Oct 1981. https://www.lds.org/general-conference/1981/10/the-honored-place-of-woman

that endlessly feeds on itself. Unhappiness is a sign that you must be doing something wrong, which leads to more shame, which leads to more internalized anger, which leads to deeper depression. For many, surfacing without medication is impossible.

In this case, medication is only masking the true problem.

Repression of anger and other unwanted feelings is also known to cause depression. This is sometimes known as "anger turned inward", and getting to the root of this anger is a common therapy technique.[1] Mormon doctrine actively encourages the repression of anger, doubts, and desires, which I will show throughout this book.

Contained pressure has to go somewhere, and like an overheated boiler, repression may explode at "safe" targets, like spouses and children, nonmembers, or members who do not seem to measure up. This can result in passive-aggression and abuse.

Inwardly-directed rage may result in self-harm, eating disorders, chronic illness, and even suicide, all noted as being problematic among Utah Mormons.

Suicide rates in Utah, and indeed, the rest of "Mormon corridor" (Idaho, Wyoming, Arizona) are much higher than the rest of the nation. According to the Utah Department of Health, 402 Utahans end their own lives every year, and another 4,152 attempt it.[2] Utah came in at the 45th worst in completed suicides, at 15.57 per capita compared to the national average of 11.05.[3] And the Center for Disease Control found Utah ranks the highest for adults having suicidal thoughts, 6.8% of the population compared to the national average of 3.7%.[4,5]

Certainly the Church cannot be blamed for all suicides in Utah; other factors should be considered. Yet LDS pressures are too large a factor to ignore. Why need the Church orchestrate a Jonestown-style mass-suicide to be considered dangerous, when every day, individual members are killing themselves due to shame and depression? What is the difference between 912 deaths in one day and thousands of deaths over decades?

## Codependency & Passive-Aggressive Culture

*Mormon psychological conditioning interferes with self-assertion in a variety of ways. Many Latter-day Saints dilute their personality because it doesn't fit the LDS concept of being nice, meek, long-suffering, and placating to Mormon authority figures (including God, as defined by Mormonism). Many members hide their assertiveness because they fear confrontation and conflict and the disapproval and possible rejection by LDS family members, leaders, and friends if they assert themselves and speak their truth...*

—**Blair Watson,**
***The Psychological Effects of Mormonism*[6]**

Many Mormons lack an understanding about setting healthy boundaries. It is difficult for most Saints to say "No" to new callings[7], charitable requests, and demands for more time. Mormons are often meddling in each other's business, judging one another and, for

---

1. Fredric N. Busch. "Anger and Depression." *Advances in Psychiatric Treatment* 15 (2009): 271-278.
2. "Utah Department of Health: Violence & Injury Prevention Program." Accessed Nov 9, 2013. http://www.health.utah.gov/vipp/suicide/
3. Mark, et al., "Ranking America's Mental Health," *Mental Health America* (Dec 11, 2007).
4. Alex E. Crosby, MD, Beth Han, MD, Ph.D., LaVonne A. G. Ortega, MD, Sharyn E. Parks, Ph.D., and Joseph Gfroerer, BA. "Suicidal Thoughts and Behaviors Among Adults Aged ≥18 Years – United States, 2008-2009." *CDC Surveillance Summaries* 60 (Oct 21, 2011): 1-22
5. Candice Madsen. "Utah at Center of 'Suicide Belt'; Youth Suicide Rate Troubling." *KSL.com*, April 25, 2013. http://www.ksl.com/?nid=148&sid=24937434
6. Watson, "Psychological Effects of Mormonism," 2008. http://members.shaw.ca/blair_watson/
7. Nearly every function at the ward-level of the Church is filled by members who are "called" of God to serve, without financial compensation. Callings include leadership roles at every level, teachers, organists and pianists, Boy Scout leaders, choir directors, and so on.

the sake of someone else's spiritual welfare, offer unsolicited advice, drop in unannounced for visits, or simply don't take no for an answer.

Often members are pecked to death with good intentions.

Codependence and enmeshment can be a big issue in many LDS families, which is especially encouraged by the Church doctrine of the Forever Family. If we cannot be saved without our children, then we'll have to drag them kicking and screaming to the Celestial Kingdom[1].

This is not what a healthy family looks like, but without any counterexamples, most Church members don't realize this.

Michael J. Stevens, Professor at Weber State University in Utah, conducted research and wrote extensively on the topic of passive-aggressive conflict resolution among Mormons:

> I often observe that mainstream LDS Church members along the Wasatch Front have a difficult time confronting any form of disagreement, even when they are clearly uncomfortable or unhappy with what's being discussed or decided. It's as if they were conflating all forms of disagreement or conflict with contention...
>
> If all conflict is viewed as the functional equivalent of having the 'spirit of contention,' what options are left to a person who disagrees, or sees things differently, or who has goals and interests different from the rest of the community? How can one raise objections or question and challenge others, or raise unpleasant topics, if doing so is tantamount to being in league with Beelzebub? If one's view of all conflict is that it must be avoided so as to avoid contention, then there is no direct, healthy, constructive strategy available for resolving conflicts and disagreements.[2]

He analyzed LDS writings to find the frequency of how often passivity is encouraged.

> ...queries at www.lds.org for variations of 'obey/obedience,' and 'submit/submission' returned over 500 hits in general conference talks since 2002, and Mosiah 3:19 (which encourages the reader to be 'submissive, meek, humble, patient, full of love, willing to submit to all things') was quoted at least once in 17 of the preceding 20 general conferences...
>
> The influences of this aspect of LDS culture works on us like the tide—repeatedly and unremittingly, year after year after year, in subtle and subconscious ways, making it difficult to ever spontaneously develop healthy coping skills for managing conflict and disagreements. It also undermines our capacity to use power ethically when we have it at our disposal, or to respond effectively to abuses of power when we are in a subordinate position. I would argue that few people who are raised Mormon are provided with good examples of what healthy disagreement and conflict management looks like or with methods of how to foster constructive, collaborative problem-solving and negotiation.

He found the highest passive-aggression scores among Mormons and people raised in Utah.

---

1. Mormons believe the afterlife is divided into three "degrees of glory," plus outer darkness. The kingdoms are: Celestial, Terrestrial, and Telestial. All three are said to be heavenly, but only admittance to the Celestial Kingdom allows you to be with God and your family forever. Your position in the afterlife is based on your repentance, growth, and works in this life. The criteria for the Celestial Kingdom is quite high. Outer darkness is reserved for the worst people, perhaps only for Sons of Perdition (those who deny the Holy Ghost). The exact criteria for each kingdom and outer darkness are unclear, i.e. What does it take to "deny the Holy Ghost"? Members are not supposed to speculate too much, because only God can judge.

2. Michael J. Stevens. "Passive-aggression Among the Latter-day Saints." *Sunstone Magazine* no. 170 (April 2013). https://www.sunstonemagazine.com/passive-aggression-among-the-latter-day-saints/

Along this same vein, abuse, especially of children, is often ignored and covered up by LDS families and by Church leadership. Victims of emotional, physical, and sexual abuse are often revictimized while perpetrators are let off with barely a slap on the hand. Church authorities are not given sufficient education to counsel abuse victims, and LDS Family Services therapists may ignore secular understandings of family dynamics when it conflicts with doctrine.

In most cases, bishops and stake presidents are in violation of the law when they fail to report abuse to authorities. This is a serious problem which could fill its own book, and indeed, The Mormon Alliance and others have written a great deal on this topic.

## Material Loss

As Church members, we were taught to not value "things of the world." Nevertheless, material goods are valuable, and the Church is happy to take these goods off the Saints' hands.

Tithing and other donations make sense from the LDS perspective, but once outside, it is easy to see it as a form of extortion under the threat of invisible consequences, namely saving your eternal soul, and buying insurance against burning at the last day.[1]

Life is short, and as far as I know, it is the only one I have. Church members are busy "storing up treasures in heaven", and often have little time to enjoy this life that we most definitely, provably, possess.

While many intangible goals are for good, such as spending time with family and doing charity work, most endeavors of the Church are make-work projects that have no lasting impact. Such demands on resources can be exhausting, and Church members are never allowed to relax or just "be."

Over-reliance on faith can lead to magical thinking and gullibility. Members tend to lean on God to solve their problems. While the Church does attempt to teach self-reliance, members may have their minds so crippled by the many mind control techniques that it makes them less capable.

The suppression of critical thinking can leave members susceptible to scams which do not directly conflict with the gospel. Members are often naive and overly trusting, taken in by manipulative individuals and multi-level marketing, pyramid schemes, and expensive self-improvement seminars.

*The Economist* ran an article on affinity fraud, a type of scam involving close friends and trusting communities. Utah received special mention:

> The state thought to have the most affinity fraud per head is Utah, where 60% of the population are Mormons. In 2010, regulators and the FBI were investigating cases there with 4,400 victims and perhaps $1.4 billion (or $500 for every Utahn) in losses. The numbers have surely climbed since, with the three largest cases alone involving combined losses of up to $700m, says one investigator.
>
> Mormons tend to be both trusting and welcoming of newcomers, says Keith Woodwell, head of Utah's Division of Securities. As soon as you pull up to your new house, neighbours appear to help you unpack. A scammer who gets his foot in the door can exploit this closeness.[2]

---

1. President Marion G. Romney Second Counselor in the First Presidency. "The Blessings of an Honest Tithe." *New Era*, Feb 1982. http://www.lds.org/new-era/1982/01/the-blessings-of-an-honest-tithe
2. "Fleecing the Flock." *The Economist*, Jan 28, 2012. http://www.economist.com/node/21543526

*Until a person leaves Mormonism, they have no idea how painful it can be.*
—**Anonymous Online Exmormon,**
quoted in ***The Pattern of the Double-Bind in Mormonism***[1]

*One of the nifty paradoxes of dysfunction is that the crazier the system in which you grow up, the more afraid and less equipped you are to leave it and stand on your own.*
—**Martha Beck,**
***Leaving the Saints***[2]

*Is it any wonder that many former cultists describe their post-cult experience as an emotional roller coaster? ...whether they 'pocket' the cult experience or confront it, it inexorably permeates their lives... Consequently, if it is not properly understood, it cannot be effectively managed.*
—**Michael Langone,**
***Recovery from Cults***[3]

# Don't Just Get Over It—Recover!

Church members are "leaving the Church in droves", according to General Authority Marlin K. Jensen speaking to Utah State University students and faculty.[4]

A 2011 survey[5] conducted by John Dehlin questioned 3,000 Mormons who had lost their testimonies and found the leading causes of disillusionment included doctrinal and theological issues, historical issues, losing faith in Joseph Smith and the Book of Mormon, and problems with the Church's stance on social issues, like homosexuality and the role of women.

Additional reasons included disliking the feeling of being judged, the emphasis on the "one true church" and perfectionism, and the organization's use of funds.

The results of this survey contradict the prevailing myths, that members leave or become inactive because they are offended or want to sin. These two reasons tied for *last* on the survey.

Easy exposure to disconfirming information on the internet is facilitating these increased losses in membership[6]. On the survey, leading historical and doctrinal problems

---

1. Stricker, *The Double-Bind in Mormonism,* 2000. 96.
2. Beck, *Leaving the Saints,* 2005. 262.
3. Langone, "Introduction," *Recovery from Cults,* 1995. 12.
4. Peter Henderson, and Kristina Cooke. "Special Report - Mormonism Besieged by the Modern Age." *Reuters*, Jan 30, 2012. http://uk.reuters.com/article/2012/01/30/uk-mormonchurch-idUKTRE80T1CP20120130
5. "Understanding Mormon Disbelief: Why Do Some Mormons Lose Their Testimony, and What Happens to Them When They Do?" March 2012. http://www.whymormonsquestion.org/wp-content/uploads/2012/05/Survey-Results_Understanding-Mormon-Disbelief-Mar20121.pdf
6. A complete list or detailed description of all controversial issues is outside the scope of this book.

include: Polygamy/polyandry[1], origins of The Book of Abraham[2], racism[3], Book of Mormon issues (DNA[4], anachronisms[5]), Masonic influences on the temple ceremony[6], conflicting versions of the First Vision[7], women and the priesthood[8], etc. A single one of these issues might be easy to think around, but for many people, the sheer volume of problems cannot be easily dismissed.

Some think that leaving the Church is the "easy way out." Believe me, it's not. The easiest way would have been for it to be true, for all promises of happiness in this life, and eternal happiness in the next to be real. To have retained the respect and love of my family. To have held on to the identity and values I was given from birth. To have all my answers given to me by a true Prophet of God, by inspired scripture, and by bishops and priesthood leaders guided by gifts of the Holy Ghost. To receive my own guidance from the Holy Ghost. To feel like a round peg in a round hole because the Church truly is the Plan of Happiness[9] for everyone.

It was a nice dream. Though I experienced a strong sense of freedom when I left, I also had a thousand new problems, with no guidebook, no leaders, and no one to help me figure it out except myself.

General Authority Glenn L. Pace said, "You can leave the Church, but you can't leave it alone. The basic reason for this is simple. Once someone has received a witness of the Spirit and accepted it, he leaves neutral ground. One loses his testimony only by listening to the promptings of the evil one, and Satan's goal is not complete when a person leaves the Church, but when he comes out in open rebellion against it."[10]

This simple dismissal distracts from our legitimate concerns. For all the negative effects of being Mormon, leaving brings its own consequences. For many, leaving can be harder than staying, especially at first.

---

1. Joseph Smith, Brigham Young, and other LDS leaders practiced polygamy up until 1890. Many controversies surround this topic, which exceed the scope of this book.
2. The Book of Abraham was purportedly translated by Joseph Smith based on a set of papyri he bought from a traveling mummy exhibit. Most Mormons accept that this document was written by the prophet Abraham, and it is now considered scripture. However, modern Egyptologists who have analyzed remaining fragments of the papyri have identified it as a common Egyptian funerary text.
3. Multiple racism controversies surround the past and present LDS Church, including the fact that men of African descent were not allowed to hold the priesthood until 1978. And the fact that black skin was considered a curse for Cain's sins. And the fact that Native Americans were also said to be cursed with dark skin. While the Church now disavows many of these doctrines, they still flourish in LDS folklore. The Book of Mormon still describes righteous people as being "white and delightsome" and still includes God cursing a whole race of people with "a skin of blackness" for their sins. (2 Nephi 5:21, 2 Nephi 30:6, 4 Nephi 1:10)
4. Members are lead to believe the Lamanites, a race of people in the Book of Mormon who originally came from Jerusalem, are modern-day Native Americans (including South American peoples). DNA evidence does not support this claim.
5. Various items mentioned in the Book of Mormon were not available to the people of the Americas during that time period. Examples include horses, steel, wheels, and silk.
6. The temple ceremony is in many ways identical to Masonic rituals. Joseph Smith joined the Freemasons and founded a Masonic lodge in Nauvoo, IL, shortly before introducing the temple ceremonies to Latter-day Saints.
7. The First Vision is the account of how Joseph Smith went to the woods to pray and was visited by God the Father and Jesus. This story is central to the founding of the LDS Church and to Joseph Smith's legitimacy as a prophet. Yet there are four different accounts written by Smith himself, all of which contain troubling contradictions.
8. Some LDS women argue that there is a power imbalance between men and women, since women cannot "hold the priesthood." Priesthood is the power and authority to act on behalf of God. It comes along with spiritual powers (like discernment and inspiration, the ability to give healing blessings, etc.) It also comes along with a great deal of leadership and organizational power. Women have little say in Church decisions, except for when it comes to leading children and other women. And even then, male priesthood-holders can overrule. There are also historical issues which most members are unaware of, that women once had more power within the Church and were also ordained with the priesthood.
9. The Plan of Happiness, or the Plan of Salvation, is the core doctrine of the Church. In a nutshell: We existed as the spirit children of God before we were born. We needed bodies and we needed to learn and be tested. In order to do so, we needed free agency. Yet freedom to act required sin, and justice demands that sin must be paid for. Our brother Jesus offered to take on the price of our sins. Our other brother Lucifer wanted to force everyone to obey. God cast out Lucifer and those who sided with him. The rest of us came to earth. We are tempted and tested, but those who keep the commandments and repent are cleansed through Christ's atonement and can return to the Father. Following this plan is supposed to bring at least some measure of happiness and comfort in this life, as well as unimaginable joy in the next.
10. Glenn L. Pace. "Follow the Prophet." In LDS General Conference, April 1989.

There's a good reason we can't leave it alone. The Church was my entire life for twenty-six years. I lived in fear and respect and love of God, the Church, the Prophet, the Book of Mormon, and had professed *knowledge* of their truth in public. I was raised to believe its tenets were as real as the mountains. The Celestial Kingdom existed just like Earth. I learned the names of latter-day prophets alongside US Presidents.

The history of the Church and the scripture stories are instilled as deep in my memory as the history of the world. Mormon culture is as familiar as American culture. The principles of the gospel are as much a foundation to my views of morality as any ethics or philosophy book I've read since.

Mormonism is an integral part of my identity and always will be. Even after writing this book, I still won't have spent as much time thinking about the Church since I've left as I did while in.

All but one other member of my family are still members. I have a very uncomfortable relationship with most of them as a result. It is difficult for them to understand me. They've been trained to think I am weak at best, evil at worst. I was told that if I ever left, I'd suffer in many ways, up to and including spiritual death.

How could I just "leave it alone"? How could anyone?

*Captive Hearts* says, "Reentering the noncult world can be painful and confusing. To some extent, time will help. But the passage of time and merely being physically out of the group are not enough. You must actively and of your own initiative face the issues of your cult involvement... We both know ex-cult members who have been out of their groups for 7, 10, 15 years, who have never had any counseling or education about cults or mind control. These individuals live in considerable emotional pain and have significant difficulties in their lives due to unresolved conflicts about their group, their leader, or their cult experience. Often they are still under the subtle effects of the group's thought-reform program."[1]

Exit counselor Carol Giambalvo agrees with many cult researchers about the best way to recover from a high-demand group: "In my experience the most helpful tool for recovering ex-cultists is learning what mind control is and how it was used in their specific cult."[2]

According to another helping professional, Paul R. Martin, "If former cultists do not understand the thought-reform program, they will not be able to resolve their tangle of emotions—guilt, fear, shame, sadness, and anxiety. They will not appreciate the extent to which these emotions result from a constricting of their relationship with self, world, and cult."[3]

In *Reflections on "Brainwashing"*, researcher Geri-Ann Galanti describes her experience attending a Moonie recruitment camp to observe their techniques. She went into the situation knowing they would try to manipulate her and the methods they would use. This only added a little to her resistance:

> The day after the camp experience I was interviewing a former deprogrammer who had spent several years in the Moonies. About halfway through the interview I asked her to describe exactly what she did during a deprogramming. She looked me straight in the eye and said, 'Exactly what I've been doing with you.'
>
> I was shocked; I didn't need deprogramming; I didn't buy their doctrine; they didn't brainwash me. Despite my protestations, I came to realize that they *had* influenced me: 'Remind me again what's so bad about the Moonies.' I knew very well the reported abuses of members by the Unification Church—the long hours of fund-raising, late at night, often in dangerous areas; the lack of proper nutrition; the

---

1. Tobias and Lalich, *Captive Hearts, Captive Minds,* 1994. 2.
2. Carol Giambalvo. "Post-Cult Problems: An Exit Counselor's Perspective." *Recovery from Cults,* ed. Langone, 1995. 148.
3. Paul R. Martin, Ph.D. "Post-Cult Recovery: Assessment and Rehabilitation." *Recovery from Cults,* ed. Langone, 1995. 211.

> suicide training; the fear and guilt; the relative poverty in which the members live, while the leaders dwell in splendor; the munitions factory owned by a church that is supposedly striving for world peace; the divisions created between family members; the deceptions—all of the horrors. But that knowledge no longer seemed important. I had a great time, the people seemed good, so by association, the group did as well. While I was with them I was unable to reconcile the emotional truth with the intellectual one, and the more immediate emotional reality won out. It was only later, when I was outside the environmental influence of the group, that what I knew began to sink in.[1]

Most ex-members retain elusive remnants of this programming. "Many former cult members selectively deny aspects of their cult experience. Some become angry and resistant at the mention of mind control, thought reform, or brainwashing, thinking that these things could not possibly have been done to them. It is very threatening to a person's sense of self to contemplate having been controlled or taken over... Yet only by confronting the reality of psychological manipulation can ex-cult members overcome its effects."[2]

Steve Sanchez recounts talking to a fellow former member of his New Age Christian cult, SLF: "I realized she was still under the spell of [Rev.] Will to some degree, even though she had left more than two years earlier. When I talked to her I could see she was hesitant to be too critical of SLF."[3]

Often when members leave, "they will tend, as do victims of other forms of abuse, to believe that they left because something was wrong with them. They do not usually view the group as a cult—at least not initially. Holding the layperson's view of cults, they think that cults are weird groups for crazy people, and since they are not crazy and their group isn't weird, it isn't a cult."[4]

This is the sort of residual programming that leads to such hardships long after being under the group's influence. The remedy is simple: "Knowledge of cults gives you the language to explain to yourself what happened."[5] *Captive Hearts* speaks of "demystifying the guru's power."[6]

Michael Langone says, "Although not necessarily caused only by the cult experience, their pain is inextricably linked to that experience. And because deception lies at the heart of the cult experience, former cult members...must be educated about cults before they can see through the deception and adequately deal with the problems."[7]

Exit counselors are expensive and hard to find. With the right tools, it is possible to help yourself.

That's why I don't "leave it alone." By reading dozens of books and papers on cults and mind control, and by reading LDS exit stories and unfiltered sources about problematic doctrines and history, I experienced the healing I needed to overcome my programming. Most of the triggers I once experienced are now gone.

Many former Mormons go through a phase where they devour anti-Mormon material. They flood internet forums designed for them, sharing with one another so they can understand their experiences and work through their anger, pain, betrayal, and ongoing hurt caused by leadership, family and friends.

As former Mormon Chris L. Morin describes, "I spent every spare moment studying Church matters. This investigation exposed subconscious biases and validated doubts that had plagued me for years."[8]

---

1. Galanti, "Reflections on 'Brainwashing,'" *Recovery from Cults,* ed. Langone, 1995. 100-101.
2. Tobias and Lalich, *Captive Hearts, Captive Minds,* 1994. 35.
3. Sanchez, *Spiritual Perversion,* 2005. 377.
4. Langone, "Introduction," *Recovery from Cults,* 1995. 11.
5. Tobias and Lalich, *Captive Hearts, Captive Minds,* 1994. 92.
6. Tobias and Lalich, *Captive Hearts, Captive Minds,* 1994. 64.
7. Tobias and Lalich, *Captive Hearts, Captive Minds,* 1994. xi. (From Foreword by Michael Langone)
8. Morin and Morin, *Suddenly Strangers*, 2004. 158.

Compare to Steve Sanchez's account: "For me it was strengthening and therapeutic to be doing all this exposing and fighting."[1]

This process is a vital part of healing and finding a new place in the world. Answers about church history and doctrine have been explored at length by many other authors. Follow your interests and trust your instincts. If you feel like reading twenty books about Joseph Smith, do it. Those who tell you it is an unhealthy obsession, or it is somehow proof that the Church is true, do not fully understand the psychological pressures involved or are making further attempts to control.

And then I did leave it alone for a few years. But I keep coming back. Why? Again, it is a part of me. Every time Mormonism comes up in the news and each time I meet a Mormon or exmormon, it all floods back. Sometimes I'm still a teenager trying to be perfect.

Today, I can't leave it alone because I know there are thousands of others like I was ten years ago, struggling to find the answers I have. I cannot hide my candle under a bushel. I wrote this book to help them move more quickly through the phases of recovery.

## Though hard to you this journey may appear...

The fact that most people who leave cults will have a high number of negative mental, emotional, and situational difficulties is noncontroversial among cult researchers. I've compiled a comprehensive list taken from multiple books:

Depression; low self-worth; anxiety; panic attacks; phobias; paranoia; flashbacks; nightmares; insomnia; eating disorders; restlessness; lack of direction; memory loss; self-blame; guilt; shame; anger & rage; confusion; sense of betrayal; loss of concentration & blurring of mental acuity; the feeling of being in a fog; feeling lost; loneliness, isolation, & alienation; indecisiveness; "floating" or slipping into dissociative or altered states; uncritical passivity; the "fishbowl effect" (feeling scrutinized or watched); no longer feeling "chosen" or special; confusion about morality; confusion about personal goodness; financial problems; excessive doubt; fear of joining new groups & distrust of professional services; distrust of personal decision-making ability; relationship issues; culture shock; identity issues; employment issues.[2,3,4,5]

EMOTIONAL ISSUES SUFFERED BY THOSE WHO LEAVE CULTS:
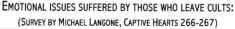
(SURVEY BY MICHAEL LANGONE, CAPTIVE HEARTS 266-267)

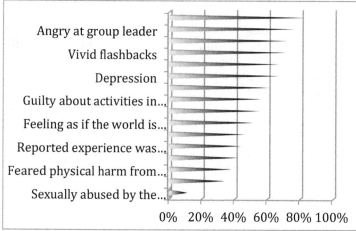

Research by Margaret Thaler Singer and Richard Ofshe found signs of temporary psychosis in otherwise healthy individuals, as well as post-traumatic stress, dissociative disorders, psychosomatic illnesses, cognitive inefficiencies, phobias, and self-harm.[6]

Effects on family relationships are particularly difficult for Mormons. Families are forever, except when

---

1. Sanchez, *Spiritual Perversion*, 2005. 380.
2. Langone, *Recovery from Cults*, 1995.
3. Singer, *Cults in Our Midst*, 1995.
4. Hassan, *Releasing the Bonds*, 2000.
5. Tobias and Lalich, *Captive Hearts, Captive Minds*, 1994.
6. Tobias and Lalich, *Captive Hearts, Captive Minds*, 1994. 267-268.

family members stray. Severing very often occurs, either because the apostate is shunned, or because the LDS family focuses so heavily on the gospel as to be alienating. As Jack B. Worthy said, "Leaving the Mormon reality dome usually damages family relationships in painful ways, so people with traits and personalities that clash with the culture suffer whether they stay or go."[1]

Self-blame can exacerbate all the negative effects. As *Captive Hearts* describes, "Already prone to much self-doubt, former cult members easily fall prey to obsessional thoughts about the nature of reality, the truth about the leader or group, and especially about whether or not they did the right thing by leaving."[2] And, "...ex-members may further berate themselves by analyzing their unhappiness according to the cult's doctrines, which always places the cult on top and the member on the bottom. All these people unknowingly participate in victim blaming because they don't understand cults."[3]

As you can see, leaving a high-demand group is not easy.

Other factors can complicate recovery. "Individuals with a prior history of emotional problems are also more likely to experience emotional problems while *in* the group. Therefore, they more commonly require psychotherapeutic interventions following their cult departure."[4]

This is compounded by the fact that members with emotional or family problems are referred to LDS Family Services, which can keep that person within the closed logic of the Church. While many find relief and modern therapeutic practices through LDS therapists, strict adherence to some doctrines might reinforce problems.

For instance, unlike mainstream psychologists, most LDS therapists still counsel that masturbation is a sin. Since this one point can be the source of severe shame and self-loathing, a client will find no relief where she ordinarily would. Likewise, a woman who is stressed from trying to follow the Church's high standards of motherhood might not receive permission to slow down and take care of herself. Victims of sexual abuse might be further victim-blamed to mirror what they've heard from their abuser, culture, family, and bishop. And addictions may continue to be moralized as sins rather than psychological disorders which respond best to treatment.

Those who suffer from extreme difficulties like self-harm, eating or sleeping disorders, panic attacks, anxiety or depression, or severe dissociative episodes, should seek help from secular mental health professionals. You don't necessarily need to find a cult exit counselor. Any good mental health professional can assist with these problems, but be sure to inform them of your background. Since experience in a high-demand group can simulate other mental disorders, treatment may not be the same. Refer professionals to books like *Recovery from Cults* as a starting resource.

# Born Under the Covenant[5]

*When a seal is put upon the father and mother, it secures their posterity, so that they cannot be lost, but will be saved by virtue of the covenant of their father and mother.*

—**Prophet Joseph Smith**[6]

Most cult recovery books assume members were converted rather than born into their

---

1. Worthy, *The Mormon Cult,* 2008. 50.
2. Tobias and Lalich, *Captive Hearts, Captive Minds,* 1994. 99.
3. Tobias and Lalich, *Captive Hearts, Captive Minds,* 1994. xi.
4. Tobias and Lalich, *Captive Hearts, Captive Minds,* 1994. 51.
5. When Mormons get married, they are sealed together in the temple for eternity. Their children will be automatically sealed to them when they are born. Such children are considered born "under the covenant," since their parents made covenants with God. Most LDS children are born to temple married parents, thus "born under the covenant" means "raised LDS."
6. Joseph Smith. *History of the Church of Jesus Christ of Latter-day Saints*. Salt Lake City: Deseret Book Co., 1978. 5:530.

high-demand group. For Mormons, this is usually reversed. Recovery books help readers remember their pre-cult identity. For most of us, the road is more difficult. We don't *have* a pre-Mormon identity.

> Children born or raised within a cult grow up in a closed, controlled environment where bizarre, unorthodox, and harmful beliefs, values, and mores are accepted. When someone raised in a cult leaves it, that person may truly feel like a stranger in a strange land, and may have difficulty adapting to the dominant, noncult society. Cult life may have delayed emotional and educational development; it may have hampered medical needs. In addition, the child may have suffered physical, emotional, and sexual abuse—a common and serious problem for children in cults.[1]

Thankfully, the LDS church allowed us some exposure to mainstream culture. Most of us were given access to medical treatment, and though familial abuse is prevalent in LDS families[2,3], it is not officially encouraged.

Though R-rated movies were verboten, we were allowed to watch other movies. While rock-and-roll might have been banned in some of our more zealous families, we could overhear enough. Most of us were educated in public schools (although I wasn't). We could participate in sports; read books and magazines (within limits); eat most normal foods; wear relatively normal clothes; and generally had enough exposure to the mainstream to make the transition.

However, the limits that *were* placed on us can make our upbringing a little odd, especially for those who did not sow wild oats, or were raised in more sheltered or abusive households, or who lived in the Mormon corridor[4] where outside culture is Mormonized.

The lack of exposure to "the world" during high school and college has effects. From *Captive Hearts*, "There are developmental tasks to be completed, such as individuation and separation from the family. There are educational and career choices to be made. And there are issues about dating, sex, and marriage to explore. Cult members do not get the opportunity to pass through these normal developmental stages and experiences, and sometimes complain of being 30- and 40-year-old teenagers when they get out of the cult."[5]

This is why many exmormons describe going through an "adolescent phase", where, no matter their age, they spend a year or two acting like teenagers, experimenting with music, movies, fashions, pastimes, sex, alcohol, and drugs. We faced moral and philosophical questions we had never before confronted.

It's a whirlwind of fresh experiences, and suddenly life is brand new again. Decisions are not always made with the wisdom of an experienced adult, because this adult has been sheltered and now must make them without the parental safety net.

Some exmormons, suddenly free from isolation and depression, may be in danger of going too far in experimenting with substances and lifestyles, and may fall to the very perils the Church warned of: Alcoholism, drug addiction, broken relationships, sexually transmitted diseases, and unwanted pregnancy.

The Church labeled many things sinful. But just because the Church exaggerated the consequences of "sin" does not mean you should do the exact opposite of everything they said once you get out... caffeine, alcohol, nicotine, revealing clothing, sex, pornography, and even drugs and new religions may be safe to explore, but only in moderation, with full awareness of the risks, and with assurance you can fulfill your responsibilities towards self, children, spouse, career, education, and safety.

---

1. Tobias and Lalich, *Captive Hearts, Captive Minds*, 1994. 50.
2. Emily Belanger. "Domestic Violence and Mormonism." *Peculiar People*, April 26, 2012. http://www.patheos.com/blogs/peculiarpeople/2012/04/domestic-violence-and-mormonism/
3. Lavina Fielding Anderson, and Janice Merrill Allred. *Case Reports of the Mormon Alliance (Volumes 1, 2, & 3)*. The Mormon Alliance, 97 1996. http://mormon-alliance.org/casereports/casereports.htm
4. The Mormon Corridor is the area of the Western US settled in the 1800's by Mormons, and it retains a high percentage of Saints to this day. The areas include Utah, Idaho, Nevada, Arizona, along with parts of Wyoming, California, Colorado, Oregon, and Washington.
5. Tobias and Lalich, *Captive Hearts, Captive Minds*, 1994. 50.

This is the time for you to learn to make your own decisions, and it can be both scary and rewarding. Consequences both positive and negative are now yours to reap. It is best to take this phase with caution. Fortunately, the internet is a great resource. I highly recommend researching any topic about which you have doubts. Awareness and education can lead to a safe, sane, and consensual life full of moderated choices.

Identity issues were perhaps the most difficult for me during this phase. I was a person held together by the glue of LDS ideology. As I proudly told the world, "I am a Mormon." I *am*. To no longer *be* that meant I didn't know who I was. The impact of disillusionment cannot be overstated, especially for those of us who knew no other identity from birth.

## We Then Are Free From Toil and Sorrow, Too…

*Know this, that ev'ry soul is free, to choose his life and what he'll be.*
—***Know This, That Every Soul Is Free**,*
**LDS Hymn #240**[1]

*Freedom is born in the moment I decide I am free to move away from what has previously imprisoned me.*
—**Sam Keen,**
***Hymns to an Unknown God***[2]

The apostle John said, "Ye shall know the truth, and the truth shall make you free." John 8:32. Lots of people like to co-opt this phrase, especially those who are selling truth.

I assert *you* are the arbiter of truth. You get to decide what is meaningful. Maybe this book is full of crap. You can judge it on its merits, along with every other thing.

Martha Beck said, "I am free, and always have been; free to accept my own reality, free to trust my perceptions, free to believe what makes me feel sane even if others call me crazy, free to disagree even if it means great loss, free to seek the way home until I find it."[3]

I resist anyone who claims exclusive coverage of truth. I retain my freedom to move away from that which imprisons me, be it religions, commercial enterprises, relationships, or fitness programs. I value my hard-won liberty way too much. I am now in charge and get to decide what works best for me and what doesn't. As they say in twelve-step groups, "Take what you like and leave the rest." By "like", I don't mean meaningless temporary pleasures. I mean I get to judge what is important to me and what offers the lasting happiness I seek.

There is life after Mormonism. I and thousands of other exmormons are living joyfully, free from guilt, shame, closed-logic structures, blinders, and monopolized time. Rather than follow rote rules, I make my own choices based on wise consideration of proven risks. I've learned what I really want from life. I am free to pursue dreams which were impossible before. I have many friends with similar interests who accept me for who I am, not who I'm pretending to be. I've got confidence, the career I want, and the family I want. I am a square peg who made my own square hole.

Joe Kelly, a former member of Transcendental Meditation and the International Society of Divine Love, recounts, "…back in the world now, I found it to be so very different from what they taught… cults had taught me that all worldly relationships were mundane and ultimately meaningless, self-centered, and based on what others could take from you… I learned how caring and helpful my true friends and family could be. They accepted me as I

---

1. Anon. "Know This, That Every Soul Is Free." In *Hymns of the Church of Jesus Christ of Latter-Day Saints*. The Church of Jesus Christ of Latter Day Saints, 1985.
2. Keen, *Hymns to an Unknown God*, 1995. 66.
3. Beck, *Leaving the Saints,* 2005. 297.

was. They didn't require absolute belief or use pressure."[1]

Adam had to break one commandment to thrive, to fulfill the purpose of all existence. He had to learn that which God had forbidden. Just as eating the fruit set Adam and Eve free from their beautiful and confining garden, so shall the truth set you free. Perhaps God's real test is this: Can you sacrifice ignorant bliss on the altar of knowledge? Will you trade milk for meat? Will you put away childish things and finally grow into adulthood?

---

1. Tobias and Lalich, *Captive Hearts, Captive Minds,* 1994. 90.

*Ironically, my parents' strong faith and loving kindness sent me contradictory messages that sent me on a quest that would carry me far from home: 'Think for yourself. But believe in the fundamental truths God has revealed in the Bible.'*
—Sam Keen,
***Hymns to an Unknown God***[1]

*Fix reason firmly in her seat, and call to her tribunal every fact, every opinion. Question with boldness even the existence of God; because, if there be one, he must more approve of the homage of reason, than that of blindfolded fear.*
—**Thomas Jefferson**

# Slippery Sources

## Truth Is Eternal (And Verifiable)

Blair Watson described integrity as "integration of ideals, convictions, standards, beliefs, and behavior."[2]

Integrity is being honest first to one's self, and then to one's world. This is my first value, and it means I try to base my beliefs as much on evidence as possible, so that when I profess those beliefs, reality supports me. Here is how I applied this philosophy while writing *Recovering Agency*.

Throughout the text, I will explain mind control techniques supported by direct quotes from secular cult researchers so you can see I have not distorted their words. These are followed with examples from Mormon sources to show each technique in practice.

I cite all references, and most are easy to find on the official LDS website (LDS.org), on academic, government, or personal websites[3], or in readily available books. I encourage you to verify any claim and supporting evidence I present.

In many ways, the Church has lightened-up since its founding in 1830. It continues to become less restrictive and demanding, and I applaud this trend. I primarily chose recent sources which have been made or restated in the last fifty years. I avoid obscure quotes except where appropriate to demonstrate deceptive practices, reveal hidden intent, or show where ongoing problematic LDS culture originated. I staunchly avoid misconstruing intended meaning by quoting out of context.

These materials are familiar to average Mormons. I wish to accurately portray the experience of a typical Latter-day Saint. In addition to scripture, I cite LDS manuals; magazines; talks; books; hymns; words from prophets, general authorities, and other high-ranking leaders; and media available from Deseret Book[4].

Due to the overwhelming amount of content, I was unable to exhibit all examples of a specific technique. I found similar concepts promoted throughout dozens and sometimes hundreds of different sources. I often selected the example near the top of the search

---

1. Keen, *Hymns to an Unknown God*, 1995. 97.
2. Watson, "Psychological Effects of Mormonism," 2008. http://members.shaw.ca/blair_watson/
3. I have included URLs for many books, articles, and LDS Conference talks that are available both on and offline. When these sources are repeated, I have removed the web address from subsequent instances to save space.
4. Deseret Book is a publisher owned by the Church. It publishes and distributes books, music, and other products related to LDS doctrine and culture. The word comes form a Book of Mormon scripture; it means "honey bee."

results, or tried to give priority to recency. Or I selected based on which quote was most concise or most closely matched the concept I wish to show. At other times, I analyzed a single talk and spread quotes from it throughout the book. Rest assured, I did not have to look far for the examples I chose.

You may not always agree with my interpretation of LDS doctrine. Nevertheless, my interpretation is shared by many others and is as valid as yours. Scripture says these are plain and precious things. (1 Nephi 13:26-40) If a specific source is so easily misinterpreted, perhaps it should be abandoned in favor of something more plain.

I also quote personal accounts from former Mormons and include personal quotes from those who have lived through other high-demand groups to show similarity with Mormonism.

I followed this methodology not only out of my own vigorous sense of integrity, but also for selfish reasons. To be less than honest would weaken my case. Since I expect criticism, I have done my best to build this work on a foundation of rock.

## Truth Is Eternal (Depends on Who You Ask)

*To know and not to know, to be conscious of complete truthfulness while telling carefully constructed lies, to hold simultaneously two opinions which cancelled out, knowing them to be contradictory and believing in both of them, to use logic against logic, to repudiate morality while laying claim to it, to believe that democracy was impossible and that the Party was the guardian of democracy, to forget, whatever it was necessary to forget, then to draw it back into memory again at the moment when it was needed, and then promptly to forget it again, and above all, to apply the same process to the process itself—that was the ultimate subtlety... Even to understand the word 'doublethink' involved the use of doublethink.*

—**George Orwell, *1984***

For each LDS source demonstrating one idea, there is another demonstrating its opposite. Scriptures are like statistics—you can always find one that makes your point. Yet somehow no one notices how many contradict one another. This is part of mind control. There are enough contradictory verses for religious leaders to preach one thing, only to deny it later with a different quote. This is a way of blaming the faithful follower for misunderstanding "the plain and precious truths."

Is God violent or peaceful? Should Mormons be proud or humble? Are we eternally punished because of justice or is a loving God teaching us? Is God forgiving or does he demand perfection? Are we meant to be happy in this life, or is suffering required for growth? Are we supposed to keep silent about sacred things (like the temple ceremony), or are we supposed to shout sacred things (like Christ's Atonement) from the rooftops?

Mormons are instructed to "let them worship how, when, or what they may", yet when a member leaves, the Church and family can't stop pestering them to return, threatening them with loss of blessings and eternal salvation. God is not a respecter of persons, yet doctrine speaks of chosen people and predestination. The Church is not political, yet it involved members in the campaigns against the Equal Rights Amendment and for Proposition 8.

The examples are endless. There are official Church sources to support each of these points, as needed. If you need to argue that the Church never taught something, just show one of the opposite quotes and you're covered.

Apostle Bruce R. McConkie wrote about this problem. "Truth is eternal and does not vary. Sometimes even wise and good men fall short in the accurate presentation of what is truth. Sometimes a prophet gives personal views which are not endorsed and approved by the Lord.

> Yes, President [Brigham] Young did teach that Adam was the father of our spirits, and all the related things that the cultists ascribe to him. This, however, is not true. He expressed views that are out of harmony with the gospel. But, be it known, Brigham Young also taught accurately and correctly, the status and position of Adam in the eternal scheme of things. What I am saying is that Brigham Young, contradicted Brigham Young, and the issue becomes one of which Brigham Young we will believe.[1]

How did he advise members to grapple with this problem? "...as Joseph Smith so pointedly taught, a prophet is not always a prophet, only when he is acting as such. Prophets are men and they make mistakes. Sometimes they err in doctrine. This is one of the reasons the Lord has given us the Standard Works. They become the standards and rules that govern where doctrine and philosophy are concerned. If this were not so, we would believe one thing when one man was president of the Church and another thing in the days of his successors."

Though McConkie here emphatically claims that the scriptures always trump the words of a modern prophet, other sources state that the prophet's new revelations supersede scripture and past prophets. In fact, in an earlier talk, McConkie contradicts himself. In the context of allowing black men to hold the priesthood:

> ...people write me letters and say, 'You said such and such, and how is it now that we do such and such?' And all I can say to that is that it is time disbelieving people repented and got in line and believed in a living, modern prophet. Forget everything that I have said, or what President Brigham Young or President George Q. Cannon or whomsoever has said in days past that is contrary to the present revelation. We spoke with a limited understanding and without the light and knowledge that now has come into the world.
>
> We get our truth and our light line upon line and precept upon precept. We have now had added a new flood of intelligence and light on this particular subject, and it erases all the darkness and all the views and all the thoughts of the past. They don't matter any more.[2]

Sometimes it is convenient to allow scripture to trump the modern prophets, and other times, the modern prophets are here to erase the darkness of the past. What is Mormon doctrine? It's a matter of who you choose to quote. Not just who, but when. This ends up being whatever the powers-that-be say it is.

In this case, McConkie says to forget any quotes supporting racism. Is that because those past leaders made mistakes? Because God wants us to forget racism? Or because racism makes the Church look bad?

Even while leaders deny past doctrines, some members still remember, which leads us to LDS culture and folklore. Mormonism is a high-demand *group*, not a high-demand set of doctrines locked in dusty books. The culture supports the doctrine, and the doctrine drives the culture, and all of it influences behavior to shape the Mormon experience.

Some elements of culture stem from older or more obscure doctrines. Others come from unofficial media, like Deseret Book publications, popular LDS musicals (like *Saturday's Warrior*), and unofficial LDS music (like Janice Kapp Perry). Sometimes cultural conclusions are *implied* by official doctrine though not directly spoken.

When it comes to convictions like, "As man is now, God once was; as God now is, man may become," the Prophet Gordon B. Hinckley can tell Time Magazine reporters things like, "I don't know that we teach it," or that he "[hasn't] heard it discussed for a long time in

---

1. Bruce R. McConkie. Letter to Eugene England. "Bruce McConkie's Letter of Rebuke to Professor Eugene England," Feb 19, 1981. http://www.mrm.org/bruce-mcconkies-rebuke-of-eugene-england
2. Bruce R. McConkie. "All Are Alike Unto God," 1978. CES Religious Educators Symposium http://speeches.byu.edu/?act=viewitem&id=1570

public discourse."[1] It doesn't need to be taught from the pulpit. Church members still believe it. I believed it. My family still believes it. We all heard it *somewhere*.

If it's told around campfires and taught by a "rogue" teacher, it's just as part of the Mormon mind as the words to "Choose the Right." Not a single Three Nephites[2] story or angels-save-the-missionaries story is told in any modern General Conference, but these urban legends reinforce official doctrine and are not outright denied—at least not where anyone can hear.

LDS culture is the slipperiest of sources, yet it is just as real to faithful Mormons. When necessary, I include these beliefs to demonstrate Mormon cultural pressures.

A popular LDS saying is, "The Church is perfect, but her members are not." Yet without her members, the Church is nothing but a bunch of shepherds with no sheep. Others say, "The Church is not perfect, but the gospel is." Yet without the Church, the gospel is just a pile of old lesson manuals.

My sources show that the Church and its doctrines are as imperfect as her people. Let's not blame the members for failing to live up to flawed teachings. Playing the accusation shell game will solve no problems. Thoughtful examination of all the parts of the machine might.

# By Their Fruits

*If Mormons are willing to do good things so eagerly, even if it's for a combination of the right and wrong reasons, it's difficult to criticize them for it.*
—**Jack B. Worthy,** *The Mormon Cult*[3]

Cult recovery books are quick to point out that even the worst cults are capable of doing good. Many teach solid values and help people overcome addictions. Many run charitable organizations to feed children, heal the sick, and house the homeless. Many are capable of enacting much-needed political change.

Likewise, the LDS Church does much to help out after natural disasters and it has service programs to aid people around the world, both members and nonmembers alike. It also teaches children and adults sound values and provides spiritual insights. Members often experience personal growth as a direct result of membership.

I am one of those members. The Church taught me to be comfortable with public speaking. It gave me opportunities to showcase my talents. It taught me how to transform my weaknesses into strengths. It inspired me to keep progressing. It taught me to stand up for truth in the face of persecution. These and many other doctrines helped me, and some I still hold dear to this day.

In writing, I have left out many of the positive aspects of LDS life, partly because the Church toots its own horn from the rooftops of every chapel. If you are looking for a glowing review of an organization with no flaws, the Church will happily provide you with one.

I shine a spotlight on specific aspects of the leadership, organization, doctrine, and culture which are harmful. These are hidden and thus need to be brought to light. Nevertheless, my criticisms are not meant to dismiss all the good the Church does for its members and those outside its sheltering walls.

Those who are recovering may feel conflicted. How can they be angry or in pain because

---

1. David Van Biema. "Kingdom Come." *Time*, Aug 4, 1997.
http://content.time.com/time/magazine/article/0,9171,986794,00.html
2. The Nephites were a group of people in the Book of Mormon. When Christ visited the Nephites after his resurrection, he blessed three particularly faithful men that they would "never taste of death." They are said to still be alive today, and many miracles that involve kind strangers helping during a time of need are attributed to them.
3. Worthy, *The Mormon Cult*, 2008. 124.

of an institution that does so much good? Internally, they may remember ways in which the gospel helped them become a better person.

This experience is normal for former members from all kinds of cults. It is important to embrace, accept, and be grateful for the positives of your experience, while also acknowledging deceptive and manipulative methods used.

## Unto Whom Much Is Given

*...a sharp line is drawn between those who will be 'saved' and those who will be 'damned' (nonmembers). In response to my questions, the Moonies openly denied this as one of their beliefs, although ex-members report that this view is taught later on. This tenet forms the basis for much of the fear and guilt that some former members say kept them in the group for so long.*

—Geri-Ann Galanti,
***Recovery from Cults***[1]

*Individuals involved in the same cult can experience vastly different levels of mind control.*
—**Steven Hassan, *Releasing the Bonds***[2]

Each Mormon may have very different experiences within the same Church. What this means for the recovering Mormon is that your process will be similar, yet unique, to that of other exmomons.

Aside from doctrine and culture, your experience in the Church might vary based on your age (what was emphasized forty years ago as opposed to today), where you grew up (the Mormon corridor vs. outside the US), your family of origin, level of involvement, etc.

It is possible that in some regions and families and eras, a Church member could have a wonderful experience your whole life. The gospel could have been interpreted only in the best light, with the fewest dogmas and spiritual abuses. Additionally, if all the doctrines fit your own personality and desires perfectly, you may have never felt inadequate. You fit in and have always been truly happy. If so, perhaps these words will only serve to help you walk a mile in the shoes of those less fortunate.

Here are some factors that may have colored your experience and affect your recovery:

- Convert vs. Born in the Church
- Age
- Temple Endowment
- Temple Marriage
- Mission
- Higher Church Callings
- Church Employment
- A degree from an LDS school
- Family
- Spousal and Child abuse
- Home schooling
- Geographical location
- Length of time in the Church
- Interpretations of doctrine
- Bishops and Stake Presidents

---

1. Galanti, "Reflections on 'Brainwashing,'" *Recovery from Cults,* ed. Langone, 1995. 94.
2. Hassan, *Releasing the Bonds,* 2000. 112.

§ Personal family stories and beliefs

As you read, you will think of examples from your own experience. Let these come to mind and maybe spend a little time reflecting on those moments. If emotions flow, let them, even if they are feelings labeled by the Church as negative, unholy, ungodly, or sinful. (There is a distinction here between feelings and harmful actions.) It is an expected and healthy part of the healing process to acknowledge sadness, loss, grief, betrayal, confusion, fear, and even anger and hate. The Church took your time, resources, money, maybe even family members. It shaped your identity and dictated your very thoughts. You may have done things in good faith which you now regret. You may have helped perpetuate what you now view as lies. You may have even been abused or mistreated by Church members, including your family, who may have used doctrine to justify their actions. Those feelings will be all mixed in. If you're reading this book, you probably have many reasons to grieve.

You may also feel positive emotions, and that's okay, too. The Church teaches many truths, and you most likely benefited in certain ways. It's healthy to integrate your uplifting experiences.

The grieving process is temporary. There are phases to exiting a high-demand group. Each phase takes a different length of time for each person, and happens in different intensities and does not follow a schedule. They do not always happen in order, and sometimes you may revisit a phase or skip a phase entirely. But know that eventually, it can all work itself out of your system. Hopefully, this book will help you better understand yourself and what happened to you, and through that, your grieving process can go more smoothly.

Please note that while your emotions are never wrong, what you do with them can be. Strong feelings might motivate you to lash out. Please keep your anger healthy by refraining from unnecessarily hurting anyone with actions or harsh words. The fact that you've left the Church will likely hurt family members and friends—that can't be helped. Do what you need to protect yourself and establish boundaries, and no more. It's highly possible you were never modeled good boundaries, so if you make mistakes, forgive yourself. Ask forgiveness of others if appropriate, and then move on.

Overall, just do your best. You no longer have to seek perfection.

# Part 2: The Science of Believing

*Every principle for personal growth, once institutionalized, shifts from serving as a vehicle for self-actualization to serving the actualization of the vehicle itself. We are no longer nurtured, but managed.*

—Matt Berry, *A Human Strategy*,
quoted in *The Pattern of the Double Bind in Mormonism*[1]

*We have learned by sad experience that it is the nature and disposition of almost all men, as soon as they get a little authority, as they suppose, they will immediately begin to exercise unrighteous dominion.*

—Doctrine & Covenants[2] 121:39

# Exploited Human Tendencies

The fields of cognitive science and behavioral psychology study why people believe and act the way they do. We can learn much from their experiments, studies, and theories.

Airplanes seem to defy the law of gravity, but in fact, wings manipulate the laws of fluid dynamics to work around gravity. Likewise, many mind control techniques can seem like magic, but in fact are leveraging ordinary human tendencies.

As human beings, we are predisposed with certain traits that help us thrive and negotiate with others. These social instincts aided the survival of our ancient ancestors. In modern times, they make us more efficient and save time and energy. They are decision-making shortcuts and automated assumptions to help us organize and make us efficient and give society a stable framework. As Robert Cialdini, compliance researcher and author of *Influence*, pointed out, "If, rather than whirring along in accordance with our prior decisions and deeds, we stopped to think through the merits of each new action before performing it, we would never have time to accomplish anything significant."[3]

The drawback of such automatic reactions is that they make us fallible while simultaneously giving us an illusion of correctness. Worse, these traits can be exploited and manipulated by cunning individuals and groups.

Science is beginning to understand these cognitive structures, to learn how we become persuaded by and retain long-term beliefs. Just as the laws of physics can be put to many uses, so can the mind's natural operation. These tools can be used to teach, liberate, entertain, build monuments, and to create a peaceful society. Or they can be used to abuse, deceive, oppress, imprison, and to incite war.

Some tools operate on the micro-level, the nuts and bolts of manipulation. These are the short-term persuasive tricks that work well one-on-one to accomplish a single goal with individual. Con men use them to swindle retirees. Computer hackers use them to tease passwords out of corporate employees. Pick-up artists use them to get laid. These methods are also used one-on-one by cult members to recruit.

Other tools work on a macro-level to support an entire system. In this book, I am more interested in these overarching structures. The same nuts and bolts go to creating that structure to be sure... They explain why you might fork over your fortune to the hustler you met last week. I want to show why you'd willingly fork over your monthly paycheck for decades.

---

1. Stricker, *The Double-Bind in Mormonism*, 2000. 143.
2. The Doctrine and Covenants (also abbreviated as the "D&C") were revelations given directly to Joseph Smith (and a couple of later prophets) in the 1800s. They are considered scripture.
3. Robert B. Cialdini. *Influence: Science and Practice*. Boston: Pearson Education, 2009. 89.

To reiterate, there is nothing magic about it. As well-known psychologist and Stanford Professor, Dr. Philip Zimbardo, was quoted so well in *Releasing the Bonds*, "We will try to understand how cults recruit members, indoctrinate them and shape their lives for noble religious deeds or ignoble secular ones. We will learn that there are no tricks or special gimmicks, only the systematic application of many techniques we have seen used and developed in other arenas of social influence—only more intensively over extended periods."[1]

Cult leaders themselves are just following instincts. Cults existed long before cult researchers, so I doubt many leaders study these techniques before wrapping people in their web. Control comes as naturally for them as following comes to their followers. These are the same dynamics used by narcissists, sociopaths, and domestic abusers, only done on a larger scale. Manipulative people experiment and notice what works. At some point, they cross an unstated ethical line, where the artifice goes a little too far. And that's where we call it a cult.

These tendencies are so natural, they also hold together all kinds of organizations, be they corporate, charitable, political, or religious. The more totalistic, deceptive, and manipulative the system, the more unhealthy it is for its participants, and for society at large.

Fortunately, the more you understand about how your brain works (how it holds tightly to existing beliefs, how it fools you, and the hidden biases it employs) the more you can put your mind to work for you, rather than handing it over to outside influencers. Think of this Part 2, and in fact, the entire book, as inoculation against unethical persuasion.

---

1. Hassan, *Releasing the Bonds,* 2000. 37.

> *I said [to the bishop], 'I guess I'd like to know why the Church keeps attacking anyone who has material evidence disconfirming Mormon scripture. I'd like to know how people who talk all day about Truth can spend all their time trying to hide it...'*
>
> *But there was no point in going on, because the good bishop had literally stuffed his forefingers in his ears. 'I can't hear you, I can't hear you, I can't hear you,' he chanted.*
>
> —Martha Beck,
> *Leaving the Saints*[1]

> *If we've been bamboozled long enough, we tend to reject any evidence of the bamboozle. We're no longer interested in finding out the truth. The bamboozle has captured us. It's simply too painful to acknowledge, even to ourselves, that we've been taken. Once you give a charlatan power over you, you almost never get it back.*
>
> —Carl Sagan,
> *Demon Haunted World*[2]

# Cognitive Consonance/Dissonance Theory

In 1959, social psychologist Leon Festinger set up a famous experiment that proved foundational to our understanding of human belief. He wanted to show that when we receive insufficient justification for behaving in a certain way, our beliefs will change to justify the behavior.

Psychology students were asked to participate in a study relating to "Measures of Performance." Before signing up, they were told that all experiments were being evaluated by an outside organization, so they should expect an unrelated survey afterwards.

During the experiment, subjects were given a boring, repetitious task. For thirty minutes, they were to move spools, one by one, from one tray to another. For another half-hour, they were to turn 48 pegs, one by one, a quarter-turn. These tasks were specifically designed to be futile, tedious, and unpleasant. And they had nothing to do with the real experiment.

At the end of the hour, the researcher lied to the subject, explaining that some subjects were told ahead of time how enjoyable the tasks would be to see if it improved their performance.

After this point, the experiment diverged. There were three groups of subjects who received different instructions.

The control group moved on to a supposedly "independent" interviewer, where they were asked a series of questions about how fun, interesting, and scientifically useful the test was.

For the other two groups, the experimenter asked the subject to wait a moment. He returned with news that the assistant, who normally would explain the tasks in positive terms to the next awaiting subject, had called in sick. The researcher then offered the subject money to fill in.

---

1. Beck, *Leaving the Saints,* 2005. 257.
2. Carl Sagan. *The Demon-Haunted World: Science As a Candle in the Dark.* New York: Ballantine Books, 1997. 241.

One group was paid $1 (in 1959 money) to extol the virtues of the tedious tasks to the next "subject" in the waiting room, while another group was paid $20. The next "subject" of course was a hired actor who pretended to be persuaded.

Afterward, all subjects were led to the "independent" interviewer and asked questions relating to enjoyability of the task.

Both the control group and those paid $20 rated the task poorly. Boring, tedious, would not recommend to my friends, would not repeat. But something different happened for those who were paid only $1. They seemingly changed their beliefs about the experiment. They found it fun, they would repeat it, and they would recommend it for their friends.

This experiment was in response to several previous, similar experiments, which showed that "...under some conditions, private opinion changes so as to bring it into closer correspondence with the overt behavior the person was forced to perform."[1] In one experiment[2], subjects were required to give a persuasive speech espousing an opinion they did not agree with. Those subjects who had to improvise the speech changed their existing beliefs more than those given a prepared speech to read, or those who merely listened to the speech.

Further work during this era studied brainwashing methods of the Chinese. Though the Chinese did not have access to this kind of research (most of it had not yet been written), they knew that offering small rewards in exchange for statements of belief would eventually win over their prisoners.[3,4]

What psychological trait could possibly account for these surprising results? Festinger's own cognitive dissonance theory helps explain not only why students talk themselves into thinking they enjoyed twisting pegs, but also why people are willing to kill and die rather than give up their beliefs.

Cognitive dissonance is not, in and of itself, a thought reform method. But because it is so central to how we think and make decisions, it becomes key to understanding manipulative techniques.

A cognition is a single belief, concept, perception, behavior, social reaction, memory, attitude, goal, value, commitment, or emotion. We carry millions of cognitions within our minds, like tiny cogs that turn with all the other gears in our minds to support an impressive thinking machine. Some of these cogs have no relationship to each other and cannot be correlated—for instance, our favorite football team has nothing to do with worries over the rising price of gas. Other cognitions are connected and reaffirm or detract from one another, like the price of gas and an economic political opinion.

We are driven to have at least an illusion of internal and external consistency. We must feel integrated. Our constructs must feel true. No one likes to be a hypocrite or liar, at least not without justification or excuse. Moreover, we want to feel sane both in our own eyes and especially in the eyes of others. Mental incongruence can threaten our sense of sanity.

This desire applies to larger spiritual and political beliefs, but also to small decisions and daily activities, like what products to purchase and how we raise our children.

The biblical James astutely observed human behavior when he said, "But let him ask in faith, nothing wavering. For he that wavereth is like a wave of the sea driven with the wind and tossed." James 1:6 We need a mechanism to filter new cognitions and keep us together, or we'd hop quickly from belief to belief.

To maintain this mental integrity, two powerful emotional forces sit in opposition to help us filter all the new information we take in. These are called "consonance" and "dissonance": the carrot and the stick.

---

1. Leon Festinger, and James M. Carlsmith. "Cognitive Consequences of Forced Compliance." *Journal of Abnormal and Social Psychology* no. 58 (1959): 203-210.
2. Irving L. Janis, and Bert T. King. "The Influence of Role Playing on Opinion Change." *The Journal of Abnormal and Social Psychology* 49, no. 2 (1954): 211-218.
3. Edgar H. Schein. *Coercive Persuasion: A Socio-Psychological Analysis of the "Brainwashing" of American Civilian Prisoners by the Chinese Communists.* W. W. Norton & Company, 1971.
4. Cialdini, *Influence,* 2009. 61.

According to Festinger, "Dissonance and consonance are relations among cognitions—that is, among opinions, beliefs, knowledge of the environment, and knowledge of one's own actions and feelings. Two opinions, or beliefs, or items of knowledge are *dissonant* with each other if they do not fit together—that is, if they are inconsistent, or if, considering only the particular two items, one does not follow from the other."[1]

When cognitions are aligned, when they reaffirm one another, you feel good. Consonance is the buzz when you know you're right. It's the thrill when your team wins, when you make a prediction and it comes true, and when your friend buys a product you recommended. It's the "I told you so" feeling. It's the elation when you preach to the choir or when the newspaper prints a story that supports your political position.

It's a kind of high, and it can be addictive. Scientist and author David Brin describes this addictive draw to consonance: "While there are many drawbacks, self-righteousness can also be heady, seductive, and even... well... addictive. Any truly honest person will admit that the state feels good. The pleasure of knowing, with subjective certainty, that you are right and your opponents are deeply, despicably wrong... many people actively seek to return to it, again and again."[2]

When cognitions clash, the exact opposite emotions are triggered. Dissonance is that sinking feeling when you think you might be wrong. It's the unrest when you realize you just did something you swore you'd never do, or the defensiveness when you're accused. It's your anger when the ref makes a bad call. The awkward tension when you realize your best friend disagrees with you. It's the driving need to explain the punchline when no one laughs at your joke, and the awkward knot in the pit of your stomach when news reports threaten to discredit the politician you voted for. It's the confusion you feel when someone you trust makes a factual claim that seems to shatter your deeply held religious faith.

Sometimes it is a mild discomfort, other times a devouring rage. Regardless of intensity, you are driven to resolve it, like thirst or hunger, and the more intense the dissonance, the more extreme the actions you may take to bring yourself back to consonance.

As your thoughts struggle to find resolution, your emotions morph. You try on various possibilities: The news report is a lie. There must be more to this story. Those factors aren't relevant.

At all costs, you must avoid the least comfortable option, the dreaded impossibility, the unthinkable, because facing it simply feels too terrible: *You've been wrong the whole time.*

Discomfort can be dodged using a number of strategies. Like water that seeks its level by flowing downhill, the path of resolution will be the one of least resistance. Most often the least comfortable option is to change existing beliefs or behavior in favor of the new cognition. We would rather justify, rationalize, and deny, than let that little piece of us die. And in some cases, we literally would rather die.

Barbara Harrison describes the aftermath when in 1914, Jehovah's Witnesses end-times prophecies failed to come to pass: "The Witnesses had nowhere else to go. Their investment in their religion was total; to leave it would have meant spiritual and emotional bankruptcy. They were not equipped to function in a world without certainty. It was their life. To leave it would be a death."[3,4]

The early Witnesses did not merely face the end of one cognition, that Christ would return in October, 1914. If that one cognition was false, all other cognitions must fall, one by one, until the collapse of the integrity of their entire mental structure.

---

1. Leon Festinger. *When Prophecy Fails: a Social and Psychological Study of a Modern Group That Predicted the Destruction of the World.* Harper & Row, 1964. 26.
2. David Brin. "An Open Letter to Researchers of Addiction, Brain Chemistry, and Social Psychology," 2005. http://www.davidbrin.com/addiction.html
3. Randall Watters. "When Prophecies Fail (Jehovah's Witnesses) A Sociological Perspective on Failed Expectation in the Watchtower Society." *Bethel Ministries Newsletter (now the Free Minds Journal)* no. May/June 1990. Accessed July 20, 2013. http://www.freeminds.org/psych/propfail.htm
4. Barbara Grizzuti Harrison. *Visions of Glory.* New York: Simon and Schuster, 1978. 167.

Knowing this, it is easy to see why wars are fought over nationalistic and religious ideals. It is easy to see why Jim Jones and his followers would rather commit suicide than let the US government destroy their community, which is what they believed would happen.

It is also easier to understand why students would come to believe that turning pegs was fun. There are four cognitions interacting in this experiment: 1) The opinion of the task, 2) The behavior of talking to another student about the task, 3) The student's desire to be honest, 4) Money.

Nearly everyone hated the task *while performing it*. Those who were not asked to lie reflected this feeling on the follow-up survey. Similarly, the $20 group also stated they did not enjoy themselves because they had been given an "out" for any feelings of dissonance. Twenty bucks is fair justification for committing a little white lie for the sake of science.

But those who were paid $1 had no easy out. They had just lied for practically nothing. In their case, the path of least resistance required them to change their opinion—to convince themselves they did indeed enjoy the task.

This is a powerful force, and it affects all of us. Since the 1950s, many experiments continue to be done in this field. In Festinger's book, *A Theory of Cognitive Dissonance*[1], he suggests three strategies we naturally tend towards for reducing dissonance. In general, most responses will be some variation on one of these, applied either to the existing or new cognitions:

1. **Alter Cognitions**

    a. **Existing cognitions**: Decrease dissonance by changing one or more existing beliefs, attitudes, behaviors, or even memories. In the face of new facts, we may change our minds. Or in the face of social pressure, we may begin to favor something we had distaste for previously.

    b. **New cognitions**: Return to consonance by rejecting the new information. If it confronts our fast-held beliefs, we may be prone to assume the bearer of information (activist, author, speaker) is a liar, is a member of an opposing group, has ulterior motives, or is morally wrong. Sometimes it is easier to deny facts out of hand than it is to change our minds.

2. **Add New Cognitions**

    a. **Mental**: We can add new concepts, ideas, or known facts to explain or justify conflicts, believe both, and transform nonsense into sense. For example, if we are a biblical literalist, we may be inclined to believe the parting of the Red Sea really happened. If this dissonates with our belief in a rational world, then we may add the idea that the sea was parted by a strong wind, or that in a translation error, the Israelites actually crossed the more shallow Reed Sea.

    b. **Behavioral**: Behaviors are also cognitions, so in the face of dissonance we may exaggerate, increase, or add new behaviors which support our beliefs. If someone calls us selfish, we may donate to charity for awhile.

    c. **Social**: Social support bolsters consonance. If we surround ourselves with those who share the challenged beliefs, the additional consonance will overwhelm the dissonance.

---

1. Leon Festinger. *A Theory of Cognitive Dissonance*. Stanford, Calif.: Stanford University Press, 1985.

## 3. Alter Importance of Cognitions

    a. **Lower the weight of dissonant cognitions**. When we can't get what we want, it is often easier to say, "Fine, I didn't really want it anyway." When a claim is proven factually wrong, we can dismiss its relevance and shift focus to a fact that continues to support our position. If we discover our favored candidate cheats on his wife, we decide fidelity is irrelevant.

    b. **Increase the importance of consonant cognitions**, to drown out the discomfort of dissonance. We may still be disappointed in our candidate's behavior, but we can elevate our candidate's work on causes we've convinced ourselves that we cared about all along.

Sometimes dissonance resolution may take some combination of all these forms, so long as it takes the path of least resistance given all our other cogs and their levels of importance. Changing, adding, or altering importance of cognitions may cause new sources of pain, loss, shame, disorientation, or fear. Which of these we choose will usually be that which causes the least discomfort.

We like to think of our minds as infallible (to think otherwise can induce dissonance), but resolution is so powerful that even memories can be altered, just enough to emphasize certain details while completely forgetting others. Deeply held beliefs will nudge one direction or another. Feelings will reverse. Minor facts will be misremembered or forgotten. The process is automatic and nearly invisible. Even if you're watching for it, it can be very difficult to observe.

Thousands of cogs end up linked together in larger systems of beliefs. Affiliations, religion, politics, culture, and other belief networks are reinforced by our social web. For some, keeping this belief system alive can become vitally important. The stakes are raised under the threat of losing livelihood, pride, social standing, or family. As the stakes go up, the more we are willing to do to protect each and every cog that supports the entire structure.

When one cog is threatened, we do just as Festinger predicted: alter the new or existing cog, add a whole different cog, or change the importance of the new or old cog. In this way, cognitive repairs can build up over time.

Many exmormons talk about the "mental gymnastics" they performed during the years leading up to their eventual departure from the Church. I've often thought of my LDS constructs as an elaborate tinker-toy of logic, or as a Rube Goldberg machine.

A Rube Goldberg machine is an overly complicated device that doesn't actually do much. You've seen them in movies, TV shows, comic strips, at science fairs, and on YouTube. To make breakfast, the clock-hand depresses a switch that releases the egg which rolls down a chute and winds back a spring-loaded metal woodpecker which has been repurposed to crack the egg and also turn on the stove. The egg's contents are dropped neatly into a frying pan. The heat from the burner ignites a fuse which launches a bottle rocket into an old skate that rolls into a series of dominoes. The final domino is attached to a string that pulls open a chute to let bread fall into the toaster, and also starts a ball bearing rotating down a spiral conduit where it drops onto the switch to turn on the toaster. When the toast pops, it fires off a ping-pong ball that tips over a cardboard sign which opens a valve letting water fall into a bucket and when the bucket is full it presses down on a scale that flips up a spatula to turn the eggs, and so on, in perpetual motion that resets itself in the end for tomorrow's breakfast.

Such a construct appears precarious from the outside, but is perfectly stable from within, so long as it receives constant tinkering and maintenance. Every piece depends on the other, and any slight change challenges smooth function.

Accepting the validity of even the smallest disconfirming cognition is like throwing out the egg-alignment or removing a domino. In order to keep believing in this unlikely, complex structure, new parts must be added, or old parts bypassed, a rubber band here, a bowling ball there, until the machine gets ever more elaborate.

It's just like I learned in Seminary: the Book of Mormon is the keystone of the Church. If it is false, then Joseph Smith wasn't the prophet, which means modern day revelation is wrong, which means the Church is not true.

Dissonance can't always be resolved, which adds to the complexity of the machine. Low-importance dissonance can be "put on the shelf" and exist there for years. Often people hold hundreds of unexamined conflicting views, by raising and lowering the importance of cogs at will. In *1984*, Orwell called this "doublethink", the ability to self-contradict without any awareness or discomfort.

Psychological totalism survives by manipulating dissonance and consonance. It's another way of describing mind control. Cognitions can be pre-installed in anticipation of external opposition to transform dissonance instantly into consonance. In this way, opposing cognitions can actually *increase* belief.

Persecution is a great example. Normally social disapproval is a dissonance-cognition that might intimidate a person into altering behavior. But if Satan hates truth and seeks to lead believers astray, persecution becomes proof. Under a persecution complex, criticism miraculously transforms into the potent emotional high of self-righteousness. Dissonance reversal is so powerful that people may even seek out contradictory cognitions. Followers may even perceive persecution where there is none.

How does the LDS belief system increase consonance and decrease dissonance to convert and retain members? This book is an exploration of the springs and strings and levers and latches of the Mormonism machine.

For some people, dissonance becomes too great to repair, and when it breaks down, you're able to see the machine for what it is. It all looks really cool but it just makes breakfast, and that's something you could more easily do yourself.

## Dissonance in Mormon Life
### Five Fictional Case Studies

Let's take a look at a few stories in the Mormon context. These specific events did not occur, but similar stories are frequently told in exit stories and online accounts.

> **Sister Brooks–**
> Sister Brooks has been semi-active in the Church for several years. Sometimes she takes her children to Church and still reads the scriptures.
>
> One day her friend, Sister DuPont, calls her in tears, ready to confide the source of her marital troubles. Her husband, a member of the bishopric, has been abusive toward her and her children. The night before, her husband gave her youngest son a black eye. Sister DuPont tried going to the bishop for help, but he insisted Brother DuPont is a righteous man and accused Sister DuPont of lying. She just needed to show her husband more Christlike love and support him in his stressful calling.
>
> Sister Brooks becomes confused, and eventually says, "I don't think your husband would do such a thing!" She hangs up.
>
> Sister Brooks abruptly increases Church activity, and tries to avoid Sister DuPont whenever possible. She has added consonance through behavior and social support. The importance of her beliefs outweighs her friendship with Sister DuPont, so she has cut off association to eliminate the dissonant memory of the uncomfortable phone call.

> **Brother Pell–**
> Brother Pell is in college with the hopes of becoming a science teacher. He had been raised to believe in the literal Genesis account of creation.
> In class, his Biology teacher, also his bishop, lays out convincing evidence for evolution. For a time, this dissonance threatens to crumble his belief in God. Then he realizes that God could easily have used evolution to create life on earth. "Seven days" could mean "seven time periods." Genesis is understandably vague about the other details, given the pre-scientific understanding of its author. Brother Pell adds cognitions to resolve his dissonance.

> **Sister Warren–**
> Sister Warren is a bishop's wife, former Relief Society President, and mother of six. At the county fair an anti-Mormon booth catches her eye. Though she ignores the pamphleteers, she can't miss a large sign which reads, "Joseph Smith married a 14 year old."
> Sister Warren senses discomfort between her image of Joseph Smith as a beloved and righteous prophet and the vile thought of a grown man marrying one of her teenage daughters.
> Sister Warren immediately dismisses the anti-Mormons as hateful liars. She changes cognitions—in this case, she rejects the new information as a lie.

> **Elder Roberts–**
> Elder Roberts is on a mission. Through converting others to the Gospel, he has finally gained a firm knowledge the Church is true.
> While proselytizing one day, an old man invites the missionaries in, where he points out conflicting passages in the Bible and the Book of Mormon. Dissonance slowly begins to niggle at Elder Roberts as the contradictions mount. When they leave, his companion shrugs it off. "The Bible wasn't translated correctly anyway, right?" Elder Roberts begins to relax. "Besides," says his companion, "That's why we have a living prophet. The Lord will reveal everything in due time."
> Elder Roberts smiles. With the help of his companion, he has reduced the importance of scriptural conflicts. The gospel as a whole is more important.

> **Brother Porter–**
> Brother Porter is an Elder's Quorum President. A few weeks ago, his wife came to him in distress about some information she found online. After much resistance, he agrees to look, and learns a few things about Church history that trouble him. He never heard these things taught in Church, and in fact on several points, the Church has stated the opposite. In light of the deception, and after a year of troubling thought and soul-searching, he and his wife put in their resignations. The Porters have changed cognitions, in this case, altering old beliefs to match the new information.

## Antidote—Cognitive Awareness

The good news is that we can choose mental constructs that help us resolve cognitive dissonance in ways that better match reality. We can ease the discomfort of uncertainty by installing one simple cognition: "I may be wrong."

I have made a number of cognitive restructuring decisions since I left the Mormon Church. I have a strong desire to never fall for falsehoods again—and to correct it as quickly as possible if I have been misled. I have chosen to make truth and reality my most important value.

That means if it turns out I've been wrong... yeah, it still hurts. But my choice is usually clear: Adopt the new information and change my beliefs to match.

When I first left the Church, I declared that if I could have one superpower, it would be to tell truth from lies, fact from fiction. Since superpowers don't exist, I settled for learning healthy cognitive tools. I continue to study the rules of logic, the scientific method, logical fallacies, skepticism, and cognitive science. I frequently debate with my partner and others to keep my wits sharp and my arguments honest.

Because I know what cognitive dissonance feels like, I can recognize it. It becomes information, itself a cognition, that I can take into account. Am I resisting this new idea because it's wrong? Or because of dissonance?

The effect is that I am less resistant to change and more open to learning. I am also more skeptical and less apt to accept new ideas without first researching opposing viewpoints.

Sometimes information simply isn't available to satisfy my criteria. In those cases, I mark them as "unknown" or "unknowable" rather than becoming certain of something I can't verify. It's possible to hold an unverifiable belief in a tentative manner. Some beliefs help me feel better or I find personal meaning in them. This is the category in which I place all my spiritual beliefs. These are preferences, not "truths." They are true for me and no one else. I do not try to convince anyone else to believe them. And they are subject to change.

If we can become aware of our cognitions and how they affect our behavior, we gain control of our own minds. We can choose cognitions that benefit us, and in that, find true cognitive freedom.

*...when the Dutch Anabaptists saw their prophesied year of destruction, 1533, pass uneventfully, they became rabid seekers after converts, pouring unprecedented amounts of energy into the cause. One extraordinarily eloquent missionary, Jakob van Kampen, is reported to have baptized 100 persons in a single day. So powerful was the snowballing social evidence in support of the Anabaptist position that it rapidly overwhelmed the disconfirming physical evidence and turned two-thirds of the population of Holland's great cities into adherents.*
—**Robert Cialdini, *Influence*** [1]

*Although there is a limit beyond which belief will not withstand disconfirmation, it is clear that the introduction of contrary evidence can serve to increase the conviction and enthusiasm of a believer.*
—**Leon Festinger, *When Prophecy Fails*** [2]

# When Prophecy Fails

I used to wonder about men who prophesied the end of the world. How could the followers continue to believe after it didn't happen?

In 1954, Leon Festinger set out to answer the same question. In historical accounts, he had noticed what he called a disbelief-disconfirmation paradigm, that groups "increase proselyting following unequivocal disconfirmation of a belief." In other words, when the world doesn't end, you'll try harder to convince other people you were right all along.

This shouldn't be too surprising given what we know about cognitive dissonance. Though the failure of one tiny part threatens to send all the gears flying off onto the floor, the Rube Goldberg construct of cogs must still be maintained.

"Disconfirmation introduces an important and painful dissonance. The fact that the predicted events did not occur is dissonant with continuing to believe both the prediction and the remainder of the ideology of which the prediction was the central item. The failure of the prediction is also dissonant with all the actions that the believer took in preparation for its fulfillment. The magnitude of the dissonance will, of course, depend on the importance of the belief to the individual and on the magnitude of his preparatory activity."[3]

Festinger observed this pattern in millennial and messianic movements going back to the second century. Montanus, the Anabaptists, Sabbati Zevi, and the Millerites, and I could argue, Christianity itself. In all cases, followers increased missionary zeal after their public claims were horribly disproven.

---

1. Cialdini, *Influence*, 2009. 109.
2. Festinger, *When Prophecy Fails*, 1964. 23.
3. Festinger, *When Prophecy Fails*, 1964. 27.

Festinger detailed criteria for his hypothesis:

1. The cognition(s) must be deeply held and related to action—the believer must act on his convictions.
2. There must be commitment on the part of the believer and he must take actions which are irreversible. The more committed the action, the deeper the conviction.
3. The beliefs must be specific, detailed, and related to reality, i.e. falsifiable or disprovable.
4. Irrefutable counter-evidence (disconfirmation) must be introduced and understood by the believer.
5. The believer cannot be isolated. He must have social ties to other believers.[1]

"…frequently the behavioral commitment to the belief system is so strong that almost any other course of action is preferable. It may even be less painful to tolerate the dissonance than to discard the belief and admit one had been wrong. When this is the case, the dissonance cannot be eliminated by giving up the belief."

Under these conditions, followers will try a number of purely cognitive attempts at finding relief. "Rationalization can reduce dissonance somewhat. For rationalization to be fully effective, support from others is needed to make the explanation or the revision seem correct…"

Eventually, "Whatever explanation is made it is still by itself not sufficient… The dissonance cannot be eliminated completely by denying or rationalizing the disconfirmation. But there is a way in which the remaining dissonance can be reduced. *If more and more people can be persuaded that the system of belief is correct, then clearly it must, after all, be correct.*"[2]

In other words, the most hardcore followers in this situation will be driven to convert others.

Every good hypothesis is itself a prediction and needs to be tested. Festinger was in luck. A UFO cult publicly predicted the end of the world before dawn on December 21, 1954. Followers had acted on their beliefs in irreversible ways. Their beliefs were specific and related to a real event. And when the date came around, the followers would have irrefutable proof of whether they were right… or wrong.

It was the perfect case study. Yet it wasn't enough for Festinger to read about the group's progress in the newspaper. He did something even more daring: His team of researchers infiltrated the group and observed their behavior *from the inside*—as fellow cult members.

The researchers established that believers had, in fact, taken irreversible actions. Members of the group had made public statements, quit jobs or gotten fired, alienated relatives, moved, and had no future plans for after the date predicted by the group's leader, "Marian Keech." (Festinger used a pseudonym. We now know her real name was Dorothy Martin.)

One follower, Kitty, remarked: "I have to believe the flood is coming on the 21st because I've spent nearly all my money. I quit my job, I quit comptometer school, and my apartment costs me $100 a month. I have to believe."[3]

Another member recounted, "Mrs. Lowell expressed…her fear that Bob was 'so deeply involved' that if the flood didn't occur he would surely 'crack up'."[4]

In spite of growing publicity, the group remained secretive, only allowing a few select members to join, and they became more insular over time. The inner circle cautioned, "be

---

1. Festinger, *When Prophecy Fails,* 1964. 4,216.
2. Festinger, *When Prophecy Fails,* 1964. 27-28.
3. Festinger, *When Prophecy Fails,* 1964. 80.
4. Festinger, *When Prophecy Fails,* 1964. 119.

discreet in talking about the beliefs, do not attempt to force people into the belief," and "by early December, an air of secrecy had enveloped the group and sentiments toward outsiders shifted to an even more extreme position—to almost an antiproselyting admonition: of those who come, speak only to the ones you are sure have been chosen."[1]

As doomsday neared, several small predictions failed to materialize. These were rationalized away, but at the same time, their stance on secrecy began to dissolve.

The first major disconfirming event occurred on December 17th, at 4pm. The faithful were supposed to be picked up by a UFO, to be spared from the coming flood. Excuses were made for the missed appointment and a new time was set. The UFO failed to land again and again, until the final deadline, midnight of December 20th.

As these smaller predictions lapsed, the group slowly lost members. For some, it was easier to throw out the whole machine than continue believing. Keech said "that now was the time to stick together, no, above all, there ought to be a 'strong group.'. The group and the support it offered were evidently very important, and the slightest sign of disintegration or defection was painful to those who remained behind."[2] Losing members clearly contributed to dissonance and became something of a disconfirmation itself.

During this phase, the group invented ceremonies, including a process that is strangely evocative of the LDS temple: "When their [Guardian] escort knocked on the door at midnight, Thomas Armstrong was to act as the sentry and ask the caller: 'What is your question?' There was a thorough rehearsal of the passwords the believers would have to use in boarding the saucer. Marian Keech temporarily took the role of the Guard at the portal of the spaceship and delivered the specific challenges he would use... The group went through the drill with intense care."[3]

Five minutes before midnight, various remaining members adjusted clocks and sat in tense silence. The shock of an uneventful midnight led to more silence, then another proclamation: There had been a slight delay.

Over the next few hours, the aliens remained absent, and the idea of a miracle began to develop. There was a prophecy that Mr. Keech, who had become disillusioned with the group over the previous week, would die. As he slept in the other room, the prediction changed. Now he would die and be resurrected. When he continued breathing, the group decided he had already *spiritually* died and been spiritually resurrected, in the sense that he had been reconverted.

The group tried on other explanations as the doomsday moment approached. Their stress clearly increased. Dr. Armstrong, one of the founders, said, "I've given up just about everything. I've cut every tie: I've burned every bridge. I've turned my back on the world. I can't afford to doubt. I have to believe. And there isn't any other truth. The preachers and priests don't have it... I've taken an awful beating in the last few months, just an awful beating. But I do know who I am and I know what I've got to do... I won't doubt even if we have to make an announcement to the press tomorrow and admit we were wrong... These are tough times and the way is not easy. We all have to take a beating. I've taken a terrific one, but I have no doubt."[4]

The nearness of dawn offered another opportunity for a miracle:

> Marian once more summoned everyone to the living room, announcing that she had just received a message which she read aloud...
> 
> "Not since the beginning of time upon this Earth has there been such a force of Good and light as now floods this room and that which has been loosed within this room now floods the entire Earth..."
> 
> The message was received with enthusiasm by the group. It was an adequate,

---

1. Festinger, *When Prophecy Fails*, 1964. 210.
2. Festinger, *When Prophecy Fails*, 1964. 157.
3. Festinger, *When Prophecy Fails*, 1964. 160-161.
4. Festinger, *When Prophecy Fails*, 1964. 168.

> even an elegant, explanation of the disconfirmation. The cataclysm had been called off. The little group, sitting all night long, had spread so much light that God had saved the world from destruction.[1]

The group decided immediately to talk to reporters they had been rebuffing all week. "The whole atmosphere of the group changed abruptly and, with it, their behavior changed too. From this point on, their behavior toward the newspapers showed an almost violent contrast to what it had been. Instead of avoiding newspaper reporters and feeling that the attention they were getting in the press was painful, they almost instantly became avid seekers of publicity."[2]

Sadly for Marian Keech, she failed to gain any new followers, unlike other prophetical groups like the Millerites (who became the Seventh-day Adventists), the Watchtower Society (Jehovah's Witnesses), or the Mormons. The group eventually dispersed, but under the name Sister Thedra, she later founded another religion, known as The Association of Sananda and Sanat Kumara, which survives after her death.[3]

Perhaps Keech's later, relative success, was owing to one slight but important change in the nature of her predictions: They became vague.

When we look at the larger body of prophecies, from scripture to horoscopes and even fictional omens used in novels and movies, they are typically indirect or metaphorical. They are designed, perhaps inadvertently, to have the widest possible range of interpretation. Religions that survive a disconfirmed prophecy tend to develop new indefinite prophecies. A specific year becomes "within a generation", and after enough time, that turns into "soon." Those who are members their whole lives never seem to notice when their generation passes away and Christ has not yet returned.

Joseph Smith's own prophecies took a turn towards ambiguity over time. In the early days, he made predictions of specific events which would happen by certain dates. In contrast, the modern Church's stance on the Second Coming has been "any day now" since I was born. In doing so, the Church avoids shedding members, though they lose the opportunity for prophecies to fuel the zeal for core members.

Yet as individual members, in the context of personal revelation, we had opportunities to create our own miniature versions of Festinger's disconfirmation paradigms.

I was nine years old, riding to camp with the Girl Scouts. One other Mormon rode in the car with me. Suddenly, the driver pulled over—a flat tire. As we waited for the tire change, a narrative unfolded in my mind, perhaps inspired by all the stories my mother told. Everything had a reason, so I became convinced our car had been protected from disaster. The other car, which had gone on, had probably met with an accident which we avoided. I loudly declared this to be true, and my fellow-Mormon agreed. Everyone else thought we were crazy.

As we got going, we passed no accident. And I experienced my first disconfirmation, the first event that threatened to shatter my childlike faith.

But my faith persevered in that moment. So the other car didn't get into an accident, but that doesn't mean we didn't avoid an accident of our own. I become convinced that God had given us a flat to protect us. And I made sure to tell everyone else. Maybe they would never agree with me, but I had right on my side.

---

1. Festinger, *When Prophecy Fails,* 1964. 169.
2. Festinger, *When Prophecy Fails,* 1964. 170.
3. "Association of Sananda and Sanat Kumara: Information from Answers.com." Accessed July 20, 2013. http://www.answers.com/topic/association-of-sananda-and-sanat-kumara

*All the truths you will learn can eventually fit together into a fervent, undoubting testimony.*
—Elder Robert D. Hales[1]

*After all, there is no need to be objective when you know you are right.*
—Chris L. Morin,
*Suddenly Strangers*[2]

# Biases, Behaviors, & Other Boogeymen

Biases. We all have them. Yes, even you.

As of this date, Wikipedia lists 168 cognitive biases, categorized by social psychologists and behavioral scientists. They affect belief, behavior, memory, social assumptions, and decision making.

The study of biases is important to the scientific community because their goals are accuracy-oriented. Scientific papers are subject to critical peer review, so researchers try (and sometimes fail) to structure experiments to eliminate them as much as possible. When the goal is to see reality for what it is, we try to set aside the human weaknesses that blind us.

In contrast, a manipulator can leverage biases to gain and retain followers, regardless of reality.

There are too many biases to cover in this book, but there are two worth mentioning.

The Bias Blind Spot is the king of all biases. In essence, it states that you have the tendency to see yourself as more objective than others. You feel that you are more open-minded and more likely to look at all the facts to form a reasonable opinion. *Other people are suckers. But not you.*

And that is an illusion. You're a sucker, too. We all are.

What is hard to accept is that biases occur unconsciously, at the level prior to conscious thought. When you encounter new information, your subconscious filters everything and offers up an interpretation as if it were the experience itself. Your conscious mind likes to pretend it is acting without bias, but the decision has already been made. All it's doing is rationalizing and trying to make that decision make sense.

Kind of scary, isn't it? We are enjoying an illusion of self-control, but more operates under the surface than we'd like to admit. I know the thought makes me extremely uncomfortable.

The only antidote is to accept it, learn about it, and to change those biases whenever possible so they work in our favor.

Then there is the one big bugaboo of a bias that deserves more attention than all the rest—Confirmation Bias.

---

1. Robert D. Hales. "The Importance of Receiving a Personal Testimony." In LDS General Conference, Oct 1994. https://www.lds.org/general-conference/1994/10/the-importance-of-receiving-a-personal-testimony
2. Morin and Morin, *Suddenly Strangers*, 2004. 44.

# Seek and Ye Shall Find—Confirmation Bias

*Every time I wash my car, it rains.*
—**American proverb**

*If there is anything virtuous, lovely, of good report or praiseworthy, we seek after these things.*
—**LDS Articles of Faith 1:13**

*...yea, and all things denote there is a God; yea, even the earth, and all things that are upon the face of it...*
—**Alma 30:44 (Book of Mormon)**

Confirmation bias is the human tendency to automatically accept information that confirms existing beliefs, while ignoring information that disconfirms existing beliefs. Instinctively, most of us start with the conclusion and then look for evidence to confirm it. It occurs on a fundamental, subconscious level, so we don't even get a chance to argue.

After the explanation of cognitive dissonance, this may seem rather obvious. Confirmation bias is an extremely useful shortcut to reduce dissonance—the disconfirming evidence simply doesn't exist. It slips past your notice into oblivion.

Confirmation bias isn't a bad thing. It lets us sift wheat from chaff and filter the signal from the noise. It is part of our human ability to notice patterns so we know what to seek out and what to avoid.

It may even be fundamental to how we learn. Brain cells (neurons) join together to form synaptic pathways, and these become our memories and knowledge. When we are first learning something new, say the alphabet, we see those shapes repeated, and with each viewing, those synaptic paths begin to form. When we see them enough, our brain decides they are important, and locks them in for good.[1] Put simply, neurons that fire together, wire together. Everything else is ignored.

Have you ever noticed that when you buy a new car, you begin to see the same model everywhere? Or when you learn a new word that you thought you'd never seen before, and then you see it four more times that week? Or when you keep hearing your favorite song being played all the time?

Repetition is the key to learning, and to some extent, this is our mind locking in important information. Without the ability to notice those patterns and ignore all non-patterns, our neurons would go on firing randomly and we would be incapable of coherent thought. Letters would be no different from squiggles, and we would never have any context for understanding how new information fits in with anything else.

Confirmation bias gives us an existing puzzle with tidy places for putting the new pieces we find.

However, it can also be a disadvantage. When the patterns are inaccurate, it will reflect a distorted view of the world. For this reason, confirmation bias needs to be understood, preferably by everyone. If I had my way, I'd have this taught in schools.

Scientist and author Carl Sagan recounts a study. "A scientist places an ad in a Paris newspaper offering a free horoscope. He receives about 150 replies, each, as requested, detailing a place and time of birth. Every respondent is then sent the identical horoscope, along with a questionnaire asking how accurate the horoscope had been. Ninety-four percent of the respondents (and 90 percent of their families and friends) reply that they were at least recognizable in the horoscope. However, the horoscope was drawn up for a

---

1. Thomas Lewis, and Richard Lannon. *A General Theory of Love*. New York: Vintage Books, 2001. P125-140

French serial killer. If an astrologer can get this far without even meeting his subjects, think how well someone sensitive to human nuances and not overly scrupulous might do."[1]

In a totalist system, many doctrines and mind control techniques encourage the use of confirmation bias, rather than discourage it. In a religious system, everyday occurrences become miracles, messages from God, fulfillment of prophecy. Disconfirming occurrences become forgotten mundane events. You pray for sun and nine times it's rainy, but that tenth time, the sun came out, and you thank God.

Remember *When Prophecy Fails*? "We have noted that following the major disconfirmation... there was a growing tendency on the part of the group to identify their visitors as spacemen...

"Though one or two visitors had been identified as spacemen in the months before the disconfirmation of December 17, after the disconfirmation not a day passed without two or three telephoners or visitors being nominated for the position."[2]

These "angels in disguise" stories take confirmation bias to an extreme, turning ordinary human beings into messengers from space who bring welcome relief from the pain of cognitive dissonance.

As a Mormon, I touted news articles which declared the dangers of coffee, alcohol, and cigarettes. Joseph Smith was right, 150 years ago! News stories about the benefits of these substances, however, simply went ignored.

Chris Morin recalls,

> Often, Mormons (myself included) pointed out how our version of the gospel was so logical, and easy to understand. Yet when a contradiction reared its ugly head, the mantra changed to, "the gospel is not supposed to be logical, it takes faith." If science supported some Church teaching, we pointed to those facts as support for our views; but in cases where science disagreed with us, we noted the flaws and inadequacies of science—"the wisdom of this world is foolishness with God."
>
> With a feeling of "by their fruits shall ye know them" we were quick to point out the humanitarian efforts of the Church as evidence of its truthfulness. However, we downplayed the good motives and humanitarian efforts of other churches.[3]

God's promise is easily fulfilled, because we are wired this way: "Ask, and it shall be given you; seek, and ye shall find; knock, and it shall be opened unto you: For every one that asketh receiveth; and he that seeketh findeth; and to him that knocketh it shall be opened." Matthew 7:7-8[4]

Examples of how the Church and its members confirm beliefs in this way are myriad. Scriptures, prayers, patriarchal blessings[5], inspired feelings, rewards for passing trials, interpretation of news stories and scientific research, interpretation of history—all information passes through the Mormon filter and comes through bearing consonance.

Anything that doesn't fit the narrative is excused away as human error or lost blessings or the effects of sin or Satan's interference. Everything becomes proof, except for what isn't, and those things are ignored.

Now that you know about confirmation bias, you'll see examples of it everywhere...

---

1. Sagan, *The Demon-haunted World*, 1997. 243.
2. Festinger, *When Prophecy Fails*, 1964. 214.
3. Morin and Morin, *Suddenly Strangers*, 2004. 49.
4. Mormons use the King James Version of the bible, and therefore, all bible quotes in this book will use the KJV.
5. All worthy members receive a patriarchal blessing. For those born in the Church, it is given during the teen years by a special member of the priesthood, the Patriarch of a stake. The blessing is pronounced verbally, and then typed up for later reference. Members are to keep their blessing secret. It contains the tribe of Israel to which the member belongs and a list of promises and commandments specifically tailored for that member. These promises are considered to be personalized prophecies, so long as the member remains worthy. The commandments are usually reiterations: attend Church regularly, read the scriptures, do genealogy work, serve a mission, magnify your callings, etc. The promises include things like: you will meet your eternal companion, you will be called to many great callings, you will have strength or other gifts and virtues to help you through life, etc. Praise of special spiritual traits may also be included. These blessings are considered the word of God, personal scripture.

## Six Compliance Practices

*All I want is compliance with my wishes, after reasonable discussion.*
—**Winston Churchill**

*Control leads to compliance; autonomy leads to engagement... While complying can be an effective strategy for physical survival, it's a lousy one for personal fulfillment. Living a satisfying life requires more than simply meeting the demands of those in control.*
—**Daniel H. Pink,**
***Drive: The Surprising Truth About What Motivates Us***

Social psychologist Robert B. Cialdini, who studies the psychology of compliance, sums up six major categories of social behaviors that leave us vulnerable to manipulation: Reciprocation, Commitment and Consistency, Social Proof, Liking, Authority, and Scarcity.

As he describes in his popular book, *Influence: Science and Practice*[1], all of these tendencies are useful. We don't always have all the information, and our busy minds need to make quick decisions. We take shortcuts, and are therefore prone to make a decision based on a single reason, rather than considering all angles. In many cases, these shortcuts are likely to lead to the best outcomes. But compliance professionals (like used car salesmen, advertisers, employers, and charismatic cult leaders) can manipulate those shortcuts to their exclusive benefit, and to the detriment of our own interests.

After making this type of decision, we often rationalize more reasons why we made it, even when these compliance pressures have short-circuited our ability to think rationally at the moment of making the choice. As always, our minds are driven to feel integrated and right. And we never like feeling suckered.

## Reciprocation

If someone gives you something, be it an object, a capitulation in negotiation, a discount, a compliment, or kindness, most people feel driven to give something in return. "By virtue of the reciprocity rule...we are *obligated* to the future repayment of favors, gifts, invitations, and the like."[2]

"...we will often go to great lengths to avoid being considered a moocher, ingrate, or freeloader. It is to those lengths that we will often be taken...by individuals who stand to gain from our indebtedness."[3]

Failing to reciprocate causes so much discomfort that we may even perform favors that far exceed the quantity or quality of the original gift.[4]

*Recovery from Cults* recounts a story of Diane Louie who escaped Jonestown on the morning of the infamous mass-suicide. How did she escape when nearly everyone else literally drank the Koolaid? Prior to that fateful day, after she had become disillusioned, she was sick in the hospital. Jim Jones came to visit and, showing concern, offered to make her

---

1. Cialdini's book includes all the science and references backing up these six social behaviors, including descriptions of the most significant studies leading to these conclusions.
2. Cialdini, *Influence*, 2009. 19.
3. Cialdini, *Influence*, 2009. 22.
4. Cialdini, *Influence*, 2009. 34.

horrible living conditions better. She refused.

"I knew once he gave me those privileges, he'd have me. I didn't want to owe him nothin'."[1]

Yet refusing an offer is also very difficult. We feel driven to accept what is given. "...it is the obligation to receive that makes the rule so easy to exploit. An obligation to receive reduces our ability to choose those to whom we wish to be indebted and puts the power in the hands of others."[2]

The social group also recognizes the unspoken reciprocity rule and will help enforce it by exerting additional pressures on anyone who refuses to comply of their own accord.[3] And an unpaid debt can result in strong feelings of guilt or shame. Moreso for a gift that we're regularly told we never can repay.

"Unto whom much is given, much is required," and what God requires (via the Church) is tithing, loyalty, and time. All in exchange for intangibles like blessings, atonement and salvation, eternal life, and spiritual gifts. It costs the Church nothing to grant us these unpayable debts.

Tangible gifts include disaster relief, service projects, and love bombing with cookies. Members and Church PR like to advertise their good works and point to the scripture, "by their fruits ye shall know them", that such acts of service ought to be proof of the Church's truthfulness.

Service activities are not bad in and of themselves, but they do generate feelings of reciprocity that can be leveraged. If members of the Church have been kind to us all our lives, we may feel a sense of obligation towards—not the members themselves—but to the Church as a whole, since we're told it is the Church that makes people so nice.

When we interpret all the good things in life as blessings from the Lord, we will desire to reciprocate by trying harder to follow the commandments.

## Commitment & Consistency

Commitment and consistency fit very well into what we've learned about cognitive dissonance. It is "...our desire to be (and to appear) consistent with what we have already done. Once we make a choice or take a stand, we will encounter personal and interpersonal pressures to behave consistently with that commitment. Those pressures will cause us to respond in ways that justify our earlier decision.

"...we all fool ourselves from time to time in order to keep our thoughts and beliefs consistent with what we have already done or decided."[4]

People are driven to be "right." Little commitments turn into larger ones. White lies turn into fervent beliefs. This mechanism is important in gaining and retaining long-term beliefs, so its various aspects will be explored throughout this book, especially as it relates to Public Commitment and Belief Follows Behavior.

It is important to note, "Social scientists have determined that *we accept responsibility for a behavior when we think we have chosen to perform it in the absence of strong outside pressure. A large reward is one such external pressure. It may get us to perform certain actions, but it won't get us to accept inner responsibility for the acts.*"[5]

In other words, if we can rationalize our behavior (dissonance) because we feel externally pressured, it will do nothing to change our internal attitude. But if we believe we have freely chosen the action, then it will become our belief. As you can see, the illusion of

---

1. Zimbardo and Andersen, "Understanding Mind Control," *Recovery from Cults*, ed. Langone, 1995. 114.
2. Cialdini, *Influence*, 2009. 31.
3. Cialdini, *Influence*, 2009. 34.
4. Cialdini, *Influence*, 2009. 52.
5. Cialdini, *Influence*, 2009. 80-81.

choice isn't just "nice." It is *necessary* to gain internal compliance and belief.

# Social Proof

Monkey see, monkey do.

People generally rely on one another to know the right thing to do in any given situation. Marketers have used this technique to sell products. It's the principle behind advertising testimonials, citing millions of happy customers, and placing that first dollar in a tip jar.

Cialdini says, "…we determine what is correct by finding out what other people think is correct… As a rule, we will make fewer mistakes by acting in accord with social evidence than by acting contrary to it. Usually, when a lot of people are doing something, it is the right thing to do."[1]

If the crowd after a concert is moving in one direction, it's probably towards the exit. If the parking lot at a restaurant is full, they probably serve good food. If all your friends are talking about the new bestseller they just read, it's probably better than a random book you pick off the shelf.

In the famous Asch Conformity Experiment in 1951, Solomon Asch tested to see how many people act against the current of social pressure. A subject was placed in a room with seven actors pretending to be fellow subjects. All were all asked to compare the length of three lines. The actors answered first, and all gave the wrong answer. Three times out of four, the subject would comply with the popular opinion rather than agree with his own perceptions about the length of the lines.[2] Many variations on this experiment have been done since.

Uncertainty makes us more likely to rely on the behavior of others. We watch what they do and mimic it. It's a useful shortcut, most of the time, until we encounter "pluralistic ignorance." "In the process of examining the reactions of other people to resolve our uncertainty, we are likely to overlook a subtle, but important fact: Those people are probably examining the social evidence, too."[3]

So if some people are wrong, everyone ends up wrong. Cialdini credits this phenomenon for what is more commonly known as "bystander apathy", when bystanders fail to assist a victim in need. Everyone assumes that someone else knows what's going on. "[One way] uncertainty develops is through lack of familiarity with a situation. Under such circumstances, people are especially likely to follow the lead of others there."[4] And if no one else is acting, then everyone continues to not act.

Pro-tip: If you find yourself in an emergency situation, it helps to give specific instructions to a *specific person*, if you are able. Bystanders will then immediately assist. It's not that they don't care, it's that they don't know what to do.

This effect is amplified by a sense of tribe. "We will use the actions of others to decide on proper behavior for ourselves, *especially when we view those others to be similar to ourselves.*"[5]

How could 15 million fellow Saints be wrong? How could all the people in your ward, many of whom you love and respect, be so fooled? If they believe it, it must be true. That is what the principle of social proof tells us.

---

1. Cialdini, *Influence,* 2009. 99.
2. Asch, S.E. "Effects of Group Pressure on the Modification and Distortion of Judgments." Edited by Harold Guetzkow. *Groups, Leadership and Men*, 1951, 177-90.
3. Cialdini, *Influence,* 2009. 110.
4. Cialdini, *Influence,* 2009. 109.
5. Cialdini, *Influence,* 2009. 118.

## Liking

It may not be surprising, but science has shown that "...we most prefer to say yes to the requests of people we know and like."[1] This affects some of our more important decisions and can overcome all other factors. For instance, when buying a product, "The strength of that social bond is twice as likely to determine product purchase as is preference for the product itself."[2]

Researchers found that a sales event performed from within the home of a friend, like a Tupperware party, is successful because it's as if we're buying from our friend. Tupperware has seen the highest sales in Asian and Latin American cultures, where ties to friends and family are even stronger than in the US.[3]

When friends aren't available, "...professionals...make use of the liking bond by employing a compliance strategy that is quite direct: They first get us to like *them*."[4] We are naturally prone to like someone who is physically attractive. "Research has shown that we automatically assign to good-looking individuals such favorable traits as talent, kindness, honesty, and intelligence..."[5] This is known as the "halo effect."

We are also unduly persuaded by the "association principle": "An innocent association with either bad things or good things will influence how people feel about us."[6]

It is no mistake that Mormons are associated with positive concepts such as God, love, Christian values, integrity, hope, virtue, blessings, children, scripture, clean-living, kindness and charity, all flaunted by well-dressed missionaries and happy families in heartwarming TV commercials.

Good food can also create a positive association. A researcher in the 1930s discovered that "...his subjects [became] fonder of the people and things they experienced while they were eating... These changes in liking seem to have occurred unconsciously, since the subjects could not remember which of the statements they had seen while the food was being served."[7] Would you like another helping of green Jell-O?

And if a person seems to like you, you will probably like them back. This is a form of reciprocity. Most people have a deep need to be liked, and have a desire to please others to accomplish this. It manifests in a technique known as "love bombing" and is a component of social pressure and other techniques.

## Obedience to Authority

We have a natural instinct to follow the instructions of someone who appears to be in authority. "...we are trained from birth to believe that obedience to proper authority is right and disobedience is wrong. This message fills the parental lessons, the schoolhouse rhymes, stories, and songs of our childhood..."[8]

There are many practical reasons for following parents, teachers, judges, academics, government officials, and other authorities. "Because their positions speak of greater access to information and power, it makes sense to comply with the wishes of properly constituted authorities. It makes so much sense, in fact, that we often do so when it makes no sense at all.

"...once we realize that obedience to authority is mostly rewarding, it is easy to allow

---

1. Cialdini, *Influence,* 2009. 142.
2. Cialdini, *Influence,* 2009. 142.
3. Cialdini, *Influence,* 2009. 142.
4. Cialdini, *Influence,* 2009. 145.
5. Cialdini, *Influence,* 2009. 146.
6. Cialdini, *Influence,* 2009. 160.
7. Cialdini, *Influence,* 2009. 164.
8. Cialdini, *Influence,* 2009. 180.

ourselves the convenience of automatic obedience. The simultaneous blessing and curse of such blind obedience is its mechanical character. We don't have to think, therefore we don't. Although such mindless obedience leads us to appropriate action most of the time, there will be conspicuous exceptions because we are reacting, not thinking."[1]

This instinct can be manipulated by con artists. "The appearance of authority [is] enough. ...our actions are frequently more influenced by a title than by the nature of the person claiming it."[2]

Other trappings of authority, such as clothing and status symbols, are equally persuasive. There is no need for proof of position. The claim is enough. If he's got the title of Bishop or Prophet and he's standing at the podium, of course you trust him. This principle (and that of social proof) is reflected in the story of the Emperor's New Clothes.

How far will people go when asked by a perceived authority? Read more below under the Milgram Experiment.

## Scarcity

That which is scarce, or which may become scarce, is more valuable to us. So if you can make something seem rare, people will want it more. Additionally, we are more motivated to prevent loss than we are to gain something new. In short, "...our typical reaction to scarcity hinders our ability to think."[3]

Early in his chapter on scarcity, Cialdini illustrates using a Mormon example: "The newspaper story reported that the Mesa temple had been recently refurbished... Thus, for the next several days only, non-Mormon visitors could see the temple area traditionally banned to them. I remember quite well the effect this had on me: I immediately resolved to take a tour...

"It became clear as I spoke [to a friend] that the special lure of the temple had a sole cause: If I did not experience the restricted sector soon, I would never again have the chance. Something that, on its own merits, held little appeal for me had become decidedly more attractive merely because it was rapidly becoming less available."[4]

Scarcity applies to intangibles as well as real goods, and also to information. If you really want to get people to agree with your message, just tell them it's been banned or that the powers-that-be want to hide it from people.

"According to the scarcity principle, we will find a piece of information more persuasive if we think that we can't get it elsewhere."[5]

The LDS claim to exclusive truth makes it more believable. It is a "Pearl of Great Price", exceedingly rare. And the people themselves are rare: "Many are called but few are chosen—and why are they not chosen?" So they will flock to the doors of the meeting house, overvaluing an artificially inflated commodity.

The scarcity principle also applies to freedom. "As opportunities become less available, we lose freedoms. And we *hate* to lose the freedoms we already have."[6]

This is called psychological reactance theory. "According to the theory, whenever free choice is limited or threatened, the need to retain our freedoms makes us want them...significantly more than before."[7]

If we have never had the freedom, we are complacent, accepting of the idea that we will never have it. But when a freedom is granted, even for a short time, and then removed, it

---

1. Cialdini, *Influence*, 2009. 181.
2. Cialdini, *Influence*, 2009. 184.
3. Cialdini, *Influence*, 2009. 221.
4. Cialdini, *Influence*, 2009. 199.
5. Cialdini, *Influence*, 2009. 212.
6. Cialdini, *Influence*, 2009. 205.
7. Cialdini, *Influence*, 2009. 205.

causes massive revolts, even on national scales.[1]

This seems to contradict the fact that cults take away freedoms, especially for those who join as adults. This tendency needs to be addressed or manipulated if the cult hopes to retain and gain members.

The LDS Church has a set of very clever doctrines which channel the fear of lost liberty to their benefit, by promising even *more* freedoms to those who follow the commandments. For those who were raised in the Church, who never actually knew the freedoms that nonmembers take for granted, the Church makes a threat: leaving will cause an additional loss of personal liberty. Moreover, without societal obedience to God's laws, everyone else's political freedom will also slip away.

## Mirror Neurons

Mirror neurons may help explain how social compliance mechanisms function. While no one has yet researched how mirror neurons act in thought-reform or cult environments, it is easy to imagine the role this plays in manipulation and coercion.

"Mirror neurons are a type of brain cell that respond equally when we perform an action and when we witness someone else perform the same action. They were first discovered in the early 1990s, when a team of Italian researchers found individual neurons in the brains of macaque monkeys that fired both when the monkeys grabbed an object and also when the monkeys watched another primate grab the same object.

"...watching an action and performing an action could also elicit the same feelings in people."[2]

One-on-one manipulation techniques, such as social proof, identification and example, and trance inducement make sense in the light of this discovery. It indicates that some types of influence occur on a cellular level, unaffected by the filter of conscious thought. When we see someone in pain, we tend to instinctively feel their pain. When we see a look of disgust, we too feel the disgust. It is how we sync up to the moods and social direction of those around us, and when guided by authority, can direct us wherever the leaders would have us go.

## Milgram Experiment

In 1961, Stanley Milgram began a series of psychological experiments, hoping to discover if Nazi war criminals could have been simply "following orders" as they claimed. The answer he found was, "Yes." Decent people will do horrible things to one another when ordered to do so by someone in authority.

The experiment purported to have two subjects: a "Teacher" and a "Learner"; but the Learner was merely an actor. The Learner sat, strapped to a chair, covered in ominous wires and electrodes, The Teacher could see him through a window and hear via intercom.

The researcher, in a lab coat and with a clipboard (both trappings of authority), instructed the Teacher to administer a memory test. If the Learner failed to answer correctly, the Teacher should press a button to deliver an increasingly intense shock.

As the voltage increased, the actor played the role. At first, he merely twitched in discomfort. But as the voltage increased, the shocks seemed to elicit real pain. Eventually, the "Learner" would scream and beg to be set free.

The real test was whether the Teacher would continue administering the shocks, or whether he would walk out, refusing to commit torture.

---

1. Cialdini, *Influence*, 2009. 214-216.
2. Lea Winerman. "The Mind's Mirror." *APA Monitor on Psychology*, Oct 2005.

Though the subjects grew increasingly uncomfortable, and in some cases, protested and questioned, most continued to electrocute the "victim." In one version, the "Learner" would complain about his heart condition and his fear he would not survive. In that, 65 percent of the subjects obeyed authority all the way to the end of the experiment.[1]

The subjects of these experiments suffered acute stress, in some cases, long-term psychological harm, even after being let in on the secret. Nevertheless, their instinct to follow authoritative commands led them to go against their morals.

As Cialdini points out, the Milgram Experiment was repeated several times throughout the bible, most notably in "...Abraham's willingness to plunge a dagger through the heart of his young son because God, without any explanation, ordered it. We learn in this story that the correctness of an action was not judged by such considerations as apparent senselessness, harmfulness, injustice, or usual moral standards, but by the mere command of a higher authority."[2]

This experiment is now considered unethical because of the psychological damage it caused its subjects, yet it is allowed to play out in the real world, and sometimes it is even celebrated. Rather than attempting to suppress this human tendency, LDS doctrine, sadly, seems to encourage it.

---

1. Cialdini, *Influence,* 2009. 176-180.
2. Cialdini, *Influence,* 2009. 180-181.

# Part 3: Thought Reform Methods

*[My doubts] were dim, as if under water, and they lacked power.*
—**Steve Sanchez, *Spiritual Perversion***[1]

*Those who can make you believe absurdities, can make you commit atrocities.*
—**Voltaire, *Miracles and Idolatry***

*Wherefore take unto you the whole armour of God, that ye may be able to withstand in the evil day, and having done all, to stand.*
—**Ephesians 6:13**

# The Whole Armor of God

If Mormonism is a machine, thought reform methods are a series of protective cognitions designed to repair and bolster continuing operation in the face of breakdown or external sabotage. Like gears in a complex device, thought reform is the sum of hundreds of moving parts with reinforcing systems to ensure that if one sprocket breaks, there are a dozen more to pick up the load.

The machine starts simple so that it will remain stable in its new environment. The outside of the machine remains the same size as pieces are crammed in tighter and tighter, added by the leaders, the group, and you. There is enough redundancy in function that any one part can break, and other mechanisms will step in.

The machine self-repairs from internal (negative emotions, personal doubts) or external damage (experiences, facts, helpful outsiders, attacks against the belief system). It is in perpetual motion, gaining energy from the group and from itself. A series of circuits establish a win-win situation for the truthfulness of the Church, and a lose-lose situation for members who question or fail to measure up. Thought reform stokes the flames of cognitive consonance while rerouting dissonance.

At first it seems the machine is external—the Church, the doctrines. But the machine isn't separate from you—it *is* you. It grows to fill the space of your mind as it pushes out other machines. You become fully invested in maintaining the machine because letting it break down means the end of *you*.

According to Singer, "As part of the intense influence and change process in many cults, people take on a new social identity, which may or may not be obvious to an outsider. When groups refer to this new identity, they speak of members who are transformed, reborn, enlightened, empowered, rebirthed, or cleared. The group-approved behavior is reinforced and reinterpreted as demonstrating the emergence of 'the new person.' Members are expected to display this new social identity."[2]

Some sources call this a "pseudopersonality", and it brings to mind the words to a song I once knew and loved, *His Image In Your Countenance* by Janice Kapp Perry, and the scripture it is based on: "And now behold, I ask of you, my brethren of the church, have ye spiritually been born of God? Have ye received his image in your countenances? Have ye experienced this mighty change in your hearts?" Alma 5:14

---

1. Sanchez, *Spiritual Perversion,* 2005. 176.
2. Singer, *Cults in Our Midst,* 1995. 77-78.

So among other things, thought-reform can be thought of as self-replacement—the leader or the group recreates the individual in the leader or group's image.

Voltaire's famous quote about atrocities comes from a longer, more illuminating paragraph: "Formerly there were those who said: You believe things that are incomprehensible, inconsistent, impossible because we have commanded you to believe them; go then and do what is unjust because we command it. Such people show admirable reasoning. Truly, whoever is able to make you absurd is able to make you unjust. If the God-given understanding of your mind does not resist a demand to believe what is impossible, then you will not resist a demand to do wrong to that God-given sense of justice in your heart. As soon as one faculty of your soul has been dominated, other faculties will follow as well. And from this derives all those crimes of religion which have overrun the world."[1]

Indeed, once you buy into all the seemingly good parts of the system, you are also compelled to buy the bad. Thought-reform methods work in tandem to accomplish this level of control. Michael Langone stated that controlling groups create a system of deception, dependency, and dread.[2] According to clinical psychologist, Margaret Singer, a thought-reform system works by:

1. Controlling an individual's social and psychological environment, especially a person's time.
2. Placing an individual in a position of powerlessness within a high-control authoritarian system.
3. Relying usually on a closed system of logic, which permits no feedback and refuses to be modified except by executive order.
4. Relying on unsophistication of the person being manipulated [that is, the person is unaware of the process], and he or she is pressed to adapt to the environment in increments that are sufficiently minor so that the person does not notice changes.
5. Eroding the confidence of a person's perceptions.
6. Manipulating a system of rewards, punishments, and experiences to promote new learning or inhibit undesired previous behavior. Punishments usually are social ones, for example, shunning, social isolation, and humiliation (which are more effective in producing wanted behavior than beatings and death threats, although these do occur).[3]

Steven Hassan organizes the structure of control in his BITE Model, which stands for Behavior, Information, Thought, and Emotion. If you can control these four elements, you control the individual.

In his book, *Releasing the Bonds*, Hassan goes into greater detail, breaking down each element into specific actions and beliefs. For example, clothing, personal affiliations, food, and use of time are dictated by the organization, to one extent or another. Exposure to outside information media is restricted, incentives and deterrents are established, and rigid rules are enforced. Access to information is limited based on how involved an individual is in the organization, criticism is curtailed, blame is reversed, guilt and fear is established, and family contact is manipulated in some way. Mormonism fits this model like a glove. I have expanded fully on *The BITE Model and Mormon Control* on my website and in a short ebook.

With this "whole armor of God", the minds of members are guarded from any threat which might shake faith and increase doubt. Even when doubt is fully justified.

---

1. Voltaire. *Miracles and Idolatry*, 1765. http://en.wikiquote.org/wiki/Voltaire
2. Langone, "Introduction," *Recovery from Cults*, 1995.
3. Tobias and Lalich, *Captive Hearts, Captive Minds*, 1994. 38

> And if your eye be single to my glory, your whole bodies shall be filled with light, and there shall be no darkness in you; and that body which is filled with light comprehendeth all things.
>
> Therefore, sanctify yourselves that your minds become single to God, and the days will come that you shall see him; for he will unveil his face unto you, and it shall be in his own time, and in his own way, and according to his own will.
>
> Remember the great and last promise which I have made unto you; cast away your idle thoughts and your excess of laughter far from you.
>
> D&C 88:67-69

Perhaps the whole system can be summed up by the words of exmormon, Brad Morin: "It is not ignorance which damns us; rather, it is the love of ignorance, the devotion to ignorance, the passionate embrace of ignorance by labeling other views as evil, then relentlessly insisting: 'See no evil. Hear no evil.'"[1]

## Breastplates, Shields, & Helmets of Faith

*Brainwashing...is an invisible social adaptation. When you are the subject of it, you are not aware of the intent of the influence processes that are going on, and especially, you are not aware of the changes taking place within you.*
—**Margaret Thaler Singer, *Cults in Our Midst***[2]

*And they all cried with one voice, saying: Yea, we believe all the words which thou hast spoken unto us; and also, we know of their surety and truth, because of the Spirit of the Lord Omnipotent, which has wrought a mighty change in us, or in our hearts, that we have no more disposition to do evil, but to do good continually.*
—**Mosiah 5:2 (Book of Mormon)**

Armor metaphors abound in scripture, lessons, and talks. The symbol is a personal defense to keep out dangerous elements. "A testimony is a shield of faith 'wherewith ye shall be able to quench all the fiery darts of the wicked.'"[3]

This magic armor is forged of links that I will name, because in myth, naming magic unravels the spell. There are thirty-one specific control mechanisms used by high-demand groups to "recruit, convert, control, and retain members."[4] They are:

✓ **Love Bombing**—Friendliness, flattery, praise, and affection are used to entice participation and attendance for potential recruits, and to retain members who may be showing less enthusiasm or are thinking of leaving.

✓ **Destabilizing the Self**—Barriers are torn down that would otherwise prevent acceptance of new beliefs. Includes those who have already been destabilized by life situations and the indoctrination of children, who have not yet formed a sense of self.

✓ **Deception**—Lies, omissions, and "front" activities cover up flaws or unusual aspects of the group, doctrine, leadership, and history. Some deceptions will be revealed later when a member is "ready."

✓ **Sacred Science (Closed System of Logic)**— The ideology and leader have the one

---

1. Morin and Morin, *Suddenly Strangers*, 2004. 150.
2. Singer, *Cults in Our Midst*, 1995. 61.
3. Robert D. Hales. "The Importance of Receiving a Personal Testimony." In LDS General Conference, Oct 1994.
4. Singer, *Cults in Our Midst*, 1995. 126.

and only truth. Members should only seek answers in group teachings. Doctrinal logic is airtight. The leaders are above criticism and those who question or criticize are immoral.

✓ **Mystical Manipulation**—Forces exist which are more powerful than the self. The group strives to fulfill a higher purpose. Ends justify the means. Events and experiences are orchestrated, manipulated, or reframed to appear supernatural and prove the leader is chosen and the doctrines are true.

✓ **Milieu Control**—Information and environment are tightly controlled. Gossip, questioning, and criticism is tightly regulated, as is access to outside information, especially that which might raise doubts or be critical of the group.

✓ **Demand for Purity (Perpetual Inadequacy)**— Lofty moral goals are set. At first the goals seem achievable, but the standards for achievement grow ever more impossible to meet, keeping the follower perpetually inadequate.

✓ **Dispensing of Existence**—The individual's literal or figurative existence is threatened as a consequence for impurity, doubt, or leaving the group. Life, the eternal soul, self-esteem, a sense of "being good", and one's identity hangs in the balance.

✓ **Doctrine Over Self**—The individual is subordinate to the group, leader, and teachings. When personal desires, goals, and values conflict with group values, they become selfish or immoral.

✓ **Loading the Language**—Existing words are loaded with new meaning. New words are added. Other words are banned or dropped from usage. This affects ability to think, as well as ability to communicate comfortably with those outside the group.

✓ **Totalist Reframing**—Situations, thoughts, or feelings are reinterpreted in a way that suits the goals of the organization. This is used to continually prove the ideology correct, to squelch doubts, and to silence outsiders.

✓ **Thought-Terminating Clichés**—Short phrases, pat answers, metaphors, and emotional reactions are pre-established to frame doubts. Doubt and questions are automatically shut down.

✓ **Social Pressure**—Social acceptance and rejection are used to reward and punish. A member becomes driven with a desire to conform.

✓ **Belief Follows Behavior**—Action generates the associated beliefs.

✓ **Public Commitment**—Commitments are expressed aloud. Public statements reinforce belief and dedication to the group.

✓ **Creating Dependency**—A member comes to depend on the group for physical, emotional, social, spiritual, or other needs. The member has a high stake in continuing to stay loyal to the group.

✓ **Black and White Thinking**—Broad spectrums of thought and morality become reduced to two options: Good vs. Evil, Love vs. Hate, Weak vs. Strong, Humble vs. Proud.

✓ **Elitism**—The members of the group are chosen people, exalted, righteous. Members are made to feel special when compared to outsiders.

✓ **Us-Versus-Them Thinking**—This is a form of black-and-white thinking wherein outsiders, ex-members, and those critical of the group are dehumanized and labeled as evil, apostate, vicious, hateful, prideful, blinded, deceived, etc. A persecution complex may exist whereby reasonable criticism is reframed as an attack.

✓ **Indirect Directives**—Certain restrictions or demands on behavior are implied rather than express. The logical elements for a given conclusion are supplied, leaving the member to draw the conclusion herself. Leadership remains innocent of issuing any unseemly teachings.

✓ **Identification and Example**—Those who behave correctly or incorrectly are used as examples. Suggested behavior can be inferred from these stories without direct commandment. Stories are told, which may be reframed or blatantly untrue, to demonstrate consequences. The human mind relates strongly to stories, and it also inspires social pressure.

✓ **Emotion Over Intellect**—Emotion is emphasized as the preferred decision-making tool. The value of using reason is downplayed. Doctrines are frequently taught in emotional contexts, such as through stories told in tearful or gentle tones.

✓ **Induced Phobias**—Fears are instilled which are either imaginary, based on real or exaggerated consequences, or on artificial effects created from group pressures.

✓ **Trance Induction & Dissociative States**—Critical thinking skills are reduced through regular encouragement of receptive mental states. Altered states can be mild and seem normal, and include concentration, fatigue, boredom, and hunger.

✓ **Time Control**—The member has little time or energy to question beliefs, associate with outsiders, or examine life too closely. Time spent on group-related activities is strongly encouraged or enforced, and usually fills every spare moment.

✓ **Double-Bind**—The member is "damned if you do, damned if you don't." She must betray the group or betray her own integrity.

✓ **Blame Reversal**—The leadership, group, and doctrine are above reproach, so any failed promises and bad situations are always the fault of the member.

✓ **Guilt & Shame**—A cycle of guilt and shame comes from repressed doubts, social pressure, and failure to meet impossible standards.

✓ **Confession**—The individual surrenders to leaders through confession, which reduces privacy and boundaries. Successful purification can grant temporary relief from guilt, which increases trust and dedication. Members are motivated to obey to avoid confession.

✓ **Euphoria Induction**—The euphoria of group participation and fulfilling the member's ideals motivates good behavior and reduces doubts while proving the validity of the group.

✓ **Proselytizing**—Members are encouraged to propagate teachings to outsiders. This not only maintains or increases the size of the group, but also soothes cognitive dissonance, consumes time, and provides opportunities for public commitment.

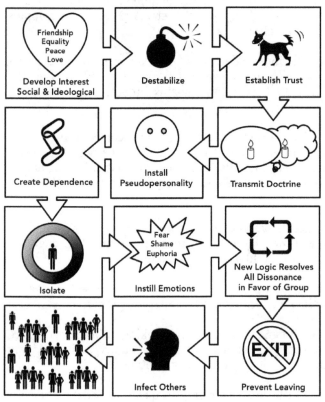

A cult may omit a few of these techniques, but most will be present. If they're not, then either it isn't a totalistic group, or the group finds no followers.

The degree to which they are used varies from group to group. Where one totalist organization may create physical dependency inside a cult compound, another may rely on emotional and spiritual dependency. One group may induce heavy and frequent trance states through the use of meditation and chanting, while another merely induces low-level trance via prayer.

Mormonism uses all thirty-one, which I will show in each associated chapter. Within the Mormon experience, the extent and effectiveness of these methods can vary from ward to ward and family to family. The varying degrees of reinforcement on the family level is a huge factor. For instance, abuse can turn what would be a mildly exploitative experience into a full-blown family-level cult, employing every controlling method at high levels.

These methods are only rough categories for understanding the complicated underlying dynamics involved. Most are dependent upon one another and sometimes it is difficult to tell where one method ends and another begins.

The techniques build foundations and enforce each other. Some would utterly fail without buttressing. Love bombing isn't very coercive unless it's used to instill dependency. No one would take demand for purity seriously without euphoria, elitism, and other incentives. Each method performs several of the following functions:

| Reward | Gives people a reason to join and stay. Heals wounds. *Creates consonance.* |
|---|---|
| Suppression | Suppresses awareness, bypasses critical thinking, and softens the mind for influence. *Reduces or prevents dissonance.* |
| Influence | The pathways for indoctrination. Teaches cognitions and behaviors. Persuades and convinces. *Increases consonance.* |
| Trust | Builds trust and likability. Proves the goodness of the group, other members, and the leader. Establishes authority. *Creates consonance.* |
| Reinforcement | Strongly reinforces other established mechanisms. *Creates consonance.* |
| Punishment | Causes avoidance of undesirable behaviors. *May cause dissonance, which is balanced by other methods.* |

| **Silencing Doubts** | Removes questions. Prevents criticism from being aired aloud. *Resolves dissonance.* |
|---|---|
| **Group Identification** | Identity becomes one with the group. Group cohesion is increased. Generates social proof. Creates a feeling of belonging. *Creates consonance.* |
| **Isolation** | Cuts members off from outside influences and sources of support. *Prevents dissonance.* |
| **Perpetuation** | Propagates the belief-system by spreading it to others. *Increases consonance.* |

The gospel is like an entrancing spell. As you try to pull away, it draws you back, even long after you've left. By naming these cantrips, you can be freed from the enchantment. You can leave the Church, and maybe soon you'll also be able to leave it alone.

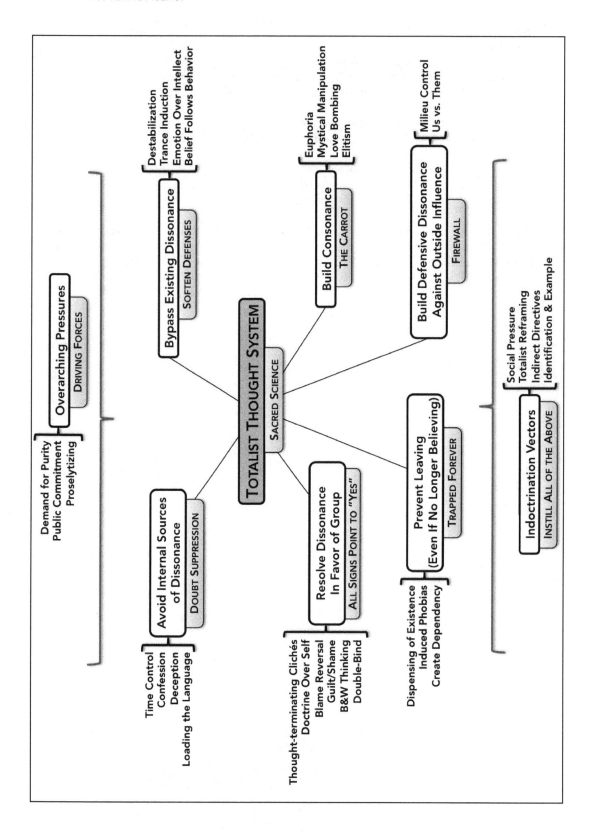

*Friendship: (verb.) To fool people into thinking you love them long enough to get them baptized. 'I've been friendshipping my neighbors for three months, and now they've suddenly put a for-sale sign on their lawn.'*

—Orson Scott Card,
**Saintspeak: The Mormon Dictionary**

*It was clear that the compassion these sweet people were offering me was real and spontaneous, that nothing I could ever do would set me outside the circle of their acceptance.*

*Looking back over the various illusions I've harbored during my lifetime, I would have to say that this was one of the very, very best.*

—Martha Beck,
**Leaving the Saints**[1]

*I understood how I had been held by chains of love in a prison that did violence to my mind and spirit.*

—Sam Keen,
**Hymns to an Unknown God**[2]

# Love Bombing

**Love Bombing**
—*Reward, Trust, Group Identification, Perpetuation*

- Attracts new members
- Builds trust
- Lowers defenses
- Makes the group seem morally good
- Overcomes resistances to strange ideas, steep learning curve, and doubts
- Establishes that member must seek approval from the group
- Establishes a reward: positive social feedback
- Pulls people back into the fold when they stray

The term "Love Bombing" was coined by the Moonies. It has since been adopted by cult researchers. New members are sought out, friendshipped, and invited to group events. Potential recruits are overwhelmed with attention, which makes them feel special.

According to psychologist Michael Langone, "As recruits lower their defenses in this 'loving' climate, intimate and seemingly caring conversations enable recruiters to assess the psychological and social status of prospects, to learn about their needs, fears, dependency potential, and actual and possible resistances. Meanwhile, testimonies from group members (who are not adverse to lying for the 'cause'), credentials (whether valid or bogus) of leaders, attacks on the group's competitors, and prospects' favorable reaction to members' seemingly warm and caring attentiveness tend to support the group's claim of benevolence and superiority, and to convince prospects that they will benefit by joining the group."[3]

Love bombing instills trust. It is difficult to think of the new group as harmful when

---

1. Beck, *Leaving the Saints*, 2005. 59.
2. Keen, *Hymns to an Unknown God*, 1995. 82.
3. Langone, "Introduction," *Recovery from Cults*, 1995. 7.

everyone is so friendly. How can such happy people be wrong?

John Goldhammer states, "Special loving attention given to new members is a common technique used by many groups and appeals to a person's innate longing to be accepted and loved. All this attention is an immediate, intoxicating, and potent hook, not only making it difficult for a new member to leave, but reinforcing the addictive need to keep returning to the group... I call this the *warm fuzzies trap*."[1]

Recruits become dependent on this social high. Geri-Ann Galanti experienced this firsthand at a Moonie recruitment camp. "A basic human need is for self-esteem. The Moonies utilize a technique known as love bombing to capitalize upon this need. Basically it consists of giving someone a lot of positive attention. For example, one morning Jane said to me, 'You know, you're really one of the most open people I've ever met. You don't put up any defenses. You're really open, I think that's so great.'... Of course I was prepared for this; immediately part of my mind flashed, 'Love bombing, love bombing.' The other part of my mind, however, said, 'Yes, but it's really true. I *am* an open person.' Even though I knew it was a manipulative technique, I *wanted* to believe she meant it, and I decided that she really did. After all, it matched my own perception of myself."[2]

Aspects of this technique include, but are not limited to flattery, verbal seduction, affectionate but usually non-sexual touching, and lots of attention.[3]

Sometimes love bombing involves sexual attraction. Many cults send males to recruit lone females, and females to recruit lone males. In the case of Mormonism, many young women become attracted to young, polished male missionaries. I don't believe this tactic is intentional, but sometimes it works. Other times, due to the commandment against dating or marrying outside the Church, young members are motivated to convert their love interests.

It also includes group participation activities, such as sports, crafts, games, projects, and service. Cooperative activities increase group cohesion and positive feelings.

Remember mirror neurons? Love bombing may cause mirror neurons to fire which would help us identify with group members on a cellular level. Desirous of love, the recruit will look for opportunities to model the behavior of his new friends so he will fit in.

"...the newcomer is surrounded by long-term members. Not only are these more experienced members trained to love bomb the potential recruit, but they are on their best behavior, proudly proclaiming the joys of membership, the advantages of the new belief system, and the uniqueness of the leader. Consciously or unconsciously, these members always speak and make their presentation in cult jargon, which they all seem to understand but which tends to make the newcomer feel out of sorts, a bit alienated, and undereducated by cult standards. The lonely visitor or seminar attendee begins to want some sense of connection to the rest of the group. With all the surrounding reinforcement, soon enough the newcomer realizes that, in order to be accepted and part of the group, she or he simply needs to mirror the behavior of other members and imitate their language."[4]

At first, these behaviors seem minor—bow your head during prayer, dress nicely for Church functions, avoid swearing. Once a potential convert gets used to the precedent of social acceptance, they must maintain the baseline by continuing to seek approval.

Remember my friend who had been through a small cult of her own? She wrote a perceptive note in the margins of one of my books: "Love bombing works as a replacement for self-esteem. When the positive attention becomes more rare, the subject will do more and more to receive that attention in particular."[5]

Over time, requirements increase, until it's paying tithing, going on missions, and attending the temple once a week. "...this apparent acceptance and love from a group is

---

1. Goldhammer, *Under the Influence*, 1996. 53.
2. Galanti, "Reflections on 'Brainwashing,'" *Recovery from Cults*, ed. Langone, 1995. 98.
3. Singer, *Cults in Our Midst*, 1995. 114.
4. Singer, *Cults in Our Midst*, 114-115.
5. Jen Havener. "Margin Note in *Spiritual Perversion*," 2005. 103.

*conditional*, which the new member quickly learns."[1] Over time, feelings of loyalty and dedication build, as does the safety net of belonging to a close-knit tribe. As we learned previously, reciprocation is a powerful force, leading the potential convert to owe increasing debts in return.

That's not to say that members are insincere or are ill-intentioned. In fact, their intentions are the purest. They believe their efforts will result in spiritual salvation and bring happiness to the potential convert. "And if it so be that you should labor all your days in crying repentance unto this people, and bring, save it be one soul unto me, how great shall be your joy with him in the kingdom of my Father!" D&C 18:15

Mormons refer to this technique as "fellowshipping." Missionaries have their own term for the process: "BRT" which stands for Build a Relationship of Trust. I'm sure the examples I've selected will seem familiar.

Teenagers are asked to bring friends to church. From the "For the Strength of Youth" pamphlet given to all Mormon teenagers: "Invite your friends of other faiths to your Church meetings and activities. Help them feel welcome and included. Many people have joined the Church through the example and fellowship of their friends. Also make a special effort to reach out to new converts and to those who are less active."[2]

And from the *New Era*[3], "Tell people in your ward or branch that your friend needs a special welcome. Introduce her to the bishop or branch president, Young Women leaders, her Sunday School teacher, your friends, and others she might share an interest with. They can help you show her around at church, explain the meetings, and let her know about upcoming activities. As you and others include her, she will begin to feel welcome.

"These efforts are important because they will let your friend know she is in the right place. It's the Lord's Church, and He invites everyone to worship and learn of Him at church."[4]

The *Gospel Principles* lesson manual states: "There are many ways we can share the gospel. Following are some suggestions: ...We can overcome our natural shyness by being friendly to others and doing kind things for them. We can help them see that we are sincerely interested in them and are not seeking personal gain."[5]

Prophet Gordon B. Hinckley advised, "With the ever-increasing number of converts, we must make an increasingly substantial effort to assist them as they find their way. Every one of them needs three things: a friend, a responsibility, and nurturing with 'the good word of God'. It is our duty and opportunity to provide these things."[6]

And Apostle M. Russell Ballard: "The likelihood of lasting conversion greatly increases when a nonmember has a friend or a relative who radiates the joy of being a member of the Church. The influence of members of the Church is very powerful. I believe that's why President Hinckley asked us to see that everyone has a friend."[7]

Members of all ages, especially home and visiting teachers, are encouraged to provide service, especially to families struggling with activity. Often the concepts of service and missionary work are overly conflated—helping means teaching the gospel:

"...we have an obligation as members of the Church to accept callings to serve in building the kingdom of God on earth. As we serve in our various callings, we bless the lives of others. In missionary work lives are changed as people learn of the gospel of Jesus Christ and receive a testimony of its truth. By the sacred work in the temple we bless the lives of those who have gone on before us. In gospel service we have the privilege to teach others, to

---

1. Goldhammer, *Under the Influence*, 1996. 191.
2. *For the Strength of Youth*, 2011. https://www.lds.org/manual/for-the-strength-of-youth/friends
3. The *New Era* is the official LDS monthly magazine for youth ages 12-18.
4. "Q&A: Questions and Answers." *New Era*, Feb 2006. https://www.lds.org/new-era/2006/02/qa-questions-and-answers
5. *Gospel Principles*. The Church of Jesus Christ of Latter-day Saints, 2011. (Chapter 33: Missionary Work)
6. Gordon B. Hinckley. "Converts and Young Men." In LDS General Conference, April 1997. https://www.lds.org/general-conference/1997/04/converts-and-young-men
7. M. Russell Ballard. "Now Is the Time." In LDS General Conference, Oct 2000. https://www.lds.org/general-conference/2000/10/now-is-the-time

strengthen the youth, and to bless the lives of the little children as they learn the simple truths of the gospel. In Church service we learn to give of ourselves and to help others."[1]

A priesthood lesson on fellowshipping says, "Although we should be friendly and neighborly and try to show our love to all people, giving help and friendship to new and less-active members is a basic priesthood responsibility... [Fellowshipping] helps new converts and other Church members feel wanted and needed and motivates them to participate in the Church."[2]

That same lesson tells two stories which show love bombing in action:

> A young man was lonely and unhappy. His church attendance was irregular, and he found difficulty being dependable in Church assignments. Two men, both widowers, invited the young man to join them for family home evenings[3].
>
> Before long, Monday evening became the most important time in his week. There he engaged in many gospel discussions and gained a desire to begin praying more diligently. It was not long before his testimony changed from a passive knowledge to a burning witness of the truth...
>
> One day as he discussed with an acquaintance the joy in his life, the other asked, "What do you think caused it to happen?"
>
> "The kindness of two friends has been the most important part," he said. "I have come to trust and feel secure in their love, which has helped me do things I never even dreamed were possible."

And this one's about Jack, whose wife is a member. Local members planned a block party.

> Jack, initially reluctant to come, was surprised and delighted with the easy, natural friendliness of the group. By the evening's end, he enthusiastically supported the idea of a second party, a picnic in two weeks. No one said anything about going to church, but Allen Westover, who had discussed Jack's house-painting project at the party, showed up on Saturday with his own ladder—and came back evenings after work. [Two other men] also helped several times...
>
> Later that month when the elders quorum had a project, Jack was anxious to help *them*... As the summer progressed, Jack spent more and more time with Church members. There were chats about fishing rods and politics and raising children... To [his wife's] great joy, Jack told her one evening that he was ready to take the next step of being taught by the missionaries and...joining the Church.

Jack was love-bombed into joining the Church. The stated goal for planning the original block party was to convert Jack. Several members befriended him. They helped him paint his house and engaged him in activities which motivated him to reciprocate. They discussed non-Church topics with him, circumventing a direct approach that may have put him off.

Had Jack not been a potential convert, I doubt any of these men would have been bothered to waste their time. They didn't host block parties for each other or offer to paint one another's houses. This story was meant to show how socializing can convert nonmembers to the gospel.

---

1. Steven E. Snow. "Service." In LDS General Conference, Oct 2007. https://www.lds.org/general-conference/2007/10/service
2. *Duties and Blessings of the Priesthood: Basic Manual for Priesthood Holders, Part B*. Lesson 10, LDS, 2000. https://www.lds.org/manual/duties-and-blessings-of-the-priesthood-basic-manual-for-priesthood-holders-part-b/priesthood-and-church-government/lesson-10-fellowshipping-a-priesthood-responsibility
3. LDS families are strongly encouraged to hold a weekly togetherness night typically held on Mondays. Family home evening often follows the form of Church meetings, with prayer, song, and a lesson taught from a special manual. Those without families sometimes get together with other families or with one another.

Mormons are encouraged to sincerely love one another, yet often this love is not, in reality, unconditional. Members, sadly, have too many Church-driven priorities to foster many genuine friendships. Too often, as soon as the member realizes her efforts are not paying off, she shifts her attentions elsewhere. She is not interested in a friend she would honestly like to get to know—she is interested in converting them to her way of life. While this is understandable behavior given the artificial pressures members are under, it can make the unconverted feel used and may lead to inactive members who feel "offended." And justifiably so.

Love is quickly withdrawn from those who fail to act in accordance with the gospel. They may be subject to the cold shoulder or may face "dis*fellowship*" and "ex*communication*." The nature of these words is no mistake—they both imply *isolation* and a failure to *be heard*. They are the opposite of love bombing, a total withdrawal of support as a punishment for going against community standards.

"The apparently loving unanimity of the group masks, and in some cases bolsters, strict rules against private as well as public dissent. Questions are deflected. Critical comments are met with smiling pleas of 'no negativity'..."[1]

This technique is even more insidious when you think of children raised in the Church. As a child, you are emotionally and physically dependent upon maintaining the love and acceptance of your family, the only people you have ever known and loved. Those are powerful pressures that one could never expect a child to withstand.

Exmormon Marion Stricker points out that "Whether one is born into Mormonism, or not, everyone's need is for *genuine*, human social relationships...*personal*, sympathetic, caring relationships... to be understood—to love and be loved."[2]

Belief is bound to follow.

---

1. Langone, "Introduction," *Recovery from Cults,* 1995. 7-8.
2. Stricker, *The Double-Bind in Mormonism,* 2000. 33.

*The individual only has power in so far as he ceases to be an individual.*
—George Orwell, *1984*

*It is not an easy thing to become a member of this Church. In most cases it involves setting aside old habits, leaving old friends and associations, and stepping into a new society which is different and somewhat demanding.*
—Prophet Gordon B. Hinckley[1]

# Destabilization

**Destabilization**
—*Suppression, Trust, Isolation, Perpetuation*
- Establishes influence through emotion
- Suppresses the self, lowers defenses
- A reward is offered—"We will restabilize you"
- Builds trust
- Fills an ongoing need
- Isolates or targets those who are already isolated
- Creates dependency
- Preys on children
- Puts adults in a regressed, childlike mindset

Cognitive dissonance prevents new beliefs from taking root. So a conversion effort must bypass defensive barriers and convince you to listen without argument.

The new beliefs must be seen as a benefit. In *Coercive Persuasion*, Psychology Professor Edgar H. Schein said, "...attitudes, values, and behavior patterns of an individual tend to be integrated with each other and tend to be organized around the person's self-image or self-concept. This integration, even if imperfect, gives continuity and stability to the person and hence operates as a force against being influenced, unless the change which the influence implies is seen to be a change in the direction of greater integration."[2]

This "greater integration" is a mighty big carrot to a mind seeking consonance. In that sense, certain dogmatic systems are more attractive to us if they seem to promise greater mental stability by enabling us to pursue our existing values more effectively.

Schein proposed three basic steps to accomplish destabilization: Unfreeze, change, and refreeze.

- ◎ Unfreezing creates specific dissonance, an unstable state in cognitive equilibrium. Suddenly, you have an induced motive to change. The message is,
  **"You are flawed..."**
- ◎ The next step promises relief, wherein the manipulator offers answers.
  **"We can help..."**
- ◎ Refreezing locks in the new belief, hopefully along with lasting commitment to the manipulator who provided relief. You never notice the manipulator caused the dissonance in the first place.
  **"Doesn't that feel better?"**

---

1. Gordon B. Hinckley. "Converts and Young Men." In LDS General Conference, April 1997.
2. Schein, *Coercive Persuasion*, 1971. 118-120.

In most simplistic terms, think of a TV ad:

| Unfreezing, cognitive dissonance. ☹ | **"You are paying too much for your car insurance!"** |
| --- | --- |
| | "Have I made a mistake?" |
| Change, promised relief from dissonance. 😐 | **"Look no further. CarHugs can save you money today."** |
| | "I can easily correct my mistake." |
| Refreezing. ☺ | **"Call now!"** |
| | You pick up the phone and all is well again. "Yes, please sign me up!" |

Margaret Singer and Richard Ofshe wrote a paper on how thought-reform attacks identity. They defined two types of self-image:

- The **periphery self** reflects "self-evaluations of the adequacy or correctness of public and judgmental aspects of a person's life", which includes things like social status, performance of roles, conformity to societal norms, political opinions, and taste.
- The **central self** reflects "self-evaluations of the adequacy or correctness of a person's intimate life and confidence in perception of reality", which includes relationship with family, personal aspirations, sexual activity, traumatic experiences, religious convictions, and estimates of the motivations of others.[1]

Singer and Ofshe note that the type of brainwashing employed on prisoners and students in China, Russia, and North Korea attacked the peripheral self, and that modern techniques used in America are directed at the central self. Moreover they estimate that these core-self attacks are far more effective and psychologically devastating, and that self-image is used to reward desired behavior and punish undesired behavior.

It is impossible to control the mind without controlling a sense of self. A group does this by dismantling certain elements of identity and rebuilding them in the group's image. As Steven Hassan points out, "...cult mind control can be understood as a system of influence that is designed to disrupt a person's authentic identity and replace it with a new identity."[2]

This process can be useful when done with fully informed consent. Military training does this, as does therapy and addiction rehab. Sometimes there are undesirable parts of ourselves we want to transform. Influential psychiatrist Carl Jung spoke of metanoia, the beneficial process of rebuilding self through a major transition or psychotic break. And when I left the Church, I had to rebuild my identity on my own.

These life phases require deep trust, and just because someone *seems* trustworthy does not make them so.

If I let anyone in on this process at all, I look for people who don't have the answers, but who are instead helping me find *my own* answers. A good therapist or spiritual leader is only a mirror to reveal myself. As soon as anyone tries to put me on "the right path" as they define it, I run away screaming.

---

1. Margaret Singer, and Richard Ofshe. "Attacks on Peripheral Versus Central Elements of Self and the Impact of Thought Reforming Techniques." *The Cultic Studies Journal* 3, no. 1 (1986). http://www.antisectes.net/singer-ofshe.htm
2. Hassan, *Releasing the Bonds,* 2000. 5.

## Put Your Self on the Shelf

*The dogma of the group reflects the psychology of the leader.*
—**Dr. Michael Welner**[1]

*We must all be alike. Not everyone born free and equal, as the Constitution says, but everyone made equal. Each man the image of every other; then all are happy, for there are no mountains to make them cower, to judge themselves against.*
—**Betty from Ray Bradbury's *Fahrenheit 451***

What would it take for you to set aside yourself?

It doesn't take much. It merely takes trust that a person or group has your best interest at heart. They must convince you that your own defectiveness is keeping you from your ideals and goals.

Once they seem to be on your side, you are on *their* side as the change-agent. You will listen intently to learn new doctrine, habits, and values. You will willingly strive to quell all parts of your old self which have been labeled as undesirable. You will be motivated to develop qualities which comply with the ideals of the group, to add whatever new cognitions, behaviors, or even personality traits are required of you.

That's it. Nothing mysterious. No one gets imprisoned, tortured, hypnotized, or drugged.

When this process is repeated alongside other manipulative techniques, eventually a "pseudopersonality" develops which matches the ideal personality as defined by the group. If it's working well, it will feel naturally a part of you.

Singer and Ofshe describe how this works. "Because the reinforcement structure of the environment is arranged to shape behavior, participation in the environment will create a history of activity which, when reviewed, would normally tend to lead the individual to conclude that perspectives and values consistent with these activities are indeed his or her own."[2]

The true self may resist being repressed or destroyed, and thus, it must be under constant attack from the totalist system. "...intense anxiety can be engendered about the worthiness and even the existence of the self. The self is under attack to merge with and identify with the offered new model..."[3]

The individual is made to blame herself for this continual discomfort, which the group promises to relieve for the low-low price of total dependence. After that, all self-measurement is done using the group yardstick. Such a restructuring of self into an externally-molded pseudopersonality carries detrimental risks to self-esteem, psychological integrity, personal autonomy, and mental health.[4]

Mormonism gets its toe in the door by identifying personal flaws, echoing your existing instincts for self-improvement with promises to make your inner world even more integrated. The gospel will replace anger with love, lies with truth, and death with eternal life. It's hard to disagree with that.

Then they teach that your natural human state leads you towards the carnal, wicked, and cruel. This feeds your worst fears, that perhaps you can't ever be good. Now you're off balance, unfrozen, and ready to accept change. Perhaps even a "mighty change of heart", as described in Alma 5. (Alma himself used this technique to convert the Nephites.)

The Church's list of personal moral defects is quite long, and all can be used to dissolve resistance. Two in particular directly attack stability: Selfishness and pride.

---

1. Welner, "Psychology of Polygamous Sects," *ABC News*, March 1, 2010.
2. Singer and Ofshe, "Peripheral Versus Central Elements of Self," *Cultic Studies Journal*, 1986.
3. Singer and Ofshe, "Peripheral Versus Central Elements of Self," *Cultic Studies Journal*, 1986.
4. Tobias and Lalich, *Captive Hearts, Captive Minds*, 1994. 45.

Just how bad is selfishness? "Selfishness is the basic substance—the raw material, if you will—of almost all other sins that Satan has introduced upon the earth. Under his skillful management, this sin manifests itself in such a myriad of ways that virtually no one escapes its influence. Its magnetic tentacles stretch out and draw to itself every indulgence that can block the path to exaltation."[1]

Yuck, tentacles. This is the part where a person, desiring to be good, might sit up in her seat and pay attention.

Apostle Neal A. Maxwell takes this track in a 1990 Conference talk. "Stubborn selfishness is actually rebellion against God, because, warned Samuel, 'stubbornness is as...idolatry.'

"Selfishness is much more than an ordinary problem because it activates all the cardinal sins! It is the detonator in the breaking of the Ten Commandments."[2]

Certainly too much selfishness is problematic. We should consider the less fortunate, share of our time and resources with those in need, and give kind words to our friends and neighbors. However in this talk, and indeed in many other references, the concept of selfishness is conflated with resistance to God's word, and by proxy, the LDS message.

"Selfishness is often expressed in stubbornness of mind. Having a 'mind hardened in pride' often afflicts the brightest who could also be the best. 'One thing' the brightest often lack: meekness! Instead of having 'a willing mind' which seeks to emulate the 'mind of Christ,' a 'mind hardened in pride' is impervious to counsel and often seeks ascendancy. Jesus, who was and is 'more intelligent than they all,' is also more meek than they all."[3]

Thus in the name of being good, which we all want to be, the softening of the will begins, pointing towards those opposite traits: humility and submissiveness.

"Jesus, stunningly brilliant, nevertheless allowed His will to be 'swallowed up in the will of the Father.' Those with pride-hardened minds are simply unable to do this."

Maxwell concludes that in order to avoid being selfish (i.e. in order to stop feeling the uncomfortable dissonance of feeling like a bad person), we have to lose not just selfishness, but the self entirely:

"One of the last, subtle strongholds of selfishness is the natural feeling that we 'own' ourselves. Of course we are free to choose and are personally accountable. Yes, we have individuality. But those who have chosen to 'come unto Christ' soon realize that they do not 'own' themselves. Instead, they belong to Him. We are to become consecrated along with our gifts, our appointed days, and our very selves. Hence, there is a stark difference between stubbornly 'owning' oneself and submissively belonging to God. Clinging to the old self is not a mark of independence, but of indulgence!"

Thus, by abandoning the self, we will realize the truth of all things: "The Prophet Joseph promised that when selfishness is annihilated, we 'may comprehend all things, present, past, and future.'... Indeed, the gospel brings glorious illumination as to our possibilities. Scales fall from our eyes with the shedding of selfishness. Then we see our luminous and true identity."[4]

In this one talk, Apostle Maxwell has led us through the process of Unfreeze-Change-Refreeze into a new self.

Preaching against pride is intended to strip away the aspects of identity that do not conform with Church teachings. Yes, it is good to avoid arrogance. But this isn't what they really mean. As you can see by the LDS definition, pride is about one's relationship with God:

"A lack or absence of humility or teachableness. Pride sets people in opposition to each other and to God. A proud person sets himself above those around him and follows his own

---

1. Elder William R. Bradford. "Selfishness Vs. Selflessness" *Ensign*. Accessed Aug 13, 2013. http://www.lds.org/ensign/1983/04/selfishness-vs-selflessness
2. Neal A. Maxwell. "Put Off the Natural Man, and Come Off Conqueror." In LDS General Conference, Oct 1990. http://www.lds.org/general-conference/1990/10/put-off-the-natural-man-and-come-off-conqueror
3. Maxwell, "Put Off the Natural Man," General Conference, Oct 1990.
4. Maxwell, "Put Off the Natural Man," General Conference, Oct 1990.

will rather than God's will. Conceit, envy, hardheartedness, and haughtiness are also typical of a proud person."[1]

By contrast, the first two listings in Free Dictionary speak to one's sense of dignity and self-respect, pleasure and satisfaction taken in one's own achievement, possessions, or associations, as in "parental pride." Then it moves on to the negative associations of arrogance and conceit, and of course it never talks of being in opposition to others or God, nor about being unteachable, nor setting one's self above God.[2]

By the Church's definition, you must become teachable. You must submit yourself to the will of God, and by proxy, to the will of the Church. You cannot hold fast to your own opinion where it differs from the Church's opinion without being guilty of this grave sin.

Scriptures abound. Here are a few:

- God hates pride. (Proverbs 8:13)
- God commanded Mormons cease from pride and its evil siblings, laughter, light-speech, light-mindedness, lustful desires, and other "wicked doings." (D&C 88:121)
- The people in Helaman's[3] day were admonished to silence their pride so they could give ear to God's counsel and walk in his path. (Helaman 12:4-5)
- The great and spacious building in Lehi's dream[4] represented the wicked and prideful of the world. All the prideful nations in the world are promised destruction. (1 Nephi 11:36)
- The proud will be burned as stubble. (Malachi 4:1)
- Pride was responsible for the final destruction of the Nephites. (Moroni 8:27)

The message is clear: Best be humble, which means open your mind to Church leaders. Unfreeze the self; open up for change.

> And ye shall offer for a sacrifice unto me a broken heart and a contrite spirit. And whoso cometh unto me with a broken heart and a contrite spirit, him will I baptize with fire and with the Holy Ghost, even as the Lamanites, because of their faith in me at the time of their conversion, were baptized with fire and with the Holy Ghost, and they knew it not.
>
> 3 Nephi 9:20

Nephi's promise is true for many people. If you lower your defenses and repress yourself, there's a good chance the message will start to make sense.

The LDS Church officially defines "humble" as: "To make meek and teachable, or the condition of being meek and teachable. Humility includes recognizing our dependence upon God and desiring to submit to his will."[5]

According to the Free Dictionary, being humble has nothing to do with being teachable or depending on God. Yet the humble Latter-day Saint is meek and passive, sets aside any objections, and trusts completely in the teacher.

---

1. The Church of Jesus Christ of Latter Day Saints. "LDS.org The Guide to the Scriptures: Pride." Accessed Aug 13, 2013. http://www.lds.org/scriptures/gs/pride
2. "Free Dictionary: Pride." *The Free Dictionary*. Accessed April 27, 2014. http://www.thefreedictionary.com/pride
3. Helaman is a Book of Mormon prophet.
4. Early in the Book of Mormon, the prophet Lehi has a dream about walking a straight and narrow path with his family, towards the Tree of Life. The only thing guiding them is an iron rod, which they must hold tight to. They are beset by many dangers and temptations, including a great and spacious building full of worldly people mocking them and causing many people to leave the Tree of Life in shame. 1 Nephi 8
5. The Church of Jesus Christ of Latter Day Saints. "LDS.org The Guide to the Scriptures: Humble, Humility." Accessed Aug 13, 2013. http://www.lds.org/scriptures/gs/humble-humility

> Behold, the Lord requireth the heart and a willing mind; and the willing and obedient shall eat the good of the land of Zion in these last days.
>
> D&C 64:34

> Nevertheless they did fast and pray oft, and did wax stronger and stronger in their humility, and firmer and firmer in the faith of Christ, unto the filling their souls with joy and consolation, yea, even to the purifying and the sanctification of their hearts, which sanctification cometh because of their yielding their hearts unto God.
>
> Helaman 3:35

With these kinds of mechanisms in place, you are ready to be converted, changed, reborn. The phrase "born again" conveys the replacement of the old self with a newborn which can be molded into a fresh personality. "And the Lord said unto me: Marvel not that all mankind, yea, men and women, all nations, kindreds, tongues and people, must be born again; yea, born of God, changed from their carnal and fallen state, to a state of righteousness, being redeemed of God, becoming his sons and daughters; And thus they become new creatures; and unless they do this, they can in nowise inherit the kingdom of God." Mosiah 27:25-26

In addition to its religious meaning, "convert" means to change a thing into something else, or to adapt to a new purpose or function. In a religious conversion, what is transformed? The self. The individual self becomes the group self, which is always striving to be recreated in the image of the group ideal.

Apostle Richard G. Scott quotes President Marion G. Romney in his 2002 Conference talk: "Converted means to turn from one belief or course of action to another. Conversion is a spiritual and moral change. Converted implies not merely mental acceptance of Jesus and his teachings but also a motivating faith in him and his gospel. A faith which works a transformation, an actual change in one's understanding of life's meaning and in his allegiance to God in interest, in thought, and in conduct. In one who is really wholly converted, desire for things contrary to the gospel of Jesus Christ has actually died. And substituted therefore is a love of God, with a fixed and controlling determination to keep his commandments."[1]

Just to be sure you're motivated to stay changed, Apostle Scott adds: "Your happiness now and forever is conditioned on your degree of conversion and the transformation that it brings to your life."

He then directs the congregation to continually apply the parable of the seeds, meaning you are to actively remove infertile ground, portions of yourself which still resist being taught.

Christ himself drove this message home: "Except ye be converted, and become as little children, ye shall not enter into the kingdom of heaven." Matthew 18:3

The idea of making oneself like a child is common in the persuasion process employed by many high-demand groups. Who is more clean-slate than a child? If you are an unconvinced adult, you need only be reminded of what it was like to be trusting and wide-eyed. The notion seems safe enough. After all, children are innocent and there is appeal to remembering that carefree time. But it also regresses your mind to a state which is more receptive and feeling, when you, too, were a clean slate. It vilifies your adult self and asks you to set aside the experiences and skepticism which protect you.

Steven Hassan said, "It is common for cult leaders to ask members to become like 'children of God.' In fact, an essential aspect of the cult identity is to possess the naiveté of a child. A child's idolization of the parent figure is precisely what a cult leader needs to be in total control. By taking advantage of the desire for childlike innocence, cult mind control

---

1. Richard G. Scott. "Full Conversion Brings Happiness." In LDS General Conference, April 2002. http://www.lds.org/general-conference/2002/04/full-conversion-brings-happiness (Quoting President Marion G. Romney.)

undermines the normal resources of a mature mind."[1]

I will revisit this concept in depth in the chapter on creating dependency, but conclude with a haunting quote from *Captive Hearts*: "Cults...induce dependency, compliance, rigid obedience, stunted thinking, and childlike behavior in their members."[2]

## Targeting Unstable Individuals

Life offers its own destabilizing events. We are more open to persuasion when we've already been unfrozen. Margaret Singer elaborates:

> Everyone is influenced and persuaded daily in various ways, but the vulnerability to influence varies. The ability to fend off persuaders is reduced when one is rushed, stressed, uncertain, lonely, indifferent, uninformed, distracted, or fatigued. Alternatively a person with a sense of clarity and sureness about his own beliefs and values, with a feeling of being embedded in meaningful relationships with other persons, and with a sense of having a role in life that gives him support is much less likely to be vulnerable to persuasion.[3]

Cults can increase success by targeting converts who are already unfrozen, particularly those who are going through significant transition.

"Certain life events or crises may enhance susceptibility to cult recruitment at any age. These include times of high stress like divorce, unemployment or a job change, entering or graduating from school, a significant loss (personal or monetary), relocation, marriage, a birth in the family, and death of a loved one. Cult membership, with its promise of relief from suffering, offers a substitute for personal mastery of these life events."[4]

Groups sometimes even have special terms for people who are "ready." Scientologists call them "raw meat", and soon-to-be Mormons are called "golden investigators."

"Cults aim their recruitment at vulnerable people because these individuals are less likely to see through the layers of deceit. Cults target friendly, obedient, altruistic, and malleable persons because such individuals are easy to persuade and manage."[5]

*Captive Hearts* lists additional traits that make one more susceptible, including a desire to belong, lack of self-confidence, unassertiveness, lack of critical thinking skills, a need for absolute answers, cultural disillusionment, desire for spiritual meaning, ignorance of manipulation tactics, and being neurologically more prone to trancelike states.

The LDS missionary manual, *Preach My Gospel*, echoes this: "You are surrounded by people. You pass them on the street, visit them in their homes, and travel among them. All of them are children of God, your brothers and sisters. God loves them just as He loves you. Many of these people are searching for purpose in life. They are concerned for their families. They need the sense of belonging that comes from the knowledge that they are children of God, members of His eternal family. They want to feel secure in a world of changing values."[6]

The manual also says, "Work with the bishop and the ward council to identify and contact people who have recently had a baby, moved to the area, or experienced a death in the family."[7]

---

1. Hassan, *Releasing the Bonds,* 2000. 118.
2. Tobias and Lalich, *Captive Hearts, Captive Minds,* 1994. 34.
3. Margaret Singer. "Group Psychodynamics and CULTS." *Merck Manual of Diagnosis and Therapy* Fifteenth Edition (1987). http://www.lermanet2.com/scientologynews/merck-singer.htm
4. Tobias and Lalich, *Captive Hearts, Captive Minds,* 1994. 50.
5. Singer, *Cults in Our Midst,* 1995. 106-107.
6. *Preach My Gospel: A Guide to Missionary Service.* 2004. The Church of Jesus Christ of Latter-day Saints, n.d. 1.
7. *Preach My Gospel,* 2004. 167.

The promise of eternal family can be extremely seductive to a family who has recently lost a child, parent, spouse, or other loved one. That's one particular niche Mormonism seems to have covered.

Of course it's easy for sincere Mormons to justify this tactic. If the gospel really has all the answers, it's a kindness to bring them the Plan of Happiness.

Unfortunately, the gospel doesn't have all the answers.

That's not to say cult converts are stupid. It may be tempting to self-blame for "falling for it." This only causes more dissonance and pain, and it simply isn't true. It is perfectly natural to trust a friendly soul who offers help during a time of crisis or who plays to a valiant sense of idealism. Good traits, like trust, innocence, kindness, morality, and idealistic passion are exploited. If anything, credit yourself for having those traits. "...people who join cults are *not* stupid, weird, crazy, or neurotic. Most cult members are of above-average intelligence, well-adjusted, adaptable, and perhaps a bit idealistic. In relatively few cases does the person have a history of a preexisting mental disorder."[1]

Young people are particularly susceptible. Singer found that two-thirds of those she studied were normal young people who joined during a time of crisis.[2]

Teenagers and college-aged adults are in an unstable place in their development cycle as they recreate themselves as autonomous from their parents. They are undergoing rapid transitions and are often seeking identity and purpose. Of all age groups within the Church, teens and young adults have the most attention paid them. The youth spend far more time participating in Church activities than any other age group, in this attempt to lock-in, or refreeze the gospel in their minds.

"O, remember, my son, and learn wisdom in thy youth; yea, learn in thy youth to keep the commandments of God." Alma 37:35

On the upside, the Church can actually solve some problems, like substance abuse and a lack of moral compass. Experts agree that all cults have benefits, and Mormonism is no exception. It teaches values and offers motivation for those who may need, at least temporarily, a rigid system of rules. An ex-member should never discount any healing or self-improvement accelerated by membership in a high-demand group.

## Born in the Covenant

Most books on cults assume the reader had a past prior to joining the high-demand group, and that they have previous beliefs, culture, friends and family to go back to. Recovery is highly geared towards remembering and integrating the pre-cult identity.

But most Mormons were born in the Church. For this reason, my book will spend less space addressing recruitment. Often when I say "conversion", I'm using the Church's definition, i.e. when a person goes from not believing to believing (or "knowing"), regardless of the length of membership.

Children are as destabilized as they get, having no identities of their own, ready to be shaped and molded into anything the parent desires. They have no cognitive defenses against new ideas, because they are still learning about reality.

"Children tend to experience things more on an emotional level rather than on an intellectual one..."[3] And, "Children usually do not have to be converted because their induction into the cultic society begins so early. The cult world may be all they have ever known."[4]

It's like a child knowing Santa is real, but never being corrected after growing up, because all the adults believe it, too. Mormon children are given a distorted view of the

---
1. Tobias and Lalich, *Captive Hearts, Captive Minds*, 1994. 28.
2. Tobias and Lalich, *Captive Hearts, Captive Minds*, 1994. 27.
3. Galanti, "Reflections on 'Brainwashing,'" *Recovery from Cults*, ed. Langone, 1995. 100.
4. Tobias and Lalich, *Captive Hearts, Captive Minds*, 1994. 244.

world and a distorted explanation of the views of others. They literally have no comparisons judge the truth for themselves. When a child has been given nothing but false options, the age of eight is *not* the age of accountability.[1]

Margaret Singer addresses the severity of this issue:

> Children adopt the cult's right-wrong, good-bad, sinner-saint starkly polarized value system. They are taught that a divided world exists—"we" are inside; "they" are outside... In this us-against-them world, children (like the rest of the members) are taught to feel paranoid about nonmembers and the outside society.
>
> Cult children have no opportunity to observe the compromising, negotiating, and meeting on middle ground demonstrated in ordinary families. They do not see people resolving disputes or adjusting to the wants and desires of others, the trade-offs that are so central to learning how to play, work, and live in a family or in groups that have been socialized in democratic ways...
>
> Instead they witness and are taught that critical, evaluative thinking; new ideas; and independent ideas get people in trouble. From this, they learn simply to obey.
>
> In many cults, normal aggressiveness, liveliness, and assertiveness in children are labeled as sinful or as signs of demons... As a result, anxious-dependent personality traits can be built into cult children's developing character.[2]

Church leaders seem to understand the need to indoctrinate children early to inoculate them against the world. Prophet Thomas S. Monson, then an apostle, acknowledged this blank slate: "Dr. Glenn Doman, a prominent author and renowned scientist, reported a lifetime of research in one statement: 'The newborn child is almost an exact duplicate of an empty computer, although superior to such a computer in almost every way... What is placed in the child's brain during the first eight years of his life is probably there to stay. If you put misinformation into his brain during this period, it is extremely difficult to erase it.' This evidence should provoke a renewal of commitment in every parent: 'I must be about my Father's business.'"[3]

Parents are asked to become agents in programming their children. This isn't a request; it's a commandment that is endlessly reiterated in lessons and conference talks. Apostle Robert D. Hales: "When we follow the prophets' counsel to hold family home evening, family prayer, and family scripture study, our homes become an incubator for our children's spiritual growth. There we teach them the gospel, bear our testimonies, express our love, and listen as they share their feelings and experiences. By our righteous choices and actions, we liberate them from darkness by increasing their ability to walk in the light."[4]

And from a 2012 Conference talk by Cheryl A. Esplin, "Teaching our children to understand is more than just imparting information. It's helping our children get the doctrine into their hearts in a way that it becomes part of their very being and is reflected in their attitudes and behavior throughout their lives."[5]

The eternal family is held up as a reward for the proper upbringing of children, and yet the implication is that failing to do so means you will *lose* them in the eternities. Your family is held hostage to your efforts as a parent to indoctrinate your children.

The First Presidency is often quoted from the 1974 Family Home Evening Manual: "In a

---

1. Children are considered unable to understand the difference between right and wrong until the age of eight. This is considered the "age of accountability," at which point, they are eligible (and expected) to be baptized.
2. Singer, *Cults in Our Midst*, 1995. 262.
3. Thomas S. Monson. "Teach the Children." In LDS General Conference, Oct 1997. https://www.lds.org/general-conference/1997/10/teach-the-children
4. Robert D. Hales. "Agency: Essential to the Plan of Life." In LDS General Conference, Oct 2010. https://www.lds.org/general-conference/2010/10/agency-essential-to-the-plan-of-life
5. Cheryl A. Esplin. "Teaching Our Children to Understand." In *LDS General Conference*, April 2012. https://www.lds.org/general-conference/2012/04/teaching-our-children-to-understand

day when the sanctity of the home is being invaded and where the care of children has been regarded lightly, we, by means of the family home evening manual, have endeavored to impress upon the parents the importance of developing a love in the home so that in the future, should those children thus taught stray away, they would eventually return again, lest they lose their place in the eternal family circle."[1]

This same principle is reiterated everywhere, including in the most recent Family Home Evening Manual: "After we come to earth we can begin to develop our own eternal families. If we succeed with our families in this life, we may return with them to our Heavenly Father. Then we will establish our own heavenly homes and be able to continue to have families."[2]

Even more oft-quoted is the proverb which I've heard attributed to various LDS prophets, "Train up a child in the way he should go: and when he is old, he will not depart from it." Proverbs 22:6

Modern scripture takes this a step further. "And again, inasmuch as parents have children in Zion, or in any of her stakes which are organized, that teach them not to understand the doctrine of repentance, faith in Christ the Son of the living God, and of baptism and the gift of the Holy Ghost by the laying on of the hands, when eight years old, the sin be upon the heads of the parents." D&C 68:25

These doctrines place family relationships in a precarious position. The outcome of the children becomes dependent upon the effort and skill of the parents, and the parents become dependent upon the behavior of their children. And many parents with wayward children are judged harshly by other Mormons. The thought is, "You must have done something wrong, because *my* children are fine."

Singer describes what can happen in families under high-demand group pressures:

> ...parents are just intermediaries who see that the children obey the will of the leader. Even in many Bible-based cults, respect for parents is not extolled as might be expected. Rather, the leader positions himself as the gatekeeper between parents and their God. Parents must get their children to submit to them and to the dictates of the leader in order to prove that they themselves are submitting to the leader.[3]

The shame and guilt and worry parents experience can build up and sometimes come out sideways in unhealthy behavior towards the child. After all, what are a few manipulative words or beatings when compared to the pain of eternal separation? Abuse in this religious context, with spiritual justifications, can be especially devastating[4].

In this dangerous environment, where so much is artificially at risk, "Children may become convinced that they are a creation of the cult, their only purpose being to serve the system and their only usefulness defined by the system's needs and functions. The child, his or her needs ignored or minimized, has no purpose other than to be used by others."[5]

LDS parents are constantly given advice on how to practice thought-reform on their children while simultaneously being reminded of the stakes, often in life-or-death terms:

> Elder Henry B. Eyring of the Quorum of the Twelve Apostles has outlined three things we can do to increase the likelihood the Holy Ghost will bear witness of sacred truth to our children: "First, we can teach some sacred truth. Then, we can testify that we know what we have taught is true. And then we must act so that those

---

1. The Church of Jesus Christ of Latter Day Saints. *Family Home Evening Manual: Love Makes Our House a Home.* The Church of Jesus Christ of Latter Day Saints, 1974. 2
2. *Family Home Evening Resource Book Lesson One: Building Our Family through Home Evenings.* The Church of Jesus Christ of Latter Day Saints, 2011. http://www.lds.org/manual/family-home-evening-resource-book/family-home-evening-lessons/lesson-one-building-our-family-through-home-evenings
3. Singer, *Cults in Our Midst,* 1995. 259.
4. It is said that we relate to God the way we related to our parents. Those with an angry father imagine an angry God. This means the behavior of our parents will be projected onto interpretations of God, thus generating a vicious psychological cycle of spiritual abuse from what might otherwise be our source of spiritual comfort.
5. Tobias and Lalich, *Captive Hearts, Captive Minds,* 1994. 249. (Quoting Anna Bowen who works with survivors of severe childhood trauma.)

> who hear our testimony see that our actions conform with what we said was true. The Holy Ghost will then confirm to them the truth of what we said and that we knew it to be true. That is how a legacy of testimony is created, preserved, and transmitted in a family."
>
> Loving, sincere parents with strong testimonies of their own are better equipped than anyone else to influence their children's testimonies. Our instructions and examples are like those given by flight attendants to passengers on commercial flights. Demonstrating the use of oxygen masks that automatically drop from the ceiling during emergency situations, flight attendants instruct parents to first put on their own masks, then assist their young children. We must be consistently seeking, developing, and bearing strong testimonies of our own in order to extend this spiritual lifeline to our children.[1]

Children are held hostage to pleasing their parents. Any small thread of cognitive dissonance in child's mind will tend to resolve according to what her loving family expects of her. Former Mormon Diana Kline expressed this well in a journal entry she wrote on the day of her baptism:

> I feel so happy to be baptized and confirmed a member of the ONE and ONLY true church. I have been looking forward to this day for the past several weeks. Heavenly Father is proud of me, and I can feel that God loves me and my mom and dad are both pleased with my decision. I want to always be faithful to the Lord and honor all of His commandments, never straying from the straight and narrow road into Satan's grasp.[2]

This quote reveals several thought-reform techniques instilled in a child of only eight, including reframing, mystical manipulation, sacred science, black and white thinking, and phobias.

Children are easily manipulated on an emotional level and parents are put into a highly-motivated position to do so. In the *Ensign*[3] article I quoted above, parents are instructed to regularly encourage children to express their feelings, but the only feelings the article seems to address are those that affirm the Church is true.

The story is told about how 14-year-old Joseph Smith felt safe enough to share the First Vision with his mother, and how he discovered Presbyterianism wasn't true. But I have to wonder, if a modern Joseph were to tell his LDS mother that Mormonism isn't true, would he get the same reaction? Or would that just give her the opportunity to talk him out of his doubts? It certainly depends on the family, but many Mormon children are unable to follow Smith's example.

# Regaining the Self

Regaining the self is one of the most difficult tasks of leaving any type of controlling situation, be it a high-demand group or even an abusive relationship.

Your path is unique only to you. Others can give you advice and share their own experiences, but in the end, you must discover who you are and what works best. Anyone who tries to tell you who you "really" are, or how you "should" be, might be trying to control you.

There is a deep inner feeling which I like to think of as my "spark." It is my sense of who I am. When I can tap into that, I am filled with a sense of joy, comfort, and rightness. It is, perhaps, a type of cognitive consonance that points the direction to my "true self." For me,

---

1. Elder Carl B. Cook. "When Children Want to Bear Testimony." *Ensign*, Dec 2002.
https://www.lds.org/ensign/2002/12/when-children-want-to-bear-testimony
2. Kline, *Woman Redeemed*, 2005. 5.
3. The *Ensign* is the official LDS monthly magazine for general membership.

having integrity means integrating with this true self as much as possible.

This feeling is your guide to self-discovery. The answers you find will be quite different from my answers. And that's the point.

*Past events, it is argued, have no objective existence, but survive only in written records and in human memories. The past is whatever the records and the memories agree upon. And since the Party is in full control of all records, and in equally full control of the minds of its members, it follows that the past is whatever the Party chooses to make it.*

**—George Orwell, *1984***

*Truth surely exists as an absolute, but our use of truth should be disciplined by other values.*

**—Apostle Dallin H. Oaks, *Ensign*** [1]

*I shudder at the list of apparent falsehoods for which I would have given my life.*
**—Brad L. Morin,**
***Suddenly Strangers*** [2]

*Don't be afraid to die... They'll torture some of our children here. They'll torture our people.*

**—Jim Jones,
moments prior to the Jonestown suicides** [3]

# Deception

**Deception**
*—Suppression, Trust, Silencing Doubts*
- Hides negative effects of the group
- Hides challenging "doctrines" which are actually just tighter control methods
- Hides negative history of the group
- Hides atrocities committed by leader and members
- Obfuscates control methods; makes the member feel in control of her own choices
- Builds trust by not causing reasons for mistrust

In a democracy cults must resort to deception to gain consent. The leader of a successful totalist group must appear kind, intelligent, and holy. Members must appear joyful at all times. They promise happiness and appeal to imagination and existing ideals.

Yet such a group can't fulfill its too-good-to-be-true promises. The leaders demand a steep price, and there may be unusual doctrines and distasteful practices that would be off-putting to outsiders. In order to gain and retain members, it becomes necessary to hide anything which can generate doubt or serious questions.

You will not be told up front just how much will be expected of you in terms of time, money, loyalty, and obedience. Objectionable doctrines are saved for later, when you're unlikely to object. Anything that might illuminate the group in a negative light is obfuscated or minimized, like facts about the organization's history; misdeeds of the leaders; conflicts

---

1. Elder Dallin H. Oaks. "Criticism." *Ensign*, Feb 1987. https://www.lds.org/ensign/1987/02/criticism
2. Morin and Morin, *Suddenly Strangers,* 2004. 168.
3. Mary McCormick Maaga. "Jonestown 'Suicide Tape Transcript'," Nov 18, 1978. http://employees.oneonta.edu/downinll/mass_suicide.htm

in dogma; financial status; and complaints from individual members.

Members unknowingly become part of the deception. They put on their happy faces (whether they are happy or not) and begin painting the same pristine picture for others.

The opposite of coercive persuasion is "informed consent." An ethical persuader educates before asking for commitment. Employment is "at will." Ethical therapists allow you to quit without questioning. Email newsletters offer an unsubscribe option. Contracts have expiration dates with reasonable consequences for early cancelation. Uncontrolling churches never pressure you to attend.

Organizations in our society run the ethical spectrum. Sometimes doctors fail to explain all the pertinent risks of a procedure, and consumer contracts push the limits on what they can squeeze into the fine print. However it is clear that our culture values fairness and honesty. False advertising is considered fraud. No matter what you sign, you can never be legally forced into indentured servitude or slavery; the law will protect you. When companies go too far in testing the reasonable edges of deception, consumers become outraged.

Deception is a major factor separating cults from ethical institutions which utilize similar persuasive techniques. Healthy organizations practice transparency, exposing their mistakes so the group can improve and so members can make informed decisions.

The LDS Church practices the opposite. Former member Marion Stricker observes, "There can be no real choice without knowledge. The Closed System of Mormonism gives 'lip service' to reality, then negates it by keeping its members in an emotional, and rationally confused state of mind from which they 'choose...without choosing'; they 'choose' the *label* that best fits their needs without being shown the contents."[1]

Like a can that says "soup" on the outside but is filled with dirt, the Church makes many promises and then forbids use of a can opener.

Each LDS covenant is a contract with God, and we are asked to sign on these dotted lines without informed consent:

**Baptism & Confirmation:**
New converts are rushed into commitments they don't understand after only the most basic of lessons. Eight-year-olds are expected to be mature enough to make eternal commitments.

**Endowment:**
Temple ceremonies are completely secret. No one understands what they are committing to until it's far too late to reasonably back out. Consequences for breaking these covenants are believed to be severe and eternal.

**Marriage:**
Most young people are pressured to marry too young and often without enough time to get to know one another. Emphasis on avoiding sexual sin increases urgency and turns it into a biological decision. The commitment is not only to God and the Church but to another adult and to your future children.

Other serious decisions, like missions, are born of compliance pressure with little information about the realities of the job. Returning missionaries are instructed to tell only positive stories, even to their close families.

Isolation, also known as milieu control, is an important tool for maintaining illusions. An ex-Moonie quoted in *Captive Hearts* said, "When a person is isolated, he is not in a good position to discover that he is being deceived. Deception and isolation reinforce each other... Perhaps more important, you are isolated from your own mind."[2]

Hassan states:

---

1. Stricker, *The Double-Bind in Mormonism*, 2000. 34.
2. Tobias and Lalich, *Captive Hearts, Captive Minds*, 1994. 30.

> Information control begins during recruitment, when cults withhold information to draw people in...
>
> People are given only the information they are deemed 'ready for'... Recruits who ask questions are often told that they are not yet mature enough to know the whole truth. Insider doctrines are reserved for people who are already thoroughly indoctrinated. In this way, assessments of cult doctrines are delayed until the recruit's ability to make them objectively is impaired.[1]

Sometimes the deceptive recruiting tactics are blatant, though because they are unpublished, the only way we know about it is when someone happens to write about it. Martha Beck recounts, from her own mission, "The local Mormon authorities [in Japan] decided to print up glossy English-language brochures, using them to lure prospective converts with the promise of English lessons."[2]

More often, these are lies of omission. LDS missionaries are instructed to limit how much doctrine they reveal to investigators. "When first teaching [the Plan of Salvation] doctrine, do not teach everything you know about it."[3]

We were taught catchphrases like "milk before meat", "line upon line", "do not cast pearls before swine", "it's sacred, not secret." They all mean the same thing: Those who learn too much too soon will reject the whole system.

But once you're in deep, when you have too much riding on your convictions, when there are enough thought-control mechanisms in place, nothing will shake your faith. Steve Sanchez tells us the leader of his group was eventually able to reveal himself as "a former con man and card-playing mechanic from the streets," without anyone batting an eye.[4]

This is how believing members can hear unvarnished details from Joseph Smith's shady history, a con man and swindler himself[5,6], and dismiss them with ease.

These deceits are not accidental oversights, but facts intentionally withheld, distorted, misrepresented, or completely rewritten. There is no telling what Church leaders talk about behind closed doors, but some leaders have given talks with a very clear message.

Apostle Boyd K. Packer spoke at a symposium for Church Education System (CES) members in 1981, which included BYU, Institute[7], and Seminary teachers. These are people who, as part of their academic jobs, may encounter some of these suppressed facts.

> Teaching some things that are true, prematurely or at the wrong time, can invite sorrow and heartbreak instead of the joy intended to accompany learning...
>
> The scriptures teach emphatically that we must give milk before meat. The Lord made it very clear that some things are to be taught selectively, and some things are to be given only to those who are worthy.
>
> It matters very much not only what we are told but when we are told it. Be careful that you build faith rather than destroy it.[8]

He goes on:

> There is a temptation for the writer or the teacher of Church history to want to tell everything, whether it is worthy or faith promoting or not. Some things that are true are not very useful...
>
> In the Church we are not neutral. We are one-sided. There is a war going on and we are engaged in it. It is the war between good and evil, and we are belligerents

---

1. Hassan, *Releasing the Bonds,* 2000. 48-49.
2. Beck, *Leaving the Saints,* 2005. 123.
3. *Preach My Gospel: A Guide to Missionary Service.* 2004. The Church of Jesus Christ of Latter-day Saints, n.d. 50.
4. Sanchez, *Spiritual Perversion,* 2005. 91.
5. "Mormon Quotes on Joseph Smith's Trial of 1826." Accessed April 8, 2014. http://www.mormonthink.com/QUOTES/js1826.htm
6. Dale R. Broadhurst. "Joseph Smith: Nineteenth Century Con Man?," July 5, 2009. http://sidneyrigdon.com/criddle/Smith-ConMan.htm
7. Institute is like Seminary for college students.
8. Boyd K. Packer. "The Mantle Is Far, Far Greater Than the Intellect." Brigham Young University, 1981.

> defending the good. We are therefore obliged to give preference to and protect all that is represented in the gospel of Jesus Christ...

Then he offers this analogy:

> Suppose that a well-managed business corporation is threatened by takeover from another corporation. Suppose that the corporation bent on the takeover is determined to drain off all its assets and then dissolve this company. You can rest assured that the threatened company would hire legal counsel to protect itself.
>
> Can you imagine that attorney, under contract to protect the company having fixed in his mind what he must not really take sides, that he must be impartial?
>
> Suppose that when the records of the company he has been employed to protect are opened for him to prepare his brief he collects evidence and passes some of it to the attorneys of the enemy company. His own firm may then be in great jeopardy because of his disloyal conduct.
>
> Do you not recognize a breach of ethics, or integrity, or morality?

And what if the lawyer found the company had caused actual harm to its employees and customers? What if the attorney discovered a lengthy list of blatant lies this company had told the public to cover up its injurious actions? Are the ethics so clear in that situation?

To ensure teachers understood the dire consequences of ignoring Packer's advice, he backed it with a threat: "The writer or the teacher who has an exaggerated loyalty to the theory that everything must be told is laying a foundation for his own judgment. He should not complain if one day he himself receives as he has given. Perhaps that is what is contemplated in having one's sins preached from the housetops."

The complete speech is available on the internet. I encourage you to read the full context.

In a more public forum, referencing a different CES talk, Apostle Dallin H. Oaks wrote in *The Ensign:*

> In a talk I recently gave to Church Educational System teachers, I urged that "the fact that something is true is not always a justification for communicating it." A letter published in the New York Times Magazine described my counsel as "contempt for the truth." I disagree. I rely on the teaching in Ecclesiastes: "To every thing there is a season, and a time to every purpose under the heaven." Specifically, there is "a time to speak," and there is also "a time to keep silence."
>
> The counsel to mute our criticism is like the counsel the Apostle Paul gave to the Corinthian Saints to abstain from eating meat offered as sacrifices to idols. In truth, he taught, the idol was nothing. But since some of the members were weak and might misunderstand, those who knew the truth needed to "take heed lest by any means this liberty of yours become a stumblingblock to them that are weak." A Protestant theologian, Krister Stendahl, concludes: "The gist of Paul's thought is that integrity is of no value in itself"...
>
> A Christian who has concern for others exercises care in how he uses the truth. Such care does not denigrate the truth; it ennobles it.[1]

More recently, General Authority Steven E. Snow spoke to this in the *New Era*, because access to uncomfortable facts is no longer restricted to Church insiders. Thanks to the internet, it is difficult to keep secrets, and the Church is rapidly losing members, including several high-ranking authorities. The next best move is damage control:

---

1. Oaks, "Criticism," *Ensign*, Feb 1987.

> Certainly, the world has changed in the last generation or two. The Internet has put all kinds of information at our fingertips—good, bad, truthful, untruthful—including information on Church history. You can read a great deal about our history, but it's important to read about it and understand it in context. The difficulty with some information online is that it's out of context and you don't really see the whole picture.
>
> Information that tries to embarrass the Church is generally very subjective and unfair. We should seek sources that more objectively describe our beliefs and our history. Some websites are very mean-spirited and can be sensational in how they present the information. Look for sources by recognized and respected historians, whether they're members of the Church or not.[1]

Unfortunately for Elder Snow, most of those authors actually *are* objective and quite fair, basing conclusions on *all* the evidence. Such authors, like myself, cite their references so sources can be freely reviewed by anyone. We are not afraid of the conclusions you may draw from our sources.

What *is* very subjective is hiding difficult facts from members. As Packer stated, the Church is like a lawyer who refuses to release evidence that could assist the other side. Hardly an objective position.

Elder Snow concludes, "The overwhelming evidence of Church history is positive and faith-promoting. In its full context, it is absolutely inspiring." The full context is exactly what this book is designed to show: a context of coercive manipulation.

George Orwell illustrated this concept well in *1984*: "...if all others accepted the lie which the Party imposed—if all records told the same tale—then the lie passed into history and became truth. 'Who controls the past' ran the Party slogan, 'controls the future: who controls the present controls the past.'"[2]

Many websites and books are dedicated to exposing LDS deceptions, especially the history from a time when Church actions and beliefs were more extreme. Learning more about the specific deceptions is helpful for recovery.

Here is a brief list of the most commonly discussed past and present controversies that are regularly concealed or distorted by the Church:[3]

- The Mountain Meadows Massacre
- The destruction of the newspaper "The Nauvoo Expositor" by Nauvoo mayor, Joseph Smith, and a mob he controlled
- The theocratic power wielded by Brigham Young in the Utah government
- Doctrines that were taught by Brigham Young which are now suppressed, such as the Blood Atonement, which justified murder
- Mormon activities in Missouri that prompted persecution
- Joseph Smith's practice of polygamy, without Emma's knowledge or permission, which included marrying women who already had husbands
- The continued secret practice of polygamy by Church leaders, including

---

1. Elder Steven E. Snow. "Balancing Church History." *New Era*, June 2013. http://www.lds.org/new-era/2013/06/balancing-church-history
2. George Orwell. *1984: A Novel*. New York, N.Y.: Signet Classic, 1984.
3. A good starting source for studying these and many other issues is www.mormonthink.com. Its articles are well-researched and well-cited, and it includes both the LDS perspective and the controversial perspectives. Many of its authors are still active and devout Latter-day Saints.

Feel free to search multiple sources and make up your own mind. Aside from Google, a few more starting points are listed in the Appendix under "Recommended Reading."

Also, while this book was in the final stages of editing, the LDS Church began to release essays on its official website, LDS.org, which describe many of the historical issues in a much more forthright and accurate way. These essays continue to be released as of May 2014. This is an encouraging trend, and if it continues, it will make significant portions of this chapter less relevant.

Prophet Joseph F. Smith, after 1890
- Mormon women once held the priesthood
- Joseph Smith was a convicted treasure hunter and con-man
- The temple ceremony has been changed multiple times over the past 150 years, in spite of claims it has not changed
- The source-scrolls for the Book of Abraham were actually common Egyptian funerary texts
- Differing accounts of how Joseph Smith translated the Book of Mormon, including the use of "peep stones" and gazing into a hat
- Striking parallels between Smith's "revealed" teachings and other written works of the time
- Joseph Smith was tricked into "translating" the Kinderhook Plates, which were fake records written in meaningless symbols
- Conflicting accounts of the First Vision
- Joseph Smith and later prophets made specific prophecies that failed to come true
- Joseph and Hyrum Smith became Freemasons months before introducing the temple ceremony, which is remarkably similar to Masonic rites
- Racist doctrines and leaders
- Archeological, historical, geographic, and DNA evidence show no signs that the Book of Mormon is literally true
- A secret "Second Anointing" temple ceremony guarantees recipients access to the Celestial Kingdom
- Sexual abuse cover-ups

Faithful Saints reading non-LDS accounts of these events often feel strong dissonance, and when it cannot be easily resolved in favor of the Church, they feel intense betrayal.

Though American corporations and secular non-profits are required by law to disclose financial information, LDS finances are largely unknown. Members assume tithing mostly goes to running the Church, caring for the needy, and building churches and temples. Separate funds are created for the needy (fast offering, Church farms, etc.), missionaries are usually required to cover their own expenses, and buildings are maintained in large part by unpaid volunteers. Yet the Church takes in a vast amount of untaxed wealth, something approximating 10% of the annual income of some undisclosed number of million active households.

We do know the Church has purchased quite a lot of prime Utah commercial real estate, including at least one operating shopping mall, and other for-profit businesses. Most Mormons do not know this. Members are also led to believe Church leadership is unsalaried, without being told that general authorities receive a very generous "living stipend." More details about Church finances can be found on websites and books dedicated to the subject.

The Church also hides the actual number of active members, the number of people leaving, and other relevant statistics, in favor of touting a steadily increasing 15 million members. These numbers do not compare well to census and survey data. Either Mormons are too ashamed to tell the truth to survey-takers, or the Church pads its numbers. Some speculate that the Church never subtracts members who have been removed from Church roles. At the very least, it is counting "inactives" who no longer believe or wish to be members.

Not all LDS deceptions are provable or even knowable. Most religious claims are what scientists call "non-falsifiable." There is no way to know if the Celestial Kingdom is real, if families are forever, or if God even exists. Most of what the Church promises can never be validated.

Philosopher Bertrand Russell demonstrated this idea by claiming there is a teapot in orbit around the sun between Earth and Mars. Scientists who attempt to disprove his claim might use telescopes and will fail to find any heavenly teapot. Russell could then argue that it is too small to be seen by telescopes. So researchers might send a probe and still fail to find the teapot. At which time, Russell will claim the teapot is *invisible*. Any subsequent tests will be met with further justifications about why the teapot is undetectable.

"Non-falsifiable" means there is no condition under which the statement can be proven false. If I claim gravity pulls objects downward, tests can be designed that could prove my claim wrong *if it wasn't true*. If I am wrong, a dropped a pen will fall upward or in some other direction.

A falsifiable statement, given the right tools and tests, is *knowable*. The field of science concerns itself with falsifiable claims, i.e. there are imagined conditions under which, if a claim is not true, it can be shown to not be true.

If the Earth is flat, we would expect to be unable to measure curvature at the horizon (we can, so it's not). If the universe is not expanding, we'd expect every star to be heading towards us (they don't). If Prozac does not effectively treat depression, we'd expect a high percentage of test subjects fail to report relief compared to placebos (they don't). These are the conditions under which we expect a thing to work, and if it doesn't work, then the statement is not true.

Even historical claims can be falsifiable to a certain extent, for instance, if Lincoln had not been shot in Ford's Theater in 1865, we would expect a number of reliable contemporary documents to reveal this controversy.

Even the overarching claim of this book is falsifiable. I propose that if I'm wrong, you can sift through a fair number of LDS doctrines and find no sign of mind control. I encourage you to seek for signs or lack of signs.

Religion frequently concerns itself with claims which are non-falsifiable: An angel appeared to Joseph Smith. He received gold plates written in an ancient language. He translated it through the power of God. The Nephites lived in the Americas two-thousand years ago. God lives in the Celestial Kingdom. We'll get to go there, too, but only if we obey.

I can't design a test that would show any of these false. Religious claims could be proven *true*, like if God came down in a busy public square and handed the gold plates over to the media for public scrutiny. But, like Russell's Teapot, we cannot design a test that would show God or the gold plates *don't* exist. They are ever-elusive, mysterious, hidden, taken up into heaven.

"With God, nothing shall be impossible." Luke 1:37 And maybe that's true. It's just that neither you or I can prove it. There is no way to prove if someone is lying about these kinds of truths. This is very convenient for cult leaders, who can claim just about anything.

From *Captive Hearts*, "...[cult] leaders have an intuitive ability to sense their followers' needs and draw them closer with promises of fulfillment. [The leader] creates conditions so that his victims cannot or dare not test his claims. How can you prove someone is *not* the Messiah? That the world *won't* end tomorrow? That humans are *not* possessed by aliens from another world or dimension? Through psychological manipulation and control, cult leaders trick their followers into believing in something, then prevent them from testing and disproving that mythology or belief system."[1]

As Carl Sagan declared in *Cosmos*, "Extraordinary claims require extraordinary evidence."[2] Yet within Mormonism, those who demand rational proof are considered sign-seekers and are vilified rather than celebrated. One of the greatest villains in the Book of Mormon, Korihor, was struck dumb by one of the greatest heroes, Alma, because he demanded evidence in order to believe in God. Korihor pleads forgiveness, which Alma does not grant, so Korihor dies as a beggar in the streets. (Alma 30) Let this be a lesson to the doubters.

Well-meaning members are regularly asked to deceive, though they usually don't realize it. The pressure is on to maintain a good front. Brad Morin wrote about his own participation in the Church's dishonesty. "During my years as a faithful Mormon, I was

---

1. Tobias and Lalich, *Captive Hearts, Captive Minds*, 1994. 67.
2. "Encyclopedia Galactica." *Cosmos*. 1:24: PBS, Dec 14, 1980.

convinced, and had stated it as fact to others, that the archaeological evidence in support of the *Book of Mormon* was substantial. Apparently, other Mormon faithful had fallen into the same trap; we believed whatever we heard that supported the *Book of Mormon*, bypassing scrutiny and representing it as fact. Total honesty had been shoved aside for the good of the cause which I *knew* to be true. As with most Mormons, it was not my intent to be dishonest; rather, my intellectual shortcuts were born of a passion for my beliefs—and the notion that some truths were tricky to establish, requiring a selective perspective."[1]

At least one scripture story shows that deception is morally acceptable. Nephi was commanded to disguise himself as Laban and lie to the servants so he could steal the brass plates [2]. The justification? Laban had threatened Nephi, he wouldn't obey God's commandments, and Laban had stolen Nephi's money. What did the angel say to finally convince Nephi? That an entire nation should not dwindle in unbelief. Murder was justified by the same reasoning. 1 Nephi 3-4

With these priorities set by an angel of God, members often come to their own very logical conclusions about how to resolve moral conflicts. As Jack B. Worthy reports, "Having grown up inside The Mormon Show, I had been indoctrinated to believe that the sin of lying was less serious than the sin of harming the reputation of the Church... It is a member's responsibility to demonstrate to nonmembers that being an obedient member of the LDS Church brings great happiness—even if this must be demonstrated through play acting."[3]

Worthy was asked to lie many times on his mission and after it. As he served in the office of the Mission President, "I was privy to all the information that officially went out of the mission. I typed a letter to the parents of every missionary who was about to go home. It was a form letter that raved about each missionary's accomplishments. It talked about his or her spiritual growth and said that he or she had learned to speak Cantonese almost like a native speaker. When I typed these exact same words to Elder Bird's parents, it made me realize that nothing in any of the letters was sincere. But they made all the mothers proud, I'm sure. (After I returned home from my mission, my mother refused to listen to me when I told her it was a form letter. She wanted to believe that her son was especially good at learning languages.)"[4]

According to Cialdini, once a lie is told, it's hard to stop believing it. "People have a natural tendency to think that a statement reflects the true attitude of the person who made it. What is surprising is that they continue to think so even when they know that the person did not freely choose to make the statement... Unless there is strong evidence to the contrary, observers automatically assume that someone who makes such a statement means it."[5] Other studies show that people will continue to believe a false news report, even when it has been corrected.

Mormon culture places a huge emphasis on "keeping up appearances." On a social level, it is more important to appear righteous than it is to actually *be* righteous. A hypocritical member can easily get away with binge drinking or other "sins", so long as he keeps his hair cut, wears a white shirt to church, and quotes a scripture now and then. Even men who are caught in adultery can get away with a slap on the wrist, so long as people perceive him as a "spiritual giant." The higher the rank (Bishop, High Council, Stake Presidency), the lighter the sentence often is, and the more people are willing to brush it off as a human mistake—if they even find out.

Because of all the pressure from countless "shoulds", emotional deception is common. For example, Mormons are supposed to be happy all the time. A Christlike countenance is a

---

1. Morin and Morin, *Suddenly Strangers,* 2004. 80.
2. According to the Book of Mormon, the brass plates contained "a record of the Jews," which is considered to be the Old Testament. Not to be confused with the gold plates, upon which Nephi and his descendants wrote the scriptures which Joseph Smith later found and translated into the Book of Mormon.
3. Worthy, *The Mormon Cult,* 2008. 177.
4. Worthy, *The Mormon Cult,* 2008. 142.
5. Cialdini, *Influence,* 2009. 68.

cheerful one. Righteousness leads to happiness, and wickedness to misery. Yet familiar to me is the bright smile under sad eyes, the stressed, unappreciated woman with seven kids who can never give enough, but she must remain perky, suppress her depression, anguish, and anger, and "do her duty with a heart full of song."

Only positive church experiences are openly discussed. In testimony meetings[1], we may hear about illnesses, the negative actions of outsiders, or the member's own spiritual weaknesses, but never about faults of the Church or how doctrine might have caused unhappiness.

You have to leave the LDS echo chamber to hear, "My missionary companions all treated me terribly, the rules were too strict, they worked me too hard, I got no converts, and I hated that I couldn't talk to my family." Likewise, family difficulties, marital issues, abuse, psychological problems, negative interactions with Church leadership, unfulfilled spiritual promises, and other important personal issues are never allowed to be seriously addressed within the rigid Church structure. Appearances must be maintained.

I remember my own lies, from my fake smile to the excuses I made whenever anyone challenged Church truthfulness. The Church had a monopoly on Truth, so the only truth I could hear had to be signed and sealed by the Church.

When the facts threaten to destroy your entire perception of reality—when the basis of your entire way of life is in danger of toppling, avoidance is sometimes the only answer. The Church and its members will avoid cognitive dissonance to the point of deception and denial, even when they cause prolonged misery within self and others.

Deception is a mildew that depends upon shadows and secrecy. Though it can be extremely painful, we should never be afraid to examine the flaws in our beliefs, nor should we avoid listening to critiques of the institutions we hold dear. If there is something ugly there, it should be brought to light. Sunlight really is the best disinfectant, and it can only serve to improve every aspect of human existence.

---

1. Once a month, a special sacrament meeting is held in which, instead of talks, a microphone is provided for members who wish to voluntarily share their testimonies with others. This is done on "Fast Sunday," when members are asked to go without food for two meals, and donate the money they would have spent on food to the Church to feed the poor.

> *I tell you Winston, that reality is not external. Reality exists in the human mind, and nowhere else. Not in the individual mind, which can make mistakes, and in any case soon perishes: only in the mind of the party, which is collective and immortal. Whatever the party holds to be truth, is truth. It is impossible to see reality except by looking through the eyes of the Party.*
> —George Orwell, *1984*

> *God's will is always whatever the leader wants or decides... Under such psychological tyranny, even one's own thoughts become suspect as potential enemies of the system.*
> —John D. Goldhammer, *Under the Influence*[1]

> *Because Mormonism is a Closed System, 'one-sided,' there can only be one view, that of the Binder, which leaves out reason, choice and universal principles.*
> —Marion Stricker, *The Pattern of the Double-Bind in Mormonism*[2]

# Sacred Science: A Closed System of Logic

**Sacred Science: A Closed System of Logic**
—Trust, Suppression, Silencing Doubts, Isolation, Influence, Reinforcement

- Establishes authority of the leader
- Establishes goodness
- Establishes the one true way, which...
- ...blocks out a desire to seek answers outside the system
- Suppresses the ability to ask questions or express doubts about core principles
- Suppresses the ability to criticize leadership

Sacred science is a philosophical narrative that weds the sublime with the sensible. Delivered in the language of logic, it excites a spiritual sense of wonder. This global, universal force for good inflames fascination and marvel, and promises ultimate fulfillment and resolution to all ills. Sacred science engenders full trust and becomes the passion driving continued participation. This technique puts the total in totalist.

Psychiatrist and early cult researcher, Robert J. Lifton, coined the term in his original list of eight mind control techniques. It accomplishes three key goals:

- ♌ The system is infallible. The doctrine is the only truth. The logic is complete and airtight.
- ♌ The leader(s) speak for God and are one with God's will. God, the leaders, the organization, and the doctrine are one and the same.
- ♌ Open expression of questions, doubt, and criticism of the system and leadership is discouraged or not allowed.

---

1. Goldhammer, *Under the Influence*, 1996. 105.
2. Stricker, *The Double-Bind in Mormonism*, 2000. 64.

According to Lifton:

> The assumption here is not so much that man can be God, but rather that man's *ideas* can be God: that an absolute science of ideas (and implicitly, an absolute science of man) exists, or is at least very close to being attained; that this science can be combined with an equally absolute body of moral principles; and that the resulting doctrine is true for all men at all times. Although no ideology goes quite this far in overt statement, such assumptions are implicit in totalist practice.
>
> At the level of the individual, the totalist sacred science can offer much comfort and security. Its appeal lies in its seeming unification of the mystical and the logical modes of experience... Since the distinction between the logical and the mystical is, to begin with, artificial and man-made, an opportunity for transcending it can create an extremely intense feeling of truth.[1]

Our post-Enlightenment culture requires a pretense of reason for all ideas. The modern mind, even the modern religious mind, demands an explanation. Yet on an intuitive level, we still crave the unexplainable. If a cult leader can successfully wrap the two together in a way that continues to make sense, the opposing concepts can amplify in a feedback loop of euphoric consonance—a spiritual experience for the present day. Such teachings will satiate a craving for answers and seem superior to any other school of thought.

"The glory of God is intelligence, or, in other words, light and truth." D&C 93:36 God's ways are scientific, or in other words, transcendent. This well-known verse conflates scientific and spiritual knowledge into one merged concept. The requirements for logic become redefined on the cult's terms.

In Steven Hassan's words, sacred science is "The belief that the group's dogma is absolutely scientific and morally true, with no room for questions or alternative viewpoints."[2]

In such a system of thought, there will be no wiggle room, no space for disagreement. The logic will not stand up to close scrutiny, so it is necessary to squelch even the smallest whisper of objection. Michael Langone said, "The apparent loving unanimity of the group masks, and in some cases bolsters, strict rules against private as well as public dissent. Questions are deflected. Critical comments are met with smiling pleas of 'no negativity', or some other 'thought-terminating cliché...' Doubt and dissent are thus interpreted as symptoms of personal deficiency."[3]

Sacred Science is about closing off all sources of internal dissonance and maintaining consistency within the group, the doctrine, and even the individual. Nothing but consonance is allowed, and any dissonance that is allowed (to create the illusion of free thought) will be minor and easily reconsonated.

Margaret Singer describes how the mind resolves any unspoken dissonance under these kinds of mental pressures. "If...a target lacks even occasional external support for doubts, it is seductively easy and conflict-resolving to, at some point, literally abandon old standards by creating the rationalization that 'I now understand' the correctness of the community's viewpoint, or even that 'I don't understand it, but I will trust the community and conform.'"[4]

If you believe you are alone in uncertainty, it is easiest to eliminate your own doubts, or at least pretend to go along. This creates a false sense of unanimity and group cohesion.

"...recruits are told that negativity is never to be expressed. Should they have any questions, hesitations, or bad feelings, they are told to consult with an upper-level person, or their trainer, helper, or guide. Isolated from others who have doubts and questions,

---

1. Robert J. Lifton. *Thought Reform and the Psychology of Totalism: A Study of Brainwashing in China.* W W Norton & Co Inc, 1961. (Chapter 22 as accessed from http://www.culteducation.com/brainwashing19.html)
2. Hassan, *Releasing the Bonds,* 2000. 34.
3. Langone, "Introduction," *Recovery from Cults,* 1995. 8.
4. Singer and Ofshe, "Peripheral Versus Central Elements of Self," *Cultic Studies Journal,* 1986.

recruits are left with the impression that everyone else agrees with what is going on."[1] Expressing misgivings directly to leaders also gives them an opportunity to rationalize away questions with ready-made answers.

*Captive Hearts* adds insights about how sacred science suppresses the self. "...the group's doctrine is seen as the Ultimate Truth. Here no questions are allowed. This reinforces personal closure and inhibits individual thought, creative self-expression, and personal development. Experience can only be perceived through the filter of the dogmatic belief."[2]

Hassan addresses this as well. "Cult members are taught that the leader is always correct, and are not allowed to doubt or question him or her. Thoughts that go along with the leader are good. Any other thoughts need to be pushed down by chanting, praying, or speaking in tongues. Any negative feelings are always blamed on the individual. Any disillusionment means the member is doing something wrong... Consequently, the member's ability to reality-test is suppressed. If you can only think positively, you bury your bad thoughts and feelings."[3]

Confirmation bias is also leveraged strongly. If you believe in the ubiquitous, true path, then all signs must point to "Yes", even when they point to "No." "Adaptation to the group, then, requires a capacity...to deceive oneself and others in order to believe that the group is always right, even if it contradicts itself."[4]

It then becomes necessary to link the leader to the doctrine so that members will follow without question. The authority of the leader is reinforced by faith in the system, and the system is reinforced by trust in the leader. Janja Lalich describes her experience as a member of the Worker's Democratic Union: "In the WDU we came to understand (and accept) that revolutionary theory = the party = Doreen Baxter. That kind of ruling principle covers a lot of territory. Moreover, that equation linked our idealism to Baxter's demands for obedience. Our highest aspirations became subservient to her whims. In day-to-day practice this meant that we had to either accept the rules or leave; the latter, of course, meant abandoning the revolutionary struggle, the ideal that animated us."[5]

In spiritual groups, you cannot actually know God's will without a human mouthpiece. Even the Bible is just a collection of men speaking for God. In order to gain unquestioning obedience, a leader must not only claim divine authority, he must make himself interchangeable with God. From a recent LDS Conference talk, "The question is simple: Do we trust our Heavenly Father? Do we trust our prophets?"[6] We must trust one in order to trust the other.

Geri-Ann Galanti's account of her experience at a Moonie recruitment camp echoes my experiences in the Church. "One of the questions I raised in discussion was whether they were presenting the Divine Principle (the bible of the Unification Church) as absolute Truth or as one truth among many. The answer I got was essentially this: All religions have elements of the truth. We believe that we have the Greater Truth. We've tried it. It works. Recruits are invited to try it for themselves and see.

"Note the emphasis on the traditional scientific method of hypothesis and testing. It is, however, only the veneer of science. What is lacking is falsifiability. The basic tenets of their beliefs must be accepted on faith; there is no way to prove them false. The corruption that exists in the world is evidence to them that Satan controls us. There is no way to scientifically prove or disprove the existence of Satan. All discussion starts from the basic assumption that the Divine Principle is true. Its veracity is not a point of discussion."[7]

---

1. Singer, *Cults in Our Midst*, 1995. 115.
2. Tobias and Lalich, *Captive Hearts, Captive Minds*, 1994. 36.
3. Hassan, *Releasing the Bonds*, 2000. 51.
4. Langone, "Introduction," *Recovery from Cults*, 1995. 8.
5. Lalich, "A Little Carrot and a Lot of Stick," *Recovery from Cults*, ed. Langone, 1995. 72-73.
6. R. Conrad Schultz. "Faith Obedience." In LDS General Conference, April 2002. http://www.lds.org/general-conference/2002/04/faith-obedience
7. Galanti, "Reflections on 'Brainwashing,'" *Recovery from Cults*, ed. Langone, 1995. 93.

She describes a presentation they gave: "I wrote down my questions and objections as the lecture progressed. I found, however, that by the end of the lecture many of my questions would have sounded stupid and picky, so I didn't ask them. If an argument is based on 15 points, and point 2 is fallacious, the whole argument falls apart. But if you cannot question point 2 until after the final conclusion has been arrived at, the objection becomes meaningless and the conclusions stands. What makes it even more difficult is that the conclusions are very general and idealistic. *Who wants to argue that the world doesn't need love?*"[1]

She said one more thing that struck me as eerily familiar. "The Moonies listen to the same lectures over and over. I asked a few if they didn't get tired of hearing them so many times. They told me no; they said they hear new things in them every time."

All three points of sacred science seem overwhelmingly present in LDS doctrine. But you don't have to take my word for it; I will oblige with examples.

## The Church Is Universally True (And Logical)

*The group displays excessively zealous and unquestioning commitment to its leader and (whether he is alive or dead) regards his belief system, ideology, and practices as the Truth, as law.*

—Janja Lalich, Ph.D. and Michael Langone, Ph.D.,
***Cults 101: Checklist of Cult Characteristics***[2]

*You will be disappointed if you expect that a spiritual quest will lead to certainty and possession of the truth, the whole truth, and nothing but the truth. Doubt and dialogue will always be with us.*

—Sam Keen,
***Hymns to an Unknown God***[3]

"I know this Church is true," goes every testimony, ever. The Church isn't "mostly" true. No one "believes" it's true. They *know*. It's True with a capital T, and its truthfulness permeates all reality and the universe itself. It's supposedly true for *everyone*.

The introduction to the Book of Mormon states Joseph Smith's own unambiguous take on the subject. "I told the brethren that the Book of Mormon was the most correct of any book on earth, and the keystone of our religion, and a man would get nearer to God by abiding by its precepts, than by any other book."[4]

Here is a smattering of quotes by Dallin H. Oaks echoing this idea in a 2006 Conference talk:

"Again and again the Book of Mormon teaches that the gospel of Jesus Christ is universal in its promise and effect, reaching out to all who ever live on the earth…"

On the Atonement: "His grace is for all. These teachings of the Book of Mormon expand our vision and enlarge our understanding of the all-encompassing love of God and the universal effect of His Atonement for all men everywhere…"

And in prophecy:

---

1. Galanti, "Reflections on 'Brainwashing,'" *Recovery from Cults,* ed. Langone, 1995. 90. (Emphasis added.)
2. Janja Lalich, Ph.D., and Michael D. Langone, Ph.D. "Cults 101: Checklist of Cult Characteristics." Accessed Oct 7, 2013. http://www.csj.org/infoserv_cult101/checklis.htm
3. Keen, *Hymns to an Unknown God*, 1995. 7.
4. Joseph Smith. *Book of Mormon: Another Testament of Jesus Christ ; Doctrine and Covenants of the Church of Jesus Christ of Latter-day Saints ; Pearl of Great Price.* Salt Lake City, UT: Church of Jesus Christ of Latter-day Saints, 2004.

> "He manifesteth himself unto all those who believe in him, by the power of the Holy Ghost; yea, unto every nation, kindred, tongue, and people, working mighty miracles, signs, and wonders, among the children of men according to their faith"...
>
> Today we are seeing the fulfillment of that promise in every nation where our missionaries are permitted to labor, even among peoples we have not previously associated with Christianity...
>
> The Lord provides a way for all His children, and He desires that each of us come unto Him.[1]

Scripture repeats this belief that in the end, all mankind will be converted.

> Yea, every knee shall bow, and every tongue confess before him. Yea, even at the last day, when all men shall stand to be judged of him, then shall they confess that he is God; then shall they confess, who live without God in the world, that the judgment of an everlasting punishment is just upon them; and they shall quake, and tremble, and shrink beneath the glance of his all-searching eye.
>
> Mosiah 27:31

Yikes, sounds a bit like Sauron from *Lord of the Rings*.

Prophet Ezra Taft Benson is oft-quoted in saying, "We are commanded by God to take this gospel to all the world. That is the cause that must unite us today. Only the gospel will save the world from the calamity of its own self-destruction. Only the gospel will unite men of all races and nationalities in peace. Only the gospel will bring joy, happiness, and salvation to the human family."[2]

Missionaries are instructed to "Help people recognize that the Church is not just another religion, nor is it an American church. Rather, it is a restoration of the 'fulness of [the] Gospel', the same as it was revealed and taught from the beginning."[3]

The sitting prophet, Thomas S. Monson, quoting Joseph Smith, teaches that to find our way through life, we only need obey. Our direction is spelled out: "There is no need for you or me in this enlightened age, when the fulness of the gospel has been restored, to sail uncharted seas or travel unmarked roads in search of the fountain of truth. For a loving Heavenly Father has plotted our course and provided an unfailing map—*obedience!*"[4]

The gospel is a prescription for happiness, so long as we view our entire life experience through its lens. "President Hunter [said]: 'I suggest that you place the highest priority on your membership in the Church of Jesus Christ. Measure whatever anyone else asks you to do, whether it be from your family, loved ones, your cultural heritage, or traditions you have inherited—measure everything against the teachings of the Savior. Where you find a variance from those teachings, set that matter aside and do not pursue it. It will not bring you happiness'.

"Why give the Lord's teachings first priority? They are your perfect handbook to happiness."[5]

In Seminary, we memorized the verse, "...I did liken all scriptures unto us, that it might be for our profit and learning." 1 Nephi 19:23, and we were meant to apply it in our lives, that we should live by the word of God.

The Church regularly sets mystical principles in a rational frame. "The Book of Mormon...is convincing evidence that Joseph Smith was a prophet and that the gospel of

---

1. Dallin H. Oaks. "All Men Everywhere." In LDS General Conference, April 2006. http://www.lds.org/general-conference/2006/04/all-men-everywhere
2. Ezra Taft Benson. *The Teachings of Ezra Taft Benson*. Salt Lake City, Utah: Bookcraft, 1988. 167.
3. *Preach My Gospel: A Guide to Missionary Service*. 2004. The Church of Jesus Christ of Latter-day Saints, n.d. 7.
4. President Thomas S. Monson. "First Presidency Message 'Finding Strength through Obedience.'" *Ensign*, Oct 2009. https://www.lds.org/ensign/2009/10/finding-strength-through-obedience
5. Richard G. Scott. "Removing Barriers to Happiness." In LDS General Conference, April 1998. http://www.lds.org/general-conference/1998/04/removing-barriers-to-happiness

Jesus Christ has been restored... [It] is evidence of the love of God for His children."[1]

Many Mormons pride themselves on the gospel's supposedly scientific approach, but as I quickly learned after leaving, the principles of logic were distorted and not those actually used by scientists, logicians, or forensic debaters. An article in the *New Era* demonstrates this distortion:

> Faith, like science, is based on evidence. It is no more subjective and ignorant of evidence than secular knowledge is objective and unbiased about evidence. Having abandoned the idea that knowledge is like an objective picture, that it is in all respects to be contrasted with faith, we can see that faith and knowledge are similar in important ways. Instead of looking away from the facts of the real world, faith is one way, among many others, of looking at the world.
>
> Thus faith need be no less intellectual and well-founded than a scientist's belief about the temporal world, provided the faithful person is pure in heart, is honest and unrationalizing about the evidence he receives, and throws his energies into blessing others' lives. When he does this, he constantly encounters and recognizes spiritual landmarks—'hidden treasures of knowledge'—that allow him with complete intellectual integrity to bear witness of the accuracy of the gospel 'map' that he has personally verified.[2]

And from another *New Era* article:

> Some people have suggested that science and religion are basically different, that they involve themselves in different questions (which is probably true), and that they are incompatible intellectually. I challenge the incompatibility part of that statement. Science and religion use different kinds of tools, but I think they are intellectually compatible, since a person who is well educated can also have a testimony. He need not be ashamed of his testimony, and he need not compromise his intellectual standards when he considers the gospel...
>
> ...the gospel is susceptible to the scientific method. The Lord gives us several examples. Concerning tithing, he said: 'Bring ye all the tithes into the storehouse,...and prove me now herewith...if I will not open you the windows of heaven, and pour you out a blessing, that there shall not be room enough to receive it'. That is just an experiment. Many people have testified that they've tried the experiment and it works. That is the process of science. It is not an intellectually different kind of a thing.
>
> Alma says, 'Experiment upon my words' (Alma 32:27) ["But behold, if ye will awake and arouse your faculties, even to an experiment upon my words, and exercise a particle of faith, yea, even if ye can no more than desire to believe, let this desire work in you, even until ye believe in a manner that ye can give place for a portion of my words."]. He then goes on to compare the word to a seed that, if we will water and feed and nurture it with faith, will let us know whether the message is good.
>
> The Savior gave us another example. He said that if we want to know whether the doctrine is true and comes from the Father, we must 'do his will.' Then we 'shall know of the doctrine, whether it be of God, or whether I speak of myself'. This is all that science asks us to do—simply judge on the basis of the data.[3]

Yet as I've discussed, none of these claims are falsifiable, and there are other, more plausible explanations for these results, such as confirmation bias and the psychological

---

1. *Preach My Gospel*, 2004. 7.
2. C. Terry Warner. "An Open Letter to Students: On Having Faith and Thinking for Yourself" *New Era*, Nov 1971. https://www.lds.org/new-era/1971/11/an-open-letter-to-students-on-having-faith-and-thinking-for-yourself
3. Don Lind. "Things Not Seen." *New Era*, Sept 1986. https://www.lds.org/new-era/1986/09/things-not-seen

factors outlined in this book. The scientific method makes every effort to account for biases and fallacies, and to offer sincere alternate explanations. The experiments suggested by scripture do not stand up these critiques or to Occam's Razor, which states that the simplest explanation that fits the evidence is most likely correct. Scientific method encourages critical examination, questioning, doubts, and challenging authoritative conclusions based on evidence.

The Church would have you believe that "God is the source, the fountain of all intelligence, no matter who possesses it, whether man upon the earth, the spirits in the spirit-world, the angels that dwell in the eternities of the Gods, or the most inferior intelligence among the devils in hell. All have derived what intelligence, light, power, and existence they have from God—from the same source from which we have received ours. Every good and perfect gift cometh from God. Every discovery in science and art, that is really true and useful to mankind has been given by direct revelation from God, though but few acknowledge it. It has been given with a view to prepare the way for the ultimate triumph of truth, and the redemption of the earth from the power of sin and Satan."[1]

There is a scripture that fits this state of affairs well, so long as I replace one word: "Having a form of [science], yet denying the power thereof: from such, turn away." 2 Timothy 3:5

## The Prophets Speak for God

*[David Koresh] had an amazing gift of fluency and conviction. His central point was that God always worked through prophets, and that God had granted him special insight into the Book of Revelation.*
—**Colin Wilson, *Rogue Messiahs***[2]

*It seems improbable to me that God would have whispered the meaning of my life into the ear of some guru or authority.*
—**Sam Keen,**
***Hymns to an Unknown God***[3]

Some principles of the gospel were so driven into my head that I find them hard to explain because of how obvious they seem. It's like explaining that the sun shines. This is one of them.

The prophet is a representative of God, and he receives revelation directly from God. There is only one living prophet at a time and he is God's only spokesman and holds all the keys to the priesthood. He is not perfect, but he is seen by many members (along with other apostles and general authorities) as being the closest to righteous purity you'll find on Earth. He is highly respected, just like the ancient and early LDS prophets like Moses, Isaiah, Nephi, Joseph Smith, and Brigham Young.

Five of the thirteen Articles of Faith establish the authority of the prophet and other leaders:

> 5: We believe that a man must be called of God, by prophecy, and by the laying on of hands by those who are in authority, to preach the Gospel and administer in the ordinances thereof.

This applies to anyone with a calling. Their authority comes from God.

---

1. *Teachings of Presidents of the Church: Brigham Young*. "Chapter 4: Knowing and Honoring the Godhead." The Church of Jesus Christ of Latter Day Saints, 1997. https://www.lds.org/manual/teachings-brigham-young/chapter-4
2. Wilson, Colin. *Rogue Messiahs: Tales of Self-Proclaimed Saviors*. Charlottesville, VA: Hampton Roads Pub, 2000. 5.
3. Keen, *Hymns to an Unknown God*, 1995. 41.

> 6: We believe in the same organization that existed in the Primitive Church, namely, apostles, prophets, pastors, teachers, evangelists, and so forth.

The Church holds the same authority and hierarchy as Christ's original church.

> 7: We believe in the gift of tongues, prophecy, revelation, visions, healing, interpretation of tongues, and so forth.

Spiritual powers exist.

> 8: We believe the Bible to be the word of God as far as it is translated correctly; we also believe the Book of Mormon to be the word of God.

God's ancient words are written in scripture.

> 9: We believe all that God has revealed, all that He does now reveal, and we believe that He will yet reveal many great and important things pertaining to the Kingdom of God.

God continues to speak to man, and scripture continues to be written.

The words of the prophet are like new portions of the bible. According to Brigham Young, "The Lord is in our midst. He teaches the people continually. I have never yet preached a sermon and sent it out to the children of men, that they may not call Scripture."[1,2]

The prophet is so in touch with the will of God, that anything he says is the same as God speaking. In Seminary, I memorized this scripture: "What I the Lord have spoken, I have spoken, and I excuse not myself; and though the heavens and the earth pass away, my word shall not pass away, but shall all be fulfilled, whether by mine own voice or by the voice of my servants, it is the same." D&C 1:38

Elder Glenn L. Pace emphasized this: "I testify to you that Ezra Taft Benson is a prophet of God and is surrounded by other special witnesses of the Savior. Jesus the Christ stands at the head of this church, and he has personally called these servants who preside over us."[3]

Before Ezra Taft Benson was called to be himself a prophet, he stated the rules very clearly in the *Liahona*[4], "Fourteen Principles in Following the Prophet."[5]

- The prophet is the only man who speaks for the Lord in everything.
- The living prophet is more vital to us than the Standard Works [scriptures].
- The living prophet is more important to us than a dead prophet.
- The prophet will never lead the Church astray.
- The prophet is not required to have any particular earthly training or diplomas to speak on any subject or act on any matter at any time.
- The prophet does not have to say 'Thus saith the Lord' to give us scripture.
- The prophet tells us what we need to know, not always what we want to know.
- The prophet is not limited by men's reasoning.
- The prophet can receive revelation on any matter—temporal or spiritual.
- The prophet may well advise on civic matters.
- The two groups who have the greatest difficulty in following the prophet are the proud who are learned and the proud who are rich.

---

1. *Journal of Discourses*. Vol. 13. 26 vols. Privately Printed, n.d. http://jod.mrm.org/1
2. *Teachings of the Living Prophets Student Manual*. The Church of Jesus Christ of Latter Day Saints, 2010. http://www.lds.org/manual/teachings-of-the-living-prophets-student-manual/chapter-2-the-living-prophet-the-president-of-the-church
3. Glenn L. Pace. "Follow the Prophet." In LDS General Conference, April 1989. https://www.lds.org/general-conference/1989/04/follow-the-prophet
4. The *Liahona* is the official LDS monthly magazine for members outside the United States and is published in 51 languages.
5. Ezra Taft Benson. "Fourteen Fundamentals in Following the Prophet." *Liahona*, June 1981. http://www.lds.org/liahona/1981/06/fourteen-fundamentals-in-following-the-prophet

- The prophet will not necessarily be popular with the world or the worldly.
- The prophet and his counselors make up the First Presidency—The highest quorum in the Church.
- The prophet and the presidency—the living prophet and the First Presidency—follow them and be blessed—reject them and suffer.

President Benson's full article references scripture and former prophets to prove that his summary has a firm foundation in doctrine, far more than I have room to cite here. He quotes President Wilford Woodruff: "I say to Israel, the Lord will never permit me or any other man who stands as president of the Church to lead you astray. It is not in the program. It is not in the mind of God."

And he quotes a story told by President Marion G. Romney:

"'I remember years ago when I was a bishop I had President Heber J. Grant talk to our ward. After the meeting I drove him home... Standing by me, he put his arm over my shoulder and said: 'My boy, you always keep your eye on the President of the Church and if he ever tells you to do anything, and it is wrong, and you do it, the Lord will bless you for it.' Then with a twinkle in his eye, he said, 'But you don't need to worry. The Lord will never let his mouthpiece lead the people astray.'"

Dallin H. Oaks cultivates complete trust, telling us that Church leaders cannot misuse power: "In contrast to government and corporate officers, who can often be high-handed and authoritarian in the use of their powers, Church leaders have strict limits on the way they can exercise their authority. The Lord has directed that the powers of heaven can be exercised only 'upon the principles of righteousness'—that is, 'by persuasion, by long-suffering, by gentleness and meekness, and by love unfeigned'. And this command is enforced:

"'When we undertake to...gratify our pride, our vain ambition, or to exercise control or dominion or compulsion upon the souls of the children of men, in any degree of unrighteousness, behold, the heavens withdraw themselves; the Spirit of the Lord is grieved; and when it is withdrawn, Amen to the priesthood or the authority of that man.'"[1]

Many Mormons will claim they are never asked to follow the prophet blindly, and yet they are, again and again, both directly and indirectly. It's in the hymns and Primary songs (several of which I've had stuck in my head while writing this chapter), in scripture stories, in lesson manuals, sacrament talks, and conference talks. The concept of "blindness" is repeatedly reframed as "faith" so members maintain an illusion of choice. Faith and obedience are spoken of together so often they are in danger of being conflated concepts.

As Gordon B. Hinckley taught before he himself was called as prophet, "How thankful we ought to be, how thankful we are, for a prophet to counsel us in words of divine wisdom as we walk our paths in these complex and difficult times. The solid assurance we carry in our hearts, the conviction that God will make His will known to His children through His recognized servants, is the real basis of our faith and activity. We either have a prophet or we have nothing; and having a prophet, we have everything."[2]

And General Authority, Elder Carlos E. Asay, "We walk in uncharted mine fields and place our souls in jeopardy when we receive the teachings of anyone except he that is ordained of God...

"*Remember that there may be many questions for which we have no answers and that some things have to be accepted simply on faith.* An angel of the Lord asked Adam, 'Why dost thou offer sacrifices unto the Lord?' He answered, 'I know not, save the Lord commanded me.' There may be times when we are called upon to climb Mount Moriahs and to sacrifice our Isaacs without a full and prior explanation. Faith is the first principle of the

---

1. Elder Dallin H. Oaks. "Criticism." *Ensign*, Feb 1987.
2. Gordon B. Hinckley. "We Thank Thee, O God, for a Prophet." *Ensign*, Sept 1991. http://www.lds.org/ensign/1991/09/we-thank-thee-o-god-for-a-prophet

gospel; it is a principle of progress."[1]

Our obedience to the prophet must be total. "There are some of our members who practice selective obedience. A prophet is not one who displays a smorgasbord of truth from which we are free to pick and choose. However, some members become critical and suggest the prophet should change the menu. A prophet doesn't take a poll to see which way the wind of public opinion is blowing. He reveals the will of the Lord to us. The world is full of deteriorating churches who have succumbed to public opinion and have become more dedicated to tickling the ears of their members than obeying the laws of God."[2]

The only method offered for confirmation of the prophet's guidance is prayer. Or so long as his words support the truthfulness of the Church. "For behold, the Spirit of Christ is given to every man, that he may know good from evil; wherefore, I show unto you the way to judge; for every thing which inviteth to do good, and to persuade to believe in Christ, is sent forth by the power and gift of Christ; wherefore ye may know with a perfect knowledge it is of God." Moroni 7:16

As long as the prophet speaks of Christ, he's the prophet. All signs point to "Yes."

And the leaders are always working for our own good even if it doesn't seem that way. "Inappropriate intellectualism sometimes leads one to testify that he knows the gospel is true but believes the Brethren are just a little out of touch. Out of touch with what? Don't confuse a decision to abstain from participating in a trend with a lack of awareness about its existence. These Brethren 'prove all things' and 'hold fast that which is good.' To accomplish this, they are in constant touch with Him who created this earth and knows the world from beginning to end."[3]

*All* Church leaders are inspired by God: "Every man and young man in the Church who lives in accordance with the Savior's teachings is ordained to the priesthood. The use of this power, however, is limited. Every father is to his family a patriarch and every mother a matriarch as coequals in their distinctive parental roles. Members, men and women, may receive inspiration by the gift of the Holy Ghost for their personal lives and for their areas of responsibility."[4]

In this way, the power of authority descends through the hierarchy of the Church, so long as you never try to overrule someone above you in the chain.

> The Lord's house is a house of order. The Prophet Joseph Smith taught that "it is contrary to the economy of God for any member of the Church, or any one [else], to receive instruction for those in authority, higher than themselves."
>
> You may receive revelation individually, as a parent for your family, or for those for whom you are responsible as a leader or teacher, having been properly called and set apart.
>
> If one becomes critical and harbors negative feelings, the Spirit will withdraw. Only when they repent will the Spirit return. My experience is that the channels of inspiration always follow that order. You are safe following your leaders.[5]

We are expected to obey anyone with the priesthood who has authority over us. But there are no checks or balances going *upward* except faith in an unseen God.

---

1. Carlos E. Asay. "Opposition to the Work of God." In LDS General Conference, Oct 1981. http://www.lds.org/general-conference/1981/10/opposition-to-the-work-of-god
2. Pace, "Follow the Prophet," General Conference, April 1989.
3. Pace, "Follow the Prophet," General Conference, April 1989.
4. James E. Faust. "The Prophetic Voice." In LDS General Conference, April 1996. http://www.lds.org/general-conference/1996/04/the-prophetic-voice
5. Boyd K. Packer. "Personal Revelation: The Gift, the Test, and the Promise." In LDS General Conference, Oct 1994. http://www.lds.org/general-conference/1994/10/personal-revelation-the-gift-the-test-and-the-promise

> Then President Lee added a warning when he went on to say that we may not always like what comes from the authority of the Church, because it may conflict with our personal views or interfere with some of our social life. However, if we will listen to and do these things as if from the mouth of the Lord Himself, we will not be deceived and great blessings will be ours.
> It brings us back to obedience. It will always be so. It's part of the plan of eternal happiness. I know of no doctrine that is more critical to our well-being in this life and the next. All scriptures teach obedience, and no apostle or prophet has ever lived who has not taught the principle of obedience.
> Sometimes it is necessary to be obedient even when we do not understand the reason for the law. It takes faith to be obedient. The Prophet Joseph Smith, in teaching obedience, said that whatever God requires is right, though we may not know the reason until much later.[1]

Children are particularly vulnerable to these teachings, and it's a simple thing to instill in them feelings of trust using simplistic manipulation.

> Have the children stand up, close their eyes, and hold hands. Take the hand of the first child in line. Lead the line of children around the room, guiding them with your voice as necessary to avoid possible injury and confusion. After several trips around the room, lead them to the picture of Jesus Christ. Explain that by following you, they were all able to find their way safely to the picture of the Savior. Ask the children to return to their seats...
> Explain that a good example could be like a leader guiding us to safety. Just as following their leader's voice brought the children safely to the picture of Jesus Christ, so too can following the words of the prophet allow them to return to Heavenly Father and Jesus someday.[2]

## Suppression of Dissent

*No legitimate group should fear an honest critique of its practices.*
—**Steven Hassan, *Releasing the Bonds*** [3]

*My uncompromising zeal closed all avenues for discovering the error in my beliefs. I refused to question God's ways, not acknowledging the difference between questioning God and questioning the man I considered to be God's spokesman.*
—**Brad L. Morin, *Suddenly Strangers*** [4]

Members are under the illusion that they are free to question. Certain questions, and even jokes, are indeed encouraged, but within unspoken, invisible limits that jolt like an electric fence when crossed. Irreverence about core doctrines is heresy; you just "know" this. Thought-terminating clichés are offered in answer for those who ask or complain, and those who persist are shunned or disciplined.

Church sources regularly silence dissent in its many forms.

Prophet Harold B. Lee tells the story of a woman who encountered this invisible fence with her question, "concerning the promise made that if one would keep the Word of

---
1. R. Conrad Schultz. "Faith Obedience." In LDS General Conference, April 2002.
2. *Primary 3: Choose the Right B (Ages 4-7)*. The Church of Jesus Christ of Latter-day Saints, 1994. Lesson 45 https://www.lds.org/manual/primary-3/lesson-45-i-can-be-a-good-example-for-my-family
3. Hassan, *Releasing the Bonds,* 2000. xx.
4. Morin and Morin, *Suddenly Strangers,* 2004. 168.

Wisdom he should run and not be weary and should walk and not faint."

> And she said, "How could that promise be realized if a person were crippled? How could he receive the blessing that he could run and not be weary, and walk and not faint, if he were crippled?"
> I answered her, "Did you ever doubt the Lord? The Lord said that."
> The trouble with us today, there are too many of us who put question marks instead of periods after what the Lord says. I want you to think about that. We shouldn't be concerned about why he said something, or whether or not it can be made so. Just trust the Lord. We don't try to find the answers or explanations. We shouldn't try to spend time explaining what the Lord didn't see fit to explain. We spend useless time.[1]

Brigham Young had several things to say on this topic:

"Whenever there is a disposition manifested in any of the members of this Church to question the right of the President of the whole Church to *direct in all things*, you see manifested evidences of apostasy—of a spirit which, if encouraged, will lead to a separation from the Church and to *final destruction*."[2]

And, "One of the first steps to apostasy is to find fault with your Bishop; and when that is done, unless repented of a second step is soon taken, and by and by the person is cut off from the Church, and that is the end of it. Will you allow yourselves to find fault with your Bishop?"[3]

Dallin H. Oaks covered the topic of criticism at length in the *Ensign*. He starts by loading the term "criticism" so it can be reframed in the LDS context:

> I do not refer to the kind of criticism the dictionary defines as 'the act of passing judgment as to the merits of anything.' That kind of criticism is inherent in the exercise of agency and freedom. In the political world, critical evaluation inevitably accompanies any knowledgeable exercise of the cherished freedoms of speech and of the press. In the private world, we have a right to expect critical evaluation of anything that is put into the marketplace or the public domain. Sports writers, reviewers of books and music, scholars, investment analysts, and those who test products and services must be free to exercise their critical faculties and to inform the public accordingly. This kind of criticism is usually directed toward issues, and it is usually constructive.
> My cautions against criticism refer to another of its meanings, which the dictionary defines as 'the act of passing severe judgment; censure; faultfinding.' Faultfinding is 'the act of pointing out faults, especially faults of a petty nature.' It is related to 'backbiting,' which means 'to attack the character or reputation of [a person who is not present].' This kind of criticism is generally directed toward persons, and it is generally destructive...[4]

He was right in that criticism is necessary in the exercise of agency. To keep the reader from asking, "Why is religion an exception?" he turns sharply to petty faultfinding and personal judgments against fellow members. This advice is hard to argue with. We should be understanding and kind to one another. These two concepts are not actually mutually exclusive—it is possible to criticize an organization and its leadership methods without

---

1. President Harold B. Lee. "Admonitions for the Priesthood of God." *Ensign*, Jan 1973. https://www.lds.org/ensign/1973/01/admonitions-for-the-priesthood-of-god
2. *Teachings of Presidents of the Church: Brigham Young*, 1997. 80. (Emphasis added.)
3. *Teachings of Presidents of the Church: Brigham Young*, 1997. 81.
4. Oaks, "Criticism," *Ensign*, Feb 1987.

being mean-spirited.

But he does not make this point. Instead, Elder Oaks quickly redirects the conversation back to leadership. "Does the commandment to avoid faultfinding and evil speaking apply to Church members' destructive personal criticism of Church leaders? Of course it does. It applies to criticism of all Church leaders—local or general, male or female. In our relations with all of our Church leaders, we should follow the Apostle Paul's direction: 'Rebuke not an elder, but intreat him as a father.'"

After reading this, church members will conflate the idea of small-minded personal attacks with legitimate criticism of an institution, its policies, and its doctrine. Perhaps this is why my mother became incredibly concerned that my book would criticize innocent members of the Church. She had a hard time understanding how I could criticize the Church as an organization without personally attacking members. Having lived outside the direct influence of the Church for so long, it is easy for me to differentiate the two, and I sometimes forget how these distinctions are erased by LDS doctrine.

Elder Oaks continues,

> Criticism is particularly objectionable when it is directed toward Church authorities, general or local. Jude condemns those who 'speak evil of dignities.' Evil speaking of the Lord's anointed is in a class by itself. It is one thing to depreciate a person who exercises corporate power or even government power. It is quite another thing to criticize or depreciate a person for the performance of an office to which he or she has been called of God. *It does not matter that the criticism is true...* [Emphasis added.]
>
> Government or corporate officials, who are elected directly or indirectly or appointed by majority vote, must expect that their performance will be subject to critical and public evaluations by their constituents...
>
> A different principle applies in our Church, where the selection of leaders is based on revelation, subject to the sustaining vote of the membership. In our system of Church government, evil speaking and criticism of leaders by members is always negative.

Yet there are thousands of religious leaders throughout the world who claim to speak for God. Does speaking for God automatically grant immunity from close examination? Is a claim to heavenly authority a license to be above reproach?

Supposedly, this teaching is for our own good.

> The counsel against speaking evil of Church leaders is not so much for the benefit of the leaders as it is for the spiritual well-being of members who are prone to murmur and find fault...
>
> In these two instances, the Bible teaches that rejection of or murmuring against the counsel of the Lord's servants amounts to actions against the Lord himself. How could it be otherwise? The Lord acts through his servants. That is the pattern he has established to safeguard our agency in mortality. His servants are not perfect, which is another consequence of mortality. But if we murmur against the Lord's servants, we are working against the Lord and his cause and will soon find ourselves without the companionship of his Spirit.

He counsels that complaints should be handled in private. "Why aren't these differences discussed in public? Public debate—the means of resolving differences in a democratic government—is not appropriate in our Church government. We are all subject to the authority of the called and sustained servants of the Lord. They and we are all governed by the direction of the Spirit of the Lord, and that Spirit only functions in an atmosphere of unity." In other words, your cognitive dissonance must be resolved without causing dissonance for others. Don't be a cognitive dissident.

In 1981, Bruce R. McConkie wrote stronger words in a private letter to LDS scholar Eugene England, who had publicly espoused a not-terribly controversial idea that Heavenly Father was still progressing and learning.

> ...it is my province to teach to the Church what the doctrine is. It is your province to echo what I say or to remain silent. You do not have a divine commission to correct me or any of the Brethren. The Lord does not operate that way. If I lead the Church astray, that is my responsibility, but the fact still remains that I am the one appointed with all the rest involved so to do. The appointment is not given to the faculty at Brigham Young University or to any of the members of the Church. The Lord's house is a house of order and those who hold the keys are appointed to proclaim the doctrines.
>
> Now you know that this does not mean that individuals should not do research and make discoveries and write articles. What it does mean is that what they write should be faith promoting and where doctrines are concerned, should be in harmony with that which comes from the head of the Church...
>
> If they err then be silent on the point and leave the event in the hands of the Lord.[1]

This is all firmly based in scripture. In the Doctrine and Covenants, we are instructed: "And see that there is no iniquity in the church, neither hardness with each other, neither lying, backbiting, nor evil speaking." D&C 20:54

And "Cursed are all those that shall lift up the heel against mine anointed, saith the Lord, and cry they have sinned when they have not sinned before me, saith the Lord, but have done that which was meet in mine eyes, and which I commanded them." D&C 121:16

The sin of "contention", aka dissent, is in good company with the worst of all sins: "The Lord God hath commanded that men should not murder; that they should not lie; that they should not steal; that they should not take the name of the Lord their God in vain; that they should not envy; that they should not have malice; that they should not contend one with another." 2 Nephi 26:32

Many scriptures repeat the fact that contention comes from the devil: "And this I do that I may establish my gospel, that there may not be so much contention; yea, Satan doth stir up the hearts of the people to contention concerning the points of my doctrine; and in these things they do err, for they do wrest the scriptures and do not understand them." D&C 10:62-63

"Satan did stir them up to do iniquity continually; yea, he did go about spreading rumors and contentions upon all the face of the land, that he might harden the hearts of the people against that which was good and against that which should come." Helaman 16:22

"He that hath the spirit of contention is not of me, but is of the devil, who is the father of contention, and he stirreth up the hearts of men to contend with anger, one with another. Behold, this is not my doctrine, to stir up the hearts of men with anger, one against another; but this is my doctrine, that such things should be done away." 3 Nephi 11:29-30

Dissent is continually associated with evil and anger. Nowhere does it allow for the concept of rational dissent, which is a natural and healthy part of running an organization. As Oaks pointed out, democratic governments and commercial enterprises consider this valuable, as do many other spiritual groups. We are just supposed to trust that the LDS Church is somehow protected from the corrupting nature of humans operating in secret, outside the accountability of earthly questioning.

In the context of the Church, dissent is the root of *all* evil. Apostle Russell M. Nelson says so: "But that spirit of inner peace is driven away by contention. Contention does not

---

1. Bruce R. McConkie. Letter to Eugene England. "Bruce McConkie's Letter of Rebuke to Professor Eugene England," Feb 19, 1981. http://www.mrm.org/bruce-mcconkies-rebuke-of-eugene-england

usually begin as strife between countries. More often, it starts with an individual, for we can contend within ourselves over simple matters of right and wrong. From there, contention can infect neighbors and nations like a spreading sore."[1]

Surely arguing and fighting for its own sake is not conducive to anyone's happiness. But Nelson is clear, "This war in heaven was not a war of bloodshed. It was a war of conflicting ideas—the beginning of contention... Whenever tempted to dispute, remember this proverb: 'He that is void of wisdom despiseth his neighbour: but a man of understanding holdeth his peace.'"

Since Satan caused contention in the war in heaven by questioning God's will, it's best to just remain quiet. Satan's motive is described as glory-seeking, self-serving, arrogant, angry, hateful, and jealous. God's only motive is love and the rearing up of all His children to His own level. Likewise, members are aligned with Satanic forces if they question Church authority. Your choice—agree with the Church in all things... or be contentious, which will align you with Lucifer.

But you cannot have freedom of choice without "contention." You must be offered multiple points of view to make an informed decision. This applies to all of life; questions of spirituality are not exempted, and I don't believe a benevolent Heavenly Father would think so either.

Not only are we supposed to keep unresolved doubts to ourselves, but also we are to push doubts out of our own minds until they can be resolved. "We must trust in the Lord with a mature faith that someday we will know the answers to the right questions. Yet, from time to time, we find an answer to a burning question that we may have put on the shelf earlier. These answers confirm our faith and our appreciation for the profound nature of the gospel."[2]

A former member of a cult known as "The Work" described it in exactly the same way, "It is as if there is a shelf where all your doubts and misgivings are placed while you are in the group... Because of the indoctrination and not being allowed to ask questions, you just put it on the shelf. Eventually, the shelf gets heavier and heavier and finally just breaks, and you are ready to leave."[3]

## An Open System of Logic

In a *totalist* system, all arrows point to the center, to the conclusion that the system is the one and only way. The questions don't matter—only The Answer.

In an *open* system, the arrows lead out in all different directions. Those directions depend very much on the question being asked. Logic leads to truth, no matter what that truth is. You start with a pile of data and see where it leads. You do not start with the conclusion and then try to make the data fit.

No organization has a monopoly on truth. Truth is woven into the fiber of the universe, and the best way to discover it is to explore that universe. Be open to doubt and to the possibility of being wrong. Be comfortable with questions that have no answers, and be suspicious of anyone who seems to know it all.

As they say, if it looks too good to be true, it probably is.

---

1. Russell M. Nelson. "The Canker of Contention." In LDS General Conference, April 1989. https://www.lds.org/general-conference/1989/04/the-canker-of-contention
2. Richard Neitzel Holzapfel. "Question, but No Doubts." In *Expressions of Faith: Testimonies of Latter-day Saint Scholars*, ed. Susan Easton Black. Salt Lake City, Utah. Deseret Book Co.; Foundation for Ancient Research and Mormon Studies, 1996. http://maxwellinstitute.byu.edu/publications/books/?bookid=107&chapid=1213
3. Tobias and Lalich, *Captive Hearts, Captive Minds,* 1994. 55.

*We were deluded by a mere human influence, which we mistook for the Spirit of God.*

**—George Storrs, Millerite (Seventh-day Adventist),**
***The Morning Watch*, Feb. 20, 1845**
***after a prophesied second coming did not occur***

*If our people want to be safely guided during these troublous times of deceit and false rumors, they must follow their leaders and seek for the guidance of the Spirit of the Lord in order to avoid falling prey to clever manipulators who, with cunning sophistry, seek to draw attention and gain a following to serve their own notions and sometimes sinister motives.*

**—Prophet Harold B. Lee**[1]

*And [the beast] doeth great wonders, so that he maketh fire come down from heaven on the earth in the sight of men, and deceiveth them that dwell on the earth by the means of those miracles which he had power to do...*

**—Revelations 13:13-14**

# Mystical Manipulation

**Mystical Manipulation**
*—Trust, Reinforcement, Silencing Doubts, Influence*

- Establishes higher purpose
- Reinforces legitimacy of authority via higher authority (God, higher goals)
- Reinforces legitimacy of authority via unexplainable events (like miracles)
- Gives mystical power to leaders and members
- Creates an aura of control that seems to go beyond physical possibility
- Builds trust via events which are perceived as proof of truth
- Suppresses cognitive dissonance when values collide
- i.e. the higher purpose supersedes all other goals
- Subordinates self to the group

Mystical Manipulation establishes a sense of higher purpose where the ends can justify any means. Forces exist which are more powerful than the self, therefore, the self must adapt at all costs. In fact, the self has no choice but to adapt. Miracles may be orchestrated, or at the very least, ordinary events come to be seen as proof of the group's reality.

As Galanti described, "The potential convert is convinced that the group is working toward a 'higher purpose' and that he will be instrumental in the attainment of that goal... The group provides a meaning for existence..."[2]

*Captive Hearts* calls it a "...claim of authority (divine, supernatural, or otherwise), which allows for the rationale that the ends justify the means since the 'end' is directed by a higher purpose. Certain experiences are orchestrated to make it seem that they occur spontaneously. The person is required to subordinate himself to the group or cause and stops all questioning—for who can question 'higher purpose'? Self-expression and

---

1. President Harold B. Lee. "Admonitions for the Priesthood of God." *Ensign*, Jan 1973.
2. Galanti, "Reflections on 'Brainwashing,'" *Recovery from Cults*, ed. Langone, 1995. 92.

independent action wither away."[1]

Hassan describes mystical manipulation as, "the contrived engineering of experiences to stage seemingly spontaneous and 'supernatural' events. Everyone manipulates everyone else for the higher purpose."[2]

As you can see, this is the natural extension of sacred science, for if a doctrine is all-encompassing and is backed by the power of God, the impossible becomes expected. A few supernatural or spiritual experiences, real or imagined, can seal the deal.

Robert J. Lifton said, "The inevitable next step...is extensive personal manipulation. This manipulation assumes a no-holds-barred character, and uses every possible device at the milieu's command, no matter how bizarre or painful. Initiated from above, it seeks to provoke specific patterns of behavior and emotion in such a way that these will appear to have arisen spontaneously, directed as it is by an ostensibly omniscient group, must assume, for the manipulated, a near-mystical quality."[3]

The manipulation may not be entirely intentional, and may arise naturally given the environment. Lifton continues, "Ideological totalists do not pursue this approach solely for the purpose of maintaining a sense of power over others. Rather they are impelled by a special kind of mystique which not only justifies such manipulations, but makes them mandatory. Included in this mystique is a sense of 'higher purpose,' of having 'directly perceived some imminent law of social development,' and of being themselves the vanguard of this development. By thus becoming the instruments of their own mystique, they create a mystical aura around the manipulating institutions - the Party, the Government, the Organization. They are the agents 'chosen' (by history, by God, or by some other supernatural force) to carry out the 'mystical imperative,' the pursuit of which must supersede all considerations of decency or of immediate human welfare. Similarly, any thought or action which questions the higher purpose is considered to be stimulated by a lower purpose, to be backward, selfish, and petty in the face of the great, overriding mission."

Mystical manipulation is also related to the concept of cognitive distortions, which are ways in which we view reality incorrectly to fit beliefs about ourselves. This concept is used widely in Cognitive Behavior Therapy, which focuses on transforming negative thought patterns into more truthful and beneficial beliefs. (i.e. "I'm so stupid," becomes, "Sometimes I make mistakes, but I can do this.")[4]

In extreme cases, distortions occur in the minds of abusers to justify heinous acts. Michael Welner of The Forensics Panel evaluated Brian David Mitchell, the kidnapper of Elizabeth Smart. He compared Mitchell to other sexual offenders in religious contexts.

"Cognitive distortions are generally accepted in psychiatry and the behavioral sciences to be a non-delusional form of how offenders and sometimes even otherwise morally sensitive individuals exploit and prey upon others."[5]

The belief is, "I am a good person, so I would never do anything wrong." The filter concocts coinciding beliefs and even perceptions to maintain the illusion, even when the offender *is* doing something wrong.

> Researchers who interviewed and catalogued fourteen such religious abusers noted such accounts divided into 'justifications' and 'excuses,' both of which serve to shift the responsibility from the offender...
>
> These religious offenders use religion-related beliefs prior to the sexual acts to enable them to overcome inhibitions to offend and...minimize the effects of their offending, to reduce guilt associated with these offenses, and to maintain a positive

---

1. Tobias and Lalich, *Captive Hearts, Captive Minds,* 1994. 36.
2. Hassan, *Releasing the Bonds,* 2000. 34.
3. Lifton, *Thought Reform and the Psychology of Totalism,* 1961. (Chapter 22)
4. Burns, David D., M. D. *Feeling Good: The New Mood Therapy.* Reprint edition. New York: Harper, 2008.
5. Michael Welner, M.D. *The Forensic Panel - U.S. Vs. Brian David Mitchell,* June 16, 2009. 167.

> self-image. The researchers determined that religious beliefs actually facilitated offending behavior rather than inhibited it.[1]

Within a religious system, these same distortions affect the victim just as strongly and can be used to manipulate them into compliance and silence. Dr. Welner calls these "spiritual coupons."

> ...recall that [Mitchell's wife] Wanda [Barzee] already had a history of having been confronted with a Brian Mitchell extramarital relationship. She knew her husband to be lustful. She also knew herself, however, to have been brought down to the dust after years of living with no possessions, estranged from her children, her family, her music, even her name. So in the same vein that a dismantled and bewildered Elizabeth Smart came to go along with the ministrations of Brian Mitchell, so did Wanda come to be invested that she must subscribe to all of the revelations, blessings, and other spiritual coupons Mr. Mitchell was touting—for these were the only ideas that lifted her above the dust. This underscores how frightening a trauma Wanda Mitchell, Elizabeth Smart and others have endured under such a misogynistic deconstruction...
>
> When the asserted 'revelation' of polygamy was chronicled, it was accompanied by the directive that Wanda must accept the law or suffer eternal damnation. At the same time, the now-infertile Wanda was promised by the prophet in whom she believed that her womb would again open and bear fruit.[2]

Such artifice can cause complete and total submission to the manipulator. Back to Lifton, "At the level of the individual person, the psychological responses to this manipulative approach revolve about the basic polarity of trust and mistrust. One is asked to accept these manipulations on a basis of ultimate trust (or faith): 'like a child in the arms of its mother.' He who trusts in this degree can experience the manipulations within the idiom of the mystique behind them: that is, he may welcome their mysteriousness, find pleasure in their pain, and feel them to be necessary for the fulfillment of the 'higher purpose' which he endorses as his own."

Eventually, the deceptions may fail to work. Man cannot be led by miracles alone, which is why there isn't just one thought-reform technique. They must work in tandem.

> When trust gives way to mistrust (or when trust has never existed) the higher purpose cannot serve as adequate emotional sustenance. The individual then responds to the manipulations through developing what I shall call the *psychology of the pawn*. Feeling himself unable to escape from forces more powerful than himself, he subordinates everything to adapting himself to them. He becomes sensitive to all kinds of cues, expert at anticipating environmental pressures, and skillful in riding them in such a way that his psychological energies merge with the tide rather than turn painfully against himself. This requires that he participate actively in the manipulation of others, as well as in the endless round of betrayals and self-betrayals which are required.[3]

The forces of cognitive dissonance do battle in the mind of the subject, who *wants* and even *needs* to believe in the miracles. Under the right pressures, he will betray himself rather than betray the leader, group, or doctrine. What Lifton describes here is known as the double-bind, which I will explore later.

---

1. Welner, *U.S. Vs. Brian David Mitchell*, 2009. 159.
2. Welner, *U.S. Vs. Brian David Mitchell*, 2009. 131.
3. Lifton, *Thought Reform and the Psychology of Totalism*, 1961. (Chapter 22)

"But whatever his response—whether he is cheerful in the face of being manipulated, deeply resentful, or feels a combination of both—he has been deprived of the opportunity to exercise his capacities for self-expression and independent action."[1] The self is once again subsumed to the group pseudopersonality.

Intangible gifts can lead to reciprocity indebtedness, and intangible dark forces can inspire phobias and halt thought. John D. Goldhammer gives us an example of mystical manipulation in his new age group.

> We were told that any criticism or doubts about Ann Ree were inspired by "ancestral negativities" or satanic forces. Conflicting ideas or philosophies from other religions or groups were the result of what Ann Ree called that particular group's "dweller action..." What's more, these dweller forces could cause accidents, mishaps, and even death.
>
> This explanation-for-everything approach prevented members from critically thinking about the dark side of life. It prevented any in-depth thinking at all.[2]

And Steve Sanchez describes this technique in play in another new age cult.

> As I sat close to [Rev. Will], I kept having the image in my mind of hitting him or even stabbing him. This was very disturbing, and it made me uneasy because I was afraid he could tell what I was thinking. It was almost like I couldn't control it. He asked me how I was doing. I felt I was obliged to be honest, so I said, "I keep having these weird thoughts of hitting your body."
>
> "I know," he acknowledged. "I can feel all the entities in your space that hate me for telling the truth. Those are all the entities that can't have this teaching."[3]

Both examples are similar to the LDS belief that Satan is constantly trying to destroy the gospel. This type of supernatural event is easily staged. Rev. Will probably noticed a change in Steve's expression. He likely had a ready response to *any* answer Steve might have given. And the words "I know" from someone you trust will spark confirmation bias.

A totalist system need only predispose your mind towards a certain meaning, and you will mystically manipulate yourself via confirmation bias. Since our natural tendency is to look for patterns to confirm what we already believe, we will notice all meaningful coincidence and forget any meaningless coincidences. For a Mormon, a chance event represents an answer to prayer or the power of the Holy Ghost. For those in other belief systems, the same coincidence is attributed to the guidance of the ancestors, the will of the gods, or the manifestation of the law of attraction.

Miracles and synchronicities happen to everyone. It is okay and even healthy to derive personal meaning from them. But they are never evidence of the veracity of any given system of dogma. If that were so, then every church, political system, and multilevel marketing scheme on the planet would be simultaneously true.

---

1. Lifton, *Thought Reform and the Psychology of Totalism*, 1961. (Chapter 22)
2. Goldhammer, *Under the Influence*, 1996. 55.
3. Sanchez, *Spiritual Perversion*, 2005. 72.

# Magical Thinking

*He related personal experiences of true modern miracles which had occurred to him...*

—LDS Lesson Manual,
Referring to Prophet Harold B. Lee[1]

*Unless we enjoy the same gifts and work the same miracles that marked the lives of those who have gone before, we are not the Lord's people. ...anytime any of us exercise the same faith that moved the ancients in their pursuit of righteousness, we will enjoy the same gifts and blessings that attended their ministries.*

—Bruce R. McConkie,
*New Era*[2]

Mormons have been conditioned towards magical thinking, which Wikipedia defines as, "the identification of causal relationships between actions and events, where scientific consensus says that there is none,"[3] or even where there is direct evidence to the contrary.

A former member of the Transcendental Meditation cult said, "The basis of the TM program is that thoughts can magically materialize into matter. If you think a thought, it has an effect... In TM subjective experience determines reality. If it feels good, it must be right."[4]

Harold B. Lee wrote to the priesthood about a problem he saw occurring in the Church: "As I say, it never ceases to amaze me how gullible some of our Church members are in broadcasting these sensational stories, or dreams, or visions, some alleged to have been given to Church leaders, past or present, supposedly from some person's private diary, without first verifying the report with proper Church authorities."

I allege this problem is of the Church's own making, and it generally serves the Church well. Within his own talk, President Lee references all manner of supernatural powers and asks members to trust wholeheartedly in the leadership. He quotes a 1913 declaration from the First Presidency:

> When visions, dreams, tongues, prophecy, impressions or an extraordinary gift or inspiration convey something out of harmony with the accepted revelations of the Church or contrary to the decisions of its constituted authorities, Latter-day Saints may know that it is not of God, no matter how plausible it may appear. Also, they should understand that directions for the guidance of the Church will come, by revelation, through the head. All faithful members are entitled to the inspiration of the Holy Spirit for themselves, their families, and for those over whom they are appointed and ordained to preside. But anything at discord with that which comes from God through the head of the Church is not to be received as authoritative or reliable.[5]

So, it isn't that one should disbelieve wild claims, but that a good Mormon will make sure the wild claims are coming from the right source. The talk continues,

---

1. *Church History In The Fulness Of Times Student Manual*. The Church of Jesus Christ of Latter Day Saints, 2003. http://www.lds.org/manual/church-history-in-the-fulness-of-times-student-manual/chapter-forty-three-an-era-of-correlation-and-consolidation
2. Bruce R. McConkie. "The How and Why of Faith-promoting Stories." *New Era*, July 1978. https://www.lds.org/new-era/1978/07/the-how-and-why-of-faith-promoting-stories
3. "Magical Thinking." *Wikipedia, the Free Encyclopedia*, Dec 6, 2013. https://en.wikipedia.org/w/index.php?title=Magical_thinking&oldid=584773356
4. Patrick L. Ryan. "A Personal Account: Eastern Meditation Group." *Recovery from Cults,* ed. Langone, 1995. 135.
5. Lee, "Admonitions," *Ensign*, Jan 1973.

> Now, if one comes claiming that he has authority, ask him, 'Where do you get your authority? Have you been ordained by someone who has authority, who is known to the Church, that you have authority and have been regularly ordained by the heads of the Church?' If the answer is no, you may know that he is an imposter. This is the test that our people should always apply when some imposter comes trying to lead them astray.

The concept of an invisible, bodiless member of the Godhead, who is ordained for the purpose of motivating people to do good through subtle promptings, is highly manipulatable. If it feels good and confirms the gospel, it's the Holy Spirit. If it feels good and doesn't confirm the gospel, it's carnal pleasure, wishful thinking, or Satan. All signs point to "Yes." It transfers the burden of proof to an emotional basis for evidence, which is extremely easy to engineer.

For instance, guilt and sadness are easily brought on with minor key hymns and sad lyrics about the Savior, who died because of you. You are to meditate on Christ's sacrifice during the preparation and passing of the sacrament, sometimes while fasting, in a room where others are crying. This situation can induce strong emotion, and before long, you may be crying, too, perhaps even out of relief that your sins have been forgiven. Once this emotional environment is interpreted as "the Spirit", mystical manipulation is accomplished.

Many members receive mini-revelations about themselves and their families. Some are based on personal interpretations of patriarchal blessings. Some on dreams or strong feelings or the still small voice[1]. Some people even have auditory promptings or visions. Most are minor revelations, like premonitions to visit a sick ward member. Others are major revelations of destiny.

My mother had a strong feeling I'd marry someone who would one day be a general authority. And I dated a guy who was certain he would be called to be one of the two witnesses from biblical prophecy. Neither of these came to pass, so they've been forgotten. But had they, these stories would have been retold again and again.

Individual members who may not have the best intentions can use these beliefs to manipulate others into marriage and business partnerships. A typical story: A young couple has been dating for three weeks when he tells her he dreamed they were meant to be married. These stories sometimes end in domestic abuse and divorce.

We are taught that what happened in the scriptures can happen today. We're supposed to retell stories of major and minor miracles. The missionary manual instructs, "As you testify of a commandment, talk about the blessings you have received from living that commandment. Promise those whom you teach that they can enjoy similar blessings."[2]

Bruce R. McConkie advised the youth, "Perhaps the perfect pattern in presenting faith-promoting stories is to teach what is found in the scriptures and then to put a seal of living reality upon it by telling a similar and equivalent thing that has happened in our dispensation and to our people and—most ideally—to us as individuals."[3]

Church members have regular access to miracles, and I don't know a single family who didn't have at least a dozen stories. My own family did, including a priesthood blessing that saved my own life.

Such tales are constantly repeated in Conference:

> In faraway Bucharest, Romania, Dr. Lynn Oborn, volunteering at an orphanage, was attempting to teach little Raymond, who had never walked, how to use his legs. Raymond had been born with severe clubfeet and was completely blind... Dr. Oborn knew that a child-size walker would enable Raymond to get on his feet, but such a

---

1. The Holy Ghost.
2. *Preach My Gospel: A Guide to Missionary Service*. 2004. The Church of Jesus Christ of Latter-day Saints, n.d. 198.
3. McConkie, "The How and Why of Faith-promoting Stories." *New Era*, July 1978.

> walker was not available anywhere in Romania. I'm sure fervent prayers were offered by this doctor who had done all he could without a walking aid for the boy...
>
> Let us turn now to Provo, Utah. The Richard Headlee family, learning of the suffering and pitiful conditions in Romania, joined with others to assemble a 40-foot container filled with 40,000 pounds of needed supplies, including food, clothing, medicine, blankets, and toys...
>
> No one involved with the project knew of the particular need for a child-size walker. However, at the last possible moment, a family brought forth a child's walker and placed it in the container...
>
> Every item it contained would be put to immediate use at the orphanage... Another family member was dispatched back into the container, crawling among all the bales of clothes and boxes of food, searching for the walker... Cheers erupted—which quickly turned to tears, for they all knew they had been part of a modern-day miracle.[1]

There's a story for every commandment, a cautionary tale to ward off every sin, and an unexpected blessing to reward every leap of faith. The sweeping promise is, "Let us consider some of God's basic instructions which, if obeyed, bring peace and prosperity,"[2] So of course, "We have in the Church an untapped, almost unknown, treasury of inspiring and faith-promoting stories."[3] Examples abound which prove each principle of the gospel is undeniably true: prophecy, prayer, tithing, priesthood blessings, the Word of Wisdom, temple work, genealogy, garments, keeping the Sabbath holy, missions, etc. Entire books published by Deseret contain nothing but faith-promoting stories.

## Wages of Sin and Miracles of Forgiveness

The Church employs many emotional setups to create self-fulfilling prophecies.

I recall a tearful fireside where a former apostate had returned after sewing her wild oats. She spoke of her sinful years and how unfulfilling they were, and how guilty and miserable she felt until she finally repented and found relief.

If you are told repeatedly by everyone you trust that shame comes from doing a certain thing, then you will feel shame in doing that thing. It doesn't matter what that thing is. You can be programmed to feel shame or guilt for killing insects, for not saying "thank you", or for failing to sacrifice a goat.

If the Church gives you a list of sins and claims they will make you feel horrible, then you will probably feel horrible if you do those things. You will come to view your guilt as proof that the Church was right all along. You are also told you can't feel the Spirit if you're unworthy. Naturally, feelings of shame and worry will prevent anyone from feeling serenity and peace. That is the effect of the prediction itself.

Another common LDS idea is that of "desensitization", that repeatedly feeling a certain way will remove the ability to feel. For instance, R-rated movies will dull your sensitivity to violence and sex, and may even cause addiction.

"Determined to walk in his own way, the natural man often persists to the point where he is 'past feeling,' having been sedated by pleasing the carnal mind. Sadly, like the drug addict, he is always in need of a fresh fix."[4]

And... "What may appear to be of little importance, such as going to bed late, not praying for a day, skipping fasting, or breaking the Sabbath—such little slips—will make us

---

1. Thomas S. Monson. "Teach the Children." In LDS General Conference, Oct 1997.
2. Marion G. Romney. "A Silver Lining." In LDS General Conference, April 1977.
3. McConkie, "The How and Why of Faith-promoting Stories." *New Era*, July 1978.
4. Neal A. Maxwell. "'Repent of [Our] Selfishness' (D&C 56:8)." In LDS General Conference, April 1999. https://www.lds.org/general-conference/1999/04/repent-of-our-selfishness-d-c-56-8

lose sensitivity little by little, allowing us to do worse things."[1]

And... "Recently I heard of a good man who, after being married in the temple and having four children, fell away from the Church. His physical appearance become shabby and his demeanor sad as he became a drug addict, an alcoholic, and then a chain-smoker."[2]

This slippery-slope argument is often told through parable. Elder Jairo Mazzagardi tells of a fencepost overcome with tiny vines because it thought, "'No problem. I am strong and big, and this small plant will do me no harm.'

"Often, becoming prey to sin starts with someone choosing friends whose standards are not consistent with the gospel; and in order to be popular or to be accepted by peers, the person then compromises gospel principles and laws, going down a path that will bring only pain and sadness to this person and to his or her loved ones..."[3]

Mormons are under the kind of psychological pressures that can turn this into a self-fulfilling prophecy. Repression of natural desires, added to the double-bind and guilt/shame cycles, can turn a minor sin into a sin-binge. Certain sins carry such a heavy weight that once you've crossed the line, it makes sense to go "all the way."

If, in a moment of weakness, we have one drink or engage in "petting", we now feel we're lost souls. We're going to suffer guilt, the embarrassment of confession, and lost social status, so we might as well enjoy it while we can. We might as well have a few more drinks until we're drunk and passed out, or might as well go all the way and have sex.

We feel so unworthy and dirty and sinful and evil anyway, we might as well surrender. The relief from not having to hold back the entire world full of its denied carnal pleasures simply takes over. Like a shipwreck survivor denied food for weeks, we gobble down the banquet with reckless abandon. It proves the slippery-slope argument that a little sin leads to alot.

While wantonly committing so many sins with naive minds, we're bound to make terrible mistakes that lead to the kinds of consequences we've been warned about: heartbreak, STDs, pregnancy, addiction, being taken advantage of by others, hurting our families, and so on.

I remember when I contemplated getting a divorce, it seemed like such a horrible sin, that I pictured myself leaving the Church, shacking up with a series of men, and becoming a drug addict. Of course I didn't do that, but the choice lay before me. I experienced this feeling in other contexts as well.

Jack B. Worthy tells of this cycle happening to him on his mission. A pattern of shame and guilt from not having any baptisms, in spite of his every effort, led to depression, and led to feelings of perpetual unworthiness and cynicism. At some point, he fell in love with a girl, Mandy, and had committed acts of consensual petting with her. Once.

> I knew I would be confessing to the mission president the next day... I was keenly aware of the eternal implications of what I had done on my first date with Mandy... I was a serious sinner and was undoubtedly under Satan's influence.
>
> Mulling over these disastrous realizations depressed me profoundly. I suddenly hated myself much more than usual, which was no easy feat since I had become expert at despising myself for every infraction of Heavenly Father's numerous commandments. I even hated myself for things I *hadn't* done. A Mormon can never do enough of what he or she is supposed to do. I hated how pitifully weak I was. I hated my dirty, worthless soul.
>
> People don't care for those they hate, so I no longer cared for myself. I no longer cared about anything at all...
>
> My self-loathing and self-disrespect were severe, and what made it dangerous

---

1. Jairo Mazzagardi. "Avoiding the Trap of Sin." In LDS General Conference, Oct 2010. https://www.lds.org/general-conference/2010/10/avoiding-the-trap-of-sin
2. James E. Faust. "Pioneers of the Future: 'Be Not Afraid, Only Believe.'" In LDS General Conference, Oct 1997. http://www.lds.org/general-conference/1997/10/pioneers-of-the-future-be-not-afraid-only-believe
3. Mazzagardi, "Avoiding the Trap of Sin," General Conference, Oct 2010.

> was that I didn't feel that way just prior to confessing, rather I felt that way before my next encounter with Mandy, the source of my sin. This was a problem. A boy who hates and disrespects himself is not going to respect his date. I had entered a vicious cycle: my feelings of despair and my 'sinful' acts were feeding on each other. I had defined myself as a loathsome sinner, and therefore I longed to sin. The more I hated myself, the more I wanted to make myself worthy of that hate.[1]

He calls it the "you-might-as-well-sin-since-you're-already-a-sinner mindset." He also uses a phrase I can relate to: "drunk with sin." I've been out of the Church for over a decade, and there's something about repression and taboo that intoxicates like nothing I've experienced since. It becomes so seductive that, given the opportunity, it seems to compel as if by some outside force.

"Mandy was not dating the same person she had been a week before. I was caught up in a religious daze. Submitting to the evil influence guiding me, I switched to autopilot and accepted the invitation I read in her eyes... I had gone so far astray that I was at risk of coming under the influence of Satan."

The Church can control you even when you're doing the opposite of what you're supposed to. He concludes that, "The very same culture that had influenced me to remain a virgin until the age of twenty had also influenced my decision to lose it in a foolish, irresponsible manner."

While I lost my virginity under entirely different circumstances, I have to agree. I happened to lose it on my wedding night, after getting married too young to someone I shouldn't have. My ideas about dating, sex, and marriage were incredibly confused.

These same mechanisms can cause abuse victims to take on the guilt and shame of a sin perpetrated against them, as if they had committed it themselves. Recall Elizabeth Smart's feelings of worthlessness after being raped by her kidnapper. It wasn't just the issue of chastity. "In the interim, remembered Elizabeth, she had nightmares of dying, and of her family hating her, thinking she was unworthy for smoking and drinking."[2]

Given all this buildup, imagine the relief the Church has to offer for all these "wages of sin", many of them manufactured by the Church itself. Forgiveness then truly becomes, itself, a miracle.

## Spiritual Surveillance

Growing up, I always had a sense of being watched that sometimes returns to this day. Between God and Satan, external forces were constantly trying to either guide me or trip me up.

The manual for teaching kids aged 4-7 states, "Remind the children that each of us is a child of Heavenly Father. He watches over us just as he watched over Jesus... Share a personal experience when you felt that Heavenly Father was watching over and protecting you, or have the invited ward or branch member share his or her experience... Point to a child and say, 'Heavenly Father will always watch over (child's name).' Repeat for each child."[3]

Even our smallest actions were being recorded, saved up to be used against us on Judgment Day:

---

1. Worthy, *The Mormon Cult*, 2008. 148-149.
2. Welner, U.S. Vs. Brian David Mitchell, 2009. 11.
3. *Primary 2: Choose the Right A*. The Church of Jesus Christ of Latter Day Saints, 1995. Lesson 8: "Heavenly Father Watches Over Me" http://www.lds.org/manual/primary-2/lesson-8

> The Lord said: "Every idle word that men shall speak, they shall give account thereof in the day of judgment. For by thy words thou shalt be justified, and by thy words thou shalt be condemned."...
>
> [President Lee:]"Every one of you...must stand before 'the judgment-seat of the Holy One of Israel...and then must...be judged according to the holy judgment of God.' And according to the vision of John, 'The books were opened: and another book was opened, which is the book of life: and the dead were judged out of those things which were written in the books, according to their works.' The 'books' spoken of refer to the 'records [of your works] which are kept on the earth. ...the book of life is the record which is kept in heaven.'"[1]

At baptism, we were promised the Holy Ghost who would be our "constant companion." We were supposed to keep our homes clean so the Spirit of God could dwell there. The popular poem, *Footprints in the Sand*, tells of a traveler who sees only one set of footprints when God had promised to walk beside him. The Lord replies that during his times of need, "I carried you."

The powers of spiritual surveillance were not limited to disembodied beings. The bishop, for instance, possessed powers of discernment.

"Have you ever wondered about this mantle which comes upon a bishop? He can sit in a sacrament meeting and look out at his flock and know who is in trouble, look at his Aaronic Priesthood[2]—the deacons, the teachers, and the priests—and know which ones need his counsel. There is a hopeless feeling when you are released as a bishop to become a General Authority, and then return to your home ward where you have been serving and realize you have lost the power of discernment with the ward members."[3]

Somehow I got the idea that a bishop would know if I was lying during an interview. The Bishop's Handbook says bishops "...should seek the power of discernment. This is a spiritual gift that will help them discern truth, as well as a member's needs."[4]

This exacerbated my feeling of being watched. Imagine what this does to a member's concepts of healthy boundaries or entitlement to privacy.

And when God wasn't watching, the role was played by the Adversary. Evil spirits were frequently alluded to, both at Church activities and in my childhood home. LDS folklore included tales of spiritual possession, devils in the waters, and Satan being cast out from this place or that. My mother and grandmother had their own frightening stories.

Evil spirits were regularly blamed for negative emotions such as anger or fear. Certain objects and activities could invite evil into the home, which in my family included rock music, playing cards, Dungeons and Dragons, and horror movies. Satan could smell fear, so just the act of being afraid could invoke him. Imagine the escalating feedback cycle of fear this caused me both as a child and an adult.

Tales of evil spirits have been longtime Church favorites. Elder Carlos E. Asay repeated a Chinese fable in conference, as originally told by Elder George A. Smith in 1857.

> A man travelling through the country came to a large city, very rich and splendid; he looked at it and said to his guide, "This must be a very righteous people, for I can only see but one little devil in this great city."
>
> The guide replied, "You do not understand, sir. This city is so perfectly given up to wickedness...that it requires but one devil to keep them all in subjection."
>
> Travelling on a little farther, he came to a rugged path and saw an old man trying

---

1. *Gospel Principles*. The Church of Jesus Christ of Latter Day Saints, 2011. (Chapter 46: The Final Judgment.) http://www.lds.org/manual/gospel-principles/chapter-46-the-final-judgment
2. There are two types of priesthood: Aaronic and Melchizedek. Aaronic is the lesser, and for those raised in the Church, it is granted at the age of twelve. These young men are then divided by age into "Deacons," "Teachers," and "Priests." The Melchizedek priesthood holders are divided into quorums, like Elders, High Priests, Patriarchs, Seventies, and Apostles.
3. Robert D. Hales. "The Mantle of a Bishop." In LDS General Conference, April 1985. http://www.lds.org/general-conference/1985/04/the-mantle-of-a-bishop
4. *Church Handbook of Instructions Book 1*. Salt Lake City, Utah: The Church of Jesus Christ of Latter Day Saints, 1998. 18.

> to get up the hill side, surrounded by seven great, big, coarse-looking devils.
> 
> "Why," says the traveler, "this must be a tremendously wicked old man! See how many devils there are around him!"
> 
> "This," replied the guide, "is the only righteous man in the country; and there are seven of the biggest devils trying to turn him out of his path, and they all cannot do it."
> 
> After relating the fable, Elder Smith added that "the devil has the world so perfectly at his disposal that it requires few devils to keep it in subjection' and that 'the whole legion of devils has nothing to do but look after the 'Mormons' and stir up the hearts of the children of men to destroy them—to put them out of existence."[1]

Jack B. Worthy, who served his mission in Hong Kong, spoke at length of the similarity between the LDS and Chinese beliefs in ever-present demons.

"…we lay in our beds scared, knowing, as all Mormons and all Chinese do, that talking about evil spirits invites them to appear. We were much more like the superstitious people we had been called to serve than we realized."[2] He tells his own tale about casting out an evil spirit, which turned out to be a medical illness.

## Missions

In the context of magical thinking, new missionaries imagine they will encounter an endless stream of spiritual experiences, perhaps because so many returned missionaries tell inspirational stories.

"Church leaders do not overlook the fact that most missionaries expect an unrealistically high level of spiritual guidance while on their missions. Therefore…there are also stories that 'prove' that spiritual guidance exists, if only one is faithful enough to receive it."[3]

Jack B. Worthy relays how his zone leader told a story with the conviction of truth:

> "There used to be a missionary in Hong Kong that never had to tract[4]," the zone leader said. "He spent all his time teaching."
> 
> "How'd he find investigators if he didn't tract?" I asked.
> 
> "He'd look at the side of a building," he said, pointing up at the building on the hill, "and he'd wait for inspiration to know which home was the right one to go to. When it came, he'd count the number of windows up and number across. Then he'd go to that floor and count the doors 'til he got to the right one."
> 
> "How often did that work?"
> 
> "Every time."
> 
> Stories like this are meant to be 'inspiring', but of course they don't inspire missionaries for long, if at all. When viewed against reality, stories like this make missionaries feel inadequate, unworthy, and guilty.

Jack B. Worthy was told constantly on his mission that miracles were right around the corner.

"[President Smith] talked about moving mountains and walking on water, saying we could actually do it if we had faith, though he never said we should try—perhaps because he knew we'd fail; and swimming is strictly forbidden because Satan has control over the

---

1. Carlos E. Asay. "Opposition to the Work of God." In LDS General Conference, Oct 1981.
2. Worthy, *The Mormon Cult*, 2008. 78.
3. Worthy, *The Mormon Cult*, 2008. 112.
4. When LDS Missionaries go door to door, they call this "tracting."

water. This reminded me of a man in my ward back home who had said he would not have failed the way Peter had when Jesus asked him to step out of the ship and walk on the water. Peter started out okay, but he became afraid and began to sink. Jesus said to him, 'O thou of little faith, wherefore didst thou doubt?' The man in our ward claimed to have more faith than Peter did, saying he could have walked on the water for as long as Jesus wanted him to, and now we were being told we could do the same by our mission president."[1]

Even the "miraculous" language-learning of missionaries has a rational explanation. "One could assume, as Mormons do, that God helped us learn Cantonese... But there was nothing unusual or outstanding about our linguistic performance. Our Cantonese-speaking abilities were exactly what one would expect considering the type and amount of language training we received, coupled with the type and amount of real-life exposure and practice we had."[2]

# Prophecy

Everywhere you look there's a prophecy to be fulfilled and vaguely worded scriptures to be put to the test. Dallin H. Oaks believes that the internet, compact disc, and fast food, "...seems to fulfill the prophet Daniel's prophecy that in the last days 'knowledge shall be increased' and 'many shall run to and fro'."[3]

President Hinckley, in 2001, stated the War on Terror was a continuation of the War in Heaven. "Now, all of us know that war, contention, hatred, suffering of the worst kind are not new. The conflict we see today is but another expression of the conflict that began with the War in Heaven."[4]

Ezra Taft Benson did likewise, 22 years earlier, regarding Communism:

> Isaiah also predicted there would be those who would "seek deep to hide their counsel from the Lord, and their works are in the dark, and they say, Who seeth us?" He saw the time when the work shall say of him that made it, "He made me not".
>
> It is well to ask, what system established secret works of darkness to overthrow nations by violent revolution? Who blasphemously proclaimed the atheistic doctrine that God made us not?... I refer to the infamous founders of Communism and others who follow in their tradition.[5]

And then he made a prediction of his own. "Never before has the land of Zion appeared so vulnerable to so powerful an enemy as the Americas do at present. And our vulnerability is directly attributable to our loss of active faith in the God of this land, who has decreed that we must worship Him or be swept off. Too many Americans have lost sight of the truth that God is our source of freedom—the Lawgiver—and that personal righteousness is the most important essential to preserving our freedom. So, I say with all the energy of my soul that unless we as citizens of this nation forsake our sins, political and otherwise, and return to the fundamental principles of Christianity and of constitutional government, we will lose our political liberties, our free institutions, and will stand in jeopardy before God."

My own family spent alot of time thinking about the end times and reading books about how modern events had or would fulfill revelation. Some of those books were written decades ago, when the world sill operated under the Cold War. Though times have changed, the adaptation of current events to millennia-old prophecy is still a common pastime for many Mormons.

---

1. Worthy, *The Mormon Cult*, 2008. 84.
2. Worthy, *The Mormon Cult*, 2008. 73.
3. Dallin H. Oaks. "Focus and Priorities." In LDS General Conference, April 2011.
4. Gordon B. Hinckley. "The Times in Which We Live." In LDS General Conference, Oct 2001. http://www.lds.org/general-conference/2001/10/the-times-in-which-we-live
5. Ezra Taft Benson. "A Witness and a Warning." In LDS General Conference, Oct 1979. http://www.lds.org/general-conference/1979/10/a-witness-and-a-warning

# Prayer

A story about a miraculous answer to prayer was as close as the latest issue of the *New Era*:

> One night before bed I was thinking about what to pray for when I felt prompted to pray for my uncle's family. I prayed that they would feel the Spirit. Two days later I learned that my uncle had lost his job and that his family would have to move.
>
> It was then I realized that what I had prayed for was a prompting from the Holy Ghost, and I felt grateful that I had listened to the still small voice. In a situation where I could not do much else to help, I felt good knowing my prayers could help. Sometimes instances like this may seem insignificant, but I know that seeking personal revelation, listening to promptings, and following them—even small ones—can increase our faith and strengthen others.[1]

And in a recent copy of the *Ensign*:

> I wanted to be a missionary ever since I was young... But life in the Philippines was difficult... Because I was helping my family financially, my savings for my mission built up slowly...
>
> My branch president interviewed me and told me afterward that the last thing I needed to do was make the initial payment and then be interviewed by the mission president. I felt so happy and excited. I would get my paycheck that week, and I would be able to give the required amount. However, when I got home, I found out that my father was in the hospital. I felt overwhelmed when I realized we had to pay the hospital the exact amount I needed for my mission payment.
>
> But Heavenly Father prepared a way. We got some help from relatives and members of the Church, including my branch president. Miraculously my father was out of the hospital after one week, and I was able to make my payment... I know that Heavenly Father made it possible for me to submit my mission papers.[2]

The Church is careful to instruct, repeatedly, that answers to prayer often aren't so obvious. As a youth, I was regularly told to use the random-scripture prayer answering method. "Sometimes answers are given but we don't recognize what they are. Recently, there was a problem before me. I prayed and asked Heavenly Father for help. Then I opened my scriptures and read. The verse I read wasn't an answer, but the thought it provoked was. You might not think that a stray thought is the answer, but it can be. You have to listen to hear it."[3]

And if a promised blessing or answer to prayer *still* fails to materialize, just wait for it. "Sometimes we will receive counsel that we cannot understand or that seems not to apply to us, even after careful prayer and thought. Don't discard the counsel, but hold it close. If someone you trusted handed you what appeared to be nothing more than sand with the promise that it contained gold, you might wisely hold it in your hand awhile, shaking it gently. Every time I have done that with counsel from a prophet, after a time the gold flakes have begun to appear and I have been grateful."[4]

---

1. Andrew P. "Instant Messages" *New Era*, Aug 2013. http://www.lds.org/new-era/2013/08/instant-messages
2. Cheenee Lagunzad. "Move Forward in Faith: Faith Precedes Miracles." *Ensign*, Aug 2013. http://www.lds.org/ensign/2013/08/move-forward-in-faith
3. Hannah Thompson "Q&A: Questions and Answers." *New Era*, April 1993. http://www.lds.org/new-era/1993/04/qa-questions-and-answers
4. Elder Henry B. Eyring. "Finding Safety in Counsel." In LDS General Conference, April 1997. https://www.lds.org/general-conference/1997/04/finding-safety-in-counsel

# Tithing

Tithing is inexorably tied to blessings.

"Would any of us intentionally reject an outpouring of blessings from the Lord? Sadly, this is what we do when we fail to pay our tithing. We say no to the very blessings we are seeking and praying to receive. If you are one who has doubted the blessings of tithing, I encourage you to accept the Lord's invitation to 'prove [him] now herewith.' Pay your tithing. Unlock the windows of heaven. You will be abundantly blessed for your obedience and faithfulness to the Lord's laws and commandments."[1]

Children as young as four are taught the blessings of tithing, as shown in this example from a Primary lesson manual: "President Heber J. Grant, one of our latter-day prophets, said that we would be blessed with a greater knowledge of Heavenly Father and Jesus Christ, a stronger testimony, and an increased ability to obey the commandments. Other latter-day prophets have also told us that when we pay our tithing, we will prosper. Prosper means that we will be blessed with material needs such as food and shelter."[2]

The concept that tithing will increase your wealth is not unique to the LDS Church. Paul R. Martin, in *Recovery from Cults*, states: "The prosperity gospel holds the conviction that if a believing person has enough faith, is completely repentant of all sin, and gives at least 10% of his or her income to the church or to some Christian ministry, then he or she will have good health, obtain financial wealth, and experience general prosperity in all areas of life."[3]

The prosperity gospel even exists in new age cults. "At every church service Rev. Will talked about tithing and how it was the true way to prosperity. All the ministers came up and told stories of how tithing prospered them... I believed that by giving I would prosper. Rev. Will constantly told stories about how if you give with true faith, you will receive back tenfold what you have given."[4]

LDS prosperity gospel stories are commonplace.

"I know of a couple who lived thousands of miles from the nearest temple. Although they earned little, they faithfully paid their tithing and saved all that they could to journey to the house of the Lord. After a year, the husband's brother—not a member of the Church—unexpectedly came forward and offered them two airplane tickets. This temporal blessing made possible the spiritual blessings of their temple endowments and sealing. An additional spiritual blessing came later as the brother, touched by the couple's humble faithfulness, joined the Church."[5]

Members are instructed to give, even when there isn't enough. They are promised that they will somehow be provided for.

> After reading these scriptures together, Bishop Orellana looked at the new convert and said, "If paying tithing means that you can't pay for water or electricity, pay tithing. If paying tithing means that you can't pay your rent, pay tithing. Even if paying tithing means that you don't have enough money to feed your family, pay tithing. The Lord will not abandon you."
>
> The next Sunday, Amado approached Bishop Orellana again. This time he didn't ask any questions. He simply handed his bishop an envelope and said, "Bishop, here is our tithing..."
>
> "Ever since then, they have been faithful tithe payers." The family received some

---

1. Robert D. Hales. "Tithing: A Test of Faith with Eternal Blessings." In LDS General Conference, Oct 2002. http://www.lds.org/general-conference/2002/10/tithing-a-test-of-faith-with-eternal-blessings
2. *Primary 3: Choose the Right B (Ages 4-7)*. The Church of Jesus Christ of Latter-day Saints, 1994. (Lesson 45: Tithing)
3. Martin, "Post-Cult Recovery," *Recovery from Cults*, ed. Langone, 1995. 212.
4. Sanchez, *Spiritual Perversion*, 2005. 71.
5. Hales, "Tithing," General Conference, Oct 2002

> commodities from the bishops' storehouse during their financial difficulties. Beyond that, the Lord blessed them to be able to care for themselves. Evelyn received a promotion, and Amado found a good job. Evelyn later lost her job, but they continued to pay tithing and to receive spiritual and temporal blessings for their faithfulness. Once Bishop Orellana asked Amado how the family was doing financially. Amado responded, "We're doing all right. Sometimes we don't have much to eat, but we have enough. And more than anything, we trust in the Lord."[1]

The stories are never repeated when the unexpected check doesn't arrive, the job offer falls through, the power gets shut off, and the children go hungry.

Yet President Gordon B. Hinckley suggested tithing as a solution to third world poverty. "I have wept as I have seen the poverty and the suffering of the people in this part of the earth. My heart reaches out to them. I do not know what the solution is, except the gospel of Jesus Christ... I believe with all my heart that if they will accept the gospel and live it, pay their tithes and offerings, even though those be meager, the Lord will keep His ancient promise in their behalf, and they will have rice in their bowls and clothing on their backs and shelter over their heads. I do not see any other solution. They need a power greater than any earthly power to lift them and help them."[2]

The prophet hoped God would give the children rice if their parents sent their widow's mite to one of the wealthiest organizations in the world. (NBC News estimates the Church brings in $7 billion a year in untaxed tithes, not counting their many for-profit investments and businesses.[3])

Forgive me for viewing the prophet's tears with skepticism.

## Word of Wisdom

The Word of Wisdom promises that whosoever keeps the dietary commandments "shall receive health in their navel and marrow to their bones" and "shall run and not be weary, and shall walk and not faint." D&C 89:18-20 For this reason, avoidance of alcohol and coffee are credited for cases of good health. The Aaronic Priesthood manual tells one such story:

> I wasn't quite 12 years old, but I worked right alongside my father in the grain harvest over 60 years ago. He cut and I bundled the grain...it was exhausting labor, day after day.
>
> One Saturday, we began [working] at daylight and stopped about 8:30 that night. I was so tired I wanted to lie down and sleep without even waiting for supper.
>
> My father looked at me and said gently, "Lee, the patch of grain I cut today was very green. If we wait until Monday..., the kernels will be shrunken. We must do it tonight..."
>
> I fought back the tears and nodded...
>
> We soon finished our bread and milk, but I was still so tired that I could hardly raise my head... I sat at the table, thinking bitterly, "I've never smoked or drank; I've always obeyed the Word of Wisdom... And now I'm so tired I can hardly raise my head." My mouth twitched as I fought to keep back the tears of exhaustion.
>
> It is impossible to describe what happened, but it seemed as though a beautiful

---

1. Aaron L. West. "Sacred Transformations." *Ensign*, Dec 2002. https://www.lds.org/ensign/2012/12/sacred-transformations
2. President Gordon B. Hinckley. "Inspirational Thoughts." *Ensign*, Aug 1997. http://www.lds.org/ensign/1997/08/inspirational-thoughts
3. Peter Henderson, and Reuters. "Mormon Church Earns $7 Billion a Year from Tithing, Analysis Indicates." *NBC News*, Aug 13, 2012. http://investigations.nbcnews.com/_news/2012/08/13/13262285-mormon-church-earns-7-billion-a-year-from-tithing-analysis-indicates

> shaft of white light entered my body, filling every fiber of my being...
> My father was a very fast worker, but he couldn't keep up with me that night, even though he worked as fast as he could. I ran for stray bundles, and tossed them, many heavier than I was, from [pile to pile]. I'll never forget the astonishment in my father's eyes.[1]

The Word of Wisdom is conveniently forgotten when there is illness or disability, unless it has been actively broken, and then it is trotted out as the cause for misfortune.

## Loops of Logic

Mystical manipulation doesn't so much require leaps of logic as much as loops of logic. Circular reasoning keeps members forever spinning. Blessings and positive events are credited to God. Lack of blessings is caused by sin, testing, growing experiences, or God's mysterious ways. All signs point to "Yes." Everything is proof of the truthfulness of the Church.

"Just when all seems to be going right, challenges often come in multiple doses applied simultaneously. When those trials are not consequences of your disobedience, they are evidence that The Lord feels you are prepared to grow more. He therefore gives you experiences that stimulate growth, understanding, and compassion which polish you for everlasting benefit."[2]

| You are... | Life is... | Cause: | Therefore the Church is: |
|---|---|---|---|
| Righteous | Great | Blessings | TRUE |
| Sinning | Great | Temptations | TRUE |
| Righteous | Terrible | Being Tested<br>Growing Experience | TRUE |
| Sinning | Terrible | Punishment<br>Lack of Blessings | TRUE |

The same truth table can be applied to many Church concepts. For instance, when praying to receive a testimony:

| Answer: | Cause: | Therefore the Church is: |
|---|---|---|
| "Yes, the Church is true." | God answers prayers. | TRUE |
| No answer. | Being Tested<br>Need More Patience<br>Weak Faith | TRUE |
| "No, the Church is not true." | Satan is deceiving you. | TRUE |

Miraculous events never need be orchestrated by the Church when members are trained to never take no for an answer.

---

1. *Aaronic Priesthood Manual 1*. The Church of Jesus Christ of Latter Day Saints, 2002. (Lesson 18: The Word of Wisdom.) http://www.lds.org/manual/aaronic-priesthood-manual-1/lesson-18-the-word-of-wisdom
2. Richard G. Scott. "Trust in the Lord." In LDS General Conference, Oct 1995. http://www.lds.org/general-conference/1995/10/trust-in-the-lord

## Grounded in Reality

The only truth that we can be sure of is that which can be seen, heard, tested, measured, and/or touched. Like many mind control techniques, mystical manipulation can be defeated by keeping a skeptical outlook and learning as much about the world as you can from multiple sources.

Some areas of knowledge can never be known. For these things, I have become comfortable with the idea of believing something in a tentative way. I have a place in my mind for beliefs I cannot fully commit to because I don't have enough evidence for them. I'd like them to be true, and they *could* be true, but I don't really *know*. I don't need definitive answers to these questions. These beliefs are helpful, but something better (and more evidence-based) could come along at any moment. I am ready to change my mind.

*When a man or quorum of men assume their word is God's word and then isolate their followers from sources that suggest alternative views, it is akin to removing free agency. They, in essence, presume that only they are wise enough, worthy enough, or inspired enough to control information. If they err in their logic or inspiration, their faithful followers are doomed to the cell of ignorance. If the followers accept that the mantle is greater than the intellect, then they yield their judgment up to another; the door is opened for Waco, Heaven's Gate, Jonestown, Mountain Meadows Massacre, the Third Reich, September 11, and an unending parade of horrors.*

—Brad L. Morin,
*Suddenly Strangers*[1]

*What a tragic loss that often we are exposed to only one religious or philosophical view. In this group-facilitated...narrow-mindedness we find the roots of prejudice, bigotry, and hatred.*

—John D. Goldhammer, *Under the Influence*[2]

*The best books, he perceived, are those that tell you what you know already.*
—George Orwell, *1984*

# Milieu Control

**Milieu Control**
—*Suppression, Group Identification, Isolation*

- Suppresses outside information
- Suppresses questions
- Builds dependency
- Limits outside relationships
- Limits choices while maintaining an illusion of choice
- Prevents complaints and open expression of doubts
- Controls the environment
- Reinforces the need for approval from the group
- Makes the group the sole source of rewards & good feelings
- Limits the range of self-expression
- Members spend increasing amounts of time with the group

Exposure to the outside world can cause regular cognitive dissonance for members of a totalist system; the kind of dissonance that can lead the member away from the group.

Some groups solve this by physically isolating members from all outsiders, while others merely limit access and reframe information. If you can control the environment, you control the very perception of reality. This technique is called milieu control.

Lifton called this "the most basic feature of the thought reform environment, the psychological current upon which all else depends...the control of human communication. Through this milieu control the totalist environment seeks to establish domain over not only the individual's communication with the outside (all that he sees and hears, reads or writes, experiences, and expresses), but also - in its penetration of his inner life - over what we may speak of as his communication with

---

1. Morin and Morin, *Suddenly Strangers*, 2004. 168.
2. Goldhammer, *Under the Influence*, 1996. 35.

himself. It creates an atmosphere uncomfortably reminiscent of George Orwell's 1984."[1]

This stems naturally from sacred science and mystical manipulation. "At the center of this self-justification is their assumption of omniscience, their conviction that reality is their exclusive possession. Having experienced the impact of what they consider to be an ultimate truth (and having the need to dispel any possible inner doubts of their own), they consider it their duty to create an environment containing no more and no less than this 'truth.'"

As *Captive Hearts* summarizes, it is "...control of all communication and information, which includes the individual's communication with himself. This sets up what Lifton calls 'personal closure,' meaning that the person no longer has to carry on inner struggles about what is true or real. Essentially, this prevents any time being spent on doubts."[2]

Margaret Singer expands: "This is total control of communication in the group. In many groups, there is a 'no gossip' or 'no nattering' rule that keeps people from expressing their doubts or misgivings about what is going on. This rule is usually rationalized by saying that gossip will tear apart the fabric of the group or destroy unity, when in reality the rule is a mechanism to keep members from communicating anything other than positive endorsements.

"Milieu control also often involves discouraging members from contacting relatives or friends outside the group and from reading anything not approved by the organization. They are sometimes told not to believe anything they see or hear reported by the media."[3]

The LDS Church does not typically isolate its members from non-LDS relatives or friends to the extent that other totalist groups like the Moonies do (a major exception to this is the sequestration of LDS missionaries). However Mormonism does teach its members to be very cautious and even fearful of media that might cause dissonance about the gospel. It is not necessary for a cult to be sequestered on-compound to create seclusion and detachment from society. A high-demand group can easily "be in the world but not of the world."

Unfortunately, access to a full banquet of choices is necessary for freedom and informed consent, as we've previously explored. Cult researchers agree with me. "It is impossible to make unbiased decisions when we are isolated from outside information."[4]

Philosophers have long tackled this question. "In his celebrated little book *On Liberty*, the English philosopher John Stuart Mill argued that silencing an opinion is 'a peculiar evil.' If the opinion is right, we are robbed of the 'opportunity of exchanging error for truth'; and if it's wrong, we are deprived of a deeper understanding of the truth in 'its collision with error.' If we know only our own side of the argument, we hardly know even that; it becomes stale, soon learned only by rote, untested, a pallid and lifeless truth."[5]

In *Under the Influence*, John D. Goldhammer said, "To blindly accept group propaganda as the truth makes one subservient to a monolithic collective structure whose basic motive is to perpetuate itself and increase its power and control over masses of individuals."[6]

Mormons like to think of themselves as a peculiar people, but they are not so different from other high-demand groups. In 1844, the Millerites, who later became the Seventh-day Adventists, printed cautions against being too worldly. "Break loose from the world as much as possible. If indispensable duty calls you into the world for a moment, go as a man would run to do a piece of work in the rain. Run and hasten through it, and let it be known that you leave it with alacrity for something better. Let your actions preach in the clearest tones: 'The Lord is coming'—'The Time is short'—'This world passeth away'—'Prepare to

---

1. Lifton, *Thought Reform and the Psychology of Totalism*, 1961. (Chapter 22)
2. Tobias and Lalich, *Captive Hearts, Captive Minds*, 1994. 36.
3. Singer, *Cults in Our Midst*, 1995.
4. Zimbardo and Andersen, "Understanding Mind Control," *Recovery from Cults*, ed. Langone, 1995. 116.
5. Sagan, *The Demon-haunted World*, 1997. 430.
6. Goldhammer, *Under the Influence*, 1996. 75.

meet thy God'."[1]

Restrictions on clothing and food are a type of milieu control in which strict culture takes root deep in daily routine. For instance, garments protect you spiritually from the world by dividing you from the world in a symbolic, physical way, and really are a "constant reminder" and "provides protection against temptation and evil."[2]

Modest dress isolates Mormons culturally. So do restrictions on caffeine, alcohol, sexuality, working on Sunday, etc. The proud declaration of being a peculiar people means, "we are happily different from you."

Members are asked to police their own thoughts and information intake, always directing our attention to the gospel.

Like Apostle Neil L. Andersen said at conference, "When faced with a trial of faith—whatever you do, you don't step away from the Church! Distancing yourself from the kingdom of God during a trial of faith is like leaving the safety of a secure storm cellar just as the tornado comes into view."[3]

Scripture tells us, "That which the Spirit testifies unto you even so I would that ye should do in all holiness of heart, walking uprightly before me, considering the end of your salvation, doing all things with prayer and thanksgiving, that ye may not be seduced by evil spirits, or doctrines of devils, or the commandments of men... Wherefore, beware lest ye are deceived; and that ye may not be deceived seek ye earnestly the best gifts, always remembering for what they are given." D&C 46:7-8

In the temple, members covenant "...to avoid all lightmindedness, loud laughter, evil speaking of the Lord's anointed, the taking of the name of God in vain, and every other unholy and impure practice, and to cause you to receive these by covenant."[4] Note that members agreeing this are unaware this is what they will promise until it's too late to back out.

We are to set aside anything which is not for our "profit and learning." "Since immortality and eternal life constitute the sole purpose of life, all other interests and activities are but incidental thereto."[5]

That we should only focus on core doctrine is also founded in scripture. "But whatsoever thing persuadeth men to do evil, and believe not in Christ, and deny him, and serve not God, then ye may know with a perfect knowledge it is of the devil; for after this manner doth the devil work, for he persuadeth no man to do good, no, not one; neither do his angels; neither do they who subject themselves unto him." Moroni 7:17

The New Testament counsels, "If any man teach otherwise, and consent not to wholesome words, even the words of our Lord Jesus Christ, and to the doctrine which is according to godliness; He is proud, knowing nothing, but doting about questions and strifes of words, whereof cometh envy, strife, railings, evil surmisings, Perverse disputings of men of corrupt minds, and destitute of the truth, supposing that gain is godliness: from such withdraw thyself." 1 Timothy 6:3-5

The gift of spiritual discernment is the gift of milieu control. Spencer W. Kimball counseled, "First, I mention the gift of discernment, embodying the power to discriminate...between right and wrong. I believe that this gift when highly developed arises largely out of an acute sensitivity to impressions—spiritual impressions, if you will—to read under the surface as it were, to detect hidden evil, and more importantly to find the good that may be concealed...

"Every member in the restored Church of Christ could have this gift if he willed to do so. He could not be deceived with the sophistries of the world. He could not be led astray by pseudo-prophets and subversive cults. Even the inexperienced would recognize false

---
1. Festinger, *When Prophecy Fails*, 1964. 21.
2. *Administering the Church: Handbook 2*. The Church of Jesus Christ of Latter-day Saints, n.d.
3. Elder Neil L. Andersen. "Trial of Your Faith." In LDS General Conference, Oct 2012. https://www.lds.org/general-conference/2012/10/trial-of-your-faith
4. "Mormon Temple Covenants." Accessed Aug 21, 2013. http://lds4u.com/lesson5/templecovenants.htm
5. Spencer W. Kimball. *The Miracle of Forgiveness*. Salt Lake City: Bookcraft, 1969. 2.

teachings... We ought to be grateful every day of our lives for this sense which keeps alive a conscience which constantly alerts us to the dangers inherent in wrongdoers and sin."[1]

Yet any inkling that the Church is deceptive is itself said to be a deception, since it persuades men to not believe in Christ. It's a vicious circle that always points back to the Church being true. All signs point to "Yes."

## Doctrine Correlation

*First, I had not studied any other religions, so my assumption that the Mormon Church possessed the best answers was based on what I had been told by the Mormon Church itself. Second, I hadn't even studied Mormonism (which is typical of the vast majority of Mormons), so I believed it to be logical and rational—again, based on what it said about itself.*

—**Jack B. Worthy,**
***The Mormon Cult***[2]

In the 1960s, the Church created the Correlation Committee, to keep all Church publications and auxiliaries in every ward in lockstep with the central Church.

> Over the years the General Authorities have taken steps to ensure that the Church and its programs were perfecting the Saints and preparing a people worthy to establish Zion on earth. Their concerns became more urgent as the Church membership doubled in just a decade and a half and passed the two million mark in 1963. Church leaders became increasingly convinced that the varied organizations had to work harmoniously together under the direction of the priesthood, that families had to be strengthened, and that administration needed to be streamlined in order to more adequately meet the complex needs of the Saints... To this end they conducted periodic reviews to be sure that all Church organizations and their activities were properly correlated...
>
> A thorough correlation effort began in 1960 when the First Presidency directed the General Priesthood Committee under Elder Harold B. Lee of the Quorum of the Twelve Apostles to conduct "an exhaustive, prayerful study and consideration" of all programs and curriculum in the light of the Church's ultimate objectives "so that the Church might reap the maximum harvest from the devotion of the faith, intelligence, skill and knowledge of our various Auxiliary Organizations and Priesthood Committees."[3]

If you've ever wondered why meetings seemed so repetitive, the goal is "'That the gospel be taught as completely as possible at least three times during these three age levels of life: children, youth, and adults.'"[4]

Periodicals are covered by the same committee. "Church magazines draw their content from a wide range of authors and contributors, in addition to those who serve as professional staff members. Those items that are published in the magazines receive not only the scrutiny and judgment of the editing staffs, but are also subject to clearance by the Correlation Review committees. Committee members are called as a result of their expertise in such areas as Church doctrine, Church history, and Church administration...

"Much care is exercised to make certain that the official publications of the Church carry messages that are sound in doctrine and fully in harmony with currently approved

---

1. Elder David A. Bednar. "Quick to Observe." *Ensign*, Dec 2006. https://www.lds.org/ensign/2006/12/quick-to-observe
2. Worthy, *The Mormon Cult*, 2008. 163-164.
3. *Church History In The Fulness Of Times Student Manual*, 2003.
4. *Church History In The Fulness Of Times Student Manual*, 2003.

policies and procedures."[1]

In my research, I've found this committee to be very thorough. I can search LDS.org for a topic, say "Prayer", and regardless of publication date or targeted age-group, each source will basically say the same thing, and it will be no different from what I was taught 15, 20, 30 years ago. Speakers and authors restate the same quotes, and sometimes quotes are embedded three-deep, say Dallin H. Oaks quoting Ezra Taft Benson quoting Harold B. Lee telling a story about Heber Grant.

Finding original sources older than 1970 through official channels is difficult. They've done an adequate job censoring the past while maintaining a veneer of transparency and openness the internet generation has come to expect.

Martha Beck, the daughter of LDS scholar, Hugh Nibley, has insider knowledge. "Mormons are discouraged from reading any materials about the Church that are not produced through official channels and approved by a panel called the Correlation Committee, notorious among Mormon authors (including my father) for its strict censorship. These are the folks who create the standardized teaching manuals for the whole worldwide Church, who carefully edit out even tangential references to the 'alternative voices' that teach things like evolutionary biology, modernist moral reasoning, and the wearing of non-standard underwear—anything, in other words, that might shed the slightest shadow of doubt in the minds of the faithful.

"When I began reading about the history and doctrine of the Latter-day Saints, I saw why the committee is so active and so vigilant."[2]

Boyd K. Packer made this principle clear at the CES Symposium: "In an effort to be objective, impartial, and scholarly, a writer or a teacher may unwittingly be giving equal time to the adversary."[3]

## Outside Friends & Media

*Members are encouraged or required to live and/or socialize only with other group members.*
—**Janja Lalich, Ph.D. and Michael Langone, Ph.D.,**
***Cults 101: Checklist of Cult Characteristics***[4]

*It is a challenge to work in the world and live above its filth... Brethren, be strong. Rise above the evils of the world.*
—**Prophet Gordon B. Hinckley,**
***"The Shepherds of the Flock", Ensign*, May 1999**

Mormons are famous for a number of things, including their aversion to R-rated movies. It seems like an innocent-enough commandment. What's wrong with keeping our minds pure?

Yet this is one way of restricting access to alternate points of view. The Church often builds straw man arguments around secular philosophies. It oversimplifies social issues so that the gospel seems a ready cure for all ills. Exposure to mature topics might reveal the man behind the curtain. Sex and violence are easily dismissed as unimportant topics, but other content is filtered out, like nuanced views of addiction, poverty, war, abuse, racism, homosexuality, depression, religion, and history.

It takes more than a Disney movie to convey complex ideas. While in the world,

---

1. Elder Dean L. Larsen. "I Have a Question - Should That Which Is Written in Church Publications and Lesson Manuals Be Taken as Official Doctrine?" *Ensign*, Aug 1977. http://www.lds.org/ensign/1977/08/i-have-a-question
2. Beck, *Leaving the Saints*, 2005. 176.
3. Boyd K. Packer. "The Mantle Is Far, Far Greater Than the Intellect." Brigham Young University, 1981. 5.
4. Lalich and Langone, "Cults 101: Checklist of Cult Characteristics."

members are still alienated from mainstream culture and competing philosophies. They are kept childlike and naive. When I finally began watching R-rated movies, I discovered a universe of intelligent films that opened my eyes on so many subjects.

I also avoided the study of other religions, even though I was curious about Eastern philosophy, ancient religions, and paganism. While the Church never banned this reading, they never encouraged it either. All religions held some truth, but only Mormonism had all truth, so they were not pertinent to my eternal salvation. The fear of deception by the cunning plan of the Evil One always lurked at the fringes of alternate spiritual views.

The Church regularly denounces popular delivery mediums which may contain diverse thought: "Modern revelation declares that 'Satan hath sought to deceive you, that he might overthrow you'. Satan's methods of deception are enticing: music, movies and other media, and the glitter of a good time. When Satan's lies succeed in deceiving us, we become vulnerable to his power."[1]

Since my time in the Church, technology has changed a bit, and the Church keeps abreast of the times: "We must be alert not to let sin grow around us. Forms of sin are everywhere—even, for example, in a computer or cell phone. These technologies are useful and can bring great benefits to us. But their inappropriate use—such as involvement in time-wasting games, programs that would drive you to carnal pleasure, or much worse things such as pornography—is destructive."[2] "Carnal pleasure" is always the justification, but the real goal is keeping you focused on the Church.

We were directly counseled to avoid material in direct opposition to the gospel. It's become a larger concern since I left—the internet gives easy, and sometimes even accidental access to what they call "anti-Mormon literature."

Apostle Quentin L. Cook admonishes, "Others spend most of their time giving first-class devotion to lesser causes. Some allow intense cultural or political views to weaken their allegiance to the gospel of Jesus Christ. Some have immersed themselves in Internet materials that magnify, exaggerate, and, in some cases, invent shortcomings of early Church leaders. Then they draw incorrect conclusions that can affect testimony."[3]

The youth are counseled to prepare ahead of time to resist dissonance:

> Some young people are surprised and shocked by anti-Mormon material on the Internet because they haven't fortified themselves against it. They may not have spent enough time on the spiritual side to prepare and strengthen themselves for whatever may come. When life experiences come to knock their legs out from under them, it's important that they do those basic things we always talk about: continuing to study the scriptures and having meaningful prayer with our Heavenly Father. Those basic things prepare people for all kinds of adversity, including anti-Mormon articles they'll come across online...
>
> If a friend came to me with an honest question about a controversial issue from Church history, I'd do my best to answer it. And if I found that he was spending a lot of time in that area, the first questions I'd want to ask him are: "Are you reading the Book of Mormon? Are you saying your prayers? Are you keeping your life in balance so that you can protect yourself against the storms of life?"[4]

This is milieu control in a nutshell. Keep believing at all costs. "If you're spending time on websites that criticize the Church and its history but aren't spending time in the scriptures, you're going to be out of balance, and those negative things may have an unduly

---

1. Dallin H. Oaks. "Be Not Deceived." In LDS General Conference, Oct 2004. http://www.lds.org/general-conference/2004/10/be-not-deceived
2. Jairo Mazzagardi. "Avoiding the Trap of Sin." In LDS General Conference, Oct 2010.
3. Elder Quentin L. Cook. "Can Ye Feel So Now?" In LDS General Conference, Oct 2012. http://www.lds.org/general-conference/2012/10/can-ye-feel-so-now
4. Elder Steven E. Snow. "Balancing Church History." *New Era*, June 2013.

strong effect on you. If you were in proper balance, they wouldn't."[1]

This seems reasonable and appeals to our sense of fairness. Until you realize it would be difficult for any active member to spend more time reading critical material than they spend weekly on Church study and activities.

Missionaries are even more restricted on their access to outside media. "The mission conference also included a dire warning about listening to music, a rule I had been breaking at the time. During President Smith's talk, he pounded his fist on the pulpit to dramatize his words: 'Every beat of the drum takes you one...step...closer to hell!' He said, 'Missionaries who listen to music are definitely going to hell.'"[2]

And, "Because we were not allowed to watch TV, read books, or read newspapers, and because we were discouraged from talking to people about much of anything except the Church, we were not affected by Hong Kong culture nearly as much as we might have been. Most of my ignorance and ethnocentricity remained intact. I didn't learn until years later that in 1982, while I was in Hong Kong, Margaret Thatcher visited Beijing to discuss Hong Kong's 1997 handover to China. Her visit was one of the catalysts that caused an economic recession and a property crash in Hong Kong, none of which entered my awareness at the time, which is incredible if you think about it. Missionaries prove beyond any doubt that it is entirely possible to live in a place and not be at all 'of it'..."[3]

And, "The mother of all rules—the one that helps to ensure that all the others are kept—requires missionaries to remain in the presence of their companions every second of every day. Being in different rooms while at the apartment is acceptable, but rarely is it considered acceptable outside the apartment. The function of this rule is obvious: Anything a missionary says or does will be witnessed by his or her companion. To make this rule as effective as possible, companionships are chosen carefully to avoid the pairing up of two notorious rule breakers, or even two missionaries who get along too well."[4]

Missionaries who violated the rules were to be reported.[5] If this is the standard on missions, then of course missionaries will bring home this attitude of lax respect for boundaries and the irrelevance of privacy. Why would God counsel anything unethical? If it's good enough for a mission, it's good enough for daily life.

Associations also come under scrutiny. Particularly, members are not allowed to associate with open apostates and those vocally critical of the Church.

"Avoid those who would tear down your faith. Faith-killers are to be shunned. The seeds which they plant in the minds and hearts of men grow like cancer and eat away the Spirit. True messengers of God are builders—not destroyers."[6]

Association with nonmembers is also discouraged, again, especially with the vulnerable young. The *For the Strength of Youth* pamphlet contains this advice: "Choose friends who share your values so you can strengthen and encourage each other in living high standards... As you seek to be a friend to others, do not compromise your standards. If your friends urge you to do things that are wrong, be the one to stand for the right, even if you stand alone. You may need to find other friends who will support you in keeping the commandments."[7]

The LDS youth website currently poses the question, "Is it OK for me to have good friends who are not members of the Church?" The fair-sounding, yet still milieu-controlling answer: "It is important that you choose friends who share your standards, but that does not mean that all of your friends will be members of the Church. President Thomas S. Monson taught: 'Everyone needs good friends. Your circle of friends will greatly influence

---

1. Snow, "Balancing Church History," *New Era*, June 2013.
2. Worthy, *The Mormon Cult*, 2008. 119.
3. Worthy, *The Mormon Cult*, 2008. 93.
4. Worthy, *The Mormon Cult*, 2008. 136.
5. Worthy, *The Mormon Cult*, 2008. 79.
6. Carlos E. Asay. "Opposition to the Work of God." In LDS General Conference, Oct 1981.
7. *For the Strength of Youth*. The Church of Jesus Christ of Latter-day Saints, 2011. "Friends." https://www.lds.org/youth/for-the-strength-of-youth/friends

your thinking and behavior, just as you will theirs. When you share common values with your friends, you can strengthen and encourage each other. Treat everyone with kindness and dignity. Many nonmembers have come into the Church through friends who have involved them in Church activities.'"[1]

In other words, we need to let kids out of the milieu just long enough to convert other kids. I had nonmember friends as a kid, too, and the thought of converting them never left my mind.

My favorite LDS musical, *Saturday's Warriors*, features the protagonist, Jimmy, being seduced away from his loving family by his sneering, immodestly-dressed, worldly nonmember friends. Propaganda at its best.

Dire warnings lurk around every corner: "Think to yourself about any situation you know in which someone followed the wrong kind of friend or group. Think about how often these situations ended in sadness, tragedy, or suffering."[2]

When advising on "Using Our Free Agency," Delbert Stapley warns, "Be suspicious of those who would put you in a compromising position. Never compromise the right, for compromise can lead to sin, sin to regret, and regret can hurt so very much."[3]

And Robert D. Hales explains the consequences: "Mother and father coyote send those little coyote pups out to play and frolic. And the little lambs who are secure in the fold look over there and say, 'Boy, doesn't that look like a lot of fun?' And they leave to go play with the coyote pups. Then the adult coyotes come down and kill them."[4]

## The Family Milieu

Families are an extension of the Church. Indeed, "Church leaders often referred to the family as the central unit in Church organization."[5]

Family members become agents of the larger institution, repeating the same control techniques they learned from the Church. Families keep an eye on one another, teach one another, and come to depend on one another. Church members don't need to live on a weird cult compound. Instead, they can have a typical family, smiling and happy with a white picket fence and a trampoline in the backyard.

This is perfect chicanery for cults trying to appear mainstream. As *Captive Hearts* describes, "If the group isn't already living communally, the cult leader creates an environment that extends into members' homes and families."[6]

Dependency is built in, since most people don't want to hurt or be rejected by loved ones. Family members, especially parents, are in a better position to indoctrinate children, monitor behavior, and isolate them from outside influences. In this way, as Elder Carl B. Cook said, "Our homes will then become spiritual fortresses."[7]

Prophet David O. McKay famously said, "Nothing can take the place of home in rearing and teaching children, and no other success can compensate for failure in the home."[8]

*The Proclamation to the World* states: "Parents have a sacred duty to rear their children in love and righteousness, to provide for their...spiritual needs, to teach them

---

1. "LDS.org - Youth - Top Questions," 2013. https://www.lds.org/youth/ask/top/friends#is-it-okay-for-me-to-have-good-friends-who-are-not-members-of-the-church
2. *The Presidents of the Church: Teacher's Manual*. The Church of Jesus Christ of Latter Day Saints, 1996. Lesson 19: Make Peer Pressure a Positive Experience http://www.lds.org/manual/the-presidents-of-the-church-teachers-manual/lesson-19-make-peer-pressure-a-positive-experience
3. Elder Delbert L. Stapley. "Using Our Free Agency." *Ensign*, May 1975. http://www.lds.org/ensign/1975/05/using-our-free-agency
4. *The Presidents of the Church: Teacher's Manual*, 1996. Lesson 19: Make Peer Pressure a Positive Experience
5. *Church History In The Fulness Of Times Student Manual*, 2003.
6. Tobias and Lalich, *Captive Hearts, Captive Minds*, 1994. 245.
7. Elder Carl B. Cook. "When Children Want to Bear Testimony," Dec 2002.
8. *Doctrine and Covenants and Church History: Seminary Student Study Guide*. The Church of Jesus Christ of Latter Day Saints, 2005.

to...observe the commandments of God... Husbands and wives—mothers and fathers—will be held accountable before God for the discharge of these obligations."[1]

Sometimes this commandment is put into life-and-death terms. Scripture says, "Ye will not suffer your children that they go hungry, or naked; neither will ye suffer that they transgress the laws of God. ...ye will teach them to walk in the ways of truth and soberness; ye will teach them to love one another, and to serve one another." Mosiah 4:14-15

And in modern times,

> [Before the age of accountability] is protected time for parents to teach the principles and ordinances of salvation to their children without interference from Satan. It is a time to dress them in armor in preparation for the battle against sin. When this preparation time is neglected, they are left vulnerable to the enemy. To permit a child to enter into that period of his life when he will be buffeted and tempted by the evil one, without faith in the Lord Jesus Christ and an understanding of the basic principles of the gospel, is to set him adrift in a world of wickedness. During these formative, innocent years, a child may learn wrong behavior; but such is not the result of Satan's temptations, but comes from the wrong teachings and the bad example of others. In this context, the Savior's harsh judgment of adults who offend children is better understood, wherein he said, "It were better for him that a millstone were hanged about his neck, and he cast into the sea, than that he should offend one of these little ones" (Luke 17:2).
>
> We offend a child by any teaching or example which leads a little one to violate a moral law; causes him to stumble, or go astray; excites him to anger; creates resentment; or perhaps even leads him to become displeasing and disagreeable. Certainly, in the context of the Savior's harsh indictment concerning anyone who "offends" a child, one guilty of such conduct is in serious jeopardy.[2]

Chris Morin describes his typical LDS upbringing. "The Church was an integral part of our family. Its teachings guided our daily family activities and our individual lives as well. Before the family prayer each morning, we usually sang a song accompanied by Mom or a sister at the piano. Then we took turns, each of us reading two verses from our individual copies of the *Book of Mormon*."[3]

The milieu of choice is definitely the home, complete with LDS memorabilia as the designated decor.

---

1. Gordon B. Hinckley. "The Family: A Proclamation to the World," Sept 23, 1995. http://www.lds.org/topics/family-proclamation
2. Merlin L. Lybert. "The Special Status of Children." In *LDS General Conference*, April 1994. https://www.lds.org/general-conference/1994/04/the-special-status-of-children
3. Morin and Morin, *Suddenly Strangers,* 2004. 11.

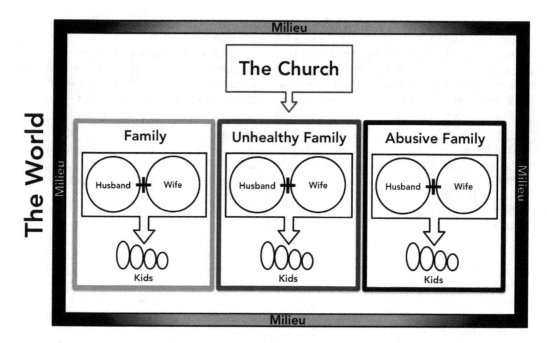

With the best of intentions, families become police-agents operating on behalf of the Church to control information. "Parents must have the courage to filter or monitor Internet access, television, movies, and music. Parents must have the courage to say no, defend truth, and bear powerful testimony. Your children need to know that you have faith in the Savior, love your Heavenly Father, and sustain the leaders of the Church."[1]

Family Home Evening became a big part of LDS life through the 1960s as a way to bring formalized and unified teaching of the gospel into the home. "Whether the family home evening was held in a New York City apartment, a Navajo hogan, or in a Polynesian thatched home, there were usually certain common elements: family members took turns conducting the program, offering prayers, leading the singing, and presenting the lesson."[2]

As I have previously quoted, parents are made responsible for all outcomes. Prophet Spencer W. Kimball reiterated this message: "The prophet Lehi, greatly concerned about his posterity, said, 'But behold, my sons and my daughters, I cannot go down to my grave save I should leave a blessing upon you; for behold, I know that if ye are brought up in the way ye should go ye will not depart from it.' Lehi went further and said, 'Wherefore, if ye are cursed, behold, I leave my blessing upon you, that the cursing may be taken from you and be answered upon the heads of your parents.' Are we, as parents, prepared to assume the curses, the responsibilities, for what our children fail to do?"[3]

If a child strays, it is the fault of the mother and father. If parents do not put in the effort, the soul of their child may be lost forever. It is difficult for parents to get away from the constant guilt-tripping. "How sad if the Lord should charge any of us parents with having failed to teach our children."[4]

So it is no surprise when well-meaning parents experience severe sorrow and guilt when their children act as free agents and leave the Church. Enough so that a counselor in the First Presidency decided to address it in Conference: "My dear brothers and sisters and friends, my message this morning is one of hope and solace to heartbroken parents who have done their best to rear their children in righteousness with love and devotion, but have

---

1. Elder Quentin L. Cook. "Can Ye Feel So Now?" In LDS General Conference, Oct 2012.
2. *Church History In The Fulness Of Times Student Manual*, 2003.
3. President Spencer W. Kimball. "'Train Up a Child' First Presidency Message." *Ensign*, April 1978. http://www.lds.org/ensign/1978/04/train-up-a-child
4. Kimball, "'Train Up a Child,'" *Ensign*, April 1978.

despaired because their child has rebelled or been led astray to follow the path of evil and destruction."[1]

Chris Morin noted this anguish in the life of his own mother. "Mom had dedicated her life to helping her children attain salvation so we could be together as a family in the afterlife. I believe that nothing brings her more joy than to see her children living to attain that goal. Thus, she believed she had failed with two of her sons; she had lost them for eternity. The blow was almost more than she could bear..."[2]

Restrictions against marrying outsiders are common in totalist groups. Mormons are strongly encouraged to only date and marry worthy members of the Church, thus enforcing this form of milieu control throughout the generations.

My patriarchal blessing reinforced this commandment: "When the time comes in your life to choose a companion and helpmate for time and for eternity, it will be necessary for you to date within the Church... make sure your companion holds the priesthood, and he will take you to the temple and there you will be sealed for time and for all eternity, and your children will be born in the new and everlasting covenant of marriage which is performed in the temple. Then your lives will be more compatible one with another; you will think the same, you will want to do the same things, and through righteous living comes joy and happiness not only for this life, but for the eternities to come..."

Imagine the painful and damaging effects when a previously "righteous" husband or wife begins to lose faith. A deeper unspoken promise is broken between them. Non-believing spouses are sometimes motivated to fake it, to go through the motions to avoid breaking home and heart.

Increased dependence on families is encouraged by the Church. As taught in a talk about transgression, "When a person has to be disciplined, remember the impact this has on his or her family. That family is already crushed by what has occurred. The family has been betrayed and abused, and individual family members often feel the taint of that transgression upon them even though they may be personally innocent. Do not abandon them in their hour of need. Never will they need friends more than at that moment. Never will they need acceptance, kindness, and understanding more than in those first few months after their betrayal."[3]

These blurrings of a healthy concept of boundaries is particularly insidious. Typically, individuals act for their own reasons, yet the Church describes sin as a "betrayal" and "abuse" of the whole family. This may naturally apply in cases of domestic abuse or infidelity, but for most other sins, this level of enmeshment is inappropriate.

## Miscellaneous Milieus

The Home Teaching and Visiting Teaching programs are another way for the Church to keep an eye on people. "The home teachers' regular visits, made at least monthly, provided a channel for two-way communication between the family and the ward priesthood leaders."[4]

Church universities are another milieu where behavior and academic freedom are strictly controlled. BYU has a zero tolerance policy on worldly practices like beards and piercings.

Former BYU faculty member Martha Beck called BYU the place where students are

---

1. James E. Faust. "Dear Are the Sheep That Have Wandered." In *LDS General Conference*, April 2003. https://www.lds.org/general-conference/2003/04/dear-are-the-sheep-that-have-wandered
2. Morin and Morin, *Suddenly Strangers,* 2004. 141.
3. Theodore M. Burton. "Let Mercy Temper Justice." In LDS General Conference, Oct 1985. http://www.lds.org/general-conference/1985/10/let-mercy-temper-justice
4. *Church History In The Fulness Of Times Student Manual*, 2003.

"able to learn about things like…evolutionary theory while still simultaneously disbelieving them."[1]

Beck tried to research Sonia Johnson in the BYU library. Johnson was excommunicated in 1979 for promoting the Equal Rights Amendment. Though Johnson's story had been highly publicized in the national media, the BYU library didn't contain a single reference. Specific newspaper articles had been removed, though the library still had microfilm of the rest of the paper. "Someone in the BYU library had spent an enormous amount of time and effort to excise every single reference to Sonia Johnson that had ever appeared in print… People really do underestimate the capacity of things to disappear."[2]

Mental health services are another milieu where it is in the Church's best interest to limit access to external philosophies. Scientists have made many great discoveries about the human mind, some which threaten to break the thought-limiting spell of the gospel. For this reason, the Church advises members to seek therapy from within LDS Social Services, or at least try to find a therapist who "shares their values." The Bishop's Handbook (concealed from members), states, "If a member needs professional counseling or therapy, the stake president or bishop should select or recommend a professional who will work in harmony with gospel teachings and principles. Leaders may work through LDS Social Services where it is available."[3]

The therapeutic relationship is very personal and based on trust. When you go to the doctor, you expect her to employ the latest advances in medicine. Likewise for mental health. Therapist John Goldhammer states, "…so called 'Christian therapy' is not therapy, but mind control, a marketing and recruitment technique for a particular religion in the guise of psychotherapy. Also called 'moralizing,' judgmental attitudes demean individual self-worth by telling clients they are right or wrong, or that they 'should' do something that reflects the therapist's personal morals and value system."[4]

Some LDS beliefs and behaviors may be harmful or unhealthy for specific members, or perhaps even for all members. For example, there has been recent controversy among LDS therapists about the Church's official stance on masturbation. Some argue the level of shame this causes is psychologically harmful to their clients.[5]

I, and others, have strong concerns over LDS therapists' objectivity in regards to issues like divorce, abuse, manipulation, overwork, boundaries, homosexuality, and unhealthy dependence on religion. The Church's control over the mental health milieu worries me deeply.

We often thought that we had some level of privacy when it came to personal sin. The choice to confess was up to us. But concerned bishops are allowed to initiate contact when they believe members are struggling with sin:

"When counseling members, the stake president or bishop helps them take preventive action to resist temptations. For example, members who are courting, are having difficulty in their marriages, are separated or divorced, or are struggling with minor moral problems may be protected and strengthened by counseling designed to help them guard against transgression. Presiding officers need not wait for members to seek such help but may call them in for counseling."[6]

Moreover, members who have been involved in transgressions may be pressured into reporting others. "Disclosure of the identity of others who participated in a transgression should be *encouraged* as part of the repentance process, especially when this can help Church leaders encourage those participants to repent."[7]

---

1. Beck, *Leaving the Saints*, 2005. 77.
2. Beck, *Leaving the Saints*, 2005. 83.
3. *Church Handbook of Instructions Book 1*, 1998. 22.
4. Goldhammer, *Under the Influence*, 1996. 217.
5. Natasha Helfer Parker. "My Official Stance on Masturbation." *The Mormon Therapist*, Aug 6, 2012. http://www.patheos.com/blogs/mormontherapist/2012/08/my-official-stance-on-masturbation.html
6. *Church Handbook of Instructions Book 1*, 2006. 26.
7. *Church Handbook of Instructions Book 1*, 2006. 107.

In these cases, or when any member accuses another, the bishop is to launch an investigation and confront the accused. If the accused denies it, the bishop may appoint two priesthood holders to find evidence:

"A bishop interviews any member of his ward who is accused of a serious transgression. If the member denies an accusation that the bishop has reliable evidence to support, the bishop (or the stake president if he will preside over the disciplinary council) gathers further evidence that would confirm or disprove the accusation. The presiding officer may conduct the investigation himself, or he may assign two reliable Melchizedek Priesthood holders to do so."[1]

It is unclear how often this happens or the methods they employ. They are specifically instructed to not do anything illegal or maintain a watch on a member's home.

## Strengthening Church Members Committee

Most Church members are unaware that a secretive committee exists, called the Strengthening Church Members Committee, which watches for heretical and critical publications. They allegedly collect files on members who are suspected of apostasy. Very little is known about this group and what they do, or how they do it. But its existence is confirmed in a leaked memo from General Authority Glenn L. Pace,[2] which was acknowledged by official spokesman Don LeFevre, and later Elder Dallin H. Oaks.

LaFevre stated the purpose of the group "is to prevent members from making negative statements that hinder the progress of the Mormon church..." He also said "the committee receives complaints from church members about other members who have made statements that 'conceivably could do harm to the church.'"[3]

According to the Mormon Alliance[4,5], feminists, environmentalists, anthropologists, historians, and journalists have been pressured by the committee. Many of these were eventually excommunicated as part of the September Six[6] purge in 1993 and at later times.

The First Presidency also confirmed the existence of this committee and quoted D&C 123:1-5:

> And again, we would suggest for your consideration the propriety of all the saints gathering up a knowledge of all the facts, and sufferings and abuses put upon them...
>
> And also of all the property and amount of damages which they have sustained, both of character and personal injuries...
>
> And also the names of all persons that have had a hand in their oppressions, as far as they can get hold of them and find them out.
>
> And perhaps a committee can be appointed to find out these things, and to take statements and affidavits; and also to gather up the libelous publications that are afloat;
>
> And all that are in the magazines, and in the encyclopedias, and all the libelous histories that are published.

---

1. *Church Handbook of Instructions Book 1*, 2006. 107.
2. Glenn L. Pace. "Strengthening Church Members Committee - Ritualistic Child Abuse," July 19, 1990. http://www.utlm.org/images/newsletters/no80pacememop1.gif
3. Religious News Services. "Mormon Church Said to Be Keeping Files on Dissenters." *The Times-News*. Aug 13, 1992. 5B.
4. Anderson, Allred. *Case Reports of the Mormon Alliance (Vol 2)*. 1996. http://mormon-alliance.org/casereports/volume2/prolog.htm
5. Lavina Fielding Andersen. "The Church and Its Scholars: Ten Years After." *Sunstone Magazine*, July 2003. https://www.sunstonemagazine.com/pdf/128-13-23.pdf.
6. In Sept 1993, six prominent LDS academics were disfellowshipped or excommunicated for publicizing material the Church deemed to be heretical or critical. Heretical topics included writings on the Heavenly Mother, interpretation of prophecy, and alternative views of Church history. Criticism included the Church's approach on abuse, homosexuality, sexism, racism, and control of its members.

The Presidency stated, "This committee serves as a resource to priesthood leaders throughout the world who may desire assistance on a wide variety of topics. It is a General Authority committee, currently comprised of Elder James E. Faust and Elder Russell M. Nelson of the Quorum of the Twelve Apostles. They work through established priesthood channels, and neither impose nor direct Church disciplinary action."[1]

## Without Milieu Control

Without restrictions on where we get information, there are abundant sources of wisdom and comfort, insight and wonder. There are millions of writers, creators, researchers, and professionals who share valuable pieces of their experience.

The world is rich with inspiration. Take what works for you. Embrace what speaks to you. If there is anything lovely, virtuous, of good report, or praiseworthy seek after those things, no matter what the origin.

---

1. "First Presidency Statement Cites Scriptural Mandate for Church Committee." *LDS Church News*, Aug 22, 1992. http://www.ldschurchnews.com/articles/22281/First-Presidency-statement-cites-scriptural-mandate-for-Church--committee.html

*The only way to purify our hearts is to receive the ordinances of the gospel and follow the Master in word, deed, and thought.*
—**Visiting Teaching Message:**
***More Purity Give Me***[1]

*No matter how hard I tried to please him, to please them, I fell flat on my face, and was always behind, trying hard to catch up.*
—**Pam Kazmaier,**
***Losing My Mind, Bit by Bit***[2]

*...you will never know until the Judgement Day whether or not you've been good 'enough'...*
—**Marion Stricker,**
***The Pattern of the Double-Bind in Mormonism***[3]

*Mormonism had taught me that 'pure' meant sexless, tame, and manageable, which is just how things had felt behind my old pane of glass.*
—**Martha Beck, *Leaving the Saints***[4]

# Demand for Purity: Perpetual Inadequacy

Mormons like to pride themselves on having high standards, as if it distinguishes them from other earthly organizations. Yet this is the mark of *most* totalist groups, to set lofty moral measures in areas like sexual purity, meditation or prayer, clean living, health, piety, and charity. All spiritual groups must appeal to the desire to rise above evil and tragedy. In addition to attracting new recruits, demand for purity firmly binds the members to the herd.

While still peculiar, Mormons are not so unique.

Geri-Ann Galanti spoke of this technique as it was used by the Moonies. "The need for purity is the need to constantly strive for perfection in order to achieve the higher goal... they are always aware of trying to be better people."[5]

Robert J. Lifton stated, "In the thought reform milieu, as in all situations of ideological totalism, the experiential world is sharply divided into the pure and the impure, into the absolutely good and the absolutely evil. The good and the pure are of course those ideas, feelings, and actions which are consistent with the totalist ideology and policy; anything else is apt to be relegated to the bad and the impure. Nothing human is immune from the flood of stern moral judgments. All 'taints' and 'poisons' which contribute to the existing

---

1. "Visiting Teaching Message: More Purity Give Me." *Ensign*, Sept 1995. http://www.lds.org/ensign/1995/09/more-purity-give-me
2. Pam Kazmaier. "Losing My Mind, Bit by Bit," Aug 13, 2005. http://questioningmormonism.wordpress.com/2011/12/02/pam-kazmaier-losing-my-mind-bit-by-bit/
3. Stricker, *The Double-Bind in Mormonism,* 2000. 90.
4. Beck, *Leaving the Saints,* 2005. 205.
5. Galanti, "Reflections on 'Brainwashing,'" *Recovery from Cults,* ed. Langone, 1995. 96.

state of impurity must be searched out and eliminated."[1]

This is a demand, not request, for purity. Purity is necessary to retain membership. And since membership is married to higher consequences, such as existence and induced phobias, the demand for purity is a very profound and intense form of control. It instills in the member a mindset of unquestioning obedience.

These standards are held too high for members to actually reach; thus the faithful can never measure up. On the surface, the goals seem reasonable and possible to attain, and thus they are never questioned; only the member who is not meeting them is questioned. After all, God will give no commandment unto the children of men save he provide a way for them to fulfill it (1 Nephi 3:7), nor will he allow anyone to be tempted beyond that which he is able (1 Corinthians 10:13).

> **Demand for Purity: Perpetual Inadequacy**
> —*Suppression, Reinforcement, Group Identification, Influence*
> - Creates impossible standards that get more difficult over time
> - Suppresses self
> - Builds foundation for Reward/Punishment cycle
> - Builds foundation for Shame/Guilt
> - Builds foundation for double-bind
> - Allows for blame reversal
> - Offers legitimacy for elitism
> - Reinforces higher purpose
> - Appeals to ideals
> - Reinforces:
>   - Black & white thinking
>   - Dispensing of existence
>   - Indirect directives
>   - Identification & example
> - Builds identification with group via shared struggle

"The philosophical assumption underlying this demand is that absolute purity is attainable, and that anything done to anyone in the name of this purity is ultimately moral."[2]

The expectation of achievability is a necessary illusion to keep members striving and to place any blame for failure on themselves.

"The demand for purity means that members will feel permanently inadequate. It keeps them in a perpetual cycle of 'trying harder' and yet never reaching the required goal. The net result of the practice of confession and purity is to severely limit the vast array of behaviors that people are normally allowed to express."[3]

Former Mormon Diana Kline writes, "I only felt loved if I was a human doing [as opposed to a human 'being'] following all of the commandments without hesitation. And even when I did jump through all the right hoops, I still didn't think that I was deserving, because I didn't jump through all the hoops perfectly enough..."[4]

And Pam Kazmaier says, "It was April 2003. I was taking notes in General Conference. There was a talk on 'Raising the Bar'. It devastated me. The gist of the message was that the expectations were being raised for missionaries. The Stake and Bishopric leaders reinforced the 'we're raising the bar' message every other week or so. It grew to encompass the mothers. I was already stretched to the max trying to meet an unbelievably impossible high standard. The church leaders had now raised the bar so high I'd never be able to reach it, let alone get Zack up there. It was impossible."[5]

Members will see others around them who *seem* to be following the standards perfectly, but in fact they are not. This reinforces the illusion. Standards become about appearances rather than reality. Each individual believes herself to be to be uniquely inadequate.

Reaching for perfection then becomes a form of misdirection, distracting each member

---

1. Lifton, *Thought Reform and the Psychology of Totalism,* 1961. (Chapter 22)
2. Lifton, *Thought Reform and the Psychology of Totalism,* 1961. (Chapter 22)
3. Martin, "Post-Cult Recovery," *Recovery from Cults,* ed. Langone, 1995. 210.
4. Kline, *Woman Redeemed*, 2005. 211.
5. Kazmaier, "Losing My Mind," Aug 13, 2005.

from the real source of their problems, like in this example from the SLF group: "We were too busy competing with each other and trying to please Rev. Will to stop and think. We were so afraid of losing standing and going to hell that we didn't pay full attention to our internal pain, lack of income, and discomfort."[1]

The qualities of perfection cannot actually be defined. We are all different, so a perfect me would be quite different from a perfect you. The totalist establishes a single target of perfection, a pseudopersonality, with qualities that don't match what would make a perfect me *or* a perfect you.

The concepts of perfection and eternal progression are incompatible. And as Goldhammer points out, "Perfection, a totalitarian-rooted idea, can never be attained and is in reality a state of death. Perfection, once achieved, would mean the end of all further development. To disengage from the collective consciousness, we must let go of such *absolutes.*"[2]

Since perfection is elusive, this thought reform method might be better named "perpetual inadequacy." Demand for purity turns into toxic perfectionism which leads quickly to self-blame. "Establishing impossible standards for performance, thereby creat[es] an environment of guilt and shame. No matter how hard a person tries, he always falls short, feels badly, and works even harder."[3]

Shame is its own thought control device, perhaps the most powerful and damaging one. Worthiness is equated to self-esteem. A good person who perpetually falls short can feel worthless in the sight of God and his fellows. Singer states, "There is no in between, and members are expected to judge themselves and others by this all-or-nothing standard. ...this ubiquitous guilt and shame creates and magnifies your dependence on the group. Thus you easily feel inadequate, as though you need 'fixing' all the time, just as the outside world is being denounced all the time."[4]

Demand for purity is "...a black-and-white world-view with the leader as the ultimate moral arbiter. This creates a world of guilt and shame, where punishment and humiliation are expected. It also sets up an environment of spying and reporting on one another. Through submission to the powerful lever of guilt, the individual loses his or her own moral sense."[5]

And in losing it, one hands control of that sense over to the group. The member becomes dependent upon leaders to tell the difference between right and wrong. And while the totalist moral compass generally matches society's values, leadership instills some morals to suit their own ends, particularly to prevent members from leaving, to extract more time and resources, and to drive recruitment.

The emotional toll, for some, is almost too much to bear. The wages of righteousness are costly indeed.

The Church endlessly lists sins of omission and commission, and every topic outlined in a conference talk is framed in hyperbolic language such as "critical", "most important", "serious", "dire", "vital", "urgent", "grave", "sacred duty", "grievous", "expedient", and "necessary." You don't have to pound the pulpit and shout hellfire to generate anxious immediacy. We leave sacrament meeting feeling like genealogy or scripture study or family home evening or temple work or tithing is now essential for our salvation, and we get fired up or guilted until the next topic is emphasized. There is no way to keep up.

Dr. Kris Doty, Associate Professor at Utah Valley University says many Utah women have a problem with perfection, with increased distress after meetings. "I used to be a crisis worker in an emergency room in a pretty busy hospital, and on Sundays, we would see LDS

---

1. Sanchez, *Spiritual Perversion,* 2005. 158.
2. Goldhammer, *Under the Influence,* 1996. 235.
3. Hassan, *Releasing the Bonds,* 2000. 34.
4. Singer, *Cults in Our Midst,* 1995. 71-72.
5. Tobias and Lalich, *Captive Hearts, Captive Minds,* 1994. 36.

women come in after church in acute anxiety or depressed states."[1]

Doty found that all twenty depressed LDS women she studied were perfectionists. Since the Church promises happiness as a reward for righteousness, perfectionism and depression become a self-reinforcing cycle.

According to member Lizza Nelson, who was interviewed for ABC4 news in Utah, "I think it gets really sticky when I have to be spiritually the best. [You] put a stigma on spirituality equals happiness, righteousness equals cheer, so if you struggle with it, of course your mind is like, I guess I'm wicked. I guess I'm doing it all wrong. I guess I'm not measuring up, I'm not righteous."[2]

The feeling of inadequacy leads to trying harder, which leads to a greater feeling of inadequacy. According to "Lindsey" cited in Doty's study, "When you're depressed, you just do anything to not feel it. So you think perfection is the answer. 'So if I have the perfect body, if I had the perfect looks, if I had the perfect kids, the perfect house, the perfect whatever, the perfect spirituality, if I somehow just loved to serve and I never felt like I was being burdened by doing this, then everything would be okay and I wouldn't have depression.'"[3]

Lindsey blames this attitude on herself. "...it's just something we do to ourselves. That's not coming down from the prophet; it's not coming down from God. That's just us comparing ourselves to each other and having that perfect standard."

But this idea *does* come from the prophet, and the scriptures, and conference talks, and lessons. As Dr. Doty claims, toxic perfectionism comes from the culture. But the culture gets it from somewhere.

This youth Sunday School lesson describes perpetual inadequacy and tries to soften the blow, but with the last sentence, still demands perfection: "Many people find the commandment 'be ye perfect' to be overwhelming. Youth especially can get discouraged easily when they make mistakes. They may feel that perfection is unattainable and thus not worth working toward. We all need to realize that perfection in this life is not expected or even possible. What is expected is that we try each day to be better than we were the day before. Help class members understand that they will someday reach perfection if they strive for it as best they can from day to day."[4]

Another woman in Dr. Doty's study, "Haylee", said, "A lot of my triggers were that I liked to be the best at everything. In high school, I was a straight-A student in school, I was in the national honor society and president of a club... In church, I wanted to be the super active one that everyone thought had it all together.

"I wanted to do everything and I wanted to do everything fantastically well. I think it for sure fuels [my depression] because no one's ever going to hit that. It's like the unobtainable. No one is ever going to be perfect. Logically I know it's unobtainable, but you are still pushing for that."[5]

As my LDS piano teacher said, "Practice doesn't make perfect... *Perfect* practice makes perfect." While this is good advice for someone learning a delicate and precise skill, there is a tendency for the LDS obsession with perfection to spill over into every aspect of life. In her exit story, Diana Kline said, "Whenever I had declined to do something well, I felt a deep inner shame for not being 'good enough.' If I received a 'B' on a school assignment instead of an 'A', if I tripped in front of the class on my way up to the blackboard, if I pronounced a word wrong, these were all misgivings of the incompetent and inadequate

---

1. "The Perfect Problem." *The Perfect Problem Special Report*. ABC4, May 13, 2013. http://www.abc4.com/content/news/perfectproblem/story/The-Perfect-Problem/2LurhsZFIESq8hDXysldXw.cspx
2. "The Perfect Problem." *The Perfect Problem Special Report*. ABC4, May 13, 2013.
3. Kristine J. Doty, Ph.D., LCSW. "Cultural Considerations for Social Work with Mormon Women Diagnosed with Depression (In the Culture But Not of the Culture)." presented at the Mental Health Symposium, Utah Valley University, Jan 31, 2013.
4. *Preparing for Exaltation: Teacher's Manual*. The Church of Jesus Christ of Latter Day Saints, 1998. Lesson 22: Striving for Perfection http://www.lds.org/manual/preparing-for-exaltation-teachers-manual/lesson-22-striving-for-perfection
5. Doty, "In the Culture But Not of the Culture," 2013.

self... I didn't want others to see my 'bad' side, or the state of my human vulnerabilities, especially in a faith which constantly demanded a 'perfecting of the Saints.'"[1]

Perfectionist attitudes are reinforced in many LDS family systems. In Dr. Doty's presentation, "Sarah" reflects, "As a kid I never felt like I was living up to [my mom's] religious expectations even though I was trying really hard to, but she struggled with...anything that would be contrary to the LDS church. It's hard for me to see her point of view and it seems like nothing is ever good enough or up to her expectations religiously, so even though I know she's happy with me I still feel like she doesn't think I'm up to her expectations...

"If I'm not reading my scriptures then I feel like I'm not doing what I should be doing and that I'm not keeping all of the commandments, so it makes me feel like my self-worth goes down. So even those little things make me feel lower than they should."[2]

Common human frailties are the most effective targets for strict compliance. The highest morals ought to involve helping others, yet these standards can't transform daily temptations into implements of control. I managed to be nice to everyone today, so I'm doing great! I don't need this church anymore. I'm already perfect.

Thus, "The prophet Alma taught that sexual sins are more serious than any other sins except murder or denying the Holy Ghost."[3]

If you've ever wondered why the Church spends more time promoting chastity than charity, and why sexual sin seems more abhorrent than fraud, extortion, and murder, this is why. Instinctual drives become demonized so that you have no choice but to fail. This proves the Church's doctrinal position, that mankind is in a fallen state and we need the help of a Savior. Sexuality, "impure" thoughts, "selfish" desires, language, clothing, food, music, personal interests, and leisure time are brought under the domain of purity.

I used to think that if the goal of a church were to gain as many members as possible, they'd promote hedonism. How much I underestimated the use of sexuality to manipulate. Every cult controls sex, either by demanding chastity, or by forcing non-consensual sex, or some mix of the two.

Orwell's *1984* examines the power of sexual control.

"The sexual act, successfully performed, was rebellion. Desire was thoughtcrime."

Why? "There was a direct intimate connection between chastity and political orthodoxy. For how could the fear, the hatred, and the lunatic credulity which the Party needed in its members be kept at the right pitch, except by bottling down some powerful instinct and using it as a driving force?"

And, "When you make love you're using up energy; and afterwards you feel happy and don't give a damn for anything. They can't bear you to feel like that. They want you to be bursting with energy all the time. All this marching up and down and cheering and waving flags is simply sex gone sour. If you're happy inside yourself, why should you get excited about Big Brother and the Three-Year Plans and the Two Minutes Hate and all the rest of their bloody rot?"[4]

By controlling our bodies, the Church controls our minds. All that potential energy is channeled towards LDS ends. Shaming sex shames the individual, who becomes dependent on the organization to become pure again.

Additionally, an over-focus on what one "should not" do further excites the desire to do it. Whatever you do, don't think of an elephant—and you think of an elephant. If I warn in a church talk that R-rated movies cause impure thoughts when you least want them, you may instantly recall a passionate love scene. If I constantly belabor that sex is sacred, sex becomes something bigger than it really is, and you become incapable of thinking rationally about it—or incapable of thinking about anything else. The Church's emphasis on sex,

---

1. Kline, *Woman Redeemed*, 2005. 2.
2. Doty, "In the Culture But Not of the Culture," 2013.
3. *For the Strength of Youth*, 2011. "Sexual Purity." https://www.lds.org/youth/for-the-strength-of-youth/sexual-purity
4. Orwell, *1984*.

especially to youth, is like setting a chocolate bar in front of a hungry child, and then telling them they can't have it.

The number of Church sources demanding purity is overwhelming. Here are a few examples. First, in scripture:

"Be ye therefore perfect, even as your Father which is in heaven is perfect." Matthew 5:48

"And we will prove them herewith, to see if they will do all things whatsoever the Lord their God shall command them." Abraham 3:25

"And that thou mayest more fully keep thyself unspotted from the world, thou shalt go to the house of prayer and offer up thy sacraments upon my holy day." D&C 59:9

Nephi lists sins at length. 2 Nephi 28 includes verses like: "And there shall also be many which shall say: Eat, drink, and be merry... there shall be many which shall teach after this manner, false and vain and foolish doctrines... the blood of the saints shall cry from the ground against them...

"O the wise, and the learned, and the rich, that are puffed up in the pride of their hearts, and all those who preach false doctrines, and all those who commit whoredoms, and pervert the right way of the Lord, wo, wo, wo be unto them, saith the Lord God Almighty, for they shall be thrust down to hell!"

I had to memorize some of these verses in Seminary. I also had to memorize this:

"For of him unto whom much is given much is required; and he who sins against the greater light shall receive the greater condemnation." D&C 82:3

The verse preceding it is: "Nevertheless, there are those among you who have sinned exceedingly; yea, even all of you have sinned; but verily I say unto you, beware from henceforth, and refrain from sin, lest sore judgments fall upon your heads."

The oft-used "cleanliness" metaphor is a set of loaded terms designed to make us feel disgust at the idea of sin. "And no unclean thing can enter into his kingdom; therefore nothing entereth into his rest save it be those who have washed their garments in my blood, because of their faith, and the repentance of all their sins, and their faithfulness unto the end." (3 Nephi 27:19) Scriptures like these abound.

Conference talks, lesson manuals, and hymns reinforce this constant need for purity.

"Too many Latter-day Saints today somehow believe they can stand with one hand touching the walls of the temple while the other hand fondles the unclean things of the world. We can't do that. As Alma said, 'Touch not their unclean things'. I plead with you, put both hands on the temple. Put your arms around the temple, and hang on for dear life to your family dream. If you don't, the tigers will come at night and tear your dreams apart."[1]

The *For the Strength of Youth* pamphlet lists the exacting requirements placed upon LDS teenagers. "We promise that as you keep the covenants you have made and these standards, you will be blessed with the companionship of the Holy Ghost, your faith and testimony will grow stronger, and you will enjoy increasing happiness...

"The standards presented in this booklet are a guide to help you make correct choices. Review the standards often and ask yourself, 'Am I living the way the Lord wants me to live?' and 'How have I been blessed by living these standards?'"[2]

Ezra Taft Benson said, "A standard is a rule of measure by which one determines exactness or perfection. The Saints are to be a standard of holiness for the world to see! That is the beauty of Zion."[3]

One-third of the Threefold Mission of the Church is "Perfecting the Saints." *Mormon Doctrine* states, "*Finite perfection* may be gained by the righteous saints in this life. It

---

[1]. Elder Bruce C. Hafen. "Your Longing for Family Joy." *Ensign*, Oct 2003. http://www.lds.org/ensign/2003/10/your-longing-for-family-joy
[2]. *For the Strength of Youth*, 2011. "Message from the First Presidency."
[3]. President Ezra Taft Benson. First Presidency Message "Strengthen Thy Stakes." *Ensign*, Jan 1991. http://www.lds.org/ensign/1991/01/strengthen-thy-stakes

consists in living a godfearing life of devotion to the truth, of walking in complete submission to the will of the Lord, and of putting first in one's life the things of the kingdom of God. *Infinite perfection* is reserved for those who overcome all things and inherit the fulness of the Father in the mansions hereafter...

"Many scriptures exhort the saints to be perfect in this life, an attainment which will lead to eternal perfection hereafter, unless by subsequent rebellion and wickedness a departure is made from the strait and narrow path."[1]

As a child, I was led to believe that Enoch's people were so righteous, their whole city was raised into heaven. "As disobedience brought on the flood, so obedience sanctified Enoch's Zion."[2] Likewise, prophets like Moses, Elijah, the apostle John, and the Three Nephites were righteous enough to gain this gift called "translation." If only we could be perfect enough, we too would be resurrected, without dying, in the twinkle of an eye. I remember trying, sometimes for months at a time, to attain this goal.

An oft-sung hymn, *More Holiness Give Me*, lists twenty-three Christlike attributes to attain. Verse three:

> More purity give me,
> More strength to o'ercome,
> More freedom from earth-stains,
> More longing for home.
> More fit for the kingdom,
> More used would I be,
> More blessed and holy—
> More, Savior, like thee.[3]

The Young Women's theme is repeated weekly in a group setting by all girls ages 12-18:

> We are daughters of our Heavenly Father, who loves us, and we love Him. We will "stand as witnesses of God at all times and in all things, and in all places" as we strive to live the Young Women values, which are: Faith, Divine Nature, Individual Worth, Knowledge, Choice and Accountability, Good Works, Integrity, and Virtue.
>
> We believe as we come to accept and act upon these values, we will be prepared to strengthen home and family, make and keep sacred covenants, receive the ordinances of the temple, and enjoy the blessings of exaltation.[4]

Virtue was recently added, as was the phrase "strengthen home and family."

Prophets from Brigham Young to Gordon B. Hinckley have delivered the same message. Young:

> If the Saints neglect to pray, and violate the day that is set apart for the worship of God, they will lose his Spirit. If a man shall suffer himself to be overcome with anger, and curse and swear, taking the name of the Deity in vain, he cannot retain the Holy Spirit. In short, if a man shall do anything which he knows to be wrong, and repenteth not, he cannot enjoy the Holy Spirit, but will walk in darkness and ultimately deny the faith.[5]

---

1. Bruce R. McConkie. *Mormon Doctrine*. Salt Lake City, UT: Publishers Press, 1966. 567.
2. Marion G. Romney. "A Silver Lining." In LDS General Conference, April 1977. https://www.lds.org/general-conference/1977/04/a-silver-lining
3. Philip Paul Bliss. "More Holiness Give Me." In *Hymns of the Church of Jesus Christ of Latter-Day Saints*. The Church of Jesus Christ of Latter-Day Saints, 1985.
4. "Young Women Theme." Accessed Aug 28, 2013. https://www.lds.org/young-women/personal-progress/young-women-theme
5. *Teachings of Presidents of the Church: Brigham Young*, 1997. 79.

Hinckley:

> We cannot indulge in swearing. We cannot be guilty of profanity; we cannot indulge in impure thoughts, words, and acts and have the Spirit of the Lord with us...
> Again Paul's counsel to Timothy, "Keep thyself pure".
> Those are simple words. But they are ever so important. Paul is saying, in effect, stay away from those things which will tear you down and destroy you spiritually. Stay away from television shows which lead to unclean thoughts and unclean language. Stay away from videos which will lead to evil thoughts. They won't help you. They will only hurt you. Stay away from books and magazines which are sleazy and filthy in what they say and portray. Keep thyself pure.[1]

Spencer W. Kimball spends the first half of *Miracle of Forgiveness* demanding purity in excruciating detail. "...every sin is against God, for it tends to frustrate the program and purposes of the Almighty. Likewise, every sin is committed against the sinner, for it limits his progress and curtails his development. In our journey toward eternal life, purity must be our constant aim. To walk and talk with God, to serve with God, to follow his example and become as a god, we must attain perfection. In his presence there can be no guile, no wickedness, no transgression."[2]

Bruce R. McConkie gave Mormons ten new commandments in a speech given at BYU in 1975:

> The first commandment: Thou shalt be morally clean and conform to every standard of virtue and chastity...
> People who live after the manner of the world are immoral and unclean—so much so that we sometimes wonder whether there are any moral standards left among men. People speak of a new morality, which is, in fact, immorality under a new name. We are confronted on every hand—on radio, on television, in the movies, and in the so-called literature that is available—with a recitation of standards that are contrary to gospel principles. They are inherent in the course that the world pursues...
> The second commandment: Thou shalt bridle thy passions and abstain from all manner of lasciviousness...
> We are here in mortality to be tried and tested; we are on probation. The great test is whether we overcome the lusts of the flesh, flee from that which is lewd, and live by gospel standards. We are to overcome the world. If we get involved in necking and petting, if we go to pornographic movies, if we read trashy and vulgar books or magazines, if we tell or enjoy vulgar stories, if we profane and are unclean in thought or word, we are living after the manner of the world. Then there is nothing peculiar about us. We are as the generality of mankind. We are outside the family circle. We lose our status as the sons and daughters of our Lord.[3]

Recently, standards were increased for young men going on missions. "The bar was raised by the leaders of the Church, and now the minimum standard for participating in missionary work is absolute moral worthiness; physical health and strength; intellectual, social, and emotional development. In every high-jumping competition there is a minimum height at which the competition starts. The high jumper cannot ask to start at a lower height. In the same way, you should not expect the standards to be lowered to allow you to

---

1. Gordon B. Hinckley. "Converts and Young Men." In LDS General Conference, April 1997.
2. Spencer W. Kimball, *The Miracle of Forgiveness*, 1969. ("Chapter 2: No Unclean Thing Can Enter")
3. Bruce R. McConkie. "The Ten Commandments of a Peculiar People." Brigham Young University, Jan 28, 1975. http://speeches.byu.edu/?act=viewitem&id=599

serve a mission."[1]

Demand for perfection is especially harmful when applied to masturbation. Attempts to resist only make it more difficult to avoid. Most people masturbate, yet as a private activity, you'd never know. A society which actively shames it can cause severe self-loathing.

A pamphlet circulating in the 1970s and 80s stated, "We are taught that our bodies are temples of God, and are to be clean so that the Holy Ghost may dwell within us. Masturbation is a sinful habit that robs one of the Spirit and creates guilt and emotional stress. It is not physically harmful unless practiced in the extreme. It is a habit that is totally self-centered, and secretive, and in no way expresses the proper use of the procreative power given to man to fulfill eternal purposes. It therefore separates a person from God and defeats the gospel plan."[2]

An LDS therapist, Natasha Helfer Parker, blogged about this problem. "...within the last 6 months I've known of two LDS adolescent boys referred to the addictions program offered by the church because they masturbate 1-3 times a week and three LDS adolescent clients tell me they believe their masturbatory behavior to be a sin next to murder! If this is what we are teaching our youth—then we are emotionally abusing them. And it needs to stop. I will no longer be a compliant witness to this type of psychological assault. I know my language is strong and I intend it to be. The numerous stories I could share about masturbatory shame run in the thousands and I find it unnecessary, harmful and life altering."[3]

Emotional demand for purity also exists and includes an emphasis on staying cheerful and positive while repressing unhappiness and anger. In a Thomas S. Monson talk entitled *School Thy Feelings*, "To be angry is to yield to the influence of Satan. No one can make us angry. It is our choice. If we desire to have a proper spirit with us at all times, we must choose to refrain from becoming angry."[4]

Since feelings are difficult to control, this definitely keeps us in a perpetual state of inadequacy. And when we do manage to control them, it suppresses healthy expression of negative emotions which, as we've discussed, may be caused by the group itself.

None of this is to say we shouldn't strive to become better people. I have never abandoned my efforts to improve myself. The difference now is that I set my own pace and hold up my own yardstick, and I use methods that work best for me. I learned to settle for good enough.

This makes it easier to rise above discouragement and value my strengths. I've made more progress this way than I ever did in the Church. This is the healthier path to happiness.

---

1. L. Tom Perry. "Raising the Bar." In LDS General Conference, Oct 2007. https://www.lds.org/general-conference/2007/10/raising-the-bar
2. Mark E. Petersen (attributed). "Steps In Overcoming Masturbation." Accessed Aug 28, 2013. http://www.ldolphin.org/mormon.html
3. Natasha Helfer Parker. "My Official Stance on Masturbation." *The Mormon Therapist*, Aug 6, 2012. http://www.patheos.com/blogs/mormontherapist/2012/08/my-official-stance-on-masturbation.html
4. Thomas S. Monson. "School Thy Feelings, O My Brother." In LDS General Conference, Oct 2009. https://www.lds.org/general-conference/2009/10/school-thy-feelings-o-my-brother

*...as many as would not worship the image of the beast should be killed.*
—**Revelations 13:15**

*Thoughtcrime does not entail death: thoughtcrime is death.*
—**George Orwell, *1984***

*Live here then, you poor, miserable curses, until the time of retribution, when your heads will have to be severed from your bodies.*
—**Prophet Brigham Young, Oct 6, 1855**[1]

*A man's ethical behavior should be based effectually on sympathy, education, and social ties; no religious basis is necessary. Man would indeed be in a poor way if he had to be restrained by fear and punishment and hope of reward after death.*
—**Albert Einstein,**
***The World As I See It***[2]

# Dispensing of Existence

**Dispensing of Existence**
*—Punishment, Silencing Doubts, Influence*
- Induces phobias
- Suppresses the self
- Reward implied by its opposite (life)
- Reinforces us vs. them, black & white thinking
- Suppresses doubts
- Reinforces demand for purity by giving a dire consequence for failure
- Reinforces the double-bind

We've already established that the demand for purity, for some, is more important than life itself. We were taught that it would be better to lose our life than lose our chastity. This thought is reinforced in the doctrine and stated in plain terms: The wicked have no right to live. God will strike them down. If you are wicked, the same fate awaits for you.

Put simply, dispensing of existence is "The belief that people in the group have the right to exist and all ex-members and critics or dissidents do not."[3]

Totalist groups require various forms of pressure to keep members in line. If you could just sleep in on Sunday with no consequence, the pews wouldn't be so full. Thus enters the grandest incentive: threat of death.

This threat can be literal, but since that could cause problems with legal authorities, non-physical death-threats work just as well. Most religious cults threaten either permanent soul-death or infinite punishment. Other forms of existence can be imperiled as well: loss of self, purpose, identity, community, or ideals are all frightening forms of figurative death. Many reason that the significance of this life is nothing compared to the next, and that some ideals are worth dying for.

Some cults imply that physical harm will come to those who leave, either through spiritual means (loss of protective blessings), or through direct action from the group. The latter only happens in the most extreme cults. To be sure, this was the case in early LDS

---

1. *Journal of Discourses.* Vol. 3. 26 vols. Privately Printed, n.d. http://jod.mrm.org/1. 50
2. Albert Einstein. *The World As I See It.* New York; Secaucus, N.J.: Wisdom Library ; Citadel Press, 1979.
3. Hassan, *Releasing the Bonds,* 2000. 34.

history. Mormon leaders have since found that figurative death is less messy and just as persuasive.

Lifton first identified this technique.

> The totalist environment draws a sharp line between those whose right to existence can be recognized, and those who possess no such right...
>
> ...one underlying assumption makes this arrogance mandatory: the conviction that there is just one path to true existence, just one valid mode of being, and that all others are perforce invalid and false. Totalists thus feel themselves compelled to destroy all possibilities of false existence as a means of furthering the great plan of true existence to which they are committed.[1]

*Captive Hearts* says, "...the group is the ultimate arbiter and all nonbelievers are considered 'evil' or nonpeople. If nonpeople cannot be recruited they can be punished, even killed. This creates an 'us-vs-them' mentality and breeds fear in the individual, who sees that one's own life depends on a willingness to obey. Here is found the merger of the individual with the belief."[2]

The core of this technique both depends upon and aids the creation of a pseudopersonality. To leave the group is death of identity. If to leave is death, then the individual must become one with the group. "Existence comes to depend upon creed (I believe, therefore I am), upon submission (I obey, therefore I am) and beyond these, upon a sense of total merger with the ideological movement. Ultimately of course one compromises and combines the totalist 'confirmation' with independent elements of personal identity; but one is ever made aware that, should he stray too far along this 'erroneous path,' his right to existence may be withdrawn."[3]

If you have placed high importance on being "spiritual" or "good", as defined by the group, your core purpose and sense of self becomes enmeshed with the group. The organization comes to represent the totality of your ideals. All sense of personal validation and justification for living are based upon continual acceptance. Ostracism becomes a terrifying possibility, and once shunned, some will wonder if life is even worth continuing.

By leaving, a member goes from being "good", "spiritual", "honest", "kind", "holy", or "enlightened", to being "wicked", "a sinner", "lost", "a liar", "hateful", or even "evil." Perceiving the loss of these attributes is nearly like dying.

The cult must merely convince you that your life has no meaning without the group. Even political cults can employ this method. Lalich reports on the WDU, "Once in this world, as awful as it was, being thrown to the outside became an unthinkable alternative: It meant failure to meet the test; even worse, it meant failing the working class, betraying the ideals that first attracted us to the party's pitch. It also meant acknowledging that we had bought into a horrible lie and, in so doing, had hurt our comrades as they had hurt us. Once caught in such a trap, decent human beings, which we were, don't easily say, 'Sorry, friends, I'm getting out of here.' Rather, they look for ways to rationalize their subservience and exploitation."[4]

This isolates and induces strong avoidance of even thinking about leaving.

> Cultists who have lost faith in the outside world and have lost faith or confidence in themselves, and who come to understand that they must be remolded by the processes and teachings of the cult are faced with a horrifying perspective when encountering dispensing of existence. Hence, if one has already lost the outside

---

1. Lifton, *Thought Reform and the Psychology of Totalism*, 1961. (Chapter 22)
2. Tobias and Lalich, *Captive Hearts, Captive Minds*, 1994. 37.
3. Lifton, *Thought Reform and the Psychology of Totalism*, 1961. (Chapter 22)
4. Lalich, "A Little Carrot and a Lot of Stick," *Recovery from Cults*, ed. Langone, 1995. 72.

> world believing it is evil and lost one's self believing it too is evil or 'bourgeois', then the prospect of losing one's affiliation with the cult presents the cultist with the phenomenon of the total annihilation of the self.
>
> The dispensing of existence accentuates members' anxiety because their often-hidden feelings of inadequacy render them vulnerable to being judged unworthy. Having been indoctrinated to believe that rejection from the cult is tantamount to personal annihilation, members will obviously do all that they can to remain in good standing.[1]

Steve Sanchez quotes his cult leader, Rev. Will, employing this method. "'I guarantee you this: if you people leave, you will do just like them. First you'll stop reading! Then you'll stop running your energy! Then you'll stop grounding! With each step your information is lost—it's *erased*! You gradually go back to sleep, and I'm telling you! You are a hundred times worse off than if you had never started this. When you go to sleep, it's spiritual death; it's exactly like a heroin addict who cuts his wrist because he can't get another fix... When you give in to the spirit of the world, you feel euphoria. It's got you... The dark angels come up and take you down just like those shadows took the evil guys down in the movie *Ghost*.'"[2]

If not being a member equals death, it becomes a driving motivation for proselytization. The unenlightened, worldly, sinful, and selfish must be converted to save them from hell.

Mormons may try to deny that they teach such doctrines, or they downplay the severity of what is taught. They try to soften words like "damned" and "death", claiming they mean the absence of God's presence or a halting of eternal progress. Other high-demand groups do the same. "Here, a sharp line is drawn between those who will be 'saved' and those who will be 'damned' (nonmembers). In response to my question, the Moonies openly denied this as one of their beliefs, although ex-members report that this view is taught later on. This tenet forms the basis for much of the fear and guilt that some former members say kept them in the group for so long."[3]

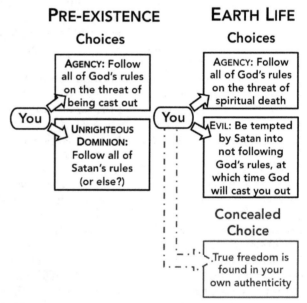

Though Mormons deny that belief in hell or other harsh punishments, fear of failure is just as strong. Martha Beck reflects, "To these good Saints, our defection from the Church was a far more horrible death than the loss of John's mother. Mormons believe that love and belonging reach easily beyond the boundaries of the grave. It just can't make it over the high-voltage electric fence of apostasy."[4]

So where do members get this idea? From Church teachings. One of the most threatening scriptures is 2 Nephi 2:27: "Wherefore, men are free according to the flesh; and all things are given them which are expedient unto man. And they are free to choose liberty and eternal life, through the great Mediator of all men, or to choose captivity and death,

---

1. Martin, "Post-Cult Recovery," *Recovery from Cults,* ed. Langone, 1995. 210.
2. Sanchez, *Spiritual Perversion,* 2005. 211.
3. Galanti, "Reflections on 'Brainwashing,'" *Recovery from Cults,* ed. Langone, 1995. 94.
4. Beck, *Leaving the Saints,* 2005. 277.

according to the captivity and power of the devil; for he seeketh that all men might be miserable like unto himself."

You are free to choose all right, but your choices are severely limited to two paths with extreme consequences: life and liberty or certain destruction. Members recognize that this refers both to the afterlife and to personal happiness and freedom during this life. Once you are under the influence of the devil, it's curtains for you.

Another oft quoted scripture is Mosiah 4:30: "But this much I can tell you, that if ye do not watch yourselves, and your thoughts, and your words, and your deeds, and observe the commandments of God, and continue in the faith of what ye have heard concerning the coming of our Lord, even unto the end of your lives, ye must perish. And now, O man, remember, and perish not." This is pretty plain. Endure to the end, or die.

Repent or be tortured: "But if they would not repent they must suffer even as I; Which suffering caused myself, even God, the greatest of all, to tremble because of pain, and to bleed at every pore, and to suffer both body and spirit—and would that I might not drink the bitter cup, and shrink—" D&C 19:17-18

In Seminary, we jokingly referred to tithing as "Fire Insurance": "...for he that is tithed shall not be burned at his coming." D&C 64:23

And from the Bible: "But there were false prophets also among the people, even as there shall be false teachers among you, who privily shall bring in damnable heresies, even denying the Lord that bought them, and bring upon themselves swift destruction." 2 Peter 2:1-2

> Enter ye in at the strait gate: for wide is the gate, and broad is the way, that leadeth to destruction, and many there be which go in thereat: Because strait is the gate, and narrow is the way, which leadeth unto life, and few there be that find it.
> Matthew 7:13-14

Joseph Smith wanted his wife to know, via direct revelation, what would happen if she didn't submit to the will of God and to Joseph's desire to marry other women: "...if she will not abide this commandment she shall be destroyed, saith the Lord; for I am the Lord thy God, and will destroy her if she abide not in my law." D&C 132:54

In scripture stories, people are struck by lightning, cities are thrown into the ocean, and entire nations are cursed or eradicated:

"And if the time comes that the voice of the people doth choose iniquity, then is the time that the judgments of God will come upon you; yea, then is the time he will visit you with great destruction even as he has hitherto visited this land." Mosiah 29:27 The Nephites were utterly wiped out for being wicked.

These scriptures are not rare; there are dozens more.

Brigham Young had perhaps the harshest words to say. "What have the Latter-day Saints got to apostatize from? Everything that there is good, pure, holy, God-like, exalting, ennobling, extending the ideas, the capacities of the intelligent beings that our Heavenly Father has brought forth upon this earth. What will they receive in exchange? I can comprehend it in a very few words. These would be the words that I should use: death, hell and the grave. That is what they will get in exchange. We may go into the particulars of that which they experience. They experience darkness, ignorance, doubt, pain, sorrow, grief, mourning, unhappiness; no person to condole [lament] with in the hour of trouble, no arm to lean upon in the day of calamity, no eye to pity when they are forlorn and cast down; and I comprehend it by saying death, hell and the grave. This is what they will get in exchange for their apostasy from the Gospel of the Son of God."[1]

But perhaps I shouldn't be quoting anything by Brigham Young that makes the Church look bad. In 1981, Bruce R. McConkie wrote a letter attempting to silence BYU academic Eugene England, who also quoted some of the prophet's more controversial words.

---

1. *Teachings of Presidents of the Church: Brigham Young*, "Chapter 12: Preventing Personal Apostasy," 1997. 82.

> I do not know all of the providences of the Lord, but I do know that he permits false doctrine to be taught in and out of the Church and that such teaching is part of the sifting process of mortality. We will be judged by what we believe among other things. If we believe false doctrine, we will be condemned. If that belief is on basic and fundamental things, it will lead us astray and we will lose our souls. This is why Nephi said: 'And all those who preach false doctrines,...wo, wo, wo be unto them, saith the Lord God Almighty, for they shall be thrust down to hell!' This clearly means that people who teach false doctrine in the fundamental and basic things will lose their souls... I repeat: Brigham Young erred in some of his statements on the nature and kind of being that God is and as to the position of Adam in the plan of salvation, but Brigham Young also taught the truth in these fields on other occasions. And I repeat, that in his instance, he was a great prophet and has gone on to eternal reward. What he did is not a pattern for any of us. If we choose to believe and teach the false portions of his doctrines, we are making an election that will damn us.[1]

So while England would be damned for quoting the false doctrines of the prophet, the prophet who taught them would be okay. According to McConkie, all LDS authorities are exempt: "If I err, that is my problem; but in your case if you single out some of these things and make them the center of your philosophy, and end up being wrong, you will lose your soul."

General authorities often make eternal-death threats. Boyd K. Packer addressed little children, and said, "There is another kind of death you should think of. That is the separation from the presence of our Heavenly Father. If we will be baptized and live his gospel, we may be redeemed from this second death."[2]

First Counselor in the First Presidency, N. Eldon Tanner: "Those who stray away and follow detours find themselves on paths leading to failure and destruction."[3]

General Authority David R. Stone: "But we also have our spiritual hurricane guardians, those whose calling it is to watch and warn, helping us avoid spiritual damage, destruction, and even death. Our watchmen on the tower are known to us as apostles and prophets."[4]

Dallin H. Oaks: "Beware of the slick package and the glitz of a good time. What the devil portrays as fun can be spiritually fatal."[5]

The temple endowment ceremony, prior to 1990, included a dramatic pantomime of the penalty of physical death should the details of the ceremony be revealed.[6] Many living Saints will remember swearing this oath. The vows still contain the wording, "even at the peril of your life."

You can say this is figurative all you want. The psychological effects are the same. They lead to fear and shame, and all the behaviors that these feelings motivate.

Last-days prophecies include imagery of the righteous being lifted into God's embrace while the wicked suffer war and natural disaster right before being consigned to Satan. "A desolating scourge shall go forth among the inhabitants of the earth, and shall continue to be poured out from time to time, if they repent not, until the earth is empty, and the inhabitants thereof are consumed away and utterly destroyed by the brightness of my coming." D&C 5:19

Apostle Marion G. Romney spoke on this topic. "He has told them that if they would

---

1. Bruce R. McConkie. Letter to Eugene England. "Bruce McConkie's Letter of Rebuke to Professor Eugene England," Feb 19, 1981. http://www.mrm.org/bruce-mcconkies-rebuke-of-eugene-england
2. Boyd K. Packer. "Behold Your Little Ones." In LDS General Conference, April 1973. https://www.lds.org/general-conference/1973/04/behold-your-little-ones
3. N. Eldon Tanner. "Why Is My Boy Wandering Tonight?" In LDS General Conference, Oct 1974. https://www.lds.org/general-conference/1974/10/why-is-my-boy-wandering-tonight
4. David R. Stone. "Spiritual Hurricanes." In LDS General Conference, Oct 1999. https://www.lds.org/general-conference/1999/10/spiritual-hurricanes
5. Dallin H. Oaks. "Be Not Deceived." In LDS General Conference, Oct 2004.
6. "LDS (Mormon) Temple Penalties." Accessed Oct 18, 2013. http://lds-mormon.com/veilworker/penalty.shtml

follow His directions, they would be blessed and flourish upon the earth. At the same time He has warned that if they persisted in disregarding His directions, they would bring upon themselves calamities and disaster."[1]

If the world is scheduled to end "someday", you must constantly remain prepared. Only LDS righteousness can stop it. "Now all the acts of governments, all the armies of the nations, all the learning and the wisdom of man together cannot turn these calamities aside. The only way they can be averted is for men to accept and conform to the way of life revealed by God our Heavenly Father."[2]

For those who are truly bad, the Mormon hell, Outer Darkness, awaits: "Behold, and lo, there are none to deliver you; for ye obeyed not my voice when I called to you out of the heavens; ye believed not my servants, and when they were sent unto you ye received them not. Wherefore, they sealed up the testimony and bound up the law, and ye were delivered over unto darkness. These shall go away into outer darkness, where there is weeping, and wailing, and gnashing of teeth." D&C 133:73

It's a bit confusing about who Outer Darkness is for. Supposedly, it's for Sons of Perdition, people who commit the unpardonable sin of denying the Holy Ghost. But what does that mean? Interpretation seems mixed. Do you have to turn away the missionaries? Do you have to hold the priesthood and then apostatize? Do you have to "know" beyond a doubt, and then deny it? Or do you just have to be a member with a testimony who stops believing?

I was under the impression you had to have incontrovertible evidence, like meeting God in person, and then openly deny him. Other Mormons believe that doubting just a little makes you Outer Darkness material.

Bruce R. McConkie does nothing to clear this up in *Mormon Doctrine*. Under "Outer Darkness", he quotes Alma: "At death, the spirits of the wicked 'shall be cast out into outer darkness; there shall be weeping, and wailing, and gnashing of teeth, and this because of their own iniquity, being led captive by the will of the devil. Now this is the state of the souls of the wicked, yea, in darkness, and a state of awful, fearful looking for the fiery indignation of the wrath of God upon them; thus they remain in this state, as well as the righteous in paradise, until the time of their resurrection."[3] He strangely has no entry on "Son of Perdition", and fails to mention sons of perdition under "Outer Darkness." So it's all of the wicked? And it only lasts until the resurrection? That's not what I heard.

The *Gospel Fundamentals* lesson manual mentions the three kingdoms and outer darkness, but only says Satan and his spirit-followers will go there.[4] The current Seminary manual claims the Alma scripture doesn't refer to the actual outer darkness, but to the spirit prison.[5] To confuse matters more, the *Doctrine and Covenants Student Manual* quotes McConkie from *Mormon Doctrine*, **and** D&C 133:73, and says it's hell.[6]

It serves the Church well to let members believe whatever they infer from this teaching. For those who fear, it motivates behavior while giving the Church an out.

Mormon folklore delivers its own stories of what happens to the wicked. Members tell urban legends of apostates or sinners who died in fatal car accidents or became drug addicts or other such extremes.

Some of these stories come from the top, General Conference: "Although warned of the dangers which lay ahead, he continued in the forbidden paths, experimenting with alcohol,

---

1. Marion G. Romney. "A Silver Lining." In LDS General Conference, April 1977.
2. Romney, "A Silver Lining," General Conference, April 1977.
3. McConkie, *Mormon Doctrine*, 1966. 551.
4. *Gospel Fundamentals*. The Church of Jesus Christ of Latter Day Saints, 2002. (Chapter 36: Eternal Life)
https://www.lds.org/manual/gospel-fundamentals/chapter-36-eternal-life
5. *Book of Mormon Seminary Teacher Manual*. The Church of Jesus Christ of Latter Day Saints, 2012. Lesson 97: Alma 40
https://www.lds.org/manual/book-of-mormon-seminary-teacher-manual-2013/alma/lesson-97
6. *Doctrine and Covenants Student Manual*. The Church of Jesus Christ of Latter Day Saints, 2002.
https://www.lds.org/manual/doctrine-and-covenants-student-manual/sections-132-138/section-133-the-lords-appendix-to-the-doctrine-and-covenants

drugs, and the gay life. Eventually he left his home and family, traveled across the country, took up residence in a community comprised of nomads, or wanderers, we might say. They were accountable to no one; they were free to come and go as they pleased; they had no responsibilities and seemingly were leading the kind of carefree lives that they thought they wanted.

"There is a sad ending to nearly every story I have heard about those who drift away from the straight and narrow path. Such a tragedy ended the life of the young man to whom I refer. Under the influence of drugs and alcohol, and motorcycling with his companions late one night, he plunged through the rails of a bridge over a murky river and was killed."[1]

Excommunication is another form of death, due to the web of dependencies members are spun into. Worthiness plays such a large part in the social role and self-image of Mormons. For those in the Mormon Corridor, where the population is highly LDS, excommunication can result in social shunning and a loss of livelihood and friendships.

Referring to the September Six excommunications, Martha Beck said,

> For a pioneer people, accustomed to a level of interdependency rare in the United States, [excommunication] was a horrifying prospect. It was similar to the penalty of *mura hachibu*, "expulsion from the village," in feudal Japan, where many people found suicide preferable to living as exiles.
>
> ...the accused heretics had broken none of the Church's commandments except for the unspoken eleventh ('Thou shalt not commit publicity')... Their real crime was excessive knowledge—having it, communicating it.[2]

Even the Church acknowledges how painful this can be. "The trauma of being disfellowshipped or excommunicated from the Church will likely never be fully understood by those who have never experienced it."[3]

Mormons believe that spiritual rewards are more valuable than life itself: "Do as He bids you to do, no matter how hard it may seem to you, and do it now. It is in doing the will of the Lord that knowledge of Him and love for Him accrue to your soul, which leads you to be ever more willing to lay down your own life and follow Him."[4]

These doctrines are not harmless. When I was young, a friend was severely depressed and suicidal, thinking he had sinned to the point where God could no longer love him. I tried to convince him to pray, but he thought himself too unworthy. What was his unforgivable sin? He had been involved in "heavy petting" with a girl. Some might say the Church does not teach sin makes one unworthy of prayer, and that no doctrine should have made my friend suicidal. They would quickly blame him for misunderstanding the "plain and precious things." Yet it is not a misunderstanding in light of these harsh doctrines and cultural pressures.

Perhaps he had heard the statement from the First Presidency: "Please believe me when I say that chastity is worth more than life itself. This is the doctrine my parents taught me; it is truth. It is better to die chaste than to live unchaste. The salvation of your very souls is concerned in this."[5]

Gordon B. Hinckley reported what a soldier in the Vietnam War once told him, "I know what my mother expects. I know what she's saying in her prayers. She'd rather have me come home dead than unclean." This anecdote was repeated as recently as 2003.[6]

---

1. Tanner, "Why Is My Boy Wandering Tonight?" General Conference, Oct 1974.
2. Beck, *Leaving the Saints,* 2005. 240.
3. M. Russell Ballard. "A Chance to Start Over: Church Disciplinary Councils and the Restoration of Blessings." *Ensign*, Sept 1990. https://www.lds.org/ensign/1990/09/a-chance-to-start-over-church-disciplinary-councils-and-the-restoration-of-blessings
4. James J. Hamula. "Winning the War Against Evil." In LDS General Conference, Oct 2008. https://www.lds.org/general-conference/2008/10/winning-the-war-against-evil
5. President Marion G. Romney. "We Believe in Being Chaste." *Ensign*, Sept 1981. http://www.lds.org/ensign/1981/09/we-believe-in-being-chaste
6. Marilyn S. Bateman, and Merrill J. Bateman. "BYU Devotional: Mortality and Our Eternal Journey." Brigham Young University, Jan 14, 2003. http://speeches.byu.edu/?act=viewitem&id=182

Death becomes, in a way, an escape hatch for depressed, overtaxed members who are enduring to the end, and can only hope for that end, who "look forward with an eye of faith, and view this mortal body raised in immortality, and this corruption raised in incorruption..." Alma 5:15

Pam Kazmaier conveys this feeling in her exit story. "I thought if I kept working hard, I'd earn God's peace. I was so focused on having eternal perspective that I lost perspective; the perspective that this life was worth living. I was living just to get to die soon, and get admitted to the celestial kingdom where all those hardy, enduring souls got to go."[1]

I can relate to her. There were moments when I, too, looked forward to my death, the Second Coming, anything to ease my pain, to get the tests and trials over with lest I fail.

This is not a misinterpretation of doctrine. In *Come, Come Ye Saints*, I sang, "And should we die before our journey's through, Happy day! All is well! We then are free from toil and sorrow, too; With the just we shall dwell!"[2]

In Pam's case, she suffered from being bipolar, and in that state of mental illness and overwork, she eventually lost all hope. "I felt it was my duty as a mother, since I had failed every which way here on earth to help Zack, to go with him to the other side. Neither Zack nor I would ever get better. If Zack was finally going to kill himself, I must somehow get over there, too... I didn't want to kill Zack, or myself, but I wanted Zack to feel relief. I didn't have the hand-eye coordination and thinking ability to effectively see my way to accomplish it. I didn't have the ability, at the time, to get us to the other side. Maybe we could just sleep. I told him we could take our meds. We could take a little extra...

"I had stopped him so many times over the years from taking his life. This time, I was going with him, so he wouldn't be alone. From the temple covenants I heard, 'It's time to sacrifice your own life if necessary.' From the New Testament I heard, 'There is no greater love than to lay down your life for a friend.'"[3]

Yes, the Church teaches that suicide is a sin. But it also teaches that not working hard enough and not being a good mother, and innumerable of other things are also sins. Eventually, some commandments have to take priority over the others, and in an unstable place of overwhelming pain, sometimes suicide seems like the best option.

In reality, the best option is to back off from the constant demand for purity and other doctrines that drive people to this state. In Pam's case, that's exactly what she did when she survived her suicide attempt. She left the Church altogether and became happier for it.

Historically, the Church leaned more heavily on the threat of physical death. Early leaders had apostates and detractors outright killed. As a kid, I remember thinking of the Nauvoo Legion, Porter Rockwell, and the Danites as wild-west frontier heroes, because they rode around smiting enemies of the Church. Later, I learned about the Mountain Meadows Massacre and other events during Brigham Young's era in which innocent people died under very suspicious circumstances.

In modern times, FLDS [4] groups and fringe Mormons commit murder using justification derived from LDS doctrine. Given the bulk of scriptures espousing violence, these conclusions are unsurprising.

There are certainly rumors and urban legends that the Danites still exist. According to Martha Beck, whenever Utah news reports certain types of murder, rumors flurry that the Danites did it.[5]

I doubt this is true, but the fear of it certainly exists, enough to make some vocal, prominent heretics a little afraid. Says Beck, "Even years later, writing this, I can feel the twinge of that old terror. I've read too much about the Danites, seen too many religious

---

1. Pam Kazmaier. "Losing My Mind, Bit by Bit," Aug 13, 2005. http://questioningmormonism.wordpress.com/2011/12/02/pam-kazmaier-losing-my-mind-bit-by-bit/
2. William Clayton. "Come, Come Ye Saints." In *Hymns of the Church of Jesus Christ of Latter-Day Saints*. The Church of Jesus Christ of Latter-Day Saints, 1985.
3. Kazmaier, "Losing My Mind," Aug 13, 2005.
4. Fundamentalist Mormons
5. Beck, *Leaving the Saints,* 2005. 190.

fanatics worship at my father's feet, taken too many death vows to think that Mormonism has no dark side. I don't think most people realize how much the Latter-day Saints' history of quietly perpetrated violence still resonates throughout the community, what a powerful agent of social control it still is."[1]

Steve Benson, another exmormon, famous for being a newspaper cartoonist and Ezra Taft Benson's grandson, was openly threatened with violence by members, often enough to get police protection.[2]

It is interesting that in the Plan of Salvation, we're told Lucifer wanted to force us all to choose the right, so there would be no sin, and no one would be lost. "Satan would have coerced us, and he would have robbed us of that most precious of gifts if he could: our freedom to choose a divine future and the exaltation we all hope to obtain."[3]

And yet, the definition of "coerce" is "to force to act or think in a certain way by use of pressure, threats, or intimidation."[4] The scriptures and the words of the prophets are full of threats, pressure, and intimidation. The message is, as Elder Keith B. McMullin said, "There is safety in being a Saint."[5]

I'm sure Elder N. Eldon Tanner intended gentle persuasion in saying, "Punishment and remorse, one way or another, will come to all who wander from the path of truth and righteousness..."[6] At least Lucifer was honest and transparent in framing his plan.

---

1. Beck, *Leaving the Saints,* 2005. 191.
2. Beck, *Leaving the Saints,* 2005. 242.
3. Howard W. Hunter. "The Golden Thread of Choice." In LDS General Conference, Oct 1989.
4. "Free Dictionary: Coerce." Accessed April 27, 2014. *The Free Dictionary*, n.d. http://www.thefreedictionary.com/coerce
5. Keith B. McMullin. "An Invitation with Promise." In LDS General Conference, April 2001. https://www.lds.org/general-conference/2001/04/an-invitation-with-promise
6. Tanner, "Why Is My Boy Wandering Tonight?" General Conference, Oct 1974.

*Let us here observe, that a religion that does not require the sacrifice of all things never has power sufficient to produce the faith necessary unto life and salvation.*
—**Joseph Smith,**
***Lectures on Faith***[1]

*Never again will you be capable of love, or friendship, or joy of living, or laughter, or curiosity, or courage, or integrity. You will be hollow. We shall squeeze you empty and then we shall fill you with ourselves.*
—**George Orwell, *1984***

*Going mute to protect the system doesn't keep you from being destroyed; it just means that you destroy yourself. 'What profiteth it a man,' Jesus said, 'if he should gain the whole world, and lose his own soul?'*
—**Martha Beck,**
***Leaving the Saints***[2]

*If you tell us we have to give our lives now, we're ready—all the rest of the sisters and brothers are with me.*
—**Unidentified man,**
**moments prior to the Jonestown massacre**[3]

# Doctrine Over Self

**Doctrine Over Self**
—*Suppression, Reinforcement, Group Identification, Influence*
- Suppresses and destabilizes the self
- Replaces identity
- Establishes total trust in leadership
- Builds dependence on the group
- Reinforces sacred science, milieu control, demand for purity
- Blinds member to deception
- Suppresses a connection with personal feelings
- Builds a foundation for the double-bind

In order for mind control to remain effective, one's personal core must not only be disintegrated (destabilization) and rebuilt in the image of the group (demand for purity), but the importance of the group must be elevated over individual needs, so that any dissonance arising from private doubts and feelings will resolve in favor of the group.

Steven Hassan defines doctrine over self simply, as "The imposition of group beliefs over individual experience, conscience, and integrity."[4]

*Captive Hearts* states, "...the goal of thought reform is for the subject to become one with the ideal."[5]

Lifton originally described this technique as "the totalist approach to changing people:

---

1. Joseph Smith. *Lectures on Faith*, 1835. http://eom.byu.edu/index.php/Lectures_on_Faith
2. Beck, *Leaving the Saints*, 2005. 191.
3. Maaga, "Jonestown 'Suicide Tape Transcript,'" Nov 18, 1978. http://employees.oneonta.edu/downinll/mass_suicide.htm
4. Hassan, *Releasing the Bonds*, 2000. 34.
5. Tobias and Lalich, *Captive Hearts, Captive Minds*, 1994. 47.

the demand that character and identity be reshaped, not in accordance with one's special nature or potentialities, but rather to fit the rigid contours of the doctrinal mold. The human is thus subjected to the ahuman."[1]

The true danger of thought reform is not that you are striving for an ideal, or that you believe in something. It is that your individuality and personality is swept away. The system is so universal and total that it ignores your unique talents, preferences, and learning styles when these differ from the ideal. The end goal is to obliterate who you are and replace you with a pseudopersonality. You can be unique, just like everyone else who is a righteous child of God.

> The underlying assumption is that the doctrine—including its mythological elements—is ultimately more valid, true, and real than is any aspect of actual human character or human experience. Thus, even when circumstances require that a totalist movement follow a course of action in conflict with or outside of the doctrine, there exists what Benjamin Schwartz described as a 'will to orthodoxy'...particularly the totalists' pattern of imposing their doctrine-dominated remolding upon people in order to seek confirmation of (and again, dispel their own doubts about) this same doctrine. Rather than modify the myth in accordance with experience, the will to orthodoxy requires instead that men be modified in order to reaffirm the myth.[2]

Allowing you to be yourself, outside certain limits, threatens everyone else's cognitive consonance. And they can't have that, because it threatens sacred science and the authority of leadership. Non-conformity can lead to doubts, and doubts can pull the whole machine apart.

> This primacy of doctrine over person is evident in the continual shift between experience itself and the highly abstract interpretation of such experience—between genuine feelings and spurious cataloguing of feelings. It has much to do with the peculiar aura of half-reality which totalist environment seems, at least to the outsider, to possess.
>
> The inspiriting force of such myths cannot be denied; nor can one ignore their capacity for mischief. For when the myth becomes fused with the totalist sacred science, the resulting 'logic' can be so compelling and coercive that it simply replaces the realities of individual experience.[3]

The forces of the system cause such a level of self-denial that perception of reality, and therefore reality itself, becomes distorted to comply with the group's beliefs. *Captive Hearts* reveals it is the "...denial of self and any perception other than the group's. There is no longer such a thing as personal reality. The past—society's and the individual's—is altered to fit the needs of the doctrine. Thus the individual is remolded, the cult persona emerges, and the person's sense of integrity is lost."[4]

Imagine how difficult it would be to leave after your very being has been restructured to become one with the group. I don't have to imagine. I went through it.

Doctrine over self causes tremendous discomfort in most individuals. "Attacking the inner person, the self, makes the person feel defective at his or her very core... The effect is that members become extremely anxious about self-worth and, at times, about their very existence. In such an environment it is easy to bring on feelings of personal disintegration."[5]

And in this environment, the individual becomes driven to resolve any discomfort by participating more zealously. "The individual person who finds himself under such

---

1. Lifton, *Thought Reform and the Psychology of Totalism*, 1961. (Chapter 22)
2. Lifton, *Thought Reform and the Psychology of Totalism*, 1961. (Chapter 22)
3. Lifton, *Thought Reform and the Psychology of Totalism*, 1961. (Chapter 22)
4. Tobias and Lalich, *Captive Hearts, Captive Minds*, 1994. 37.
5. Tobias and Lalich, *Captive Hearts, Captive Minds*, 1994. 37.

doctrine-dominated pressure to change is thrust into an intense struggle with his own sense of integrity, a struggle which takes place in relation to polarized feelings of sincerity and insincerity. In a totalist environment, absolute 'sincerity' is demanded; and the major criterion for sincerity is likely to be one's degree of doctrinal compliance—both in regard to belief and to direction of personal change."[1]

The group becomes the source of salvation from the perceived sins of self. "A systematic attack on the person's central self...tears apart the inner equilibrium and perception of reality. For some, the 'easiest way to reconstitute the self and obtain a new equilibrium is to 'identify with the aggressor' and accept the ideology of the authority figure who has reduced the person to a state of profound confusion. In effect, the new ideology...functions as a defense mechanism...and protects the individual from having to further directly inspect emotions from the past which are overwhelming."[2]

To what extent can a personality be replaced? This depends on the group and the individual. No study has been done of Mormonism specifically, but Steven Hassan observes that, "Cult mind control dissociates a person from his authentic identity... The cult member actually comes to exhibit symptoms of a 'dissociative disorder,' as defined in the...DSM-IV[3]. His behavior can also resemble that of a person with a dependent personality disorder..."[4]

Inner changes are assisted by outer changes. "The make-over often includes a new name, new clothes, new hair style, new manner of speech, new mannerisms, a new 'family,' new 'friends,' new thoughts, new emotions, and a new relationship with God."[5]

The authors of *The Guru Papers* say, "What is requisite...is a core of deep self-mistrust and even fear of oneself. Authoritarian moralities that denigrate the carnal and the self-centered implant the mind control that is necessary for such self-control. All mind control operates under the guise of self-control."[6]

In the Workers Democratic Union, Janja Lalich describes her experience with a haunting level of familiarity. "Self-denial was glorified as the only road to purification—that is, the ideal must always come before the individual. The message was: Be harsh to find goodness. Suffer to find happiness. Work hard to find freedom. Ruthlessness is kindness. Change yourself to fit the mold or be banished to the selfish fate of the rest of the world."[7]

And describing her brief encounter with the Moonies, Geri-Ann Galanti said, "...group doctrine is made to take precedence over everything a person has previously learned. The value of the individual is subordinated to the value of the group, its work, and its doctrine. In the context of the Unification Church, you're made to see how selfish it is to place yourself and your individual needs and wants first. We must think of others and of God before we think of ourselves. Individuality becomes linked with the notion of selfishness, the group with the concept of unselfishness. Our culture has taught us to believe that being selfish is bad and being unselfish is good; therefore, it is natural to learn to subjugate yourself for the good of the group in the name of being a 'good' person."[8] As she insightfully points out, the doctrine leverages an existing societal value.

As John Goldhammer remarks, "...the doctrine, the program, the mission, and the beliefs are *superior to the individual and always come first*. This is precisely the reverse of a healthy group where the individual comes first and the group fulfills a supportive role."[9]

The Utah state seal is Deseret, the beehive, representing the hard work and industry of the honeybee towards the building of the kingdom. It is important to note this symbol's

---

1. Lifton, *Thought Reform and the Psychology of Totalism*, 1961. (Chapter 22)
2. Tobias and Lalich, *Captive Hearts, Captive Minds*, 1994. 37-38.
3. The Diagnostic and Statistical Manual of Mental Disorders (4th Revision)
4. Hassan, *Releasing the Bonds*, 2000. 55.
5. Hassan, *Releasing the Bonds*, 2000. 56.
6. Joel Kramer, and Diana Alstad. *The Guru Papers: Masks of Authoritarian Power*. Berkeley, Calif.: North Atlantic Books/Frog, 1993. 225.
7. Lalich, "A Little Carrot and a Lot of Stick," *Recovery from Cults,* ed. Langone, 1995. 66-67.
8. Galanti, "Reflections on 'Brainwashing,'" *Recovery from Cults,* ed. Langone, 1995. 94.
9. Goldhammer, *Under the Influence,* 1996. 103.

collective nature. These are not individuals working together—they are subordinate to the central commander, mere extensions of the queen's mind. Never stopping to rest, they build the walls of the hive and care for larval children, who in turn grow up to serve the collective.

Marion Stricker writes, "In The Pattern, all individuals become an 'other' and are reduced to the lowest common denominator; individuals not keeping up with the herd are expendable... In Mormonism, no one leaves the 'ninety and nine to save one.'"[1]

Exmormons describe well what this feels like. Shauna Adix in *Leaving the Fold* said, "That's one of the problems about church membership—that it calls you to ignore your own truths so much of the time to heed what the brethren say."[2]

Martha Beck describes this prioritization of values: "I realized that the only way I'd kept from feeling angry as a child and adolescent was to believe that my natural reactions to these issues were hopelessly defective, innately wrong."[3] She later addressed the level of control members give up. "The belief in the unassailable virtue of helplessness runs very deep in Mormonism, as it does in any culture that tries to instill absolute obedience in its members."[4]

Online, "Chris" wrote, "I felt a vague sense that whatever I wanted, what I felt must be against God. I learned to alienate myself from myself. I learned to suppress my feelings, to shut myself down emotionally. That's perhaps the thing I'm most angry about now as I try to reconnect to myself, to repair all those years of psychic abuse and emotional neglect."[5]

And Pam Kazmaier wrote, "I lost my identity. I lost all sense of who I was as an individual with a right to sleep, pleasure, fun, joy. Being a mormon, de-humanized me. I was just a worker-bee, like in that beehive thing they use as their symbol. Rather than rest, I plodded on, just like a good pioneer woman... I was obedient to every rule... There had been so little time over the years, for myself, I had forgotten that I was even there at all."[6]

A large number of LDS teachings support doctrine over self, including:

- ⇅ The central Plan of Salvation: As sinners we cannot be redeemed without Jesus.
- ⇅ Obedience is vital for salvation.
- ⇅ Rigid roles for men and women were assigned in the preexistence[7].
- ⇅ Seek happiness through serving others.
- ⇅ Pray about everything. All decisions need God's approval.
- ⇅ Bishopric and Stake leaders hold power over personal decisions. (Some bishops do not abuse this power; others do.)
- ⇅ God gives each of us a special mission that we must fulfill on his behalf.

Doctrine over self is often presented alongside all other doctrines. Commandments such as tithing are taught using previously-instilled concepts of obedience, faith, humility, or selflessness.

A scripture I memorized in Seminary made the priorities very clear: "For the natural man is an enemy to God, and has been from the fall of Adam, and will be, forever and ever, unless he yields to the enticings of the Holy Spirit, and putteth off the natural man and becometh a saint through the atonement of Christ the Lord, and becometh as a child, submissive, meek, humble, patient, full of love, willing to submit to all things which the Lord seeth fit to inflict upon him, even as a child doth submit to his father." Mosiah 3:19

---

1. Stricker, *The Double-Bind in Mormonism*, 2000. 62.
2. James W. Ure. *Leaving the Fold: Candid Conversations with Inactive Mormons*. Salt Lake City, Utah: Signature Books, 1999. 162.
3. Beck, *Leaving the Saints*, 2005. 181.
4. Beck, *Leaving the Saints*, 2005. 195.
5. Stricker, *The Double-Bind in Mormonism*, 2000. 128. (Original quote from: http://www.exmormon.org/whylft65.htm)
6. Pam Kazmaier. "Losing My Mind, Bit by Bit," Aug 13, 2005.
http://questioningmormonism.wordpress.com/2011/12/02/pam-kazmaier-losing-my-mind-bit-by-bit/
7. Mormons believe that before we were born, we existed as spirits in heaven. This is known as the "preexistence."

Alma said, "Yea, I know that I am nothing; as to my strength I am weak; therefore I will not boast of myself, but I will boast of my God, for in his strength I can do all things..." Alma 26:12

Our purpose is to submit ourselves to God (and by proxy, the Church). "Your entire lives on earth are intended to give you the opportunity to learn to choose good over evil, service over selfishness, kindness and thoughtfulness over self-indulgence and personal gratification. By comparing your behavior and thoughts with your Father's standards, you are in a better position to govern yourselves and make the right choices. God's commandments (standards) are constant, unwavering, and dependable."[1] This quote originally came from the copy of *For the Strength of Youth* distributed during my teen years.

From Anne C. Pingree, Second Counselor in the Relief Society General Presidency: "I bear witness, my beloved sisters, that in order to truly be an instrument in the hands of God, in order to fully have that blessing bestowed upon us in 'the day of this life' in which we 'perform [our] labors,' we must, as Elder Maxwell says, 'finally submit ourselves' to the Lord...'

"In even the smallest details of each day, I submitted my will to the Lord's, for I so needed His help, His guidance, and His protection."[2]

The concept of being an instrument in God's hands is an oft-repeated dehumanizing metaphor. God will not let us be tools if we give any thought to ourselves. "For although a man may have many revelations, and have power to do many mighty works, yet if he boasts in his own strength, and sets at naught the counsels of God, and follows after the dictates of his own will and carnal desires, he must fall and incur the vengeance of a just God upon him." D&C 3:4

Neal A. Maxwell vilifies selfishness in a Conference talk:

> In one degree or another we all struggle with selfishness. Since it is so common, why worry about selfishness anyway? Because selfishness is really self-destruction in slow motion. No wonder the Prophet Joseph Smith urged, "Let every selfish feeling be not only buried, but annihilated." Hence annihilation—not moderation—is the destination!
>
> Surging selfishness, for example, has shrunken some people into ciphers; they seek to erase their emptiness by sensations. But in the arithmetic of appetite, anything multiplied by zero still totals zero! Each spasm of selfishness narrows one's universe that much more by reducing his awareness of or concern with others. In spite of its outward, worldly swagger, such indulgent individualism is actually provincial, like goldfish in a bowl congratulating themselves on their self-sufficiency, never mind the food pellets or changes of water.[3]

Certainly, it's not good to be too selfish. To what extent does Elder Maxwell believe we should take self*less*ness? Pretty far:

> ...consider unselfish Melissa Howes, whose comparatively young father died of cancer several months ago. Just before, Melissa, who was then nine, was voice in family prayer, pleading, "Heavenly Father, bless my daddy, and if you need him more than us, you can have him. We want him, but Thy will be done. And please help us not to be mad at you".
>
> What spiritual submissiveness for one so young! What an unselfish understanding of the plan of salvation! May unselfish submissiveness be our path too...

---

1. *Preparing for an Eternal Marriage Teacher Manual*. The Church of Jesus Christ of Latter Day Saints, 2003. Chapter 4. https://www.lds.org/manual/preparing-for-an-eternal-marriage-teacher-manual/4-the-lords-standards-for-dating
2. Anne C. Pingree. "Knowing the Lord's Will for You." In LDS General Conference, Oct 2005. http://www.lds.org/general-conference/2005/10/knowing-the-lords-will-for-you
3. Neal A. Maxwell. "'Repent of [Our] Selfishness' (D&C 56:8)." In LDS General Conference, April 1999.

Like Abraham, we should be willing to sacrifice our family members, somehow in the name of altruism.

Self-denial is a high virtue in Mormonism. As the hymn says, "'Tis better far for us to strive, Our useless cares from us to drive."[1]

In Conference, we heard, "Possibly the most lost of all is the wanderer who has failed through lack of desire or determination to discipline himself. His wilderness is dark and desolate indeed, and he will stumble and fall again and again until he emerges as master of himself."[2]

And, "A young mother once turned to a wise old man for advice. "What should I teach my son?" she asked. The man replied, 'Teach him to deny himself.'"[3]

Boyd K. Packer spoke to the All-Church Coordinating Committee, asking specialists to obey the counsel of the Brethren and the Correlation Council, even if it goes against their own expert opinions. "Could you believe other than it is critical that all of us work together and set aside personal interests and all face the same way?"[4]

More subtle methods can stir up subconscious social pressures to promote a collective sense that the needs of the many outweigh the needs of the one.

For instance, many cults give members a new name, or discourage use of first names. Lalich describes that in her political group, she was instructed to give herself a new first name. "For the new member, taking on a party name was the first stage in losing his or her preparty identity and taking on a party-molded one."[5]

The LDS tradition of calling people by their last name is a way of accomplishing the same thing. All signs of personal intimacy become inaccessible except in families or in the closest of friendships. The formal system of "Brother Young" and "Sister Smith" creates a barrier between individuals and further enforces the sense that everyone is merely an extension of the group. Even co-workers generally don't establish this kind of distance or depersonalization.

It's worse for missionaries. "Our first names were strictly off limits at all times throughout our mission. We all had a drastic new look and a new identity, which was, I suppose, a purposeful attempt to make us believe we were all different from the boys we had been back home, in the hope that it would cause us to behave differently as well."[6]

Receiving a new name in the temple is another way of washing away the old identity. The granting of a new or secret name is a common practice in many initiation ceremonies worldwide. A new name reminds the member he has an identity to strive for that he himself may not be familiar with, but that God knows more intimately. A new name encourages disassociation from the member's true identity, and enables self-definition to be directed by an outside authority.

Loss of selfhood can also be implied in how ideas are framed. For example, the Young Women's value of Individual Worth seems to speak positively to the idea of having your own personality. "I am of infinite worth with my own divine mission, which I will strive to fulfill."[7] Yet in the related Personal Progress chapter, a girl's value is couched mostly in terms of her relationship to Heavenly Father, her patriarchal blessing, her future in the Church, family history, and in her ability to make others feel worthy. Talents are discussed as God-given gifts. Based on this, a teen girl may draw the conclusion, either consciously or subconsciously, that without God and the Church, she isn't worth much at all.

The Young Women's lesson on how to choose a career advises that girls first learn about themselves, and then immediately says, "We should avoid vocations that would

---

1. Clayton, "Come, Come Ye Saints," *Hymns*, 1985.
2. N. Eldon Tanner. "Why Is My Boy Wandering Tonight?" In LDS General Conference, Oct 1974.
3. Bruce C. Hafen, and Marie K. Hafen. "'Bridle All Your Passions.'" *Ensign*, Feb 1994. http://www.lds.org/ensign/1994/02/bridle-all-your-passions
4. Elder Boyd K. Packer. "Talk to the All-Church Coordinating Council," 1993. http://lds-mormon.com/face.shtml
5. Lalich, "A Little Carrot and a Lot of Stick," *Recovery from Cults,* ed. Langone, 1995. 67.
6. Worthy, *The Mormon Cult,* 2008. 83.
7. *Young Women Personal Progress*. The Church of Jesus Christ of Latter Day Saints, 2009.

require us to compromise our values or turn us from our eternal goals."[1] "Our values" means group values, not individual values. This of course comes after young women are firmly instructed that their primary vocation is to raise a family.

Homosexual Mormons undergo an extreme suppression of the self. Current church policy (as of 2012) is that having "same sex attraction" is not a choice. But under no circumstances should a faithful Mormon act on it.[2] Though one of the greatest blessings the Church promises is a temple marriage, homosexuals are not allowed to have relationships or marry who they want. If you are LDS and gay, you are denied these blessings, and instead are asked to make a straight marriage work.

Your position in the eternal scheme, when it comes to tithing, is unquestionable. "When a friend of President George Albert Smith asked him what he thought of his friend's personal plan to take what would have been tithing and donate his tenth in charitable donations of his own choice, President Smith's counsel was:

> "I think you are a very generous man with someone else's property... You have told me what you have done with the Lord's money but you have not told me that you have given anyone a penny of your own. He is the best partner you have in the world. He gives you everything you have, even the air you breathe. He has said you should take one-tenth of what comes to you and give it to the Church as directed by the Lord. You haven't done that; you have taken your best partner's money, and have given it away."[3]

As we were instructed, tithing is training wheels for the eventual full implementation of the Law of Consecration, which we committed to in the temple:

> You and each of you covenant and promise before God, angels, and these witnesses at this altar, that you do accept the Law of Consecration as contained in the Doctrine and Covenants, in that you do consecrate yourselves, your time, talents, and everything with which the Lord has blessed you, or with which he may bless you, to the Church of Jesus Christ of Latter-day Saints, for the building up of the Kingdom of God on the earth and for the establishment of Zion.[4]

And in the Law of Sacrifice:

> ...as Jesus Christ has laid down his life for the redemption of mankind, so we should covenant to sacrifice all that we possess, even our own lives if necessary, in sustaining and defending the Kingdom of God...

As discussed in the previous chapter, some sins are worse than death. Virtue is valued higher than life because eternity hangs in the balance. President J. Reuben Clark, in a 1938 Conference talk, said, "Please believe me when I say that chastity is worth more than life itself. This is the doctrine my parents taught me; it is truth. Better die chaste than live unchaste. The salvation of your very souls is concerned in this."[5]

Spencer W. Kimball repeated this sentiment in *The Miracle of Forgiveness*, in several places, including on the topic of rape. "Your virtue is worth more than your life. Please, young folk, preserve your virtue even if you lose your lives."[6]

Church members also learn to deny themselves through fasting, which teaches self-sacrifice on a visceral level. "Each time we fast, we gain a little more control over our worldly appetites and passions."[7]

---

1. *Young Women Manual 3*. The Church of Jesus Christ of Latter Day Saints, 1994. "Lesson 45: Choosing a Vocation" http://www.lds.org/manual/young-women-manual-3/managing-personal-resources/lesson-45-choosing-a-vocation
2. "Love One Another: A Discussion on Same-Sex Attraction." Accessed April 10, 2014. http://www.mormonsandgays.org/
3. Robert D. Hales. "Tithing: A Test of Faith with Eternal Blessings." In LDS General Conference, Oct 2002.
4. "Mormon Temple Covenants." Accessed Aug 21, 2013. http://lds4u.com/lesson5/templecovenants.htm
5. President Marion G. Romney. "We Believe in Being Chaste." *Ensign*, Sept 1981.
6. Spencer W. Kimball, *The Miracle of Forgiveness*, 1969. 63, 196.
7. Joseph B. Wirthlin. "The Law of the Fast." In LDS General Conference, April 2001. http://www.lds.org/general-conference/2001/04/the-law-of-the-fast

But it isn't really "self" control when the coercive influence comes from the group. "Nevertheless they did fast and pray oft, and did wax stronger and stronger in their humility, and firmer and firmer in the faith of Christ, unto the filling their souls with joy and consolation, yea, even to the purifying and the sanctification of their hearts, which sanctification cometh because of their yielding their hearts unto God." Helaman 3:35

Fasting is directly tied to the concept of selflessness. "Fasting can help us become more humble, less prideful, less selfish, and more concerned about the needs of others. It can help us see more clearly our own mistakes and weaknesses and help us be less prone to criticize others."[1]

The practice of fasting reinforces the spirit/body duality concept, the idea that the carnal is evil and the spirit is sublime. "For we know that the law is spiritual: but I am carnal, sold under sin." Romans 7:14

"And I would not that ye think that I know of myself—not of the temporal but of the spiritual, not of the carnal mind but of God." Alma 36:4

We were taught that all personal suffering is for the greater good. In the *New Era*,

> Elder Orson F. Whitney wrote: "No pain that we suffer, no trial that we experience is wasted. It ministers to our education, to the development of such qualities as patience, faith, fortitude, and humility. All that we suffer...builds up our characters, purifies our hearts, expands our souls, and makes us more tender and charitable, more worthy to be called the children of God...and it is through sorrow and suffering, toil and tribulation, that we gain the education which will make us more like our Father and Mother in heaven..."
>
> Obedience may be learned from suffering... Superior blessings from God are dependent upon our being severely tried and tested. Suffering may lead us to put our trust in the Lord and to keep his commandments. Of course, Alma suggests we can learn obedience without first being humbled by experiences, but many of us need help.[2]

Philosophies like this teach that suffering, sorrow, pain, and distress are fine, because the greater reward will come after this life. When combined with ideals of selflessness and spirit/body duality, it can lead to depression and self-destructive behaviors. While there are commandments against being idle, there is no commandment against self-abasing thoughts, sleep deprivation, eating disorders, cutting, and wishing for death.

Many times I wished I could just hurry up and die. But there was a commandment against doing the job myself, so I could find relief nowhere but in following the commandments even harder than before. The solace I found there was fleeting.

No doctrine is more important than the health and happiness of each member. You cannot fill the cup of others if your own cup is empty. No matter your beliefs, you exist independently of any group. Your value is derived from being you, not from earning the approval of those you associate with.

---

1. Carl B. Pratt. "The Blessings of a Proper Fast." In LDS General Conference, Oct 2004. http://www.lds.org/general-conference/2004/10/the-blessings-of-a-proper-fast
2. Kenneth H. Bessley. "What Is the Purpose of Suffering?" *New Era*, April 1975. http://www.lds.org/new-era/1975/04/what-is-the-purpose-of-suffering

*Then the face of Big Brother faded away again and instead the three slogans of the Party stood out in bold capitals:*

*WAR IS PEACE*
*FREEDOM IS SLAVERY*
*IGNORANCE IS STRENGTH*

—George Orwell, *1984*

*Obedience to Law is Liberty.*

—Title of a General Conference talk
given by Apostle L. Tom Perry, April 2013

*Recently I received a letter from a friend of over 50 years who is not a member of our church. I had sent him some gospel-related reading, to which he responded: 'Initially it was hard for me to follow the meaning of typical Mormon jargon, such as agency. Possibly a short vocabulary page would be helpful.'*
*I was surprised he did not understand what we mean by the word agency.*

—Robert D. Hales,
*Agency: Essential to the Plan of Life*[1]

# Loading the Language

**Loading the Language**
—*Suppression, Silencing Doubts, Group Identification, Influence*
- Creates new pathways of thought to circumvent criticism, doubt, contradiction, awareness of options
- Isolates the member from the outside world
- Bolsters group identification via common linguistic culture
- Suppression and reframing of emotions
- Enables manipulation of thoughts

Each word is an entire package filled with implication, emotion, metaphor, and experience.

A high demand group uses its own complex vocabulary, a mix of invented words and phrases to convey complicated symbolism and doctrines, and existing words which have been redefined either subtly or dramatically.

Loaded language serves several purposes:

- Reframes meanings accepted by greater society
- Shuts down critical thinking
- Isolates members, making it difficult to communicate with outsiders

Mormons believe totalitarianism is evil, but through loaded language, they are deluded into accepting their own dictators as benevolent. As George Orwell demonstrated through the fictional language "newspeak", words are thinking tools. "Don't you see that the whole aim of Newspeak is to narrow the range of thought? In the end we shall make thoughtcrime

---

1. Robert D. Hales. "Agency: Essential to the Plan of Life." In LDS General Conference, Oct 2010.

literally impossible, because there will be no words in which to express it."[1]

If there was no word for "freedom" or "truth", no one could think about these things, much less fight for them. People would be imprisoned without any means of escape, or even understanding that there was anything to escape from. Orwell's dystopia takes this concept to an extreme, where the authoritarian government eliminates all words not required for production and survival. Cults do not have this level of total influence; nevertheless, loading the language is very effective. Altering the meanings of "freedom" and "truth" serve just as well.

Loaded language is the "...use of jargon internal to—and only understandable by—the group. Constricting language constricts the person. Capacities for thinking and feeling are significantly reduced. Imagination is no longer a part of one's actual life experiences; the mind atrophies from disuse."[2]

Words are often the filters through which we experience the world. By loading the language, the filter changes. Through this, "Our thoughts automatically interpret what we experience and feel."[3]

Robert J. Lifton, who originally identified this method, goes into further detail. "For an individual person, the effect of the language of ideological totalism can be summed up in one word: constriction. He is, so to speak, linguistically deprived; and since language is so central to all human experience, his capacities for thinking and feeling are immensely narrowed. This is what Hu meant when he said, 'using the same pattern of words for so long...you feel chained.' Actually, not everyone feels chained, but in effect everyone is profoundly confined by these verbal fetters. As in other aspects of totalism, this loading may provide an initial sense of insight and security, eventually followed by uneasiness. This uneasiness may result in a retreat into a rigid orthodoxy in which an individual shouts the ideological jargon all the louder in order to demonstrate his conformity..."[4]

To some extent, words always serve these purposes, to filter, to unify, to persuade, and shape thought. "...this kind of language exists to some degree within any cultural or organizational group, and all systems of belief depend upon it. It is in part an expression of unity and exclusiveness..." But Lifton makes an important distinction. "The loading is much more extreme in ideological totalism...since the jargon expresses the claimed certitudes of the sacred science."[5]

Steven Hassan draws this line at the level of control, where "The use of vocabulary constrict[s] members' thinking into absolute, black-and-white, 'thought-terminating clichés' understood only by insiders."[6]

Indeed, another manipulation tool, the thought-terminating cliché, is a specific implementation of loaded language, as is its use for reframing and manipulating of emotions.

Emotionally charged labels can make a concept seem inherently positive or inherently negative. It is impossible to use certain words without passing instant moral judgment. People who are "righteous", "spiritual", or "faithful" are automatically good. Those who are "stiffnecked", "inactive", or "immodest" are automatically bad. Thoughts around these topics become restricted.

Goldhammer states, "Language becomes the collective weapon of choice. By naming the enemy, we infer they are guilty, judged and sentenced without trial."[7]

According to Lifton, "The most far-reaching and complex of human problems are compressed into brief, highly reductive, definitive-sounding phrases, easily memorized and easily expressed. These become the start and finish of any ideological analysis. In [Chinese

---

1. Orwell, *1984*.
2. Tobias and Lalich, *Captive Hearts, Captive Minds*, 1994. 37.
3. Tobias and Lalich, *Captive Hearts, Captive Minds*, 1994. 95.
4. Lifton, *Thought Reform and the Psychology of Totalism*, 1961. (Chapter 22)
5. Lifton, *Thought Reform and the Psychology of Totalism*, 1961. (Chapter 22)
6. Hassan, *Releasing the Bonds*, 2000. 34.
7. Goldhammer, *Under the Influence*, 1996. 177.

Communist] thought reform, for instance, the phrase 'bourgeois mentality' is used to encompass and critically dismiss ordinarily troublesome concerns like the quest for individual expression, the exploration of alternative ideas, and the search for perspective and balance in political judgments. And in addition to their function as interpretive shortcuts, these clichés become what Richard Weaver has called 'ultimate terms': either 'god terms,' representative of ultimate good; or 'devil terms,' representative of ultimate evil. In [Chinese Communist] thought reform, 'progress,' 'progressive,' 'liberation,' 'proletarian standpoints' and 'the dialectic of history' fall into the former category; 'capitalist,' 'imperialist,' 'exploiting classes,' and 'bourgeois' (mentality, liberalism, morality, superstition, greed) of course fall into the latter. Totalist language then, is repetitiously centered on all-encompassing jargon, prematurely abstract, highly categorical, relentlessly judging, and to anyone but its most devoted advocate, deadly dull: in Lionel Trilling's phrase, 'the language of nonthought.'"[1]

Goldhammer writes, "By using a unique vocabulary, the group mind reaches its tentacles deep inside the individual's psyche, limiting one's ability to express any feelings, ideas, and emotions except in ways that substantiate the group's viewpoint. This mental reprogramming also has the effect of making previously acquired knowledge useless unless it happens to fit within group parameters and definitions."[2] He also calls this "polarizing jargon."

In Lalich's political group, they said, "Ours is a hard calling and a stern discipline: It is also liberation."[3] Straight is the gate, narrow is the way. Put your shoulder to the wheel. Obedience is liberty.

As Lalich shows, loaded language restricts criticism. "...questions, should there be any, had to be couched within an overall agreement. After years of this process, party members became incapable of any kind of critical thinking. They could only parrot one another and had shrunken vocabularies riddled with arcane internal phraseology."[4]

Very thought-limiting indeed. And isolating. "Loaded language...creates barriers to communication with others."[5] This isolation technique helps you be in the world but not of it. You can interact with nonmembers, but your mind is apart from them, because your very words are different from theirs. With all the talk of Nephites, endowments, priesthood, wards and stakes, sweet spirits, temples, dispensations, cultural halls, mutual, callings, ordinances, quorums, atonements, sacraments, and garments, outsiders may have difficulty relating to Mormons. Likewise, Mormons will tend to better enjoy the company of other people who understand their dialect.

On the lighter side, Orson Scott Card defined "prayerspeak" in his satirical Saintspeak dictionary: "A highly elevated language used in Mormon prayers. It consists of a limited repertoire of incantatory phrases, a mystical vocabulary of long or archaic words that are rarely understood by anyone, and a grammar built around the misuse of the second person singular pronoun... The mystical vocabulary consists of frequently repeated words like which, preserve, gracious, endeavor, numberless, and bounteous. Especially daring speakers even venture to use the really potent words: wast, wouldst, shalt, hath, hast, and art, to name a few. These words all derive from the English language, but they have lost all meaning. Rather, they are used to impart an aura of spirituality and exaltation to the prayer, and, when used, someone fluent in Prayerspeak, can make a perfectly common public prayer into an ecstatic musical experience."[6]

It's funny because it's true.

All humor aside, the effect of loaded words can be powerful. In some cases, "...changing

---

1. Lifton, *Thought Reform and the Psychology of Totalism*, 1961. (Chapter 22)
2. Goldhammer, *Under the Influence*, 1996. 74.
3. Lalich, "A Little Carrot and a Lot of Stick," *Recovery from Cults*, ed. Langone, 1995. 67.
4. Lalich, "A Little Carrot and a Lot of Stick," *Recovery from Cults*, ed. Langone, 1995. 70.
5. Tobias and Lalich, *Captive Hearts, Captive Minds*, 1994. 94.
6. Orson Scott Card. *Saintspeak, the Mormon Dictionary*. Salt Lake City, Utah: Orion Books, 1981.

the meanings of words produces anxiety and self-doubt..."[1] For those who leave the group, these words can later trigger a negative emotional response. "Sometimes when a former member unexpectedly encounters the cult's language, she or he may dissociate or experience a variety of feelings: confusion, anxiety, terror, guilt, shame, or rage."[2]

Ex-members may need to examine, work through, and release these pent-up feelings. Among other things, this can be done by exploring the coercive use of those words.

Words are my passion, and I'd love the space to dissect all LDS phrases. I've selected some of the more obvious examples, but the list is not inclusive.

From a Conference talk entitled, "Obedience to Law is Liberty", L. Tom Perry said, "Men and women receive their agency as a gift from God, but their liberty and, in turn, their eternal happiness come from obedience to His laws."[3] To anyone outside the Church, this sounds downright Orwellian, a contradictory redefinition, "doublespeak."

Here, Elder Perry sounds like Jareth the Goblin King from the movie *Labyrinth*, who said, "I ask for so little. Just let me rule you, and you can have everything that you want... Just fear me, love me, do as I say, and I will be your slave." As seductive as this sounds, we know that the roles will be reversed, that Sarah will be enslaved by Jareth. This scene very effectively portrays manipulation in action: the doublespeak, double-binds, reversal of logic, guilt-tripping, and empty but beguiling promises.

In defense, Sarah responds, "For my will is as strong as yours, my kingdom as great..." She struggles to remember the last line, almost as if some enchantment occludes it. Then she summons the powerful reply, "You have no power over me." These are magic words, because through them, Sarah asserts her own authority and declares her independence. The clock strikes thirteen and the world turns right-side-up. Sarah is home.

Supposedly God designed every commandment to maximize free agency. Obedience to authority then becomes synonymous with freedom. In fact, the word "commandment" is often avoided. Conference talks often employ phrases like, "I invite you to..." or "I encourage you..." but everyone hears, "You'd better do it, or else," especially in the context of the rest of the talk, which is padded in very serious terms.

Sentences like, "I invite you to pay your tithing to the Lord first, before you meet any other financial obligations," is in a talk entitled "The *Law* of Tithing" (emphasis added), which also includes sentences like, "To fail to meet this obligation in full is to deny ourselves the promises and is to omit a weighty matter. It is a transgression, not an inconsequential oversight."[4]

Similar forms of doublespeak abound throughout the doctrine. "In marriage, neither the man nor the woman is more important than the other—they are equal partners, although the man is the head of the house."[5]

The Church's discipline arm is called the Court of Love, which seems like a warm, caring place... and for some it is. Others have found harsh judgment, attacks on character, accusations without evidence, and intimidation. This is reminiscent of *1984*'s "Ministry of Love", the discipline arm of Big Brother, where dissidents are reeducated and brought into line.

The LDS concept of discipline is reframed in many ways. Here is another example of the word being softened: "It saddens me when I hear how some of our members and even sometimes our local leaders treat people who have to be disciplined for transgression. I realize there is a tendency to equate the word discipline with the word punish, but there is a difference between these words. In English, at least, the word discipline has the same root as the word disciple. A disciple is a student, to be taught. In dealing with transgressors, we

---

1. Tobias and Lalich, *Captive Hearts, Captive Minds,* 1994. 95.
2. Tobias and Lalich, *Captive Hearts, Captive Minds,* 1994. 94.
3. L. Tom Perry. "Obedience to Law Is Liberty." In LDS General Conference, April 2013. http://www.lds.org/general-conference/2013/04/obedience-to-law-is-liberty
4. Daniel L. Johnson. "The Law of Tithing." In LDS General Conference, Oct 2006. http://www.lds.org/general-conference/2006/10/the-law-of-tithing
5. *Gospel Principles.* The Church of Jesus Christ of Latter Day Saints, 1985. 226.

must remember that they desperately need to be taught."[1] Yet the primary definition of "discipline" in Merriam-Webster is, "control that is gained by requiring that rules or orders be obeyed and punishing bad behavior." Often Church leaders use the root of a word to help redefine it, ignoring the importance of common modern usage.

Perhaps in this chapter I am twisting the words of God's servants, or perhaps they twisted them in the first place and I am untwisting them. "Twisting" and "the Lord's servants" are two more loaded phrases that terminate thought.

Missionary "discussions" imply interactive dialog, but instead, memorized prefab lessons are given by rote. Questions are allowed, but the answers are listed in the manual.

Members are cautioned not to "entertain" doubts—this word implies two things: That doubts are trivial, like entertainment, and that doubts shouldn't be allowed even guest-entry into the home of the mind. There is no acknowledgement that doubt often leads to discovery, invention, correction, and self-improvement.

To nonmembers, "eternal life" means to live forever. To Mormons, it specifically means exalted life with Heavenly Father. Everyone else gets to live forever, too, but not with God. The implication is that non-exalted people have "non-eternal life." But since "eternal" still means forever, this implies imperfect people aren't actually immortal. Confused yet? Loaded language confuses thinking and obfuscates contradictions. If you ask a Mormon if unrighteous people will live forever, they will say yes. Is the afterlife like heaven, even for the unrighteous? Yes. Yet Mormons are still terrified of missing the mark. Scriptures bolster this implied meaning by explicitly stating that to fail God is death. It's a shell game of words.

"Your body is a temple." First, "temples" are beautiful, sacred, holy, white, the House of the Lord, a dwelling for the spirit. Anyone entering a temple is stepping into heaven where no impurity is allowed. Now we apply that one word, with its concepts, images, and emotions, to "your body." It must be sacred and pure all the time. The Holy Ghost belongs there every moment. It should be heaven on earth constantly. What pressure! If you don't feel the Spirit right this very minute... Well, it's not the temple's fault. It must be something unclean you allowed in.

Emotions are easily manipulated by linking concepts. Disgust is a powerful emotion of avoidance that can be evoked by using words like "filth", "unclean", and "toxic." "Thus, excess of ego is like a spreading, toxic spill from which flow all the deadly sins."[2] By equating sin with disgust, we can replace natural feelings of desire and love with revulsion.

"Uplifting" is a term that refers to books, movies, and music that support faith and evoke the Spirit. Uplifting experiences include Church meetings, temple attendance, and sometimes the family camping trip. Uplifting books include scriptures, Deseret publications, Church magazines, Ann of Green Gables, some classic literature (like Charles Dickens), and any self-help book as long as it is written by Steven Covey. Uplifting movies include anything from the ward library and almost anything rated G or PG, especially if it involves horses. Uplifting music is severely limited to hymns, classical, and the Janice Kapp Perry genre. All other media are considered "unclean" and may "desensitize" the mind.

"Father" is also an emotive word, which projects existing feelings for our earthly father onto God. So we either love God, or respect him, or even fear him. God "loves you"—if you reject him, you reject love.

"Endure to the end" is something all Mormons must do. This implies a life of constant suffering and temptation. I always envisioned a torture rack, and that all I had to do was hold on to my principles until I finally died. It implies passive acceptance rather than action. Things are being done to you which need resisting. It never seemed to imply active, conscious participation in life. The best strategy involved deadening emotions and awareness.

---

1. Theodore M. Burton. "Let Mercy Temper Justice." In LDS General Conference, Oct 1985.
2. Neal A. Maxwell. "'Deny Yourselves of All Ungodliness.'" In LDS General Conference, April 1985.
http://www.lds.org/general-conference/1995/04/deny-yourselves-of-all-ungodliness

"Immorality" is a Church euphemism for sexual impurity. In the outside world, immoral acts include lying, cheating, stealing, killing, and abusing others. When the Church limits this word specifically to sexual acts, discussion of the moral aspects of other acts is restricted and the depravity of sex is overemphasized.

"Reverent" means receptive, and "receptive to the Spirit" means ready to trust and believe what is about to be said. "Forgiveness" seemed to be more about enabling abusive behavior than anything else. "Faith" means to rely on emotion and remain gullible to anything coming from ordained men who claim to speak for God.

A "calling" is an unpaid Church job. It implies divine command, a special request from on high. To refuse is to defy God's will. A calling is "ordained" and "sacred." So you'd better accept it. Saying "no" to what is actually an "unpaid job" is not an option.

The Church refers to "gifts", which may be talents and skills, or blessings. Being LDS itself is a "gift", so unhappy feelings must not be coming from the Church. Be grateful. After all, it's a gift.

"Dissent" literally means to "differ in opinion or feeling; disagree", or "to withhold assent or approval." Yet to Mormons, this is a harsh word, implying outright rebellion and hatred against God and the Church.

Those who criticize the Church are "persecuting", which implies hatred. The dictionary says persecution is to "oppress or harass with ill-treatment" or to "annoy persistently."[1] Mormons consider critical books, websites, and support groups to be persecution. Others might call it "public discourse."

Many LDS words are loaded with elitism, for instance, "Saint", "elder", "high priest", "elect", and "child of God."

Other words denote shame. The word "worthy" implies self-worth; "unworthy" implies worthless, and you must be "purified" to be clean again. This requires the "Redeemer", aka the "Savior", who will save you from your "lost and fallen state." Then you will be "sanctified", which means to be made holy.

To go against the "Word of Wisdom" automatically means you are acting unwisely. Your spouse is an "eternal companion." Secret is "sacred." Weird is "peculiar" or "elect." Submission is "meekness." Giving time to the Church is "service." Criticism is "contention" or "murmuring" or "backbiting" or "tearing down God's Church." Listening to your inner voice is "selfish pride" or "hardening your heart" or "stiffnecked" or "backsliding." Being normal is "worldly." Homosexuality is "same-sex attraction" (formerly known as "a choice"). Following the commandments is to have "standards", to set an "example."

A "forever family" looks perfect from the outside. "Sustaining authority" means you commit to follow and support a leader, even if you don't agree. Your "lot in life" is either your personal mission or your burdens and temptations, depending on when you ask. And of course, you will only receive a witness after a "trial of your faith" which is a biased way to say "doubt and questioning." The Church wasn't "founded", instead the gospel was "restored." Joseph Smith didn't write the Book of Mormon, he "translated" it.

There are hundreds of other loaded words. If you find triggering or confusing terms, look them up in the dictionary and search online to see how mainstream society and other groups use them. Think about how the word may have been used to stifle thought, manipulate your feelings, reframe ideas, or filter your worldview.

---

1. "Free Dictionary: Persecute." Accessed April 27, 2014. *The Free Dictionary*, n.d. http://www.thefreedictionary.com/persecute

*Woe unto them that call evil good, and good evil; that put darkness for light, and light for darkness; that put bitter for sweet, and sweet for bitter!*
—Isaiah 5:20

*Why should we mourn or think our lot is hard? 'Tis not so, all is right... And should we die, before our journey's through, Happy day! All is well!*
—*Come, Come, Ye Saints*,
LDS Hymn #30[1]

*Some months I've tried to keep this thing from happening. But I now see it's the will—it's the will of Sovereign Being that this happen to us... That we lay down our lives to protest at what's being done.*
—Jim Jones,
moments before the Jonestown massacre[2]

# Totalist Reframing

**Totalist Reframing**
*—Suppression, Influence, Silencing Doubts*

- Context of events and emotions are controlled
- Explains cognitions in a new light to change meaning
- Similar to mystical manipulation, loading the language
- Dismisses or alters disconfirming information
- Reinforces existing beliefs
- Assists in indoctrination
- Suppresses or changes emotions
- Twists logic and reality to fit the expectations of the group
- Can reframe events to support the group
- Can reframe emotions to seem as though they are coming from some other source
- Can redirect negative emotions, such as anger, away from the intended target
- Suppresses critical thinking
- Confuses reality
- A type of deception
- Reinforces many other mechanisms

It is human nature to assign meaning wherever we can. We find patterns based upon our own experiences and cognitive frame.

Reframing is when others infuse events and concepts with their own meanings in an attempt to persuade. A new frame casts matters in a different light. This is normally a healthy part of social discourse, a persuasive and artistic tool that can lead to new insights. For instance, in chapter one, I reframed the Garden of Eden story as a dystopia to provoke thought and shake up old beliefs.

*Totalist* reframing attempts to imbue everything with group meanings. The frame is continually directed by a single source guiding you exclusively towards their all-encompassing conclusion. It is the force that turns each sign to "Yes." It can be rooted in deception, though it often arises naturally as the resolution to dissonance. When reframes are detached enough from reality, they become cognitive distortions.

Cult researchers have not identified this as a mind control technique, but reframing is

---

1. Clayton, "Come, Come Ye Saints," *Hymns*, 1985.
2. Maaga, "Jonestown 'Suicide Tape Transcript,'" Nov 18, 1978. http://employees.oneonta.edu/downinll/mass_suicide.htm

essential to coercive persuasion. In order to manipulate, you must get people to see the world through your filter, and that can only be done by shifting the frame of all incoming cognitions—experiences, information, feelings, and events—to the exclusive benefit of the group. This thread underlies all other methods. Some, like loaded language, mystical manipulation, and black and white thinking, *are* reframes.

The Church tries to frame everything into the context of itself and puts members into the habit of doing the same. Even events, ideas, and beliefs that occur outside LDS context always have to be about the Church. "Everything that is good in this world is part of the gospel of Jesus Christ."[1]

Mormons believe modern advances in communication fulfill prophecy to bring the gospel to the four corners of the earth. They carefully pattern-match news from the Middle East to revelations about the Second Coming. They believe the Constitution was divinely inspired so that religious freedom could pave the way for Joseph Smith's restoration. Every time a country moves towards democracy, it's so God can open a mission there. The Communists were inspired by Satan, trying to play out his evil plan to enforce righteousness. The Civil Rights Movement is an extension of that plot. The War on Terror is a continuation of the War in Heaven.

"In short," observes Chris Morin, "Mormons were at the center of the universe, the focus of both good and evil forces."[2]

Emotions are regularly reframed by the Church. All good feelings (except sexual desire) come from God, and bad feelings are signs of evil. Warmth, peace, love, certainty, humility, and serenity aren't *yours*, they're God's. Doubt, confusion, unhappiness, anger, hatred, fear, and guilt are all your own, or if not, they're Satan's.

"For behold, at that day shall he [the devil] rage in the hearts of the children of men, and stir them up to anger against that which is good." 2 Nephi 28:20

Romantic love is reframed as "feelings of forever", a sure sign you've discovered your eternal companion whom you must have known in the preexistence. *Saturday's Warrior* poked fun at this idea, when Julie falls for different men, each time sure that he is The One. Then she finally meets Tod, who really *is* her preordained companion. It made me cry every time. It *still* does.

All forms of love are regularly defined as "The Spirit. " Here is blatant emotional reframing in a family home evening lesson:

> When we do what is right, we get that good, warm feeling...That is the Holy Ghost letting us know that Heavenly Father and Jesus Christ are real...
>
> Direct your children...toward a time when they had a special experience that made them feel good. If they can't think of anything, tell the following story...
>
> Would you like to hold your new brother?' grandmother asked Lindsay as she placed the baby on her lap. 'Lindsay, you know this baby boy was with Heavenly Father just a few short days ago. Heavenly Father sent him to our family to love, guide, and train. You must always be kind and good to him.'
>
> As Lindsay held her new brother and looked at him, she had a good, warm feeling inside. She knew Heavenly Father had sent her little brother to their family.[3]

This little girl simply felt love for her brother, which the Church compels parents to use in a frame of testimony-building.

Other normal emotions encompass "The Spirit", like excitement, consonance, and peace. "The [youth] conference ended with many of the youth expressing gratitude for

---

1. "Article of Faith 13." *Friend*, Dec 2011. https://www.lds.org/friend/2011/12/article-of-faith-13
2. Morin and Morin, *Suddenly Strangers,* 2004. 126.
3. *Family Home Evening Resource Book*. The Church of Jesus Christ of Latter Day Saints, 1997. Lesson 16
https://www.lds.org/manual/family-home-evening-resource-book/family-home-evening-lessons/lesson-sixteen-gaining-a-testimony-through-the-holy-ghost

having feasted at a spiritual banquet. I said nothing to discredit their view, yet I could not shake the feeling that the youth had simply felt some powerful emotions, which—with a little help from a few adult leaders—they had interpreted as spiritual experiences. "[1]

Lumping together such a broad spectrum of feelings severely limits thought. It can take years to sort out after leaving, which can be aided with the help of a dictionary, emotion lists, and conscious observation.

It becomes necessary for a totalist group to reframe any discomfort that arises from all the money tithed, work performed, time wasted, sleep lost, tuna casseroles consumed, and long boring repetitive talks endured.

"In a cult, happiness is often redefined as sacrifice or suffering."[2] We must endure all these tests to the end. Our pioneer role models cheerfully died on the plains in service to God. Toil and strife are cause for rejoicing.

Hymns are great at emotional reframing because singing is a visceral experience, where melodies reinforce poetic language. In this state, we never question the contradiction.

"When upon life's billows you are tempest-tossed," you count your many blessings.[3]

And...
> Come, come, ye Saints, no toil nor labor fear;
> But with joy wend your way.
> Though hard to you this journey may appear,
> Grace shall be as your day.[4]

And...
> More holiness give me,
> More strivings within,
> More patience in suff'ring,
> More sorrow for sin,
> More faith in my Savior,
> More sense of his care,
> More joy in his service,
> More purpose in prayer.[5]

And...
> Put your shoulder to the wheel; push along,
> Do your duty with a heart full of song,
> We all have work; let no one shirk.
> Put your shoulder to the wheel.[6]

*Let Us All Press On* is another one, which even manages to merge the joy-in-work trope with the battle themes we will examine in the us-versus-them chapter.[7]

The concept of the refiner's fire inspired analogies about pressure turning coal into diamonds. One story told of a child helping a chicken hatch by peeling back pieces of the egg, but the chick died. This lesson taught that we have to struggle to grow. There must be opposition in all things.

Mormons aren't alone in this belief. The leader of a new age cult taught the same reframing doctrine. "[Rev. Will] said he had a rough personality because he was meant to 'refine' others' personalities so they could have a more spiritual life, 'like sandpaper refines wood.'"[8]

---

1. Morin and Morin, *Suddenly Strangers*, 2004. 48.
2. Hassan, *Releasing the Bonds*, 2000. 116.
3. Johnson Oatman. "Count Your Blessings." In *Hymns of the Church of Jesus Christ of Latter-day Saints*. Hymns of the Church of Jesus Christ of Latter-day Saints, 1985.
4. Clayton, "Come, Come Ye Saints," *Hymns*, 1985.
5. Bliss, "More Holiness Give Me," *Hymns*, 1985.
6. Will L. Thompson. "Put Your Shoulder to the Wheel." In *Hymns of the Church of Jesus Christ of Latter-day Saints*. The Church of Jesus Christ of Latter-day Saints, 1985.
7. Evan Stephens. "Let Us All Press On." In *Hymns of the Church of Jesus Christ of Latter-day Saints*. The Church of Jesus Christ of Latter Day Saints, 1985.
8. Sanchez, *Spiritual Perversion*, 2005. 89.

We all face adversity, so managing it is advantageous. However, too much adversity can wear you down or break you. As Viktor Frankl, psychiatrist and Nazi concentration camp survivor, observed, "Let me make it perfectly clear that in no way is suffering necessary to find meaning... If [suffering] were avoidable...the meaningful thing to do would be to remove its cause, be it psychological, biological or political. To suffer unnecessarily is masochistic rather than heroic."[1]

The Church also reframes agency and freedom, for obvious reasons. Pam, in *Saturday's Warrior*, says, "Freedom is knowing who you are... the rest can straighten out itself, if you really know who you are. Oh Jimmy, I pray for the day that you will know you *are* a child of God, with endless potential. Know it so strongly it burns in your heart as it does in mine now."[2]

This isn't just a cognitive reframing, but an emotional one. Couched in themes of familial bonds, celestial potential, and divine identity, this quote packs a powerful punch. Freedom is living up to your promise... Which means following Church leaders without question.

Janja Lalich recounts how reframing was used to conceal the brainwashing in her political cult: "Shortly after the Jonestown massacre a Central Committee member dared to question what we were creating. 'I'm afraid we're a cult,' he said. 'How are we different from the Moonies?' he rather painfully asked. 'We are not a cult,' [the leader] professed, 'and we're not brainwashed. Why? Because we willingly and consciously submit to cadre transformation. Transformation is our goal!'"[3]

We're not brainwashed because we choose to be here. Obedience to the law is liberty, right?

This talk reframes submission:

> One of the sneaky ploys of the adversary is to have us believe that unquestioning obedience to the principles and commandments of God is blind obedience. His goal is to have us believe that we should be following our own worldly ways and selfish ambitions. This he does by persuading us that "blindly" following the prophets and obeying the commandments is not thinking for ourselves. He teaches that it is not intelligent to do something just because we are told to do so by a living prophet or by prophets who speak to us from the scriptures.
>
> Our unquestioning obedience to the Lord's commandments is not blind obedience. President Boyd K. Packer...taught us about this: "Latter-day Saints are not obedient because they are compelled to be obedient. They are obedient because they know certain spiritual truths and have decided, as an expression of their own individual agency, to obey the commandments of God... We are not obedient because we are blind, we are obedient because we can see."[4]

In another Conference, we learn exactly why obedience is liberty. "A useful way to think about the commandments is they are loving counsel from a wise, all-knowing Heavenly Father."[5]

Either they are commandments, or they are loving counsel. They cannot be both. Loving counsel would not come with the punishment of eternal separation from a Father who loves you. They say God cannot tolerate being in the presence of sin, and yet he is all-knowing and carries us through tribulations, during which someone might be committing a sin against us. When examined within a different frame, the logic falls to pieces.

As Lalich pointed out, cult members risk making note of similarities from other cults and making the connection. It helps to speak openly about the topic and reframe it. When

---

1. Viktor E. Frankl. *Man's Search for Meaning: An Introduction to Logotherapy.* New York: Simon & Schuster, 1984.
2. Williams, Bob. *Saturday's Warrior.* Drama, Family, Musical, 1989.
3. Lalich, "A Little Carrot and a Lot of Stick," *Recovery from Cults,* ed. Langone, 1995. 69.
4. R. Conrad Schultz. "Faith Obedience." In LDS General Conference, April 2002.
5. L. Tom Perry. "Obedience to Law Is Liberty." In LDS General Conference, April 2013.

this happened in Sanchez's cult, members were already inoculated: "It was the first time I had ever heard anyone say that SLF was a cult in this way. In fact, Rev. Will used the word all the time, but in a very sardonic manner so that no one would ever think of thinking that SLF was a cult."[1]

And Geri-Ann Galanti, in describing her experience at a Moonie recruitment camp, recounts: "...I heard the word *brainwashing* four or five times, always used in a joking context... He said it was because people often accused them of being brainwashed. 'People are so cynical. They can't believe that we can be happy and want to help other people and love each other, so they think that we must be brainwashed to feel this way,' he explained, with a good-natured laugh afterward to underscore the ridiculousness of the charge. ...my answer to their frequent query, 'We don't *look* brainwashed, do we?' was always no."[2]

As Mormons, we often joked that we were a cult, that we had horns, that we were secretly devil worshippers, because that ridiculous definition was so easy to deny. The Church's official website states that any unorthodox religion is a cult, so it's no big deal.[3]

The Church reframes its own past. "The overwhelming evidence of Church history is positive and faith-promoting. If you choose to spend much of your time studying only the controversial chapters of our history, you'll see a few threads, but you'll miss the whole quilt. And you need to understand the whole picture of our history. In its full context, it is absolutely inspiring."[4]

And also to reframe why people leave the Church or fail to follow the commandments. "It is most astonishing to every principle of intelligence that any man or woman will close their eyes upon eternal things after they have been made acquainted with them, and let the...things of this world, the lusts of the eye, and the lusts of the flesh, entangle their minds and draw them one hair's breadth from the principles of life."[5]

Why indeed, when the commandments are so easy and the rewards are so great, and the lusts of the world so trifling? This comes from Brigham Young, a man who had fifty-five wives.

Legitimate reasons for falling away are dismissed through reframing. Shortly after I left the Church, I told my mother I was happy. She said I only thought I was happy, that I had confused pleasure with happiness.

Since members are constantly having their own emotions reframed, they don't see how it could be offensive or hurtful to do this to others. It is an invalidating boundary violation that damages relationships. However, to accept another's feelings at face value would cause too much dissonance when they conflict directly with totalist doctrine—in this case, with "wickedness never was happiness."

The LDS Church isn't the only one to propagate this type of belief. A letter from the leader of SLF stated, "There are some here that enjoy their wicked delights so much that they would rather risk [violating] the sanctification of this place for a few moments of stolen pleasure. These people are making excuses for their ill temperament, prideful in their insolence toward the reverence of the Holy."[6]

Outside the LDS frame, those who receive a service or gift should thank the giver. Inside the frame, general authorities request gratitude for giving members "opportunities" to serve. Recently, the Church made a "wonderful gesture" for elderly couples on full-time missions:

---

1. Sanchez, *Spiritual Perversion,* 2005. 135.
2. Galanti, "Reflections on 'Brainwashing,'" *Recovery from Cults,* ed. Langone, 1995. 88.
3. "Why Do Some Call Mormonism a Cult?" *Mormon.org.* Accessed Oct 11, 2013. http://mormon.org/faq/mormon-church
4. Elder Steven E. Snow. "Balancing Church History." *New Era,* June 2013.
5. *Teachings of Presidents of the Church: Brigham Young,* 1997. 79-80.
6. Sanchez, *Spiritual Perversion,* 2005. 110.

> To encourage more couples to serve, [we] have made one of the boldest and most generous moves seen in missionary work in the last 50 years. In May...priesthood leaders in the field received a notice that housing costs for couples (and we speak only of housing costs) would be supplemented by Church missionary funds if the cost exceeds a predetermined amount per month. What a blessing! This is heaven-sent assistance toward the single largest expense our couples face on their missions. The Brethren have also determined that couple missions can be for 6 or 12 months as well as the traditional 18 or 23. In another wonderful gesture, permission is given for couples, at their own expense, to return home briefly for critical family events. And stop worrying that you are going to have to knock on doors or keep the same schedule as the 19-year-olds! We don't ask you to do that, but we have a host of other things you can do, with a great deal of latitude in how you do them.[1]

How many Saints hearing this realized that the elderly couple is dedicating six to twenty-three months of their lives, at their own financial expense, after having paid tithing all their lives? Aren't *they* the ones making a wonderful gesture? Any financial assistance and time off to visit family should simply be assumed. In this reframe, the Church reverses the roles and takes all the credit of generosity for itself.

After all this external reframing, we learned to reframe on our own. Chris Morin explains how he reframed interactions with nonmembers: "I thought of occasions when a non-Mormon had complimented the Mormon Church. How many times had the compliment been given in an attempt to find some common ground, an attempt to make a peace offering in the midst of conflicting claims to truth? How many times had I interpreted these compliments as evidence that even the non-Mormons recognize us as a cut above the rest?"[2]

And this mission story: "Some of the fabric at both the foot and the head of the mattress had rotted away, exposing the foam inside. Where the foam was exposed it had oxidized and crumbled into crusty brown powder. The sight of that pleased me immensely. It gave me a deep sense of satisfaction to know that I would be sacrificing the luxuries I had enjoyed from the day I was born. My service to the Lord would thus be more difficult, and, therefore, more meaningful. Such open-armed acceptance of sacrifice makes excellent fodder for faith-promoting mission stories."[3]

Reframed, this is the essence of mind control in action.

---

1. Jeffery R. Holland. "We Are All Enlisted." In LDS General Conference, Oct 2011. http://www.lds.org/general-conference/2011/10/we-are-all-enlisted
2. Morin and Morin, *Suddenly Strangers,* 2004. 125.
3. Worthy, *The Mormon Cult,* 2008. 88.

> *The collective personality, like a recorded message, replies with programmed responses for everything.*
> —**John D. Goldhammer, *Under the Influence*** [1]

> **Spirit of Contention:**
> *What it is when you disagree with a Church leader. (See Spirit of Love)*
> **Spirit of Love:**
> *What it is when a Church leader disagrees with you. (See Spirit of Contention)*
> —**Orson Scott Card,**
> ***Saintspeak: The Mormon Dictionary*** [2]

> *Why should my doubts and questions upset the faithful? IF God created me, did He not also create my mind? And if He created my mind, wouldn't it be irreverent to refuse to question and think clearly?*
> —**Sam Keen,**
> ***Hymns to an Unknown God*** [3]

# Thought-Terminating Clichés

**Thought-Terminating Clichés**
—*Suppression, Silencing Doubts, Group Identification, Reinforcement*

- Provides easy answers to circumvent critical thought
- May transform thoughts into emotions
- Leverages loaded language
- Some clichés trigger trance states (when in doubt, pray or sing a hymn)
- Creates identification with the group via a familiar linguistic culture
- Reinforces double-binds
- Relies on other mechanisms; reinforces other mechanisms

Picture a forest path advertised as a wilderness adventure. According to the map, there are many forks ahead. A sign at the trailhead tells you, "Stay on the trail and follow the rules." Seems fair enough.

You reach the first fork. The sign on the left reads, "Trail closed due to landslide." Of course nature is unpredictable. So you continue right.

At the next fork, the sign on the left reads, "Danger: Bears." It's for your own safety. So you take the right fork again.

The next lefthand path has a sign that reads, "Restricted access. Park service only."

Each fork greets you with more signs, forcing you down right turns until you're back at the trailhead. You fail to realize that your only *real* choice was to go around in a circle.

Each sign represents a thought terminating cliché, an inner voice to keep you from taking the left path. Technically, you could have veered left at any time. You didn't even need to stay on the path at all! Nevertheless, thanks to your willingness to follow the rules, you always chose the right path.

Your access to choices became illusion. Likewise, the Church gives you the illusion of agency by displaying a map full of choices. But when it comes time to make them, they've erected signposts in your mind to keep you on the straight and narrow.

---

1. Goldhammer, *Under the Influence,* 1996. 203.
2. Orson Scott Card. *Saintspeak, the Mormon Dictionary.* Salt Lake City, Utah: Orion Books, 1981.
3. Keen, *Hymns to an Unknown God,* 1995. 80.

A thought-terminating cliché is a phrase that halts argument or prevents clear thought. It can be a short "bumper sticker slogan", seeming to deliver a profound message without really meaning much. Or it can represent a larger concept that can't be expressed in words. In either case, it is a shortcut to prevent deeper exploration or discussion.

Mainstream society presents thought-terminating clichés as well, and some of them employ logical fallacies or manipulative techniques such as black and white thinking or doctrine over self.

"You're either with us, or against us," is used to quickly silence dissent in many situations. At first glance, it's difficult to argue with. It takes extra mental effort to dismantle so you can say, "Actually, I can be on your side and still disagree on your methods."

Other common examples are:

- Because I said so.
- You're just being selfish.
- Don't be unpatriotic.
- Nobody's perfect.
- Sellout.
- Visualize world peace.
- Property is theft.
- Taxes are theft.
- How can anyone know for sure?
- Don't worry so much.
- It's only a theory.
- It's no big deal.
- You're being politically correct.
- Guns don't kill people, people kill people.
- It's a conspiracy.
- "u mad bro?"
- Just trust me.
- Some things just can't be explained.
- You can't do anything right.
- That woman only wants attention.
- He's overreacting.
- Those people are only doing it for the money.
- Science doesn't know everything.
- Do or do not; there is no try.

Sometimes, these phrases are valid. It's only a thought-terminating cliché if it's used to stop debate or silence further thought within yourself.

Here's one used in the SLF: "Rev. Will laughed infectiously, 'If people are not grounded in God, they are confused and will accept any thought that comes to them.'"[1]

And, "It says right in scripture—what you do in mind, you do in spirit, or in other words, it's as if you actually did it."[2]

Both of these thoughts cripple further reflection. If you become confused, it's because you're not following God. If you think something bad, you might as well have done it.

The Unification Church just comes right out and calls it what it is. "In the Moonies, I was told thought stopping would help me grow spiritually, and allow me to remain centered and focused on God. I didn't know it was a mind control technique. I had been indoctrinated to believe that thinking negative thoughts would allow 'evil spirits' to invade

---

1. Sanchez, *Spiritual Perversion*, 2005. 261.
2. Sanchez, *Spiritual Perversion*, 2005. 123.

me... Frequently, in many Bible-based cults, the 'devil' or 'Satan' is the source of the member's doubts. Reciting scripture, speaking in tongues, and humming can be used to stop critical thinking."[1]

Mormons are also told that Satan is the source of doubt, and they should sing a hymn or say a prayer to avoid problematic thoughts. Hassan says, "Meditation or prayer, used in an automatic way, can shut off critical thinking. Through a technique called 'thought stopping,' these ordinarily useful and valuable actions are programmed to become mechanical whenever the member feels doubt, anxiety, or uncertainty."[2]

Many of the examples in other chapters reflect LDS thought-terminating clichés. Here are more. This list is by no means all-inclusive:

1. Is it pertinent to your eternal salvation?
2. Don't place stumbling blocks in your path.
3. The church is perfect, man is not.
4. Don't be close-minded.
5. The hardhearted hate the truth.
6. Satan is raging in the hearts of men.
7. Choose the right.
8. Love the sinner, hate the sin.
9. This is a trial of your faith.
10. Be of good cheer.
11. Be in the world but not of the world.
12. Avoid the appearance of evil.
13. "Can ye be angry, and not sin?" Ephesians 4:26 (Joseph Smith Translation)
14. These are plain and precious things.
15. Cast not your pearls before swine.
16. He without faith is driven on the waves and tossed.
17. Would the prophet approve of this movie?
18. Would the Holy Ghost feel welcome in your heart?
19. Would The Savior be ashamed in your home?
20. Milk before meat.
21. Line upon line, precept on precept.
22. It will be sorted out in the next life.
23. Wickedness never was happiness.
24. Be not ashamed of the gospel of Christ.
25. The only reason you do X is because of Y...
26. All will be revealed in due time.
27. Have you prayed about it?
28. You will not be tempted more than you are able to bear.
29. Are those feelings/thoughts/teachings in line with the gospel?
30. Don't seek for signs.
31. Get thee behind me, Satan.
32. Leaving the Church is the easy way out.
33. "Trust in the Lord with all thine heart; and lean not unto thine own understanding." Proverbs 3:5
34. "I never said it would be easy, I only said it would be worth it."
35. Endure to the end.
36. I'll go where you want me to go, dear Lord.
37. God's ways are not man's ways.
38. Everything happens for a reason.

---

1. Hassan, *Releasing the Bonds*, 2000. 52.
2. Hassan, *Releasing the Bonds*, 2000. 51.

39. Even the very elect will be deceived.
40. Don't delve too deeply into the mysteries.
41. "To be learned is good if they hearken unto the counsels of God."
    2 Nephi 9:29
42. "When the prophet speaks, the debate is over."[1]
43. "It is foolish to suppose that men can be left to their own devices and accomplish what God intended for them."[2]
44. "Where your treasure is, there will your heart be also."
    Matthew 6:21
45. "He who hath ears to hear, let him hear."
    Matthew 13:9
46. "Those who lose the Spirit are filled with darkness and confusion."[3]
47. Satan is the author of confusion.
48. The spirit of contention is of the devil.
49. "Ye receive no witness until after the trial of your faith."
    Ether 12:6

Other thought-terminators aren't so much clichés but images or feelings based on stories or principles. For instance, the fear of losing the Spirit by thinking even one "bad thought" leads members to never question.

I remember a story of how the devil schemed to not tell complete lies, but instead to tell half-truths because these were more deceptive. This story prevents the consideration of new information if even one part of it seems wrong.

Another story was about the dangers of tolerating sin. A wandering nomad and his camel saw a sandstorm coming. The nomad pitched his small tent and crawled inside. The camel begged to just put in his nose so he could breathe. The nomad figured there was room for a nose, and allowed it. Then the camel complained of sand in his eyes, so the nomad scooted over to let in the camel's head. Before long the nomad is sitting outside the tent because the camel has taken over.

Aside from feeling bad for the camel, I remembered this story as a good reason to never watch a single R-rated movie or listen to any philosophy not stamped with the LDS Seal of Approval.

Many of the parables have this same effect, like the prodigal son: Don't be the prodigal son. (But if you are, God will welcome the repentant home.) The parable of the wheat and the chaff: Don't be the chaff. The parable of the ten virgins: Always be spiritually prepared.

Another visual thought-terminating trope: "...it is upon the rock of our Redeemer, who is Christ, the Son of God, that ye must build your foundation; that when the devil shall send forth his mighty winds, yea, his shafts in the whirlwind, yea, when all his hail and his mighty storm shall beat upon you, it shall have no power over you to drag you down to the gulf of misery and endless wo..." Helaman 5:12

War and battle metaphors also terminate thought. "Today we find ourselves in another war. This is not a war of armaments. It is a war of thoughts, words, and deeds. It is a war with sin, and more than ever we need to be reminded of the commandments. Secularism is becoming the norm, and many of its beliefs and practices are in direct conflict with those that were instituted by the Lord Himself for the benefit of His children."[4]

The Church encourages members to police their own thoughts: "When evil thoughts arise—Stop! Think! Control your mind! Visualize a large EXIT sign in your mind's eye.

---

1. President N. Eldon Tanner First Counselor in the First Presidency. "The Debate Is Over." *Ensign*, Aug 1979. https://beta.lds.org/ensign/1979/08/the-debate-is-over
2. Tanner, "The Debate Is Over," *Ensign*, Aug 1979.
3. *Teachings of Presidents of the Church: Brigham Young*, 1997. 81.
4. L. Tom Perry. "Obedience to Law Is Liberty." In LDS General Conference, April 2013.

Immediately change your thoughts. Get off of that avenue of thinking."[1]

Camilla Eyring Kimball was the well-respected wife of Prophet Spencer W. Kimball. "Camilla had a philosophy about religious problems... She said that when things troubled her, she put them on the shelf; later when she looked at them again, some were answered, some seemed no longer important, and some needed to go back on the shelf for another time."[2]

Prophet Harold B. Lee: "If you would teach our people to put periods and not question marks after what the Lord has declared, we would say, 'It is enough for me to know that is what the Lord said.'"[3]

And Apostle James E. Faust: "The new aristocracy will not be seeking to eliminate thoughtful inquiry, or be a board of censors as it were, but rather seek to teach right concepts and to replace bad ideas with enlightened thought."[4]

And a recent *New Era* article reflects yet another common thought-terminating cliché to help the youth who may find troubling information on the internet: "There are sad or confusing episodes in our history that we seek to understand better, but some of these questions might not be answered on this side of the veil. And that's fine."[5]

There are a number of thought-stopping ideas about exmormons that keep members from paying much attention to us, including:

- You can't trust them.
- Satan is trying to destroy the Church.
- They are liars who want to tear down the Church.
- You can leave the Church but you can't leave it alone.
- They're angry and hateful.
- They have a chip on their shoulder.
- They're twisting the gospel.
- They're misled.

Here is a thought-terminating cliché in action, in a passage written by Brad L. Morin: "I wanted to read his book [on polygamy in church history] and debunk it or verify the claims. On several occasions I almost purchased the book, but each time the guilt welled up: Where was my faith? How could God support me if I so acted on these doubts? I renewed my efforts to build my faith with good works, study, and prayer, but my concerns did not go away."[6]

And from an article in an apologetics book, the question is asked, "When I started my graduate work, I firmly believed in the infallibility and inerrancy of the Bible. Now, after several years of study, I no longer believe in the Bible and have stopped attending my church. You, however, are still committed to your faith and still believe in the inspiration of scripture. How is that possible after all you have been exposed to in graduate school?"

BYU professor Richard Neitzel Holzapfel answers: "I have thought about this situation and similar circumstances many times during the past few years. On such occasions, I often recall what Peter told the early Christian Saints: 'Be ready always to give an answer to every man that asketh you a reason of the hope that is in you with meekness and fear'. I have found 'a reason' for the hope that is in me and for why I continue to be a committed disciple

---

1. Rulon G. Craven. "Temptation." In LDS General Conference, April 1996. http://www.lds.org/general-conference/1996/04/temptation
2. Caroline Eyring Miner, and Edward L. Kimball. *Camilla, a Biography of Camilla Eyring Kimball*. Salt Lake City, Utah: Deseret Book Co., 1980. 110.
3. President Harold B. Lee. "Admonitions for the Priesthood of God." *Ensign*, Jan 1973.
4. James E. Faust. "A New Aristocracy." In LDS General Conference, Oct 1974. https://www.lds.org/general-conference/1974/10/a-new-aristocracy
5. Elder Steven E. Snow. "Balancing Church History." *New Era*, June 2013.
6. Morin and Morin, *Suddenly Strangers,* 2004. 69.

after years of study and thought."[1]

If you have a reason, you will continue to believe, no matter what the facts say. Thought-terminating clichés are those reasons.

In contrast, some clichés are far more thought-liberating. Here are a few:

> ↻ Question authority.
> ↻ Question everything.
> ↻ Moderation in all things.
> ↻ The truth will set you free.
> ↻ Your best is good enough.
> ↻ I could be wrong.

---

1. Richard Neitzel Holzapfel. "Question, but No Doubts." In *Expressions of Faith: Testimonies of Latter-day Saint Scholars*, ed. Susan Easton Black. Deseret Book Co., 1996.

*How could someone not fit in? The community was so meticulously ordered, the choices so carefully made.*
—**Lois Lowry, *The Giver*** [1]

*He wondered, as he had many times wondered before, whether he himself was a lunatic. Perhaps a lunatic was simply a minority of one. At one time it had been a sign of madness to believe that the earth goes round the sun; today, to believe that the past is unalterable... the thought of being a lunatic did not greatly trouble him; the horror was that he might also be wrong.*
—**George Orwell, *1984***

# Social Pressure

**Social Pressure**
*—Group Identification, Influence, Suppression, Reinforcement, Punishment, Perpetuation*

- Influences via culture as opposed to official teachings...
- ...which is a type of indirect directive
- Influence through identification and example
- Creates a powerful yet subtle reward/punishment dynamic based on group approval
- Reinforces created dependency
- Reinforces all doctrines directly taught
- Reinforces all culture indirectly taught
- Prompts mimicking of behavior which builds towards belief follows behavior
- Encourages filtering of expression to gain approval, i.e. only recounting positives
- Encourages white lies (exaggerating positive feelings & experiences)
- Such filtering reinforces the mechanism of public commitment, transforming exaggerations into belief
- Reinforces **all** other established mechanisms
- Member mimics love bombing behavior towards others
- Member mimics other mind control techniques towards others

Social pressure is perhaps the most powerful tool of group mind control. Group dynamics can subjugate an individual by leveraging shame, embarrassment, the desire to fit in, group euphoria, cohesion, exemplification, and fear of rejection.

When we belong to a group, we often model the behavior of others. We don't need to hear commandments preached from the pulpit. According to the principle of social proof, we repeat what we see others say and do. Social proof contributed to humanity's survival—successful behaviors are quickly passed along without dangerous and time-consuming delays.

Very complex social messages can be conveyed entirely without words. John Goldhammer writes, "The raised eyebrows, a certain expression, are all that we need to immediately know we have deviated from the collective norm... any feelings or thoughts that are not in alignment with our social group are censored and repressed. Like a child who becomes acutely aware of a parent's disapproving glance, we are taught to repress unacceptable behavior, ideas, and language." [2]

When used unethically, social pressures incite emotional forces which can be used to promote compliance to

---

1. Lois Lowry. *The Giver*. New York: Random House/Listening Library, 2006. 48.
2. Goldhammer, *Under the Influence*, 1996. 79.

manipulative expectations. According to Margaret Singer, "Since esteem and affection from peers is so important to new recruits, any negative response is very meaningful. Approval comes from having your behaviors and thought patterns conform to the models put forth by the group. Your relationship with peers is threatened whenever you fail to learn or display new behaviors. Over time, an easy solution to the insecurity generated by the difficulties of learning the new system is to inhibit any display of doubt and, even if you don't understand the content, to merely acquiesce, affirm, and act as if you do understand and accept the new philosophy or content."[1]

All groups, to some extent, have their own customs. Coercive groups take this a bit further.

> Peer pressure is an effective means to get people to fit their behavior to group norms. In cults, this works for new and old members alike, going far beyond what is generally seen in society at large. In an atmosphere that states or implies that there is only one way to be and this is it, it is most important to have models around to imitate. Robert Lifton speaks of the totalism of the person meeting the totalistic ideology of a group, an idea that suggests why adaptation filters down to the clothing, the smiles, the language—all the details of behavior that are either approved or shunned.
>
> For example, a number of women, particularly those from religious and political cults, told me that without being aware of it and without ever being told to do so, they slipped from dressing in ordinary clothes into wearing dark colors, long skirts, flat heels, and no makeup...
>
> In these activities, there is no need for cult leaders to fuss and belabor followers... The clever cult leader or mind manipulator manages to use the innate tendencies toward group conformity that we bring with us as a powerful tool for change. No one has to announce the rules to us. Most of us look around and discern what they are and how we should behave.[2]

Robert Cialdini implied that social pressure is a form of delegation. "[Jim Jones'] real genius as a leader was his realization of the limitations of individual leadership. No leader can hope to persuade, regularly and single-handedly, all the members of the group. A forceful leader can reasonably expect, however, to persuade some sizable proportion of group members. Then the raw information that a substantial number of group members has been convinced can, by itself, convince the rest. Thus, the most influential leaders are those who know how to arrange group conditions to allow the principle of social proof to work in their favor."[3]

It is easier to like and trust those close to us, even if we may not like or trust the central leader. As Boyd K. Packer said, regarding testimony, "I have that certain witness. It came to me in my youth. During those early periods of doubt, I leaned on the testimony of a seminary teacher. Although I did not know, somehow I *knew* that he *knew*."[4]

Cognitive dissonance plays a role. One cognition is, "I want to belong." The other is, "These people act differently than I do." To resolve it, the individual merely changes her actions and becomes accepted.

Social pressure is then motivated out of a group-wide desire to maintain maximum consonance for everyone. According to Festinger in *When Prophecy Fails*, "It is reasonable to believe that dissonances created by unequivocal disconfirmation cannot be appreciably reduced unless one is in the constant presence of supporting members who can provide for one another the social reality that will make the rationalization of disconfirmation

---

1. Singer, *Cults in Our Midst*, 1995. 67-68.
2. Singer, *Cults in Our Midst*, 1995. 168.
3. Cialdini, *Influence,* 2009. 131.
4. Boyd K. Packer. "Personal Revelation: The Gift, the Test, and the Promise." In LDS General Conference, Oct 1994.

acceptable."[1] Cultural trappings, along with members "preaching to the choir", can generate enough consonance to drown out disconfirming events as dissonant as unfulfilled prophecy.

Researchers studying brainwashing in communist states found that, for US prisoners of war who were beaten and deprived of food, brainwashing was less effective compared with Chinese students who were influenced by communist peers. Singer and Ofshe observed, "In these programs, it appears that aversive arousal [guilt and anxiety], coupled with peer rejection, became the driving force through which the target was coerced... Social and psychological punishment by peers became the workhorse of the system. For many individuals this process induced psychological breakdown."[2] POWs, conversely, suffered no breakdowns.

How can social pressures be more powerful than torture?

Perhaps because rejection feels just as bad as severe physical pain. Scientists simulated the sensation of spilling hot coffee on subjects and examined their brain patterns using an fMRI. Then they had the subject look at a photo of someone who had recently broken up with them. The patterns matched one another, activating the same areas of the brain, but did not match controls (pictures of good friends and low-heat stimulation).

The author of the study, Ethan F. Kross, assistant professor of psychology at the University of Michigan, said, "When we sat around and thought about the most difficult emotional experiences, we all agreed that it doesn't get any worse than social rejection."[3]

Elizabeth Smart said, regarding her forced loss of chastity, "If you can imagine the most special thing being taken away from you and feeling like that, not that that was your only value in life, but something that devalued you, can you imagine turning around and going back into society where you're no longer of value, where you're no longer as good as everybody else?"[4]

While it's true that "no one can make you do it", the threat of ostracization can be as frightening as the threat of violence. The risk of not fitting in can be more coercive than taking a beating. When you're being physically hurt, it's hard to like the person causing you pain. When you're being socially coerced, you *already* like them. They couldn't cause you pain otherwise.

Moreover, when we have a reason for why our actions are out of discord with our beliefs, there is no motive to resolve dissonance by altering belief. Remember the students who were given $20 to lie in Festinger's dissonance study? They knew that $20 was a good reason to lie, so unlike the students only given $1, they did not come to believe the tedious task was fun. The same happens when we know someone is trying to change our beliefs by force. Torture is a poor change-agent, because, even though we may *say* what our captor wants to hear, our hearts know exactly why.

Social pressures are just as painful and scary, yet more subtle and subconscious, and therefore much harder to be aware of. Under these conditions, it is easier to resolve the dissonance by adopting the new beliefs.

Most people will go to great lengths to fit in—from the small things, like learning to make green Jell-O and using fake swearwords, to the big things, like repressing sexual orientation. If all you have to do is bear your testimony or sit through an awkward temple ceremony, well of course you'll do it. Especially if everyone smiles and congratulates you afterwards.

It is difficult to find scriptural support that men must wear suits and keep their hair cut and face shaved; in fact Jesus himself is portrayed as rather scruffy in all his portraits. Nevertheless, these pious fashion trends have become a cultural force all on their own

---

1. Festinger, *When Prophecy Fails,* 1964. 205.
2. Singer and Ofshe, "Peripheral Versus Central Elements of Self," *Cultic Studies Journal,* 1986.
3. Pamela Paul. "Is Rejection Painful? Actually, It Is: Studied." *The New York Times,* May 13, 2011, sec. Fashion & Style. http://www.nytimes.com/2011/05/15/fashion/is-rejection-painful-actually-it-is-studied.html
4. *Child Trafficking Symposium: Elizabeth Smart.* Johns Hopkins Bloomberg School of Public Health, 2013.

among Latter-day Saints. The extent to which the leadership drives these norms, or follows them, isn't quite clear, nor is it a very important question. The trappings of culture are powerful regardless of their source.

The clean-cut, traditional, Sunday look serves to present a certain brand to outsiders, but the specifics of the culture don't matter for this mind control technique. As we'll see later, the clothing and diet and little customs aren't harmless; they are a vector for inducing belief.

Members seek signs of approval by keeping the many commandments, both express and implied. They magnify callings, try to outdo one another in public prayers and talks, participate in class, and offer praise to one another for doing such a great job (and subtle shunning of those who falter). There are dozens of outward manifestations of righteousness, including clothing, temple garments, Word of Wisdom compliance, affluence, rank of callings, display of talents, and performing as a super-mom. Members are expected to keep up appearances at all times, and in all places. The stars are those who succeed at being the most holy.

According to Beck, "It is unheard of to refuse a call, especially since a lot of social currency accrues from one's ward rank. From the top-dog rank of bishop, to the mid-prestige senior Sunday school teachers, to the lowly child-care specialists in the junior Sunday school, ward members are assigned to care for each other in sickness, teach each other in health, and communicate a mutual sense of belonging and respect on a continual basis."[1]

The Church emphasizes setting and following a good example. Youth are repeatedly told the importance of choosing friends and role models who maintain "high standards."

*For the Strength of Youth* counsels, "Everyone needs good and true friends. They will be a great strength and blessing to you. They will influence how you think and act, and even help determine the person you will become. They will help you be a better person and will make it easier for you to live the gospel of Jesus Christ."[2]

The Church is correct in this regard—if it wants its members to follow strict practices, it needs to isolate members from observing the behavior of outsiders, because they really *will* get the idea that it's okay.

The Church also focuses on peer pressure, especially to the youth. For a teen, pressure from non-LDS friends can be pretty steep, especially outside the Mormon Corridor. Such social proof can cause dissonance unless handled ahead of time.

The *Presidents of the Church* lesson on the subject says, "Class members will see that peer pressure can be both a negative and a positive experience, and they will choose to follow the positive influences that help them to return to Heavenly Father."[3]

Students are taught how to resist it. "Try to show that it is important what influences us. Also, emphasize how important it is for them to influence their friends and families to go in the right direction...

"'What is the definition of a friend? Friends are people who make it easier to live the gospel of Jesus Christ.'"

The lesson then quotes David O. McKay: "One of the principal reasons which the Lord had for establishing His Church is to give all persons high and low, rich and poor, strong and feeble an opportunity to associate with their fellow men in an atmosphere of uplifting, religious fellowship. This may be found in priesthood quorums, Auxiliaries, Sacrament meetings. He who neglects these opportunities, who fails to take advantage of them, to that extent starves his own soul."

The teacher is asked to "bear your testimony that there is safety and happiness in choosing positive influences, especially in following the Savior and his prophets," and then to "challenge the class to seek positive influences, to become positive influences in the lives

---

1. Beck, *Leaving the Saints,* 2005. 54.
2. *For the Strength of Youth*, 2011. "Friends." https://www.lds.org/manual/for-the-strength-of-youth/friends
3. *The Presidents of the Church: Teacher's Manual*, 1996. (Lesson 19.)

of their friends and family, to shun negative influences."

The ultimate outward expression of righteousness, clothing, will forever be the mark of an upright Mormon. "Never lower your standards of dress. Do not use a special occasion as an excuse to be immodest. When you dress immodestly, you send a message that is contrary to your identity as a son or daughter of God. You also send the message that you are using your body to get attention and approval... The fashions of the world will change, but the Lord's standards will not change."[1]

How people are treated, social cues, and folklore all send messages of what is acceptable. The Sunday School teacher may teach, "Love one another," but then later gossip about a gay ward member who got what was coming to him by being excommunicated. A Seminary teacher may give a lesson about how the spirit of the law is more important than the letter, and then scold a student for saying "fetch" because it sounds too much like a swear word. These types of cues are more likely to influence behavior, emotion, and self-image than Sacrament talks and scripture references.

Indoctrination via culture also gives the Church plausible deniability for awful behaviors or culpable doctrines passed along in this manner. For example, apologists often claim members are not restricted from thinking for themselves. Indeed, there are a lot of written quotes declaring the merits of reason and freedom of thought, action, and speech. But the social and behavioral records tell us otherwise.

The scriptures instruct members to not judge, but they do it anyway. I know I sure did. I also felt judged, just like "Tracie" does in this case study cited in a study on LDS depression. "I feel like everything is judgmental. I have never seen people judge so harshly on clothing, hair, the things that [others are] doing. But that's what Utah is. I don't get it. What's wrong with me? What am I doing so wrong? For some reason, people just judge me really harshly. I don't know why. I just have come to the conclusion that it's Utah, and I hate it here."[2]

Tracie blames herself and Utah culture in equal measure, yet words from the pulpit are constantly condemning this or that form of wickedness. The members are merely following the example of their leaders, just as they've been instructed to do by the sitting prophet. "My brethren, I reiterate that, as holders of the priesthood of God, it is our duty to live our lives in such a way that we may be examples of righteousness for others to follow."[3] If priesthood leaders are judgmental, then so will be the members, even when they're told elsewhere not to be. It is interesting to note that this problem seems much worse in Utah than it is in regions where there is a smaller concentration of members. It would seem that social proof tends to amplify with more people.

Brad L. Morin comments on how toxic this type of culture can be. "While greatly concerned about the infectious influence of others' lifestyles upon our children, we frequently seemed oblivious to the highly contagious nature of our own intolerance. At times, the practical side of goodness was shoved aside for the intense emotional or spiritual experience or in the interest of maintaining a *pure* society."[4]

Jack B. Worthy notes how difficult these pressures are for some. "The Mormon community can be a source of serious misery for those with traits or personalities that clash with its clearly defined norms of acceptable behavior and its endless list of expectations."[5]

It's a common problem. I always felt like a square peg in a round hole for being a geek girl, interested in science fiction, who unknowingly had Asperger's Syndrome, which made me a naturally unorthodox thinker and less socially savvy than my peers. Nevertheless, I kept trying to fit that mold, and it became a great source of depression, social anxiety, and

---

1. *For the Strength of Youth*, 2011. "Dress and Appearance." https://www.lds.org/manual/for-the-strength-of-youth/dress-and-appearance
2. Doty, "In the Culture But Not of the Culture," 2013.
3. President Thomas S. Monson. "Examples of Righteousness." In LDS General Conference, April 2008. https://www.lds.org/general-conference/2008/04/examples-of-righteousness
4. Morin and Morin, *Suddenly Strangers,* 2004. 59.
5. Worthy, *The Mormon Cult,* 2008. 50.

deflated self-worth for most of my life.

Others may be gay or transgender, or they have interests outside the Church norm. Some people would rather identify with some other subculture like punk or hip hop or emo or whatever it is kids are into these days. Some members prefer loud music or art films. Maybe they're politically liberal. Maybe they're academics in scientific fields or other faith-challenging careers. Maybe their racial background is incompatible with apple pie, white middle-class illusions. Maybe they struggle with mental illnesses or disabilities that make conformity impossible. Maybe they're simply free spirits who don't like to be hemmed in or put on a schedule.

The Church claims God loves all his children, and then makes it clear these personalities and perspectives are not compatible with LDS culture.

"Leaving the Mormon reality dome usually damages family relationships in painful ways, so people with traits and personalities that clash with the culture suffer whether they stay or go. Sadly, members are taught to believe that Mormonism is right for every single human on the planet—that the Church is perfectly compatible with every person who has all the good traits of human nature. If a person has trouble fitting in, therefore, there is something seriously wrong with that person."[1]

LDS culture is right for some people. In its current rigid form, it can never be right for everyone. It's not you, it's *them*, and you've got to find your own path and make your own choices.

There are many stresses on young people to make important life decisions according to God's will, whether or not they truly want that path for themselves. As Bran Morin describes, "Young men face tremendous pressure to go on missions, and young women are taught they should marry a returned missionary. As a result, those young men who do not serve successful missions often feel inferior and have little chance to win the heart of a nice Mormon girl. Some missionaries serve only because of the expectations of others, not because they want to be there or because they are genuinely convinced of or committed to the gospel. Some of them struggle with the lie they are living, uncomfortable with both their belief and unbelief."[2]

Members are also encouraged, via doctrine, home teaching programs, and emphasis on family, to take care of one another. This can lead to a tendency to ignore healthy boundaries in the name of love. When fellow members believe they are looking out for your spiritual welfare, all other ethics get pushed aside. Sometimes this results in overt pressuring, spying, preaching, and uninvited visits. There is no more coercive social pressure than that which uses friends and family to trample an individual's right to respect, freedom, and privacy.

Effective boundary-setting is the answer to social pressure. You have the right to stand up for yourself and draw lines to keep people from hurting you or pushing you into doing things you don't want. It can be difficult to learn, but there are many books on this topic. Even just being aware of the mechanics of this dynamic can reduce its power.

---

1. Worthy, *The Mormon Cult*, 2008. 50.
2. Morin and Morin, *Suddenly Strangers*, 2004. 152.

*Monkey see, monkey do, [monkey believe].*

—**American proverb**

*...I would show unto the world that faith is things which are hoped for and not seen; wherefore, dispute not because ye see not, for ye receive no witness until after the trial of your faith.*

—**Ether 12:6 (Book of Mormon)**

# Belief Follows Behavior

**Belief Follows Behavior**
*—Suppression, Group Identification, Reinforcement, Influence, Isolation*

- Unusual behaviors are unique to the group
- The behaviors reinforce isolation
- Leverages cognitive dissonance by reshaping beliefs after behaviors are followed
- Requires social pressure to motivate the behavior
- Behaviors can modify or limit thought, create group cohesion, and limit access by outsiders
- Reinforces us vs. them thinking, because the behavior is easy to observe
- Reinforces indirect directives and milieu control because members can judge if the behavior is being followed
- Relies on influence through identification and example, as many behaviors are not dictated but observed and copied
- Reinforces demand for purity as behavior-mirroring is part of being "good"
- Very closely related to public commitment
- Some behaviors may generate shame if not performed for the benefit of the group
- Some behaviors may generate shame when judged by outsiders

Seeing isn't believing; doing is believing.

As we've seen, all the cultural trappings of Mormondom exert social pressure to get people to act in certain ways. But to what end? Where's the harm in the good clean fun, modest clothing, and odd ways of talking during prayers?

To gain acceptance, a prospective member may go through the motions without knowing why. A new member, not wanting to appear out of place, quickly catches on to the routine of a typical sacrament meeting: wear a dress or a white shirt and tie, close your eyes and bow your head during prayer, remember to say "Amen", sit quietly, sing the hymns (remember to stand up!), partake of the sacrament, raise your hand to the square[1] to show support for leaders, shake hands, and refer to everyone as "Brother Y" and "Sister X." People are reading their scriptures and listening to the speakers intently. So you do, too.

Those born into it experience the same acculturation, only with the loving guidance and instruction from parents.

Simple behaviors are repeated mindlessly at first. As time goes on, complex behaviors are added, like fasting, Home Teaching, missionary work, callings, and temple work. New Mormon women excitedly learn that they are free to create any kind of Jell-O salad they want, so long as it's green.

---

1. When members sustain, or show support for, a leader or a point of business, they raise their right arm outward, bent to a right angle at the elbow, with the hand pointing up. This is known as "raising your hand to the square."

You don't have to believe to participate, as evidenced in the Church's many talks and lessons on testimony. "Don't live on borrowed light" is repeated enough to know that many members must be relying on the collective social testimony. All LDS children start with behaviors, not beliefs. Everyone is promised they will gain more understanding in time.

And they will.

Remember cognitive dissonance? The author of that theory, Leon Festinger, said, "If you change a person's behavior, his thoughts and feelings will change to minimize the dissonance."[1] His research bore this out.

Dissonance is the force behind this thought reform technique. As a new member goes through motions that seem a little bit odd (but not overly so), she begins to wonder why. Members and investigators usually want to believe at this point anyway, so her mind will take the path of least resistance. Under most conditions, the dissonance will resolve to, "I am acting like a Mormon because I am one of them, so I will believe what they believe." She will come to know on a deep and profound level that the basis of her actions (the doctrines of the Church) are true.

Of course this is a subconscious process. If you were aware of it, it wouldn't work. Which is probably why you're reading this book—knowing is, as they say, half the battle.

Singer said, "If you say it in front of others, you'll do it. Once you do it, you'll think it. Once you think it (in an environment you do not perceive as coercive), you'll believe that you thought it yourself."[2]

The most obvious example of belief follows behavior is how often we're told to gain a testimony by bearing it. In that case, there are additional forces at play, so it gets its own chapter: public commitment.

Researchers who studied American POWs found that "...the Chinese set about arranging the prison-camp experience so that their captives would consistently *act* in desired ways. Before long, the Chinese knew, these actions would begin to take their toll, causing the prisoners to change their views of themselves to align with what they had done.

"Writing was one sort of committing action that the Chinese urged incessantly upon the captives. It was never enough for prisoners to listen quietly or even to agree verbally with the Chinese line; they were always pushed to write it down as well."[3]

It is very important to reiterate that for this to work, you must not perceive the environment as coercive. If you feel you are being tricked, defrauded, or threatened, you will have an outlet for your cognitive dissonance. Brainwashing techniques only worked on POWs when they felt certain choices were voluntary. Decisions made under the illusion of freedom are binding.

Even when you are prepared, however, it's hard to remember this when surrounded by nice people. After researcher Geri-Ann Galanti attended a Moonie recruitment camp to study techniques, she discovered, "...contrary to what I once believed[,] it is *not* the mind that is first affected by the influence. Rather, if there is any time lag between changes in our beliefs and behavior, our behavior changes first and then our beliefs follow; in that way, we maintain a consistency between the two."[4] She found herself surprised at how taken in she was, even with her defenses up.

I highly recommend reading her entire account in *Recovery from Cults*. It's eye opening to see how a cult researcher, fully aware of the abuses committed by this group, became sympathetic and wanted to spend more time with them.

The little things matter. Singer said, "If you really want to change people, change their appearance. Thus cult members can be asked or told to cut their hair or wear it in a particular style, wear different clothes, take on new names, and assume certain gestures or

---

1. Hassan, *Releasing the Bonds,* 2000. 40.
2. Singer, *Cults in Our Midst,* 1995. 76.
3. Cialdini, *Influence,* 2009. 67.
4. Galanti, "Reflections on 'Brainwashing,'" *Recovery from Cults,* ed. Langone, 1995. 87.

mannerisms."[1]

Church callings are also powerful generators of behavior dissonance, especially those that might seem menial or below one's abilities. In her political cult, Lalich describes jobs they had to perform. "Work assignments had little to do with a person's skills, training, or preferences. Doctors could be given production work, intellectuals put in typing pools. This was supposed to teach humility. In later years, however, such assigning was used only for punishment… Over time there came to be an obvious distinction between mental and manual labor, resulting in a somewhat privileged group of intellectuals and administrative leadership and another somewhat disregarded group of lower-level workers. This rather glaring class division would never have been admitted to since the party thought of itself as a microcosm of a perfect socialist society—with equality and justice for all members."[2]

Anyone who's been LDS for long knows that teaching Primary holds a lower social status, though if asked, leadership will avidly deny it. And God forbid you've been called to nursery. If your faith is wavering because of pride, this might be just the thing to correct your testimony.

This principle is official doctrine. The Church instructs that the best way to gain a testimony is to act. Follow the commandments first, then believe:

"If any man will do his will, he shall know of the doctrine, whether it be of God, or whether I speak of myself." John 7:17 I memorized this in Seminary. We are to experiment upon the word, by planting the seed and nourishing it, to see if it is true (Alma 32:26-43). We were constantly told to immerse ourselves in the converting fire of obedience, service, callings, and church activities. There is certainly no shortage of commandments to obey. I made a list containing about seventy, and I might have missed some.

Apostle Richard G. Scott said, "You will receive from the Holy Ghost a confirming witness of things you accept on faith by willingly doing them."[3]

President Harold B. Lee said, "No person knows the principle of tithing until he pays tithing."[4]

General Authority Loren C. Dunn spoke about it in the April 1971 Conference. "If we are going to experiment with the things of Christ, then we are going to have to put these things to a spiritual test—a test that the Savior himself has outlined for all those who wish to know, a test of doing."[5]

He tells of how two young men came to his office with questions about the doctrine. He challenged them to keep all the commandments for three months: Go to church (and take notes), pray, keep the Word of Wisdom, remain morally clean, and read the Book of Mormon. Dunn doesn't say what happened to the boys, but we are to assume they got their testimony.

M. Russell Ballard said, "We know that both members and nonmembers are more likely to be thoroughly converted to the gospel of Jesus Christ when there is a willingness to experiment upon the word. This is an attitude of both mind and heart that includes a desire to know the truth and a willingness to act on that desire."[6]

The girl in this story received her testimony through behavior: "…both the Relief Society and the priesthood had been working with [an inactive] family in their stake but had failed to make progress with the parents. Primary leaders found the answer. Permission was given by the parents for their young daughter to attend Primary. Their one condition was that she had to want to go badly enough to get there on her own. Rides to church could not be provided. Because she had to go through a rough part of town, the

---

1. Singer, *Cults in Our Midst*, 1995. 117.
2. Lalich, "A Little Carrot and a Lot of Stick," *Recovery from Cults,* ed. Langone, 1995. 81.
3. Richard G. Scott. "Full Conversion Brings Happiness." In LDS General Conference, April 2002.
4. *Family Home Evening Resource Book*. The Church of Jesus Christ of Latter Day Saints, 1997. https://www.lds.org/manual/family-home-evening-resource-book/lesson-ideas/tithing
5. Loren C. Dunn. "Drink of the Pure Water." In LDS General Conference, April 1977. https://www.lds.org/general-conference/1971/04/drink-of-the-pure-water
6. M. Russell Ballard. "Now Is the Time." In LDS General Conference, Oct 2000.

ward council saw to it that someone would drive along beside her as she rode an old bicycle to church. Through summer heat, through rain and even snow, she persisted in going to church. One young man, who with his family was assigned to escort her on a snowy morning, was so touched as he watched the commitment of this little girl pedaling through the snow and cold that he decided to serve a full-time mission, citing this experience as the turning point in his life. At Christmastime, a family in the ward gave this faithful little girl a new 10-speed bicycle. This so touched the parents that they too began attending church. In May 1999 this young girl was baptized. What made the baptism even more special was that it was performed by the newest priest in the ward, her recently activated father."[1]

This repeated act not only led to the girl's and her family's conversion, but also the young man who drove alongside her, who needed an explanation for his own incomprehensible behavior of not simply giving the poor girl a ride.

At least one prophet clearly behaved before he believed. "President Lorenzo Snow had studied the gospel for several years before joining the Church. But he did not receive a witness until two or three weeks after his baptism when he retired in secret prayer. 'The Spirit of God descended upon me,' he said. 'O, the joy and happiness I felt, [for] I then received a perfect knowledge that God lives, that Jesus Christ is the Son of God, and of the restoration of the holy Priesthood, and the fulness of the Gospel.'"[2]

Doubting young men (and sometimes women) are often told they will gain their testimonies on their mission. Why else would one sacrifice two years, possibly career, school, girlfriends, and other opportunities, if one doesn't know for certain that it is for a legitimate higher cause? And so the seed of belief grows.

Behavior can also perpetuate faith even after a testimony is gained. Dallin H. Oaks spoke to this. "I will conclude by describing another subtle form of deception—the idea that it is enough to hear and believe without acting on that belief. Many prophets have taught against that deception. The Apostle James wrote, 'Be ye doers of the word, and not hearers only, deceiving your own selves'. King Benjamin taught, 'And now, if you believe all these things see that ye do them'. And in modern revelation the Lord declares, 'If you will that I give unto you a place in the celestial world, you must prepare yourselves by doing the things which I have commanded you and required of you'."[3]

For those whose testimonies are at risk, the general authorities recommend more doing. "How do you remain 'steadfast and immovable' during a trial of faith? You immerse yourself in the very things that helped build your core of faith: you exercise faith in Christ, you pray, you ponder the scriptures, you repent, you keep the commandments, and you serve others."[4]

My own patriarchal blessing gave me personal advice that reflects this mechanism: "...inasmuch as you will be called to many positions to fulfill in the Church, your testimony will increase by the preparation that you put forth to magnify all the callings that our Father in Heaven will call you to in this life here on earth."

Very often these promises are fulfilled, not just in the LDS Church, but in any totalist group, because this is how the human mind has always worked.

---

1. Ballard, "Now Is the Time," LDS General Conference, Oct 2000.
2. Robert D. Hales. "Personal Revelation: The Teachings and Examples of the Prophets." In LDS General Conference, Oct 2007. http://www.lds.org/general-conference/2007/10/personal-revelation-the-teachings-and-examples-of-the-prophets
3. Dallin H. Oaks. "Be Not Deceived." In LDS General Conference, Oct 2004.
4. Elder Neil L. Andersen. "Trial of Your Faith." In LDS General Conference, Oct 2012.

*Public commitments tend to be lasting commitments.*
—**Robert B. Cialdini,** *Influence*[1]

*When we say we will do something, we do it. When we make a commitment, we honor it. When we are given a calling, we fulfill it... When we enter into an agreement, we keep it.*
—**Elder Sheldon F. Child,**
**General Conference, April 1997**[2]

# Public Commitment

**Public Commitment**
*—Suppression, Group Identification, Reward, Reinforcement, Perpetuation*
- Leverages cognitive dissonance to turn agreements, statements, and unbelieved testimonies into strong beliefs
- Relies on social pressure to motivate

**Testimony**
- Has potential to convert new members via social proof
- May include elements of confession
- Spreads loaded language, thought-terminating clichés
- Shared struggle with others increases dependency and group identification
- Positive stories promise rewards
- May enkindle group euphoria

**Covenants**
- Sense of contract leverages ideals of integrity to keep member trapped in belief system
- Leverages deception by not fully informing the member of commitments beforehand
- Leverages destabilization by covenanting children before the age of consent
- Reinforces covenants with dispensing of existence
- Reinforces covenants with threat of separation from the group, leveraging dependency

Just as belief follows behavior, public commitment leverages cognitive dissonance to convert actions into beliefs. This technique is defined not so much by a rote activity, but on social visibility and open declarations.

Public displays carry not only the force of internal cognitive integrity, but also outward social pressures which drive to protect esteem and reputation. No one wants to be called a hypocrite. Voiced intention is the soul of this technique: intention to act, intention to comply, intention to believe.

Singer states, "As social psychology experiments and observations have found for decades, once a person makes an open commitment before others to an idea, his or her subsequent behavior generally supports and reinforces the stated commitment. That is, if you say in front of others that you are making a commitment to be 'pure', then you will feel pressured to follow *what others define as the path of purity.* "[3]

Commitment leads to behavior, which then leads to belief. There is nothing wrong with committing to a desired goal, but in a totalist milieu, you give up control over the definition of your commitment. Once you've

---

1. Cialdini, *Influence,* 2009. 71.
2. Sheldon F. Child. "As Good As Our Bond." In LDS General Conference, April 1997. http://www.lds.org/general-conference/1997/04/as-good-as-our-bond
3. Singer, *Cults in Our Midst,* 1995. 75-76. (Emphasis added.)

committed to vague ideas of being pure, kind, loving, or faithful, a group can later say, "This is what it means to be faithful," and you are stuck with it, even if you started with something else in mind.

In this way, public commitment is instrumental in developing a group identity, of letting the doctrine begin its work redefining who you *are*.

Cialdini cautions, "...be very careful about agreeing to trivial requests, because that agreement can influence our self-concepts. Such an agreement can not only increase our compliance with very similar, much larger requests, it can also make us more willing to perform a variety of larger favors that are only remotely connected to the little one we did earlier. ...once a person's self-image is altered, all sorts of subtle advantages become available to someone who wants to exploit that new image."[1]

Once the identity ball is rolling, "There is no need for the compliance professional to undertake a costly and continuing effort to reinforce the change; the pressure for consistency will take care of all that. ...they will automatically begin to see things differently. They will convince themselves that it is the correct way to be and will begin to pay attention to facts they hadn't noticed before... They will make themselves available to hear arguments they hadn't heard before...and will find such arguments more persuasive than before."[2]

But you will never notice the process happening. "...when you engage in cooperative activity with peers in an environment that you do not realize is artificially constructed, you do not perceive your interactions to be coerced. And when you are encouraged but not forced to make verbal claims to 'truly understanding the ideology and having been transformed,' these interactions with your peers will tend to lead you to conclude that you hold beliefs consistent with your actions. In other words, you will think that you came upon the belief and behaviors yourself."[3]

The illusion of freedom is vital. If you commit to action under the point of a gun, it will do nothing to alter your beliefs. Overt coercion gives dissonance a release valve; you can reason that you're doing it under duress. But if you feel you're doing it on your own, then you will come to think those beliefs are also your own.

If you say it, you'll do it. When you do it, you think it. When you think it, you believe it. And when you believe it, you own it.

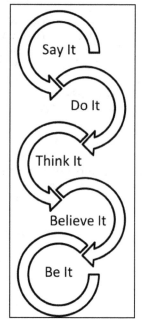

This works whether your commitment is made in front of a congregation, or one-on-one with a missionary or parent or bishop, or even when done only in the presence of God. An honest person will keep that commitment no matter what.

But when honesty is one-way, when you are consenting under deception, the contract is broken the moment you sign it, just as it would be if you signed under duress.

Of course Mormons are asked to commit publicly in lots of ways. "We are a covenant-making people."[4] That's what all the ordinances are all about. Elder Sheldon F. Child elaborates: "We make covenants at the waters of baptism. We renew those covenants each week as we worthily partake of the sacrament. We take upon ourselves the name of Christ; we promise to always remember Him and to keep His commandments. And in return He promises us that His Spirit will always be with us. We make covenants as we enter into the temple, and in return we receive the promised blessings of eternal life—if we keep those sacred covenants. Covenants with God are not to be taken lightly."

Mormons are people of the covenant, and covenants are

---

1. Cialdini, *Influence*, 2009. 65-66.
2. Cialdini, *Influence*, 2009. 83.
3. Singer, *Cults in Our Midst*, 1995. 76.
4. Child, "As Good As Our Bond," General Conference, April 1997.

promises to God. Apostle Russell M. Nelson explains this important gospel principle: "One of the most important concepts of revealed religion is that of a sacred covenant. In legal language, a covenant generally denotes an agreement between two or more parties. But in a religious context, a covenant is much more significant. It is a sacred promise with God. He fixes the terms. Each person may choose to accept those terms. If one accepts the terms of the covenant and obeys God's law, he or she receives the blessings associated with the covenant."[1]

When you accept those terms, you are accepting whatever terms the Church wishes to impose, as Henry B. Eyring shows. "He always keeps His promises offered through His authorized servants, but it is the crucial test of our lives to see if we will make and keep our covenants with Him."[2] Again, leadership stands in proxy for God's will. We're not committing to God, but to them.

There are many ways to publicly display commitment to the Church. When we accept a calling, we are "set apart" in the presence of witnesses. There are CTR rings[3], hymns, awards programs like Personal Progress and Faith in God, recitation of mottos, sustaining leaders with our arms to the square, public solo performances and talent shows, talks and teaching Sunday School. As Mormons, we were constantly reaffirming our commitment to the gospel and had ample opportunities to shout our beliefs from the rooftops.

The greatest of all these opportunities is bearing testimony. This is a common practice in totalist groups. From *Captive Hearts*, "Actions that are public...tend to reinforce the conditions necessary for lasting commitment. Hence the value of 'testifying' or group self-criticism sessions."[4]

The Church makes the promise, repeatedly, that if you don't have a testimony, you can gain one by bearing it. Robert D. Hales said, "You will find when you share your testimony it becomes stronger..."[5]

Boyd K. Packer wrote, "A testimony is to be found in the bearing of it. Somewhere in your quest for spiritual knowledge, there is that 'leap of faith,' as the philosophers call it. It is the moment when you have gone to the edge of the light and step into the darkness to discover that the way is lighted ahead for just a footstep or two."[6]

The general authorities are asking you to lie in front of others, to say, "I know this Church is true," when you *don't* know. This is literally bearing false witness of the truthfulness of the gospel, and it ignites dissonance to transform lies into truth. A testimony really is to be found in bearing it.

And a testimony is total. "Simply stated, testimony—real testimony, born of the Spirit and confirmed by the Holy Ghost—changes lives. It changes how you think and what you do. It changes what you say. It affects every priority you set and every choice you make."[7]

In this talk by Russell M. Nelson, and in many others, general authorities direct *what* we should say in our sincere and freely given testimony. He continues, "Although we can have testimonies of many things as members of the Church, there are basic truths we need to constantly teach one another and share with those not of our faith. Testify God is our Father and Jesus is the Christ. The plan of salvation is centered on the Savior's Atonement. Joseph Smith restored the fulness of the everlasting gospel of Jesus Christ, and the Book of Mormon is evidence that our testimony is true." This one-size-fits-all testimony ensures that all Mormons believe the same thing.

---

1. Russell M. Nelson. "Covenants." In LDS General Conference, Oct 2011. http://www.lds.org/general-conference/2011/10/covenants
2. Henry B. Eyring. "Witnesses for God." In LDS General Conference, Oct 1996. http://www.lds.org/general-conference/1996/10/witnesses-for-god
3. "Choose the Right." CTR rings are given to children about the time they are baptized at age 8. Older kids and adults often buy nicer versions. They are a constant outward reminder to keep the commandments.
4. Tobias and Lalich, *Captive Hearts, Captive Minds*, 1994. 29.
5. Robert D. Hales. "The Importance of Receiving a Personal Testimony." In LDS General Conference, Oct 1994.
6. Boyd K. Packer. *That All May Be Edified*. First Edition. Bookcraft Pubs, 1982. 340.
7. M. Russell Ballard. "Pure Testimony." In LDS General Conference, Oct 2004. http://www.lds.org/general-conference/2004/10/pure-testimony

All testimonies should reinforce the milieu, as shown by Elder Carl B. Cook: "In fast and testimony meetings, our Church leaders invite us to 'bear brief, heartfelt testimonies and to relate faith-promoting experiences.' When guided by the Holy Ghost, we will refrain from...saying and doing anything that detracts from the Spirit."[1]

Social pressures reinforce a milieu of unanimous testimony. Goldhammer notes that in high-demand groups, "Flattery and praise are given to members whose testimony supports the group mission, while the rare antidoctrinal sharings are met with icy silence and ostracism. A mass of people who all think alike exerts an awesome influence on the individual."[2]

Signs of spirituality improve status, and some bear testimony to impress others and gain acceptance. Someone struggling in their faith may bear testimony just to prove their belief, which, as we've seen, can lead to actual belief. Even if it doesn't, it gives others in the group the false impression of total agreement.

Galanti observed this at the Moonie recruitment camp. "I experienced a direct example of a display of reference power on Saturday evening when we gathered in our small groups to discuss 'what we liked best about the day'—not what we thought about the day, but what we liked best. As we went around the circle, people mentioned things like the lecture on the Reverend Moon, the movie about the Unification Church, or a point made in a lecture. Personally, what I liked best about the day was the volleyball game. But I realized if I said that I would sound quite shallow. I liked these people and I didn't want them to think I was shallow, so I searched for something that would make me look better in their eyes, yet would still be true. When my turn came, I said, 'I really enjoyed meeting a lot of really nice people.' Already, in this small way, my behavior was being influenced."[3]

These social pressures are potent. Many seemingly heartfelt testimonies may be entirely faked. Diana Kline tells a story in *Woman Redeemed* almost identical to my time at Girl's Camp around a campfire testimony meeting. Everyone else was crying and she wished she could cry, too. Instead, she felt nothing. When her turn came, she stood and said the usual, trying to put enough quiver into her voice to be convincing, because it was expected of her and she wanted to be liked. Afterwards, by herself, she couldn't *stop* crying because of how alone she felt.[4]

Those who struggle to gain faith may feel secretly alienated, not realizing how many others around them are also pretending. It is the Emperor's New Clothes of emotion, heartbreaking and manipulative to the extreme.

The habit of testimony-bearing begins in childhood. Anyone raised LDS can probably remember a parent or teacher whispering a testimony into their ear. Obediently, with childlike faith, she stumbles over unfamiliar words, repeating them into a microphone. "I know this Church is true. I know Joseph Smith was a prophet of God. I know President Kimball is a prophet, too. I know my Heavenly Father loves me. I know the Book of Mormon is the word of God." I was so young, I thought I was "burying" my testimony.

Now, they even give children a "testimony glove" to help them remember the five points they "know" to be true.[5]

This practice is systematic and intentional. "Parents are responsible to teach their young children how to bear their testimonies in public settings such as youth conferences, seminary, Primary, or fast and testimony meetings. The principles that govern appropriate testimony bearing should be learned and applied at home, thus preparing children to share their heartfelt thoughts with others. Public testimony-bearing is most often a natural extension of the testimony bearing experiences family members have at home."[6]

This has a powerful effect on children. As Chris L. Morin recollects, "...our bishop

---

1. Elder Carl B. Cook. "When Children Want to Bear Testimony." *Ensign*, Dec 2002.
2. Goldhammer, *Under the Influence*, 1996. 108.
3. Galanti, "Reflections on 'Brainwashing,'" *Recovery from Cults*, ed. Langone, 1995. 98.
4. Kline, *Woman Redeemed*, 2005. 28-29.
5. "Testimony Glove." *Friend*, Oct 2008. http://www.lds.org/friend/2008/10/testimony-glove
6. Cook, "When Children Want to Bear Testimony," *Ensign*, Dec 2002.

wanted each person in the congregation to bear his or her testimony. Starting with those in the back of the chapel, each member...stood up and bore testimony. As my turn drew closer, I became increasingly uneasy, afraid of speaking in front of the whole congregation and unsure of what to say. 'I believe the Church is true' seemed to be the only acceptable testimony. In retrospect, the pressure I felt was probably more imagined than real. However, being six or seven years old at the time, and wanting to fit in, I stood and said that I knew the Church was true."[1]

Children quickly learn that good testimonies earn praise. All they have to do is repeat the mantra. As they grow they learn to embellish.

> A very young boy... proceeded to the pulpit with my approval, stretched tall so he could see over it, and shared his sincere feelings about the restored gospel. He declared that Joseph Smith had been called of God and that the Church today is led by a prophet. He expressed his appreciation for Jesus Christ, for his blessings, and for a loving family. Young Brian spoke spontaneously from his heart, with conviction, and without rehearsal or memorization. Hearts were touched and testimonies strengthened because this young boy was prepared to bear his testimony at a moment's notice.
>
> Contrast this with the child who goes to the microphone less prepared with his own feelings and convictions who must be prompted on what to say, or who is primarily looking for the approval of others.[2]

But it starts with looking for approval, first of parents, then of peers, teachers, and priesthood leaders. This young boy learned how easily he could bring all those around him to tears, and be praised for it, just as this general authority praised him.

It's no mistake missionaries are given a list of commitments to ask investigators for at the end of every lesson. The missionary manual states:

> Commitment is an essential part of repentance. It is the act of obligating oneself to a course of action and then diligently following through on that decision. When people are genuinely committed, they have real intent, meaning that they fully intend to do what they become committed to do. They make an unwavering and earnest decision to change. They become devoted to Christ and dedicate themselves to His gospel...
>
> Extending and following up on commitment invitations is vital because...people become converted as they live the principles they learn...and feel the Spirit confirm that what they are doing is pleasing to their Father in Heaven...
>
> Rarely, if ever, should you talk to people or teach them without extending an invitation to do something that will strengthen their faith in Christ.[3]

Missionaries are to state the request in a way that makes it difficult to refuse or express doubt: "A commitment invitation often takes the form of a 'will you' question, which requires a *yes* or *no* response."[4]

Missionaries are then expected to follow up. "Make frequent contact, daily if possible, to find out how people are progressing with their commitments... There may be times when you call the investigators to remind and encourage them to keep a commitment... Express concern and disappointment when people fail to keep their commitments and thus fail to experience the blessings."[5]

This advice seems manipulative and pushy now, but inside the LDS echo chamber, these seem like reasonable efforts to save someone's soul and bring them the happiness of the gospel.

---

1. Morin and Morin, *Suddenly Strangers,* 2004. 33.
2. Cook, "When Children Want to Bear Testimony," *Ensign,* Dec 2002.
3. *Preach My Gospel: A Guide to Missionary Service*. 2004. The Church of Jesus Christ of Latter-day Saints, n.d. 196.
4. *Preach My Gospel*, 2004. 197.
5. *Preach My Gospel*, 2004. 200.

From the very first meeting, these are the commitments the missionary is encouraged to elicit from the investigator:

- ☑ Will you read and pray to know that the Book of Mormon is the word of God?
- ☑ Will you pray to know that Joseph Smith is a prophet?
- ☑ Will you attend church with us this Sunday?
- ☑ May we set a time for our next visit?
- ☑ Commandments from lesson 4 that you choose to include.[1]

Note that some of these seem like commitments to do a thing, but in a way are commitments to *believe* a thing. Praying is a behavior, but what are you praying for? To know Joseph Smith is a prophet.

Later, more commitments are added, including: "Will you pray to know that what we have taught is true?" By the second lesson, missionaries are already asking for a baptismal commitment.[2]

The effects of testimony-bearing are also brought into play. "Bear testimony several times in each lesson, not just at the end. Bear testimony that what your companion has taught is from God. Bear testimony that the principle you are going to teach will bless the investigators' lives if they will follow it. Talk about how living a principle has blessed your life."[3]

This exerts a number of pressures on everyone involved. The investigator is asked to believe within the context of committing to follow gospel principles by two polite, well-dressed youths who reinforce one another's statements with confident assurance. Remember social proof?

But the mind control works in both directions. The young missionary, who may himself have a weak testimony, thinks through times when he followed a commandment and had something good happen. He publicly declares the connection between the deed and the positive effect while his companion testifies it is true. Any doubts he may have started with will slowly fade.

This is one of the many reasons that "every member is a missionary." Bearing testimony and teaching outsiders strengthens convictions, lest you feel hypocritical or foolish.

Jack B. Worthy noted, "Why was my testimony ('I know these things are true') written into the memorized discussions? My testimony was supposed to be real, personal, and expressed with conviction from the heart; it wasn't supposed to be a piece of memorized text."[4]

Sincerity would be nice, but that isn't what's important.

Youth are told that if they don't have a testimony, they will have one by the end of a mission. "In my own teenage years I didn't completely understand the importance of developing spiritually. I was probably more interested in becoming a good football player than in becoming a good student of the Book of Mormon. It wasn't until I reached the mission field that, like many young men, I had that transformation and understood what happiness is really about. It's the joy, the peace that comes from serving the Lord, from studying and from praying, from loving and helping others."[5]

After regularly bearing testimony and teaching gospel principles, it's no surprise when many young men and women come home with a testimony. Depending on the mission president, this technique can be reinforced at levels much more severe and obvious than the general membership is aware of. "President Clark decided we should be 'hungry' for baptisms. He concluded that yelling, 'I am hungry!!' at the top of our lungs would be a good

---

1. *Preach My Gospel*, 2004. 43.
2. *Preach My Gospel*, 2004. 58.
3. *Preach My Gospel*, 2004. 199.
4. Worthy, *The Mormon Cult*, 2008. 124.
5. Elder Steven E. Snow. "Balancing Church History." *New Era*, June 2013.

way to start off each day."[1]

Returned missionaries (RMs) often report miracles and profound spiritual experiences. But many of these are embellished and hand selected to be faith-promoting.

> The first thing any RM has to do after returning home is to stand up in front of the entire congregation and give a homecoming talk in his or her ward, usually addressing several hundred members... RMs are expected to include at least one or two spiritually uplifting stories from their mission experience...
>
> "One of the most important components of a successful welcome-home sacrament meeting message will be [the returned missionary's] testimony..."[2] I would have received praise for the spiritual portions of my talks, and would have been increasingly praised each time my reports of divine guidance increased in number and vividness. If I had gone through this process, perhaps today, more than twenty years after my mission, I would truly believe that my mission was filled with miracles.[3]

Jack B. Worthy quotes from the 1998 Church Handbook of Instructions:

"'The stake president counsels returned missionaries to teach the gospel in talks they give. As they speak in sacrament meetings, they should share experiences that strengthen faith in Jesus Christ, build testimonies, encourage members to live and share the gospel, and illustrate gospel principles. They should avoid travelogues, inappropriate stories about their companion or others, disparaging remarks about the area in which they served, and other matters that would be inappropriate for a servant of the Lord to discuss in the sacred setting of a sacrament meeting.'"

Given these requirements, Worthy observes, "There are two choices for those who literally don't have any spiritual, faith-promoting material, or, for that matter, a testimony: 1) give talks in church void of any spiritual, faith-promoting material, and without bearing one's testimony; or 2) begin the process of emphasizing and exaggerating some facts, while de-emphasizing and omitting others, and then adding, 'I know the Church is true.' They must choose between feeling uncomfortable about lying, or feeling uncomfortable about not living up to their families' and ward members' expectations. It is not hard to guess what virtually all RMs choose to do. Can you blame them?"[4]

This is an example of a double-bind, a win-win for the Church. All missions seem like spiritually enlightening experiences, even when many are not. Eventually, those who must lie will come to believe in the miracles.

Like the computer, Joshua, said in *War Games*, "The only winning move is not to play." Unfortunately for many, that isn't much of a choice, either.

---

1. Worthy, *The Mormon Cult,* 2008. 129.
2. Joe J. Christensen. "Welcome Home! Advice for the Returned Missionary," 1989.
3. Worthy, *The Mormon Cult,* 2008. 168-169.
4. Worthy, *The Mormon Cult,* 2008. 169-170.

*The thought of leaving remotely occurred to me, but this place was my whole life. I was tied into it by everything—my marriage, my job, my friends, my church, my teacher, my daughter.*

—**Steve Sanchez,**
***Spiritual Perversion***[1]

*This is so effective on many people who were raised in Mormonism as children because it plays on a child's sense of dependency on his or her parents and community, causing a sense of separation anxiety at the thought of going against the system.*

—**Online Exmormon "Chris",**
quoted in ***The Pattern of the Double-Bind in Mormonism***[2]

# Creating Dependency

**Creating Dependency**
—*Group Identification, Silencing Doubts, Reinforcement, Isolation*

- Establishes punishment for failure
- Prevents any thoughts of leaving the group
- Prevents criticism, doubts
- Dependency can be real or imagined (physical dependence on family support, or emotional dependence on group approval)
- Established by social pressure; reinforces social pressure
- Established by:
    o Destabilization
    o Loaded language
    o Sacred science
    o Love bombing
    o Mystical manipulation
    o Doctrine over self
    o Dispensing of existence
    o Public commitment
    o Us vs. them
    o Induced phobias
    o Elitism
- Heavily reinforced by milieu control & deception
- Leads to double-binds

Many cults completely remove a member's support system, including outside friends and family and means of earning income, causing physical dependence on the group. In many cults, members live with other members, sometimes in completely closed environments. It becomes physically impossible to slip away without notice. And once escaped, how can the ex-member make a living?

Mormonism encourages self-reliance for temporal needs, so on the surface dependency seems irrelevant. But upon reflection, it surprised me the number of members physically dependent upon remaining in good standing. And as we'll see, material dependence isn't the only type.

*Captive Hearts* states, "Threats of excommunication, shunning, and abandonment by the group become powerful forces of control once members become fully dependent on the group and alienated from their former support network. If a person is completely estranged from the rest of the world, staying put appears the only

---

1. Sanchez, *Spiritual Perversion*, 2005. 236.
2. Stricker, *The Double-Bind in Mormonism*, 2000. 120. (Original quote from: http://www.exmormon.org/whylft65.htm)

option. Members come to dread losing what they consider to be the group's psychological support, regardless of how controlling or debilitating that support may be in reality."[1]

Church employees, BYU faculty, and current full-time missionaries are economically dependent upon the Church, essentially sequestered from the mainstream. Some BYU faculty report that BYU tenure is not respected by other universities, so it is difficult to find work elsewhere.[2] Church Education System (CES) employees have spent their lives teaching the gospel, a skill not in high demand in secular circles.

Often members living within the Mormon Corridor are physically dependent upon appearing righteous, as their jobs and businesses require acceptance by Mormons employers and customers. Many exmormons have reported lost business and jobs after leaving or being excommunicated.

Where the Church really creates physical dependency is in families. The majority of women, who have been obedient to LDS teachings, have avoided a career. The wife is entirely dependent upon her husband, and if she loses faith, she may as well be living on a cult compound. Same for the children. Counting this way, well over half of active Saints are physically dependent upon following or pretending to follow the gospel.

Men aren't free, either. They may have means of physical support, but they are emotionally and socially dependent upon their wives, children, and extended family.

The emphasis on family milieu creates a circle of interlocked dependent members, a mini-compound with the same dynamics of living assignments in a cult. The Church's entrenchment into the family unit enforces LDS control on a daily basis.

There are other forms of dependency, and as we've seen previously, mental forces can be as strong as physical ones. The Church creates a system of psychological, spiritual, social, and emotional dependence. On this level, dependence is a theme running throughout all the mind control methods.

*Recovery from Cults* states that the cult systematically creates a sense of powerlessness.[3] As *Captive Hearts* puts it, "The superiority of the group is established through the combination of peer pressure and constant reminders of the new member's weaknesses and vulnerabilities. The new member begins to rely on the beliefs of the group or leader for his or her future well-being."[4]

Once a recruit is hooked, continuing acceptance is oriented to compliance with group rules and culture. The doctrine begins to entangle with the individual's self-image, emotional stability, cultural filter, purpose for living, salvation from evil, direction towards ideals, and sense of being special.

For those who are born in the Church, this is all we know. We began physically dependent upon the entire system, so the psychological dependence runs as deep as family roots. "...culturally, I will always be a Mormon and will always feel most at home and in tune with other Americans raised as Mormons. Ironically, the religious beliefs of Mormons prevent many of them from having a close and meaningful relationship with someone like myself, which is why there is a community of ex-Mormons. We associate with each other to replace the relationships we've lost."[5]

We can leave the Church, but on some level, we can never leave it alone. We are emigrants forced to completely abandon the culture of our homeland, expected to never speak of it again. Even if our new lives are better, the culture of our birth will always be a part of us.

The Forever Family is part of this system of dependency. Mormons aren't the only ones told they cannot be saved without their ancestors. I was surprised to read Hassan's words about his former group. "...the Moonies tell members that ten generations of their ancestors

---

1. Tobias and Lalich, *Captive Hearts, Captive Minds,* 1994. 43.
2. Beck, *Leaving the Saints,* 2005. 231-234.
3. Langone, "Introduction," *Recovery from Cults,* 1995. 3.
4. Tobias and Lalich, *Captive Hearts, Captive Minds,* 1994. 42.
5. Worthy, *The Mormon Cult,* 2008. 59.

are stuck in the spirit world and are depending on them for salvation. If they don't do what the leadership tells them, all of their relatives in the spirit world will accuse them throughout eternity of lacking faith and betraying the Messiah."[1]

As former Mormon, Shauna Adix, observes, "The power of the promise of families together for eternity is so great that should one member of the family decide to leave the system, that person could destroy the whole family's capacity for future glory... It's one thing to take risks and possibly ruin things for yourself, but to ruin something for everybody else is a huge burden to bear."[2]

Children generally follow in parental footsteps. Bertrand Russell wisely noted that, "With very few exceptions, the religion which a man accepts is that of the community in which he lives, which makes it obvious that the influence of environment is what has led him to accept the religion in question."[3]

Here's that effect in action on a teenage boy, trying to gain a testimony:

> Considering my lifelong indoctrination, the result of my fast was inevitable... If I had received no answer from the Holy Ghost, I would have remained stuck in limbo without having resolved that "integral part of [me that] must be dealt with." And if I had concluded the Church to be false, there would have been serious difficulties at home. A dependent, sixteen-year-old Mormon cannot expect his or her parents to accept such a conclusion without their applying plenty of pressure to go back and ask the Lord again and again until the right answer is reached.
>
> Ultimately, the easiest choice for LDS children is to discover that the Church is true, and they subconsciously know it. Many Mormon boys miraculously gain strong testimonies just before they are to serve their mandatory missions. This enables them to survive the sacrifice of two years of their lives.[4]

There's that cognitive dissonance again...

Since children are so susceptible to influence, it is in the organization's best interest to regress adults to a state of innocence. As Margret Singer explains, "Through the cult experience and all those influences, an *enforced dependency* is developed. You may have started out as a completely autonomous independent individual, but after a certain amount of time, even though you may not want to admit it, you become completely dependent on the group for all your social needs, your family needs, your self-image, and your survival. To varying degrees, you are told every day what to do, and so you regress. You become like a child for whom any thought of independent action is totally confusing and unbearably overwhelming."[5]

Hassan reveals some of the methods for invoking regression. "During recruitment and indoctrination, cult members sometimes share activities—like sitting around the campfire, enacting skits, playing games or sports, and singing songs—that bring new recruits back to a childlike state. Leaders encourage members to talk about what they were thinking and feeling when they were little children."[6]

Galanti describes how the Moonies employ regression: "...the experience of being a child again during the training weekend serves to intensify the experience by psychologically bringing the person back to the period in his or her life when socialization first occurred."[7]

---

1. Hassan, *Releasing the Bonds*, 2000. 53.
2. Ure, *Leaving the Fold*, 1999. 175.
3. Russell, Bertrand, and Rouben Mamoulian Collection (Library of Congress). *Why I Am Not a Christian: And Other Essays on Religion and Related Subjects*. New York: Simon and Schuster, 1957.
4. Worthy, *The Mormon Cult*, 2008. 63.
5. Singer, *Cults in Our Midst*, 1995. 277-278.
6. Hassan, *Releasing the Bonds*, 2000. 117.
7. Galanti, "Reflections on 'Brainwashing,'" *Recovery from Cults*, ed. Langone, 1995. 101.

Sincere Mormons are instructed to have childlike faith. Even adults sing the Primary song, "I am a Child of God." We are taught to think of God as our loving Heavenly Father, and therefore submit to His guidance the way we submitted to parents. This places adults in a dependency mindset.

From Conference: "These children are providing examples of some of the childlike qualities we need to develop or rediscover in ourselves in order to enter into the kingdom of heaven. They are bright spirits who are untarnished by the world—teachable and full of faith."[1]

And scripture:

> Therefore, whoso repenteth and cometh unto me as a little child, him will I receive, for of such is the kingdom of God...
>
> 3 Nephi 9:22
>
> Except ye be converted, and become as little children, ye shall not enter into the kingdom of heaven.
>
> Matthew 18:3
>
> [He] becometh as a child, submissive, meek, humble, patient, full of love, willing to submit to all things which the Lord seeth fit to inflict upon him, even as a child doth submit to his father.
>
> Mosiah 3:19

Just like the Mormons, Moonies use family terms to refer to fellow members: "One major example of this is the use of the terms *mother, father, sister,* and *brother*. Rather than referring to blood relationships, they reflect church ties. 'Brother' refers to all male Moonies, 'sister' to all female Moonies. ...the use of these particular terms de facto turns the recruit into the 'child.' The Moonies never call you that outright, but if they are your spiritual mother and father, what else can you be but their child? The implication is that you are someone who does not know very much, someone who needs to be taught. Along with the childlike nature of other activities...it serves to psychologically transport you to the time when socialization first occurred, thus facilitating the resocialization process."[2]

Another form of submission comes through spiritual dependency. The only way to overcome the emphasized sins and weaknesses (demand for purity) is to lean on the group, doctrine, or leader.

I was taught that I never could attain perfection on my own. I would always fall short of the mark. No matter how hard I tried, I would need the redeeming power of Jesus Christ to pull me the rest of the way up. My best would literally never be good enough.

That is the essence of the doctrine of the Atonement. In this dynamic, we're first made to believe we're incapable of saving ourselves. This causes fear. Hope is then offered, but it is contingent upon the big "if" of faith, submission, and obedience.

Thus reciprocity is stretched to infinite extremes. Jesus bled from every pore and hung on the cross for you. This is central to LDS teachings. "How Jesus loves us, to suffer such spiritual and physical agony for our sake! How great the love of Heavenly Father that he would send his Only Begotten Son to suffer and die for the rest of his children."[3]

How much bigger a sense of obligation can we have than that? This concept of unpayable debt is repeated over and over, from the pulpit, in lessons, at family home evening, in hymns, and during the Sacrament.

One of my favorite scriptures was, "And if men come unto me I will show unto them

---

1. Jean A. Stevens. "Become as a Little Child." In LDS General Conference, April 2011. http://www.lds.org/general-conference/2011/04/become-as-a-little-child
2. Galanti, "Reflections on 'Brainwashing,'" *Recovery from Cults,* ed. Langone, 1995. 96.
3. *Gospel Principles*. The Church of Jesus Christ of Latter Day Saints, 2011. (Chapter 12: The Atonement.)

their weakness. I give unto men weakness that they may be humble; and my grace is sufficient for all men that humble themselves before me; *for if they humble themselves before me, and have faith in me, then will I make weak things become strong unto them.*" Ether 12:27 [Emphasis added]

It doesn't say strength will come from your own hard work. The grace of the Lord is required, and only after you've submitted.

Another way to create dependency is to strip away confidence in perceptions. This weakens an individual's ability to interpret the world on his own. He requires the cult paradigm to think and make daily decisions.

There is a strong doctrinal focus on "Choice and Accountability." It is true that every decision has a consequence. Wisdom comes from reality-based understanding of cause and effect. But Church doctrine exaggerates the consequences of even mundane and personal decisions.

Many members, both adults and children, wear CTR rings (Choose the Right) to remind them constantly of their eternal responsibilities. Stories are told of choices that turned out miraculously or disastrously. This or that small decision will lead to grand cosmic outcome. Something as simple as an accidentally blurted swear word could cause someone to apostatize because of your bad example. One kind word to a random stranger may save her life because she is about to die of lonely despair.

Richard G. Scott quoted Church President Hunter in his talk *Removing Barriers to Happiness*: "Throughout your life, you will be faced with many choices. How well you select among the alternatives will determine your success and happiness in life. Some of the decisions you will make will be absolutely critical and can affect the entire course of your life. Please measure those alternatives against the teachings of Jesus Christ."[1]

That's alot of pressure. But there is a guiding light to help. We were commanded to keep constantly in tune, open to spiritual promptings. "Be believing and your faith will be constantly replenished, your knowledge of the truth increased, and your testimony of the Redeemer, of the Resurrection, of the Restoration will be as 'a well of living water, springing up unto everlasting life.' You may then receive guidance on practical decisions in everyday life."[2]

Decision-making skills include scripture reading, praying, and listening for the Holy Ghost. Members are promised certainty through following emotions and leadership.

However, for many, it leads to confusion and perpetual self-doubt. What is the difference between my own thoughts and the still small voice? Am I feeling good about this because it's my desire, or God's? Let alone that third influence: Satan and his followers seek to tempt us and can counterfeit thoughts and feelings.

In the midst of this confusion, the only fallback plan is to follow the scriptures and the general authorities. Barbara Thompson of the Relief Society General Presidency counsels, "Most often personal revelation will come as we study the scriptures, listen to and follow the counsel of prophets and other Church leaders, and seek to live faithful, righteous lives."[3]

But what if they have nothing to say on a particular matter, or if authoritative sources contradict one another? "Sometimes inspiration will come from a single verse of scripture or from a line in a conference talk. Perhaps your answer will come when the Primary children are singing a beautiful song. These are all forms of revelation."

The scriptures say that a decision to act wrongly will cause a stupor of thought. That's how we're to know if a message is from God or someplace else. It is more likely that stupors are caused by dissonance in an environment with so many conflicting sources of unverifiable emotions and messages hidden in plain sight, with allegedly drastic consequences for choosing incorrectly.

---

1. Richard G. Scott. "Removing Barriers to Happiness." In LDS General Conference, April 1998.
2. Boyd K. Packer. "Personal Revelation: The Gift, the Test, and the Promise." In LDS General Conference, Oct 1994.
3. Barbara Thompson. "Personal Revelation and Testimony." In LDS General Conference, Oct 2011. http://www.lds.org/general-conference/2011/10/personal-revelation-and-testimony

Chris Morin reflects, "The more I ignored my own thoughts in order to align my thinking to prescribed ideas, the more I lost touch with my own sense of right and wrong, and the more I lost confidence in my own judgment. I became more dependent on the source of authority as to the correct course of action. At times, I asked not: 'What is right?' or 'What is wrong?' but 'What do the authorities say on the matter?'"[1]

In cases where the morality of a decision is unclear or irrelevant, it helps to imagine realistic consequences instead of dire good vs. evil outcomes. Usually the results of our actions aren't so drastic as the Church led us to believe. This is the beginnings of self-reliance and the essence of any effort to untangle emotional and spiritual dependency on the Church.

Sadly, physical and economic dependency is not so easily resolved.

---

1. Morin and Morin, *Suddenly Strangers,* 2004. 38.

*No man can serve two masters: for either he will hate the one, and love the other; or else he will hold to the one, and despise the other. Ye cannot serve God and mammon.*

—Matthew 6:24

*In the Church we are not neutral. We are one-sided. There is a war going on, and we are engaged in it. It is a war between good and evil, and we are belligerents defending the good.*

—Boyd K. Packer,
*The Mantle Is Far Greater Than The Intellect*[1]

# Black and White Thinking

**Black and White Thinking**
—*Suppression, Silencing Doubts, Reinforcement, Isolation, Influence, Trust*

- Establishes underlying polarizing logic which can be applied in many ways
- Severely limits ability to think
- Severely limits range of choices
- Limits ability to criticize and question—a doctrine is all true or all false
- Instantly reshapes incoming information to fit the mold of the belief system
- Reframes complex thought into simple thought
- Reinforces us vs them thinking
- Reinforces dispensing of existence (life vs death)
- Reinforces thought-terminating clichés, which are often built on B&W logic
- Reinforces the closed logic of sacred science
- Causes confusion when facing ambiguity, i.e. contradictory doctrines and denied indirect directives
- Confusion is easily short-circuited by mystical manipulation, loaded language, reframing, blame reversal, etc.

High-demand groups instill black and white thinking. Choices are either right or wrong, good or evil. All or nothing, aligned with God or Satan.

Thinking habits form around regular polarization of diametrically opposed concepts: Mormon or gentile[2]. Righteous or wicked. Humble or proud. Weak or strong. Blessed or cursed. Clean or unclean. Holy or unsanctified. Loving or hateful. Perfect or sinful. Obedient or rebellious. Eternal life or death. Spiritual or material. Sacrificing or selfish. Godly or sensual. The Church of the Lamb of God vs. the Great and Abominable Church.

There is no in between, and God says he prefers it that way. "So then because thou art lukewarm, and neither cold nor hot, I will spue thee out of my mouth." Revelations 3:16

Steven Hassan calls these "simplistic dichotomies."[3] Those who study informal fallacies of logic call it the "false dichotomy" or "false choice." It is a forked question, multiple choice with only two answers. And it is incredibly thought-limiting.

---

1. Boyd K. Packer. "The Mantle Is Far, Far Greater Than the Intellect." Brigham Young University, 1981.
2. Mormons consider anyone who is not LDS to be a gentile, though in some contexts, it means the same as it does to the rest of the world: Someone who is not Jewish.
3. Hassan, *Releasing the Bonds,* 2000. 50.

John Goldhammer says, "...collective vocabulary promotes *binary thinking*: everything is either yes or no, on or off, wiring in a monocratic dualism through one's vocabulary. Such language-bound groups, whether religious, economic, or political, are full of *rules*, doctrine, and dogma, saturated with 'shoulds' and 'should nots'."[1]

Black and white thinking serves several purposes:

- It contributes to the feeling of being right, one of the "good guys."
- It further isolates the member from those who think differently.
- It closes the mind to influence from outside information. Nuances can be instantly labeled "good" or "evil", rather than processed and fully understood.
- It makes direction very simple. Leaders don't need to explain or logically present a case. They merely need to say, "This is bad because we said so", or because God said so, and the followers, who are already in the habit of thinking this way, will accept the leader at his word.

There are some benefits for members as well. In this mindset, some decisions are very clear. You don't need to hear or understand all sides. There is only good and evil, and since you side with good, there is no need for further consideration.

*Captive Hearts* says that "cults create a world in which all the answers are known—and the cult supposedly has them. This type of thinking also serves a protective function, saving members from the anxiety of thinking for themselves. It keeps members functioning and cooperative."[2]

Harsh self-reproach can come into play. The instant you waver from exact gospel teachings, you're a bad person. Such condemnation will also be projected onto outsiders. Cult members often sound very judgmental against those who don't share their views. This leads to us-versus-them mentality and further isolates members.

In reality, there are usually three or four sides to every story. Life is a series of essay questions. Some answers are sort of right, or neither right nor wrong. Most situations are very complicated, and there are few easy problems.

Imagine painting with a watercolor set that only has pink and forest green. There's not much you can do, is there? Creativity requires the ability to think of all possibilities. *Captive Hearts* entitles a section "The Poverty of Black and White Thinking", which is apt. It's like voluntarily draining your brain-bank of thought-cash. Those who limit their choices and their worldview limit their ability to come up with practical, fair solutions.

The Church instills this habit so deeply that it's difficult to shake even when we stop believing the doctrine. Adapting to the real world from this environment is difficult. "Sometimes when people first leave a cult they temporarily reverse their values so that everything that was bad is now good and vice versa. This thinking is still limiting, simply a different version of the black-and-white formula. In fact, truth is made up of many shades of grey, a realization that can be frightening for it forces people to accept that there are not easy answers. Eventually, however, there is joy in discovering the vast array of colors as the mind opens to the richness of life."[3]

The thread of polarized logic runs through many of the other mind control techniques, so examples from other chapters illustrate this model well. Let's explore a few more ways the Church utilizes this technique.

Black and white logic can reframe the concept of "choice" and confuse the true meaning of free agency. "There is no middle road. Our position must be one of strength in order to overcome the evil that Satan would have us do."[4] This comes from a talk entitled "Using Our Free Agency", but it actually seems to be about good versus evil. In it, Apostle Delbert

---

1. Goldhammer, *Under the Influence*, 1996. 75.
2. Tobias and Lalich, *Captive Hearts, Captive Minds*, 1994. 101.
3. Tobias and Lalich, *Captive Hearts, Captive Minds*, 1994. 100.
4. Elder Delbert L. Stapley. "Using Our Free Agency." *Ensign*, May 1975.

L. Stapley proclaims freedom for all, then immediately limits choices to either A or B. A is following the gospel in every way, and B is succumbing to Satan's evil.

"How far does our agency extend? Brigham Young answered this question by saying: 'There are limits to agency, and to all things and to all beings, and our agency must not infringe upon that law. A man must choose life or death. ...the agency which is given to him is so bound up that he cannot exercise it in opposition to the law, without laying himself liable to be corrected and punished by the Almighty.'"[1]

Bruce R. McConkie established the false dichotomies of free will in *Mormon Doctrine*: "Four great principles must be in force if there is to be agency: 1. Laws must exist, laws ordained by an Omnipotent power, laws which can be obeyed or disobeyed; 2. Opposites must exist—good and evil, virtue and vice, right and wrong—that is, there must be an opposition, one force pulling one way and another pulling the other; 3. A knowledge of good and evil must be had by those who are to enjoy the agency, that is, they must know the difference between the opposites; and 4. An unfettered power of choice must prevail.'[2]

Black and white thinking is central to LDS doctrines, particularly to agency and the Plan of Salvation, where it is used to argue for complete submission. "Korihor [a Book of Mormon villain] was arguing, as men and women have falsely argued from the beginning of time, that to take counsel from the servants of God is to surrender God-given rights of independence. But the argument is false because it misrepresents reality. When we reject the counsel which comes from God, we do not choose to be independent of outside influence. We choose another influence. We reject the protection of a perfectly loving, all-powerful, all-knowing Father in Heaven, whose whole purpose...is to give us eternal life, to give us all that He has, and to bring us home again in families to the arms of His love. In rejecting His counsel, we choose the influence of another power, whose purpose is to make us miserable and whose motive is hatred. We have moral agency as a gift of God. Rather than the right to choose to be free of influence, it is the inalienable right to submit ourselves to whichever of those powers we choose."[3]

In reality there are millions of influences in the world, your own inner sense of self being central among them. LDS leaders want you to believe that any influence contrary to their position is from a single source: Satan.

This doctrine has a basis in scripture. The prophet Moroni said:

> Wherefore, a man being evil cannot do that which is good; neither will he give a good gift.
>
> For behold, a bitter fountain cannot bring forth good water; neither can a good fountain bring forth bitter water; wherefore, a man being a servant of the devil cannot follow Christ; and if he follow Christ he cannot be a servant of the devil.
>
> Wherefore, all things which are good cometh of God; and that which is evil cometh of the devil; for the devil is an enemy unto God, and fighteth against him continually, and inviteth and enticeth to sin, and to do that which is evil continually.
>
> But behold, that which is of God inviteth and enticeth to do good continually; wherefore, every thing which inviteth and enticeth to do good, and to love God, and to serve him, is inspired of God.
>
> Moroni 7:10-13

In a talk on resisting the devil, James E. Faust hoped to emphasize the dire need to constantly choose the right. "Someone once said, 'If you come to a fork in the road, take it.' But it doesn't work that way."[4] Actually, it *usually* works that way. A fork in the road

---

1. Stapley, "Using Our Free Agency," *Ensign*, May 1975.
2. McConkie, *Mormon Doctrine*, 1966. 26.
3. Elder Henry B. Eyring. "Finding Safety in Counsel." In LDS General Conference, April 1997.
4. President James E. Faust. "Serving the Lord and Resisting the Devil." *Ensign*, Sept 1995.
https://www.lds.org/ensign/1995/09/serving-the-lord-and-resisting-the-devil

usually has no moral consequences. If you're only sightseeing, does it matter which fork you take? Relative to how drastically the Church framed the outcome of every little choice, most of life's decisions have no spiritual implications.

President Faust goes on to quote Marion G. Romney from 1955: "The consequences of [mortal man's] choices are of the all-or-nothing sort. There is no way for him to escape the influence of these opposing powers. Inevitably he is led by one or the other."

According to the Old Testament, you can choose to either have a good day, or a bad day, depending on your obedience: "Behold, I set before you this day a blessing and a curse; A blessing, if ye obey the commandments of the Lord your God, which I command you this day: And a curse, if ye will not obey the commandments of the Lord your God." Deuteronomy 11:26-28

Dallin H. Oaks said, "If we choose the wrong road, we choose the wrong destination."[1] Boyd K Packer: "Doctrines can be spiritual or secular, wholesome or destructive, true or false."[2] And Brigham Young: "There is no such thing as confusion, division, strife, animosity, hatred, malice, or two sides to the question in the house of God; there is but one side to the question there."[3]

All-or-nothing logic can easily lead to binge-sinning. When you commit a minor sin, it's easy to feel like a "bad" person. At that moment, the fight feels lost. If you cannot conceive of any middle ground, and you've crossed the line, what's the point in keeping the rest of the commandments? This heightened depression and shame can lead to the very sins that the Church is trying to prevent; irresponsible behavior, moral abandon, and ill consequences become a self-fulfilling prophecy. As Steve Sanchez said of his new age cult, "Nothing really mattered now. I was already in hell anyway."[4]

As I've pointed out previously, there is rarely any clear cut polarity to any given issue. The complexities of any situation, action, belief, or value must be considered and weighed. This can be done without dumping everything into "good" and "evil" buckets. It may take a little more time and effort, but the outcome leads to greater freedom of thought.

---

1. Dallin H. Oaks. "Be Not Deceived." In LDS General Conference, Oct 2004.
2. Elder Boyd K. Packer. "Little Children." *Ensign*, Nov 1986. https://www.lds.org/ensign/1986/11/little-children
3. *Teachings of Presidents of the Church: Brigham Young*, 1997. 81.
4. Sanchez, *Spiritual Perversion*, 2005. 228.

*Called to serve Him, heav'nly King of glory,*
*Chosen e'er to witness for his name...*
*Called to know the richness of his blessing—*
*Sons and daughters, children of a King.*

—**Called to Serve, LDS Hymn #249**[1]

*Leaving the group was like ending my life as I knew it—like the prospect of dying. I could not imagine my life without the spiritually 'chosen' inflated self-image that was maintained by belonging to the group.*

—**John D. Goldhammer,**
**Under the Influence**[2]

*We are born before our time. They won't accept us... We've lived...as no other people lived and loved. We've had as much of this world as you're gonna get. Let's just be done with it.*

—**Jim Jones,**
**moments before the Jonestown massacre**[3]

# Elitism

**Elitism**
—*Group Identification, Reward, Trust, Isolation*

- Gives member a sense of pride and good feelings, of being elite, chosen
- Good feelings offset punishments, shame/guilt, and other negative side effects
- Provides strong group cohesion
- Reinforces social pressure
- Reinforces us vs. them
- Motivates demand for purity
- Eases doctrine over self, if the member feels she is made better by the group
- Supplants personal self-image with group-image
- Causes double-binds
- Can be used as a reward for good behavior

Most people don't like feeling dependent. They also don't like guilt and shame, repression of self, and other negative emotions generated by these controlling techniques. If that were all there were to cult membership, more people would walk out.

In order to distract from feeling powerless, totalist organizations spend significant time boosting you back up and making the group itself your primary source of pride. Elitism makes members feel special and offers a high to balance the many deep lows that come from membership. Additionally, elitism is a form of milieu control, preventing members from being influenced by outsiders who are "evil" or "don't know anything." This high is conditional upon you remaining in good standing and meeting the demand for purity.

Church members are elevated in two ways: collectively (as members of the group), and as individuals compared to others within the group.

The group's elevation over the world is a logical extension of sacred science. If the cult

---

1. Grace Gordon. "Called to Serve." In *Hymns of the Church of Jesus Christ of Latter-Day Saints*. The Church of Jesus Christ of Latter-Day Saints, 1985.
2. Goldhammer, *Under the Influence,* 1996. 58.
3. Maaga, "Jonestown 'Suicide Tape Transcript,'" Nov 18, 1978. http://employees.oneonta.edu/downinll/mass_suicide.htm

is the only true path to happiness or salvation, and if the leader is a messenger, a prophet, or savior, then by extension, the followers are chosen people, enlightened, gifted, or exceptionally intelligent. Whatever the words used, or whatever the doctrine supporting it, members are superior to outsiders.

Steve Sanchez said, "This was the kind of tough love that we were convinced made SLF and Rev. Will special and real. It made all of us special too, because we were among the few who could be around him and handle a truly enlightened and tough teaching."[1]

Nearly every cult teaches its members are special. Lalich and Langone's cult checklist states, "The group is elitist, claiming a special, exalted status for itself, its leader(s) and members."[2]

Singer states, "Most cults claim their members are the elite of the world, even though individual members may be treated subserviently and degraded. While in the cult, members identify with this claim and display moral disdain toward others."[3]

Goldhammer outlines the emotional dichotomy of extreme ups and downs: "...a destructive group directly erodes the individual's self-esteem and sense of worth while at the same time paradoxically maintaining the illusion of elitism and superiority... Persons trapped in this dynamic derive their self-worth and sense of identity from a group and their position in the group."[4]

This becomes a natural extension of sacred science. "...the individual members of a group so completely identify with a collective mission that they, too, experience tremendous ego-inflation, viewing themselves, through their association with their group, as anointed persons, uniquely gifted and appointed as emissaries of a world-saving cause which, of course, all others must be converted to."[5]

Social pressure and love bombing (in the form of flattery) leverage elitism during conversion. A fellow former member of Janja Lalich's political cult reflects, "I thought to myself that this was all pretty weird and I probably would not have joined except I knew that two of my best friends were going through the same investigation and were expecting and hoping to join. They were both mature and level-headed individuals whom I respected, so I thought it must be all right and worth a try. At the same time I was being treated with a lot of favor... The words of praise overshadowed my inner doubts and fears."[6]

Another quote from Lalich's account also made me think of the Church: "Study group members had the sense that they were being observed, watched; participation was encouraged, praised. All of this added to a growing sense of being special, of being part of an elite, of being 'chosen'."[7]

The feeling of being constantly watched can lead to a sense of pride. In her case, she thought the cult leader might be watching her. In the case of Mormonism, we were being looked after by God himself.

Latter-day Saints are elevated above the world. It is built into the name: Saints. Members are the "elect": "And even so will I gather mine elect from the four quarters of the earth, even as many as will believe in me, and hearken unto my voice." D&C 33:6

All worthy men are granted the priesthood, and given titles like Elder and High Priest, which signifies authority to act on behalf of God. These are not mere titles, but powers granted directly from God to ordain, dedicate, heal, discern, and cast out evil. All members are elect, but priesthood holders all the more so. From a Conference talk for men only, Elder William R. Bradford began: "My dear brethren, this is a thrilling hour. At no time has there been a gathering such as this of the elect sons of God. Were it not for the power of the

---

1. Sanchez, *Spiritual Perversion*, 2005. 91.
2. Lalich and Langone, "Cults 101: Checklist of Cult Characteristics."
3. Singer, *Cults in Our Midst*, 1995. 325.
4. Goldhammer, *Under the Influence*, 1996. 210.
5. Goldhammer, *Under the Influence*, 1996. 103.
6. Lalich, "A Little Carrot and a Lot of Stick," *Recovery from Cults*, ed. Langone, 1995. 65.
7. Lalich, "A Little Carrot and a Lot of Stick," *Recovery from Cults*, ed. Langone, 1995. 63.

Spirit, I could not bear up the weight of this moment."[1]

Women are singled out for praise, too. As Ezra Taft Benson addressed the Relief Society, "This is an inspiring and glorious sight. I am most honored and uplifted to be in your presence."[2] This type of flattery is a fairly common way to begin a talk.

Women are considered more spiritual and endowed with spiritual gifts just for being women. I was often told men were given the priesthood to make up for a lack of gifts that women naturally possessed. Motherhood itself is a power on par with the priesthood. Prophet David O. McKay said, "The noblest calling in the world is motherhood. True motherhood is the most beautiful of all arts, the greatest of all professions. She who can paint a masterpiece, or who can write a book that will influence millions, deserves the plaudits and admiration of mankind; but she who rears successfully a family of healthy, beautiful sons and daughters whose immortal souls will exert influence throughout the ages long after paintings shall have faded, and books and statues shall have decayed or been destroyed, deserves the highest honor that man can give, and the choicest blessings of God."[3]

The youth and single adults are also singled out for praise: "In great contrast to the low scenes in some of the streets...where 4,000 members of this Church had assembled, there was a completely different spirit and appearance. The youth and young adults at this great conference, along with the others participating, sang, danced, and demonstrated the best of themselves and their culture in a most delightful and uplifting manner. As we looked into their happy, clean, and appealing countenances and felt their enlightened presence, they radiated great moral strength and beauty. They reflected an inner light... These youth and young adults are part of an almost worldwide new aristocracy—as the elect of God—who know that the source of all light is divine."[4]

Elder Faust's talk here is entitled, "A New Aristocracy", and seems to argue for a modern aristocracy run by the Church, with members as agents for good to rule the world with a kind and virtuous hand. This may be an innocent metaphor, but if so, it is a poorly chosen one, with odd statements that smack of doublespeak: "The new aristocracy will not be seeking to eliminate thoughtful inquiry, or be a board of censors as it were, but rather seek to teach right concepts and to replace bad ideas with enlightened thought." As long as you're among the righteous, you'll have some say in which thoughts are enlightened, I suppose? At any rate, it succeeds in conveying a sense of elitism to the youth at whom the talk is addressed.

Missionaries are also praised. Jack B. Worthy recounts, "During our time at the MTC, we Hong Kong-bound missionaries were repeatedly told that missionaries assigned to serve in Hong Kong were extra special—the elite of the elite. I was almost convinced of it after the fifth or sixth time I heard it. Mormon culture traditionally propagates the concept of being a chosen race in a chosen place... But it wasn't only me; all LDS children are made to feel like they are the chosen of the chosen."[5]

Latter-day Saints pride themselves on being "a peculiar people." "...we are a congregation of true believers who are unique and different from all others; we are the Saints of the Most High who are assembling together in many nations to build up Zion and to prepare a people for the second coming of the Son of Man...

"We glory in our designation as a peculiar people. It is our desire to be unique—different from other men—because we have forsaken the world and have made a covenant

---

1. William R. Bradford. "The Governing Ones." In LDS General Conference, Oct 1979. https://www.lds.org/general-conference/1979/10/the-governing-ones
2. Ezra Taft Benson. "The Honored Place of Woman." In LDS General Conference, Oct 1981. https://www.lds.org/general-conference/1981/10/the-honored-place-of-woman
3. *Teachings of Presidents of the Church: David O. McKay*. The Church of Jesus Christ of Latter Day Saints, 2011. (Chapter 16: The Noble Calling of Parents.) https://www.lds.org/manual/teachings-david-o-mckay/chapter-16
4. James E. Faust. "A New Aristocracy." In LDS General Conference, Oct 1974. https://www.lds.org/general-conference/1974/10/a-new-aristocracy
5. Worthy, *The Mormon Cult,* 2008. 79.

to live godly lives and to walk in paths of truth and virtue."[1]

This is not without scriptural basis. "For thou art an holy people unto the Lord thy God, and the Lord hath chosen thee to be a peculiar people unto himself, above all the nations that are upon the earth." Deuteronomy 14:2

Scripture is replete with praise from God to his people. "Therefore, let your hearts be comforted; for all things shall work together for good to them that walk uprightly, and to the sanctification of the church. For I will raise up unto myself a pure people, that will serve me in righteousness." D&C 100:15-16

God's chosen are called to usher in Christ's Second Coming. Mormons believe that all other churches have corrupted the truth. We were always supposed to feel lucky for having been born LDS in modern times. Like President Hinckley iterated: "Our membership in The Church of Jesus Christ of Latter-day Saints is a precious thing... This is the kingdom of God on earth. This is His work in which we are engaged, and there is no more important work in all the world than this work. It concerns the eternal salvation of the sons and daughters of God, those living, those who have lived upon the earth, and those who will yet live. No people have ever been charged with a greater, more inclusive mandate than have we, you and I. Our work, given to us by the Lord, encompasses all of mankind."[2]

Members believe they are gods themselves in training. "Jesus answered them, Is it not written in your law, I said, Ye are gods?" John 10:34

Children are taught to sing, "I Am a Child of God" in Primary. This is central to the LDS identity, as reflected by the character Pam in the musical, *Saturday's Warrior*: "If I didn't know I am a child of God, I'd feel very lost."

This feeling isn't an accident, as parents and teachers are instructed: "First, make sure all of our youth understand who they are... Help them to know what it really means to be a child of God. Remind them that they are here at this particular time in the history of the world, with the fullness of the gospel at their fingertips, because they made valiant choices in the premortal existence. Our youth need to stand firm for righteousness and truth."[3]

Notice that specialness is contingent upon righteousness. These concepts are often wed. When Elder William R. Bradford praised the priesthood holders, he reminded them, "Your status as the governing ones has been, and remains, conditional upon compliance with the terms set forth by the Father and his Son, Jesus Christ, in our premortal life... Nothing about this is casual. It is serious business. It is so serious that God's affairs on earth and the salvation of all mankind rest upon it."[4]

In scripture, we read: "For whoso is faithful unto the obtaining these two priesthoods of which I have spoken, and the magnifying their calling, are sanctified by the Spirit unto the renewing of their bodies. They become the sons of Moses and of Aaron and the seed of Abraham, and the church and kingdom, and the elect of God." D&C 84:33-34

Elite status becomes contingent upon behavior, a motivation for the demand for purity. Stay worthy or lose your worth.

Battle themes are often used in the Church, throughout the scriptures, talks, lessons and hymns. Soldiers are also made to feel elite—"the few, the proud"—and this feeling is carried over through metaphor.

A number of LDS hymns get members to imagine fighting in God's select army, and are sung with great gusto to a triumphant beat: "True to the faith that our parents have cherished, true to the truth for which martyrs have perished." And in *We Are All Enlisted*, "Soldiers in the army, there's a bright crown in store, we shall win and wear it by and by." *Everyone* gets a crown.

---

1. Bruce R. McConkie. "The Mystery of Mormonism." In LDS General Conference, Oct 1979. https://www.lds.org/general-conference/1979/10/the-mystery-of-mormonism
2. Gordon B. Hinckley. "Recurring Themes of President Hinckley" *Ensign*, June 2000. https://www.lds.org/ensign/2000/06/recurring-themes-of-president-hinckley
3. M. Russell Ballard. "One More." In LDS General Conference, April 2005. https://www.lds.org/general-conference/2005/04/one-more
4. Bradford, "The Governing Ones," General Conference, Oct 1979.

All of these hymns, for me, are associated with a doctrine designed to make the youth feel extra special (since teens are particularly prone to wander). This doctrine has been preached generation after generation. In my time, *Saturday's Warrior* spoke of children coming down from heaven in glory, saved for the last dispensation, the world's metaphorical "Saturday", when only the most valiant, the strongest of God's children would fight against Satan's final rally. The Second Coming was just around the corner, so stay righteous and ready at all times.

We were the rising generation, and it was up to us to save the world. Firesides, Seminary, youth conferences, and Mutual activities reinforced a very strong warm feeling of being special. Celestial material for sure. We had what it took to withstand the overpowering attacks from the outside, and in this sense, it became a thought-terminating cliché.

The following scripture was said to apply both to the prophets of old, and to us, reserved for the last days:

> Now the Lord had shown unto me, Abraham, the intelligences that were organized before the world was; and among all these there were many of the noble and great ones; And God saw these souls that they were good, and he stood in the midst of them, and he said: These I will make my rulers; for he stood among those that were spirits, and he saw that they were good; and he said unto me: Abraham, thou art one of them; thou wast chosen before thou wast born.
>
> Abraham 3:22-23

And no one seems to notice when they grow old with the promise unfulfilled, when they make the same promise to their children. Kids were told this in the generations before mine, as is the generation younger than me. Ezra Taft Benson taught the following on March 4, 1979 at a BYU Fireside talk:

> For nearly six thousand years, God has held you in reserve to make your appearance in the final days before the Second Coming of the Lord. Every previous gospel dispensation has drifted into apostasy, but ours will not. True, there will be some individuals who will fall away; but the kingdom of God will remain intact to welcome the return of its head—even Jesus Christ. While our generation will be comparable in wickedness to the days of Noah, when the Lord cleansed the earth by flood, there is a major difference this time. It is that God has saved for the final inning some of his strongest children, who will help bear off the Kingdom triumphantly. And that is where you come in, for you are the generation that must be prepared to meet your God.
>
> All through the ages the prophets have looked down through the corridors of time to our day. Billions of the deceased and those yet to be born have their eyes on us. Make no mistake about it—you are a marked generation. There has never been more expected of the faithful in such a short period of time as there is of us. Never before on the face of this earth have the forces of evil and the forces of good been as well organized. Now is the great day of the devil's power, with the greatest mass murderers of all time living among us. But now is also the great day of the Lord's power, with the greatest number ever of priesthood holders on the earth. And the showdown is fast approaching.[1]

That was 35 years ago. As a child, I remember an elderly woman in our ward being sure the Second Coming would happen any day, because her patriarchal blessing promised she'd

---

1. Ezra Taft Benson. "In His Steps." BYU Fireside, March 4, 1979. http://speeches.byu.edu/?act=viewitem&id=89

live to see it. You'd think after all these generations passing away that this lie would stop working. But the youth are still being taught this doctrine. In 2001, James E. Faust said, "I salute you young people as chosen, special spirits who have been reserved to come forth in this generation."[1]

And in 2004, General Young Women's President Elaine S. Dalton made reference to a prophet's revelation from 1918: "In the vision of the redemption of the dead given to President Joseph F. Smith, he saw many of the noble and great prophets who had been on the earth prior to the Savior's coming. He also saw the Prophet Joseph Smith, Hyrum Smith, his father, and 'other choice spirits who were reserved to come forth in the fulness of times to take part in laying the foundations of the great latter-day work.' Who were those other choice spirits? Our generation was somewhere there among those 'noble and great' leaders, prepared in the world of spirits to be on the earth at this time!"[2]

And again, in 2008 Conference, when General Authority James J. Hamula spoke to the young men: "Now, my young friends of the Aaronic Priesthood, you are these valiant and noble sons of our Father! You are the strength of the Lord's house, His warriors! You are those who chose good over evil and who exhibited 'exceedingly great faith' and 'good works.' And because of your personal history, you were entrusted to come to the earth in these last days to do again what you did before—to once again choose good over evil, exercise exceedingly great faith, and perform good works—and to do so in behalf of the kingdom of God on the earth and your fellowman!"[3]

Needless to say, we felt very special indeed.

Patriarchal blessings are another way to make members feel special throughout their lives. It's a personalized prophecy to imply you are more than a nameless cog among millions. God speaks to you directly and itemizes your talents and potential. You are assigned a tribe of Israel, a lineage straight from the Bible. Particular blessings are promised for your continued obedience.

The exclusivity of the temple ceremony continues this theme. Not everyone is allowed into the temple (much to the sorrow of unworthy family members excluded from weddings), so being pure enough for it is a special feeling indeed.

The ceremonies themselves also convey elitism through secret signs and tokens, special clothing, and being called a "Priest and King", or "Priestess and Queen." Furthermore, you receive a sacred name that only you get to know. Few members know that the same name is given to everyone who goes through the temple the same day.[4]

At the end of the ceremony, you are granted access to the most exclusive place in the world: the Celestial Room, which is designed to make you feel as though you are in the highest tier of heaven. It doesn't get any more elite than that.

Unofficial ranks or forms of praise are available to members who prove worthy. There are sweet spirits, special spirits, spiritual people, and the greatest of the great: spiritual giants. This can subtly motivate members to strive harder.

Higher callings can be a source of pride. Lalich noticed this dynamic in her political cult: "Being asked to do more was a sign of greater acceptance and trust on the part of the leadership; agreeing to do more was a show of willingness to make the commitment on the part of the new member. Any resistance was met with criticism, signaling a weak link."[5] Accept your callings and magnify your callings, because many are called, but few are chosen.

But status is not all based on merit. "The social structure of the Latter-day Saint community is more aristocracy than democracy. Descendants of the early pioneers enjoy a

---

1. President James E. Faust. "Who Do You Think You Are?" *New Era*, March 2001. https://www.lds.org/new-era/2001/03/who-do-you-think-you-are
2. Elaine S. Dalton. "We Did This for You." In LDS General Conference, Oct 2004. https://www.lds.org/general-conference/2004/10/we-did-this-for-you
3. James J. Hamula. "Winning the War Against Evil." In LDS General Conference, Oct 2008.
4. "Temple Name Oracle." Accessed May 4, 2014. http://www.fullerconsideration.com/templenameoracle.php
5. Lalich, "A Little Carrot and a Lot of Stick," *Recovery from Cults,* ed. Langone, 1995. 66.

subtly but distinctly higher status than new converts and are more likely to be promoted to high rank in the Church's lay ministry."[1]

The saddest part of all this elitism is the effect it has on members' attitudes towards those outside the faith. Chris Morin observed, "Believing that only your group has the complete truth does not cultivate a willingness to learn from others. Believing that God has given you a special gift of discernment does not foster respect for the judgment of those who have no such gift. Being among God's chosen people does not increase your sense of brotherhood with the rest of humanity."[2]

Elitism helps keep members from straying, but ironically, this can make members less Christlike. It binds minds against learning from others, when others have so much to teach.

You don't need a group to make you into a good person. You can take pride in yourself, in your own accomplishments and sense of selfhood. Be cautious when relying on anyone else for affirmation, and make sure there are no hidden strings attached.

---

1. Beck, *Leaving the Saints,* 2005. 31.
2. Morin and Morin, *Suddenly Strangers,* 2004. 39.

*Fighting for a kingdom, and the world is our foe;*
*Happy are we! Happy are we!*
*Glad to join the army, we will sing as we go;*
*We shall gain the vict'ry by and by.*
—**We Are All Enlisted, LDS Hymn #250**[1]

*We have always been at war with Eastasia.*
—**George Orwell, *1984***

*These, these are the people—the peddlers of hate. All we're doing is laying down our lives. We're not letting them take our lives.*
—**Jim Jones,
during the Jonestown massacre**[2]

# Us-Versus-Them Thinking

**Us-Versus-Them Thinking**
*—Isolation, Group Identification, Reward, Suppressing, Silencing Doubts, Trust, Reinforcement, Perpetuation*

- Relies on black and white logic
- Creates isolation from the rest of the world
- Reinforces milieu control
- Increases trust in the group and leadership
- Decreases trust in the outside world, in criticism and doubts
- Creates a reward via a sense of elitism
- Establishes a persecution complex
- Allows for easy blame reversal
- Helps establish shame and guilt
- Influences through identification and example
- Strongly reinforces social pressure
- Subtly reinforced by doctrine over self (you don't want to be "Them")
- Ties "Them" to dispensing of existence—they are dead, going to hell, excommunicated
- Ties "Them" to a demand for purity—they are immoral, evil, lazy, weak, stupid, etc.
- Reinforces group identification via belief follows behavior & loaded language-they do not behave as we do, speak like we do

When elitism loves black and white thinking very much, they have a baby. That baby is us-versus-them thinking. It is deeply controlling and carries with it potential for deadly outcomes.

Michael Langone explains that "people outside the group are viewed as spiritually, psychologically, politically, or socially inferior, or as impediments to the members' development."[3] And according to Singer, "[Members] internalize the group's value system and its sense of moral pretentiousness, intellectual superiority, and condescension toward the outside world. In the cult, members get points for showing moral disdain for nonmembers and for members who faltered or left the group."[4]

This mechanism is a form of "othering", which paints all outsiders as enemies. It serves

---

1. Anon. "We Are All Enlisted." In *Hymns of the Church of Jesus Christ of Latter-Day Saints*. The Church of Jesus Christ of Latter-Day Saints, 1985.
2. Maaga, "Jonestown 'Suicide Tape Transcript,'" Nov 18, 1978. http://employees.oneonta.edu/downinll/mass_suicide.htm
3. Langone, "Introduction," *Recovery from Cults,* 1995. 8.
4. Singer, *Cults in Our Midst*, 1995. 325.

several purposes.

First, it thought-limits by casting automatic favor on the group's position. From *Recovery from Cults*, "While we/they dichotomies cut us off from others and suggest we think of them in terms of dehumanizing labels, such as animals, sinners, queers, rednecks, women's libbers, the teaming masses, and so forth, nothing is so simple as the labels 'good' and 'evil' suggest. They foster utter vulnerability to whatever system is the 'good' one—naturally the one that wants our support."[1]

Secondly, this isolating power keeps us from associating or listening to anyone outside the group. Continuing the previous quote, "Persuaders bring us to their place of power and separate the 'we' who are righteous and good from the 'they' who are ignorant and evil. By limiting our access to ideas that they find heretical or traitorous, they phase out other versions of reality."

Third, members themselves are strongly motivated to avoid becoming the enemy at all costs. Singer explains, "The pariah image takes on enormous proportions and coming to fit that image seems a fate worse than death."[2]

And finally, it keeps members from feeling free to walk away. Hassan says, "From the point of view of a mind control cult, there is never a legitimate reason to leave. The only people who leave are weak, selfish, or cannot control their need for sex, drugs, or other addictive substances. In the mindset of the group, people who leave are incapable of sacrificing or transcending spiritually."[3]

Steve Sanchez said of his new age cult, "[Rev. Will] painted all those who had left SLF as having fallen into karmic ruin, or as power-tripping fools whom he had completely defeated mentally, or as people who had basically become psychologically debilitated or insane from messing with the teaching. When we heard this, part of us was vengefully delighted that we were doing so much better than those who had left, and the other part of us was full of dread and determined to never suffer such an unthinkable fate."[4]

Lifton reveals how this dynamic revolves in an ongoing cycle: "The individual thus comes to apply the same totalist polarization of good and evil to his judgments of his own character: he tends to imbue certain aspects of himself with excessive virtue, and condemn even more excessively other personal qualities—all according to their ideological standing. He must also look upon his impurities as originating from outside influences—that is, from the ever-threatening world beyond the closed, totalist ken. Therefore, one of his best way[s] to relieve himself of some of his burden of guilt is to denounce, continuously and hostilely, these same outside influences. The more guilty he feels, the greater his hatred, and the more threatening they seem. In this manner, the universal psychological tendency toward 'projection'[5] is nourished and institutionalized, leading to mass hatreds, purges of heretics, and to political and religious holy wars."[6]

Thus, as individual identity gets bound up with the cult, the dehumanization of outsiders becomes personal and emotional. This was made evident in a 1971 experiment at Stanford University that quickly spiraled out of control.

Researchers asked what they thought was a harmless question: What would happen if 24 students were divided into two groups, prisoner and prison guard, and were asked to live that way for two weeks?

Even though subjects knew participation was voluntary, the guards got carried away, submitting the prisoners to escalating acts of cruelty and humiliation, including enforced nudity, sleep deprivation, and solitary confinement. The prisoners, who continued to

---

1. Zimbardo and Andersen, "Understanding Mind Control," *Recovery from Cults,* ed. Langone, 1995. 116.
2. Singer, *Cults in Our Midst,* 1995. 277.
3. Hassan, *Releasing the Bonds,* 2000. 52.
4. Sanchez, *Spiritual Perversion,* 2005. 337.
5. Projection is a psychological concept meaning the mental impulse to "project" subconscious fears about our own flaws onto others. Examples: A compulsive liar may regularly accuse others of dishonesty. A man repressing his own homosexual attractions may become a militant homophobe.
6. Lifton, *Thought Reform and the Psychology of Totalism,* 1961. (Chapter 22)

consent, became so dehumanized that they suffered short-term psychological trauma. Researchers had to end the experiment early.[1]

Hassan remarked, "This experiment, which lasted less than a week, demonstrates in a frightening way how much a person's identity depends on what role he is playing, how others treat the person, what uniforms or clothing the person wears, and so on."[2]

Roles are very important to how we behave, and totalist groups are motivated to rigidly and narrowly define everyone's part. By creating a superior LDS persona, the Church builds in automatic dismissal of other legitimate points of view. As exmormon Chris Morin confessed, "To preserve my belief in the fallen nature of those foreign to me, I must remain ignorant of who they really are—ignorant of their hopes and fears, ignorant of their unselfish deeds, and ignorant of their noble desires."[3]

Former members are the biggest potential threat to existing members, because ex-members have the most to complain about. Their insider information must be combatted to prevent dissonance in the ranks. Hassan says, "A popular argument among cult defenders is that the testimony of former members, or 'apostates,' should not be considered reliable, because such people may have been prejudiced by their departure from the group."[4]

A prominent apologist, J. Gordon Melton, has defended many modern cults, including extreme groups that have committed atrocities. "According to Melton, 'hostile ex-members invariably shade the truth. They invariably blow out of proportion minor incidents and turn them into major incidents.'" He indicates here that the survivors of the Jonestown massacre, and others, merely have a chip on their shoulders.

Sound familiar? Hassan follows up with an excellent point about objectivity. "Ironically, cult defenders appear to ignore the possibility that the testimony of cult members and leaders might be partisan." Indeed, one cannot get more biased than the scriber of scripture, the bearer of benediction, and the professor of prophecy. Their interests are *never* neutral.

Apostates from cults are actively ostracized, both to punish and to resolve the dissonant question, "If the group is so great, why would someone *leave*?"

Lalich described the multistage shunning process for expelled members of her political cult, similar to the LDS "discipline" levels of disfellowshipping and excommunication. Some, expelled "without prejudice", could still associate with the group and eventually prove themselves. Others were shunned to the fullest. "These isolationist techniques were used to create a feeling of superiority among members, as well as a sense of paranoia and hostility, as though these 'enemies' truly posed a threat."[5]

Us-versus-them language implies "they" are just as polarized and attacking back with the same or greater intensity. Which establishes a group-wide persecution complex. *Captive Hearts* explains that "paranoia may be evident in simple or elaborate delusions of persecution. Highly suspicious, they may feel conspired against, spied upon, or cheated, or maligned by a person, group, or governmental agency. Any real or suspected unfavorable reaction may be interpreted as a deliberate attack upon them or the group."[6]

This sense of persecution, usually imagined or exaggerated, serves to bolster that sense of being special. "To all of us SLF members, being persecuted by the outside galvanized the feeling of being elite and righteous in all our endeavors."[7]

Sanchez describes how SLF members responded to a newspaper article which referred to their group as a "cult": "The article had the effect of making a few of the more fringe members of SLF suspicious of Rev. Will, but most of the hardcore members just huddled

---

1. Romesh Ratnesar. "The Menace Within." *Stanford Magazine*, July/Aug 2011. http://alumni.stanford.edu/get/page/magazine/article/?article_id=40741
2. Hassan, *Releasing the Bonds,* 2000. 37.
3. Morin and Morin, *Suddenly Strangers,* 2004. 42.
4. Hassan, *Releasing the Bonds,* 2000. 170-1.
5. Lalich, "A Little Carrot and a Lot of Stick," *Recovery from Cults,* ed. Langone, 1995. 76.
6. Tobias and Lalich, *Captive Hearts, Captive Minds,* 1994. 71.
7. Sanchez, *Spiritual Perversion,* 2005. 310.

more tightly together, reassuring each other of their goodness as they were persecuted by the outside world."[1]

The Church actively cultivates a persecution complex. In the *New Era*, youth are told, "The true Church has always been a minority, and it seems like we've always had a target on our back. We'll always face adversity, and we might as well get used to that."[2]

FreeDictionary defines "persecute": 1. To oppress or harass with ill-treatment, especially because of race, religion, gender, sexual orientation, or beliefs; 2. To annoy persistently; bother.[3] Merriam-Webster uses words like "punish", "grieve", "afflict", and "to cause to suffer because of belief."[4]

*Actual* persecution against most modern Mormons is uncommon. But the myth must be maintained to deflect legitimate criticism. It transforms (reframes) a source of potential dissonance into proof that the Church is true, via the doctrine that Satan wants to destroy the One True Church. The more criticism, the better.

Yet for some reason, Satan spends the same effort trying to demolish other fringe groups, like the Jehovah's Witnesses, Scientologists, and LDS Fundamentalists. Does that make them all equally true?

To reference actual widespread persecution, Mormons must go back more than a century, to Joseph Smith's martyrdom, Haun's Mill, the Missouri Extermination Order, and the Utah War. Even then, the controversy surrounding Mormonism was complex and not without provocation. What happened to the Branch Davidians in Waco, TX in 1993 is perhaps the best modern equivalent.

Martha Beck reflects,

> The word *persecution* comes up over and over again in Mormon discourse, especially discussions of the early male Saints. The image of the slandered patriarch, accused of sexual misconduct by malicious villains, is one of the central archetypes in Mormonism...
>
> I [had] never heard anything that explained why anyone might have been justifiably angry at the Mormon organization or its leaders. The history of my people was taught to me, and to all my childhood peers, as a tale of pure victimization. The Latter-day Saints had always been a placid, sexually boring people, inexplicably tormented by liars both within and outside the Church...[5]

What Mormons now "endure" waters down what real persecution is like. Yes, people (like me) publish criticisms of the Church, its leadership, and its doctrines. That's the price (and benefit) of free speech: everything is subject to both positive and negative comment.

Yes, now and then a Mormon is teased for wearing garments or not drinking coffee. You might see the odd ignorant question about the temple or polygamy. Sometimes members have a hard time getting Sunday off work (along with everyone else who wants specific days off). Many think Mormons are a bit weird, but that is not persecution.

Conversely, Mormons are quick to brag when praised for honesty, clean living, and strong family values. The Saints are generally respected, and in many cases quite wealthy and politically powerful. It's hard to have it both ways.

There may be individual anecdotes of Mormons being persecuted in some religiously or culturally intolerant corners of the world. But Mormons as a whole are hardly "oppressed" or "harassed." However I can think of several groups that Mormons themselves persecute. The Church has often punished, harassed, and oppressed homosexuals, polygamists,

---

1. Sanchez, *Spiritual Perversion,* 2005. 316.
2. Elder Steven E. Snow. "Balancing Church History." *New Era*, June 2013.
3. "Free Dictionary: Persecute." Accessed April 27, 2014. *The Free Dictionary*, n.d. http://www.thefreedictionary.com/persecute
4. "Free Merriam-Webster Dictionary." Accessed Oct 10, 2013. http://www.merriam-webster.com/dictionary/persecute
5. Beck, *Leaving the Saints,* 2005. 180-181.

feminists, intellectuals, and critics.

The flames of a persecution complex can be fanned enough to turn into a conflagration of group paranoia. Self-defense becomes justification for atrocity. It's easy for good people to do horrible things when they believe they are protecting themselves and their families.

That is exactly what happened in the Mountain Meadows Massacre in Utah in 1857. In modern history, it happened in Waco and Jonestown.

In the case of Jonestown, we have audio tapes of the final moments as men, women, and children drank Flavor Aid tainted with poison. We know how Jim Jones countered the arguments of those who resisted.

A US Congressman, responding to allegations of imprisonment, cruelty, and inhumane conditions, visited and was shot and killed by a Jonestown security team. Three reporters were also killed. Jones convinced his followers that more government officials were on their way and would soon imprison everyone.

"Don't be afraid to die," Jones said. "You'll see, there'll be a few people land out here. They'll torture some of our children here. They'll torture our people. They'll torture our seniors. We cannot have this."[1] Compared to that, imposed suicide seemed a compassionate option.

Somehow, Jones saw mass suicide as a punishment against oppressors. "They'll pay for it. This is a revolutionary suicide. This is not a self-destructive suicide. So they'll pay for this. They brought this upon us. And they'll pay for that."[2]

This is the extreme result of us-versus-them thinking, of reframing and whitewashing the organization's actions. If the government was out to do anything to Jones and his followers, it was to help extricate those members who had decided the cost of membership was too high and had no other way out.

Critics of high-demand groups are generally not out to get anyone, and they have honest and genuine motivations. Hassan says, "Naturally, when there are many [former members] telling of similar experiences with a particular group, the information usually proves to be trustworthy. Most ex-members speak out at great personal risk and with little or no personal gain, other than the therapeutic effects of standing up to expose an injustice, and perhaps to help others."[3] The complaints of exmormons are fairly consistent.

One such ex-member, Marion Stricker points out, "...Mormonism causes the problems which it *claims to hate*. Mormonism needs enemies to fight as a *cloak* to hide the roots of the *cause*."[4] Misdirection calls it a wolf in sheep's clothing, when really the wolf is disguised as the shepherd.

The Church frequently uses war metaphors to define ideological conflicts between the gospel and the rest of the world. From General Conference in 2008, "We are entering the final stages of a great war. This war commenced before the foundations of the world and has been pursued with awful consequence throughout the world's history. I speak of the war between the followers of Christ and all those who deny Him as their God."[5]

While everyone knows it's "just" an analogy, it does exactly what analogies are supposed to do: it conjures relevant emotions, like valor, bravery, strength, endurance, and hatred against enemies. It implies a willingness to die. And a willingness to kill.

LDS hymn #254 boisterously declares, "Shall the youth of Zion falter in defending truth and right? While the enemy assaileth, shall we shrink or shun the fight? No!"[6]

Glenn L. Pace quotes this hymn, and then says, "Now that's exciting! What adventure in that great and spacious building would you trade for the thrill and excitement of building

---

1. Maaga, "Jonestown 'Suicide Tape Transcript,'" 1978.
2. Maaga, "Jonestown 'Suicide Tape Transcript,'" 1978.
3. Hassan, *Releasing the Bonds,* 2000. 173.
4. Stricker, *The Double-Bind in Mormonism,* 2000. 62.
5. James J. Hamula. "Winning the War Against Evil." In LDS General Conference, Oct 2008.
6. Evan Stephens. "True to the Faith." In *Hymns of the Church of Jesus Christ of Latter-day Saints*. The Church of Jesus Christ of Latter-day Saints, 1985

the very kingdom the Savior will come to the earth to govern?"[1]

Hymn #19 says, "The wicked who fight against Zion will surely be smitten at last."[2]

Hymn # 260 asks, "Who's on the Lord's side, who?" And hymn #243, "Fear not, though the enemy deride; Courage, for the Lord is on our side. We will heed not what the wicked may say, But the Lord alone we will obey."[3]

How wicked is the modern world outside of Mormonism? Boyd K. Packer was quoted in Conference as saying, "I know of nothing in the history of the Church or in the history of the world to compare with our present circumstances. Nothing happened in Sodom and Gomorrah which exceeds in wickedness and depravity that which surrounds us now."[4]

These are pretty strong words, considering the men of Sodom and Gomorrah wanted to rape Lot's angelic visitors. Lot was willing to give them his daughter instead, and he was the *good* guy. Vilification and demonization at its best.

The wide variety of philosophies and religions is reduced to two camps: "Behold there are save two churches only; the one is the church of the Lamb of God, and the other is the church of the devil; wherefore, whoso belongeth not to the church of the Lamb of God belongeth to that great church, which is the mother of abominations; and she is the whore of all the earth." 1 Nephi 14:10

Doctrine and Covenants goes into further detail about this abominable church: "And after they have fallen asleep the great persecutor of the church, the apostate, the whore, even Babylon, that maketh all nations to drink of her cup, in whose hearts the enemy, even Satan, sitteth to reign—behold he soweth the tares; wherefore, the tares choke the wheat and drive the church into the wilderness." D&C 86:3

Delbert L. Stapley summarizes LDS doctrine on this point: "All things good come from God. All things evil come from Satan." Then he quotes Brigham Young, "'There are but two parties on the earth, one for God and the other for the world or the Evil One. No matter how many names the Christian or heathen world bear, or how many sects and creeds may exist, there are but two parties, one for heaven and God, and the other will go to some other kingdom than the celestial kingdom of God.'"[5]

And Dallin H. Oaks: "They will come at you in classrooms and hallways, in what you read, and in what you see in popular entertainment. Many in the world deny the need for a Savior. Others deny that there is any right or wrong, and they scoff at the idea of sin or a devil. Still others rely on the mercy of God and ignore His justice. The prophet said, 'There shall be many which shall teach after this manner, false and vain and foolish doctrines'."[6]

In the musical *Saturday's Warrior*, Jimmy is faced with a choice between his loving family and his worldly, pleasure-seeking friends. In a climactic musical number where the two forces compete for his attention, his friends sneer and belittle his family. His parents helplessly plead and promise endless love. His sisters warn that his friends will take him from his family and then abandon him.

The choice between nonmember friends and one's own family is not a false dichotomy in Mormonism. It's a *real* choice, but not because of villainous friends. The Church regularly promotes us-versus-them doctrines that divide rather than bring together.

Apostle Oaks continues his above talk and quotes Paul's divisive language: "'For men shall be lovers of their own selves...disobedient to parents, unthankful, unholy, without natural affection...despisers of those that are good...lovers of pleasures more than lovers of God'. [Paul] also said that 'evil men and seducers shall wax worse and worse, deceiving, and being deceived.'"

---

1. Glenn L. Pace. "'They're Not Really Happy.'" In LDS General Conference, Oct 1987. http://www.lds.org/general-conference/1987/10/they-re-not-really-happy
2. William Fowler. "We Thank Thee O God For a Prophet." In *Hymns of the Church of Jesus Christ of Latter-day Saints*. The Church of Jesus Christ of Latter-day Saints, 1985.
3. Stephens, "Let Us All Press On," *Hymns*, 1985.
4. Hamula, "Winning the War Against Evil," General Conference, Oct 2008.
5. Elder Delbert L. Stapley. "Using Our Free Agency." *Ensign*, May 1975.
6. Dallin H. Oaks. "Be Not Deceived." In LDS General Conference, Oct 2004.

When it comes to apostasy, the Church doesn't hold back. Apostates are the worst of the worst. Martha Beck said, "As far as the Latter-day Saints are concerned, I've already committed the only sin worse than murder: I left the Church."[1]

Apostates fall into a limited number of stereotypes. One is the misled follower of the false doctrines outlined above by Apostle Oaks. Another is the lazy, filthy sinner chasing cheap thrills, also described by Oaks. This apostate doesn't care about the *true* happiness that can only be found in the gospel.

Rather than listen to exmormons to find out why we really left, the Church offers plenty of dismissive rationales, including weakness; temptation; unrepentant attitude; sin; anger; pride; taking personal offense; neglect of testimony; rebellion; laziness; taking the easy way out; and being deceived by fundamentalists, other apostates, or Satan himself.

Elder N. Eldon Tanner said, "They wander because of weakness of character. The spirit is willing, but the flesh is weak. These wanderers are in the wilderness of frustration and discontent. They know the law, but they succumb to temptation for a fleeting moment of pleasure to satisfy their appetites and passions."[2]

We were recently slandered in the *Ensign*:

> Apostasy frequently results when a person commits serious sin but does not repent. To silence his conscience or justify his sinful actions, the individual moves away from the truth, looking for imperfections in others or questioning Church doctrine with which he no longer agrees.
>
> Conflicts between Church members can also lead to apostasy. Some individuals begin to think the Church is not true when they feel that a leader did not treat them well. They become offended and, without considering what they are losing, they stray from the Church...
>
> Faultfinding can be another source of personal apostasy. When we look for faults in others or begin to think we could make better decisions than our leaders, we should remember the experience of Oliver Cowdery, the second elder of the Church... In time, sadly, Oliver rebelled against Joseph [Smith]...and he fell.[3]

Brigham Young compared apostates to a drunken man who thinks he is the only one sober. He also said, "Men begin to apostatize by taking to themselves strength, by hearkening to the whisperings of the enemy who leads them astray little by little, until they gather to themselves that which they call the wisdom of man; then they begin to depart from God, and their minds become confused."[4]

These are straw man arguments. This is a logical fallacy wherein a weak version of the real reasoning is constructed and then attacked. It can be quite convincing to those who don't recognize it for what it is.

Cognitive dissonance develops when a loved one leaves the Church. Why would they do it? Is the Church really not true? The belief that apostates are deceived or wicked easily answers these questions. Discomfort remains, yet that explanation is sadly easier to make peace with.[5]

To be considered temple worthy, family members of open apostates may have to renounce their actions and assert their loyalty. From the Church Handbook: "Bishops and

---

1. Beck, *Leaving the Saints,* 2005. 20.
2. N. Eldon Tanner. "Why Is My Boy Wandering Tonight?" In LDS General Conference, Oct 1974.
3. Elder Claudio D. Zivic. "Avoiding Personal Apostasy." *Ensign*, June 2009. http://www.lds.org/ensign/2009/06/avoiding-personal-apostasy
4. *Teachings of Presidents of the Church: Brigham Young*, "Chapter 12: Preventing Personal Apostasy," 1997. https://www.lds.org/manual/teachings-brigham-young/chapter-12
5. These levels of dissonance are not generated in non-totalist systems, even those that use manipulation tactics. Consider the marketing arm of a beverage company. Now imagine them treating their former customers this way, accusing all those who stop using its products of being weak, foolish, prideful, selfish, and rebellious. "You don't like our soda anymore because it has corn syrup? You're a hard-hearted, faultfinding, backbiting, anti-Pop!™"

their counselors must take exceptional care when issuing recommends to members whose parents or other close relatives belong to or sympathize with apostate groups. Such members must demonstrate clearly that they repudiate these apostate religious teachings before they may be issued a recommend."[1]

Those of us who criticize the Church are known as "anti-Mormons" and we are the worst of the worst: "Since the spring of 1820, Lucifer has led a relentless attack against the Latter-day Saints and their leaders. A parade of anti-Christs, anti-Mormons, and apostate groups have appeared on the scene. Many are still among us and have released new floods of lies and false accusations. These faith-killers and testimony-thieves use personal contacts, the printed word, electronic media, and other means of communication to sow doubts and to disturb the peace of true believers."[2]

For comparison, here is how the Jehovah's Witnesses feel about their enemies: "Jehovah hates sin, and so should we. Indeed, we ought to move as far away from wrongdoing as possible and not see how close we can get to it without being overcome by sin. For instance, we need to guard against succumbing to apostasy, a sin that would make us unfit to glorify God. Let us therefore have nothing to do with apostates or anyone who claims to be a brother but who is dishonoring God. This should be the case even if he is a family member. We are not benefited by trying to refute the arguments of apostates or those who are critical of Jehovah's organization. In fact, it is spiritually dangerous and improper to peruse their information, whether it appears in written form or it is found on the Internet."[3]

The *New Era* warns, "...you should never take the claims of anti-Mormon literature at face value. Although some critics of the Church may be doing what they sincerely believe to be right, too many of them are either misinformed about the Church or downright antagonistic toward it. This latter group is often all too willing to rely on deception and dishonesty to achieve their goals. The literature they produce often uses lies or half-truths; it distorts, sensationalizes, or misinterprets Church teachings and history; its intent is to tear down the Church and scare people away from it."[4]

These assumptions have a source in scripture. Doctrine and Covenants denounces and curses those who speak against Church:

> Cursed are all those that shall lift up the heel against mine anointed, saith the Lord, and cry they have sinned when they have not sinned before me, saith the Lord, but have done that which was meet in mine eyes, and which I commanded them. But those who cry transgression do it because they are the servants of sin, and are the children of disobedience themselves. And those who swear falsely against my servants, that they might bring them into bondage and death—
>
> Wo unto them; because they have offended my little ones they shall be severed from the ordinances of mine house. Their basket shall not be full, their houses and their barns shall perish, and they themselves shall be despised by those that flattered them. They shall not have right to the priesthood, nor their posterity after them from generation to generation. It had been better for them that a millstone had been hanged about their necks, and they drowned in the depth of the sea.
>
> D&C 121:16-22

General authorities want you to bolster yourself to stand against those slings and arrows: "Do not think that it is easy to maintain a testimony. Others will test you. Sometimes they will point the finger of mockery and scorn. Sometimes they may persecute you openly. Be prepared. Know in advance that the best of God's children have had the

---

1. *Church Handbook of Instructions Book 1*, 2006. 78.
2. Carlos E. Asay. "Opposition to the Work of God." In LDS General Conference, Oct 1981.
3. "Are You Reflecting the Glory of Jehovah?" *Watchtower*, May 15, 2012. http://wol.jw.org/en/wol/d/r1/lp-e/2012364
4. "Q&A: Questions and Answers." *New Era*, July 2007. http://www.lds.org/new-era/2007/07/qa-questions-and-answers

courage of true conviction and were willing to suffer ridicule, deprivation, and even death for the sake of true testimony. Is each of us willing to do likewise?"[1]

Martha Beck recalls the attitude of her father, Hugh Nibley, one of the most prominent LDS apologists who ever lived. "'This is how Satan works,' my father continues. 'And he's always taken a special interest in me, I can tell you that.' He shakes his head mournfully. 'It's the price you pay for defending the Gospel.'"[2]

Or perhaps criticism is the price anyone must pay for taking a controversial stand in a free democracy.

In the end, we are all human beings, all equally flawed and amazing in our own unique ways. We don't suddenly become evil or justified because of the groups we join. Everyone is worthy of love and understanding—yes, even people who have committed genuinely horrible acts. As Christ said, "Inasmuch as ye have done it unto one of the least of these my brethren, ye have done it unto me." Matthew 25:40

When we close our ears because an authority has dehumanized one group or another, we limit our ability to learn and grow. When we remember that we're all the same, we increase our ability to empathize and treat our fellow travelers with charity and kindness.

---

1. Robert D. Hales. "The Importance of Receiving a Personal Testimony." In LDS General Conference, Oct 1994.
2. Beck, *Leaving the Saints,* 2005. 123.

> *Nice everything you have there. It would be a shame if anything were to happen to it...*
> —**Internet meme**

> *...nobody spoke of such things, yet everybody knew of them...*
> —**George Orwell, *1984***

> *Throughout my childhood, through continuous indirect communication, I learned that a good Mormon girl doesn't ever travel in the dimension of direct communication.*
> —**Martha Beck, *Leaving the Saints*[1]**

# Indirect Directives

**Indirect Directives**
*—Suppression, Influence, Reinforcement*
- Influences members via indirect instruction, implication, and cultural forces
- Creates plausible deniability to defend leadership, group
- Feeds the double-bind
- Directs negative, critical thought away from the group and its leadership
- Reinforced by sacred science (the leader is the authority)
- Reinforced by social pressure
- Aids in deception
- Reinforces influence by identification and example
- Helps establish phobias
- Helps establish dispensing of existence

As human beings, we are capable of drawing conclusions from incomplete information. Those conclusions seem as real to us as plain writing on the wall. It allows cult leaders to issue doctrines and give commands without expressly committing or leaving any trace of their own culpability.

Like the story of Thomas Becket in the 12th century England, who had gained a little political power and rank in the Catholic Church. After Becket started to rock the boat, the King Henry II famously asked, "Will no one rid me of this turbulent priest?"

Four knights took it upon themselves to dispose of Becket. Whether the king really wanted him assassinated will never be known. Historical accounts of the king's actual words are even less clear: "What miserable drones and traitors have I nourished and brought up in my household, who let their lord be treated with such shameful contempt by a low-born cleric?"

Hardly a kill order. But within a certain context, such words could be damning while providing plausible deniability for the one who utters them. King Henry got his way free of consequence, except for the loss of four good knights, who were excommunicated and exiled to fight in the crusades.

An indirect directive is a euphemistic means of making a suggestion or threat without just coming out and saying it. It makes use of inference, connotation instead of denotation, the implicit rather than explicit. In daily life, we may employ the double entendre to flirt or we may hint when we'd like to remain tactful. Movies use this method of communication as a plot device during drug deals and assassination orders.

---

1. Beck, *Leaving the Saints*, 2005. 207.

When used within a totalist context, insinuations are highly manipulative, and can convince people to commit acts they would otherwise find abhorrent. Margaret Singer wrote, "Cult members often say to their families and friends, 'No one orders me around. I choose to do what I do.' Getting members to think that way is one of the manipulations mastered by cult leaders who have become skillful at getting acts carried out through indirection and implication."[1]

She tells of one cult where "...the leader often said during lectures that people who don't obey must be punished. This was a repetitious theme backed up with many examples. Shortly after such a lecture...one woman began to shake and slap another woman who wasn't working hard enough. Later she said, 'It was his words and how much I wanted him to like me. I saw myself doing as he would. He didn't have to be there, he didn't have to tell me when or who or where. I wanted to do just what he wanted... I realized I was flailing away at her. It was as if he and I were one at the moment.'"[2]

In another example, Steve Sanchez's leader, Rev. Will, once told the group, "'If you take a left turn somewhere along the way, like Steve, then the false god, or the Antichrist can take over the center of your head. Then you will have thoughts of killing yourself...'" Sanchez recalls that, "Killing myself was a powerfully attractive idea."[3]

Indirect directives can convey unusual or harsh doctrines that might make the public unsympathetic or turn off new recruits. Multiple doctrines taken together may imply conclusions which lead to mistakes, unhealthy behaviors, or even harm. The institution can then blame the member for misunderstanding. In any case, the organization benefits the same as if it had issued the command.

Indirect directives leverage a strong desire to please God, the leader, or others in the group. As Rev. Will bragged, "'Katie's...a perfect subject. She wants to please me so bad I can't get her off me like a booger. All you have to do with her is put a tape in her head and she will act it out for you perfectly whether she is in or out of trance. Actually a waking suggestion is the strongest kind. I've been doing that with all you people for years.'"[4]

Under other totalist pressures like demand for purity, black and white thinking, sacred science, and us-versus-them thinking, "advice" can carry tremendous weight and come across as a commandment. According to Singer, "...this task is easier when the member is in an altered state, fatigued, or otherwise anxious or under stress."[5] Influence states include guilt, shame, depression, fasting, prayerfulness, and humility.

Social pressure and culture play a huge part, too. Philip Zimbardo suggested one way to ascertain the extent of invisible forces in a group: "Testing for the presence of stated and unstated rules that unnecessarily restrict freedom of speech, action, and association can be done by subtly violating some of the rules and then observing the consequences. How much latitude is allowed for idiosyncrasy, for creative or eccentric self-expression?"[6]

What would happen if you wore jeans to sacrament meeting next week?

Example is yet another way to imply teachings, which we will explore in the next chapter.

Indirect directives help us understand the Mountain Meadows Massacre, where an LDS militia, disguised as Native Americans, attacked a wagon train of settlers passing through southern Utah, killing roughly 120 men, women, and children. Brigham Young denied issuing the order, though militiaman John D. Lee insisted he did. Perhaps he did, or perhaps he didn't, but it hardly matters. Given the fervor that the Saints were whipped into, and the logic behind the doctrine of Blood Atonement, those men had all the necessary ingredients to reach the conclusion on their own.

These days, Blood Atonement is an erased memory. It listed certain sins which could

---

1. Singer, *Cults in Our Midst*, 1995. 159-160.
2. Singer, *Cults in Our Midst*, 1995. 161.
3. Sanchez, *Spiritual Perversion*, 2005. 224-225.
4. Sanchez, *Spiritual Perversion*, 2005. 218.
5. Singer, *Cults in Our Midst*, 1995. 160.
6. Zimbardo and Andersen, "Understanding Mind Control," *Recovery from Cults*, ed. Langone, 1995. 111.

only be cleansed through the blood of the sinner. Some fundamentalists still teach it, but thankfully, this violent doctrine has vanished from the minds of most Mormons.

There are still many other indirect directives. Quotes throughout this book reveal beliefs LDS leaders claim not to teach. The Church can even claim to teach the opposite. That's because the Church teaches *both*. Their attempts to paint it otherwise is psychological manipulation.

For example, I grew up with the doctrine of eternal progression, that our purpose is to be exalted and perfected like God. Aside from explicit statements ("As man is, God once was; as God is, man may become"), the logic of all the doctrines put together (eternal progression, children of God, striving to be like our Father) can bear no other conclusion. Yet when the prophet was asked by *Time Magazine*, "Is this the teaching of the church today, that God the Father was once a man like we are?" Gordon B. Hinckley replied, "I don't know that we teach that."[1]

Bloggers and apologists scrambled to find sources that prove the Church both teaches and doesn't teach that, with controversial results. It is hard to find an *official* Church source that expressly and clearly states this principle. It's a convenient omission of what to me was an exceedingly clear and central teaching.

Likewise, many Mormons hold controversial political views, thinking of them as official teachings when they aren't. But they have official roots. "I grew up with strong sentiments against the Civil Rights Movement. I felt certain my feelings reflected the teachings of Church leaders, though I could not recall any specific sermons to that effect. I often wondered, in later years, about my *spiritual conviction* against this movement."[2]

Though I am separated from this author by a generation, I too somehow came away with moral distaste for the Civil Rights Movement, and for Martin Luther King, Jr., even though I can find no official references, and though those events happened twenty years before I was born. This sentiment spread throughout the flock, unofficially. Ezra Taft Benson spoke of it at General Conference *once* in 1967, and the idea lived on as a sort of semi-doctrine that require no further propagation by LDS authorities.[3,4]

To this day, I sometimes catch myself wondering, quite irrationally, if Rev. King was in fact a communist conspirator. That is how deeply unofficial cultural doctrines can run.

Through these influences, racism continues to thrive in Mormon culture, despite the lack of directly promoted doctrines. It is implied in certain scripture stories, like when the wicked Lamanites were cursed with dark skin, and in the unwritten meta-stories. Cain's Mark makes him the first black man. Ham's wife passed Cain's Mark to all Africans after the flood. The less valiant in the war in heaven were born black. The Lamanites (Native Americans) will be "purified" once they accept the gospel. Jews were the only people wicked enough to kill the Messiah. It goes on.

The LDS Church, like Pontius Pilate, washes its hands clean of racism and other distasteful beliefs, yet the ideas continue to be passed from mind to mind as surely as if preached from the pulpit. Many other political issues are thus indirectly directed from the top down. These tendrils reach into the areas of feminism, homophobia, and attitudes towards government, social programs, mass media, liberalism, and more[5].

Since leaving the Church, I have talked with members about various beliefs I once held. Under doctrinal deniability, they can say, "No one ever told you to do that," or "We don't

---

1. David Van Biema. "Kingdom Come." *Time*, Aug 4, 1997. http://content.time.com/time/magazine/article/0,9171,986794,00.html
2. Morin and Morin, *Suddenly Strangers*, 2004. 27.
3. Ezra Taft Benson. *Civil Rights, Tool of Communist Deception*. Deseret Book Co, 1969.
4. Ezra Taft Benson. "137th Semi-Annual General Conference Report." 35-39, 1967.
5. If the Church were serious about stamping out these problematic beliefs, it could easily do so by officially announcing at General Conference the historical sources of these doctrines, and renouncing them in direct and simple terms. i.e., "We *no longer* believe Cain was the father of the black race. We do *not* believe people of color were less valiant in the preexistence. Anyone continuing to espouse these notions hold heretical beliefs contrary to God's purpose." They have taken this clear stance on polygamy; perhaps they should do the same with other outdated and harmful folk-doctrines.

believe that", or "You must have misunderstood." But I attended the same meetings they did, and read the same scriptures. It was no problem when I expressed those beliefs and behaviors as a believing member, but when those doctrines come from the mouth of a critic who casts them as dubious, contradictory, or questionable, it's easier to deny they ever existed.

General authorities are always "counseling" and "imploring" and "advising" in a tone that leaves no room for refusal. Boyd K. Packer speaks of being "invited": "I was asked to write an article for the Improvement Era. It was returned with the request that I change some words... I balked a bit... I remembered Brother [Harold B.] Lee's counsel. I had to submit. Now...I'm glad, very glad, that if someone digs it out, I was 'invited' to change it."[1]

Another deflection is the phrase, "You should have taken it in the spirit it was given." Nice people can say some pretty mean and offensive things, so long as they do it out of love, right? Members can shun friends and family for apostasy or homosexuality, and do it out of "concern." This is the modern form of Blood Atonement. Ostracization, lectures, shaming, and boundary violations are all done for the wayward sinner's own good. Anything is justifiable when eternal life is on the line.

Just because a doctrine exists does not mean it is emphasized over other conflicting doctrines by church and family. "I am a child of God", "God loves you", and "individual worth" mean nothing when talks and lessons otherwise dwell on performance and when members experience personal rejection for not keeping up. The Church can then claim to be uplifting and to be promoting self-esteem, while simultaneously, the members feel worthless.

If it's true that the gospel makes some people unhappy, the Church would seems less than perfect. Since it claims to be perfect, admitting to this problem would evoke dissonance.

Blame reversal is the best way out of this loop. Evidence of this kind of reversal appears in a presentation written about LDS depression by researchers who were themselves LDS. The following phrases were written regarding a case study of "Jill":[2]

> - After desperate attempts to find the sin to explain her suffering could not find one
> - Common misinterpretation of Alma 41:10 'Behold, wickedness never was happiness'
> - Misinterpreted as 'if I'm unhappy, I must be wicked'
> - Well-meaning LDS leader confirmed her belief
> - After much soul-searching together they realized that Jill's suffering must be due to a lack of faith, and with sufficient faith her depression would remit
> - After months of trying to increase her faith, her depression did not remit
> - Ashamed, she quit attending her beloved congregation

Jill is not the only faithful Mormon to arrive at this logical conclusion. Nor is she the first to feel shame for a perception of not measuring up.

Fortunately for Jill, she had therapy from an intelligent LDS therapist to help her reframe her reasoning using other, more healthy LDS principles. Jill was able to stop beating herself up for her own suffering and return to a normal life.

She was one of the lucky ones. Not all Church members have access to leadership who can provide this level of wisdom, as the example illustrates—a "well-meaning leader confirmed her belief."

Another (presumably) LDS psychology researcher, Kristine Doty, and a news reporter

---

1. Elder Boyd K. Packer. "Talk to the All-Church Coordinating Council," 1993. http://lds-mormon.com/face.shtml
2. Draper, et al., "Helping Depressed Mormon Clients," Utah Valley University, 2013.

also tried to deflect mental health blame away from the Church. Speaking on toxic perfectionism, the reporter described the "perfect family" dynamic, and women who try to project an image of perfection, and then went on to say, "It's not synonymous with spiritual teachings."

Doty replies, "It is not the doctrine. I've looked at General Conference addresses in recent years and there's nobody who's lashing these women on their backs. I'm not even sure why it self-perpetuates, but it does."[1]

Doty is half-right. It's hard to find any general authority say, "Work yourself to death. Hate yourself. Feel ashamed and depressed until you're perfect." In fact, they often say the opposite.

Yet the steady demand for perfection marches on, both implied and express, in ways that may seem innocent, like this quote given in a Conference address by Julie B. Beck: "Home is where women have the most power and influence; therefore, Latter-day Saint women should be the best homemakers in the world."[2]

But... no pressure or anything.

Beck's talk is very specific about the high-demand criteria for being a good LDS mother and woman, including stories of women in poor, dusty countries who manage to dress their children nicely and walk for miles to get to Church. Descriptions of mothers who are good leaders, teachers, and nurturers. Mothers who set aside their own needs, who keep an orderly house, who rid their homes of distracting entertainment. Women who faithfully keep *all* their covenants, who prepare their children for missions, and who never give up. This and other talks given to women indicate where toxic perfectionism might come from. This is in addition to the other demands for purity assigned to *every* member.

Scripture passages and doctrines direct members to should do more than they're commanded, which leads proactive Saints to actively seek out indirect directives. Following the spirit of the law means it's not enough to simply go through the motions.

Moroni said, "For behold, if a man being evil giveth a gift, he doeth it grudgingly; wherefore it is counted unto him the same as if he had retained the gift; wherefore he is counted evil before God." Moroni 7:8

In the D&C, we memorized, "For behold, it is not meet that I should command in all things; for he that is compelled in all things, the same is a slothful and not a wise servant; wherefore he receiveth no reward." D&C 58:26

"Go the extra mile", "put your shoulder to the wheel," and "magnify your calling." And don't forget the all-encompassing temple covenant to keep the Law of Consecration, which "requires dedicating all of one's time, talents, and possessions to the Church and its purposes."[3] The parable of the talents illustrated that the more effort we put in to using our agency for good, the better. These all created additional internal pressure to obey commandments above and beyond that which was expressly spelled out.

When Nephi was commanded to kill Laban (or maybe God just implied, "It sure would be nice if Laban wasn't around anymore... Oh, he's asleep... How convenient,"), Nephi said, "I will go and do the things which the Lord hath commanded, for I know that the Lord giveth no commandments unto the children of men, save he shall prepare a way for them that they may accomplish the thing which he commandeth them." 1 Nephi 3:7

Another doctrine implies that some commandments, such as tithing, are baby steps, the milk before the meat, for "greater things", stricter commandments to come, like full implementation of the Law of Consecration. There is always some higher bar to meet.

All these add up to certain conclusions. Maybe some pay a little extra in tithing, maybe even more than is wise for their budget. Maybe some work harder, or attempt to be a

---

1. "The Perfect Problem." *The Perfect Problem Special Report*. ABC4, May 13, 2013.
2. Julie B. Beck. "Mothers Who Know." In LDS General Conference, Oct 2007. https://www.lds.org/general-conference/2007/10/mothers-who-know
3. Frank W. Hirschi. "The Encyclopedia of Mormonism: Consecration," 1992. http://eom.byu.edu/index.php/Consecration#Law_of_Consecration

Supermom, or acquire an eating disorder from over-fasting. If I endure to the end by driving myself into depressive martyrdom, all the better. Right?

And what if it leads parents to conclude they should be more strict with their kids, which leads to abuse? While some scriptures speak against abuse, there are others to promote it:

> Reproving betimes with sharpness, when moved upon by the Holy Ghost; and then showing forth afterwards an increase of love toward him whom thou hast reproved, lest he esteem thee to be his enemy.
>
> D&C 121:43
>
> He that spareth his rod hateth his son: but he that loveth him chasteneth him betimes.
>
> Proverbs 13:24

These passages are wide open to interpretation, themselves indirect directives. Add to that the emphasis on how dependent we are upon our families for salvation, how responsible parents are for their children's eternal welfare, and all the demands for purity and dispensing of existence. Suddenly a few sharp words, manipulative gestures, shunning, or even physical violence seems like the loving thing to do.

Sometimes all this indirect direction inspires members to give more than they can bear. And when they do, the Church blames them for it, for their misunderstanding of the doctrine.

Other members, those with a little less stability, might take it even further. To suicide, or to falling away into reckless sin because they've given up. They may wish to "follow the prophet" more literally by joining fundamentalist or polygamist groups.

And when they do, the Church can say, "I don't know that we teach that." Because they don't...yet at the same time, they do.

*Ye are the light of the world. A city that is set on an hill cannot be hid.*
—**Matthew 5:14**

*...the image [General Authority Paul H. Dunn] presented to me, an impressionable youth, was fake. It did not contain the full elements of humanity, only a sanitized, glorified and truly fictitious image of a superman. Living up to that image would require a denial or splitting off of much of our humanity.*
—**Ed Gardiner,**
***Shame and the Destruction of Agency***

*Jesus doesn't want me for a sunbeam.*
—**Kurt Cobain**

# Influence Through Identification & Example

**Identification and Example**
—*Group Identification, Influence, Suppression, Punishment*
- Related to social pressure and indirect directives
- Allows for plausible deniability ("I'm not sure we teach that")
- As much a cultural influence as a taught one
- Prompts behaviors that lead to belief follows behavior
- Establishes phobias indirectly via examples, stories, observed events, social pressure
- Do as I do, not as I say
- Mystical manipulation via reframing, i.e. "Something bad happened because she was sinning."
- Justification for blame reversal
- Gives seemingly real consequences to dispensing of existence, demand for purity
- Affirms black & white logic, us vs. them
- Establishes personal shame
- Used to punish, ostracize, exclude
- Used to reward, include, promote elitism
- Reinforces demand for purity because now you're an example to others

As we've seen previously, people are influenced through more than words. The more we merge with the group pseudopersonality, the more we can be swayed via role models and stories.

Even early on, recruiters leverage identification. Geri-Ann Galanti describes the ways Moonie recruiters used this technique. Members told her she looked familiar. Her cover story was that she was a school teacher, and one of them said he was a teacher, too. "It was rather transparent to me that this was merely a technique to make me feel that we were not so different and that I could be a part of their group."[1]

Of course it is normal to find common ground when making new acquaintance. But during recruiting, identification is deceitfully employed as a manipulation tactic. When we come to identify with totalist group members, we become connected to them—I *am* them,

---

1. Galanti, "Reflections on 'Brainwashing,'" *Recovery from Cults,* ed. Langone, 1995. 99.

and they *are* me. Their behaviors become my behaviors—a standard to mimic. An example.

> [The Moonies] also practiced the technique of shaping behavior through example. One way they did this was to constantly serve me. One of my secret desires is to have someone follow me around, picking up after me. That's exactly what happened that weekend...
> If I got hungry, it seemed I only needed to think of eating something and someone would bring me a plate of food. They were constantly serving me, getting things for me, trying to carry my things for me. At first, I liked it. Soon, however, it made me feel uncomfortable. The only way I could get over this discomfort was to model their behavior: I began doing things for them. Again, resocialization, while at the same time teaching subordination of person to doctrine.[1]

After recruitment, identification leads to behaviors, then beliefs, then to deepening dependency as the member's personality begins to reflect others in the group. "...most of the techniques members learn are not taught directly or consciously, but rather through the process of behavioral modeling. They learn by watching older members, listening to the leader, and modeling themselves after their behavior. Eventually, they unconsciously pick up some of the leader's behaviors, including speech patterns and gesticulations."[2]

This brings to mind the famous "Mormon accent", the "Christlike countenance", and other mannerisms that are difficult to explain to anyone who doesn't just "know." Many of these cultural trappings are the mind control techniques members unconsciously use on one another.

Steven Hassan describes how he learned to manipulate: "When I was being taught how to lecture in the Moon group, I learned by attending countless lectures, observing, listening, and praying to God to let His spirit come into me so that I could be like the older brother who was teaching. Four years after I got out of the Moonies, I started learning more about hypnosis and I realized I had been trained to use hypnotic processes without even knowing what hypnosis was."[3]

Joseph Smith instinctively knew how to manipulate people. Early Mormons emulated him. His methods were passed down, generation after generation, keeping the culture alive without conscious effort.

Under these pressures, we pay careful attention to those who are held up as examples. Anything that happens to another member could happen to me.

Steve Sanchez describes Reverend Will using example to control.

> There was at this time a big crisis about Rev. Renee wanting to leave the school... She seemed to be getting weirder and weirder as she became more and more distant, sad, and shut down. She was like a person drowning in pain, yet occasionally she reached out with an anger that was sometimes bold and sometimes feeble. I didn't know what was going on, but we all perceived her as unworthy, a renegade, and a betrayer of Rev. Will and the teaching. Personally, I felt sorry for her and regretted that she was being mistreated...
> [He said,] "She wants to take me down because misery loves company. She doesn't realize I have a mission I can't jeopardize... The entities are taking over in her head. She can't handle the truth..."
> We all believed this story and now looked at Renee as a nut case, a slime ball whose soul had been consumed by the world.[4]

---

1. Galanti, "Reflections on 'Brainwashing,'" *Recovery from Cults*, ed. Langone, 1995. 100.
2. Hassan, *Releasing the Bonds*, 2000. 50.
3. Hassan, *Releasing the Bonds*, 2000. 50.
4. Sanchez, *Spiritual Perversion*, 2005. 104-105.

A few pages later, Steve describes his own feelings when he's suddenly on the outs: "I couldn't stand to be talked to this way. At the same time it was a devastating blow—to be told I wasn't a student of his was unthinkable. I thought I was special. I was mortified with embarrassment in front of my fellow students. I was so caught up in the teaching, it never even occurred to me to question Rev. Will. I felt like slime, and that there was something inherently wrong with me, and that I had to try harder. As crushed as I felt, I still knew I would get back into good standing somehow, because I was special."[1] Steve knows he's like Renee and uses the same words against himself that had previous been applied to her.

Example works as a carrot, too. Here, Reverend Will offers members a positive illustration: "At any time you could have undergone the training as easily as Woisha. She never asked me of anything for which she wasn't ready, willing, and able to appreciate and to effectually put into her life... She has a heart of gold... She did what I said."[2]

In this way, members are actively encouraged to compare themselves to others, to avoid, at all costs, becoming the bad example, and to ever strive for the coveted position of "good guy."

Diana Kline conveys the pressure she felt. "I...had every noble hope of growing up active in the Mormon church, marrying a missionary in the temple, and having lots of children while serving in ward axillary [sic] positions. I had been taught that if I did what was right, followed my leaders advice, stayed close to the Lord, and followed God's commandments, my life would resemble a picture-perfect Molly Mormon..."[3]

Chris Morin expresses the "carrot" feeling most of us are familiar with. "As a youth, I envied fellow Mormons who could point to a certain special spiritual experience and say unequivocally: 'That is when God gave me a witness of the truthfulness of the Church.'"[4]

And the "stick":

> Although nobody formally taught me to do so, I developed a habit of identifying those who were not temple-worthy Church members and judging them as not being on the path to salvation as was I.
>
> As for Mormons who suffered a divorce in this family-oriented church, I judged them as falling short. Although I considered my judgment to be measured and merciful, my inclination was to belie that—as my wife Connie had been taught in a religion class—"Failure in marriage is almost total failure."
>
> I did not acknowledge the arrogance of the judgments I passed upon others; indeed, for the most part they were subconscious thoughts. Neither did I consider how the judgmental Mormon doctrine must have induced anguish in some Mormons who did not measure up.[5]

As a single mother, divorced at age 21, I knew this anguish and ostracism all too well. I judged myself with almost as much fervor as the "perfect" kids in the young single adult ward judged me. I was constantly aware of their scrutiny.

Mormons feel pressure to perpetually project outward signs of happiness to create a facade of righteous living. UVU Professor Kris Doty, author of a study on perfectionism, reported to Deseret News, "'There's such a huge population of LDS people here [in Utah]. They practically live on top of each other,' she said. 'People get a sense that they're always on display, so that their neighbors will see the best of them rather than who they really are.'"[6]

Identification and example are actively encouraged in doctrine. In Seminary, we

---

1. Sanchez, *Spiritual Perversion*, 2005. 109.
2. Sanchez, *Spiritual Perversion*, 2005. 112.
3. Kline, *Woman Redeemed*, 2005. 3-4.
4. Morin and Morin, *Suddenly Strangers*, 2004. 34.
5. Morin and Morin, *Suddenly Strangers*, 2004. 41.
6. Lockhart, "LDS Women and Depression," *DeseretNews.com*, Jan 31, 2013.

memorized the scripture, "Let your light so shine before men, that they may see your good works, and glorify your Father which is in heaven." Matthew 5:16

My patriarchal blessing repeats what I had often heard in lessons and talks: "You are an example unto those in whom you associate with and those in whom you come in contact with. Be not ashamed of the gospel of Jesus Christ, but speak out, uphold and sustain those in authority over you, and appreciate the blessings of being a member of the Church..."

The Prophet Thomas S. Monson told the men to be examples. "If your so-called friends urge you to do anything you know to be wrong, you be the one to make a stand for right, even if you stand alone. Have the moral courage to be a light for others to follow." He quoted N. Eldon Tanner, "Always remember that people are looking to you for leadership and you are influencing the lives of individuals either for good or for bad, which influence will be felt for generations to come."

Then he told a story to demonstrate the level of influence he has. "I have thought of an experience I had some years ago while attending a stake conference... I observed a young boy sitting with his family on the front row... I was seated on the stand. As the meeting progressed, I began to notice that if I crossed one leg over the other, the young boy would do the same thing. If I reversed the motion and crossed the other leg, he would follow suit. I would put my hands in my lap, and he would do the same. I rested my chin in my hand, and he also did so... I decided to put him to the test. I looked squarely at him, certain I had his attention, and then I wiggled my ears. He made a vain attempt to do the same, but I had him! He just couldn't quite get his ears to wiggle."[1]

Talks, *Ensign* articles, and Sunday School lessons are replete with stories reflecting those who exhibited good behavior and were rewarded, and those who committed sins and were punished. Sometimes the reward is simply praise from the speaker, and the punishment merely verbal condemnation. This is enough.

I always looked forward to stories at church. They broke up the monotony of hearing the same scriptures and gospel principles reiterated. At Conference, stories were delivered in kind voices, the gentle Mormon accent of certainty and conviction. It was the kind of voice we'd all strive to emulate when giving our own talks.

Teachers are encouraged to use examples. From the Aaronic Priesthood Manual: "If time permits, you might tell of someone you know whose life has been affected by abuse of dangerous substances, without giving names. Emphasize that the Lord has given us the Word of Wisdom to help us take care of our bodies and avoid the sorrow that comes with substance abuse."[2]

It's a habit, running like a tape when we're not even teaching or hearing lessons. Any event in the real world was a lesson to be learned. Diana Kline recalls, "Whenever anything tragic happened, such as a flood or natural disaster, it was because all of those people involved were not Mormons and thus did not live a righteous life. The fallacies and prejudices in this type of cognition led me to believe that if I lived a perfect virtuous life as a Mormon, nothing treacherous would ever happen to me."[3]

Likewise, members are driven to preach to one another with this constant internal dialog. Martha Beck writes, "When neighbors came for a visit, it was always an undisguised effort to convince us to repent, followed by stories about others who had left the fold and lived (though not long) to regret it. 'My nephew did what you're doing,' one neighbor told me, 'and a week later he died of a ruptured spleen.' 'Our bishop's son left the Church,' said another, 'and now he's bankrupt in prison.'"[4]

As a Mormon, we were constantly aware of trying not to be "like that guy." Instead, we tried to be perfect, following the example of Christ, who in turn, was following the example of the Father. We didn't always have to be told what to do when we could show and be

---

1. President Thomas S. Monson. "Examples of Righteousness." In LDS General Conference, April 2008.
2. *Aaronic Priesthood Manual 1*, 2002. (Lesson 18: The Word of Wisdom.)
3. Kline, *Woman Redeemed*, 2005. 209.
4. Beck, *Leaving the Saints,* 2005. 251.

shown.

The problem is that the role models we identified with were not realistic. They did not represent idealized versions of our unique selves, but instead the pseudopersonality envisioned by the group which embodied totalist standards. We only got to see the best sides of the good examples, and the worst sides of the bad examples. Leaders spoke often of having weaknesses themselves, but those presented were relatively tame and slightly endearing, like making minor mistakes as children or being bad at singing. Even their ugly sides were intended to make us like them more.

But we knew too well every excruciating blemish we had in our own closets. Identification not only wields the power of gentle influence, but hidden within it lies the weapon of stinging shame. And therein, it is tempered as an implement of control.

*...the prevailing mental condition must be controlled insanity.*
—George Orwell, *1984*

*If you'd rise above the thinking you'd know that you need to realize the truth. And in most cases you'd find that you hate the truth, which is the light of love that comes from the Divine...*
—From a letter by Reverend Will, the SLF cult leader, *Spiritual Perversion*[1]

*...faith can serve as a shortcut to truth, but it cannot justify persistence in error.*
—Anonymous Online Exmormon, quoted in *The Pattern of the Double-Bind in Mormonism*[2]

# Emotion Over Intellect

**Emotion Over Intellect**
*—Influence, Suppression, Silencing Doubts, Reinforcement*
- Suppresses critical thinking skills
- Encourages reliance on emotion for making decisions, determining truth
- Amplifies the power of influence
- May lead to minor trance states
- Allows for reframing of emotions
- Allows for belief and trust in mystical manipulation
- Reinforces trust in leadership and group
- Answers doubts with more emotion
- Situations can be created where emotions themselves become fulfillment of prophecy (mystical manipulation)

Cognitive scientists have studied how emotional states affect our reasoning methods. Initial motivation will change the outcome of decision-making. Researchers call this "motivated reasoning."

We can approach reasoning with "goal orientation" or "accuracy orientation." Goal oriented motivated reasoning is where we are driven to make conclusions that resolve to our existing beliefs. This is where we are most likely to use biases and jump to conclusions.

Researchers found they could direct subjects towards "accuracy oriented motivated reasoning" by instructing them to defend their eventual conclusions to another person. They found subjects were far more thoughtful and thorough, and they were less prone to bias.[3] The author of this paper, social psychologist Ziva Kunda, proposed that in order for subjects to be accuracy-motivated, they must: 1. Have appropriate reasoning strategies, 2. View them as superior to other strategies, and 3. Be capable of using them at will.

These two states are also described as "hot cognition" vs "cold cognition." A hot state is emotional, quick, and tends to confirm existing biases, whereas a cold state takes more time and relies on rational and analytical thinking.[4]

It stands to reason that if subjects in an experiment can be directed into a state of cold cognition, spiritual followers could be trained in the opposite direction, particularly when

---

1. Sanchez, *Spiritual Perversion*, 2005. 112.
2. Stricker, *The Double-Bind in Mormonism*, 2000. 89.
3. Ziva Kunda. "The Case for Motivated Reasoning." *Psychological Bulletin* 108, no. 3 (Nov 1990): 480-498.
4. Alice G. Brand. "Hot Cognition: Emotions And Writing Behavior." *Journal of Advanced Composition* (1985). http://www.jstor.org/stable/20865583

beliefs might be easily disconfirmed by pure logic. Their thinking becomes goal-oriented and they are primed to rely heavily on emotion.

Cult researchers have long understood that emotions are easier to influence than thoughts. "The most potent persuasive appeals get their wallop by reaching beyond reason to emotions, beyond awareness to unspoken desires and fears, beyond trivial attitudes to basic concerns about self-integrity and survival."[1]

Previous chapters discussed how childhood regression makes an individual more trusting. It also serves to place the mind in a more emotional state. Geri-Ann Galanti said her experience with the Moonies was like being a child again. Many of the activities were those children usually do, like singing and playing games. "Children tend to experience things more on an emotional level rather than on an intellectual one. Certainly that particular approach was stressed during the weekend; it places the recruit in a vulnerable position and helps strip him or her of the power to resist those in authority, those who are trying to influence him or her."[2]

Emotions are easily reframed and manipulated. They can't be written down or even easily thought about. They pass through our bodies like sand, and thus are easily blown this way or that. *Captive Hearts* tells us, "Cult members are taught to distrust this vital part of their being, to suppress certain emotions and encourage others. Guilt, shame, and fear are all used to foster compliance and control. Most other feelings are punished, suppressed, or forbidden."[3]

Cults can reroute suppressed anger and other negative emotions towards outsiders—in this case, exmormons, anti-Mormons, nonmembers, inactives, and sinners. All good feelings are reframed as being from God, creating, as Jack B. Worthy called it, a "feeling-based reality."[4]

Over time, this manipulation can lead to a lack of self-trust and emotional confusion, because, according to *Captive Hearts*, "for so long, feelings were defined for you by the group: good or bad, acceptable or unacceptable, pure or evil... members are taught that certain thoughts and feelings are sinful."[5]

Taking back ownership of those feelings is part of recovery. *Captive Hearts* continues: "After leaving such a group you need to recognize that having human thoughts and feelings is okay. Instead of continually confessing or suppressing feelings, you discover how to evaluate them and choose the ones you want to act upon... For some former cult members, rediscovering the world of feelings is a big portion of the healing process. If this is not addressed, they may lead a narrow, unsatisfying existence."

Let's take a look at exactly how LDS doctrines stifle intellect in favor of emotional reasoning.

> O that cunning plan of the evil one! O the vainness, and the frailties, and the foolishness of men! When they are learned they think they are wise, and they hearken not unto the counsel of God, for they set it aside, supposing they know of themselves, wherefore, their wisdom is foolishness and it profiteth them not. And they shall perish. But to be learned is good if they hearken unto the counsels of God.
> 2 Nephi 9:28-29

This scripture is a form of enforced confirmation bias. As long as you only learn that which complies with the gospel, you're fine.

Glenn L. Pace counseled against thinking too much about the wrong things. "One activity which often leads a member to be critical is engaging in inappropriate intellectualism. While it would seem the search for and discovery of truth should be the goal of all Latter-day Saints, it appears some get more satisfaction from trying to discover

---

1. Zimbardo and Andersen, "Understanding Mind Control," *Recovery from Cults*, ed. Langone, 1995. 113-114.
2. Galanti, "Reflections on 'Brainwashing,'" *Recovery from Cults*, ed. Langone, 1995. 100.
3. Tobias and Lalich, *Captive Hearts, Captive Minds*, 1994. 117.
4. Worthy, *The Mormon Cult*, 2008. 16.
5. Tobias and Lalich, *Captive Hearts, Captive Minds*, 1994. 115.

new uncertainties. I have friends who have literally spent their lives, thus far, trying to nail down every single intellectual loose end rather than accepting the witness of the Spirit and getting on with it. In so doing, they are depriving themselves of a gold mine of beautiful truths which cannot be tapped by the mind alone."[1]

He continues, "Elder Faust describes this type of intellectual as 'a person who continues to chase after a bus even after he has caught it.' We invite everyone to get on the bus before it's out of sight and you are left forever trying to figure out the infinite with a finite mind."

Boyd K. Packer addressed Church educators in a talk appropriately entitled, *The Mantle is Far, Far Greater than the Intellect*:

> There is no such thing as an accurate, objective history of the Church without consideration of the spiritual powers that attend this work.
>
> There is no such thing as a scholarly, objective study of the office of bishop without consideration of spiritual guidance, of discernment, and of revelation. That is not scholarship. Accordingly, I repeat, there is no such thing as an accurate or objective history of the Church which ignores the Spirit.[2]

"The Spirit" is another way to describe a package of emotions that the Church has defined for its members. Like all general authorities, Packer advises the Saints to study under the influence of emotions, and those emotions must always point to the truthfulness of the Church, or they aren't, by definition, the Spirit.

Scripture tells us, "But, behold, I say unto you, that you must study it out in your mind; then you must ask me if it be right, and if it is right I will cause that your bosom shall burn within you; therefore, you shall feel that it is right. But if it be not right you shall have no such feelings, but you shall have a stupor of thought that shall cause you to forget the thing which is wrong..." D&C 9:8-9 Any cognitive dissonance is reframed as a stupor, and any consonance is clearly a sign from God. All signs point to "Yes."

Faith is emphasized over knowledge and direct perceptions, in this example, by Elder Richard C. Edgley: "We do not need to rely upon intellect or our physical senses. We study, we pray, and, like Alma of old, we may even fast, and then comes a still, small voice and a throbbing heart. Imagine a personal revelation from God that these things are true. The very thought of it makes my heart throb."[3]

Elder Edgley asks the listener to "imagine" what it must feel like. This is the power of suggestion in action. It is easy to evoke emotions, and when it succeeds, that person now believes she has felt the Spirit.

Boyd K. Packer put emphasis on these feelings: "The Holy Ghost speaks with a voice that you *feel* more than you *hear*. It is described as a 'still small voice.' And while we speak of 'listening' to the whisperings of the Spirit, most often one describes a spiritual prompting by saying, 'I had a *feeling*...'

"Revelation comes as words we *feel* more than *hear*. Nephi told his wayward brothers, who were visited by an angel, 'Ye were past *feeling*, that ye could not *feel* his words.'"[4]

He then suggests that we actively try to believe, which should lead to an almost mystical experience:

---

1. Glenn L. Pace. "Follow the Prophet." In LDS General Conference, April 1989.
2. Boyd K. Packer. "The Mantle Is Far, Far Greater Than the Intellect." Brigham Young University, 1981. 2.
3. Richard C. Edgley. "A Still, Small Voice and a Throbbing Heart." In LDS General Conference, April 2005. http://www.lds.org/general-conference/2005/04/a-still-small-voice-and-a-throbbing-heart
4. Boyd K. Packer. "Personal Revelation: The Gift, the Test, and the Promise." In LDS General Conference, Oct 1994.

> The flow of revelation depends on your faith. You exercise faith by causing, or by making, your mind accept or believe as truth that which you cannot, by reason alone, prove for certainty…
>
> As you test gospel principles by believing without knowing, the Spirit will begin to teach you. Gradually your faith will be replaced with knowledge.
>
> You will be able to discern, or to see, with spiritual eyes…

Then Packer gives us the motivation to remain in a state of feeling constantly. "Ignore or disobey these promptings, and the Spirit will leave you." As soon as you neglect this method of understanding, perhaps to try some other method, the emotional method will stop working.

The Holy Ghost is promised as a *constant* companion, the only dependable guide to truth, and thus, its influence expands beyond the spiritual sphere. "…by the power of the Holy Ghost ye may know the truth of all things." Moroni 10:5

This doctrine was described in beautiful, emotion-evoking and reality-encompassing language by Parley P. Pratt: "The gift of the Holy Ghost…quickens all the intellectual faculties, increases, enlarges, expands, and purifies all the natural passions and affections, and adapts them, by the gift of wisdom, to their lawful use. It inspires, develops, cultivates, and matures all the fine-toned sympathies, joys, tastes, kindred feelings, and affections of our nature. It inspires virtue, kindness, goodness, tenderness, gentleness, and charity. It develops beauty of person, form, and features. It tends to health, vigor, animation, and social feeling. It invigorates all the faculties of the physical and intellectual man. It strengthens and gives tone to the nerves. In short, it is, as it were, marrow to the bone, joy to the heart, light to the eyes, music to the ears, and life to the whole being."[1]

It gets to the point where the *only* valid means of testing truth is through the Spirit, even though testing via the Spirit requires a belief in the Spirit. After he left the Church, Brad L. Morin received a letter from his concerned niece: "Upon choosing to leave the church did you pray to God? And if so, was the answer a feeling of peace and joy and confirmation, stronger than any you have ever felt? Did it outweigh all those feelings you received during a testimony meeting, your mission, a new convert's baptism, the temple, every priesthood blessing you have ever received or given, and the reality that God was listening as you prayed at night and your repentance on various occasions had been accepted? Did you pray with an earnest heart to know if you should leave a church you once swore to strangers was the only true gospel— And did that answer knock you to [the] floor with such an incredible force of assurance that it erased all doubts or sick feelings you had over such a choice?"[2]

And this all makes it remarkably difficult to prove much of anything, other than what the Church wants you to believe. "Mormons teach children that the truth of Mormonism is proved through feelings. This means that no evidence is required, and that no amount of conflicting empirical evidence could ever prove the Church to be false."[3]

In this Conference quote, originally spoken by Brigham Young, the meaning of the word "fact" is loaded to mean "feeling":

> There is no other experience known to mortal man that can be compared with the testimony or witness of the Holy Ghost. It is as powerful as a two-edged sword and burns in the breast of man like a consuming fire. It destroys fear and doubt, leaving in their stead absolute unqualified, and incontrovertible knowledge that a principle or thing is true…

---

1. L. Tom Perry. "That Spirit Which Leadeth to Do Good." In LDS General Conference, April 1997. https://www.lds.org/general-conference/1997/04/that-spirit-which-leadeth-to-do-good
2. Morin and Morin, *Suddenly Strangers*, 2004. 95.
3. Worthy, *The Mormon Cult*, 2008. 17.

> The effect of this testimony reaches above and beyond all physical or earthly things and makes relationship with God the Father a literal, pulsing fact. Every fiber of both body and spirit respond to the witness of that testimony and the soul knows and lives the truth.[1]

---

1. Loren C. Dunn. "Drink of the Pure Water." In LDS General Conference, April 1977.

## How to Know Truth the LDS Way

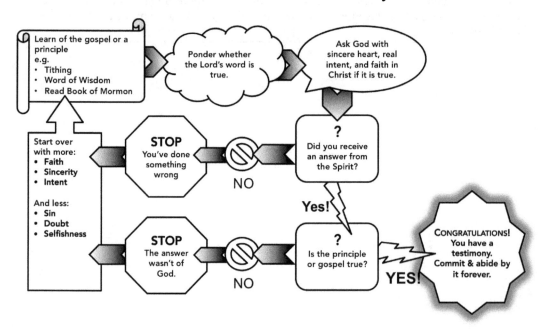

## How to Know Truth Through Reason

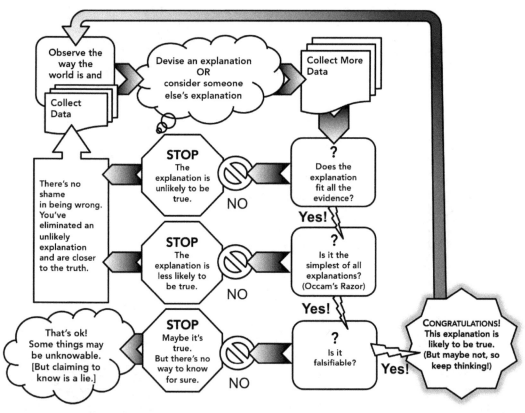

*Notice how reason allows that all proposed explanations may be wrong.*

The Church is there to help parents and teachers induce spiritual feelings in children. Elder Carl B. Cook suggests a list which is probably quite effective: "Home activities such as scripture study, prayer, family home evening, and wholesome family activities provide us, as parents, with the opportunities to teach and help our children feel the Holy Spirit. As they learn to recognize the Spirit and receive a personal witness of truth from the Holy Ghost, they will be blessed with 'a feeling of calm, unwavering certainty' regarding eternal truths."[1]

In the context of a loving family, a child might learn to mistake the warm, comforting sensation of love for the Spirit. "Cristina watched President Thomas S. Monson on the screen in her stake center during general conference. He was talking about being kind to others. Cristina had a warm feeling as she listened. She knew President Monson was a prophet of God."[2]

An emotionally-born testimony is very likely to evoke emotions, and the general authorities agree with me. "Learning how to appropriately express heartfelt feelings is a prelude to inspirational testimony bearing."[3]

That's because empathy is a human tendency. Mirror neurons help us sync emotions with those we identify with. The cracking voice of a tearful testimony is bound to draw a few tears from others. After three or four such testimonies in a row, the meeting is suddenly a "spiritual experience" for everyone.

It is difficult to argue with emotional convictions. The missionary manual advises, "People may sometimes intellectually question what you teach, but it is difficult to question a sincere, heartfelt testimony."[4]

The Holy Ghost is credited for causing other emotions as well, like in this story in the *Friend*[5] about a girl tempted to wear an immodest sleeveless shirt. "Stacey was about to pick up the shirt to try it on when she noticed she felt uncomfortable. She knew what she was about to do wasn't right and that the Holy Ghost was warning her not to do it. She knew that dressing modestly was an important way of respecting her body and being a good example."[6]

And in the *New Era*, "Think of how you feel when you read the Book of Mormon, pray, or bear your testimony. How do those feelings compare with the feelings that come from reading anti-Mormon literature? Which is guiding you to the truth?"[7]

Watch out, however, because spiritual feelings can be counterfeit. How can we tell the difference? Elder Packer answers, "If ever you receive a prompting to do something that makes you feel uneasy, something you know in your mind to be wrong and contrary to the principles of righteousness, do not respond to it!"[8] All roads lead to the gospel; all signs point to "Yes."

Other emotions are easily reframed, including anger, shame, love, compassion, serenity, peace, sexual attraction, doubt, and fear. Storytelling can facilitate this. Many Conference talks begin by evoking strong emotions, through a story about tragedy or acts of charity, before moving to a tangential topic. Listeners who are put into an emotional state will be less critical and more receptive to whatever follows.

Russell M. Nelson's April 2005 talk does exactly this. He begins with three touching paragraphs about the recent passing of his wife, which he is understandably emotional about. But the actual theme is repentance. He reminds us that tomorrow will be too late. It

---

1. Elder Carl B. Cook. "When Children Want to Bear Testimony." *Ensign*, Dec 2002.
2. "Living Prophets Teach Me to Choose the Right" *Friend*, March 2002. http://www.lds.org/friend/2012/03/living-prophets-teach-me-to-choose-the-right
3. Cook, "When Children Want to Bear Testimony," *Ensign*, Dec 2002.
4. *Preach My Gospel: A Guide to Missionary Service*. 2004. The Church of Jesus Christ of Latter-day Saints, n.d. 199.
5. The *Friend* is the official LDS monthly magazine for children under the age of twelve.
6. Annie Beer. "The Orange Shirt." *Friend*, May 2013. http://www.lds.org/friend/2013/05/the-orange-shirt
7. "Q&A: Questions and Answers." *New Era*, July 2007. http://www.lds.org/new-era/2007/07/qa-questions-and-answers
8. Packer, "Personal Revelation," General Conference, Oct 1994.

is in this sympathetic, and possibly fearful state, we are called to repent.[1]

General Primary President Coleen K. Menlove's talk[2] does the same thing. She begins by referring to the tsunami that had recently devastated South East Asia, killing 230,000 people and leaving millions without homes, electricity, water, or food. She describes in heart-wrenching detail the suffering of the children and how we yearn to help them. This evokes feelings of empathy and a desire to aid helpless little ones on the other side of the world.

Then she moves closer to home. We're overlooking our own children, she says. They are *spiritually* starving.

Logically, this makes absolutely no sense. But in an emotional context, it's perfectly rational. By telling us that teaching our children is just as vital as the starvation abroad, she creates a motivating emotional link. Images of dying toddlers are superimposed on our own well-fed but possibly spiritually impoverished kids. Plenty of guilt should follow.

Emotional manipulation is everything. According to *Captive Hearts*, "Controlling someone's emotions means controlling the person..."[3]

A totalist must have the ability to get you to suppress your own emotions and we can clearly see that being done throughout LDS doctrine.

Alma said, "Use boldness, but not overbearance; and also see that ye bridle all your passions, that ye may be filled with love..." Alma 38:12 In this context, incorrect emotions become the enemy.

Self-mastery is regularly emphasized. From an article in the *Liahona*, "Just what is this elusive word 'self-control'? Webster defines it as 'restraint exercised over one's own impulses, emotions, or desires'. These three: impulses, emotions, and desires must be put in subjection by anyone human if he is to anticipate peace and harmony in his life, if he is to acquire the sterling embodiments of perfection and godship in the eternities."[4]

Sexual control is emotional control. Nearly every cult controls sex. Whether it is no sex, or too much sex, or unwanted sex, the *person* is objectified and turned into a tool of the leader. Sexual feelings are an inseparable part of being a human. If you can reframe sexuality, you can lead a person wherever you want. It is a way of taking control of the mind by controlling the body.

The Church has an unhealthy obsession with sex. By repressing your sexuality, it caused *you* to overly focus on sex as well. As a Mormon, I couldn't think about marriage without thinking about sex. I couldn't think of dating without thinking of sex, of gay people without thinking of sex, of R-Rated movies, of bedrooms, or even of my own body. The more the Church said, "Don't think about sex," the more I thought about it, and the more I blamed myself for doing so.

This exploitation constitutes a form of sexual abuse that can leave lasting sexual issues and hang-ups, body shame, confusion, dissociation, lingering emotional repression, communication issues, and other barriers to healthy sexuality and relationships, even within the bonds of a proper LDS marriage.

*Captive Hearts* reiterates, "In a broad sense, reproductive and sexual control through enforced celibacy or mandated relationships are also forms of sexual abuse...

"At first glance such rules may provide a relief from the confusion of trying to master the intricacies of sexuality and intimate relationships. In reality, however, they merely serve as yet another cult manipulation. By controlling sex, marriage, and procreation, the cult is better able to control its membership..."[5]

---

1. Russell M. Nelson. "Now Is the Time to Prepare." In LDS General Conference, April 2005. https://www.lds.org/general-conference/2005/04/now-is-the-time-to-prepare
2. Coleen K. Menlove. "All Thy Children Shall Be Taught." In LDS General Conference, April 2005. https://www.lds.org/general-conference/2005/04/all-thy-children-shall-be-taught
3. Tobias and Lalich, *Captive Hearts, Captive Minds*, 1994. 116.
4. Melecio Vir V. Emata. "Self-Control: The Kingly Virtue." *Liahona*, July 1978. http://www.lds.org/liahona/1978/07/self-control-the-kingly-virtue
5. Tobias and Lalich, *Captive Hearts, Captive Minds*, 1994. 172-173.

Unfettered access to your own full spectrum of emotions is essential to emotional health. Emotions are a sense, just like eyesight, to convey information about your reactions to the world. Attempting to force them onto a narrow track leads to fear, depression, inadequacy, dependency, and shame, which further binds you inseparably to a totalist group.

Taking back ownership of your emotions is crucial to recovery. Otherwise you unwittingly let others have control, even after you've left the Church. Learning to accept and trust your internal emotional world—all of it—will help you regain your freedom and sense of self. Moreover, you must learn to trust your mind, with all of its niggling doubts and observations of contradiction.

*He thought with a kind of astonishment of the biological uselessness of pain and fear, the treachery of the human body which always freezes into inertia at exactly the moment when a special effort is needed.*

—George Orwell, *1984*

*Fear is the great 'dragon' that Latter-day Saints need to face within themselves and defeat.*

—Blair Watson,
*The Psychological Effects of Mormonism*[1]

# Induced Phobias

**Induced Phobias**
*—Suppression, Silencing Doubts, Punishment*

- Fears are created by:
    - Dispensing of existence
    - Dependency
    - Social pressure
    - Sacred science
    - Mystical manipulation
    - Milieu control
    - Demand for purity
    - Doctrine over self
    - Black and white thinking
    - Us vs them
    - Influence through identification
- Can create a double-bind
- Leverages guilt and shame
- Can motivate confession
- Blame reversal can deflect cause of the phobia, reinforcing the fear
- Strongly suppresses negative thoughts, criticism, doubts, and the possibility of leaving

We all know what a phobia is, right? An irrational, extreme, and persistent fear of something that doesn't exist, is unlikely to occur, or is unlikely to cause harm.

A phobic reaction can come along during the normal course of life. Hassan says, "All phobias are triggered by a cue that initiates a closed cycle of fearful images, thoughts, and feelings. The cue can be any internal or external stimulus, such as a thought, image, word, smell, taste, feeling, or behavior."[2]

Phobias are thought-stopping on a brain chemistry level. It's a closed loop, much like a depressive or anxious cycle that in our household, we call "the hamster wheel." You get on that emotional wheel and just keep running around in the same circle of anxiety thoughts, which overwhelms the rational mind and activates the amygdala, the "fight, flight, freeze, or appease" response. According to *Captive Hearts*, "A phobia is an intense reaction of fear to someone or something that, in effect, can immobilize a person from doing something."[3]

This reaction can be anything from a mild fear to a severe panic attack. In the extreme, "This panic response causes a number of physiological symptoms, including a racing heart, a shortness of breath, dry mouth, cold, clammy hands, and sometimes nausea. The most common coping mechanism for a phobic individual is avoidance of the provoking

---

1. Watson, "Psychological Effects of Mormonism," 2008. http://members.shaw.ca/blair_watson/
2. Hassan, *Releasing the Bonds,* 2000. 235.
3. Tobias and Lalich, *Captive Hearts, Captive Minds,* 1994. 130.

stimulus."[1] While the trigger itself isn't dangerous, the response to it can have short- or long-term ill effects on health.

Avoidance of the trigger is key, which is incredibly useful to a totalist system. Hassan says, "Phobias destabilize and undermine a person's view of reality, emotional and intellectual control, self-confidence, and judgment."[2]

But can a phobia be created where previously there was none? According to cult researchers, yes. "Today's cults know how to effectively implant vivid negative images deep within the members' unconscious minds, making it impossible for the member to even conceive of ever being happy and successful outside of the group... Members are programmed either overtly or subtly...to believe that if they ever leave, they will die of some horrible disease, be hit by a car, be killed in a plane crash, or perhaps even cause the death of loved ones."[3,4]

Imaginary fears can be quite vivid. "When they think of leaving the group, they imagine themselves being destroyed, along with all other nonbelievers, by the fiery judgment of Armageddon. When they picture another member leaving the group, they see him...falling deathly ill, being locked up in a mental hospital, or committing suicide... They can generate only negative images of life outside of the cult."[5]

According to *Captive Hearts*, "In some groups, members are told that they will be possessed by the devil, die, or become psychotic if they leave the group. Since some cult members believe their leader has supernormal powers, they take such predictions seriously. In other groups, members are told that the outside world is cruel, unbearable, unsympathetic, and they will never survive out there."[6]

We've previously discussed the pseudopersonality, where your identity becomes part of, and dependent upon, the group. This itself is a foundation for fear, because leaving can be a kind of death. A cult checklist says, "The most loyal members...feel there can be no life outside the context of the group. They believe there is no other way to be..."[7]

Excommunication combines two spiritually deadly concepts that evoke dispensing of existence. *Captive Hearts* states, "Some groups deliberately use threats of expulsion as a means of controlling the membership," plus, "Some [people] may believe that they are condemned not only in this life but also in the hereafter..."[8]

All acts running counter to prescribed behaviors come at the risk of fear, pain, and death. It is the stop-gap measure when all other techniques are failing. In Hassan's opinion, "Phobia indoctrination is the single most powerful technique used by cults to make members dependent and obedient. I have encountered innumerable individuals who had long ago stopped believing in the leader and the doctrine of the group, but were unable to walk away... They were psychologically frozen with indoctrinated fears, which often functioned unconsciously."[9]

These fears become independent of the doctrines, instinctual response that bypasses all conscious thought or cognitive belief. You can believe that Heavenly Father loves you, but still fear the spiritual punishment of a tyrannical God. You can stop believing in God but still fear God's wrath. These fears can exist without you even knowing, because avoiding and responding to them comes automatically.

It is the exactly the same as how you reflexively respond to danger while driving. If something unexpected occurs, instinct kicks in and without thinking, you swerve out of harm's way. Induced phobias create those same involuntary responses.

---

1. Hassan, *Releasing the Bonds,* 2000. 235.
2. Hassan, *Releasing the Bonds,* 2000. 235.
3. Steven Hassan. *Combatting Cult Mind Control*. Rochester, Vt.: Park Street Press, 1990. 45.
4. Tobias and Lalich, *Captive Hearts, Captive Minds,* 1994. 131.
5. Hassan, *Releasing the Bonds,* 2000. 241.
6. Tobias and Lalich, *Captive Hearts, Captive Minds,* 1994. 131.
7. Lalich and Langone, "Cults 101: Checklist of Cult Characteristics."
8. Tobias and Lalich, *Captive Hearts, Captive Minds,* 1994. 56.
9. Hassan, *Releasing the Bonds,* 2000. 233.

Margaret Singer writes, "Reflective, critical, evaluative thought, especially that critical of the cult, becomes aversive and avoided. The member will appear as you or I do, and will function well in ordinary tasks, but the cult lectures and procedures tend to gradually induce members to experience anxiety whenever they critically evaluate the cult. Soon they are conditioned to avoid critical thinking, especially about the cult, because doing so becomes associated with pangs of anxiety and guilt."[1]

Such fears lead to the complete inability to rely on our *own* instincts. In Hassan's own experience, "...cult leaders implanted the fear that I couldn't trust my own thinking capacities due to unseen negative spiritual forces (Satan) that were supposedly affecting my mind and spirit."[2]

Steve Sanchez writes vividly about what this paralysis feels like. "As I walked out the door, I was suddenly seized with intense fear; my heart pounded fiercely and my body was shaking. The trees, street, and walkway around me started swimming. I felt like I was walking in slow motion with a camera on me, and I was about to cross an invisible line into hell. I felt that Rev. Will and Maggie could psychically see what I was doing, and that the heavens were recording the moment that I passed the line of no return. I almost went back in to undo the deal, but I didn't."[3]

It's hard to relate to this feeling unless you've experienced it yourself. But I felt it many times when I made conscious decisions contrary to the gospel, including the moment when I knew I'd never go back.

Joe Kelly writes of his experience with the International Society of Divine Love, also known as Barsana Dham: "Thoughts of the Swami, God, Hell, my mortality rushed through my head. It took months for these thoughts to pass. I constantly questioned myself: Was I making the right choice? Am I going to have to descend to lower animal forms? Will I spend many lifetimes searching for God before I am given another chance at a human birth? Over time I began to realize that these thoughts were phobias induced by the group."[4]

Mormons going through the exit process will have many similar fears: Maybe I'm throwing away an eternity with my family in the Celestial Kingdom. Maybe God disapproves. Maybe I'm setting a bad example for my family. Maybe I've been misled. Maybe I'm in the grip of Satan's power. Maybe I'll end up dead in the gutter with a needle sticking out of my arm.

*Releasing the Bonds* details the methods for inducing phobias. To summarize:

1. **Direct Suggestion:** With the mantle of authority and firm confidence in their stance and tone of voice, the leadership makes clear statements about what happens to those who fail to obey.
2. **Indirect Suggestion:** Horrible consequences are implied, and followers are allowed to fill in the gaps with their imaginations.
3. **Stories and Testimonials:** Examples portray what happens to bad people. Former members who have returned are allowed to speak graphically about the consequences of sowing wild oats. Gossip, rumor, and urban legends effectively spread phobias.
4. **Media:** News stories are reframed in totalist context. Natural disasters and wars are reframed as consequences of sin or impending apocalypse. The group may use outside media or create their own movies about death, destruction, sin, violence, or evil.
5. **Leveraging Existing Fears:** A convert's previous weaknesses may be used against them, either implied or stated. For example, "If you leave, you'll become an alcoholic again."

---

1. Singer, *Cults in Our Midst*, 1995. 118.
2. Hassan, *Releasing the Bonds*, 2000. 236.
3. Sanchez, *Spiritual Perversion*, 2005. 210.
4. Tobias and Lalich, *Captive Hearts, Captive Minds*, 1994. 89.

Specific doctrines contain the keys to phobias, like the examples in chapters on dispensing existence, mystical manipulation, and us-versus-them thinking. If you believe those teachings are literal, the world can seem like an incredibly dangerous place.

Elder Russell M. Nelson uses all of these techniques in a talk about repentance. Amidst calls to repentance, he juxtaposes his deceased wife's promised rewards with the afterlives of unrepentant sinners, including a wealthy man who died of cancer: "His priorities were set upon things of the world. His ladder of success had been leaning against the wrong wall. I think of him when I read this scripture: 'Behold, your days of probation are past; ye have procrastinated the day of your salvation until it is...too late.'"[1]

He makes reference to worldly turbulence: "Because of frequent and frightening calamities in the world, some people doubt the existence of God. But, in fact, He is trying to help us. He revealed these words: 'How oft have I called upon you by the mouth of my servants, and by the ministering of angels, and by mine own voice, and by the voice of thunderings, and...tempests,...earthquakes,...great hailstorms,...famines and pestilences of every kind,...and would have saved you with an everlasting salvation, but ye would not!'"

Elder Nelson calls upon the Saints to obey all of God's laws, but he *specifically* mentions paying tithing, to link these phobias to the commandment that brings financial gain for the Church.

After inducing phobias, he finishes with the promise of relief: "If we are well prepared, death brings no terror. From an eternal perspective, death is premature only for those who are not prepared to meet God."

*Captive Hearts* gives us insights about how phobias are leveraged in children born in the Church. "Ordinary childhood fears such as fear of the dark, of strangers, and of being alone are often magnified and retained throughout childhood, and sometimes are never outgrown. Children in cults may fear the devil, outsiders, their parents leaving the group, and displeasing the leader."[2]

At a very young age, I remember a video. The missionaries were visiting and they showed it to investigators. It depicted end times calamities with images of earthquakes and hurricanes. I became very frightened. My mother rushed me out and said I was too young. She promised me that as a Mormon, I would be kept safe. This calmed my momentary fears, but my safety came with a price tag attached—that I devote my entire life to the gospel.

It took me several years after leaving the Church to overcome my fear of evil spirits, even though I no longer believed in them. I slept with the lights on, even as a thirty-year-old.

I wasn't the only Mormon with this phobia. Jack B. Worthy recounts: "From the night I gave him a blessing onward, Elder Metcalfe regularly feared that he was in imminent danger of becoming possessed by an evil spirit. When I was still his companion...we slept each night with the light on in our room...

"Living with Elder Metcalfe was especially helpful to me because my wife has also insisted a couple of times on sleeping with the light on to keep away the same kinds of nasty spirits...those that are afraid of light."[3]

Sometimes I still imagine someone is watching me. A Utah government administrator, speaking in anonymity, said, "I think the whole concept of the Holy Ghost looking after your every move is something very powerful to grow up with, because that means any time you're in any kind of mischief, no matter how harmless, then somebody's looking over your shoulder. Someone's always watching. I certainly felt *that* growing up."[4]

It wasn't just the Holy Ghost. I used to think the bishop's power of discernment meant

---

1. Russell M. Nelson. "Now Is the Time to Prepare." In LDS General Conference, April 2005.
2. Tobias and Lalich, *Captive Hearts, Captive Minds*, 1994. 252.
3. Worthy, *The Mormon Cult*, 2008. 143.
4. Ure, *Leaving the Fold*, 1999. 245.

he could see me. I definitely felt like God was watching me. I used to frequently get the creepy feeling of evil spirits or ghosts watching me.

This is what Hassan means by "indirect suggestion." My imagination took doctrines like "spirit of discernment" and "God's eye is on the sparrow" and turned it into something bigger. Sometimes it was comforting, but more often, I felt scrutinized, anxious, or haunted.

Moreover, Mormons believe that all of our actions are being recorded in the Book of Life, where they will be reviewed on Judgment Day. We will have a perfect memory of everything we've ever done and how much we've hurt others. Dallin H. Oaks reminds us that "God always knows. And He has repeatedly warned that the time will come when '[our] iniquities shall be spoken upon the housetops, and [our] secret acts shall be revealed'"[1] Talk about phobia-inducing.

The current temple vow includes a death threat: "We desire to impress upon your minds the sacred character of the First Token of the Aaronic Priesthood, with its accompanying name and sign, as well as that of all the other tokens of the Holy Priesthood, with their names, and signs, which you will receive in the temple this day. They are most sacred, and are guarded by solemn covenants and obligations made in the presence of God, Angels and these witnesses to hold them sacred and under no condition, even at the peril of your life, will you ever divulge them, except at a certain place in the temple that will be shown you hereafter."[2]

This adds a whole new layer to the dispensing of existence technique. In the set and setting of the surrounding ritual, it is phobia induction.

The pre-1990 ceremony took it much further, because the recipient of the ordinance had to pantomime being killed.

> The Execution of the Penalty is represented by placing the thumb under the left ear (Officiator demonstrates), the palm of the hand down, and by drawing the thumb quickly across the throat to the right ear (Officiator demonstrates) and dropping the hand to the side (Officiator drops his right hand to his side)...
> "I, John, covenant that I will never reveal the First Token of the Aaronic Priesthood with its accompanying name, sign and penalty. Rather than do so I would suffer (the right hand, palm down, is now placed near the throat so that the thumb is under the left ear)—my life—(the thumb is now drawn under the jaw-bone and across the throat to the right ear)—to be taken (the hand is now dropped to the side)."[3]

Reading about exmormons who have overcome this totalist-induced phobia is liberating. If they lived through it, so can I, though I still experience a twinge of fear even as I write these words. Because I swore that if I revealed these things, my life would be in peril.

Apprehension can last long after the old beliefs have been shed. Many exmormons report fear of committing "sin" though they no longer believe certain acts are sinful. Even simple things, like drinking coffee; after years, they fear taking that first sip.

Here is a list of things Mormons may fear:

- The last days, the Second Coming, The Great and Terrible Day of the Lord. Great for worthy members, terrible for the wicked.
- Fires, floods, earthquakes, storms, volcanoes, plagues, famines.
- Authoritarian governments.
- Unseen evil spirits or ghosts.
- Being possessed.

---

1. Dallin H. Oaks. "Be Not Deceived." In LDS General Conference, Oct 2004.
2. "Mormon Temple Covenants." Accessed Aug 21, 2013. http://lds4u.com/lesson5/templecovenants.htm
3. "LDS (Mormon) Temple Penalties." Accessed Oct 18, 2013. http://lds-mormon.com/veilworker/penalty.shtml

- Satan will gain power over you.
- God and angels are watching, recording every action, every thought.
- Ancestors and deceased loved ones are watching.
- Loss of eternal salvation.
- Loss of eternal family. Loss of temporal family.
- Being rejected, shunned, or ostracized.
- Loss of employment (especially in Utah).
- Loss of financial stability.
- Loss of the Spirit.
- Loss of blessings.
- Loss of health.
- Unspecified life disasters.
- Loss of ancestors' salvation.
- Bishop will know if you're lying.
- Having to go to the bishop to repent.
- People finding out about your sins.
- Being unable to succeed in life.
- Not getting into the Celestial Kingdom.
- Being unable to find someone to marry.
- Disfellowshipping and excommunication
- Fear of making wrong choices without the guidance of the Spirit.
- Succumbing to a life of addiction and debauchery.
- Loss of purpose and meaning.
- Being deceived.
- Death.
- Eternal guilt.
- Your actions are "crucifying Christ anew."
- God will be displeased.

And here are a few triggers, or actions, that can lead to the above results:

- Anti-Mormon material
- Losing faith
- Sinning
- Drugs
- Going into bars
- Conflict
- Contradicting authority
- Failing to pay tithing
- Not going on a mission
- Taking off your garments
- Dating or associating with nonmembers
- Questioning and having doubts
- Having a weak testimony
- Not working hard enough
- Sex
- Masturbation
- Making major or even minor decisions
- Rock music, horror movies, playing cards, D&D, tarot, the occult, paganism, and witchcraft
- The dark
- Being raped
- Going shopping on Sunday
- Being gay

- Swearing
- Uncertainty
- Revealing secrets that might make you or your family look bad
- Seeing a naked body, even on accident
- Being yourself and following your real desires

LDS folklore helps to propagate these fears. Stories are told about evil spirits, Satanism, accidents, diseases, and deaths. Urban legends and ghost stories are given a doctrinal spin, and become about angels, ouija boards, the Three Nephites, Lucifer, and Cain. While never distributed through official channels, very little effort is made to stop their spread. They were told around the campfire at Girl's Camp and during social activities, and my own family had plenty of personalized tales about encounters with the unseen world. These visions kept me awake many a night.

If you still struggle with phobias, remember that nonmembers can live normal, happy lives doing things Mormons are taught not to do. You will still be a good person and there is no punitive, obsessive, codependent, jealous God watching your every move.

*Captive Hearts* offers practical comfort: "Because you have been warned about the dangers of leaving the group, you may still be blaming yourself for everything bad that happens. Do some reality checking. If the cult is responsible for the bad things that have happened to you since leaving, then who is responsible for the good?"[1]

Steven Hassan recommends a three-step method:

- Understand the difference between a phobia and a fear of something actually dangerous.
- Understand how the phobia was induced for the purpose of compliance.
- Reason through the phobia. Ask yourself questions, research, and look for real examples of people who act without the feared consequence occurring.[2]

The phobia is a thing separate from yourself, just a feeling and not reality. It's not even *your* feeling; it was given to you from the outside in an attempt to control your actions. Understanding where your fears come from will help.

The best way to beat a phobia is to act against it and prove you will come out okay. Reason with your phobia. "I no longer believe in a vengeful God who will punish me for my sins. I've done the research and coffee isn't really going to lead me to a life of uncontrolled addiction. So I'm going to just take one sip today. If I like it, I'll take two sips tomorrow. Then I'll see that I'm not really going to hell or dying of cancer for tasting something millions of Americans consume every day."

Hassan's book, *Releasing the Bonds*, spends a whole chapter on this topic. If you are still struggling with phobias, I recommend checking it out. You may also benefit from the help of a therapist.

---

1. Tobias and Lalich, *Captive Hearts, Captive Minds*, 1994. 131.
2. Hassan, *Releasing the Bonds*, 2000. 248-255.

> *Until they become conscious they will never rebel, and until after they have rebelled they cannot become conscious.*
> —**George Orwell, *1984***

> *For my soul delighteth in the song of the heart; yea, the song of the righteous is a prayer unto me, and it shall be answered with a blessing upon their heads.*
> *Wherefore, lift up thy heart and rejoice, and cleave unto the covenants which thou hast made.*
> —**Doctrine & Covenants 25:12-13**

> *Everything he said was extraordinarily mysterious and profound in our minds, though his descriptions and definitions were nebulous.*
> —**Steve Sanchez, *Spiritual Perversion*** [1]

# Trance Induction & Dissociative States

> **Trance Induction & Dissociative States**
> —*Suppression, Influence, Group Identification, Trust*
>
> - Creates a state of being more open to influence
> - Creates a state of being influenced by emotion
> - Can create euphoric states
> - Suppresses critical thinking
> - Creates openness to indirect directives
> - Creates a better environment for inducing phobias

*What?* you may say. Trance induction? Mormons don't even have a favorable view of hypnosis. They especially don't do trances. Those are only for weird new age cults and Eastern mediation groups.

This notion comes from a misunderstanding of altered states. Most people assume that during a typical day, there are only two forms of consciousness: awake and asleep. Anything else requires weird rituals, drugs, or mesmerism.

In fact, we have many natural states of consciousness and dissociation, within which, our minds are more or less skilled at certain activities, like learning, logic, emotion, empathy, creativity, and automatic action. Parts of your awareness go slack so your mind can focus on other things.

For example, when you drive, you are not focused on operating the car. You are dissociated from the act of driving so your mind can wander. This is a form of trance known as "highway hypnosis."

Likewise, while watching a movie or reading a novel, your senses become one with the story. Reality fades out and you suspend disbelief, temporarily able to accept fictional impossibilities. In this state, logic goes on the shelf, and you are receptive (very slightly) to the underlying theme and message of the story. In this mindset, you are more easily persuaded of emotional, social, and artistic concepts that logic would otherwise reject.

For instance, a story that puts you into the head of an impoverished character struggling against adversity is much more persuasive than a logical argument which dryly states, "Help the poor because they suffer." Fiction writers call this, "Show, don't tell."

These are just two examples of common "trances" that you are used to experiencing.

---

1. Sanchez, *Spiritual Perversion*, 2005. 98.

Because altered states feel so natural, they are easy to manipulate without arousing suspicion. Like every other topic in this book, trance induction only becomes a problem when used to manipulate you in a closed, totalist system.

Galanti writes, "...our society does not recognize the full range of altered states of consciousness available to human beings... If people could get past the idea that a person must feel 'stoned' or at least 'high' to be in an altered state of consciousness, they would accept the reality of brainwashing far more easily."[1]

She describes her own misapprehension while observing the Moonies. "Not taking into account the subtlety of different phases of consciousness, I was looking for glassy-eyed zombies as an indication of brainwashing. I didn't find any... The only trait that struck me as strange was a kind of false overenthusiasm... I began to see this response as more charming than odd."[2]

Singer defines hypnosis in the cult context as, "...essentially a form of highly focused mental concentration in which one person allows another to structure the object of the concentration and simultaneously suspends critical judgment and peripheral awareness. When this method is used in a cultic environment, it becomes a form of psychological manipulation and coercion because the cult leader implants suggestions aimed at his own agenda while the person is in a vulnerable state."[3]

She defines trance as, "...a phenomenon in which our consciousness or awareness is modified. Our awareness seems to split as our active critical-evaluative thinking dims, and we slip from an active into a passive-receptive mode of mental processing. We listen or look without reflection or evaluation. We suspend rational analysis, independent judgment, and conscious decision making about what we are hearing or taking in. We lose the boundaries between what we wish were true and what is factual. Imagination and reality intertwine, and our self and the selves of others seem more like one self. Our mental gears shift into receptivity, leaving active mental processing in neutral."[4] In this state, the mind defaults to what some call "trance logic."

John D. Goldhammer lists a number of trance-inducing activities: "Hypnosis...is a major factor in the indoctrination process, especially for religious groups where members repeat mantras, prayers, affirmations, chants, songs, and practice lengthy meditations. In addition, many groups commonly have lengthy meetings, weekend conclaves, and seminars, which last for many hours without a break where people sit passively listening to highly repetitious material."[5]

Other consciousness-altering activities include speaking in tongues, guided imagery, drugs, fatigue, fasting, sensory deprivation, focused study, repetitive behaviors, creative acts (like making art), and performing music.

It is through these states that we learn. It allows suspension of cognitive dissonance long enough to take in new information. It becomes dangerous when what we're taking in is directed towards totalist ends. "It is a testament to the learning potential of a focused mind that hypnosis can be so effective in influencing behavior. An individual going through 'training' in a cult is put in an environment where all attention is focused on the cult's beliefs and behaviors. There are no conflicting messages, no non-cult distractions."[6]

So depending on which of our former beliefs we are asked to set aside, and how much of our core self we lose in the process, altered states can either aid learning or be a manipulative exploitation tool.

Some teachers induce deeper trance states than others. Singer argues, "It is my contention that a number of speeches given by certain cult leaders, and some group chants, fit the criteria for producing transient levels of trance. ...one of my graduate students made

---

1. Galanti, "Reflections on 'Brainwashing,'" *Recovery from Cults,* ed. Langone, 1995. 86.
2. Galanti, "Reflections on 'Brainwashing,'" *Recovery from Cults,* ed. Langone, 1995. 88.
3. Singer, *Cults in Our Midst*, 1995. 151.
4. Singer, *Cults in Our Midst*, 1995. 151.
5. Goldhammer, *Under the Influence,* 1996. 109.
6. Galanti, "Reflections on 'Brainwashing,'" *Recovery from Cults,* ed. Langone, 1995. 86.

a comparison of the taped speeches of charismatic cult leaders, television evangelists, and mainstream church leaders, looking for persuasive and trance-inducing qualities. Her findings, based on the evaluations of trained raters, showed that the speeches by cult leaders and fundamentalist evangelists had more hypnotic qualities than those of the mainstream church leaders."[1,2]

Dissociation is another type of altered state, and like trance-states, it occurs naturally and to varying degrees. Types of dissociation include detachment from reality, disconnections of related thoughts or events from one another, over-compartmentalization, memory blocking, and various levels of identity segregation, up to and including dissociative identity disorder (DID). In its lesser forms, it is a normal and healthy experience. For instance, we all play slightly different roles around our families than we do when talking to bill collectors or meeting new people—this is a healthy form of identity dissociation. And when a really good novel causes your external awareness to shut down, that is reality dissociation.

In its extremes, dissociation can impede a functional and enjoyable life. Severe dissociation is a psychological defense, and a symptom of post-traumatic stress disorder (PTSD).

All forms of dissociation, including the extreme forms, can be induced and used as a manipulation tool. *Captive Hearts* describes this process:

> ...unbearable emotional reactions to traumatic events can produce an altered state or dissociation. Dissociation is an 'abnormal state, set apart from ordinary consciousness,' wherein the normal connections of memory, knowledge, and emotion are severed. "If overwhelmed by terror and helplessness, a person's perceptions become inaccurate and pervaded with terror, the coordinative functions of judgment and discrimination fail..."
>
> Lifton refers to dissociation as "psychic numbing," or a sequestering of a portion of the self... Dissociation, then, is a kind of fragmentation of the self, sometimes referred to as a "splitting" and considered an "altered state of consciousness..." This state can be brought about through techniques such as chanting or meditating or achieved through a combination of long hours of lecture or criticism sessions, fatigue, and fear...
>
> ...a person in a dissociated state is not functioning at full capacity and is highly suggestible and compliant...[3]

*Recovery from Cults* says, "In dissociation cultists don't suppress facts or memories; they simply do not have access to them—even if only temporarily—because these facts or memories are 'split off' from consciousness."[4]

Dissociation makes the dots hard to connect. Awareness of the big picture is suppressed. *Recovery* continues, "The cultist's saying, during an exit counseling, that the leader was not being manipulative during a particular event under discussion may indeed be absolutely honest from the cultist's perspective. There is no denial of an unpleasant truth. There simply was never any awareness of manipulation inherent in the event."

Added elements of trauma can compound these issues into full-blown dissociative

---

1. Out of curiosity, I conducted a minor analysis of my own. I randomly picked speeches from three political figures, three religious leaders, three LDS conference talks, and three academics. Differences in the timing of the speakers' pauses really stood out. Most of the political & religious speakers (and *all* the Conference speakers) would pause at regular intervals every 3-6 words. (In the most extreme case, JFK paused every 2-3 words.) Academic lecturers paused at intervals identical to conversational speaking, like at sentence ends and natural commas, with no regular rhythm. I did not document my findings, and my sample size was super small, so it could hardly be called scientific. Take it with a grain of salt.
2. Singer, *Cults in Our Midst*, 1995. 154-155.
3. Tobias and Lalich, *Captive Hearts, Captive Minds*, 1994. 39-40.
4. David Clark, Carol Giambalvo, Noel Giambalvo, M.S., Kevin Garvey, and Michael D. Langone, Ph.D. "Exit Counseling: A Practical Overview." *Recovery from Cults*, ed. Langone, 1995. 167

disorders, especially if occurring within the context of group doctrines, for instance, when religious justification is used in child abuse or when sexual assault is denied and covered up by leadership.

Heightened altered states can generate surreal, otherworldly experiences. When this happens, the totalist always has a ready explanation. "When groups use rituals and spiritual practices that trigger transcendental mystical experiences, collective interpretation typically follows that validates the group's belief system instead of individual reality. Religious groups interpret spiritual experiences as confirming the group's unique knowledge, when in fact, spiritual experiences usually happen *in spite of* collective influences."[1]

In the LDS context, the following methods are commonly used to induce trance states:

- Vocal rhythm and soft tones of voice
- Stories
- "Be reverent"
- Logical illogic
- Hymns
- Sacrament meditation
- Repetition of concepts
- Long meetings
- Boredom
- Faith (focused trance)
- Openness to the Spirit
- Prayer
- Fasting
- Lack of sleep
- Poor diet
- Overwork

The topic of focus while in a trance is important. It's the "payload" to be delivered into the mind. Prayer puts a person into a suggestive state, and Sacrament service is a type of focused meditation. *Captive Hearts* says that while in these states, "Giving a meditator [or person praying] instructions about exactly what to look for...can be equivalent to posthypnotic suggestion. It is said among therapists that Freudian patients dream in Freudian symbolism while Jungian patients dream in Jungian symbolism."[2]

Likewise when Mormons receive answers to prayer in the form of "the still small voice," promptings, or dreams, they will encounter Mormon symbology. In this context, even visions can be induced, and they will comply with what the supplicant expects, as Singer illustrates: "I described a woman who saw an orange fog and another who spoke to the deities who appeared in her daily life like dream figures. These women's visions were the constructions of cult practices that combined trance induction with the suggestion that seeing deities or fog was a good thing. Cult members may be trained to have specific visualizations and then be praised and rewarded and feel self-fulfilled when they achieve the goal."[3]

It follows, then, that intelligent and creative people are actually *more* vulnerable to manipulation. Hassan asserts that "Individuals with good concentration and with vivid imaginations are more susceptible to hypnotic suggestion."[4]

We've already discussed the power of identification and empathy, and in fact, this can be used to create altered states. "One widely used trance induction process...is to evoke universal experiences... Evoking a feeling of universality in a person helps the speaker

---

1. Goldhammer, *Under the Influence*, 1996. 228.
2. Tobias and Lalich, *Captive Hearts, Captive Minds*, 1994. 97.
3. Singer, *Cults in Our Midst*, 1995. 316.
4. Hassan, *Releasing the Bonds*, 2000. 87.

solicit cooperation from that person."[1]

The most insidious form is the use of contradiction to overwhelm and shut down the rational centers of the mind. As Singer describes, "Sometimes the induction method is speech filled with paradox and discrepancy—that is, the message is not logical, but it is presented as though it were logical. Trying to follow what is being said can actually detach the listener from reality."[2]

I call this "logical illogic." The mind becomes so overwhelmed with immediate and inescapable dissonance that it simply gives up. I've experienced it while being bullied in personal encounters, even via email. One listed, in a rational and self-assured structure, things about me that could not possibly be true. As he continued, the less sense it made, yet it was *supposed* to make sense. I could feel my mind shut down, and I quickly turned emotional, ready to believe his every claim. Only after stepping away was I able to sort out the manipulation. These memories are still painful and confusing years later.

As I've shown, many LDS doctrines are self-contradictory, and doublespeak is employed throughout conference talks. Many hymns, especially Sacrament hymns, are full of contradictions laid out in a logical order.

The message in *I Stand All Amazed* is, "I am not worthy, yet the sinless one, God himself, sacrificed himself for me." Other Sacrament hymns repeat themes of "He died" and "He lives." Some of my favorite hymns were the most discrepant and manipulative, including *More Holiness Give Me* and *How Gentle God's Commands*, and hymns which conflated toil and suffering with joy and happiness (*Put Your Shoulder to the Wheel*; *Come, Come Ye Saints*; *Count Your Blessings*). And many others.

Emotions in any setting are contagious, but especially when they are encouraged and bolstered by other techniques. According to Singer, "Guided imagery can have any content, and the group process of hearing others cry and sob as they recall past traumas has a powerful impact, for it induces a contagion of feeling and participation that can be heady for most persons."[3]

And on the dissociative power of stories:

> Indirect trance induction also grows out of storytelling and other verbal experiences. Cult leaders often speak repetitively, rhythmically, in hard-to-follow ways, and combine with these features the telling of tales and parables that are highly visualizable. They use words to create mental imagery...
>
> In these guided-imagery exercises, the listener is urged to picture the story being told... Those who stop reflecting on their nearby circumstances and go with the picture suddenly feel absorbed, relaxed, and very focused...
>
> As a result, they enter a trancelike state in which they are more likely to heed the suggestions and absorb the content of what is being said than if they were listening in an evaluative, rational way.[4]

The use of stories isn't inherently wrong. I write fiction, and it is very much my goal to persuade and immerse my readers in the worlds I create. This is the goal of every writer. I have used stories persuasively in this book, to evoke emotion and relay concepts. However, I do not aim to deliver a totalist message. My goal is quite the opposite: I want my audience to retain the freedom to reach their own conclusions. I want to guide my readers to a path of self-actualization, which I know will be very different from my own path. I want to liberate people to see more options, not fewer.

Singer describes historical poetic forms which were known to induce "sublime ecstasy" when read aloud by a skilled reader. "Students of this phenomenon have listed six qualities

---

1. Singer, *Cults in Our Midst*, 1995. 155.
2. Singer, *Cults in Our Midst*, 1995. 154-155.
3. Singer, *Cults in Our Midst*, 1995. 159.
4. Singer, *Cults in Our Midst*, 1995. 156.

of trance-inducing poetry: (1) freedom from abruptness, (2) marked regularity of soothing rhythm, (3) refrain and frequent repetition, (4) ornamented harmonious rhythm to fix attention, (5) vagueness of imagery, and (6) fatiguing obscurities. It is these very qualities that can be identified in analyzing the speech of many cult leaders..."[1]

I've analyzed many Conference talks and found they used several or all of these techniques, often a series of stories told smoothly in a rhythmic, peaceful voice, evoking imagery and symbols.

Boyd K. Packer and Thomas Monson spring foremost to mind when I think of this technique. My favorite speakers, the ones I looked forward to listening to, the ones that made me "feel the Spirit", were those who used the most trance-induction techniques.

As Singer notes, "One leader of a Bible cult repeated long, colorful tales of his childhood as the content for his guided imagery. The history he told was later found by ex-members to be mostly fictional. The main thrust of his tales was to point out how pure and clean and innocent he was as a child. He explained that these traits led him to his special mission as a leader. Ex-members recalled that they spaced out during his tales and left the meetings feeling subdued and obedient. Interestingly, they said his guided imagery often was about achieving a mind such as he had had as a child."[2]

The Mormon accent is so lyrical, soft, soothing, calm. In Conference talks especially, their voices say, "I am at peace. I love you all. I am concerned. I care about you."

I couldn't help but notice, when listening to the Jim Jones tapes, that he had that same voice, the sound of a sweet-spirited old man with nothing but kindness in his heart. He used that voice even as he coaxed parents into feeding poison to their children. Now when I listen to Conference talks, that's all I can hear.

In Seminary, we used to joke that "Pray, fast, and read the scriptures" seemed to be the answer to every question or problem. Is it any mistake that the general authorities have said, "...members are encouraged to fast whenever their faith needs special fortification..."?[3]

It's not just the subdued state we enter due to hunger, which is powerful enough. It's the state of mind we're instructed to hold: "If we want our fasting to be more than just going without eating, we must lift our hearts, our minds, and our voices in communion with our Heavenly Father. Fasting, coupled with mighty prayer, is powerful. It can fill our minds with the revelations of the Spirit. It can strengthen us against times of temptation."[4]

Bruce R. McConkie put it very plainly. "Proper fasting, with prayer as its companion, increases spirituality, fosters a spirit of devotion and love of God, increases faith, encourages humility, teaches man his dependence upon God, and provides an opportunity for the spirit to take control over the body."[5]

Translated: Proper fasting and prayer places you in a weakened mental and physical state, reduces your cognitive ability, fosters devotion, increases dependence, and provides an opportunity for the Church to control your mind by controlling your behavior.

Music is another big part of trance induction. Galanti describes how music was used by the Moonies. "The songs were very beautiful, with upbeat lyrics. Most of them were about love and happiness and God and family. Singing is a right-brain function; critical analysis is largely the work of the left hemisphere. Thus, the singing not only served to surround the lectures with an aura of 'goodness,' but also managed to stimulate the nonanalytical portions of the brain."[6]

Here's what the Church's position on music is:

---

1. Singer, *Cults in Our Midst*, 1995. 157-158.
2. Singer, *Cults in Our Midst*, 1995. 158.
3. Joseph B. Wirthlin. "The Law of the Fast." In LDS General Conference, April 2001.
4. Wirthlin, "The Law of the Fast," General Conference, April 2001.
5. McConkie, *Mormon Doctrine*, 1966. 276.
6. Galanti, "Reflections on 'Brainwashing,'" *Recovery from Cults*, ed. Langone, 1995.

> Make wholesome music of all kinds a part of your life...
>
> Secular music may be inspiring in a classical or popular sense, but it will not prepare your mind to be instructed by the Spirit as will sacred music...
>
> The Apostle Paul counseled the Ephesians to "be filled with the Spirit; speaking to yourselves in psalms and hymns and spiritual songs, singing and making melody in your heart to the Lord."
>
> Prelude music, reverently played, is nourishment for the spirit. It invites inspiration. That is a time to, as the poet said, "go to your bosom...and ask your heart what it doth know." Do not ever disturb prelude music for others, for reverence is essential to revelation.[1]

Conversely, "Some music is spiritually very destructive. You young people know what kind that is. The tempo, the sounds, and the lifestyle of those who perform it repel the Spirit. It is far more dangerous than you may suppose, for it can smother your spiritual senses..."[2]

When we get into the habit of falling into totalist trance states, especially when we're trained to think they're healthy, we can become triggered into that state when something reminds us to do so. According to Joe Kelly, a former member of two eastern meditation groups, "I would sometimes get confused that these floating experiences were signs from God directing me back to the path."[3]

His experience included profound and lengthy meditations that left him with frequent involuntary dissociation. This phenomenon is known as "floating." Mormons are less prone to it than members from groups which foster deeper trances. But the tendency to automatically slip back into a lowered level of consciousness is still something to be aware of.

We may also be more prone to a trancelike state of fear. Singer writes, "If allowed to break into consciousness, suppressed memories or nagging doubts may generate anxiety which, in turn, may trigger a defensive trance-induction, such as speaking in tongues, to protect the cult-imposed system of thoughts, feelings, and behavior."[4]

This is similar to the dissociative "stupor of thought" we've been programed to expect when faced with information that threatens to rip apart our closed system of logic.

---

1. Boyd K. Packer. "Personal Revelation: The Gift, the Test, and the Promise." In LDS General Conference, Oct 1994.
2. Packer, "Personal Revelation," General Conference, Oct 1994.
3. Tobias and Lalich, *Captive Hearts, Captive Minds,* 1994. 90.
4. Tobias and Lalich, *Captive Hearts, Captive Minds,* 1994. 45.

*...they now live only for admittance into the Celestial Kingdom, and for that privilege they must obey and work incessantly. They are no longer individuals. No one is supposed to get sick or stop working; this would be a sign of a lack of Faith. This leads to the 'sacrifice' of all that you humanly have or own.*

—Marion Stricker,
***The Pattern of the Double-Bind in Mormonism***[1]

*We all have work; let no one shirk.*
*Put your shoulder to the wheel.*

—***Put Your Shoulder to the Wheel***,
LDS Hymn #252[2]

*'...so many meetings, I've been to so many meetings and I no longer can figure out what is real information; what is true information.'*

—Bob Eastman,
**inner circle UFO cult member in *When Prophecy Fails***[3]

*I felt suicidal and I had a deep fear that I would die with a little plaque around my neck that read 'Perfect Attendance.'*

—John D. Goldhammer,
***Under the Influence***[4]

# Time Control

**Time Control**
—*Suppression, Influence, Reinforcement, Silencing Doubts, Group Identification, Isolation*
- Limits resources for thinking critically
- Isolates member from outsiders
- Immerses member fully in group
- Creates dependency
- Exhaustion leads to trance states
- Leaves little time for self
- Makes the member more open to suggestion

Time is of the essence. The essence of control, that is.

According to Steven Hassan, "Cults often impose an oppressive time schedule on their members' lives in order to control behavior. When members are not engaged in cult rituals and indoctrination activities, they are typically assigned to specific goals that restrict their free time and behavior—anything to keep them busy. In a destructive cult, there is always work to be done."[5]

Michael Langone agrees. "In order to 'advance' at a satisfactory pace, members must...spend long hours involved in various tasks or practices the leadership deems necessary. In short, members spend more and more time with and under the direction of the group..."[6]

This is partly done to ramp up indoctrination of new members. According to *Recovery From Cults*, "The more time spent exclusively within the new culture, the more rapid and complete acculturation is likely to be... What is different in the cult context, perhaps, is that

---

1. Stricker, *The Double-Bind in Mormonism*, 2000. 93.
2. Thompson, "Put Your Shoulder to the Wheel," *Hymns*, 1985.
3. Festinger, *When Prophecy Fails*, 1964. 198.
4. Goldhammer, *Under the Influence*, 1996. 57.
5. Hassan, *Releasing the Bonds*, 2000. 46.
6. Langone, "Introduction," *Recovery from Cults*, 1995. 8.

it is done with the specific intent of acculturating someone who may or may not at that point *want* to be acculturated."[1]

The steady push to work creates fatigue and sleep deprivation that can effectively make an individual more susceptible to influence and leaves little room for awareness and self-examination.

Goldhammer says, "...destructive groups fill members' infrequent spare time with an endless series of projects... When we are exhausted and worn out we are far more vulnerable to hypnotic influences."[2] Later he says, "Lack of sufficient rest and sensory overload contribute to the inability of the individual to have time to *think* about the validity of information being received."[3]

Singer elaborates.

> Exhaustion and confusion increase cult members' inability to act. In most groups, members are made to work morning, noon, and night. It's no wonder they become exhausted and unable to think straight. After several years of sixteen to twenty-hour workdays, seven days a week, no vacations, no time off, no fun, no hobbies, and no real, intimate relationship with your spouse, even if you have one, you're living in a fog world. Some former members describe feeling as though there were a veil over their eyes, as if they were not in touch with the physical world. They functioned by rote...
>
> When you can't think, when you feel as though you can barely survive each day, all you want to do is get through that day without getting battered in whatever form that takes in your group... You plod and plod along and plod along. You are incredibly confused but don't know any way of dealing with your confusion.[4]

Energy and time for doubts, questions, and association with outsiders vanishes, so it is, in effect, a form of milieu control without physical isolation.

When pressed, LDS leadership and members may deny such demands for time, claiming the Church teaches moderation and balance. Individual Saints should fill their own cup before trying to fill others.

But in reality, most members push themselves hard. There are pressures from peers and a steady stream of demands for purity. This commandment is dire, and that one is vital. God's will is open-ended: "It is not meet I should command in all things." Members are driven ever onward to prove the worker bee reputation, ever standard-bearers of the Protestant work ethic.

This reputation was a point of pride for President Gordon B. Hinckley: "They are put to work. They are given responsibility. They are made to feel a part of the great onward movement of this, the work of God... They soon discover that much is expected of them as Latter-day Saints. They do not resent it. They measure up and they like it. They expect their religion to be demanding, to require reformation in their lives. They meet the requirements. They bear testimony of the great good that has come to them. They are enthusiastic and faithful."[5]

According to scripture, "...we should waste and wear out our lives in bringing to light all the hidden things of darkness..." D&C 123:13

And D&C 88:124 cautions us to "Cease to be idle... cease to sleep longer than is needful..."

In a Conference talk, Dallin H. Oaks sets our modern day *Focus and Priorities*:

---

1. Galanti, "Reflections on 'Brainwashing,'" *Recovery from Cults*, ed. Langone, 1995. 92.
2. Goldhammer, *Under the Influence*, 1996. 110.
3. Goldhammer, *Under the Influence*, 1996. 191.
4. Singer, *Cults in Our Midst*, 1995. 274.
5. President Gordon B. Hinckley. "What Are People Asking About Us?" *Ensign*, Nov 1998. http://www.lds.org/ensign/1998/11/what-are-people-asking-about-us

"Because of increased life expectancies and modern timesaving devices, most of us have far more discretionary time than our predecessors. We are accountable for how we use that time. 'Thou shalt not idle away thy time', and 'Cease to be idle', the Lord commanded the early missionaries and members."[1]

Time spent on other activities is, at best, wasteful. Elder Apostle Quentin L. Cook counseled that "some addictions or predilections, while not inherently evil, can use up our precious allotment of time which could otherwise be used to accomplish virtuous objectives. These can include excessive use of social media, video and digital games, sports, recreation, and many others."[2]

Examples of those who sacrifice are regularly held up for others to emulate. A series of hymns sing about constant labor and toil, including *Come, Come Ye Saints, I Have Work Enough to Do, Let Us All Press On, As Sisters in Zion,* and *Put Your Shoulder To the Wheel.* In the temple we covenanted to consecrate our time to the Church.[3]

In a talk on consecration, Apostle D. Todd Christofferson quotes from the famous LDS film, *Man's Search for Happiness.* "Every day, every hour, every minute of your span of mortal years must sometime be accounted for. And it is in this life that you walk by faith and prove yourself able to choose good over evil, right over wrong, enduring happiness over mere amusement. And your eternal reward will be according to your choosing."[4] How we should use our time is clear. "True success in this life comes in consecrating our lives—that is, our time and choices—to God's purposes."

For my paper, *The BITE Model and Mormon Control*,[5] I estimated a typical "good Mormon" would spend a *minimum* of 22 hours a week fulfilling Church duties, in addition to normal occupational and household obligations. Here's my breakdown:

> - 3 hours/week Sunday church meetings
> - Average 8 hours/week for callings
> - 2 hrs/week additional meetings
> - 2 hrs Monday for family home evening
> - 1 hr/day scripture reading & prayer

This does not include extras, like:

> + Extra meetings, classes, and events like:
>   - General and Stake Conferences
>   - Girl's Camp
>   - Scouting
>   - Dance festivals
>   - Ward gatherings
>   - Special conferences
>   - Training for callings
>   - Talent shows
>   - Seminary
>   - Others

---

1. Dallin H. Oaks. "Focus and Priorities." In LDS General Conference, April 2011. http://www.lds.org/general-conference/2001/04/focus-and-priorities
2. Quentin L. Cook. "Lamentations of Jeremiah: Beware of Bondage." In LDS General Conference, Oct 2013. https://www.lds.org/general-conference/2013/10/lamentations-of-jeremiah-beware-of-bondage
3. "You and each of you covenant and promise before God, angels, and these witnesses at this altar, that you do accept the Law of Consecration as contained in the *Doctrine and Covenants*, in that you do consecrate yourselves, your time, talents, and everything with which the Lord has blessed you, or with which he may bless you, to the Church of Jesus Christ of Latter-day Saints, for the building up of the Kingdom of God on the earth and for the establishment of Zion." http://lds4u.com/lesson5/templecovenants.htm
4. Elder D. Todd Christofferson. "Reflections on a Consecrated Life," Oct 2010. http://www.lds.org/ensign/2010/11/reflections-on-a-consecrated-life
5. Luna Flesher Lindsey. "The BITE Model and Mormon Control." *Rational Revelation.* Accessed Dec 22, 2013. http://www.rationalrevelation.com/library/bite.html

> + Highly demanding callings (Bishop, Relief Society President, etc.)
> + Supporting your spouse's calling
> + Missions
> + Member missionary work
> + Temple attendance
> + Genealogy and family history
> + Cleaning the meetinghouse and temple grounds
> + Service
> + Gardening
> + Food storage
> + Journaling
> + Pursuing Boy Scout badges & achievements
> + Studying Church publications
> + Magnifying your talents
> + Having a large family

As part of the temple ordinances, Mormons covenant to sacrifice and consecrate all to the Church. This implies that there is always something more that can be done. If 30 minutes of scripture study per day is acceptable, then an hour is better. Why stop at five children when you could have seven or eight? Wouldn't it be better to attend the temple weekly?

Members express guilt regarding things they believe they should be doing or doing better. The pressure to perform can lead to burnout, depression, and strained family relations.

Pam Kazmaier shares how the Church consumed her life when she tried to be a good Mormon:

> I was serious about doing all my new religion asked. Callings, babies, meetings, ward activities, family history work, temple work, family home evenings, prayer and scripture reading (both individual and family, both morning and night), fasting, tithing, fast offerings, relief society work, visiting teaching, kept me pretty occupied.
>
> Food became a huge all-consuming deal. Mormon women are supposed to keep everyone fed in a big way. Buying huge white containers of food, constructing food storage rooms, cooking and baking the food from scratch, then storing, freezing or re-using the food was a big task. It wasn't just for your family either... Food became like a large, looming mountain I could never overcome. It was constantly overwhelming and defeating me...
>
> I lost my identity. I lost all sense of who I was as an individual with a right to sleep, pleasure, fun, joy...
>
> I'd sign up to do extra work on those clipboards that went around the room in Relief Society: feed the missionaries, work in the cannery, take a meal into the three sick sisters, put up the temple lights, take down the temple lights, clean the church building, sew something for the humanitarian project, donate used items for the Deseret Industries, etc. Of course, there was always some meal to prepare for the Elder's Quorum function because Men are so busy acting for God they can't cook. Temple attendance was encouraged once a month, at least, twice a month was even better. Those who were celestial material attended once a week. Yes, that's right, I went every week for years...
>
> Then there were Sundays. Oh, my god, the Sundays. Depending on what time my ward got assigned the building; I was up either at 5am or 7am. Forget sleeping late on Sundays, there's just too much to do. There are meetings before and after the normal 3-hour stretch of mandated meetings of Sacrament, Sunday school and

> Relief Society, Primary or Young Women's. Depending what callings I had, there were the meetings to plan what to do in the next meeting. I would have such a splitting headache on Sundays.[1]

Just reading this list leaves me feeling exhausted. Perhaps members like Kazmaier have mistaken the doctrine. Yet when they can endure, those who sacrifice as she did are praised: "I am grateful for the marvelous examples of Christian love, service, and sacrifice I have seen among the Latter-day Saints. I see you performing your Church callings, often at great sacrifice of time and means. I see you serving missions at your own expense. I see you cheerfully donating your professional skills in service to your fellowmen."[2]

As Kazmaier put it, "Every day of the week belongs to the church..."[3]

---

1. Pam Kazmaier. "Losing My Mind, Bit by Bit," Aug 13, 2005. http://questioningmormonism.wordpress.com/2011/12/02/pam-kazmaier-losing-my-mind-bit-by-bit/
2. Dallin H. Oaks. "Sacrifice." In LDS General Conference, April 2012. http://www.lds.org/general-conference/2012/04/sacrifice
3. Kazmaier, "Losing My Mind," Aug 13, 2005.

*I had been cornered by my own words. To decline her offer at that point would have meant facing a pair of distasteful alternatives.*
—**Robert B. Cialdini, *Influence*** [1]

*I was told that God had saved me above all others for a special purpose and that now I owed Him for it.*
—**"Mitchell",**
quoted in *The Pattern of the Double-Bind in Mormonism* [2]

*The more I learned about Mormonism that tempestuous year, the more I came to believe that to be loyal to my family and religion, I would have to slaughter either my mind or my soul.*
—**Martha Beck,**
***Leaving the Saints*** [3]

# The Double-Bind

**Double-Bind**
—*Suppression, Silencing Doubts, Punishment, Reinforcement*

- Creates logical, emotional and behavioral traps
- Creates lose-lose situations where no choice is a good choice
- Very similar to blame reversal
- Leads to self-betrayal or betrayal of the group, the leader, group values
- Depends on demand for purity
- Heavily based on guilt and shame
- Can leverage induced phobias
- Reinforced by doctrine over self
- Reliant on deception

The next three chapters cover the most important and intense levers of manipulation: the Double-Bind, Blame Reversal, and Guilt/Shame. These thought-reform methods sink the deepest and affect the psyche the most negatively. Bind, blame, and shame work in tandem. Because of their emotional and dynamic nature, it is very difficult to draw clear lines between them.

A double-bind is a "damned if you do, damned if you don't" scenario, the thought-terminating setup for the landslide of blame and shame. To illustrate how it works, let's begin with a sci-fi metaphor.

You've heard of a delightful vacation planet called Kolob. The planet is many hundreds of light years away, but Happy Hyperspace Lightyears Delivery Service, Inc. proudly advertises their exclusive faster than light ships. Though you cannot ask any vacationer directly, LDS assures you that Kolob is so wonderful that people who visit never wish to return. Their salesman beamingly reports they've never had an unhappy customer.

This sounds like the best trip ever, so you sign a waiver, hand them cash, and climb aboard your automated personal rocket. You gaze excitedly out the porthole as you watch Earth get smaller and smaller.

After a week, it seems the ship has stopped accelerating. You expected a flash of light when the rocket powered into hyperspace, but there was none.

You push the "help" button on the console. The computer is slow but finally announces mechanical difficulties and prints repair instructions. You find the toolbox and repair panel,

---

1. Cialdini, *Influence,* 2009. 90.
2. Stricker, *The Double-Bind in Mormonism,* 2000. 128.
3. Beck, *Leaving the Saints,* 2005. 174.

but the directions are incomprehensible. In one place it says you should never cut the blue wire, and in another, it tells you it will be necessary to cut the blue wire.

Eventually, you decide to cut the blue wire.

The hyperdrive begins to make a clanking sound and immediately a call comes from a support technician. You prepare to chew him out for sending you in this rusty tin can and for making you repair the ship yourself. But he interrupts. In a calm and level voice, he accuses you of being a really bad repair technician.

"The instructions are very simple," he self-assuredly explains. "Just put the green wire in the port ejector. And whatever you do, don't cut the blue wire." He halts transmission.

Everything suddenly makes sense. Burning with shame, you awkwardly splice the blue wire back together and put the green wire in the port ejector. The ship accelerates. You feel like an idiot. You blast into hyperspace in the twinkling of an—

What's this? The fuel gage blinks. Sighing, you press "help", this time less sure of yourself. The exasperated technician answers. "I have other customers," he says. "Why must you keep bothering me?"

Panicking slightly, you explain that the ship is out of fuel.

"Well that's because you flew for a whole week without jumping into hyperspace," he grumbles, and then smiles, suddenly friendly.

Of course. You should have asked for help sooner. He tells you not to fear and invites you to press the orange button.

Relief at last. A panel slides away. Behind it, you see pedals.

Your mouth falls open. "How long is this trip supposed to take, anyway?" you ask. You forgot to ask before departure. Nor did you bring a copy of the contract, which you didn't really read because LDS had such a good reputation and the salesman seemed like an honest, well-dressed young man.

The technician puts you on hold. For a few days. In the meantime, you start pedaling. It's a long way home, and you have no idea where Kolob is.

The answer finally comes—pedal harder.

A month later, the pedals break. The technician kindly suggests you stop depending on him and become self-reliant. He politely implies that maybe you did something wrong. The pedals don't normally break. Maybe you got a little too eager... pedaled too hard.

You lose it. You scream and yell and rant and rave. The technician calmly asks you to relax. After all, you got yourself into your own mess. Sighing, you apologize and manage to fix the pedals yourself by weaving together spare wires.

Years go by. Sometimes you pass another ship, and inside, you see a fellow traveler, vigorously pedaling away, or tangled in cables with a screwdriver in hand.

Sometimes, another ship passes you, trailing the bright lights of their hyperdrive... At least you assume. They go by too fast to tell. You radio tech support to ask them why some ships go faster. He patiently informs you that everyone has to pedal, just like you. Those customers are simply pedaling harder.

You're sick of the bull crud. But what can you do? When you timidly ask if you can leave, the technician crosses his arms, and stiffly informs you, "You're free to return home, but you can't do it in our ship."

You look out the window into dead, empty space. There's no way out. Well, at least you brought a year's supply of food.

A closed, totalist system creates situations that are win-win for the group, and lose-lose for the member. These catch-22s are myriad. All signs must point to, "The Church is true." The answer to every serious question must be, "Yes, but..." where "but" actually means, "No." "Can I leave?" Yes, but... "Am I free to choose?" Yes, but... "Will the gospel make me happy?" Yes, but...

These are double-binds. As *Captive Hearts* describes, "This emotional cul-de-sac is defined as a 'psychological dilemma in which a usually dependent person receives conflicting interpersonal communication from a single source or *faces disparagement no matter what his response to a situation.'* It imparts a message of hopelessness: You're damned if you do and damned if you don't."[1]

Some members will encounter double-binds more than others, particularly square pegs and those who struggle with their faith. Double-binds cause instability, which leads, ironically, to total trust of the manipulator. "Double binds magnify dependence by injecting an additional element of unpredictability into cult members' relationships to their leadership. Consequently, members can never become too comfortable. Fear prevents them from challenging those on whom they have become dependent... The mere act of living creates insecurity and induces fear and withdrawal.

"When this type of manipulation...is used, cult members spend most of their time feeling as though they are walking on eggs, knowing that they must act—and yet to act may bring rebuke, punishment, or worse."[2]

The power of the double-bind is in its invisibility. "...part of the victims' denial system is the inability to believe that someone they love so much could consciously and callously hurt them. It therefore becomes easier to rationalize the leader's behavior as necessary for the general or individual 'good.' The alternative for the devotee would be to face the sudden and overwhelming awareness of being victimized, deceived, used. Such a realization would wound the person's deepest sense of self, so as a means of self-protection the person denies the abuse. When and if the devotee becomes aware of the exploitation, it feels as though a tremendous evil has been done, a spiritual rape."[3]

*Recovery from Cults* calls this the "loyalty/betrayal funnel." "If [members] remain loyal to their own perceptions about self and world, they betray the group on which they have become inordinately dependent; if they remain loyal to the group, they betray their own perception of what is real, good, and true. Dissent thus places members in a 'funnel' from which there is no escape and which inevitably leads to betrayal, either of themselves or the group."[4]

Philosopher Sam Keen describes it using a poetic Garden of Eden metaphor: "If we experiment and break the taboos, we may be punished and we will certainly feel guilt and be cast out of the Garden. But if we do not, if we remain obedient children, we will feel the shame that comes from never exercising our freedom and from living our own lives within the Garden of the Authorities. If we disobey, we will have to wrestle with guilt and autonomy; if we obey, we will have to wrestle with shame and dependency."[5]

Double-binds occur when promises cannot be fulfilled. In *Influence*, Cialdini says, "Because we build new struts to undergird choices we have committed ourselves to, an exploitative individual can offer us an inducement for making such a choice. After the decision has been made, the individual can remove that inducement, knowing that our decision will probably stand on its own newly created legs."[6]

The double-bind may arise naturally out of black and white doctrines which construct mutually exclusive false dichotomies. When there is no room for middle ground, reason becomes the enemy of faith; questioning is the enemy of obedience. Integrity becomes impossible—you can either be true to yourself, or true to your LDS ideals. There are times when you cannot be both. "The result of this process, when carried to its consummation, is a pseudopersonality, a state of dissociation in which members are 'split' but not 'multiple,' in which they proclaim great happiness yet hide great suffering."[7]

The LDS answer to all objections, failed promises, and personal struggles is some form of "keep trying harder." A scripture embodies this switcheroo: "I, the Lord, am bound when ye do what I say; but when ye do not what I say, ye have no promise." D&C 82:10

---

1. Tobias and Lalich, *Captive Hearts, Captive Minds*, 1994. 43.
2. Tobias and Lalich, *Captive Hearts, Captive Minds*, 1994. 44.
3. Tobias and Lalich, *Captive Hearts, Captive Minds*, 1994. 76.
4. Langone, "Introduction," *Recovery from Cults*, 1995. 9.
5. Keen, *Hymns to an Unknown God*, 1995. 38-39.
6. Cialdini, *Influence*, 2009. 84.
7. Langone, "Introduction," *Recovery from Cults*, 1995. 9.

And, "There is a law, irrevocably decreed in heaven before the foundations of this world, upon which all blessings are predicated— And when we obtain any blessing from God, it is by obedience to that law upon which it is predicated." D&C 130:20-21

These vague and demanding conditions can never be met, so the destination will never be reached. My patriarchal blessing says, "He will care and watch over and bless you with righteous blessings all the days of your life if you will only serve Him and keep His commandments." All these promises are yours, when you complete a long list of tasks. Unlike Cinderella, no fairy godmother comes down to finish the work, and we never get to go to the ball.

The famous promise in Moroni 10:4 is a double-bind: "...if ye shall ask with a sincere heart, with real intent, having faith in Christ, he will manifest the truth of it unto you, by the power of the Holy Ghost." That's a big open-ended "if." This is not a *real* contract where well-defined requirements can be assessed. Who can measure sincerity, intent, and faith?

Diana Kline was told, "'You aren't fasting with a pure and selfless heart, nor being humble enough for the Lord to bless you so that you will reap the blessings of your fast. You must try harder to live more righteously.'"[1]

Promises like "Wickedness never was happiness" imply that if you're not happy it must be your fault. Depression means you've lost the spirit. Again, you should try harder. We were also promised: "...God is faithful, who will not suffer you to be tempted above that ye are able; but will with the temptation also make a way to escape, that ye may be able to bear it." 1 Corinthians 10:13 So, if we *do* fall, it's our failing. We could have passed that test, if only we'd made the attempt.

Chris Morin gives this example. "From my childhood, the question had never been, 'Is the Church true?' Rather, it had been: 'Have you made the necessary effort to gain a testimony? If not, you need more diligence in your scripture study; you need to ponder and pray more sincerely.' I was the one, never the Church, on trial."[2]

Thus the Church avoids having to answer to those for whom the gospel isn't working. If the contract isn't fulfilled, toil until it is. As Marion Stricker says, "The reason 'work' is demanded of individuals who 'fail' is that their minds have not yet been 'converted' to the upside-down world of programmed 'Yes, but' thinking..."[3]

Stricker wrote an entire book on *The Pattern of the Double-Bind in Mormonism*. She lists a number of double-binds, including:

| | |
|---|---|
| ◊ | Yes, the leaders are *inspired*, But, no, they are "*only human.*"[4] |
| ◊ ◊ | If I obey authority and do not think for myself then I have "chosen" Good. <br> If I do not obey authority and think for myself then I have chosen Evil.[5] |
| ◊ ◊ ◊ | Yes, faith is the most important thing for a missionary. <br> No, obedience is priority. <br> Yet, faith *is* the most important...you fail because you don't have enough faith. |
| ◊ ◊ | If you *do* have faith, and relinquish your brain, you cannot, in reality, reach a confirmation of a truth. *The means have been taken away.* <br> If you *don't* have faith, and rely on your brain, you will *not* find the confirmation of the 'truth' of something that is false.[6] |

---

1. Kline, *Woman Redeemed*, 2005. 12.
2. Morin and Morin, *Suddenly Strangers*, 2004. 112.
3. Stricker, *The Double-Bind in Mormonism*, 2000. 56.
4. Stricker, *The Double-Bind in Mormonism*, 2000. 146.
5. Stricker, *The Double-Bind in Mormonism*, 2000. 67-68.
6. Stricker, *The Double-Bind in Mormonism*, 2000. 55.

> ◯ If you trust you are *naive*... If you use *reason* you have lost your faith.[1]

Some double-binds are doctrinal, and some are situational. As "Frances" tells in his exit story, "While in the mission home...we had a question and answer session with Pres. Lee... Being shy, I felt doubly intimidated when we were admonished that since Pres. Lee was giving up time in his busy schedule to be there that our questions needed to be important enough for him to spend his time on. Well, either many others were scared also or they already knew it all because there were not many questions..."[2]

*Yes*, we're making the prophet available and you can ask anything, *but* don't be selfish. If you're a considerate person, the choice is made for you.

More situational double-binds:

- ◯ If you don't feel worthy to take the Sacrament, and let it pass, people will notice and judge you. If you take it, you'll feel twice as guilty.
- ◯ If you have friends outside the Church, you are pressured to try to convert them. If you cannot convert them, and remain friends, they may set a bad example for you or distract from your Church duties. If you stop spending time with them, your friendship was insincere.
- ◯ If you don't go on a mission, you will let God down, will be shamed by your family, and will let souls suffer in unbelief. If you do go, you go against your own goals in schooling, career, and relationships.
- ◯ If you're gay, you can deny yourself healthy, fulfilling relationships while still being (more or less) accepted by your family, friends, and the Church. Or you can be yourself and be utterly rejected.
- ◯ If you don't have a testimony, you must bear it anyway, and feel like a liar.
- ◯ If you reveal that you can't gain a testimony, you risk bonds to your family and community. If you stay LDS and pretend, you deny your own spiritual path.
- ◯ If a family member leaves and you continue to associate with them, it may reflect badly on you. Or you can distance from them and remain accepted by your community.

Worthiness to feel the Spirit is one of the most common double-binds in the Church. The Spirit will help you "Choose the Right" but you have to choose the right to be worthy of its presence. When we partake of the Sacrament, we renew our covenant to keep the commandments, and in return we are promised the Spirit to help us. To do what? Well, to keep the commandments. But even this promise is contingent upon behavior, and, as it happens, even thoughts.

Jack B. Worthy expresses this bind while on his mission. "We were supposed to be examples of righteousness and purity to the entire world's nonmember population... Yet we were put into situations under which any nineteen-year-old male would find it almost impossible not to have at least a flash of an impure thought, and all it takes is a flash to make one unworthy of the Spirit, and therefore to ignite guilt."[3]

Double-binds also apply to choices about how to prioritize time, energy, and resources. If you do temple work, your ancestors will be saved, but you won't have time to volunteer to feed the missionaries. If you accept the calling, you'll have even less time to spend with your family, but if you don't accept it, you're denying God's will. If you're poor, you can pay a full tithe but won't have money for food storage—you'll either be burned at the Second Coming, or you'll starve. There are simply too many commandments on the list to be able to keep

---

1. Stricker, *The Double-Bind in Mormonism,* 2000. 148.
2. Stricker, *The Double-Bind in Mormonism,* 2000. 44.
3. Worthy, *The Mormon Cult,* 2008. 123.

them all.

Martha Beck describes the mindset created for well-meaning Mormons: "'Utterly confused' is exactly how I felt most of the time I was Mormon, because the 'seek your own truth but believe In the Gospel' tradition was one huge double bind. It goes like this: Before you accept any religious claim, you must scrutinize it to see if you really believe it's true. However, if it's an official Church doctrine and you feel that it *isn't* true, this is the work of a sloppy soul or, worse, the devil. On the other hand, if you accept the advice of a Church leader, which then turns out to be wrong, it's your own fault for not 'discerning' that in this particular case, the leader was mistaken."[1]

In short, "If you profess that the Mormon Church is true, that's because you know it's true; if you profess that it isn't true, that, too, is because you know it's true."[2] All signs point to "Yes."

There are gratitude double-binds. You should be grateful to be born in the Church. If you're not, then there's something wrong with you, because the Church makes everyone happy. It's a contract you never signed. As Beck's parents said, "'We raised you in the Gospel. You might want to think about how you're repaying us.'"[3]

But of course parents will try any tactic, given the double-bind they are themselves under. Remember D&C 68:25 that says parents must teach their children or "...the sin be upon the heads of the parents"? Combine this with the promise that trained children will never depart from the gospel (Proverbs 22:6; 2 Nephi 4:5) and you have an open-ended contract. Try as you might, it will still be your fault if they stray.

Boyd K. Packer illustrated another broken contract that puts members in a double-bind. In his talk to the All-Church Coordinating Council, he read several letters from members who expressed frustration when policies and counsel worsened their problems. Then he advises leaders, "When members are hurting, it is so easy to convince ourselves that we are justified, even duty bound, to use the influence of our appointment or our calling to somehow represent them. We then become their advocates—sympathize with their complaints against the Church, and perhaps even soften the commandments to comfort them. Unwittingly we may turn about and face the wrong way."[4] Leaders who show compassion by defending them or who try to improve conditions are going against the counsel of their superiors. This is a double-bind of love vs. obedience, mercy and charity vs. submission to the will of God. Commandments in conflict.

Which leaves no one to turn to for members who suffer, even though their contract supposedly promised solace. As Henry B. Eyring tearfully expressed in a video clip on LDS.org called *A Promise of Comfort*, (from a 2012 Conference talk, "Mountains to Climb"), "We have the gospel of Jesus Christ to shape and guide our lives if we choose it. And with prophets revealing to us our place in the plan of salvation, we can live with perfect hope and a feeling of peace. We never need to feel that we are alone or unloved in the Lord's service because we never are. We can feel the love of God. The Savior has promised angels on our left and our right to bear us up. And He always keeps His word."[5]

And bishops were designated as "the presiding high priest of the ward, a counselor to the people, a defender and helper of those in trouble, a comfort to those in sorrow, a supplier to those in need."[6]

We are also promised agency and the ability to question. Yet when members go to their leaders in search of relief or with questions, and the usual advice does not help, they are told it is *not* the Church's job to comfort. When the gospel fails to deliver results, and the Comforter fails to manifest, and angels are nowhere to be found, we *are* left utterly alone.

---

1. Beck, *Leaving the Saints*, 2005. 229.
2. Beck, *Leaving the Saints*, 2005. 253.
3. Beck, *Leaving the Saints*, 2005. 283.
4. Elder Boyd K. Packer. "Talk to the All-Church Coordinating Council," 1993. http://lds-mormon.com/face.shtml
5. Henry B. Eyring. *A Promise of Comfort*. Accessed Dec 28, 2013. https://www.lds.org/youth/video/a-promise-of-comfort
6. Gordon B. Hinckley. "The Shepherds of the Flock." In *LDS General Conference*, 1999. https://www.lds.org/general-conference/1999/04/the-shepherds-of-the-flock

Packer's talk makes it clear that LDS leadership is authoritarian and top-down. There is no dialog, only monolog and one-size-fits-all policies. In reference to working mothers who complained about admonishment of working mothers, he asked, "How can we give solace to those who are justified without giving license to those who are not?" The preference is for teachings that keep the majority on the straight and narrow, and never mind the lost black sheep or the widows or orphans or Samaritans or Prodigal Sons who simply can't make the system work. Never mind the "least of these" that Christ sought to protect. The outcasts are acceptable collateral damage.

I was a working, divorced mother for many years. Those talks always filled me with guilt and despair. I couldn't find a husband, I was an imperfect mother, and to some extent I actually *liked* my career. I found little comfort in the Church when my life was its most difficult; when I needed it most.

Packer counsels that comfort should be administered individually, in private, presumably by the bishops. Which kicks off a whole new set of double-binds. It ignores the fact that for many, these conflicted feelings are unexamined and subconscious. It requires that a hurting or confused member "waste" their bishop's time. It requires that untrained, overburdened bishops be equipped and willing to deal with these highly complex issues. Many bishops immediately dismiss such concerns or pile on more guilt or provide additional impractical double-bindy "answers" that solve nothing.

I resolved this particular double-bind by writing to my leaders, being ignored, and eventually repressing misgivings and going it alone. Which is the opposite of comfort for a single mother with a special-needs child.

The Church's view on agency is itself a whole package of double-binds.

Elder Delbert L. Stapley said, "While Satan would like us under his control, God does not control the actions of men."[1] God doesn't control, yet he threatens punishment, which is a method of control. Only it's not "punishment", it's a kindly warning about natural consequences... never mind the fact that many scriptures and general authorities call it a punishment.

All this doublespeak allows blame to be deflected using blame reversal. Whatever happens is *your* fault. This misdirection blinds you to the controlling aspects of the gospel, and in looking away from the Church, you can only look to yourself.

He continues, "[Satan] does not believe in free agency, and would like to control our minds, thoughts, and acts. We can see his workings more and more in the movies, television shows, magazines, and in the actions of men and nations." At least Satan uses gentle persuasion, whereas God makes outright threats. To further tighten the bind, if worldly media is persuasive, you are following Satan. If you *dismiss* persuasive arguments, then you must deny reality, yourself, and any view that does not comply with Mormonism. All signs point to "Yes."

Leaders teach that the more we use our agency to do anything *other* than closely follow the commandments, we lose it. Apostle Robert D. Hales said, "...when we don't keep the commandments or follow the promptings of the Holy Ghost, our opportunities are reduced; our abilities to act and progress are diminished."[2]

This made sense to my Mormon mind, but it no longer adds up. To paraphrase, "Obey completely, and when you do not obey, you lose your ability to choose for yourself." It means I *never* have the power to choose. I'm either obeying God or Satan. In this reality, no matter who I follow, my own will has nothing to do with it.

It's true that some choices will limit further choices. If you sign a contract, you limit your ability to act without penalties. If you become addicted to a dangerous drug, you become enslaved to the drug.

---

1. Elder Delbert L. Stapley. "Using Our Free Agency." *Ensign*, May 1975.
2. Robert D. Hales. "Agency: Essential to the Plan of Life." In LDS General Conference, Oct 2010.

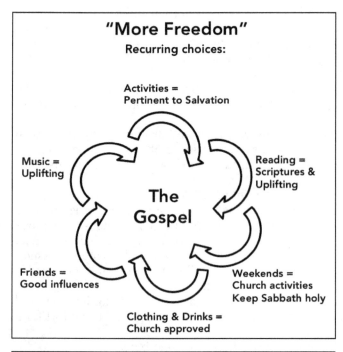

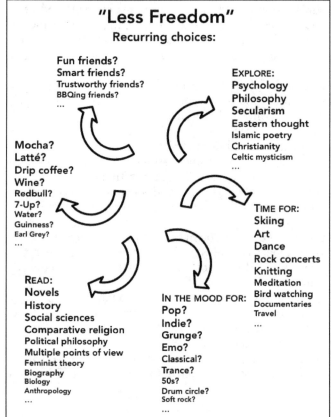

But this is not true of most choices, as the Church would have us believe. Drinking tea *increases* my choices. I use it to medicate my attention disorder and to stay energized to keep writing. And there are health benefits.

R-rated movies increase my knowledge of the world and my range of thought because I'm exposed to new points of view and ways of looking at the world. That gives me *more* freedom, not less.

Now that I'm not in the Church, I don't have to limit my associations. I have a diverse set of friends from a wide range of backgrounds. None wish to entrap me in their belief systems... and if someone tries (it has happened), I ditch them pretty quickly.

Few of the Church's commandments lead to greater agency. Most constrict it.

Now let's explore the doubly-tragic double-bind of abuse. Too many victims face this choice: Speak up and be called a liar and be blamed and invalidated by your supposed support network, or remain silent, in isolation and pain, and allow the abuse to continue.

Diana Kline reports her first interview with Bishop Smith at age 12. At home, her mother and brothers had been physically abusive, and her sisters emotionally abusive. "Bishop Smith continued the interview by then asking me if I honored and respected my parents, and how well I got along with my siblings.

"For a moment I didn't know how to respond, because if I said anything negative about my family, would he call my church membership into question? Would he look down on me with spiritual disarray? Would I still be righteous enough to go to the Celestial Kingdom...? After all, everyone throughout my life has always said what a wonderful family I had been given. Am I not supposed to feel the same? Why don't I feel this way? Why do I always wish to be in other families, with a different set of brothers, sisters, and parents that all seemed to be much happier than ours?"[1]

She did decide to tell him about her brother beating her up, and the bishop dismissed it, because her brother was an Eagle Scout. Instead, Diana was told to be more tolerant and turn the other cheek. She was told to not provoke him. Bishop Smith told Diana how special and talented she was, and that she needed to serve the Lord. Diana remained trapped in the double-bind.

Unfortunately, revictimization is far too common in the LDS Church. Thousands of personal accounts retell this story in books and online, with different little girls, sometimes little boys, with varying levels of abuse, including sexual abuse, and with different bishops or stake presidents. Sure, you might get a bishop who handles it appropriately, but who can say? For the trusting lambs of God, this should *never* be a significant risk. Spiritual leaders should be held to a higher standard. To the *highest* standard.

A properly trained clergy or therapist will intervene on a child's behalf. In fact, in most states, it is clergy's legal duty to inform civil authorities in cases of abuse. When they fail to do this, Christ's admonishment should apply, at least figuratively: "It were better for him that a millstone were hanged about his neck, and he cast into the sea, than that he should offend one of these little ones." Luke 17:2

The Church is often the very source of the unhappiness it promises to abolish, in large part because of the enslaving control techniques. Double-binds keep followers guessing, since the goalpost keeps moving. Stricker observes, "The Bound is left with the implicit demand to intuit the 'intelligent' *higher* Mind of the Binder...as to when she should...obey rules...or when she should already *know* when rules are not necessary... When she follows the rules...she is 'guilty,' When she doesn't follow the rules, she is also 'guilty.' She walks on 'egg shells' looking for a sign that would indicate *in advance* the Binder's illusive whim."[2]

The price of exit from this labyrinth is steep. "By this time, the investment in Mormonism has been so total that it would be a form of 'death' to walk away 'penniless' from it."[3] This is a "throwing good money after bad" double-bind, which causes dissonance to shut down thoughts of trying to escape. The path of least resistance says, "Stay put. No matter what it takes, stay."

There is only one gospel-approved way out: "Since the entrance into the Binder's Celestial Kingdom is through the death of the human body, the Bound yearns to die...to be released from this earthly 'veil of tears.'"[4]

So much for "men are that they might have joy." 2 Nephi 2:27

Even death isn't really a way out, at least not one that's under your control. The Church doesn't want members killing themselves, so "...the last Double-Bind usually stops these suicidal thoughts. You would be damned if you took your own life...because the Binder forbids the taking of your own life. Your life doesn't belong to you any longer... [You are] subjected to the continuation of a life of pathological mental and emotional pain."[5]

Despite all these seemingly real barriers, there *is* a way out. To grossly paraphrase scripture, in order to find my life, I had to lose it, and through that, I gained my freedom. I cast off the fictitious chains that crisscrossed through my whole existence.

Yet even then, double-binds continue to cast long shadows. Being out for twelve years, I still face them. Like writing this book—I want to "share my gifts" to help other former members who are struggling just like me, but I risk, among other things, further distancing my family. I risk being vilified by the Church and having my motives questioned, and possibly worse.

I do it anyway, because I see the bind for what it is, and I do not like being controlled.

---

1. Kline, *Woman Redeemed*, 2005. 14.
2. Stricker, *The Double-Bind in Mormonism*, 2000. 71.
3. Stricker, *The Double-Bind in Mormonism*, 2000. 123.
4. Stricker, *The Double-Bind in Mormonism*, 2000. 122.
5. Stricker, *The Double-Bind in Mormonism*, 2000. 124.

*Every dispensation of the gospel since the beginning of time has come to a close, not because God has failed, but because man has failed God by the improper use of his free agency.*
—**Apostle Delbert L. Stapley,** ***Using Our Free Agency***[1]

*A woman wrote to me a short time ago with a great sense of frustration. She indicated that she had been defeated or had failed in most of what she had tried to do. She then asked, 'What does God expect of me?'*
—**Gordon B. Hinckley, (as Second Counselor in the First Presidency)**[2]

*My main symptom was that I could never quite think, or do things 'right'—I felt and thought that something must be terribly wrong with my mind, because significant* ***others*** *could always set things 'right' for me; therefore I must be 'stupid'.*
—**Marion Stricker,** ***The Pattern of the Double Bind in Mormonism***[3]

*If I could have thought clearly, I could have handled the whole situation differently...but I was obsessed; I was hooked. I couldn't see the trap I was in; I blamed myself.*
—**Steve Sanchez,** ***Spiritual Perversion***[4]

# Blame Reversal

After myriad double-binds are established, the logic of failure is implied: If you don't receive blessings, or aren't happy, or if something bad happens, it can't be God's fault, and it's certainly not the Church or leadership. Or your fellow brothers and sisters.

So it must be *your* fault.

All promises, like "ask and ye shall receive", are negated by blame reversal. The double-bind leads you to keep trying until you succeed. If you succeed, then good for you. But if you get no results, you must have done something wrong. Even if you are innocent of all wrongdoing, your sin of omission or commission is implied by circumstance. Your unhappiness or confusion or lack of reward is proof of failure.

Blame reversal (sometimes known as "blame the victim") prevents you from questioning the broken contract. With each protestation, whether verbalized or silent, the promise is twisted around, back to your shortcomings. Accusations are either implied or made directly: You're lying, angry, selfish, unreasonable, thoughtless, accusatory (ironically), sinful, prideful, or otherwise bad. Each objection is met with counter-objections which seem perfectly reasonable, yet they reverse the original concern and place it back on the objector. Reality is flipped on its head.

A reversal is stealthy because it immediately triggers defensive barriers in the person it is used against. It instantly, silently redirects and stops thought. The double-bind sets up the subject to blame herself instinctively. The causes of failure were previously conditioned,

---

1. Elder Delbert L. Stapley. "Using Our Free Agency." *Ensign*, May 1975.
2. Gordon B. Hinckley. "'If Thou Art Faithful.'" In LDS General Conference, Oct 1984. https://www.lds.org/general-conference/1984/10/if-thou-art-faithful
3. Stricker, *The Double-Bind in Mormonism*, 2000. 9.
4. Sanchez, *Spiritual Perversion*, 2005. 154.

inherent in the wording of the original promise.

In fact, self-blame is a suitable coping mechanism for the victim. *Captive Hearts* states, "As a defense against the high level of anxiety that accompanies being so acutely powerless, people in cults often assume a stance of self-blame. This is reinforced by the group's manipulative messages that the followers are never good enough and are to blame for everything that goes wrong."[1] At least when you blame yourself, you have *some* sense of control.

But the feeling is an illusion to cover the sins of others: "In cults and abusive relationships, those in a subordinate position usually come to accept the abuse as *their* fault, believing that they deserve the foul treatment or that it is for their own good. They sometimes persist in believing that they are bad rather than considering that the person upon whom they are so dependent is cruel, untrustworthy, and unreliable. It is simply too frightening for them to do that: it threatens the balance of power and means risking total rejection, loss, and perhaps even death of self or loved ones. This explains why an abused cult follower may become disenchanted with the relationship or the group yet continue to believe in the teachings, goodness, and power of the leader."[2]

> **Blame Reversal**
> *—Suppression, Silencing Doubts, Punishment*
> - Reframes the source of problems
> - Suppresses criticism, complaints, doubts
> - Induces phobias
> - Deflects blame from the group and leadership
> - Perpetuates guilt and shame
> - Heightened by demand for purity
> - A major ingredient for the double-bind
> - Used as rationale for why promises fail, prophecies do not come true, blessings are unfulfilled
> - Used to dismiss all disconfirming evidence
> - Reinforced by the higher purpose and purity of the group (sacred science and mystical manipulation)
> - Reinforced by doctrine over self-the group is more important than the victim
> - Reinforced by us vs them & black and white logic
> - Influence by identification and example adds subtly to blame reversal and generates plausible deniability

The phrase "it's for your own good" is meant to set up the reversal of virtue, to steal it from the individual and place it upon the group and leaders. Stricker writes, "The Binder in this stage claims all of the good characteristics of the Bound and conversely projects onto the Bound all of His negative characteristics."[3]

In this state, serious questions become impossible. Langone observes, "They are indoctrinated to believe that disagreement with or doubt about the group's teachings or practices is always their fault, as are any personal problems... The very core of their sense of self is attacked as deficient... They are subjected to high and sometimes impossible and contradictory demands, which tend to leave them feeling like failures. Yet they are commanded not to express any negativity that may reflect badly on the group."[4]

Dissent itself gets pivoted about. An exit counselor noted that "Most cults respond to any criticism of the cult itself by turning the criticism around onto the individual member. Whenever something is wrong, it's not the leadership or the organization, it's the individual."[5]

Patrick L. Ryan, a former member of Transcendental Meditation, recounts that he was promised that he would learn to levitate. It never occurred to him to question TM. Instead,

---

1. Tobias and Lalich, *Captive Hearts, Captive Minds*, 1994. 64.
2. Tobias and Lalich, *Captive Hearts, Captive Minds*, 1994. 65.
3. Stricker, *The Double-Bind in Mormonism*, 2000. 91.
4. Langone, "Introduction," *Recovery from Cults*, 1995. 10-11.
5. Giambalvo, "Post-Cult Problems," *Recovery from Cults,* ed. Langone, 1995. 149.

he questioned himself. "We were sent to the flying hall, a room covered with foam rubber mattresses. A few in our group began to hop like rabbits. Those of us who remained grounded began to reflect on our transgressions of movement rules. I thought of the time I ate popcorn after 10:00p.m.—that must be the reason I was not flying."[1]

Mormons were never promised the power of flight. But we were promised joy, success, healing, marriage, children, and limitless blessings. We were told that we could walk on water and move mountains.

We had the faith of an entire storehouse of mustard seeds. We built up treasures in heaven with righteousness, obedience, and hard work. Yet there was always something more to be done, some stubborn weakness, some impure thought, one more lesson to be learned or another trial to overcome. We were *good* people. Yet how often did we blame ourselves for somehow not measuring up?

Ryan wasn't a bad person, but the twisted thinking instilled in him by TM led him to be cruel to his mother. "I had so thoroughly absorbed the Maharishi doctrine that when my mother was taken to the hospital with a heart attack, I called her and said, 'Mom, you have the solution to all problems at hand (she had learned TM) and you chose not to use it, thus you chose to suffer. When you don't want to suffer anymore, you will end it.' I then hung up the telephone."[2]

It is with these good intentions that otherwise good LDS leaders say unthinkable things. Marion Stricker sought relief from her chronic depression in the Stake President's office. "I came right out with it. I said that I was frightened because I had suicidal thoughts. [The Stake President] leaned closer towards me and looking directly into my eyes, asked, 'Marion, what *terrible* thing have you *done*?' At that moment, there was a flash of light, an explosion in my head... Here was this man of 'God,' who held an office as a 'spiritual' leader, with 'spiritual' insight, and *he had judged me without knowing the reason why* I wanted to commit suicide."[3]

This is totalist thinking at work. If the gospel is 100% correct, then there is no choice but to blame members when it fails. "The Church's stance...is that the Church is perfect...the individual is not. The Church projects its own guilt to the faithful, obedient, individual members."[4]

Steve Sanchez recounts how this blame reversal was used by his spiritual leader: "Rev. Will said that the gates of heaven would open for everyone who tithed, unless we didn't do it with a good attitude... Whenever a problem came up in our lives, he usually said it was because we weren't tithing correctly."[5]

This kind of conditioning becomes a mental habit. Stricker writes, "Like all Mormon women that I knew, I felt that I was just not trying hard enough; if I was unhappy, it was my own fault somehow."[6]

A teenager wrote to the *New Era* asking, "I've never had a prayer answered. Everybody tells me it can't be the Lord's fault, so it must be mine. What am I doing wrong?"[7]

And Jack B. Worthy recalls, "I knew if I felt uncomfortable about anything, it was my problem and was something that I needed to overcome."[8]

Doubts are reframed as a test of faith. Which means *you* have to pass the test, not the Church. Sadly, "...the ones who 'can't get it' are the ones who *are* sincere, and authentic...the ones who are earnestly trying to keep the integrity of their own minds."[9] Perhaps many of those who seem to have it easy have figured out that it's a sham and are

---

1. Patrick L. Ryan. "A Personal Account: Eastern Meditation Group." *Recovery from Cults,* ed. Langone, 1995. 132.
2. Ryan, "Eastern Meditation Group," *Recovery from Cults,* ed. Langone, 1995. 134.
3. Stricker, *The Double-Bind in Mormonism,* 2000. 147.
4. Stricker, *The Double-Bind in Mormonism,* 2000. 97.
5. Sanchez, *Spiritual Perversion,* 2005. 157.
6. Stricker, *The Double-Bind in Mormonism,* 2000. 146.
7. "Q&A: Questions and Answers." *New Era,* April 1993. http://www.lds.org/new-era/1993/04/qa-questions-and-answers
8. Worthy, *The Mormon Cult,* 2008. 69.
9. Stricker, *The Double-Bind in Mormonism,* 2000. 54.

playing along, guilt-free.

According to leaders, members often tend to misunderstand, twist things, or hear incorrectly. As former member Brad Hudson recounted online:

> [The mission president] then said something that still rings in my head... "Elder Hudson, by the authority of the Melchizedek Priesthood, and in the name of Jesus Christ, I command you not to leave the mission. And if you do, something will happen." Stunned, I flatly said "What?" (pause) "I'm not telling you Elder, and I say it in the name of Jesus Christ, Amen..."
>
> My brain exploded and my soul cried out that this was wrong... I told the assistants what had happened, and they were stunned. They said I must have misunderstood.[1]

Mystical manipulation promises miracles that often don't come to pass. Blame reversal is a way to reframe these events, thanks to a legally binding Faith Clause: "...it is by faith that miracles are wrought; and it is by faith that angels appear and minister unto men; wherefore, if these things have ceased wo be unto the children of men, for it is because of unbelief, and all is vain." Moroni 7:37

Jack B. Worthy relays how he used the Faith Clause against himself when all other self-blame was impossible:

> [The mission president] said our success depended on our obeying all the mission rules, but I was obeying them at the time, so I didn't understand why I was unable to do what he was claiming I could.
>
> I didn't think he was lying, or even exaggerating. Instead, I felt I was inadequate for some unknown reason. I logically assumed I wasn't spiritual enough, but I didn't know how to change that. Obviously I lacked faith, but there was no instruction manual that explained how to build my faith up.[2]

Priesthood blessings sometimes fail to heal. As one former member recounts, "If the person got better right away, it could be attributed to the priesthood blessing. Otherwise, I could conclude that one or more of us involved in the blessing did not have the faith to heal or be healed. Or, perhaps it was not the Lord's will that the person be healed right away."[3]

Patriarchal blessings also promise miracles. Perhaps there is a reason we had to keep them private, not because they were sacred, but so we could never compare notes to discover just how many people were promised greatness or blessings that never transpired. Instead, we kept worries quiet, and blamed ourselves because of the many contingencies we could never fulfill.

Blame reversal is most heartbreaking when a victim is blamed for her own pain.

Marion Stricker describes a story of a woman who went to her bishop after years of depression related to childhood sexual abuse. She had been abused repeatedly both by her uncles and by a bishopric counselor. When she told of her uncles, the bishop was supportive and caring. He recommend she pray and read the Book of Mormon. When that didn't resolve her depression, she "confessed" the counselor's abuse. The bishop grew suddenly cold, told her to get professional help, and stopped taking her calls.

"This is a classic reversal when the church is confronted with facts against its leaders. Instead of the counselor being advised to get psychiatric help, the victim, by silent consent, is no longer innocent but, judged 'guilty' and labeled 'mentally ill.' Mormonism causes the problem, seeks to cure it by the use of the same means that caused it, then if the member

---

1. Stricker, *The Double-Bind in Mormonism,* 2000. 108.
2. Worthy, *The Mormon Cult,* 2008. 105-106.
3. Morin and Morin, *Suddenly Strangers,* 2004. 47.

isn't 'cured,' it is the victim who is mentally ill, not the church leaders or the doctrine."[1]

In all honesty, the bishop should have referred her to a professional *immediately* and then continued to counsel and support her on a spiritual level. More importantly, he should have sought Church discipline and legal reporting against her abusers. Bishops have been called shepherds.[2] Aren't shepherds supposed to protect the flock?

Therapist Ed Gardiner, commenting on yet another case of abusive blame reversal, said, "The abuse she received, coupled with a child's egocentrism impressed a belief that she was 'bad.' This belief was not a cognitive one. It was affective in nature and out of her awareness until we worked to see it in therapy... When the condemnation was made complete by a 'priesthood holder,' one of high standing, and in a way that denied the reality of her abuse, her psyche not only split but her ability to stay connected to reality was compromised and she often was not in touch with the real world. Who understood her reality? Who acted with enough compassion and understanding to nurture a real sense of agency?"[3]

In these tragic cases, perceptions are dismissed and used to painfully silence the victim. "In each stage, the Bound's own perceptions and emotions have been invalidated, *trapped in a cul-de-sac*, which effectively walls off the ability to reason."[4] Instead of "blessed are the meek", they become the most controlled and oppressed by the very system intended to bless them.

The fact is, the Church *doesn't* have all the answers to issues like mental health, abuse, and depression. But because it claims to, well-meaning leaders are at a loss. In Pam Kazmaier's exit story, she describes how she continued to be depressed after her suicide attempt, even though she was keeping all the commandments. "The Bishop and the Stake President interviewed me for my temple recommend within a few months of my discharge and arrest. I was able to answer every question honestly and easily renewed it. Neither of them knew what to do for me. Here I was keeping all the commandments and was still uneasy and felt something was wrong."[5]

How easily such helplessness could be relieved for everyone involved, if the Church could be humble enough to admit it can't solve every problem, and in fact, in some cases, may be the cause.

Instead, when the Saints try *too hard* and become depressed over their perpetual inadequacy, they are blamed for being perfectionist. In the *New Era*, "Some...become so obsessed or consumed with their every thought, action, and response, that they may become far too extreme in their own perceptions of what is expected of them."[6] While the Church should be given credit for trying to ease the burden of perfectionism, let's not forget that the Church placed that burden in the first place, both through the demand for purity and for blaming members for a lack of effort.

Blame reversal is established throughout official doctrine. In addition to examples cited in previous chapters, Apostle Stapley said, "Satan exerts his greatest power when God has a work to do among his children on earth. Every dispensation of the gospel since the beginning of time has come to a close, not because God has failed, but because man has failed God by the improper use of his free agency."[7] It's not God's fault, and it isn't even Satan's fault... It's your fault.

If it seems here like individuals are being blamed for society's failings, it's true. Neal A.

---

1. Stricker, *The Double-Bind in Mormonism*, 2000. 98.
2. Gordon B. Hinckley. "The Shepherds of the Flock." In *LDS General Conference*, 1999.
3. Ed Gardiner, Ph.D. "Shame and the Destruction of Agency," 2003.
http://web.archive.org/web/20030821013451/http://www.post-mormons.com/shame.htm
4. Stricker, *The Double-Bind in Mormonism*, 2000. 28.
5. Pam Kazmaier. "Losing My Mind, Bit by Bit," Aug 13, 2005.
http://questioningmormonism.wordpress.com/2011/12/02/pam-kazmaier-losing-my-mind-bit-by-bit/
6. Elder Cecil O. Samuelson Of the Seventy. "What Does It Mean to Be Perfect?" *New Era*, Jan 2006.
https://www.lds.org/new-era/2006/01/what-does-it-mean-to-be-perfect
7. Elder Delbert L. Stapley. "Using Our Free Agency." *Ensign*, May 1975.

Maxwell taught, "For what happens in cultural decline both leaders and followers are really accountable. Historically, of course, it is easy to criticize bad leaders, but we should not give followers a free pass. Otherwise, in their rationalization of their degeneration they may say they were just following orders, while the leader was just ordering followers! However, much more is required of followers in a democratic society wherein individual character matters so much in both leaders and followers."[1] I'm inclined to place the bulk of the blame on the leaders, on the doctrines, and on the system itself; which is what this book attempts to do. The leaders are in a position to correct and guide the ship. They can listen to honest criticism from their followers and seek to improve. They have asked for the trust of their members, who have, in good faith, granted it. They should honor that trust.

But for blame reversal to work as a tool of control, it is important for members to know that it's for their own good:

> And now, my son, I would to God that ye had not been guilty of so great a crime [fornication]. I would not dwell upon your crimes, to harrow up your soul, if it were not for your good.
>
> Alma 39:7
>
> Verily, thus saith the Lord unto you whom I love, and whom I love I also chasten that their sins may be forgiven, for with the chastisement I prepare a way for their deliverance in all things out of temptation, and I have loved you—
>
> D&C 95:1

We are constantly reminded how much God, Church leadership, and our parents love us, and how this love excuses just about any behavior. Dallin H. Oaks taught, "God's love is so perfect that He lovingly requires us to obey His commandments because He knows that only through obedience to His laws can we become perfect, as He is. For this reason, God's anger and His wrath are not a contradiction of His love but an evidence of His love."[2]

There are many things manipulators can say to make themselves look like the good guys. If you believe he is sacrificing for your benefit, you will feel shame for falling short or complaining or being unable to trust or for asserting your rights. The victim becomes ashamed to call the manipulator out for abuse.

The following accusatory words are used by manipulators to reverse blame and ignite shame: Annoying, drama, crazy, selfish, self-centered, unsympathetic, unloving, unChristlike, not meek, aggressive, wicked, misled, uppity, sinful, rebellious, contentious, stirring up trouble, a chip on your shoulder, angry, hateful, prideful, insane, mentally ill, mixed-up, tarnished, unclean, seduced, uncaring, temporal, carnal, dishonest, unfeeling, hard-hearted, close-minded, vicious, ungrateful, slanderous, cowardly, ungenerous, and disloyal.

These kinds of accusations often fit better if you turn them back in the direction they belong: at the accuser. Sometimes "selfish" more accurately applies to the one leveling blame. Those who use harsh judgments to manipulate seem pretty selfish to me.

---

1. Neal A. Maxwell. "'Repent of [Our] Selfishness' (D&C 56:8)." In LDS General Conference, April 1999.
2. Dallin H. Oaks. "Love and Law." In LDS General Conference, Oct 2009. http://www.lds.org/general-conference/2009/10/love-and-law

*Know ye not that if ye [reject the words of the prophets], that the power of the redemption and the resurrection, which is in Christ, will bring you to stand with shame and awful guilt before the bar of God?*
—**Jacob 6:9 (Book of Mormon)**

*Come, Saints, and drop a tear or two*
*For him who groaned beneath your load;*
*He shed a thousand drops for you,*
*A thousand drops of precious blood.*
—***He Died, The Great Redeemer Died,***
**LDS Hymn #192**[1]

*As a professional teacher for the LDS Church, I saw for years the parade of those who did good because, faced with the power of shame, there was no other choice. In this I saw no virtue, only self-protection and numbness of mind.*
—**Ed Gardiner, Ph.D.,**
***Shame and the Destruction of Agency***[2]

*Within myself I tightly guarded and protected my feelings, which helped against the pain but kind of paralyzed me from action.*
—**Steve Sanchez, *Spiritual Perversion***[3]

# Guilt & Shame

**Guilt/Shame**
—*Silencing Doubts, Punishment, Group Identification, Influence, Reinforcement*
- Dependent upon demand for purity
- Punishment for failure to measure up
- Shame is public knowledge of your failure (or fear of public knowledge)
- Guilt is personal knowledge of your failure
- Creates pressure for influence or behaviors
- A large part of the double-bind
- Amplified by blame reversal
- Reinforced by influence through identification and example, and us vs them
- Reinforces destabilization

The repetitious stanzas of the double-bind and blame reversal culminate emotionally in a coda of guilt and shame. To cite the *Checklist of Cult Characteristics*, "The leadership induces feelings of shame and/or guilt in order to influence and/or control members. Often, this is done through peer pressure and subtle forms of persuasion."[4]

Shame and guilt are natural extensions of other thought control techniques. According to Lifton:

---

1. "He Died! The Great Redeemer Died." In *Hymns of the Church of Jesus Christ of Latter-Day Saints*. The Church of Jesus Christ of Latter-Day Saints, 1985.
2. Ed Gardiner, Ph.D. "Shame and the Destruction of Agency," 2003. http://web.archive.org/web/20030821013451/http://www.post-mormons.com/shame.htm
3. Sanchez, *Spiritual Perversion*, 2005. 209.
4. Lalich and Langone, "Cults 101: Checklist of Cult Characteristics."

> ...by defining and manipulating the criteria of purity, and then by conducting an all-out war upon impurity, the ideological totalists create a narrow world of guilt and shame. This is perpetuated by an ethos of continuous reform, a demand that one strive permanently and painfully for something which not only does not exist but is in fact alien to the human condition...
>
> Since each man's impurities are deemed sinful and potentially harmful to himself and to others, he is, so to speak, expected to expect punishment...he is expected to expect humiliation and ostracism...
>
> Since ideological totalists become the ultimate judges of good and evil within their world, they are able to use these universal tendencies toward guilt and shame as emotional levers for their controlling and manipulative influences.[1]

Certainly it is good to be virtuous, yet the *group* has the power to define good and evil. This conditioning applies to sins no matter how large or small, right or wrong. Goldhammer states that "A destructive group discourages individual autonomy creating feelings of selfishness, guilt, and shame for even thinking of one's own desires and needs."[2] It becomes yet another means to suppress self in favor of the group.

Singer shows how guilt is used to entrap followers while maintaining illusion of freedom. "Even more guilt is induced as recruits are set up to believe that if they ever leave the group all their ancestors and descendants will be damned or they themselves will die a pitiful death or become losers or lost souls. In this way, anxiety is heaped upon the guilt. Just as the initial love bombing awakened feelings of warmth, acceptance, and worthiness, now group condemnation leaves recruits full of self-doubt, guilt, and anxiety. Through this kind of manipulation, they are convinced that they can be saved only if they stay within the group."[3]

All the good feelings of community, elitism, and euphoria are juxtapositioned against shame. Steve Sanchez illustrates how these interplayed in his group: "Rev. Will occasionally praised one of us for something we had done, and we felt the same validation as Peter did, [a fellow member being praised,] and this was something only Rev. Will could make us feel. He also often compared us to Judas, which brought on an equally intense feeling, but in an utterly devastating way. It was unthinkable to all of us to be a Judas, but we knew it was possible because we were all under a lot of pressure and were pounded on all the time."[4]

These emotions can have a lasting impact long after leaving the toxic environment that originated them. It is important for exmormons to understand these emotions in order to recover from them. From *Captive Hearts*, "Even after leaving...many former devotees carry a burden of guilt and shame while they continue to regard their former leader as paternal, all-good, and godlike."[5]

And from *Recovery from Cults*, "...when someone is told to leave a cult, that person carries a double load of guilt and shame. Sometimes walkaways also carry a sense of inadequacy. Often they can think through these feelings intellectually, but emotionally such feelings are difficult to handle."[6]

It is important to understand that, while guilt and shame are often equated and the words used interchangeably, they are two very different emotions with distinct sources and implications. Shame is more toxic, though guilt can also be used to manipulate. The two can be felt simultaneously.

Guilt tends to be private, i.e. it is independent from others knowing or fearing they'll find out. It is a personal knowledge that you've done something that you know is wrong. It

---

1. Lifton, *Thought Reform and the Psychology of Totalism*, 1961. (Chapter 22)
2. Goldhammer, *Under the Influence*, 1996. 195.
3. Singer, *Cults in Our Midst*, 1995. 119.
4. Sanchez, *Spiritual Perversion*, 2005. 128.
5. Tobias and Lalich, *Captive Hearts, Captive Minds*, 1994. 65.
6. Giambalvo, "Post-Cult Problems," *Recovery from Cults*, ed. Langone, 1995. 149.

is related to remorse.

Shame tends to be public, i.e. it depends upon others knowing or your fear that they will find out. You've done something that *other people* think is wrong, regardless of your view of it. You don't even have to *do* anything. You can feel shame just for thinking thoughts or being accused. It is related to humiliation. As *Captive Hearts* states, "Shame requires an audience."[1]

*Captive* makes another distinction between the two: "Shame is felt when you see yourself as bad through the eyes of others; guilt is felt when you do something you believe to be bad."[2] In other words, guilt requires *doing*. Shame is a state of *being*.

Vulnerability researcher Brené Brown defines shame as "the intensely painful feeling or experience of believing we are flawed and therefore unworthy of acceptance and belonging."[3] And, "Shame makes us feel like we're alone."[4]

According to Brown, guilt has a solution. Shame does not. "Shame is a focus on self; guilt is a focus on behavior. Shame is I am bad, guilt is I did something bad."[5] And, "Guilt is when we hold something we've done or maybe failed to do up against who we want to be... Shame corrodes the piece of us that believes that we can change."[6] In this sense, if the goal is self-improvement, shame is very counterproductive.

Ed Gardiner, who researched shame in the context of Mormonism, has a similar take. "Guilt is characterized by an innate understanding that the self is good but the *behavior* is defective in some way. Shame is...characterized by an understanding that the behavior does not matter as the very core of the self is what is defective."[7]

Clearly, of the two, shame is the most damaging to the soul. I will cover the topic of misplaced guilt briefly, then spend the rest of the chapter on shame.

# Guilt

Sometimes we do bad things. And sometimes, we can be made to believe something is right or wrong when it actually isn't.

I base moral decisions around fairness, around trying to ease suffering, and around the avoidance of committing unnecessary, direct harm to myself or others. Generally speaking, all other morals are arbitrary. For instance, I feel guilty when I forget to send my mother a birthday card, but there is nothing inherently moral about birthday cards; I can show my love in other ways. Likewise, not offering a gift to the gods on certain days causes guilt in some religions.

Social science is showing that there are few universal triggers for guilt. Even murder can be justified and condoned by individuals and society. Guilt can, therefore, be both quelled and instilled, i.e. manipulated. It is inconstant and can never be proof of eternal law or even inbred instincts. If it were proof, then every religion on earth is equally true.

Under demand for purity, we saw how the Church has created an impossibly long list of sins, both of omission and commission, many of which don't have much to do with how people treat one another. Nevertheless, they can make members feel guilty.

A loving God will not be offended if you sometimes miss church. Your ancestors are dead and will be just fine if you fail to do their genealogy and temple work. Your neighbors will survive if you don't convert them. You are not "crucifying Christ anew" if you drink a little tea or let a swear word slip.

---

1. Tobias and Lalich, *Captive Hearts, Captive Minds,* 1994. 127.
2. Madeleine Landau Tobias, M.S., R.N., C.S. "Guidelines for Ex-Members." *Recovery from Cults,* ed. Langone, 1995. 309.
3. Brené Brown. *Defining Shame*. Connection: A Psychoeducational Shame Resilience Curriculum, 2007. http://vimeo.com/4620966. 3:20.
4. Brown, *Defining Shame*, 2007. 8:48.
5. Brené Brown. *Listening to Shame*. TED, 2012. http://www.ted.com/talks/brene_brown_listening_to_shame.html. 14:05.
6. Brown, *Defining Shame*, 2007. 9:18.
7. Gardiner, "Shame and the Destruction of Agency," 2003.

These are not part of an inborn moral compass that all humans have. These morals were implanted. This is what I would call "misplaced guilt."

As Chris Morin wrote, "Feelings of inadequacy and guilt for not doing enough were substantial byproducts of my Church membership. With the time commitments to the Church and with my mind continually focused on the afterlife, I often found it difficult to enjoy the moment and savor the good things in this life."[1]

As Jack B. Worthy points out, "This guilt is not only caused by proactive sins. Just believing that you don't live up to God's standards, which is practically a given in Mormonism, can depress a person. I was never comfortable looking in the mirror until I rid myself of that large baggage of guilt that very many Mormons feel, which is something that took me several years after my departure to do. This type of guilt is difficult to understand unless it's experienced first hand."[2]

In spite of lip service to the idea that our repented sins are "washed clean", the Church encourages dwelling on error, particularly in the redemption doctrine that you need a savior because you can never measure up, and in sacrament meeting, where we are to meditate on the sacrifice of the Savior and all the things we've done wrong which required such sacrifice. And we are supposed to feel some mixture of guilt and gratitude for the sacrifices of our forefathers, the pioneers, Joseph Smith, the biblical prophets, and parents, too.

Secular advice is quite different. From *Recovery from Cults*, "Forgiving yourself is essential to eliminating shame and reducing guilt. Shame is toxic: It cripples self-esteem and retards emotional healing. Although guilt may help us avoid making the same mistakes again, excessive amounts of it prevent us from growing and learning from those mistakes."[3] In the LDS context, forgiving oneself only works for so long before we are reminded once again of how inadequate we are.

# Shame

When there is nothing more we can do, repeated focus on our sins during Sacrament can transform guilt into shame. If we believe it is in our nature to sin, then it's our nature we must hate, not our actions. "With his stripes we are healed"[4], yet it might be *better* if God would "beat us with a few stripes"[5] and get it over with than to have an eternal scapegoat keeping us perpetually guilty for infinite sin we can never atone for.

"Endless punishment is God's punishment... if they would not repent they must suffer even as I. Which suffering caused myself, even God, the greatest of all, to tremble because of pain, and to bleed at every pore..." D&C 19:12,17-18

And Jacob 7:18, "...he spake plainly unto them, that he had been deceived by the power of the devil. And he spake of hell, and of eternity, and of eternal punishment."

If you really think about it, how many earthly sins could justify eternal punishment, even for the unrepentant? Even strict "eye-for-an-eye" justice might warrant a lifetime or two of punishment for each person you have hurt. Not eternity. Yet the Savior offers his "unconditional" love in trade for eternal obligation.

After striving to complete that endless list of commandments, members become depressed or exhausted and simply can't keep up. When leaders keep saying, "You can do it!" and you can't, the message is, "I must be broken." It is a message of hopelessness. How can one fix a broken self? Particularly if God, who is supposed to help, refuses to answer

---

1. Morin and Morin, *Suddenly Strangers,* 2004. 51-52.
2. Worthy, *The Mormon Cult,* 2008. 62.
3. Tobias, "Guidelines for Ex-Members," *Recovery from Cults,* ed. Langone, 1995. 309.
4. Isaiah 53:5
5. 2 Nephi 28:8

prayers? The lack of answers itself becomes a source of shame, because it suggests the Holy Ghost has withdrawn. This doctrine only reinforces the toxic cycle.

| Demand for Purity + Blame Reversal = Shame ||
|---|---|
| Worthy | Unworthy |
| Sacred | Unholy |
| Pure | Unclean |
| Righteous | Carnal |
| Humble | Selfish |
| Perfect | Sinful |

The implication, for many, is, "Not even God loves me." How can you be acceptable to your family and friends, your community, your "brothers and sisters in Zion", if you never feel "worthy"? This is where shame becomes most acidic. Brené Brown's conclusion is that "Shame is really easily understood as the fear of disconnection. Is there something about me, that if other people know it or see it, that [means] I won't be worthy of connection?" And yet, "In order for connection to happen we have to allow ourselves to be seen—really seen."[1]

According to Kristen Weir writing for the American Psychological Association, "Humans have a fundamental need to belong. Just as we have needs for food and water, we also have needs for positive and lasting relationships."[2]

Using an fMRI brain scan, researchers found that rejection activates the same part of the brain where physical pain is registered and processed. "As far as your brain is concerned, a broken heart is not so different from a broken arm," Weir says.[3]

Researchers also found that hurt feelings reduced when subjects took Tylenol. In this sense, shame is literally painful, yet it is an internal torture that leaves no marks.

Steve Sanchez, who spent years in a new age cult, calls this kind of pain and self-doubt "conditioned unworthiness."[4] Rather than giving us metaphorical Tylenol to relieve our pain, the LDS Church fosters an environment where shame thrives and we become ever more dependent upon the gospel for relief.

Like an addiction, the relief only lasts so long. As Stricker points out, a balancing act must be maintained for the illusion to be secure:

> These are the two faces of the Binder, the Guardian and the Enforcer, the "Yes" personality and the "No" ("but") personality. The effect is that we, as members of the church, become emotionally battered "children"; we can never totally be "good" because of the "But", and we are continually "Evil"...
>
> However, you are not allowed to be totally either! If you were totally "Good", you couldn't be "Saved"; if you were totally "Evil," you would be an outcast and not be a contributor to the 'upbuilding of the Kingdom...'"[5]

Sadly, those most likely to feel perpetual shame are people with the most honest and best intentions. LDS therapist Ed Gardiner observed, "Over many years of teaching and counseling...I have become convinced of the connection between the use of shame in efforts to control behavior and the destruction of the agency of the person so controlled. I have seen this be most true with those people who have an innate desire to be good, to have faith and to do the will of God as they honestly see it."[6]

And the toll is steep.

Gardiner studied a group of troubled LDS teens. "These adolescents manifest a wound

---

1. Brené Brown. *The Power of Vulnerability*. TEDx, 2010. http://www.ted.com/talks/brene_brown_on_vulnerability.html. 4:43.
2. Kirsten Weir. "The Pain of Social Rejection." *APA Monitor on Psychology* no. Vol 43, No. 4 (April 2012): 50. http://www.apa.org/monitor/2012/04/rejection.aspx
3. Weir, "The Pain of Social Rejection," *APA Monitor*.
4. Sanchez, *Spiritual Perversion*, 2005. 372.
5. Stricker, *The Double-Bind in Mormonism*, 2000. 90.
6. Gardiner, "Shame and the Destruction of Agency," 2003.

in their very core that resists discovery and efforts to heal. They cannot act from a fully authentic, personal self. That self is covered by a protective shield, the very existence of which the young person is unaware...because it [is] merely a facet of their emotional life... These dysfunctional patterns...formed a barrier, a sort of emotional armor that deflected the sting of further shaming. These patterns also had the effect of *controlling* perception and the interpretation of all perceived stimuli."[1]

The armor protects from the outside. Inside, a war is raging. "Authoritarian systems, by their very nature, enforce a mis-trust of the self. This, in order that they, the authoritarian system, may stay in power. The result of this self mis-trust is a divided psyche with an inner war that is fought with weapons forged by shame and steeped in self-loathing."[2]

The Church intentionally sets up "good examples" that everyone must follow. But these examples are whitewashed, and it fuels this inner war with disastrous results. "I was told, as a Seminary teacher, to never discuss any mistakes that I had made lest the students believe that it would be 'okay' to make similar mistakes. This practice...portrays a view of humanity that is entirely false and inherently shaming, especially if there is an attempt by a person to actually reach the ideal image presented. ...a child establishes an ideal image of the self that is impossible to reach. The person then attempts to reach it and is inevitably frustrated and shamed. This then leads to the need to split off those parts that do not fit the ideal image."[3]

This effort to live up to an impossible ideal results in dissociation. The false examples "prove" perfection is possible, so in order to feel okay, you must surgically remove parts of yourself that seem to make you bad. Unfortunately, those parts are what make you human.

Blair Watson writes that,

> The result of splitting-off and burying aspects of one's humanity is a sense/feeling of being in conflict with oneself and not whole. This personal reality can be extremely painful, so much so that some Mormons have committed suicide. Their suffering was the result of how Mormonism psychologically conditioned them...
>
> As Dr. [Nathaniel] Branden explained, self-acceptance is the refusal to be in an adversarial relationship to oneself. Self-acceptance involves non-judgmentally embracing ourselves in our minds and hearts...just as we are, and as we used to be. Self-acceptance involves understanding that everyone acts according to their level of awareness. Mentally beating ourselves up...does not make "better" people... Self-acceptance involves letting go of negative judgments about ourselves, our thoughts and behavior, the things that we have and have not achieved so far in life...[4]

It is unclear just how many Mormons suffer from toxic shame. Enough that it's a problem that ought to be addressed. Three exmormons shared their feelings online:

Helen: "They told me I needed to pray more and to be sincere. I felt embarrassed that they were telling me I was not sincere..."[5]

Ralph: "Everyone around me was so sure Mormonism was the right religion... I felt that I was just a bad person who wasn't getting it... This made me feel even worse."[6]

Anonymous woman: "Since I could never seem to achieve Moroni's promise of the burning in my bosom, I thought something was wrong with me and that God didn't love me anymore."[7]

Gardiner describes two case studies:

---

1. Gardiner, "Shame and the Destruction of Agency," 2003.
2. Gardiner, "Shame and the Destruction of Agency," 2003.
3. Gardiner, "Shame and the Destruction of Agency," 2003.
4. Watson, "Psychological Effects of Mormonism," 2008. http://members.shaw.ca/blair_watson/
5. Stricker, *The Double-Bind in Mormonism,* 2000. 42.
6. Stricker, *The Double-Bind in Mormonism,* 2000. 45.
7. Stricker, *The Double-Bind in Mormonism,* 2000. 41.

Barry constantly tried to measure up. Fearing rejection by his LDS family, he became righteous in every way, serving on a mission, going to BYU, marrying in the temple, and having several children. But to his family, his efforts weren't good enough, and the shaming continued.

Melinda was sexually abused starting at age 8. After growing older and learning more about chastity, she blamed herself for her "sin." When she revealed her abuse to her bishop, he dismissed it, saying her father would never do that, and she should stop lying. She hated herself, and became promiscuous, and then a prostitute. She was eventually excommunicated.

Gardiner asserts that neither Barry or Melinda had any agency, either to be a saint or a sinner. They were both being controlled via shame. He asks, "Is a child who totally conforms and is 'righteous' out of sheer fear any less out of the 'bondage of Satan' than the one who does the opposite in response to the shaming?"

He answers, "To be *free*, agency must imply a free choice; a choice unhindered by threats of destruction, abandonment, annihilation or misery. Such threats, which at an emotional level are felt as shaming, will condition and control responses and behavior in ways that do not bring to mind an image of a loving God."[1]

Love itself becomes distorted under the lens of shame. "In the face of shame there is no way to believe in a *loving* God. Destruction is imminent, always. Unconditional love does not exist... This is why, with shame-based people, I see the formation of a reactive identity that protects and destroys ability to live and grow in a way that honors choice and freedom. There is only one choice; doing whatever keeps me safe from shame-pain."[2]

True unconditional love requires acceptance of who a person actually is, not who they pretend to be, nor the fantasy we construct about who they are: a perfect being with at most only small weaknesses.

It is impossible to hate the sin while loving the sinner. In spite of the wording, we condemn a part of who that person *is* without understanding, love, or acceptance. Some sins are not behaviors, but aspects of personality, such as homosexuality or being a woman passionate about her career. Or they are permanent attributes acquired in the past, like a divorce or being a convert. Or emotional ailments with no easy cure, like depression that leaves your home a constant mess; or invisible disabilities like fibromyalgia or social anxiety that makes it harder to magnify callings and attend meetings; or toxic shame that keeps you trapped in a cycle of self harm. Scrutiny from the community—inspired by doctrine and leaders—makes these issues worse, not better. It adds to the member's burdens rather than ease them.

There is such a narrow definition of what a "good Mormon" looks and acts like, that it is hard to "be" acceptable.

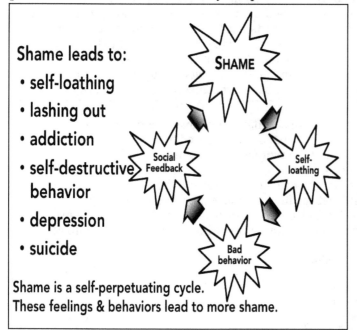

Shame leads to:
- self-loathing
- lashing out
- addiction
- self-destructive behavior
- depression
- suicide

Shame is a self-perpetuating cycle. These feelings & behaviors lead to more shame.

---

1. Gardiner, "Shame and the Destruction of Agency," 2003.
2. Gardiner, "Shame and the Destruction of Agency," 2003.

Some sins are actually harmful behaviors that need to be corrected, such as compulsive lying, neglect, addiction, or abuse. Merely labeling them as sins that we should "hate" diminishes the complexity of the behavior. If it were easy to stop, the person would, especially with the pressures they're under.

Shame is a poor deterrent for bad behavior. In fact, for some behaviors, it exacerbates a cycle that can actually *cause* addictions. The person feels shame, vows to stop, and can't. The failure proves the shame: "I *am* a terrible person." And the cycle starts over. Eventually, a person in this situation will give up trying, or be driven into more harmful behaviors or even suicide.

There are specific ways to address such conduct, something psychological and psychiatric sciences have been getting better at over the years. They don't involve much prayer, fasting, or reading scriptures. It has more to do with therapy, support groups, and becoming self-aware so that you can love and forgive and grow in an environment of shame-free self-care.

Unconditional love requires acceptance. It is healthy to erect boundaries to prevent harm, but it is not healthy to control another person's behavior or to make assumptions about the source of their problems. It is especially unhealthy to pass judgment on behaviors which are not *actually* harmful.

## Understanding & Love

Brené Brown said, "If you put shame in a petri dish, it needs three things to grow exponentially: Secrecy, silence, and judgment. If you put the same amount of shame in a petri dish and douse it with empathy, it can't survive."[1]

Understanding is the opposite of shame. It acknowledges the struggle we all go through to improve. It does accept what it is to be human.

In order to love someone and show compassion and empathy, you must know who they *truly* are, not who they pretend to be while keeping up the appearance of righteousness. True understanding leads to unconditional love, closeness, and intimacy.

Gardiner recalls, "I watch people hunger for understanding. Just to be understood, is for some people the most healing thing I can offer. When one's humanity is understood at an empathic level, with a full measure of mercy, marvelous growth can happen. I often wanted my father to listen to me, nod his head and say, 'I understand'... Instead there was always an answer, a reason and a pointed elucidation of my ability to mess things up... Many times I knew these painful things, I didn't need to be reminded of them. What I needed was someone who...could show mercy and understanding sufficient to let me be me."[2]

Brown conducted hundreds of interviews. She came up with only one common element among people with a strong sense of love and belonging: those who believe they are *worthy* of love and belonging.[3]

Certainly some leaders and members of the Church are capable of helping people feel acceptable, but given the demand for purity, us-versus-them, doctrine over self, and other pressures, these cases seem to be the exception, not the norm. This is especially problematic since parents have doctrinally been put in a position of responsibility for their child's salvation. The child's behavior becomes mixed up with the parents' intentions. It becomes impossible to separate parent from child. Control and boundary violations inevitably ensue.

Shame prevents open discussion and authenticity. Online, "Mitchell" said, "You don't share your personal beliefs, fears, doubts, dreams, concepts, theories, discoveries, attitudes,

---

1. Brown, *Listening to Shame*, 2012. 19:06.
2. Gardiner, "Shame and the Destruction of Agency," 2003.
3. Brown, *The Power of Vulnerability*. 2010. 6:50.

opinions, and views because it will just upset mom and dad. You keep your personal, family, and marital problems locked tightly away from prying eyes until they fester into a cancer that eats away at your will to live because you don't want to upset mom and dad."[1]

Secrecy pressures prevent the discussion of problems that are healthy to reveal to trusted friends, therapists, and even clergy; issues like marital conflict, questions about the meaning of life, moral confusion, spiritual doubts, suicidal thoughts, depression, anxiety, mental illnesses, and abuse.

Moreover, it creates distance and loneliness under the illusion of community. John D. Goldhammer wrote, "The ultimate effect of all this 'false self-building' are people who, in spite of being close friends or in the same group, do not actually know each other."[2]

Too many "shoulds" lead to a sense of emotional numbness. We "shouldn't" feel negative: sadness, anger, and depression. But you "should" have joy, happiness, and the Spirit. If you can't make yourself feel the positive, the only thing left is to feel nothing.

Like Diana Kline.

> I was incapable of connecting to anything or anyone, and I prided myself on the idea that I never cried, expressed anger, or felt emotional... In fact, I never felt anything, anything at all besides a constant dullness and persistent fatigue...
>
> Tears were foreign material, and any emotions except happy cordial pleasantries in a perfect Mormon world seemed strictly prohibited...
>
> Because I so desperately wanted others to like me and accept me, I tried relentlessly to engage in such humble, low-profile behavior and hide behind the fake smile that my church leaders wanted to see... My real feelings were buried so deep into so many fragmented pieces—and I had repeatedly repressed them for so long—that it almost seemed like they weren't there anymore.[3]

It gets to the point where even our emotions are a source of deep, unresolvable shame. And if you can't see a person's real emotions, how can you love them?

## Unintended Consequences of Shame

I've already mentioned the consequences of shame include addiction, suicide, anxiety, and depression. For young people, shame may actually drive them into the arms of those outside the group who are more understanding. "The power to differ in the face of this pain is obtained by banding together with others who are also locked in the same struggle. Every rebellion has witnessed the same scene; groups of people who view themselves as oppressed, disenfranchised or marginalized, banding together to validate their felt needs and pains by telling the stories, making the music, writing the poems that tell their collective story."[4]

It isn't necessarily the crowd that motivates young people to act out. It is their acting out that forms the culture of the crowd, their need be accepted as they are, and have their genuine feelings acknowledged, just as Jimmy sings in *Saturday's Warrior* when he finds acceptance among his "wicked" peers. He longs for someone to take him as he is, who will lift him up, who will make him feel like he's good enough. That's all he wants, and his family has failed to provide it. Yet the story casts aspersions against his perfectly understandable position. He doesn't run so much as he is driven away from sky-high expectations and a lack of understanding.

---

1. Stricker, *The Double-Bind in Mormonism*, 2000. 142.
2. Goldhammer, *Under the Influence*, 1996. 211.
3. Kline, *Woman Redeemed*, 2005. 35-36.
4. Gardiner, "Shame and the Destruction of Agency," 2003.

As Gardiner says, "We want children to have agency as long as they use it to identify with us."

Shame may also result in abusive behavior. Feelings are cognitions, and as such, are subject to dissonance. Shame begets shame, and can transform into other harmful feelings, such as anger. For example, a father, not wanting to reveal his vulnerability, may project or lash out, humiliating, accusing, or punishing others around him, to hide his own unacknowledged secrets.

Freud called this defense mechanism "projection." Those who feel shamed will dish out shame in return, to resolve their own constant dissonance and deflect suspicion away from themselves.

Shame also leads leaders and members to cover for those who have done real harm. Parents, friends, and bishops are willing to lie to let the true sinners have a free pass, because it's all about protecting the image.

## The Shame of Sex

No aspect of sex is left unaddressed by the shaming finger of LDS leadership. Sex is regularly preached from the pulpit, expounded upon in scripture, and interrogated about in interviews. Sex is bad, sex is bad, sex is bad. And anything tangentially related to sex is just as bad. Talking about sex is bad. Thinking about sex is bad. Your body is bad.

Eventually, it's hard to avoid the thought that *you* are bad for having a body.

Stricker writes that "The two most basic needs of the human species are sex and survival. Mormonism controls both... There is no personal ownership of one's body in Mormonism; it belongs to the Binder. Each step of the Pattern creates more guilt and hatred against the Self and the human body. Yet, members are commanded to 'love thy neighbor, as thyself!' Where there is no love of Self, there can be no love for others!"[1]

Sexual sins are a very serious. In the *Miracle of Forgiveness*, Spencer W. Kimball said, "...while one may recover in large measure from sexual sins they are nevertheless heinous, and because of their gravity the Lord has placed them very close to the unpardonable ones in order of seriousness."[2]

All that weight, yet sexual feelings and thoughts and even actions are unavoidable for most everyone. The lie is that they *are* avoidable, and something is wrong with you if you can't avoid them. "The natural man is an enemy to God."[3] You can't avoid being human. Therefore, you are an enemy to God. This mind/body duality is divisive to the self.

"The effect of this conditioning is to try to benumb...through 'guilt'...all sensual perceptions by fostering a hatred of the body and labeling it 'evil'."[4]

Throughout their teens, Mormons are subjected to increased pressures to obey the law of chastity, including regularly held special meetings in *addition* to regular church meetings. Diana Kline describes the negative effects: "Sadly, these Standards Night gatherings only reinforced my branded feeling of sexual shame, much like a scarlet letter of transgression to be worn visibly on my breast. Whatever good my leaders were trying to accomplish in teaching us sexual boundaries at these meetings was surpassed by a global ambiance of doom that sex was bad and dirty, and if you sexually sinned then you would flounder in outer darkness forever."[5]

And it wasn't just her. I and many others became adults with the exact same impression constantly lurking in our minds.

---

1. Stricker, *The Double-Bind in Mormonism,* 2000. 104.
2. Spencer W. Kimball. *The Miracle of Forgiveness*, 1969. (Chapter 14.)
3. Mosiah 3:19
4. Stricker, *The Double-Bind in Mormonism,* 2000. 141.
5. Kline, *Woman Redeemed,* 2005. 23.

> *"[Ideological totalists] become the arbiters of existential guilt, authorities without limit in dealing with others' limitations. And their power is nowhere more evident than in their capacity to 'forgive.'"*
> —**Robert J. Lifton,**
> ***Thought Reform and the Psychology of Totalism***[1]

> *The Thought Police would get him just the same... Thoughtcrime was not a thing that could be concealed forever. You might dodge successfully for a while, even for years, but sooner or later they were bound to get you.*
> —**George Orwell, *1984***

> *We have ways of making you talk.*
> —**Popular misquote from the 1935 movie,**
> ***The Lives of a Bengal Lancer***

# Confession

**Confession**
*—Punishment, Suppression, Silencing Doubts*
- Reinforces guilt and shame
- May reinforce public commitment
- Interplays with doctrine over self
- Reinforces sacred science and deep trust in leadership
- Can be used to create acts of mystical manipulation
- Destabilizes self
- Can be used to reverse blame
- Can be used in a double-bind
- Is something to be afraid of in induced phobias

After all this blame and shame, there comes a need for relief. And so members are motivated to repent. The cult has established itself as the one-and-only way, and through that, they claim to hold a monopoly over the path to absolution. They get to control the burning hoops that a member must jump through in order to be cleansed of acts that the totalist has defined as sins.

One of those hoops is confession.

Confession itself isn't problematic. It's healthy to have a trusted person to share our secrets, our flaws, and our griefs with. But the context of confession can turn it into a tool of coercion.

John D. Goldhammer outlines the complete cycle:

> Confession, in a destructive group milieu, implies forgiveness, which means the core authority in an organization becomes the judge and jury over one's existence. This existential control gives groups limitless power and control over individuals who *surrender* themselves to popular deities, whether persons, ideas, or images...
>
> ...destructive groups pervert [the] innate human need for unburdening. The act of confession implies guilt and shame, which groups use to further polarize the psyche into extremes: one centered around feelings of self-reproach and self-hatred, and the other caught into feelings of superiority and self-righteousness.[2]

This dynamic is clear in the LDS repentance process. Marion Stricker observes, "The Binder causes the Bound to be 'evil,' punishes the Bound for being 'evil,' then steps in to

---
1. Lifton, *Thought Reform and the Psychology of Totalism*, 1961. (Chapter 22)
2. Goldhammer, *Under the Influence*, 1996. 185.

become the 'Comforter' who 'forgives' upon the Bound's confession of 'guilt.' After all, if the Bound had been completely obedient punishment would not have been necessary; therefore, the Bound 'asked for it.'"[1]

Lifton calls this, "The Cult of Confession", which *Captive Hearts* describes as "...an act of surrender, of total exposure. The individual is now owned by the group. The person no longer has a sense of balance between worth and humility, and there is a loss of boundaries between what is secret (known only to the inner self) and what is known by the group."[2]

Singer describes how the need to confess makes a member dependent upon the group. "Confession is used to lead members to reveal past and present behavior, contacts with others, and undesirable feelings, seemingly in order to unburden themselves and become free. However, whatever you reveal is subsequently used to further mold you and to make you feel close to the group and estranged from nonmembers. (I sometimes call this technique *purge and merge*.) The information gained about you can be used against you to make you feel more guilty, powerless, fearful, and ultimately in need of the cult and the leader's goodness."[3]

This reinforces the member's dependency upon the group to be a good person. It further places the group in a position of power over the individual's definition of existence. Baptism, repentance, confession to the bishop, all drive to this conclusion. Stricker says, "The Bound has now 'chosen' to be 'good', which becomes the 'hook'...and receives 'Praise' from the Binder for being obedient. A true 'conversion' has taken place; all 'guilt' of the Self has been 'washed' away; a new life with no history begins. All that is needed to keep being 'Good' is to obey the Binder in all things and to reflect his mind."[4]

Totalist confession—and its related psychological dynamics—is evidence for just how completely one has given up possession of the self. It goes far beyond the simple (yet sometimes frightening) act of sitting in the bishop's office. As Lifton so powerfully puts it:

> [Confession] is first a vehicle for the kind of personal purification which we have just discussed, a means of maintaining a perpetual inner emptying or psychological purge of impurity; this purging milieu enhances the totalists' hold upon existential guilt. Second, it is an act of symbolic self-surrender, the expression of the merging of individual and environment. Third, it is a means of maintaining an ethos of total exposure—a policy of making public (or at least known to the Organization) everything possible about the life experiences, thoughts, and passions of each individual, and especially those elements which might be regarded as derogatory.
>
> The assumption underlying total exposure (besides those which relate to the demand for purity) is the environment's claim to total ownership of each individual self within it.[5]

Even for those sins we are not required to confess aloud, we were confessing in our hearts to an omniscient God. The angels were always watching, writing our secret desires and our hidden acts in the Book of Life. The Holy Ghost hovered just out of sight, judging whether we were worthy of his presence. Through "*living* the gospel", the Church possessed our minds night and day. A visit to the bishop's office was just punctuation in a longer paragraph: We had no right to privacy—our shameful secrets were already exposed.

Without this sense of personal rights, our relationship to others becomes confused, enmeshed, codependent. Lifton continues: "Each person becomes caught up in a continuous conflict over which secrets to preserve and which to surrender, over ways to reveal lesser secrets in order to protect more important ones; his own boundaries between

---

1. Stricker, *The Double-Bind in Mormonism*, 2000. 27.
2. Tobias and Lalich, *Captive Hearts, Captive Minds*, 1994. 36.
3. Singer, *Cults in Our Midst*, 1995. 72.
4. Stricker, *The Double-Bind in Mormonism*, 2000. 69.
5. Lifton, *Thought Reform and the Psychology of Totalism*, 1961. (Chapter 22)

the secret and the known, between the public and the private, become blurred…"

Mormons are under the illusion that confessions are kept in confidence; sometimes this is followed, and sometimes it isn't. Additionally, one's overall outward expression of demand for purity is visible to all, a type of public confession under the constant watchful eye of the *community*. For many, it is difficult to maintain privacy under these conditions without blatant deception.

Demand for purity divides the soul into the highs of elitism and the lows of shame, and never the two shall meet in a healthy, centered person. Which Lifton points out: "Finally, the cult of confession makes it virtually impossible to attain a reasonable balance between worth and humility. The enthusiastic and aggressive confessor becomes like [one] whose perpetual confession is his means of judging others… The identity of the 'judge-penitent' thus becomes a vehicle for taking on some of the environment's arrogance and sense of omnipotence. Yet even this shared omnipotence cannot protect him from the opposite (but not unrelated) feelings of humiliation and weakness…"

In this, we all become our brothers' keepers, subtly exerting social pressures and doling out shame based on perceptible behaviors which don't meet the totalist standards. When there isn't someone else to do it, we do it to ourselves, one self-inflicted lash for each of our hidden inner blemishes.

As you can infer, all the previously described techniques are involved in establishing this cult of confession. Let's also look at confession-specific doctrines.

The LDS doctrine of repentance is repeated throughout scripture: "Therefore I say unto you, Go; and whosoever transgresseth against me, him shall ye judge according to the sins which he has committed; and if he confess his sins before thee and me, and repenteth in the sincerity of his heart, him shall ye forgive, and I will forgive him also." Mosiah 26:29

And, "Behold, he who has repented of his sins, the same is forgiven, and I, the Lord, remember them no more. By this ye may know if a man repenteth of his sins—behold, he will confess them and forsake them." D&C 58:42-43

This is backed up with a threat: "Wherefore, I command you again to repent, lest I humble you with my almighty power; and that you confess your sins, lest you suffer these punishments of which I have spoken…" D&C 19:20

Confession works as a both a deterrent and punishment. The act of revealing shame to a spiritual leader creates a level of vulnerability that some must avoid at all costs. In my life, I was more afraid of confessing sexual sins to the bishop than I was that the Lord would not forgive me. There was an immediacy to this fear that kept me in line more than the risk of afterlife consequences ever could.

I wasn't the only member who felt that way. A teen writes to the *New Era*: "I went through a period when I had been involved in some bad things that I knew required a confession to the bishop. I was very fearful of going through with what I new was right. Instead of just confessing, I quit going to church because I didn't feel comfortable there. I quit praying because I felt unworthy. I got involved in other more serious activities that would also require a confession."[1]

Mormons don't have to sin to find themselves in confession. Regular interviews are held—at baptism, once a year for the youth (twice annually for older teens), plus tithing settlement, at every new calling, for a temple recommend, and for other occasions. Bishops are instructed to interview potentially troublesome teens more frequently, as inspired.[2] The bishop, and sometimes a member of the stake presidency, ask worthiness questions to which we are supposed to answer truthfully. Fathers can also conduct regular interviews with their children, though this isn't practiced in every family.

Bishops are instructed to, "encourage youth to talk rather than doing most of the talking themselves," and, "Matters of discussion should include the growth of the young person's testimony of Heavenly Father…" and, "The importance of sustaining the President

---

1. "Q&A: Questions and Answers." *New Era*, Oct 1989. https://www.lds.org/new-era/1989/10/qa-questions-and-answers
2. *Church Handbook of Instructions Book 1*, 2006. 24.

of the Church and other general and local Church leaders..." Emphasis should be placed on discussion of obedience to the commandments.

Not everyone may know this, but "Presiding officers need not wait for members to seek such help [to guard against transgression] but may call them in for counseling."[1]

In the Milieu Control chapter, I quoted the Church Handbook on how members are pressured to rat out other participants when they're confessing their own sins, and on how the bishop has the power to investigate such people when the sin is denied.

Discipline at confession ranges from being told to go and sin no more, to probation, to disfellowshipping, to excommunication. When disfellowshipped or put on probation, you are not to participate in activities such as public prayer, taking the Sacrament, officiating in ordinances, and attending the temple. Through this mechanism, auxiliary leaders, and possibly everyone in the ward, knows you've committed a grave sin. This transforms what otherwise might be well-placed guilt into public embarrassment and shame.

Cases of serious sin are escalated to the stake level, and these members are required to sit through a Court of Love (now often referred to by the less Orwellian name, "Disciplinary Council"), in which their sins are recounted to a large number of men, usually from the stake presidency and high council.[2] While a long list of sins are severe enough to be considered, at the bishop's discretion, for this level of discipline, only murder, incest, and *apostasy* (coming to conclusions not in line with the gospel) are grievous enough to *require* this step.[3]

In *The Mormon Cult*, Jack B. Worthy describes what followed his sexual transgressions on his mission:

> An important, ever present part of Mormon culture is guilt and confessions. This could be what caused me to share the details of my experience with Elder Sharp a few days later on the phone...
>
> [Elder Sharp and his companion] felt that they had no choice but to turn me in. They decided to give me the option of confessing my own sin, but that if I didn't, they would do it for me...
>
> They did what they had been indoctrinated to do, and they did it out of love and concern for me—as well as for their own eternal salvation, of course. It's difficult to blame people for acting according to their beliefs...
>
> I had never had my peers sit in moral judgment of me before that day (or since) and it felt strange. Only an indoctrinated prisoner would willingly allow such a thing... Now I was admitting my sins to fellow missionaries, not as friends and confidants, but as judges...
>
> At the time I had absolutely no harsh feelings against the Church. I had been programmed to blame myself for my unhappiness, and that's what I did. I wasn't angry at the Church or any of its members, but I hated my life, and wanted to stop play acting. Something had to change and confessing was the only way I knew to change things. Asking to have my name removed from Church records and my membership canceled never crossed my mind. I was still following the programming from my life-long indoctrination and was ready and willing to accept whatever judgment the Church pronounced on me...
>
> The first counselor of the stake presidency led the hearing... He explained the charges, after which he asked me to confirm my guilt. After going over what I had confessed, I was then subjected to questions from all of the men, as if I were at a press conference. The questions involved actions going back even before my mission

---

1. *Church Handbook of Instructions Book 1*, 2006. 26.
2. "Church Disciplinary Councils." *Gospel Topics*. Accessed May 6, 2014. https://www.lds.org/topics/church-disciplinary-councils
3. M. Russell Ballard. "A Chance to Start Over: Church Disciplinary Councils and the Restoration of Blessings." *Ensign*, Sept 1990.

> and were mostly related to masturbation, pornography, and sex. I went through the robotic motions of the indoctrinated and answered them all, which is something I now regret very much. My hearing was a perverted and bizarre expression of power by some men over another—in this case me.[1]

As this story illustrates, old sins are not really forgotten, as we're promised. They're subject to future interrogations. This happened to me, too. In a temple recommend interview, a stake counselor asked if I had committed any transgressions. I said, "Not that I've not repented of and resolved with the bishop." He then proceeded to question me about those sins, asking for far more details than my bishop had. I felt very violated and creeped out, almost as if he were getting off on it. It never occurred to me to refuse to answer the questions. I never realized I had a right to.

At the time, I thought this was an isolated case, one bad apple who had risen to a leadership role by mistake. But since I've left, I've read many stories of it happening to others.

As Steven Hassan suggests, it is never the group's intention to forget: "The destruction of personal boundaries, and the expectation that every thought, feeling, or action—past or present—that does not conform to the group's rules be shared or confessed. This information is not forgotten or forgiven but, rather, used to control."[2]

There can be healing in the act of confession. Be sure you can truly trust the person with whom you share, that you are sharing out of your own personal motives rather than from external pressures, and that it is someone who will give back as much as they take.

---

1. Worthy, *The Mormon Cult,* 2008. 147-148, 154-155, 163, 166.
2. Hassan, *Releasing the Bonds,* 2000. 34.

*People need a reason to change their thoughts and actions. Promised blessings often provide powerful motivation to obey God.*

—LDS Missionary Manual,
*Preach My Gospel*[1]

*It is morally as bad not to care about whether a thing is true or not, so long as it makes you feel good, as it is not to care how you got your money as long as you have got it.*

—Edmund Way Teale,
*Circle of the Seasons*

*There is sunshine in my soul today,
More glorious and bright
Than glows in any earthly sky,
For Jesus is my light.*

—*There is Sunshine In My Soul Today*,
LDS Hymn #227[2]

# Euphoria Induction

**Euphoria**
—Reward, Trust, Suppression, Group Identification, Influence

- Generated by trance states
- Generated by social cohesion, love bombing, and testimonies (public commitment)
- Establishes and reinforces trust in the leadership and group
- Generates a shared experience to reinforce group identity and cohesion
- Suppresses critical thinking and doubts
- Proves truth and legitimacy of the group via mystical manipulation
- Balances negative emotions from the group by providing positive reinforcement
- Reinforces the sense of shared purpose established in sacred science and mystical manipulation
- Obscures the negative doctrines and actions of the group

This complex system of control via negative pressures can generate overwhelming "low" feelings like shame, depression, and anxiety. So why do people put up with it?

It helps that the negative feelings are counterbalanced by equally intense feelings of well being and euphoria. Sometimes the euphoria occurred in the distant past, and the memory is enough to sustain the believer. Or it is a recurring bliss.

As the famous LDS hymn goes, "Come, come, ye saints, no toil not labor fear; but with joy, wend your way."[3] This is the joy that leads to a sense that indeed, "All is well", in spite of the toil and labor. And fear.

According to *Captive Hearts*, "...many former [cult] members confess that at first they felt a kind of wonder, as if they

---

1. *Preach My Gospel: A Guide to Missionary Service*. 2004. 197.
2. Eliza E. Hewitt. "There Is Sunshine in My Soul Today." In *Hymns of the Church of Jesus Christ of Latter-Day Saints*. The Church of Jesus Christ of Latter-Day Saints, 1985.
3. Clayton, "Come, Come Ye Saints," *Hymns*, 1985.

had drawn near something awesome. They experienced a sense of exhilaration, excitement, passion or expectation that was almost overwhelming... Members literally describe themselves as being 'enthralled' with an ideal, a group, or a person..."[1]

Lifton originally described this phenomenon in 1961. "...ideological totalism itself may offer a man an intense peak experience: a sense of transcending all that is ordinary and prosaic, of freeing himself from the encumbrances of human ambivalence, of entering a sphere of truth, reality, and sincerity beyond any he had ever known or even imagined. But these peak experiences, carry a great potential for rebound, and for equally intense opposition to the very things which initially seem so liberating. Such imposed peak experiences—as contrasted with those more freely and privately arrived at by great religious leaders and mystics—are essentially experiences of personal closure. Rather than stimulating greater receptivity and 'openness to the world,' they encourage a backward step into some form of 'embeddedness' - a retreat into doctrinal patterns more characteristic...of the child than of the individuated adult."[2]

Being around people who have similar goals will naturally elevate emotions in an uplifting positive feedback loop. As with the other techniques, group-induced euphoria is not *inherently* manipulative. The other techniques reframe the euphoria into the totalist message that the organization has a monopoly on such spiritual elation and that it's a sign of truth.

According to Paul R. Martin in *Recovery from Cults*,

> There are many group processes that can make people feel wonderful, even euphoric. And it is to be noted that these processes or euphoric feelings are not unique to cults or fringe churches. What becomes troublesome for the recovering ex-member is coming to understand that such processes are not unique to their group. Moonies have told me of the tremendous feelings of rapture, love, and warmth they have experienced at some of their services. Members from The Way International have told me how they sensed the presence of God at some of their conferences. Ex-members of Great Commission International long for the 'fellowship' and feelings they experienced while in the group. Former members of fringe churches tell of how good they felt after attending one of their services... A woman I counseled continued to go to a charismatic sect even after it had nearly destroyed her family. She admitted the people there skillfully used many techniques to induce guilt, even causing her to become estranged from her family; yet she had to go [to] the service because she 'felt so good' when she was there.[3]

How good can this feeling be? Martin continues...

> Consistently, former drug addicts who later joined cultic groups referred to the experiences as a "high" or as "getting high"...
>
> The longing to duplicate such experiences can be one of the most difficult problems for ex-cultists to overcome... It then resembles an addiction. Just like the drug addict they maintain that there is no greater feeling in the world.

Not every Mormon is capable of tapping into this high. I often found myself wishing I could feel the Spirit when others around me professed to. Square peg, round hole. But all those round pegs get easily lifted up, and swept away, in the current.

A number of factors can help stoke the flames of empathic emotional syncing: Ideals, Loss of Individuality, and Trance Inducement.

---

1. Tobias and Lalich, *Captive Hearts, Captive Minds,* 1994. 11.
2. Lifton, *Thought Reform and the Psychology of Totalism,* 1961. (Chapter 22)
3. Martin, "Post-Cult Recovery," *Recovery from Cults,* ed. Langone, 1995. 207.

## Ideals

*Captive Hearts* says, "The idea of being One with the Truth gives believers a sense of security and a feeling of superiority over others of 'lesser' beliefs. Feeling you have found the Ultimate Answer...can be a potent high."[1]

This sense of higher cause and elitism is a powerful mix, even outside an organized totalist system. Galanti recalls, "...some of my most memorable recollections of college include my participation in antiwar protests. The sense of community I felt during the candlelight moratorium, the sense of being involved in something much larger than myself was an incredible feeling that I've rarely had since. Young people today have few causes to inspire them. Cults provide a cause."[2]

The LDS Church espouses ideals of all kinds. Some coincide with the mainstream, like love, charity, family, self-reliance, and honesty; and some do not, like striving for perfection, Celestial marriage, avoiding fornication, and preparing for the end of the world.

In the song *Paper Dream* from the musical *Saturday's Warrior*, unconverted Tod sings of his desire to be part of something bigger. He is alone, directionless, and he wants a cause worth dying for. Something that will make him strong and brave, free, confident, and passionately driven. He's "golden." Fortunately, the missionaries find him in time, and Tod sings about his eternal purpose in the song *Feelings of Forever*, where he and his predestined companion experience elusive flashbacks to their valiant days in the preexistence. It ends with him quoting Moroni 10:5, "Ye may know the truth of all things."

This is a powerfully emotional scene, and it still gets me every time I watch it. It makes me wish it were all true so that I could be in the Celestial Kingdom with my eternal companion and we'll be so happy forever and ever.

Though there is little evidence Joseph Smith actually said it, he is commonly quoted as saying that if we knew the glory of even the lowest Telestial Kingdom, we'd kill ourselves just to get there.[3] To get in the *highest* kingdom, we simply have to follow the Plan of Happiness. Now who *doesn't* want to comply with that euphoric plan?

## Loss of Individuality

Totalist group identification, becoming one with the pseudopersonality, can itself cause a high. Paul Martin writes, "Cults alter the boundary between members and the world by essentially erecting a psychological wall... mystical manipulation and sacred science also contribute significantly. The euphoria that mystical manipulation produces—for example through chanting, speaking in tongues, and so forth—creates a sense that the group is radically different from the outside world. This difference is, of course, interpreted positively, for example, as 'the presence of God', 'the moving of the Holy Spirit', 'the signs of God's presence', 'bliss consciousness', or 'inner enlightenment'. They doubt if this feeling can be found outside the group."[4]

The fewer personal boundaries, the better. In *Recovery from Cults*, "The recruit is unable to differentiate his or her thoughts and feelings from those of the group, as boundaries between the individual and others in the cult have merged. Ex-cultists report that at this point they experienced a sense of peace, a euphoric feeling. The cults attribute this to a mystical or religious experience."[5]

---

1. Tobias and Lalich, *Captive Hearts, Captive Minds,* 1994. 122.
2. Galanti, "Reflections on 'Brainwashing,'" *Recovery from Cults,* ed. Langone, 1995. 93.
3. Blair Dee Hodges. "Life On Gold Plates: Committing Suicide to Get to the Telestial Kingdom?," Dec 16, 2008. http://www.lifeongoldplates.com/2008/12/committing-suicide-to-get-to-telestial.html
4. Martin, "Post-Cult Recovery," *Recovery from Cults,* ed. Langone, 1995. 209.
5. Goldberg, "Guidelines for Therapists," *Recovery from Cults,* ed. Langone, 1995. 244.

Steve Sanchez describes the feelings he got in his new age cult: "I took solace in being close to Rev. Will, probably the most enlightened man on the planet. I felt the cozy comfort of being in a community of spiritual seekers who were always there when I needed them... I believed that the world didn't understand us. I knew that my family's and the world's definition of success was bogus. I had spiritual success."[1]

In our personal time, we were to consume only "uplifting" media, movies, books, and music, keeping exclusively heartwarming and peaceful content in our minds at all times. No matter the source, the Church takes credit for any peace we feel.

Our self-worth is sacrificed to the group. We live for any acknowledgement that our efforts are recognized. Praise, both in public and private, can positively reinforce desired behavior and lift the spirits. You're a member of an elite group with difficult rules and someone tells you you're doing a good job.

We were praised for compliance, not being selfish, and letting others walk all over us. As Marion Stricker said, "The Bound live only for acceptance and praise for their obedience to the Guardian-Binder. They are to *deny* themselves completely; they *blank-out* what they can't understand...and enter a state of 'no-mind'..."[2]

Jack B. Worthy describes this spiritual upside to belonging to the Church. "Whenever I felt that I was in good standing with Heavenly Father, life was hard to beat. I felt totally at peace with myself."[3]

## Trance Inducement

We've already discussed manipulation of members via trance induction. Praying, meditating, singing, storytelling, and focused states can also contribute to euphoria. As *Recovery from Cults* describes, "The technique of guided imagery is a potent tool. It can turn a person's response to stress and anxiety into a control device. The leaders...and the subject together identify what prove to be stress-laden thoughts and activities for that person and counter the stress by focusing on soothing images. Through repeated practice, condition comes into play in that the stressful sensation or idea prompts a desire to return to the solace of the trance state brought on by the guided imagery. The individual is now locked into a prescribed, noncognitive, noncritical response pattern, not only *not* of the person's choosing but also beyond his or her immediate understanding."[4]

This process reminds me of Conference talks, which often begin by evoking guilt or fear through chastisement and vivid descriptions of dire consequences. They conclude with positive stories and flowing language about love and goodness and promised blessings, relief from the uneasiness which was drummed up just minutes before.

This pattern extends to sacrament meeting talks, Sunday School lessons, and family home evening. Even the Sacrament ritual itself plays on these dynamics: We are to imagine the suffering of the Savior, contemplate our own guilt, and feel relief at his redeeming power. Up and down like a roller coaster, on a track that someone else has built.

Spiritual highs often happen after moments of great stress. The power of suggestion combined with the power of prayer can produce powerful states of mind, endorphins rushing to the rescue. Steve Sanchez relays an experience he had after being overworked, shamed, and praised in alternating cycles, and then had his wife and daughter taken away from him by the leader:

---

1. Sanchez, *Spiritual Perversion,* 2005. 156.
2. Stricker, *The Double-Bind in Mormonism,* 2000. 22-23.
3. Worthy, *The Mormon Cult,* 2008. 63.
4. Kevin Garvey. "The Importance of Information in Preparing for Exit Counseling: A Case Study." *Recovery from Cults,* ed. Langone, 1995. 189.

> *Father, please give me some comfort, help me to find some peace within myself; help me to get out of the hellhole I am in... Help me to be what I need to be a good minister and a good father...* My heart burned with desire and pain. I began to breathe very deeply in the rocking motion until I began to feel the tingling in my whole body. I kept up the breathing in a steady pattern, although more moderately than before. I began to feel relaxed and pain free. I felt wonderful; the pain in my heart began to turn to joy...
>
> All of a sudden I felt and heard a humming. It was very distinct and beautiful, like the wings of a humming bird. At first I wondered where it was coming from because I could hear it all around me. Then it became louder, and I could feel it inside my ears and my whole body... I loved it and as I relaxed I began to feel loved. Then, as the humming continued, with my eyes closed, I could distinctly see light. It came closer and became larger. I was thrilled and ecstatic. The light was everywhere. I was utterly astounded by the distinctness of it. It was brighter than day. My body gladly received it as it all came within me. I breathed it in, my whole body and being thankful and fulfilled as I savored every millisecond. Everything was pervaded with this light now. It hummed steadily inside me. My heart was no longer constricted in pain but radiated and expanded with love and joy...
>
> I felt the presence of God, and I remembered that I had known it before. I felt an instinctual confidence that I as a human soul was cared for by God. I knew I had a connection to God and that I was of value to God.[1]

This account reminds me of my own experience, in the depths of my despair, when I reached out to God in fervent prayer, and finally received the answer which had been eluding me for years. I felt the presence of God and a sense of love. And a message—what I took as a promise in exchange for getting my life back on track.

In my case, I know it wasn't really God, because I fulfilled my part of the bargain and the promise did not come to pass. It was a response to extreme stress in the context of a religious backdrop. The mind cannot endure pain forever—we have neurological chemicals to help us, sometimes abruptly, suddenly, and profoundly. While in a trance-state (like fervent prayer), and with a little mystical manipulation and reframing, the experience is interpreted in the context of the belief system.

Mystical manipulation creates the trance, manufactures stress, and provides an explanation for its remedy. For example, the concept of sin is reinforced so much that by the time I got to the temple, the pronouncement that I was "cleansed of the sins of this generation" gave me a great sense of comfort, which itself was a spiritual experience. In the context of weariness, fasting, prayer, the new name, being dressed like everyone else, going through the same motions, making public commitments, and the otherworldliness of the setting, all led to my eventual sobbing in the Celestial Room, with my mother asking if I was alright.

Goldhammer states, "Many of these trance-inducing practices are highly addictive, producing drugged-like states and the *illusion* of a spiritual high... Immersion in and total identification with a group ideology paradoxically can be a 'peak experience.'"[2]

The peak is authentic, but the meaning is contrived. Peak experiences should direct one towards one's own inner authenticity, not be externally guided by deceitful hands towards *their* goals of totalist compliance.

---

1. Sanchez, *Spiritual Perversion*, 2005. 192.
2. Goldhammer, *Under the Influence*, 1996. 110-111.

*...in our willing participation, we become the genetic material used by groups to clone obedient servants for their collective ideologies.*
—**John D. Goldhammer,**
***Under the Influence***[1]

*My young friends, we need tens of thousands of more missionaries in the months and years that lie ahead.*
—**Apostle Jeffery R. Holland**[2]

*I did not at all expect my mission to be what it was: a sales job.*
—**Jack B. Worthy, *The Mormon Cult***[3]

# Proselytizing

**Proselytizing**
—*Suppression, Perpetuation, Influence, Group Identification*

- Suppresses cognitive dissonance
- Public commitment to outsiders increases beliefs
- Time spent proselytizing distracts from free time to think, increases exhaustion
- Increases sense of group cohesion by displaying behaviors and beliefs to outsiders
- Recruitment perpetuates the group
- Doctrines are reinforced as the member teaches them to outsiders
- Contact with outsiders is confined within a frame of preaching (milieu control, reframing)

Many organizations have an almost lifelike need to self-perpetuate. The more totalist and universal the system, the more it is driven to spread.

The Cults 101 Checklist includes the following checkbox: "The group is preoccupied with bringing in new members; The group is preoccupied with making money."[4] And *Captive Hearts* says, "Members are encouraged to spend a great deal of time proselytizing."[5]

Goldhammer writes, "Psychologically, individuals who identify with a group's agenda believe that 'what's good for us must be good for everyone else.' Their own blind conformity and one-sidedness extends itself to any and all situations. Exemplifying the *missionary consciousness*, they will not rest until all others outside their group are 'saved' or enlightened as to the obvious benefits of their program."[6]

Proselytization provides new blood and slows attrition. It also calms dissonance through steadily-increasing numbers. As the saying goes, "Millions of people can't be wrong."

Which isn't exactly true. Millions of people are frequently wrong. Nevertheless, it's a soothing thought, and it's powerful enough that it drives people to spread the word even more zealously when their core beliefs are threatened.[7]

Cialdini offers commentary on the UFO cult described in *When Prophecy Fails*: "If they

---

1. Goldhammer, *Under the Influence*, 1996. 176.
2. Jeffery R. Holland. "We Are All Enlisted." In LDS General Conference, Oct 2011.
3. Worthy, *The Mormon Cult*, 2008. 125.
4. Lalich and Langone, "Cults 101: Checklist of Cult Characteristics."
5. Tobias and Lalich, *Captive Hearts, Captive Minds*, 1994. 15.
6. Goldhammer, *Under the Influence*, 1996. 204.
7. Festinger, *When Prophecy Fails*, 1964.

could spread the Word, if they could inform the uninformed, if they could persuade the skeptics, and if, by so doing, they could win new converts, their threatened but treasured beliefs would become *truer*. The principle of social proof says so: *The greater the number of people who find any idea correct, the more a given individual will perceive the idea to be correct.*"[1]

The act of missionary work itself bolsters belief. Hassan stated, "Proselytizing is a powerful method for reinforcing new beliefs and behavior in the person doing the proselytizing." [2] It helps reinforce the other thought-reform techniques, like keeping members heavily focused on the group. It forces followers to make public commitments and gives them opportunities to exercise thought-terminating clichés.

It also contributes to the dehumanization of outsiders, who are perceived as either as worldly "enemies" or future members. In Janja Lalich's political cult, "New members were taught that previous acquaintances—no matter how intimate—were to be treated as potential recruits. If someone wasn't a potential recruit, there was no reason to maintain the relationship."[3]

As Marion Stricker observed about Mormonism, "A Binder is concerned with *numbers* and must have many followers, many 'purchasers,' as there are a few who may wake up, begin to question, find answers, and revolt by *standing up*, no longer *supplicant*."[4]

There is no question that the LDS Church "encourages" missionary work by way of outright commandment. Door-to-door missionaries are stereotypically the first thing most nonmembers think of when you say either "Jehovah's Witness" or "Mormon." Young men are expected, even commanded, to serve a full time mission, two years of their life away from home doing nothing but preaching the gospel.

Prophet Spencer W. Kimball's talk to regional representatives is often quoted in talks, Church magazines, and lesson manuals. It is the source of the title of the Aaronic Priesthood lesson, "Every Young Man Should Serve a Mission":[5]

> The question is frequently asked: Should every young man fill a mission? And the answer has been given by the Lord. It is 'Yes.' Every young man should fill a mission. He said:
>
> "Send forth the elders of my church unto the nations which are afar off...unto the islands of the sea; send forth unto foreign lands; call upon all nations, first upon the Gentiles, and then upon the Jews"...
>
> The answer is "yes." Every man should also pay his tithing. Every man should observe the Sabbath. Every man should attend his meetings. Every man should marry in the temple and properly train his children, and do many other mighty works. Of course he should.[6]

It is clear this commandment is on par with all other commandments.

The Gospel Doctrine lessons express this imperative: "Through his prophets, the Lord has repeatedly commanded every worthy, able young man to serve a full-time mission. He has also encouraged senior couples to serve as full-time missionaries if they are able."[7]

Mission worthiness is yet another motivation driving the demand for purity, especially for young men. As President Kimball iterates, "I am asking for missionaries who have been

---

1. Cialdini, *Influence*, 2009. 108.
2. Hassan, *Releasing the Bonds*, 2000. 275.
3. Lalich, "A Little Carrot and a Lot of Stick," *Recovery from Cults,* ed. Langone, 1995. 69.
4. Stricker, *The Double-Bind in Mormonism*, 2000. 24.
5. *Aaronic Priesthood Manual 3*. The Church of Jesus Christ of Latter Day Saints, 1995. http://www.lds.org/manual/aaronic-priesthood-manual-3/lesson-25-every-young-man-should-serve-a-mission 97.
6. President Spencer W. Kimball. "'When the World Will Be Converted.'" *Ensign*, Oct 1974. http://www.lds.org/ensign/1974/10/when-the-world-will-be-converted
7. *Old Testament: Gospel Doctrine Teacher's Manual* Lesson 33. The Church of Jesus Christ of Latter-day Saints, 2001. http://www.lds.org/manual/old-testament-gospel-doctrine-teachers-manual/lesson-33-sharing-the-gospel-with-the-world 162.

carefully indoctrinated and trained through the family and the organizations of the Church, and who come to the mission with a great desire. I am asking for better interviews, more searching interviews, more sympathetic and understanding interviews, but especially that we train prospective missionaries much better, much earlier, much longer, so that each anticipates his mission with great joy."[1]

Members of all ages are constantly told to be "every member a missionary", meaning we should look for opportunities to convert nonmember acquaintances. My own patriarchal blessing commanded, "...it will be necessary for you to fulfill the measure of your creation here on earth as a missionary of the Church of Jesus Christ." I was constantly on the lookout for friends I could bring to the gospel, and I imagined some unknown eternal destiny I was fulfilling.

Prophet David O. McKay said, "Every member is a missionary. He or she has the responsibility of bringing somebody: a mother, a father, a neighbor, a fellow worker, an associate, somebody in touch with the messengers of the gospel. If every member will carry that responsibility and if the arrangement to have that mother or that father or somebody meet the authorized representatives of the Church, no power on earth can stop this church from growing."[2]

We were told to be like Paul when he said, "For I am not ashamed of the gospel of Christ: for it is the power of God unto salvation to every one that believeth; to the Jew first, and also to the Greek." Romans 1:16

In a recent conference talk, Jeffery R. Holland told all priesthood holders, "Do I need to hum a few bars of 'We Are All Enlisted'? You know, the line about 'We are waiting now for soldiers; who'll volunteer?' Of course, the great thing about this call to arms is that we ask not for volunteers to fire a rifle or throw a hand grenade. No, we want battalions who will take as their weapons 'every word that proceedeth forth from the mouth of God.' So I am looking tonight for missionaries who will not voluntarily bind their tongues but will, with the Spirit of the Lord and the power of their priesthood, open their mouths and speak miracles. Such speech, the early brethren taught, would be the means by which faith's 'mightiest works have been, and will be, performed.'"[3]

And in the Doctrine & Covenants:

> Wherefore, you are called to cry repentance unto this people.
> And if it so be that you should labor all your days in crying repentance unto this people, and bring, save it be one soul unto me, how great shall be your joy with him in the kingdom of my Father!
> And now, if your joy will be great with one soul that you have brought unto me into the kingdom of my Father, how great will be your joy if you should bring many souls unto me!
>
> D&C 18:14-16

This may bring joy, but it also brings new tithe-payers. According to an online personal recollection, "We were told in no uncertain terms by our mission president...that our most important job as a missionary was to see people baptized, period. In addition, the regional representative at the time, Gene R. Cook...told us in various meetings that our job was to BAPTIZE, and that we were not to worry about whether or not they were Truly ready—that was between them and God... the leaders would get up and tell the Elders & Sisters that we should be focusing on NUMBERS."[4,5]

---

1. Kimball, "'When the World Will Be Converted.'" *Ensign*, Oct 1974.
2. *Teachings of Presidents of the Church: David O. McKay*. The Church of Jesus Christ of Latter Day Saints, 2011. 49. (Chapter 6: Every Member a Missionary.)
3. Jeffery R. Holland. "We Are All Enlisted." In LDS General Conference, Oct 2011.
4. Stricker, *The Double-Bind in Mormonism*, 2000. 85.
5. "Life as a Young Mormon Missionary Then Afterwards." Accessed Nov 1, 2013. http://www.exmormon.org/whylft19.htm

This isn't done just by means of the Spirit and miracles. The Church employs the latest in sales tactics. Jack B. Worthy says, "[On our mission] we were using polished techniques to sell our product. The product was club membership. The selling price was one baptism, ten percent of one's income, and a lifetime of commitment."[1]

A bible cult referenced by Margaret Singer experimented with various methods for conversion, first by sending out a single woman to target college students sitting alone. "One day, her cult leader abruptly changed procedures. Up to that point, individual members had gone out seeking people of the same sex. 'Now,' the leader proclaimed, 'we will have team gathering and reaping. From now on, two sisters or two brothers will go out as pairs to gather and reap, and that way they can approach both men and women.' The leader said it was 'too sexual' for a man to be approached by a lone woman, or a woman to be approached by a lone man, but two women or two men made such an approach 'friendship,' and the teams would be able to recruit both male and female students faster. The woman said the new method worked."[2]

That they send two missionaries is no mistake. It is sound science, the most successful way to put potential converts at ease.

When you're part of a totalist religion, it's hard to imagine *not* trying to convert everyone to your ways. The projected assumption is that all spiritual beliefs are driven by self-perpetuation. To a small extent this is true, but not to the degree emulated by high-demand groups like Mormonism.

I have spiritual convictions now, pieced together from a wide variety of traditions and schools of thought. When studying spiritual matters, I am hypervigilant of, and avoid, any that seem obsessed with propagation, those who try to convince me their system is the One True Way.

As for sharing what I believe? Mine are deeply personal conclusions that are especially tailored by me, to me. I now take a "live and let live" attitude. My spiritual impressions and conclusions are my own, and I only share with those who express interest. I have no need to convert anyone to the intangible beliefs I have for which I have no proof. While they give me great satisfaction and joy, I don't expect them to provide the same fulfillment for anyone else.

If I preach anything, it is that each person needs to seek her own path, adopting beliefs that lead to inner awareness, acceptance, and self-actualization. By necessity, all such paths will be very different from one another.

---

1. Worthy, *The Mormon Cult,* 2008. 126.
2. Singer, *Cults in Our Midst,* 1995. 109.

*I think I have said enough in this letter so that if you are receptive and pliable, you will get the message. If you are not, rebellion will well up in your heart.*
—**Bruce R. McConkie,
in a letter to Eugene England**[1]

*We thank thee, O God, for a prophet
To guide us in these latter days.
We thank thee for sending the gospel
To lighten our minds with its rays.*
—***We Thank Thee, O God, for a Prophet*,
LDS Hymn #19**[2]

*Only as long as we follow the group's agenda are we allowed to feel good about ourselves.*
—**John D. Goldhammer, *Under the Influence***[3]

# Bait, Hook, Line, & Sinker

In *The Mormon Cult*, Jack B. Worthy tells this mission story which demonstrates several thought-reform techniques working in tandem:

> President Smith gave an especially fiery talk. Emphasizing the word 'nothing' with pounds of his fist on the pulpit, he told us that we were just that: nothing. We were as the dust of the earth, and the only way we could accomplish anything was with God's help. Tapping into that source of help required faith, of course, but once we had enough of that, we could do anything. This made me as determined as ever to perform miracles, to convert lots of people quickly and easily through the power of the Spirit.
>
> I had always known that such miracles were possible because I was a product of Mormon culture. I believed everything the mission president said, which was very much in line with what I'd been told my whole life. I believed I hadn't been guided by the Spirit up to that point because of some unknown fault of my own. I thought that could change if I just had enough faith... After all, I knew that if I wasn't sufficiently worthy of spiritual guidance, I would never have been called by the Lord to be district leader.
>
> Predictably, the reality in the streets and doorways of Hong Kong shattered my illusions. But the extra buildup this time made me fall significantly harder.[4]

Brother Worthy was operating under the following forces: destabilization, the shame/elitism dynamic, sacred science, demand for purity, the double-bind and blame reversal, social pressure, doctrine over self, emotion over intellect, mystical manipulation, reframing, and black & white thinking, all in the context of heavy milieu control, public

---

1. Bruce R. McConkie. Letter to Eugene England. "Bruce McConkie's Letter of Rebuke to Professor Eugene England," Feb 19, 1981. http://www.mrm.org/bruce-mcconkies-rebuke-of-eugene-england
2. Fowler, "We Thank Thee O God For a Prophet," *Hymns*, 1985.
3. Goldhammer, *Under the Influence*, 1996. 45.
4. Worthy, *The Mormon Cult*, 2008. 111.

commitment, and belief follows behavior, worked into exhaustive and prayerful trance states, with every moment of his time controlled, while on a mission for the purpose of proselytizing.

Another great example to demonstrate the layered techniques appears in *Preach My Gospel*, the manual used by missionaries to teach the gospel. The second discussion, taught to potential converts, tells the Garden of Eden story, which shows God himself using mind control. I have added each technique within brackets:

> Adam and Eve were the first of God's children to come to the earth. [**Elitism**] God created Adam and Eve and placed them in the Garden of Eden. [**Milieu Control**] Adam and Eve were created in God's image, with bodies of flesh and bone. [**Influence Through Identification**] While Adam and Eve were in the garden, they were still in God's presence and could have lived forever. [**Euphoria, Love Bombing, Mystical Manipulation**] They lived in innocence, and God provided for their needs. [**Creating Dependency, Sacred Science**]
>
> In the Garden of Eden, God gave Adam and Eve their agency. [**Loaded Language**] He commanded them not to eat the forbidden fruit, or the fruit of the tree of knowledge of good and evil. [**Demand for Purity, Milieu Control**] Obeying this commandment meant that they could remain in the garden, but they could not progress by experiencing opposition in mortality. They could not know joy because they could not experience sorrow and pain. [**Double-Bind, Deception, Indirect Directive, Doctrine Over Self**]
>
> Satan tempted Adam and Eve to eat the forbidden fruit, [**Us vs. Them**] and they chose to do so. This was part of God's plan. [**Totalist Reframing, Sacred Science**] Because of this choice, [**Blame Reversal**] they were cast from the garden and out of God's physical presence. [**Shame, Social Pressure**] This event is called the Fall. [**Loaded Language**] Separation from God's presence is spiritual death. Adam and Eve became mortal—subject to physical death, or separation of the body and spirit. [**Mystical Manipulation, Dispensing of Existence**] They could now experience disease and all types of suffering. [**Induced Phobias**] They had moral agency or the ability to choose between good and evil. [**Black and White Thinking**] This made it possible for them to learn and progress. [**Demand for Purity, Double-Bind**] It also made it possible for them to make wrong choices and to sin. [**Guilt and Shame**] In addition, they could now have children, so the rest of God's spirit children could come to earth, obtain physical bodies, and be tested. [**Mystical Manipulation, Sacred Science, Thought-Terminating Cliché**] Only in this way could God's children progress and become like Him. [**Doctrine Over Self, Identification & Example**][1]

On the very next page, the missionary manual presents the LDS teachings on the meaning of life, and it, too, conveys a number of mind control methods which were apparently established by Heavenly Father:

> Life on earth is an opportunity and a blessing. [**Sacred Science, Totalist Reframing**] Our purpose in this life is to have joy and prepare to return to God's presence. [**Euphoria Induction, Demand for Purity**] In mortality we live in a condition where we are subject to both physical and spiritual death. [**Dispensing of Existence**] God has a perfect, glorified, immortal body of flesh and bones. To become like God [**Elitism, Identification and Example**] and return to His presence [**Social Pressure**], we too must have a perfect, immortal body of flesh and bones. However, because of the Fall of Adam and Eve, every person on earth has

---

1. *Preach My Gospel: A Guide to Missionary Service*. 2004. The Church of Jesus Christ of Latter-day Saints, n.d. 49.

> an imperfect, mortal body and will eventually die. [**Phobia Induction, Blame Reversal**] If not for the Savior Jesus Christ, death would end all hope for a future existence with Heavenly Father. [**Sacred Science, Dispensing of Existence, Creating Dependency, Mystical Manipulation**]
>
> Along with physical death, sin is a major obstacle that keeps us from becoming like our Father in Heaven and returning to His presence. [**Blame Reversal, Guilt & Shame, Mystical Manipulation**] In our mortal condition we often yield to temptation, break God's commandments, and sin. [**Demand for Purity, Doctrine Over Self**] During our life on earth each of us makes mistakes. Although it sometimes appears otherwise, sin always leads to unhappiness. [**Destabilization, Thought-Terminating Cliché, Emotion Over Intellect**] Sin causes feelings of guilt and shame. [**Guilt and Shame, Totalist Reframing, Mystical Manipulation**] Because of our sins, we are unable to return to live with Heavenly Father unless we are first forgiven and cleansed. [**Demand for Purity, Induced Phobias, Shame, Confession**]
>
> While we are in mortality, we have experiences that bring us happiness. [**Euphoria Induction**] We also have experiences that bring us pain and sorrow, some of which is caused by the sinful acts of others. [**Phobia Induction**] These experiences provide us opportunities to learn and grow, to distinguish good from evil, and to make choices. [**Black and White Thinking, Totalist Reframing**] God influences us to do good; Satan tempts us to commit sin. [**Us vs. Them, Mystical Manipulation**] As with physical death, we cannot overcome the effects of sin by ourselves. We are helpless without the Atonement of Jesus Christ. [**Creating Dependency, Sacred Science**][1]

This doctrine is core to Mormon teachings. The rest of the Plan of Salvation, even as it is described in the simplest terms for new members, can be similarly broken down into manipulative threads. I cannot bring myself to believe in a loving omnipotent being who would establish a plan of coercive persuasion and call it free agency.

Yet it's impossible to see it in this frame while entangled in its web. Which is why it works so well. As Goldhammer said, "...we can best see a group or an entire culture for what it really is by removing ourselves from it."[2]

The above examples illustrate how any single mind control device would not work well on its own. They must all work together in a cohesive whole. Being able to recognize these techniques dispels their power, whether the technique was used on you in the past, or will be in the future. Even if you cannot name each technique when you see it, understanding them will give you an inner "cultdar", a radar that warns you of incoming danger. So you know when to back away slowly, and when to run for your life.

---

1. *Preach My Gospel*, 2004. 50.
2. Goldhammer, *Under the Influence*, 1996. 258.

# Conclusion

*There may be intelligence or sparks of the divinity in millions—but they are not Souls till they acquire identities, till each one is personally itself.*
— **John Keats**

*Binders always punish with what they fear most...abandonment and independence.* ***They*** *are the ones who most need others... For the Bound, if they have the courage to leave, it becomes possible for them to reclaim all the humanness that was stolen from them...to live freely in the Real World which is the true home of all possibilities for understanding and love.*
— **Marion Stricker,**
***The Pattern of the Double-Bind in Mormonism***[1]

*Only the individual can initiate the hero's journey.*
— **John D. Goldhammer,** *Under the Influence*[2]

# Fleeing the Garden

If you have recently left the Church, a whole world now awaits you. You have bitten into the sweet fruit and tasted freedom and finally have an inkling of what you want *for yourself*. Now you can begin to get it.

In tasting the fruit, you have perhaps discovered that bondage in the name of agency is not freedom. Hopefully this book has increased your understanding, to light your way in making better choices—not between good and evil, but between a thousand shades of gray and millions of shades of color.

As you pass through Eden's gates, you see the thorns and thistles growing at your feet. Each crumb of spiritual bread you must now earn through the sweat of your own brow, rather than handed to you from on high.

I wish I had room enough in these pages to map the journey out, to further ease your burdens. It is certainly a grieving process, beset with anger, guilt, fear, depression, and worst of all: uncertainty. You may have conflicts with loved ones and face accusations; you *will* be misunderstood. The manipulative tactics from members may ramp up for awhile—anything to get you back.

If only I could outline the uncomfortable stages of the exit process, assist you with pointers on building new beliefs and discovering your own identity, finding new communities, re-establishing self-worth, overcoming fears, developing independence, and dealing with all the other monumental problems exmormons face.

Perhaps in a future book.

Meanwhile, there are many websites and online communities that offer support and guidance (anonymously if needed); post-Mormon groups who meet in person and offer shoulders to cry on and ears to rant at; and books about exiting cults in general, particularly *Captive Hearts, Captive Minds* and *Releasing the Bonds*.

You should accept your emotions and allow them to exist within you (while refraining from hurtfully lashing out, of course). Satiate your need to consume information on topics like LDS history—members will try to tell you it is not healthy, but it is a kind of purging, of recataloging, of grappling with the differences between illusion and reality to reach a new

---

1. Stricker, *The Double-Bind in Mormonism*, 2000. 113.
2. Goldhammer, *Under the Influence*, 1996. 37.

sense of stability after your world has been shattered. This desire is not unique to exmormons. According to *Captive Hearts*, "Most ex-members go through a period where they read everything they can get their hands on."[1]

Allow yourself to explore religions, philosophies, and media you once avoided. Pursue that which "clicks" with you. This is part of discovering your new identity. Indulge in pastimes you never had room for before. Take time off. Enjoy yourself. Invent yourself.

You must also develop your own moral compass, which can be confusing when you've spent your whole life with someone else telling you how to choose the right. In my case, my whole reality had been pulled out from under me, and I found myself questioning literally *everything*. Did I exist? Did the world exist? What made sex wrong? What made lying wrong? What made murder wrong? Over the months after my exit, I had to address each terrifying question that came into my mind.

These questions were not signs that I had fallen into Satan's grasp. I wasn't ready, at any moment, to go on a killing spree; though this was among my cult-instilled fears. I ended up using logic to assemble my new value system. For instance, I decided that if I accepted that I could harm others, then I was allowing them the right to harm me.

That became a basic measure of morality for me. As the Wiccans say, "An it harm none, do as ye will." This seems like a good minimum bar to set: "First, do no harm." Everything else is up to you.

It is possible to be both spiritual and morally good without joining any organized religion, and even without believing in a deity. The power to choose is completely up to you. I give you permission to borrow from multiple belief systems and personal experiences. Do what works. As they say in 12-step programs, "Take what you like and leave the rest."

Integrity and openness is the antidote for closed, controlling systems. Goldhammer stated, "By creating meaning in our lives, we add meaning and integrity to the universe. Life becomes a process to be lived, not a problem to be solved. And *individual integrity* becomes a soul relationship with the rest of humanity."[2] Make your own meaning. That is what it is to self-actualize, and what it means to be a spiritual human being.

If you are having an exceptionally difficult time, especially with shame, depression, anxiety, low self-esteem, or if you are also dealing with compounding issues like mental illness, past abuse, present abuse, LGBT issues, eating disorders, self-harm, recurring dissociation, abandonment or isolation from your family, marital issues, etc., you may need additional counseling from either a therapist or a cult exit counselor.

You may find an additional sense of closure by officially resigning from the Church—having your name removed from the records. There is a powerful sense of relief knowing that this last vestige of control is dissolved. Information on how to successfully resign without further pressures or harassment can be found at www.mormonnomore.com.

You have already taken a great step on your journey by reading this book. With a better understanding of how you were controlled, you should be better prepared to loose your own shackles and venture out of the Garden without shame, armed with knowledge to avoid the snares of other totalist systems. When you view it in its proper frame, the world can be more exciting than dangerous, more beautiful than sinful. More liberating than frightening.

So go, and do thou likewise. Lay down your yoke, and graze in the fields of your choosing.

---

1. Tobias and Lalich, *Captive Hearts, Captive Minds,* 1994. 183.
2. Goldhammer, *Under the Influence,* 1996. 47.

# Acknowledgements

I wish to express sincere gratitude.

I am extremely grateful to my parents, who are both still true-believing Mormons, who asked me not to write this book. Nevertheless, they both accept me, even though they vehemently disagree with me. That is the measure of true unconditional love, and we have learned and practiced that skill together.

To them and to my extended family, I am very sorry if this book hurts you. You were first on my mind when I decided to write this. You may think many things of me, which may or may not be true, but please never think I wanted to hurt you on purpose. There were truths I needed to say and I decided saying them was too important.

Thanks to my beta readers. Several wished to remain anonymous because they need to protect their families. I am grateful to them, even though I cannot mention them by name. Those I can name are Diane Thompson, Paul Witte, Alex McDavid, Josalyn Hanson, and Rebekah Davis.

Ana Cruz designed yet another a beautiful, eye-catching cover, and patiently endured my many requests for changes and tweaks, and nitpicks. A thousand thanks to her.

To all my Twitter followers who listen to my steady stream-of-consciousness, in many ways you were with me as I wrote this book. Your presence and support and retweets and mentions sustain me.

And to all who cheered me on. Writing a book like this wasn't easy in any way. The long hours and monumental effort was one thing, but on top of that were all the risks involved in writing on this topic. I have opened myself up to very harsh criticism. To everyone who called me "brave," or who told me they were looking forward to reading this, or who reminded me how much this work is needed, you bolstered me through burnout and fear.

Lastly, to all my writing influences, my favorite authors, all the people who have supported me over the years, and everyone and anyone else I forgot to mention.

**Most of all, thank YOU for reading. Triple-thanks if you leave me a review or feedback somewhere online.**

# Appendix

# Recommended Reading

Resources are cited in footnotes throughout this book. Further reading can be found by following up with any of those. Particularly useful books and other resources are listed here.

## Cults & Mind Control

Cialdini, Robert B. *Influence: Science and Practice*. Boston: Pearson Education, 2009.

Festinger, Leon. *When Prophecy Fails: A Social and Psychological Study of a Modern Group That Predicted the Destruction of the World*. Harper & Row, 1964.

Goldhammer, John D. *Under the Influence*. Prometheus Books, 1996.

Hassan, Steven. *Freedom of Mind: Helping Loved Ones Leave Controlling People, Cults, and Beliefs*. Newton, MA: Freedom of Mind Press, 2012.

Hassan, Steven, *Releasing the Bonds: Empowering People to Think for Themselves*. Somerville, MA: Freedom of Mind Press, 2000.

Langone, Michael D., ed. *Recovery from Cults: Help for Victims of Psychological and Spiritual Abuse*. New York: W.W. Norton & Company, 1993.

Tobias, Madeleine Landau and Janja Lalich. *Captive Hearts, Captive Minds: Freedom and Recovery from Cults and Abusive Relationships*. Alameda, CA: Hunter House, 1994.

Stricker, Marion. *The Pattern of The Double-Bind in Mormonism*. Universal Publishers, 2000. http://exmormon.org/pattern

Singer, Margaret Thaler, *Cults in our Midst*. San Francisco: Jossey-Bass Publishers, 1995

## Official LDS Sources

LDS.org –
All LDS lesson manuals, General Conference talks, Church magazines, scriptures, and other official Church publications are available and searchable online at LDS.org.

## LDS Controversies

Anderson, Duwayne. *Farewell to Eden: Coming to Terms with Mormonism and Science*. Bloomington, IN: AuthorHouse, 2003.

Bagley, Will. *Blood of the Prophets: Brigham Young and the Massacre at Mountain Meadows*. Norman: University of Oklahoma Press, 2004.

Bigler, David. *Forgotten Kingdom: The Mormon Theocracy in the American West, 1847-1896*. Logan, Utah: Utah State University Press, 1998.

Brodie, Fawn M. *No Man Knows My History: The Life of Joseph Smith*. New York: Vintage, 1995.

Buerger, David J. *The Mysteries of Godliness: A History of Mormon Temple Worship*. San Francisco; Salt Lake City, Utah: Signature Books, 2002.

Bushman, Richard Lyman. *Joseph Smith: Rough Stone Rolling*. New York: Vintage, 2007.

Compton, Todd M. *In Sacred Loneliness: The Plural Wives of Joseph Smith*. Salt Lake City: Signature Books, 1997.

Cowdrey, Wayne L., Howard A. Davis, and Arthur Vanick. *Who Really Wrote the Book of Mormon?: The Spalding Enigma*. St. Louis, MO: Concordia Publishing House, 2005.

Hanks, Maxine. *Women and Authority: Re-Emerging Mormon Feminism*. Salt Lake City, Utah: Signature Books, 1992.

Krakauer, Jon. *Under the Banner of Heaven: A Story of Violent Faith*. New York: Anchor, 2004.

Larson, Charles M. *By His Own Hand Upon Papyrus: A New Look at the Joseph Smith Papyri*. S.l.: Inst for Religious Research, 1992.

Newell, Linda King, and Valeen Tippetts Avery. *Mormon Enigma: Emma Hale Smith*. 2 Sub edition. Urbana, Ill.: University of Illinois Press, 1994.

Palmer, Grant. *An Insider's View of Mormon Origins*. First Edition. Salt Lake City: Signature Books, 2002.

Quinn, D. Michael. *Early Mormonism and the Magic World View*. 2nd Edition. Salt Lake City: Signature Books, 1998.

Quinn, D. Michael. *The Mormon Hierarchy: Origins of Power*. Salt Lake City: Signature Books, 1994.

Southerton, Simon G. *Losing a Lost Tribe: Native Americans, DNA, and the Mormon Church*. Salt Lake City: Signature Books, 2004.

**Websites:**

20 Truths about Mormonism – http://20truths.info

LDS-Mormon.com – http://www.lds-mormon.com

The Mormon Curtain – http://mormoncurtain.com

MormonThink.com: An Objective Look at the LDS Church – http://mormonthink.com

Wikipedia, the Free Encyclopedia – http://en.wikipedia.org

## LDS Exit Stories

Beck, Martha Nibley. *Leaving the Saints: How I Lost the Mormons and Found My Faith.* New York: Crown Publishers, 2005.

Kline, Diana. *Woman Redeemed.* Bloomington, Ind.: AuthorHouse, 2005.

Lamborn, Lyndon. *Standing For Something More: The Excommunication of Lyndon Lamborn.* Bloomington, Ind.: AuthorHouse, 2009.

Morin, Brad L. and Chris L. Morin. *Suddenly Strangers: Surrendering Gods and Heroes.* Chula Vista, CA: Aventine Press, 2004.

Worthy, Jack B. *The Mormon Cult: A Former Missionary Reveals the Secrets of Mormon Mind Control.* Tucson, Ariz.: See Sharp Press, 2008.

**Websites:**

Personal Accounts of Leaving Mormonism | Post-Mormon Scrapbook –
http://www.postmormon.org/exp_e/index.php/pomopedia/Personal_Accounts_of_Leaving_Mormonism/

Reddit – Stories of Individuals Leaving the Mormon Church –
http://www.reddit.com/r/ExitStories/

Why We Left – Personal Accounts of Leaving Mormonism –
http://www.exmormon.org/stories.htm

## Liberal Mormon Resources

There are organizations and publications that seek to work within Mormonism to explore intellectual thought free from orthodoxy or to enact social change. These are sometimes known as "liberal Mormons". Below is a list of these sources, including a description in their own words.

Affirmation — LGBT Mormons, Families & Friends –
http://affirmation.org

"Affirmation supports LGBTQ/SSA Mormons and their families, friends and Church leaders in seeking to live productive lives consistent with their faith or heritage."

Dialogue – A Journal of Mormon Thought –
https://www.dialoguejournal.com

"An independent quarterly journal of 'Mormon thought' that addresses a wide range of issues on Mormonism and the Latter Day Saint Movement."

Mormon Stories Podcast –
http://mormonstories.org

"Exploring Mormon and LDS culture, history and doctrine, Mormon Stories Podcast seeks to explore the Mormon experience through personal stories."

New Order Mormon –
  http://www.newordermormon.org

  "New Order Mormons are those who no longer believe some (or much) of the dogma or doctrines of the LDS Church, but who want to maintain membership for cultural, social, or even spiritual reasons. New Order Mormons recognize both good and bad in the Church, and have determined that the Church does not have to be perfect in order to remain useful. New Order Mormons seek the middle way to be Mormon."

Ordain Women –
  http://ordainwomen.org

  "Based on the principle of thoughtful, faith-affirming strategic action, Ordain Women aspires to create a space for Mormon women to articulate issues of gender inequality they may be hesitant to raise alone."

Sunstone Magazine –
  https://www.sunstonemagazine.com

  "The Church of Jesus Christ of Latter-day Saints is a vibrant religious tradition with a diverse membership that has widely differing needs. For many Latter-day Saints, one of these needs is free and frank exploration of gospel truths as they relate to the complexities of today's society. Some crave stimulating discussions of contemporary scholarship, literature, and social issues. Others find great comfort being able to read, hear, and share personal faith journeys, including all their twists and turns and occasional uncertainties... Sunstone brings together traditional and non-traditional Latter-day Saints, promoting an atmosphere that values faith, intellectual and experiential integrity."

## Support and Communities for Former Mormons

Exmormon Foundation –
  http://www.exmormonfoundation.org

Facebook groups, many of which are listed at –
  http://www.mormonspectrum.org/post-ex/facebook/

Further Light and Knowledge –
  http://www.furtherlightandknowledge.net

Life After Mormonism – The Social Network Serving the Exmormon Community –
  http://www.lifeaftermormonism.net

Mormon Discussions –
  http://mormondiscussions.com

Mormon Spectrum –
  http://www.mormonspectrum.org/

Mormon Transitions –
  http://www.mormontransitions.org/

PostMormon.org - Support for People as They Leave or Consider Leaving the LDS Church –
http://www.postmormon.org

Recovery from Mormonism –
http://www.exmormon.org

Reddit Exmormons –
http://www.reddit.com/r/exmormon

Recovering Agency Blog –
http://recoveringagency.com/blog/

## What Now?

There are hundreds of good books on self-actualization, personal growth, developing rational thinking skills, and spirituality outside the bonds of coercive religions. Here a few suggestions to get started.

Armstrong, Karen. *A History of God: The 4,000-Year Quest of Judaism, Christianity, and Islam.* New York: Gramercy, 2004.

Bach, Richard. *Illusions: The Adventures of a Reluctant Messiah.* London: Arrow Books Ltd, 2001.

Beattie, Melody. *Codependent No More: How to Stop Controlling Others and Start Caring for Yourself.* Center City, MN: Hazelden, 1986.

Branden, Nathaniel. *The Art of Living Consciously: The Power of Awareness to Transform Everyday Life.* New York: Touchstone, 1999.

Burns, David D., M. D. *Feeling Good: The New Mood Therapy.* New York: Harper, 2008.

Campbell, Joseph, and Bill Moyers. *The Power of Myth.* New York: Anchor, 1991.

Hanh, Thich Nhat, and Jack Kornfield. *Being Peace.* Berkeley, CA: Parallax Press, 2005.

Keen, Sam. *Hymns to an Unknown God: Awakening The Spirit In Everyday Life.* New York: Bantam, 1995.

McElroy, Wendy. *The Reasonable Woman: A Guide to Intellectual Survival.* Amherst, N.Y: Prometheus Books, 1998.

O'Donohue, John. *Anam Cara: A Book of Celtic Wisdom.* New York: Harper Perennial, 1998.

Paine, Thomas. *The Age of Reason.* Aziloth Books, 2011.

Sagan, Carl, and Ann Druyan. *The Demon-Haunted World: Science as a Candle in the Dark.* New York: Ballantine Books, 1997.

# Index

*1984* (George Orwell), 13, 21, 46, 59, 90, 101, 105, 110, 142-143, 160, 165, 174, 182, 185, 200, 234, 243, 254, 262, 269, 306

abuse (*See also* addiction; children; codependency; discipline; family; mental health; passive-aggression; trauma; unhealthiness; unrighteous dominion), 9, 16, 20, 24-25, 27, 33-35, 39, 42, 49-50, 52, 59, 82, 99-100, 109, 126, 130, 133, 146, 152-154, 164, 177, 187, 248, 272, 283, 288-289, 291, 294-295, 303-305, 325; sexual, 14, 20, 24, 34, 41-42, 106, 126, 160, 180, 202, 239, 260, 267, 272, 283, 289, 293, 302, 309; spiritual, 5, 13, 49, 99
acceptance (*See* belonging, sense of; love bombing; self-acceptance; social pressure; unconditional love).
addiction, 30, 41-42, 48, 91, 97, 131-132, 146, 164, 167, 252, 264, 267-268, 278, 300, 303-304, 312, 315
ADHD, 7
agency (*See* free agency).
angels, 6, 8, 68, 107-108, 116, 118, 144, 167, 180, 256, 265-268, 286, 293, 307
anger, 7, 9, 20, 31, 32, 33, 39-40, 48, 50, 56, 92, 109, 123-124, 134, 150, 162, 164, 177, 185, 188-189, 196, 198, 237, 240, 250, 255, 259, 290, 295, 304-305, 309, 324
anti-Mormon, 7, 39, 60, 147, 241, 255, 259, 267
anxiety (*See also* depression; induced phobias), 7, 20, 29-31, 38, 40-41, 92, 98, 158, 167, 175, 185, 196, 202, 204, 217, 224, 262, 264, 275, 291, 297, 302, 304, 311, 314-315, 325
apostasy (*See also* excommunication; leaving the Church; Outer Darkness), 41, 81, 121, 131, 148, 154, 167-170, 172, 231, 236, 239-241, 246, 309
apostle (*See* general authority).
Asch, S.E., 71
Atonement, 37, 70, 113, 178, 212, 220, 299, 322
authority (*See also* general authority; leadership; Milgram experiment; obedience to authority), 3-4, 13, 28, 33, 37, 52, 72-75, 82, 94, 110, 112, 116-125, 130, 175-176, 179, 185, 187, 221, 228, 242-243, 252, 255, 264, 284, 293, 306
autism, 29, 204
awareness, 18, 26, 42, 59-60, 119, 255, 269-272, 277, 294, 301; suppression of, 12, 27, 35, 82, 148, 182, 186, 227, 243, 249, 254, 262, 269-271, 276, 281-283, 291, 304-306, 311, 314, 316

Ballard, Russell M., 87, 208
baptism, 99-102, 134, 209, 211, 215, 257, 307-308, 318-319
Beck, Martha Nibley, 13, 21, 30, 36, 43, 54, 85, 103, 146, 152-153, 156, 167, 171, 172, 174, 177, 203, 237, 240, 242, 243, 247, 252, 281, 286
beehive, 177
behavior (*See* belief follows behavior; cognitive behavior therapy; cognitive dissonance theory).
belief follows behavior, 45, 47, 54-59, 70, 80, 86, 89, 161, 200, 204-210, 234, 249-250, 300, 317, 321
beliefs, 4-19, 23-32, 42, 45, 48-49, 52-70, 77-82, 90, 92, 96-97, 108-109, 112, 126, 130, 141, 153, 167, 175-176, 181, 188-189, 202, 206-207, 210-212, 218, 237, 245, 254, 266, 270, 303, 305, 316-319, 324
belonging, sense of (*See also* creating dependency; shame), 19, 43, 80, 83, 85-89, 96, 152, 166-167, 201, 203, 206, 213, 218-219, 227, 232, 297-298, 302-304, 314, 324
Benson, Ezra Taft, 32, 114, 117, 118, 136, 146, 161, 173, 229, 231, 245
Benson, Steve, 173
biases, 15, 39, 53, 66, 116, 236, 254; bias blind spot, 66; confirmation bias (*See also* cognitive dissonance theory; mystical manipulation), 10, 67-68, 109, 112, 115, 119, 128, 166, 175, 216, 255, 257, 291
Bible (*See* scripture).
bipolar, 29, 172
bishops, 23, 27, 35, 41, 54, 59, 60, 73, 87, 96, 134, 138, 153-154, 177, 203, 211, 213, 252, 256, 265, 267, 286-289, 293-294, 302, 305, 307-310
BITE Model (*See also* Hassan, Steven), 78, 278
black and white thinking, 11, 80, 100, 158, 165, 167, 183, 189, 195, 223-226, 234, 244, 249, 262, 278, 283-284, 291, 297, 320, 321
blame reversal, 6-7, 15-16, 29-30, 40-41, 48, 78, 81, 92, 96, 111-112, 133, 157-159, 169, 171, 204, 223, 234, 244-249, 260, 262, 281-284, 287-288, 290-296, 302, 306, 309, 320-322
blessings, 11, 21, 37, 46, 68, 70, 72, 120, 127, 129, 130-131, 137-140, 162, 165, 180-181, 187, 190, 211-212, 214, 229, 232, 252, 257, 267, 284, 290-293, 311, 314
Blood Atonement doctrine, 7, 105, 244, 246
Book of Abraham, 37, 106
Book of Mormon (*See* scripture).
boundaries (*See also* mental health; recovery; therapy), 33, 50, 81, 98, 134, 148, 152-153, 192, 205, 246, 295, 303, 307, 310, 313-314
brain cells (*See* neurons).
brainwashing (*See also* mind control), 10, 13-14, 17-18, 20, 38-39, 55, 91, 191-192, 202, 270
Brandon, Nathaniel, 27, 301
Brin, David, 56

Brown, Brené, 298, 300, 303
BYU, 6, 103, 152-153, 218, 302

callings, 24, 32-33, 49, 59, 87, 116, 184, 187, 203, 206, 208-212, 229-232, 247, 278-280, 285, 302, 308
Card, Orson Scott, 2, 85, 184, 194
career issues (*See also* creating dependency), 26, 42-43, 63, 103, 139, 171, 180, 205, 209, 217-218, 267, 285, 287, 302
Celestial Kingdom (*See also* heaven; hell; Outer Darkness), 34, 38, 106-107, 232, 264, 267, 276, 288-289, 313
chanting (*See also* hymns; music; trance induction), 18, 82, 112, 270-271, 313
chastity (*See also* sexual control; shame: sexual), 23, 133, 160, 163, 165, 171, 180, 202, 302, 305
child abuse (*See* abuse).
children (*See also* abuse; creating dependency; milieu control: family), 14, 23-25, 33-35, 42, 48, 72, 79, 88-90, 95, 97-102, 120, 133-134, 139, 145, 149-152, 160, 169, 177, 189, 200, 204, 206-207, 210, 212-213, 217-221, 229, 231, 238, 244, 248, 251, 257-260, 265, 272, 274, 279, 286-287, 289, 292, 294, 301-305, 308, 321
choice, 2-12, 21, 27, 29, 69-70, 73, 102, 110, 118, 124, 143, 153, 160, 164, 180, 187, 194, 212, 216, 219, 223-226, 239, 257, 264, 281, 283, 285, 288, 292, 296, 302, 309, 321, 324
Church Correlation Committee, 145
Church discipline (*See also* discipline; disfellowshipment; excommunication), 152, 154-155, 185, 236, 294, 309
Church Education System (CES), 103, 104, 146, 218
Church history (*See* LDS history).
Cialdini, Robert, 52, 62, 69, 71, 73, 75, 108, 201, 210, 211, 281, 283, 316
Civil Rights Movement, 189, 245
clothing, 27, 42, 73, 78, 144, 160, 176, 201, 203-207, 232, 236, 315
codependency, 33-35, 99, 268, 307
coercion, 4, 10, 12-14, 17, 37, 64, 70, 74, 82, 102, 127, 173, 175, 181, 185, 189, 202, 205, 207, 211, 217, 253, 270, 287, 296, 306, 322
cognitions (*See* beliefs; cognitive dissonance theory; motivated reasoning).
cognitive behavior therapy, 126
cognitive dissonance theory (*See also* When Prophecy Fails), 55-70, 77, 81-83, 90-93, 97, 100, 106, 109, 111, 122, 125, 127, 142-143, 147, 174-175, 188-189, 192, 201-203, 206-212, 219, 221, 236-237, 240-241, 246, 254, 256, 270, 273, 289, 305, 316
cognitive distortions (*See also* cognitive dissonance theory; justification), 126, 188
cogs (*See* cognitive dissonance theory).
commandments (*See also* obedience to authority), 2, 5-6, 9, 23, 37, 68, 70, 74, 81, 86, 93, 95, 97-100, 108, 122, 130-132, 138-139, 144, 146, 148, 150, 152, 157, 159, 160, 163, 168, 171-172, 178, 181, 185, 187, 191-192, 197, 200, 203, 208-209, 211-212, 215, 226, 244, 247, 251, 265, 277, 284-288, 294-295, 299, 309, 317, 321, 322
commitment (*See* public commitment).
commitment and consistency (*See also* public commitment), 70, 90, 98, 102, 111, 113, 210
Communism, 4, 136, 189
community, 16, 28, 34, 89, 111, 165, 173, 200, 217-219, 232, 285, 297, 300, 302, 304, 308, 313-314
compassion (*See also* acceptance; unconditional love), 3-4, 30, 45, 69, 72, 88, 97, 113, 121, 140, 149, 152, 242, 259, 286, 294, 301-304, 324
compliance, 52, 69-74, 95, 102, 160, 176, 200, 211, 218, 230, 255, 268, 314-315
confession (*See also* Church discipline), 81, 114, 132, 153, 157, 210, 262, 267, 306-310, 322
confirmation bias (*See* biases: confirmation bias).
confusion, 8, 20, 40, 50, 56, 58, 59, 102, 120, 133, 176, 185, 189, 195, 197, 221, 223, 226, 240, 255, 260, 275, 277, 286, 287, 290, 304, 307
consecration (*See also* time control; temples; tithing), 93, 180, 247, 278-279
consent, 13, 15, 91, 101-102, 143, 210, 235, 293
consonance (*See* cognitive dissonance theory).
contention, spirit of, 33-34, 123-124, 136, 187, 194, 197, 267
converts, 5, 29, 62, 86-88, 95-96, 102-103, 109, 125, 138, 232, 302, 319
coping mechanisms, 176, 262, 271, 291, 296, 302, 305
creating dependency, 15-18, 78, 80, 82, 85, 90-95, 98-99, 142, 149, 152-153, 158, 160, 171, 174, 200, 210, 217-222, 227, 248, 250, 261-263, 274, 276, 283, 300, 307, 321-322
creativity, 15, 29, 112, 116, 269, 270, 272
critical thinking skills, 6, 10, 18, 26, 28, 35, 66, 81-82, 96, 98, 116, 121, 128, 182, 184, 188, 194, 196, 223, 243, 254, 259, 264, 269-274, 276, 311, 314
CTR (choose the right), 11, 173, 212, 221, 225, 285, 325
cult leader, 10, 14-15, 19-20, 24, 38-41, 53, 63, 69, 74, 78-80, 85-86, 92, 95, 99-103, 107, 110-113, 116, 127, 149, 158, 167, 190-192, 201, 218, 224, 228, 236, 243-244, 250, 260, 263-265, 270-271, 274, 281, 283, 291-292, 297, 307-308, 314, 319
cultdar, 322
cults (*See also* FLDS; high-demand group; totalism), 4, 9, 10, 13-23, 38-43, 48, 49, 53, 63, 65, 74, 77, 82, 86, 95, 97-99, 101-103, 124, 138, 143, 149, 160, 165, 166, 176, 179, 190, 192, 201, 217-218, 224, 227, 228, 234-236, 244, 260, 263, 265, 270, 276, 291, 297, 306, 307, 312, 313, 324; Aum Shinrikyo, 17, 22; Bible-based, 4, 39, 99, 196, 271, 274, 319; Branch Davidians (*See also* Koresh, David), 16, 17, 23, 142, 237, 238; commercial, 19, 43, 123; compounds, 16, 82, 149, 218; Hare Krishna, 17; Heaven's Gate, 17, 142, 352; International Society of Divine Love, 13, 43, 264; Jehovah's Witness, 4, 56, 65, 237, 241, 317; LGATs, 19; Moonies, 13, 14, 17, 30, 38, 49, 85, 86, 102, 112, 113, 143, 156, 167, 176, 191, 192, 195, 213, 218-220, 249, 250, 255, 270, 274, 312; myths of, 17-20; New Age, 15, 17, 39,

128, 138, 190, 226, 235, 269, 300, 313; Niscience (Ann Ree), 128; political, 19, 26, 166, 179, 184, 191, 201, 208, 228, 232, 236, 317; Scientology, 96, 237; Seventh-day Adventists, 4, 65, 125, 143; SLF, 21, 39, 103, 128, 138, 157, 167, 190, 192, 195, 228, 235, 236, 244, 250, 251, 254, 264, 292, 297, 314; Transcendental Meditation, 17, 43, 129, 291, 292; Worker's Democratic Union, 112, 166, 176
culture, influence via, 4, 13, 47, 49, 58, 97, 133, 144, 176, 177, 200, 203, 204, 218, 243, 244, 249, 250, 264, 276, 304, 308
culture, LDS, 24, 25, 27, 29, 30, 32, 34, 38, 41, 42, 45, 47, 48, 108, 144, 159, 202, 204-206, 218, 229, 245, 250, 309, 320

Danites, 172
death (*See* dispensing of existence; spiritual death).
deception (*See also* disillusionment; illusion), 6, 10, 13-15, 18, 39, 46, 50, 60, 61, 70, 78, 79, 92, 101-109, 145-147, 174, 188, 197, 200, 207, 210-212, 217, 238, 241, 243, 256, 274, 281, 286, 308, 321
decisions (*See* choice; indecisiveness).
defense mechanism (*See* coping mechanisms).
Dehlin, John, 36
dehumanization (*See also* us-versus-them thinking), 166, 175, 177, 178, 234, 235, 317
demand for purity, 29, 30, 80, 82, 92, 156-164, 165, 172, 174, 206, 210, 220, 227, 230, 234, 244, 248, 249, 262, 281, 291, 292-296, 298, 300-303, 307, 308, 314, 317, 320-322
demon (*See* evil spirits).
dependency (*See* creating dependency).
depression, 20, 26, 30, 31-33, 41, 42, 107, 109, 132, 146, 159, 181, 204, 226, 244, 246, 247, 261, 279, 292-294, 302, 304, 311, 324-325; medication, 31
deprogramming (*See* exit counseling).
destabilization, 7, 79, 90, 174, 210, 217, 263, 296, 306, 320, 322
diet, 26, 42, 78, 139, 144, 160, 203, 272

discernment, 37, 134, 144, 233, 256, 265, 266
discipline (*See also* abuse; Church discipline; punishment), 185, 248, 295, 309
disfellowshipment (*See also* Church discipline; discipline; excommunication), 89, 154, 171, 236, 267, 309
disgust, 74, 161, 186
disillusionment (*See also* deception; illusions), 8, 36, 43, 96, 112
disorders (*See* ADHD; addiction; anxiety; autism; bipolar; depression; eating disorders; mental health; neurodiversity; suicide; trauma).
dispensing of existence, 11, 18, 80, 150, 165-173, 210, 217, 219, 223, 234, 243, 248, 249, 255, 262-266, 291, 302, 307, 308, 321
dissent (*See also* contention, spirit of; milieu control; sacred science), 89, 111, 120, 123, 187, 195, 291
dissociation (*See also* hypnosis; trance induction), 20, 40, 176, 260, 269, 271, 275, 283, 301, 302, 305, 306, 325
dissonance (*See* cognitive dissonance theory).
divorce, 6, 9, 29, 96, 130, 132, 153, 251, 287, 302
doctrine over self, 15, 29, 58, 80, 90-95, 118, 161, 165, 174-181, 187, 189, 195, 208, 217, 227, 234, 240, 244, 262, 274, 276, 277, 281, 285, 291, 295, 297, 303-308, 314, 320, 321
dogma (*See* ideology).
domestic violence (*See* abuse).
Doty, Kristine J., 32, 158, 159, 160, 246, 247, 251
double-bind, 81, 127, 132, 157, 165, 174, 216, 217, 227, 243, 262, 281-289, 290, 291, 296, 306, 320, 321
doublespeak, 185, 229, 273, 287
doublethink, 46, 59
doubt, 2, 4, 7, 10, 12, 27, 33, 39, 40, 43, 64, 77-81, 100, 101, 111, 116, 120, 121, 124-125, 128, 136, 142-148, 168, 170, 174-175, 182, 186, 187, 191, 194, 196, 198, 201, 214, 217, 228, 236, 241, 254, 257, 259, 261, 262, 267, 275, 277, 282, 286, 291, 303, 304, 311, 317; suppression of, 7, 12, 34, 80, 83, 85, 101, 102, 110-113, 120-125, 143, 147, 165, 182, 188, 194, 197, 198, 215, 217,

223, 234, 251, 254, 262, 276, 277, 281-283, 290, 291, 296, 306
dystopias, 3, 21, 183, 188

eating disorders, 20, 27, 33, 40, 41, 181, 247, 325
elitism, 18, 80, 82, 126, 143, 157, 187, 217, 218, 224, 227-229, 232-234, 249, 297, 308, 313, 314, 320, 321
emotion over intellect, 81, 221, 254-261, 320, 322
emotions (*See also* anger; anxiety; depression; emotion over intellect; euphoria induction; fear; grieving process; induced phobias; shame), 4, 9, 13, 15, 21, 22, 27, 31, 32, 38, 40, 50, 55, 56, 77, 90, 95, 98, 100, 111, 112, 119, 126, 130-134, 164, 169, 174-177, 182-192, 194, 197, 204, 213, 221, 238, 254-261, 269, 271, 273, 294, 296, 304, 311, 324
empathy, 259, 260, 269, 273, 303, 312
Emperor's New Clothes, 22, 73, 213
*Ensign*, 100, 101, 104, 121, 137, 145, 146, 240, 252
Equal Rights Amendment, 46, 153
ethical persuasion, 14, 15, 53, 91, 102
ethics, 38, 104, 205
euphoria induction (*See also* trance induction), 6, 18, 68, 81, 82, 86, 111, 142, 167, 189, 200, 210, 227, 257, 259, 269, 274, 297, 311-315, 321-322
evil spirits (*See also* induced phobias; Satan), 9, 20, 98, 134, 135, 144, 195, 265, 266, 268
example (*See* identification & example).
excommunication (*See also* apostasy; Church discipline; exmormons; inactivity; leaving the Church), 89, 153, 154, 171, 204, 217, 218, 234, 236, 243, 263, 267, 302, 309
exhaustion (*See* time control).
exit counseling (*See also* therapy), 9, 10, 38, 39, 41, 271, 325
exit stories, 5, 39, 59
exmormons (*See also* anti-Mormons; apostasy; excommunication; leaving the Church), 4, 5, 9, 28, 40, 42, 43, 58, 79, 173, 198, 218, 236, 238, 240, 255, 266, 297,

301, 324, 325, 330
Eyring, Henry B., 99, 212, 286

faith, 5, 7, 12, 19, 22, 27, 29, 32, 35, 45, 55, 56, 65, 68, 78, 79, 94, 95, 99, 103, 112, 114, 115, 118-124, 127, 129, 131, 135-138, 144, 145, 148-159, 161, 162, 168, 172, 174, 177, 181, 186, 187, 190, 196-198, 206, 208, 209, 212-221, 232, 233, 246, 254, 256, 267, 272, 274, 278, 283-285, 292, 293, 295, 300, 318, 320
falsifiability, 63, 107, 112, 115, 284
family (*See also* abuse; children; creating dependency; marriage; milieu control: family), 11, 15-21, 26, 29, 34, 33–35, 37-46, 49, 50, 58, 72, 78, 89, 91, 96-100, 106, 109, 114, 119, 127, 130-133, 149-152, 176, 179, 180, 187, 189, 203, 205, 214, 217-219, 232, 238-241, 244, 246-248, 252, 259, 264, 267, 274, 279, 285, 288, 289, 300, 304, 312-314, 325
family home evening, 88, 98, 99, 151, 158, 189, 220, 259, 278, 279, 314
fasting, 130, 131, 180, 181, 206, 244, 270, 272, 274, 279, 284, 303, 315
Faust, James E., 155, 198, 225, 226, 229, 232, 256
fear (*See also* induced phobias), 9-11, 14, 16, 20, 25, 33, 38, 40, 45, 49, 50, 58, 74, 75, 85, 92, 134, 147, 160, 165, 166, 167, 170, 176, 185, 186, 189, 197, 198, 200, 220, 235, 236, 255, 259, 261-266, 268, 271, 275, 296, 298, 303, 314, 324
feminism, 29, 154, 235, 237, 245
Festinger, Leon, 54-58, 62-65, 201, 202, 207
First Vision, the, 37, 100, 106
fishbowl effect (*See also* dissociation; surveillance, spiritual), 40
FLDS (fundamentalist Mormons), 24, 25, 248
floating (*See* dissociation).
folklore, LDS, 37, 47, 134, 170, 204, 268
For the Strength of Youth, 87, 148, 161, 178, 203
forgiveness, 50, 107, 131, 133, 160, 299, 306, 308
free agency, 5, 9-13, 15, 21, 37, 43, 61, 73, 74, 121, 122, 124, 136, 142, 143, 149, 162, 167, 168, 173, 176, 182, 183, 185, 191, 194, 205, 207, 211, 224, 225, 244, 247, 261, 273, 283, 286-290, 294, 297, 300, 302, 305, 321-324
free will (*See* free agency).
Freemasons, 37, 106
friends (*See also* milieu control), 6, 10, 15-17, 20, 26, 33, 35, 39, 43, 71, 72, 81, 86-88, 90, 97, 132, 143, 148, 149, 152, 176, 181, 203, 205, 217, 218, 228, 239, 246, 252, 285, 288, 300, 304, 305, 309, 318

Galanti, Geri-Ann, 14, 15, 30, 38, 49, 86, 112, 125, 156, 176, 192, 207, 213, 219, 249, 255, 270, 274, 313
Garden of Eden, 2–3, 8, 12, 188, 283, 321
garments, temple, 7, 27, 131, 144, 184, 203, 237, 267
general authority (*See also* authority; leadership; prophet; sacred science), 12, 32, 45, 106, 116, 120, 130, 145, 169, 192, 209, 212, 214, 221, 241, 246, 247, 256, 259, 274, 287
General Conference, 48, 170, 210, 245, 247, 278
Giambalvo, Carol, 38
Goldhammer, John D., 15, 22, 29, 86, 110, 128, 142, 143, 153, 158, 176, 183, 184, 194, 200, 213, 224, 227, 228, 270, 276, 277, 297, 304, 306, 315, 316, 320, 322-325
Grant, Heber J., 118, 138, 146
grieving process (*See also* recovery), 9, 50, 324
guided imagery (*See also* storytelling, trance induction), 14, 17, 19, 263, 273, 274, 314
guilt & shame (*See also* shame), 6, 15, 16, 20, 26, 30, 32, 38, 40, 43, 49, 70, 78, 81, 99, 126, 130-133, 151, 157, 158, 164, 167, 185, 189, 198, 202, 227, 234, 235, 244, 260, 262, 264, 267, 279, 281, 283, 285, 287, 291-292, 296-305, 306-309, 312, 314, 321, 322, 324

Hales, Robert D., 66, 98, 149, 182, 212, 287
happiness (*See also* mental health), 11, 21, 26, 28-32, 37, 43, 87, 95, 96, 101, 108, 109, 114, 120, 124, 152, 159, 161, 164, 168, 176, 177, 181, 185, 190, 192, 196, 203, 209, 214, 215, 221, 228, 240, 246, 251, 273, 274, 278, 283, 284, 289, 292, 304, 311, 322

Hassan, Steven, 10, 13, 15-17, 19, 49, 78, 91, 95, 102, 111, 112, 120, 126, 174, 176, 183, 196, 218, 219, 223, 235, 236, 238, 250, 262, 263, 264, 266, 268, 272, 276, 310, 317
heaven (*See also* Cestial Kingdom), 7, 35, 95, 104, 107, 115, 118, 124, 125, 134, 138, 161, 162, 177, 186, 231, 239, 292
hell (*See also* Outer Darkness), 15, 116, 148, 158, 161, 167-170, 234, 264, 268, 299
high-demand group (*See also* cults; totalism), 4, 5, 13, 14, 22, 26, 31, 38, 41, 46, 47, 50, 79, 95, 97, 99, 100, 143, 167, 213, 238, 247, 319
Hinckley, Gordon B., 47, 87, 90, 118, 136, 139, 146, 162, 171, 230, 245, 277, 290
history of the Church (*See* LDS history).
Holland, Jeffery R., 316, 318
Holy Ghost, 27, 34, 37, 79, 94, 99, 114, 118, 119, 122, 125, 128-131, 134, 137, 144, 148, 160-164, 170, 178, 186, 187, 189, 196, 197, 208, 209, 211-214, 219, 221, 229, 230, 248, 256-259, 265, 267, 272-275, 284, 285, 287, 300, 304, 307, 312, 313, 318-320
home teaching, 87, 152, 205, 206
homosexuality (*See* LGBT).
hot cognition (*See* motivated reasoning).
human tendencies, 52, 66, 67, 68, 74, 75, 108, 128, 160, 188, 235, 259, 305
humility (*See* doctrine over self).,
Hunter, Howard W., 3, 12, 221
hymns (*See also* euphoria induction; trance induction), 29, 45, 118, 130, 161, 186, 190, 206, 212, 220, 230, 231, 270-275, 278, 314
hypnosis (*See also* dissociation; mystical manipulation; trance induction), 17, 18, 250, 269-272, 277

idealism, 45, 57, 81, 92, 96, 97, 101, 112, 126, 156, 157, 165, 166, 175, 210, 218, 235, 267, 312, 313
identification & example, 25, 74, 81, 87, 100, 120, 150, 157, 163, 187, 194, 200, 203, 204, 206, 221, 234, 243, 244, 249-252, 259, 262, 264, 273, 278, 285, 291, 296, 301, 315, 321
identity (*See also*

pseudopersonality), 14-19, 27, 30, 37-43, 49, 50, 77, 79, 80, 90-93, 95, 97-100, 165, 166, 171, 174-179, 191, 204, 211, 218, 219, 225-236, 250, 261, 263, 271, 279, 283, 291, 301, 302, 308, 311, 324, 325
ideology, 10, 15, 27, 62, 79, 80, 92, 102, 111, 113, 126, 128, 156, 176, 201, 211, 224, 235, 297, 306, 315
illusions (*See also* deception; disillusionment), 9-13, 21, 52, 55, 66, 70, 85, 102, 111, 118, 120, 126, 142, 157, 194, 205, 207, 211, 228, 291, 297, 300, 304, 308, 315, 320, 324
inactivity (*See also* apostasy; excommunication), 5, 29, 31, 36, 87, 89, 183, 208, 246
indecisiveness, 11, 20, 26, 28, 40, 43, 55, 102, 143, 177, 205, 221, 222, 240, 254, 267
indirect directives, 23, 47, 81, 179, 186, 200-203, 206, 223, 243-248, 249, 264, 269, 290, 296, 321
indoctrination, 13, 18, 27, 79, 82, 98, 124, 149, 188, 219, 270, 276, 309, 318
induced phobias, 9-11, 15, 20, 27, 38, 40, 49, 78, 81, 100, 157, 165, 167, 169, 172, 217, 243, 249, 255, 262-268, 269, 275, 276, 281, 283, 291, 300, 302, 306, 308, 314, 321, 324, 325
influence (*See* persuasion).
integrity, 45, 46, 55, 56, 72, 81, 90, 92, 100, 104, 115, 174, 175, 176, 210, 255, 283, 292, 325
intellect (*See* logic).
intellectuals, 29, 168, 205, 208, 237, 256
internet, 7, 36, 39, 43, 59, 60, 104-106, 146, 147, 151, 187, 198, 241, 301, 324
interviews, LDS, 7, 27, 38, 134, 154, 288, 305, 308, 310, 318
intolerance, 204, 237
invalidation, 294
isolation (*See also* milieu control), 16, 26, 40, 42, 63, 78, 83, 89, 90, 102, 110, 111, 142-144, 149, 166, 182, 184, 203, 206, 217, 223, 224, 227, 234, 236, 276, 277, 288, 325

Johnson, Sonia, 153
Jones, Jim (*See* Jonestown).
Jonestown (*See also* mass suicide), 17, 22, 33, 57, 69, 101, 142, 174, 188, 191, 201, 227, 234, 236, 238, 274
judgmentalism, 6, 27, 36, 75, 91,
99, 134, 153, 167, 169, 183, 204, 206, 224, 251, 292, 293, 302, 303, 308, 309
Jung, Carl, 22, 91, 272
justification (*See also* cognitive distortions), 25, 50, 54-57, 70, 96, 104, 108, 125, 126, 143, 147, 166, 172, 238, 240, 272

Keech, Marian (*See* Martin, Dorothy).
Keen, Sam, 5, 43, 45, 85, 113, 116, 194, 283
Kimball, Spencer W., 144, 151, 163, 180, 198, 213, 305, 317
Kinderhook plates, 7, 106
Kline, Diana, 5, 100, 157, 159, 213, 251, 252, 284, 288, 304, 305
Kolob, 5, 281, 282
Koresh, David (*See also* cults: Branch Davidians), 17, 116

Lalich, Janja, 16, 23, 26, 38, 39, 41, 42, 95, 96, 102, 107, 112, 113, 125, 143, 146, 149, 166, 174, 175, 176, 179, 184, 191, 208, 212, 217, 218, 224, 228, 232, 236, 255, 260, 262, 263, 265, 268, 271, 272, 282, 291, 297, 298, 307, 311, 313, 316, 317, 325
Langone, Michael, 15, 16, 36, 39, 78, 85, 111, 113, 146, 228, 234, 276, 291
Last Days (*See also* mystical manipulation; prophecy; When Prophecy Fails), 22-24, 62-65, 94, 125, 136, 169, 172, 189, 229-232, 264, 266, 285, 313
LDS history, 23, 36, 38, 40, 60, 103, 105, 145, 147, 154, 166, 172, 192, 198, 237, 239, 256, 324
LDS Social Services, 153
leadership (*See also* authority; cult leader), 16, 23, 26, 28, 33, 34, 37, 39, 45-48, 77-81, 94, 98, 101, 103, 105, 106, 109, 110, 116, 118-122, 125, 129, 135, 145, 147, 151-154, 157, 166, 172, 175, 177, 185, 190-193, 201, 202, 204, 206, 212-214, 225, 232, 237, 240-246, 251, 252, 254, 264, 272, 273, 276, 277, 283-287, 289-296, 299, 302-306, 309-311, 314, 318
leaving the Church (*See also* apostasy; excommunication; inactivity), 4, 9, 16, 20, 29, 36-40, 42, 46, 50, 61, 83, 91, 124, 132, 151, 166, 172, 192, 217, 218, 224, 235, 236, 240,
245, 252, 257, 261, 264, 265, 297, 309, 324
Lee, Harold B., 120, 125, 129, 145, 146, 198, 208
LGBT, 24, 29, 36, 146, 153, 154, 180, 187, 202, 204, 235, 237, 245, 246, 267, 285, 302, 325; Affirmation, 29; Evergreen International, 24, 29; North Star International, 29
Lifton, Robert J., 110, 111, 126, 127, 142, 143, 156, 166, 174, 183, 201, 235, 271, 296, 306, 307, 308, 312
liking, influence of, 69, 72
loading the language, 26, 80, 86, 182-187, 188, 189, 194, 210, 217, 223, 234, 309, 321
logic, 8, 15, 45, 46, 61, 81, 110-113, 115, 140, 142, 188, 191, 204, 211, 223, 224, 245, 254, 255, 256, 258, 268, 269, 283, 285, 290, 325
logic, closed (*See also* mystical manipulation; sacred science; totalism), 13, 25, 41, 43, 78, 79, 110, 111, 140, 175, 185, 223, 270, 275, 281, 294
logical illogic, 272-273
love bombing, 70, 72, 79, 82, 85-89, 200, 207, 217, 228, 297, 311, 321

magical thinking, 27, 35, 129, 135
manipulation, 4, 5, 10, 13, 15, 19, 20, 23, 39, 52, 69, 74, 96, 99, 105, 107, 120, 126, 127, 153, 183, 185, 189, 214, 240, 244, 245, 249, 250, 255, 260, 270-273, 281, 283, 297, 313, 314
marriage (*See also* family), 9, 11, 26, 29, 42, 96, 102, 109, 130, 133, 152, 180, 185, 217, 251, 260, 292, 313, 325
Martin, Dorothy (*See* When Prophecy Fails).
Martin, Paul L., 313
mass suicide, 17, 22, 33, 57, 101, 236, 238
masturbation (*See also* sexual control; shame: sexual), 41, 153, 163, 164, 267, 310
Maxwell, Neal A., 93, 178, 294
McConkie, Bruce R., 46, 47, 123, 129, 130, 163, 168, 169, 170, 225, 274, 320
McKay, David O., 149, 203, 229, 318
meditation (*See also* prayer; trance induction), 17, 18, 82, 156, 196, 270-272, 275, 299, 314
mental gymnastics, 58

mental health (*See also* abuse; anxiety; depression; dissociation; fear; self-awareness; suicide; therapy; trauma; unhealthiness), 4, 29, 40, 41, 63, 91, 92, 97, 109, 153, 172, 176, 205, 246, 271, 272, 288, 294, 304, 325
metanoia, 91
Milgram experiment (*See also* authority), 73, 74, 75
milieu control (*See also* cults: compounds), 80, 97, 102, 126, 142-155, 174, 206, 210, 213, 217, 227, 234, 262, 270, 277, 306, 307, 316, 320, 321; family milieu, 28, 42, 49, 82, 98-100, 119, 129, 134, 145, 149-152, 160, 162, 189, 203, 213, 216-219, 229, 259, 260, 268, 281, 285, 302, 308, 318
mind control, 7-22, 27, 35, 38, 39, 46, 49, 59, 77, 91, 95, 107, 142, 153, 156, 174-176, 184, 193, 200, 215, 321, 322
mind control techniques, 4, 19, 31, 45, 52, 55, 68, 74, 77, 79, 82, 95, 100, 103, 110, 127, 133, 141, 149, 158, 188, 194, 195, 200, 203, 207, 218, 224, 227, 250, 289, 296, 317, 320, 321
mind control, overcoming (*See also* recovery), 20, 39, 60, 100, 265, 266, 268, 312, 324
miracles, 7, 48, 64, 68, 114, 125, 127, 129, 130, 133, 135, 216, 293, 318-320
mirror neurons, 74, 86
missions (*See also* proselytizing), 3, 60, 68, 86, 87, 96, 102, 103, 108, 109, 114, 131-132, 135-137, 148, 163, 179, 189, 192, 193, 205, 206, 209, 211, 215-219, 229, 247, 257, 267, 278, 280, 284, 285, 293, 302, 309, 316-321
Mitchell, Brian David, 25, 126, 127, 281
modesty (*See also* sexual control; shame: sexual), 21, 144, 149, 183, 204, 206, 259
Monson, Thomas S., 98, 114, 148, 164, 252, 259, 274
morality (*See also* ethics), 2–5, 11, 17, 18, 21, 38, 40, 42, 46, 75, 80, 92, 95, 97, 104, 108, 111, 153, 156-160, 163, 184, 187, 222, 225, 226, 228, 229, 234, 252, 298, 299, 304, 309, 321, 325
Morin, Brad and Chris, 13, 39, 66, 68, 79, 101, 107, 120, 142, 150, 152, 189, 193, 198, 204, 205, 213, 221, 233, 236, 251, 257, 284, 299

Mormon Alliance, 35, 154
Mormon Corridor, 33, 42, 49, 171, 203, 218
Mormon Gulag, 24
motivated reasoning (*See also* cognitive dissonance theory), 254, 255
Mountain Meadows Massacre, 105, 142, 172, 238, 244
movies, R-rated, 7, 42, 131, 146, 147, 160, 197, 288
*mura hachibu*, 171
murder, 24, 105, 123, 160, 164, 172, 236, 240, 298, 309
music (*See also* euphoria induction; hymns; trance induction), 4, 6, 18, 29, 42, 45, 47, 121, 127, 134, 147, 148, 151, 160, 186, 205, 267, 270, 274, 275, 314
mystical manipulation, 10, 80, 100, 126, 128, 130, 141, 143, 188, 189, 216, 217, 221, 223, 249, 254, 256, 265, 268, 272, 291, 293, 306, 311, 313, 315, 320-322

names, 5, 79, 127, 176, 179, 206, 207, 211, 220, 228, 232, 266, 315
Nauvoo (*See also* LDS history), 37, 105, 172
Nelson, Russell M., 123, 124, 155, 159, 212, 259, 265
neurodiversity, 29
neurons (*See also* mirror neurons), 67, 74, 86, 259
*New Era*, 87, 104, 115, 129, 137, 145, 181, 198, 237, 241, 259, 292, 294, 308
newspeak, 182
Nibley, Hugh, 146, 172, 242

Oaks, Dallin H., 11, 101, 104, 113, 118, 121, 122, 123, 136, 146, 154, 169, 209, 226, 239, 240, 266, 277, 295
obedience, 6, 34, 74, 114, 120, 138, 162, 177, 181, 185, 191, 208, 284, 292, 295, 309
obedience to authority, 15, 72, 75, 95, 98-101, 112, 118-119, 157, 166, 169, 177, 185, 186, 191, 219-221, 226, 232, 244, 263, 264, 267, 283, 284, 286, 287, 289, 307, 314
Occam's Razor, 116
occult, 19, 20, 267
Ofshe, Richard, 40, 91, 92, 202
Orwell, George, 13, 21, 46, 59, 90, 101, 105, 110, 142, 143, 160, 165, 174, 182, 183, 200, 234, 243, 254, 262, 269, 306
ostracism, 80, 89, 149, 166, 167, 171, 202, 203, 210, 217, 236, 246, 248, 249, 251, 263, 267, 285, 291, 297, 302
Outer Darkness, 34, 170, 305

Pace, Glenn L., 37, 117, 154, 238, 255
Packer, Boyd K., 103-105, 146, 169, 179, 191, 201, 212, 223, 226, 239, 246, 256, 257, 259, 274, 286, 287
panic attacks (*See also* anxiety; trauma), 20, 40-41, 262
parents, 9, 17, 23, 28, 41, 45, 72, 95, 97-100, 108, 119, 139, 149-151, 171, 180, 189, 200, 206, 213, 214, 217-220, 230, 239, 241, 248, 259, 265, 274, 286, 288, 289, 295, 299, 303
passive-aggression (*See also* abuse; codependency; unhealthiness), 27, 33–35
Patriarchal blessing, 68, 152, 179, 209, 231, 232, 252, 284, 293, 318
peak experience (*See also* euphoria induction), 8, 111, 190, 312, 315
peer pressure (*See* social pressure).
perfection, 30, 32, 46, 50, 156-159, 161-163, 220, 246, 247, 260, 294, 301, 313
perfectionism, 27, 31, 32, 36, 158, 159, 247, 251, 279, 294
Perry, Tom L., 182, 185
persecution, 17, 48, 59, 81, 105, 187, 234, 236-238, 241
persuasion, 10-18, 38, 47, 53, 72-74, 77, 79, 82, 87, 90, 91, 95, 96, 99, 102, 118, 148, 173, 183, 188, 189, 203, 204, 207, 211, 213, 219, 224, 249, 252, 253-255, 269, 277, 287, 296, 322
phobias (*See* induced phobias).
Plan of Salvation, 37, 96, 103, 173, 177, 225, 313, 322
plausible deniability, 10, 204, 243, 245, 249, 291
polygamy (*See also* FLDS), 7, 23, 37, 60, 105, 127, 168, 198, 237, 245
Ponder, Kent, 28, 32
pornography (*See also* addiction; masturbation; shame: sexual), 31, 42, 147, 310
poverty, 38, 139, 146
prayer (*See also* euphoria induction; trance induction), 6, 10, 82, 86, 98, 112, 119, 128, 131, 137, 140, 144, 147, 150, 156, 171, 177, 178, 184, 190, 196, 198, 206, 209, 221, 244, 259, 270, 272, 274, 278, 279, 292, 303, 314, 315
preexistence, 177, 189, 230,

245, 313
pride (*See* doctrine over self).
priesthood, 7, 37, 47, 68, 88, 106, 116, 118, 119, 129-131, 134, 145, 152, 154, 170, 203, 204, 228-232, 241, 252, 257, 266, 293, 294
prisoners of war, 18, 91, 202, 207
projection, 235, 291, 305
prophecy, 24, 64, 65, 68, 113, 116, 117, 129-131, 136, 154, 189, 202, 232, 236
prophecy, self-fulfilling, 131, 132, 226, 254, 272
prophet (*See also* authority; cult leader; general authority; sacred science), 8, 10, 12, 17, 23, 24, 37, 38, 46, 47, 59, 60, 73, 114, 116-120, 127, 137, 139, 159, 169, 191, 196, 197, 204, 214, 215, 228, 245, 248, 259, 285, 286, 320
Proposition 8, 46
proselytizing (*See also* missions), 60, 62, 81, 87, 316, 317, 321
prosperity gospel, 138, 267, 292
pseudopersonality (*See also* identity), 14, 15, 27, 33, 77, 91, 92, 95, 128, 158, 166, 171, 174, 175, 182, 194, 210, 211, 218, 230, 234-236, 249, 253, 263, 279, 283, 302, 307, 312, 313
psychology (*See also* mental health; therapy), 52, 69, 92, 202, 210, 246, 303
public commitment (*See also* belief follows behavior), 8, 18, 63, 70, 80, 81, 102, 200, 206-209, 210-217, 232, 257, 306, 311, 315-317, 321
punishment (*See also* abuse; Church discipline; discipline), 11, 20, 78, 80, 82, 89, 91, 114, 140, 157, 158, 165, 167, 173, 185, 191, 200, 202, 208, 217, 227, 236-238, 244, 249, 252, 255, 262, 263, 268, 281, 283, 287, 291, 296, 297, 299, 306-308, 324

racism, 29, 37, 47, 146, 154, 205, 237, 245
rape (*See* abuse: sexual).
reason (*See* logic).
reciprocation, 69, 70, 87, 88, 220, 299
recovery (*See also* boundaries; mind control, overcoming), 5, 9, 20, 24, 38, 40, 41, 48, 49, 60, 97, 100, 105, 255, 261, 268, 297, 324
recruitment (*See also* missions; proselytizing), 13-15, 38, 52, 63, 79, 86, 88, 92, 95-97, 103, 149, 153, 158, 206, 207, 210, 213, 219, 228, 249, 250, 285, 298, 317-321
reframing (*See* totalist reframing).
regression, 2, 20, 26, 90, 95, 127, 147, 178, 219, 220, 255, 283, 312
reinforcement, 41, 48, 80, 82, 86, 92, 102, 110, 125, 157, 174, 194, 200, 206, 210-213, 217, 223, 234, 243, 254, 276, 281, 296, 306, 311, 314, 317
rejection (*See* shame: rejection).
relationships, 16, 19, 26, 40, 42, 43, 89, 96, 142, 180, 192, 205, 218, 220, 260, 277, 279, 285, 300, 307
Relief Society, 5, 60, 229, 279
repentance, 30, 34, 99, 153, 161, 214, 257, 259, 265, 267, 299, 306-308
reverence, 272
rewards, 55, 68, 70, 78, 80, 82, 85, 90, 91, 98, 131, 142, 157, 159, 165, 169, 171, 181, 192, 200, 210, 213, 214, 227, 234, 249, 251, 252, 265, 272, 278, 290, 307, 311, 314
Romney, Marion G., 95, 118, 169, 226
Rube Goldberg machine, 58, 62, 77
Russell's Teapot, 106, 107
Ryan, Patrick L., 291

Sabbati Zevi, 62
Sacrament, 5, 109, 118, 130, 134, 203, 206, 211, 216, 220, 244, 272, 273, 279, 285, 299, 309
sacred science, 79, 100, 110-124, 126, 143, 174, 175, 183, 217, 223, 227, 228, 243, 244, 262, 291, 292, 306, 311, 313, 319-322
sacrifice (*See also* doctrine over self), 94, 118, 130, 172, 174, 179, 180, 190, 193, 209, 219, 276, 278-280, 299
Sagan, Carl, 54, 67, 107
Sanchez, Steve, 21, 39, 77, 103, 128, 167, 192, 217, 226, 228, 235, 236, 244, 250, 264, 269, 290, 292, 296, 297, 300, 313, 314
Satan (*See also* evil spirits; black & white thinking), 9, 11, 37, 59, 68, 93, 100, 112, 116, 123, 124, 128, 130-135, 140, 144, 147, 150, 164, 168-170, 173, 189, 196-198, 221, 223-225, 231, 237, 239-242, 263-268, 286, 287, 294, 299, 302, 321, 322, 325

Satanism, 20, 268
*Saturday's Warrior*, 47, 149, 189, 191, 230, 231, 239, 304, 313
scarcity, influence of, 69, 73
Schein, Edgar H., 90
science, 4, 18, 52, 57, 60, 61, 68, 69, 72, 107, 112, 115, 116
scientific method, 61, 112, 115, 116
Scott, Richard G., 95, 208, 221
scriptures, 5, 6, 8, 11, 19, 24, 25, 36-38, 45, 47, 52, 54, 59, 60, 65, 68, 70, 72, 77, 79, 98, 99, 103, 106-108, 112-114, 116-118, 120, 122, 123, 130, 136-138, 144, 147, 150, 158-162, 168, 172, 173, 186, 187, 191, 195, 196, 198, 204, 206, 208, 209, 212, 213, 215, 221, 230, 236, 241, 245, 246, 248, 252, 259, 274, 278, 279, 284, 293, 303, 305
Second Anointing, 106
Second Coming (*See* Last Days).
secrecy, 13, 29, 63, 64, 102-106, 109, 123, 154, 164, 213, 232, 268, 303-307
FLDS (fundamentalist Mormons), 24, 172, 237, 240, 245
self-acceptance, 100, 268, 273, 285, 301, 303, 319, 324
self-awareness (*See also* identity; recovery), 15, 27, 30, 91, 100, 176, 268, 273, 292, 303, 315, 319, 324
self-care, 303
self-control, 15, 66, 176, 179, 181, 260
self-destruction, 30, 33, 40, 41, 132, 181, 301, 302, 308, 325
self-esteem (*See also* shame; worthiness), 27, 28, 40, 80, 86, 90-92, 100, 127, 153, 158, 160, 175, 187, 204, 218, 227, 228, 230-233, 246, 299, 314, 324, 325
self-expression, 112, 128, 142, 244, 294, 301, 303
selfishness (*See* doctrine over self).
selflessness (*See* doctrine over self).
self-reliance, 20, 35, 217, 222, 313
self-righteousness, 56, 59, 306
Seminary, 6, 9, 23, 59, 103, 114, 117, 161, 168, 170, 177, 204, 208, 231, 251, 274, 278, 301
September Six, 154, 171
sexual abuse (*See* abuse: sexual).
sexual assault (*See* abuse: sexual).
sexual control, 132, 156, 160,

171, 260, 267, 295, 310
sexual issues (*See also* shame: sexual), 20, 30, 260
shame (*See also* anxiety; depression; guilt & shame; mental health; sexual control; unconditional love), 11, 18, 27, 30-33, 38, 40, 41, 43, 58, 70, 99, 131-133, 159, 169, 185, 187, 200, 206, 226, 227, 234, 244, 246, 249, 253, 255, 259, 261, 281-283, 295, 296-305, 306, 308, 309, 311, 320, 325; rejection, 33, 80, 200, 202, 246, 285, 300, 302; sexual (*See also* doctrine over self; sexual control), 102, 153, 160, 164, 171, 202, 260, 305
sin, 11, 21, 27, 30, 36, 37, 41, 42, 68, 92-94, 99, 102, 104, 108, 116, 123, 130-133, 136, 138, 140, 145, 147, 149, 150, 152-154, 158-164, 170-173, 176, 180, 181, 185, 186, 190-192, 196, 197, 220, 225, 226, 239-241, 244, 246, 248, 252, 264, 266-268, 286, 290-292, 295, 297-299, 302, 303, 305-310, 315, 321, 322
Singer, Margaret Thaler, 5, 14, 40, 77, 78, 79, 91, 92, 96, 97, 99, 111, 143, 158, 201, 202, 207, 210, 219, 228, 234, 235, 244, 264, 270, 271, 272, 273, 274, 275, 277, 297, 307, 319
single parents, 6, 29, 251, 287
Sister Thedra (aka Dorothy Martin, *See* When Prophecy Fails).
sleep deprivation, 177, 181, 190, 235, 272, 277, 279
Smart, Elizabeth, 25, 126, 127, 133, 202
Smith, Joseph, 6-8, 13, 15, 23, 24, 25, 27, 36, 37, 40, 41, 47, 52, 59, 60, 65, 68, 93, 100, 103, 105-108, 113, 114, 116, 119, 120, 168, 174, 178, 187, 189, 212-215, 232, 237, 250, 299, 313
Smith, Joseph F., 106, 232
Snow, Steven E., 104
social pressure, 10, 18, 57, 71, 72, 80, 81, 86, 89, 171, 179, 200-205, 206, 210, 213, 217, 218, 227, 228, 234, 243, 244, 249, 262, 296, 302, 308, 320, 321
social proof, 71-74, 83, 200, 201, 203, 204, 210, 215, 316, 317
Spirit, the (*See* Holy Ghost).
spiritual coupons, 127
spiritual death (*See also* dispensing of existence; hell; Outder Darkness), 11, 38, 167, 263, 321
spiritual gifts, 25, 37, 68, 70, 116, 117, 119, 128, 129, 134, 144, 162, 179, 187, 229, 233, 257
square pegs (*See also* LGBT; mental health; perfectionism), 28-29, 37, 43, 204, 283
stake presidents, 35, 153, 154, 216, 289, 294
Stanford Prison Experiment, 235
storytelling, 49, 72, 81, 130, 131, 197, 249, 252, 264, 272-274, 314
Strengthening Church Members Committee (*See* surveillance).
Stricker, Marion, 89, 102, 110, 156, 177, 238, 276, 284, 289, 290, 291, 292, 293, 300, 305, 306, 307, 314, 317, 324
stupor of thought, 221, 256, 275
suffering, 11, 22, 31, 46, 96, 109, 139, 149, 168, 181, 186, 190, 191, 246, 273, 283, 286, 293, 298-302, 314, 321
suicide (*See also* depression; mass suicide; mental health), 27, 33, 38, 171, 172, 181, 238, 248, 263, 289, 292, 294, 301-304
surveillance, 149, 153, 154; spiritual (*See also* fishbowl effect; Holy Ghost), 133, 228, 265-267
suspension of disbelief, 269

temples, 6, 7, 9, 37, 41, 46, 64, 73, 86, 87, 102, 106, 131, 132, 138, 144, 152, 158, 161, 162, 169, 172, 179, 180, 186, 202, 203, 206, 211, 232, 237, 240, 247, 251, 257, 266, 278, 279, 285, 294, 298, 302, 308-310, 315, 317
testimony, 5, 8, 9, 36, 37, 66, 79, 85, 87, 88, 98, 99, 109, 113, 115, 138, 140, 147, 151, 161, 170, 189, 201-203, 207-216, 219, 221, 236, 240, 241, 257, 259, 267, 277, 284, 285, 308, 311
therapy (*See also* cognitive behavior therapy; mental health; psychology), 9, 14, 33, 91, 153, 246, 268, 289, 293, 294, 303, 304, 325
thought police, 15, 151, 306
thought reform (*See* mind control).
thought-terminating clichés, 80, 111, 183, 194-199, 210, 223, 231, 317, 321
time control, 6, 9, 14, 26-29, 33, 35, 38, 43, 50, 70, 78, 81, 88, 97, 101, 108, 121, 136, 139, 142, 143, 147, 148, 158, 172, 177, 180, 187, 190, 192, 207, 208, 247, 267, 270-272, 276-280, 285, 299, 314, 316, 321
tithing, 9, 14, 50, 70, 86, 101, 106, 115, 131, 138, 139, 158, 168, 177, 180, 185, 193, 208, 247, 265, 267, 279, 292, 308, 317
Tobias, Madeleine Landau, 16, 23, 38, 39, 41, 42, 95, 96, 102, 107, 112, 125, 143, 149, 166, 174, 175, 212, 217, 218, 224, 236, 255, 260, 262, 263, 265, 268, 271, 272, 282, 291, 297, 298, 307, 311, 313, 316, 325
torture, 18, 74, 101, 168, 186, 202, 238, 300
totalism (*See also* cults; high-demand group; mind control), 6, 13, 15, 59, 68, 82, 92, 101, 110-111, 124, 126, 128, 142, 143, 152, 156, 158, 165, 166, 174-176, 183, 190, 192, 201, 209, 210, 212, 227, 235, 236, 244, 249, 253, 260-264, 270-275, 282, 292, 297, 301, 306, 308, 312-316, 319, 325
totalist reframing, 80, 81, 100, 114, 118, 121, 142, 179, 182, 183, 185, 187, 188-193, 223, 224, 237, 238, 246, 249, 254-256, 259, 260, 264, 291-293, 312, 315, 316, 320, 321
trance induction & dissociative states (*See also* hymns; hypnosis; music; prayer), 14, 18, 20, 74, 81, 82, 96, 194, 244, 254, 269-275, 276, 311-315, 321
transgender (*See* LGBT).
trauma (*See also* abuse), 20, 40, 91, 99, 127, 171, 235, 262, 271-272
triggers (*See also* dissociation; trauma), 39, 159, 185, 194, 263, 267, 272, 275, 290, 298
trust, building, 6, 10, 18, 19, 25, 35, 73, 81-94, 97, 101, 110-112, 118, 120, 123-125, 127-129, 139, 174, 181, 187, 196, 201, 223, 227, 234, 254, 255, 269, 283, 295, 306, 311

UFOs (*See* When Prophecy Fails).
unconditional love, 6, 27, 43, 85, 86, 89, 152, 298, 299, 302-305, 314, 319, 324
unhealthiness (*See also* abuse; addiction; codependency; mental health; passive-

aggression), 16, 53, 99, 153, 244, 260, 301, 303, 308
Unification Church (*See* cults: Moonies).
unrighteous dominion, 52, 99
uplifting, as a form of milieu control, 29, 50, 186, 203, 216, 229, 246, 274, 312, 314
us-versus-them thinking, 80, 98, 165, 166, 172, 206, 217, 223, 227, 234, 238, 244, 249, 255, 262, 265, 296, 303, 317, 321
Utah, 31-35, 42, 105, 106, 131, 159, 172, 177, 204, 238, 244, 251, 267

violence (*See also* abuse; coercion), 20, 85, 128, 172, 173, 202, 244, 245, 248, 264
visting teaching, 87, 152, 205, 206, 279
Voltaire, 77-78
vulnerability, 10, 25, 28, 29, 69, 96, 120, 148, 167, 218, 235, 255, 270-272, 277, 298, 305-308

war themes, 79, 103, 124, 197, 223, 230, 234, 238, 245, 297
Watson, Blair, 26-28, 30, 33, 45, 262, 301
Welner, Michael, 24, 92, 126, 127
West Ridge Academy, 23
*When Prophecy Fails* (*See also* cognitive dissonance theory; prophecy), 62, 68, 201, 276, 316
women, LDS, 5, 6, 28, 30, 32, 36, 37, 86, 105, 106, 158, 159, 177, 180, 201, 205, 206, 209, 218, 229, 247, 279, 292, 302
Word of Wisdom (*See also* addiction), 27, 121, 131, 139, 140, 187, 203, 208, 252
worthiness, 6, 7, 11, 12, 27, 32, 68, 92, 103, 131-133, 135, 142, 145, 152, 158, 163, 167, 171, 179, 181, 187, 228, 230, 232, 240, 242, 250, 266, 273, 285, 297, 298, 300, 303, 307, 308, 317, 320
Worthy, Jack B., 28, 41, 48, 108, 132, 135, 145, 204, 215, 216, 229, 255, 265, 285, 292, 293, 299, 309, 314, 316, 319, 320

Young Women, 5, 87, 162, 179, 180, 232, 279
Young, Brigham, 2, 47, 105, 116, 117, 121, 123, 162, 165, 168, 169, 172, 192, 225, 226, 239, 240, 244, 257
youth, 19, 24, 87, 88, 97, 130, 137, 145-148, 159-161, 164, 179, 189, 198, 203, 215, 219, 229-232, 237, 249, 300, 304, 305, 308

Zimbardo, Philip, 9, 53, 244

*Nonfiction by Luna Lindsey Corbden*

THE BITE MODEL AND MORMON CONTROL

*Fiction Titles by Luna Lindsey Corbden*

## DREAMS BY STREETLIGHT

MAKE WILLING THE PREY, Prequel
EMERALD CITY DREAMER, Book One

Coming soon:
EMERALD CITY IRON, Book Two

## NOVELETTE

GUARDIAN AT THE GATE

CPSIA information can be obtained
at www.ICGtesting.com
Printed in the USA
LVHW101124050721
691852LV00008B/328